The Food Substitutions Bible

More than 5,000 Substitutions for Ingredients, Equipment & Techniques

David Joachim

Robert ROSE

The Food Substitutions Bible
Text copyright © 2005 David Joachim
Photographs copyright © 2005 Robert Rose Inc.
Cover and text design copyright © 2005 Robert Rose Inc.

Disclaimer

The recipes in this book have been carefully tested by our kitchen and our tasters. To the best of our knowledge, they are safe and nutritious for ordinary use and users. For those people with food or other allergies, or who have special food requirements or health issues, please read the suggested contents of each recipe carefully and determine whether or not they may create a problem for you. All recipes are used at the risk of the consumer.

We cannot be responsible for any hazards, loss or damage that may occur as a result of any recipe use.

For those with special needs, allergies, requirements or health problems, in the event of any doubt, please contact your medical adviser prior to the use of any recipe.

Library and Archives Canada Cataloguing in Publication

Joachim, David
    The food substitutions bible : more than 5,000 substitutions
for ingredients, equipment & techniques / David Joachim.

ISBN 0-7788-0119-5

1. Ingredient substitutions (Cookery) I. Title.

TX652.J62 2005   641.5   C2005-902567-0

Design & Production: PageWave Graphics Inc.
Editor: Carol Sherman
Copy Editor: Karen Campbell-Sheviak
Cover image: Mark T. Shapiro

We acknowledge the financial support of the Government of Canada through the Book Publishing Industry Development Program (BPIDP) for our publishing activities.

Published by Robert Rose Inc.
120 Eglinton Avenue East, Suite 800, Toronto, Ontario, Canada M4P 1E2
Tel: (416) 322-6552   Fax: (416) 322-6936

Printed in Canada

1 2 3 4 5 6 7 8 9 FP 13 12 11 10 09 08 07 06 05

For Bonnie, earth mother extraordinaire

Introduction

Ain't nothing like the real thing, Baby
Ain't nothing like the real thing

> — Nickolas Ashford and Valerie Simpson,
> *Ain't Nothing Like the Real Thing*

Substitute me for him
Substitute my coke for gin
Substitute you for my mum
At least I'll get my washing done

> — The Who, *Substitute*

BOTH OF THE SONGS QUOTED above summarize my general philosophy of cooking. The lyrics of the first song make an impassioned plea to accept no substitutes, while the second song essentially says, "do whatever works."

When it comes to cooking, I truly believe that there "ain't nothing like the real thing." For instance, nothing tastes or acts quite like butter in cooking. But I am also a realist. I know from experience that sometimes you just have to get by with a substitute. Most cooks have, at one time or another, been in the middle of making a meal or special dish and found that they have run out of a key ingredient or don't have that special pan called for in the recipe. Other times, cooks simply want to create a different flavor or texture by experimenting with something new and exciting.

The answer to these dilemmas? Substitute.

Some of the greatest cooking discoveries have been and continue to be made by substituting one ingredient for another, one piece of equipment for another, or one cooking technique for another. Thousands of years ago, when our ancestors experimented with cooking food in clay pots rather than directly over an open flame, they opened the door to a slew of new moist-heat cooking methods, such as boiling, blanching, poaching, stewing, and steaming. Today, innovative cooks make all kinds of substitutions to suit their preferences. Those who like the taste of deep-fried food but don't care for the extra calories may turn to oven-frying, a lower-fat technique that simulates deep-frying by lightly coating the food in oil then baking it in a very hot oven. Other cooks improvise in a pinch by using whatever they have on hand. They substitute vinegar for lemon juice, oil for butter, and hot sauce for ground red chile peppers. Don't have the mirin called for in the recipe? Use a mixture of sherry and sugar instead. Can't find your fondue pot? Use a heavy stoneware dish set on a warming tray or a heating pad. Cooks make these sorts of last-minute adjustments all the time. Whether you change your ingredients, equipment, or techniques, substituting is a matter of tailoring your cooking to meet your immediate needs.

This book compiles a wide range of substitutions into one comprehensive, easy-to-use guide organized from A to Z. Beginning with Abalone and ending with Zwieback, it offers alternative ingredients, equipment, and techniques, including emergency substitutions, time-saving substitutions, healthy substitutions, alternatives for hard-to-find ingredients, alternatives for vegetarians, and ideas for varying the flavor of a dish in countless ways.

Many of the substitutions yield results that are remarkably similar to those you would achieve with the "real thing." For instance, 1 cup (250 mL) all-purpose flour mixed with $1\frac{1}{2}$ teaspoons (7 mL) baking powder and $\frac{1}{2}$ teaspoon (2 mL) salt makes a very close approximation of 1 cup (250 mL) store-bought self-rising flour. For those seeking a less-rich alternative to whipped cream, evaporated milk whips up surprisingly well and makes a creamy, lower-fat substitute that you can dollop onto your favorite desserts.

Other substitutions in the book are not intended to imitate the original item. Instead, they are meant to inspire creativity or stimulate experimentation in the kitchen. For example, replacing apple butter with pumpkin butter will not approximate the original. But it may provide a flavor variation that takes your recipe where you want it to go.

Just keep this cardinal rule in mind: Substitutes will always produce slightly different results. Sometimes the results will be fabulous. Sometimes they may be even closer to what you are going for (if you are experimenting). No matter what you anticipate, expect the results to be at least slightly different when substituting one ingredient, piece of equipment, or technique for another. For instance, using all-purpose flour instead of cornstarch as a thickener produces a slightly coarser, fluffier texture and faintly wheat-like, somewhat earthy flavor. Cornstarch produces a finer, smoother texture and an ever-so-slightly sweet flavor.

Keep in mind, too, that food and cooking are subject to myriad minute variables of time and temperature; ingredient and equipment type, quality, age, and handling; and, of course, user skill level. Whenever you alter one of these variables by substituting, the results, however microscopic, are bound to be different. The fact is that in the ever-changing world of food production, there are few absolutes. And these are mostly mathematical equivalents. For example, 3 teaspoons (15 mL) will always equal 1 tablespoon (15 mL). But, believe it or not, many other mathematical measurements change, depending upon variables such as time, temperature, ingredients, cooking technique and even location. For instance, the boiling point of water is 212°F (100°C), right? Well, that's only at sea level. Go up 5,000 feet (1,525 meters) and water actually boils at about 203°F (95°C) because there is less atmospheric pressure on the surface of the water as it heats. Cooks who bake cookies and cakes at such elevation often increase their oven temperature by 25°F (14°C) and slightly reduce cooking times. The higher oven temperature helps batters and doughs set before the leavening gases overexpand as a result of the thin, dry air at that altitude.

As you can see, substituting is something that certain cooks do all the time without even thinking about it. If you live at high altitude, you are probably used to substituting amounts and temperatures for those given in recipes. If you are lowering your saturated fat intake, you probably substitute oil for butter when sautéing. If the herb cilantro tastes soapy to you, then you probably substitute another more agreeable herb such as parsley.

Substitutions can solve many problems in the kitchen. But they can't work magic. If you have run out of an ingredient and really want to replicate the original exactly, my advice is simple: don't substitute. If you absolutely must have the flavor of cardamom in a recipe, go buy some cardamom instead of substituting another spice such as cinnamon. Cinnamon will taste like cinnamon and not like cardamom. However, if you want to experiment with changing the flavor of your recipe, cinnamon may be an acceptable substitute.

Often, that's the reason I substitute one thing for another: just to try something new. With that in mind, I hope you find this book both practical and enjoyable, a reference that inspires you with fresh ideas and gives you all the information you need to improvise with confidence at home or in a commercial kitchen.

I have tried to make the book as comprehensive as possible, but reference books like this one are rarely "finished" in the final, complete, over-and-done-with sense of the word. Undoubtedly, I have overlooked many fascinating items and substitutions. If you would like to suggest any additions (or point out any errors), please contact me through the publisher. The e-mail address is: foodsubstitutions@robertrose.ca.

I hope you have as much fun experimenting in your kitchen as I have in mine. Happy substituting!

— David Joachim

How To Use This Book

①

②

⑤

Annatto Oil

③ *Also known as manteca de achiote. Food coloring made from the hard reddish pulp that surrounds the seeds of the annatto, a tropical American tree. In Jamaica, annatto oil is used to color codfish cakes.*

④
1 cup (250 mL) = 4 oz (125 mL)

If You Don't Have It

Substitute 1 tbsp (15 mL) annatto oil with:
- 1 tbsp (15 mL) Homemade Annatto Oil: Sauté 1½ tsp (7 mL) annatto seeds in 1 tbsp (15 mL) **⑥** vegetable oil in a saucepan over medium heat, until oil turns a deep orange color, 8 to 10 minutes. Remove seeds with slotted spoon and discard.
- 1 tbsp (15 mL) vegetable oil + 2 drops yellow food coloring + 1 drop red food coloring mixed **⑦** into 1 tbsp (15 mL) water or other non-oily liquid in recipe (food coloring will not mix with oil; add to watery liquids)

⑧ *See also* ANNATTO SEEDS.

① The entries in this book are arranged alphabetically and cross-referenced like an index. The entries are alphabetized by the letter rather than by the word so that multiple word entries are treated like single words. For example, the entry Applejack appears after Apple Corer and before Apple Juice.

② Each entry has been arranged into two columns. The left-hand column contains introductory and reference information. The right-hand column contains the substitutions.

③ The introductory information in the left-hand column begins with a brief description, useful tip, or interesting fact about the item. If the item is known by any alternate names, these alternate names appear just before the description. For example, the entry for Annatto Oil begins, "Also known as manteca de achiote." These alternate names are followed by the item's description, in this case, "Food coloring made from the hard reddish pulp that surrounds the seeds of the annatto, a tropical American tree. In Jamaica, annatto oil is used to color codfish cakes."

4 In many entries, the introduction is followed by a box of useful measurement equivalents, such as $\frac{1}{2}$ cup (125 mL) = 4 oz (125 mL). In some cases, the equivalents have been rounded for ease of measuring.

5 The substitutions in the right-hand column appear in bulleted lists and have been categorized under one of five subheadings. Most substitutions fall under the subheading "If You Don't Have It," which appears in a shaded box at the top of the right-hand column. These substitutions are intended to replace items that you have run out of or cannot find in your market. However, in some cooking situations, you may want to intentionally vary the flavor of the finished dish, save time when preparing it, or improve its healthfulness. These types of substitutions appear under the subheadings "To Vary the Flavor," "To Save Time," and "For Better Health." If a particular item, such as Eggplant, has several varieties, those varieties and their characteristics appear beneath a fifth subheading, in this case, "Eggplant Varieties."

6 In some entries, the suggested substitution is a basic recipe that may replace a common store-bought item. For instance, in the Annatto Oil entry, the first suggested substitution is a simple recipe for Homemade Annatto Oil. Every entry lists the preferred substitutions first, followed by those that less closely match the replaced item but still make a fair substitute. In most entries, canned, jarred, and frozen versions of fresh ingredients are not listed as substitutions. It is assumed that the reader will use discretion and preferences when choosing these common substitutes. In those few cases in which a canned, jarred, or frozen substitution is listed, the item being replaced is listed as fresh. For instance, in the Bell Pepper entry, the first substitution appears as follows:

"Substitute 1 cup (250 mL) chopped fresh bell pepper with 1 cup (250 mL) chopped fresh, canned, or bottled pimiento."

7 Every substitution includes proportions such as "Substitute 1 tbsp (15 mL) annatto oil with 1 tbsp (15 mL) vegetable oil + 2 drops yellow food coloring + 1 drop red food coloring mixed into 1 tbsp (15 mL) water or other non-oily liquid in recipe (food coloring will not mix with oil; add to watery liquids)." In some cases, additional adjustments are suggested in parentheses. Metric equivalents for each measurement, such as milliliters and Celsius, appear in parentheses after the Imperial measurement.

8 Cross-references appear throughout the book in CAPITAL LETTERS. In most cases, cross-references direct the reader to the book entry that contains all of that item's information. For instance, readers looking up Active Dry Yeast will be referred to the entry for Yeast, Baker's. Cross-references may also direct readers to entries that provide related information. For example, under Annatto Oil, readers will find a cross-reference to see also the entry for Annatto Seeds. These "see also" cross-references appear in the right-hand column after the bulleted list of substitutions.

Reference charts and tables appear at the back of the book. The first set of tables, called Ingredient Guides (page 564), profiles the different varieties of a particular food such as apples. The profiles include alternate names for the food, texture and flavor characteristics, and the food's best uses or substitutes. The second set of tables, called Measurement Equivalents (page 605), offers Imperial and Metric equivalents for volume, weight, temperature, and pan sizes. It also includes charts of adjustments for cooking and baking at high altitude. Many of the entries in A to Z section of the book refer you to these charts for more detailed information.

Abalone to Azuki

Abalone

Also known as awabi, loco, muttonfish, ormer, and paua. A mollusk sold in many Asian markets. Smaller ones taste better.

If You Don't Have It
Substitute 1 lb (500 g) abalone meat with:
- 1 lb (500 g) canned or frozen abalone (thaw and add juices to dish)
- 1 lb (500 g) clam or conch meat

Absinthe

See ANISE LIQUEUR.

Accent

See MONOSODIUM GLUTAMATE.

Acerola

Also known as West Indian cherry. A dark red fruit that's similar to cherries, higher in vitamin C than most other fruits, and slightly acidic.

> 1 cup (250 mL) whole = 100 g
> 1 pitted acerola = 5 g

If You Don't Have It
Substitute 1 cup (250 mL) pitted acerola with:
- 1 cup (250 mL) pitted cherries

Achee

See ACKEE.

Achiote Seeds

See ANNATTO SEEDS.

Acidophilus Milk

See MILK, WHOLE.

Acidulated Water

Water made slightly acidic by adding an acid ingredient, such as lemon juice or vinegar. Used to prevent the browning of cut foods such as apples and artichokes.

If You Don't Have It
Substitute 4 cups (1 L) acidulated water with:
- 4 cups (1 L) water + 1 tbsp (15 mL) salt (prevents browning without making the water acidic)
- 4 cups (1 L) Homemade Acidulated Water: Combine 4 cups (1 L) water, 1½ tbsp (22 mL) vinegar or 3 tbsp (45 mL) lemon juice or ½ cup (125 mL) white wine.
- 4 cups (1 L) water + 2 tablets (each 500 mg) vitamin C, crushed to a powder

Acitrón

See NOPALE.

Ackee

Also known as achee and akee. A tropical fruit often served with salt cod in Jamaica. Only the ripe pale flesh of the fruit is edible.

If You Don't Have It
Substitute 1 cup (250 mL) fresh ackee with:
- 1 cup (250 mL) canned ackee

Acorn

Nuts produced by oak trees, some of which are edible by humans. Can be ground into meal, eaten raw, or roasted and eaten.

If You Don't Have It
Substitute 1 cup (250 mL) shelled white oak acorns with:
- 1 cup (250 mL) hazelnuts
- 1 cup (250 mL) chestnuts

Acorn Squash

Dark green winter squash, with orange spots, is deeply ridged and shaped like an acorn. For easy peeling, prick hard shell before cooking.

1 lb (500 g) = 1 cup (250 mL) cooked and mashed

If You Don't Have It
Substitute 1 cup (250 mL) acorn squash with:
- 1 cup (250 mL) butternut squash (more easily peeled; creamier)
- 1 cup (250 mL) buttercup squash (less moist)
- 1 cup (250 mL) pumpkin (creamier)

Active Dry Yeast

See YEAST, BAKER'S.

Adobo Sauce

Traditional Mexican seasoning sauce or paste made from toasted and rehydrated chiles, garlic, cumin, oregano and other spices. Also used as the canning liquid for canned chipotle chiles.

If You Don't Have It

Substitute 1 cup (250 mL) adobo sauce with:
- 1 cup (250 mL) Homemade Adobo Sauce: Toast 8 to 10 unpeeled garlic cloves in a large dry skillet over medium heat, shaking occasionally, until skins are blackened, 10 to 15 minutes. Let cool and peel. Tear open and discard seeds from about 4 dried ancho chiles (2 oz/60 g), about 4 dried guajillo chiles (2 oz/60 g), and about 2 dried chipotle chiles ($\frac{1}{2}$ oz/15 g) (wear gloves to protect your hands). Toast chiles in the same skillet, pressing flat with spatula, until fragrant and lightly browned, about 2 minutes per side. Put chiles in a large bowl, cover with hot water, and let stand for 20 to 30 minutes. Transfer chiles to a blender or food processor. Add $\frac{1}{2}$ cup (125 mL) beef, chicken, or vegetable broth, $\frac{1}{4}$ cup (50 mL) chile soaking liquid, toasted garlic, 1 to 2 tsp (5 to 10 mL) dried oregano, $\frac{1}{2}$ tsp (2 mL) ground black pepper, $\frac{1}{8}$ to $\frac{1}{4}$ tsp (0.5 to 1 mL) ground cumin, a pinch of ground coriander, and a pinch of ground cinnamon. Purée until smooth, scraping down sides. Strain mixture through a medium-mesh sieve into a bowl and discard solids. Stir in salt to taste. Makes about 1 cup (250 mL).

Advocaat

Dutch liqueur made from egg yolks and brandy. Similar to thick eggnog, advocaat is often dolloped into coffee or hot chocolate.

If You Don't Have It

Substitute 2 tbsp (25 mL) advocaat with:
- 2 tbsp (25 mL) nonalcoholic eggnog + $\frac{1}{4}$ to $\frac{1}{2}$ tsp (1 to 2 mL) brandy
- 2 tbsp (25 mL) Irish cream liqueur

Adzuki Bean

See THE WIDE WORLD OF DRIED BEANS (PAGE 566).

African Horned Cucumber

See KIWANO.

Agar

Also known as kanten. An odorless sea vegetable used as a gelling agent. Use 1 tsp (5 mL) agar powder to gel 1 cup (250 mL) liquid.

1½ tbsp (22 mL) agar flakes = 1 tsp (5 mL) agar powder = ½ kanten bar

If You Don't Have It
Substitute 1 tsp (5 mL) agar powder with:
- 1½ tsp (7 mL) gelatin powder

Aguardiente

See GRAPPA.

Ahi

See TUNA, FRESH.

Aïoli

See MAYONNAISE.

Aji-no-moto

See MONOSODIUM GLUTAMATE.

Ajwain

Also known as ajowan, Bishop's weed, and carom seed. A southern Indian spice that tastes somewhat like thyme. The seeds contain antioxidant and preservative qualities.

If You Don't Have It
Substitute 1 tsp (5 mL) ajwain with:
- 1¼ tsp (6 mL) dried thyme
- ½ tsp (2 mL) dried thyme or oregano + scant ½ tsp (2 mL) dried celery seeds + scant ¼ tsp (1 mL) ground black pepper
- ¾ tsp (4 mL) cumin seeds
- ¾ tsp (4 mL) caraway seeds

Akala

A large Hawaiian berry, varying in color from red to purple. Akala is eaten raw or cooked in pastries and jams.

1 pint fresh = 2⅔ cups (650 mL)

If You Don't Have It
Substitute 1 cup (250 mL) akala with:
- 1 cup (250 mL) raspberries

Akee

See ACKEE.

Akule

A Hawaiian fish that is often salted and dried like cod.

If You Don't Have It

Substitute 1 lb (500 g) akule with:
- 1 lb (500 g) salted and dried mackerel
- 1 lb (500 g) salt cod

Akvavit

See AQUAVIT.

Alaska King Crab

See CRAB; CHOOSING AMONG CRABS (PAGE 597).

Alaska Smoked Cod

See KIPPERED BLACK COD.

Albacore

See TUNA, CANNED; TUNA, FRESH.

Alcohol

See BEER; LIQUEUR; WINE; SPECIFIC TYPES.

Ale

See BEER.

Alfalfa Sprouts

Germinated seeds of a green leafy forage crop, alfalfa sprouts are eaten as a salad vegetable or sandwich topping.

If You Don't Have It

Substitute ¼ cup (50 mL) alfalfa sprouts with:
- ¼ cup (50 mL) sunflower sprouts
- ¼ cup (50 mL) mung bean sprouts (thicker and more crisp)

Alligator

Alligator meat tastes similar to chicken or mild white fish. Tail meat is white and tender while body meat is somewhat tougher and darker. It is usually sold frozen as tail steak, stew meat, burger, wings (legs), or sausage.

If You Don't Have It

Substitute 1 lb (500 g) alligator tail meat with:
- 1 lb (500 g) crocodile tail meat
- 1 lb (500 g) turtle meat
- 1 lb (500 g) chicken breast
- 1 lb (500 g) swordfish

Alligator Pepper

See GRAINS OF PARADISE.

All-Purpose Flour

See FLOUR, ALL-PURPOSE.

Allspice

Also known as Jamaica pepper and pimento. A tiny dried, dark brown berry used often in desserts and Jamaican cooking.

40 whole berries = 1 tsp (5 mL) ground

If You Don't Have It
Substitute 1 tsp (5 mL) ground allspice with:
- ½ tsp (2 mL) ground cinnamon + ½ tsp (2 mL) ground cloves + pinch of ground nutmeg (optional)

Almond

Commercially available almonds are known as sweet almonds. Most markets sell them with the natural brown skin intact or blanched (skin removed). Bitter almonds, on the other hand, contain a toxic acid and are generally unavailable to consumers. When heated, the toxin in bitter almonds is destroyed, making bitter almonds safe for use in almond extracts and liqueurs.

1 lb (500 g) in shell = 1½ cups (375 mL) whole = ⅓ cup (75 mL) ground meal

1 lb (500 g) shelled = 3 cups (750 mL) whole = 4 cups (1 L) slivered = 4½ cups (1.125 L) sliced

If You Don't Have It
Substitute 1 cup (250 mL) blanched almonds with:
- 1 cup (250 mL) almonds with skin (if you don't mind the amber color and mildly bitter flavor)
- 1 cup (250 mL) Homemade Blanched Almonds: Drop 1 cup (250 mL) almonds in boiling water for 2 minutes. Drain and rub off skins in a kitchen towel.
- 2 to 4 tbsp (25 to 60 mL) almond oil (for baking and cooking; will add nut flavor but not texture of whole nuts; reduce fat in recipe by 2 to 4 tbsp/ 25 to 60 mL)
- 2 to 4 tbsp (25 to 60 mL) almond liqueur (for baking and cooking; adds nut flavor and alcohol but not texture of whole nuts; reduce liquid in recipe by 2 to 4 tbsp/25 to 60 mL)

To Vary the Flavor
Substitute 1 cup (250 mL) shelled almonds with:
- 1 cup (250 mL) walnuts
- 1 cup (250 mL) pecans
- 1 cup (250 mL) hazelnuts
- 1 cup (250 mL) pistachios

See also NUT MEAL.

Almond Butter

A spread of ground roasted almonds, oil, and salt, almond butter is slightly grainier than peanut butter. Usually stocked in the jam and jelly section or refrigerated case of supermarkets and health food stores.

If You Don't Have It

Substitute 1 cup (250 mL) almond butter with:
- 1 cup (250 mL) Homemade Almond Butter: Combine 2 cups (500 mL) roasted almonds and ¼ tsp (1 mL) salt in a blender or food processor fitted with metal blade. Process, gradually adding 6 tbsp (90 mL) almond or vegetable oil, until the mixture forms a paste, 1 to 2 minutes. Makes 1½ cups (375 mL).
- 1 cup (250 mL) peanut butter or cashew butter
- 1 cup (250 mL) tahini (pronounced sesame flavor)

Almond Extract

A concentrated flavoring, used mostly for desserts and pastries. It's made by combining bitter almond oil and ethyl alcohol.

If You Don't Have It

Substitute ½ tsp (2 mL) almond extract with:
- 1 drop almond oil + ¼ tsp (1 mL) vodka
- 1 tbsp (15 mL) almond liqueur

To Vary the Flavor

Substitute ½ tsp (2 mL) almond extract with:
- ¾ tsp (4 mL) vanilla extract

Almond Liqueur

A cordial widely used in Italy. Amaretto di Saronno is a popular brand.

If You Don't Have It

Substitute 2 tbsp (25 mL) almond liqueur with:
- ½ to ¾ tsp (2 to 4 mL) almond extract (add 2 tbsp/25 mL water if necessary to replace lost liquid volume)

To Vary the Flavor

Substitute 2 tbsp (25 mL) almond liqueur with:
- 2 tbsp (25 mL) hazelnut liqueur, coffee liqueur, or chocolate liqueur
- 2 tbsp (25 mL) crème d'amande or crème de noyaux (sweeter flavor, thicker texture, pink color)

Almond Milk

The liquid strained from ground blanched almonds, sugar, and water. It is gelled to make the classic French pudding blancmange.

If You Don't Have It

Substitute 1 cup (250 mL) almond milk with:
- 1 cup (250 mL) rice milk or sweetened soy milk

Almond Oil

See OIL OF BITTER ALMONDS; SUBSTITUTING OILS (PAGE 598).

Almond Paste

A smooth blend of ground almonds and sugar used to make marzipan, macaroons, and fillings for Danish and other pastries.

If You Don't Have It

Substitute 1¼ cups (300 mL) almond paste with:
- 1¼ cups (300 mL) bitter almond paste (more intense almond flavor from oil of bitter almonds; often used for amaretti cookies)
- 1¼ cups (300 mL) marzipan (sweeter and more pliable)
- 1¾ cups (425 mL) ground blanched almonds + 1½ cups (375 mL) confectioner's sugar + 1 egg white + 1 tsp (5 mL) almond extract + ¼ tsp (1 mL) salt

Aluminum Foil

Also known as foil or tin foil. Around the turn of the 20th century, sheet foil manufactured from aluminum began to replace foil made from tin, which imparted a tinny aftertaste to foods wrapped in it.

If You Don't Have It

Substitute aluminum foil with:
- plastic wrap, especially sealable plastic wrap (for covering and refrigerating foods)
- parchment paper (for lining baking sheets, covering roasts, and wrapping foods)
- wax paper (for lining baking pans and wrapping foods)

To Vary the Flavor

Substitute aluminum foil (as a food wrapper) with:
- corn husks (adds mild corn aroma)
- hoja santa leaves (adds aromas of root beer and fennel)
- banana leaves (adds herby-green flavor)

Amaranth Flour

See CHOOSING AMONG WHOLE-GRAIN AND ALTERNATIVE FLOURS (PAGE 586).

Amaranth Leaves

Also known as Chinese spinach and yin choy. The leaves are similar to spinach but sweeter and more delicate, and with beautiful pinkish purple veins. The seeds are used as cereal or ground to make amaranth flour.

If You Don't Have It

Substitute 1 lb (500 g) amaranth leaves with:
- 1 lb (500 g) red chard leaves (firmer leaves)
- 1 lb (500 g) baby spinach
- 1 lb (500 g) callaloo (taro leaves)
- 1 lb (500 g) Chinese kale

Amaretti

Also known as Italian macaroons. The name means "little bitter," a reference to the bitter almond flavor. Often crushed for use in desserts and savory dishes.

If You Don't Have It
Substitute 1 lb (500 g) amaretti with:
- 1 lb (500 g) almond biscotti

To Vary the Flavor
Substitute 1 lb (500 g) amaretti with
- 1 lb (500 g) graham crackers, ladyfingers, or other crisp cookies (especially for crushing)
- 1 lb (500 g) macaroons (softer; lighter)

Amaretto

See ALMOND LIQUEUR.

Amasake

Japanese fermented rice milk. May be as thin as skim milk or as thick as a smoothie, depending upon the intended use.

If You Don't Have It
Substitute 1 cup (250 mL) amasake with:
- 1 cup (250 mL) sweetened rice milk, soy milk, or almond milk
- 1 cup (250 mL) milk

Amchur

See MANGO POWDER.

American Bacon

See BACON.

American Cheese

Also known as processed cheese. Produced with up to 51% natural cheese that is combined with emulsifiers and other liquid.

1 oz (30 g) = 1 slice

If You Don't Have It
Substitute 1 oz (30 g) with:
- 1 oz (30 g) processed cheese, such as Velveeta
- 1 oz (30 g) Cheddar cheese (sharper, deeper flavor)
- 1 oz (30 g) Swiss cheese (sharper, deeper flavor)

See also PROCESSED CHEESE.

Amer Picon

Also known as Picon. Very bitter reddish brown French apéritif produced with gentian, orange, and cinchona bark (also used to make quinine). Popular mixed with soda water or added to various cocktails.

If You Don't Have It
Substitute 2 tbsp (25 mL) Amer Picon with:
- 2 tbsp (25 mL) Byrrh, Dubonnet blanc, or Lillet (each less bitter than Amer Picon)

Ammonium Bicarbonate

Leavener that preceded modern baking powder and baking soda.

If You Don't Have It
Substitute 1 tsp (5 mL) ammonium bicarbonate with:
- 1 tsp (5 mL) baking powder
- 1¼ tsp (6 mL) baking soda
- ¾ tsp (4 mL) baking powder + ¾ tsp (4 mL) baking soda

Anago

See EEL.

Anaheim Chile

See CHOOSING DRIED CHILES (PAGE 578); CHOOSING FRESH CHILES (PAGE 582).

Anasazi Bean

See THE WIDE WORLD OF DRIED BEANS (PAGE 566).

Ancho Chile

See CHOOSING DRIED CHILES (PAGE 578).

Anchovy

Small silver fish of many species found in warm oceans around the globe. Most popular in countries that rim the Mediterranean. Historically salted or canned in oil, fresh anchovies are gaining popularity.

> 2 oz (60 g) =
> 10 to 12 anchovies =
> 3 to 4 tbsp (45 to 60 mL)
> anchovy paste

If You Don't Have It
Substitute 2 anchovy fillets with:
- 1 tsp (5 mL) anchovy paste
- ½ oz (15 g) smelt
- ½ oz (15 g) sardines

Anchovy Paste

A savory condiment of mashed anchovies, vinegar, spices and water available in tubes near the canned fish in most supermarkets.

> 2 oz (60 g)
> = 4 tbsp (60 mL)

If You Don't Have It
Substitute 1 tsp (5 mL) anchovy paste with:
- 1 mashed anchovy fillet (stronger anchovy flavor)

To Vary the Flavor
Substitute 1 tsp (5 mL) anchovy paste with:
- 1 tsp (5 mL) shrimp paste (more pungent)

Andouille

French tripe-based large rustic sausages, smoked and eaten cold. In Louisiana, descendants of French Acadians created a spicy, smoked ground pork sausage of the same name.

If You Don't Have It
Substitute 1 lb (500 g) andouille with:
- 1 lb (500 g) spicy smoked kielbasa
- 1 lb (500 g) hot links
- 1 lb (500 g) other spicy or smoked sausage

Andouillette

Small French fresh sausages most commonly made from tripe. Grilled andouillettes garnished with mustard and served with puréed potatoes are a classic bistro specialty.

If You Don't Have It
Substitute 1 lb (500 g) andouillette with:
- 1 lb (500 g) French andouille (larger)

To Vary the Flavor
Substitute 1 lb (500 g) andouillette with:
- 1 lb (500 g) sweet Italian sausage

Anesone

See ANISE LIQUEUR.

Angel Food Cake

Slice with a serrated knife or tines of a fork to prevent squashing the airy cake.

If You Don't Have It
Substitute 1 lb (500 g) angel food cake with:
- 1 lb (500 g) sponge cake
- 1 lb (500 g) pound cake (richer flavor; denser texture)

Angelica

Also known as French rhubarb. A tall, thick-stemmed, temperate plant sometimes eaten as a vegetable. Often used in European confectionery, the stalks are cut in short pieces and candied.

If You Don't Have It
Substitute 1 tbsp (15 mL) chopped fresh angelica with:
- 1 tbsp (15 mL) chopped fresh lovage (similar celery-like flavor)
- 1 tbsp (15 mL) chopped fresh tarragon (more licorice-like flavor)

Angled Loofa

See LOOFA, ANGLED.

Anglerfish

See MONKFISH.

Angostura Bitters

See BITTERS.

Anise Extract

A concentrated flavoring used for breads and pastries in European and Middle Eastern kitchens. Made by combining anise oil and ethyl alcohol.

If You Don't Have It
Substitute 1 tsp (5 mL) anise extract with:
- ⅛ to ¼ tsp (0.5 to 1 mL) anise oil
- 1 to 2 tbsp (5 to 10 mL) anise liqueur (reduce liquid in recipe by 1 to 2 tbsp/5 to 10 mL)
- 2 tsp (10 mL) ground anise seeds

To Vary the Flavor
Substitute 1 tsp (5 mL) anise extract with:
- 1 tsp (5 mL) almond or vanilla extract

Anise Liqueur

Also known as arak, ouzo, and pastis. Cordial flavored with anise seeds. When mixed with water, clear anise-flavored liqueurs turn cloudy and white.

If You Don't Have It
Substitute 2 tbsp (25 mL) anise liqueur with:
- 1 to 1½ tsp (5 to 7 mL) anise extract (add 1½ tbsp/22 mL liquid to recipe if necessary)
- 2 tsp (10 mL) ground anise seeds (add 2 tbsp/ 25 mL liquid to recipe if necessary)
- 1 whole star anise (add 2 tbsp/25 mL liquid to recipe if necessary)

Anise Liqueur Varieties
Choose 2 tbsp (25 mL) anise liqueur from these varieties:
- 2 tbsp (25 mL) anisette (French anise liqueur; sweet flavor; low alcohol)
- 2 tbsp (25 mL) anesone (Italian anise liqueur)
- 2 tbsp (25 mL) sambuca (Italian anise liqueur; more pronounced licorice flavor; higher alcohol)
- 2 tbsp (25 mL) ouzo (Greek anise liqueur; higher alcohol)
- 2 tbsp (25 mL) arak (anise-flavored liqueur of Middle Eastern origin; higher alcohol)
- 2 tbsp (25 mL) raki (anise-flavored liqueur of Middle Eastern origin; higher alcohol)
- 2 tbsp (25 mL) absinthe (anise-flavored liqueur popularized in France; contains narcotic wormwood and is banned in most countries; green color; higher alcohol)
- 2 tbsp (25 mL) herbsaint (anise-flavored liqueur originating in New Orleans; similar to absinthe but without the narcotic; higher alcohol)
- 2 tbsp (25 mL) Ricard, Pernod, or other pastis (French anise liqueur; more pronounced licorice flavor; higher alcohol)

Anise Oil

Flavoring oil extracted from anise seeds.

If You Don't Have It

Substitute ¼ tsp (1 mL) anise oil with:
- 1 tsp (5 mL) anise extract
- 1 to 2 tbsp (5 to 10 mL) anise liqueur (reduce liquid in recipe by 1 to 2 tbsp/5 to 10 mL)
- 2 tsp (10 mL) ground anise seeds

Anise Seeds

Seeds produced by a culinary herb in the parsley family. The anise plant has been cultivated since ancient Roman times. Popular in Europe, the Middle East, and India, the sweet, distinctive flavor of anise comes from the essential oil anethole.

If You Don't Have It

Substitute ½ tsp (2 mL) anise seeds with:
- 1 small crushed star anise (bolder flavor)
- ½ tsp (2 mL) fennel seeds (milder, sweeter flavor)
- ½ tsp (2 mL) caraway seeds (milder, more nutty flavor)
- 1 tsp (5 mL) chopped fresh tarragon (adds green color)

See also STAR ANISE.

Anisette

See ANISE LIQUEUR.

Annatto Oil

Also known as manteca de achiote. Food coloring made from the hard reddish pulp that surrounds the seeds of the annatto, a tropical American tree. In Jamaica, annatto oil is used to color codfish cakes.

> 1 cup (250 mL)
> = 4 oz (175 g)

If You Don't Have It

Substitute 1 tbsp (15 mL) annatto oil with:
- 1 tbsp (15 mL) Homemade Annatto Oil: Sauté 1½ tsp (7 mL) annatto seeds in 1 tbsp (15 mL) vegetable oil in a saucepan over medium heat, until oil turns a deep orange color, 8 to 10 minutes. Remove seeds with slotted spoon and discard.
- 1 tbsp (15 mL) vegetable oil + 2 drops yellow food coloring + 1 drop red food coloring mixed into 1 tbsp (15 mL) water or other non-oily liquid in recipe (food coloring will not mix with oil; add to watery liquids)

See also ANNATTO SEEDS.

Annatto Seeds

Also known as achiote seeds. To extract the rich yellow orange color, steep the seeds in boiling water for about 20 minutes, then discard the seeds. Or make annatto oil for cooking (see page 23).

If You Don't Have It

Substitute 1½ tsp (7 mL) annatto seeds with:

- ½ tsp (2 mL) turmeric + ½ tsp (2 mL) mild paprika (for yellow orange color; adds more pungent flavor)
- ½ to 1 tsp (2 to 5 mL) crushed dried safflower florets
- 2 drops yellow food coloring + 1 drop red food coloring mixed into water or other liquid in the recipe (for yellow orange color)

See also ANNATTO OIL.

Antelope

Ruminant mammals of Africa and Asia including gazelle, springbok, and wildebeest. The so-called North American antelope, the pronghorn, is also eaten as game meat. The lean meat can be larded for additional moisture and flavor.

If You Don't Have It

Substitute 1 lb (500 g) antelope with:

- 1 lb (500 g) gazelle
- 1 lb (500 g) caribou
- 1 lb (500 g) reindeer
- 1 lb (500 g) red, fallow, or white-tailed deer
- 1 lb (500 g) moose
- 1 lb (500 g) elk

See also VENISON.

Appaloosa Bean

See THE WIDE WORLD OF DRIED BEANS (PAGE 566).

Appenzeller

Also known as Appenzell. Unpasteurized whole-milk cow's cheese from eastern Switzerland. The mildly fragrant flavor is partially due to washing the rind with spiced wine or cider.

If You Don't Have It

Substitute 1 oz (30 g) Appenzeller with:

- 1 oz (30 g) Emmental (nuttier flavor; large holes)
- 1 oz (30 g) Gruyère (sweeter, nuttier flavor; semifirm texture)
- 1 oz (30 g) raclette (sweeter, nuttier flavor; semifirm texture)

Apple

Apple varieties number between 7,000 and 8,000. Modern cultivated apples differ dramatically from their tiny, sour ancestors, which excelled botanically at producing seeds for propagation.

1 lb (500 g) = 3 medium
= 3 cups (750 mL) sliced

If You Don't Have It
Substitute 1 lb (500 g) apples with:
- 1 lb (500 g) pears (generally softer flesh)
- 1 lb (500 g) Asian pears (generally crisper and juicier texture; tart flavor)
- 1 lb (500 g) quinces (best for cooking; more tart flavor)

See also PICKING APPLES (PAGE 564).

Apple Brandy

Also known as apple, applejack, Calvados (French), cider brandy, cider spirits and cider whiskey. Distilled apple cider was a popular beverage in Colonial America and, as Calvados, it enjoys a distinguished history in the French apple-growing region of Normandy.

If You Don't Have It
Substitute 2 tbsp (25 mL) apple brandy with:
- 2 tbsp (25 mL) pear brandy
- 1 tbsp (15 mL) cognac or brandy + 1 tbsp (15 mL) apple juice concentrate

Apple Brandy Varieties
Choose 2 tbsp (25 mL) apple brandy from these specific types:
- 2 tbsp (25 mL) Calvados (French apple brandy in varying degrees of good quality)
- 2 tbsp (25 mL) applejack (American apple brandy; generally of lesser quality than Calvados; look for straight instead of blended versions for higher quality)

Apple Butter

A preserve served as a bread topping or condiment. Prepared by slowly simmering apples with sugar, cider, cinnamon, cloves, and allspice.

If You Don't Have It
Substitute 1 tbsp (15 mL) apple butter with:
- 1 tbsp (15 mL) Homemade Apple Butter: Combine 1 cup (250 mL) sliced apples, 2 tbsp (25 mL) granulated sugar, and 2 tbsp (25 mL) apple juice or cider in a pot. Bring to a boil over high heat. Reduce heat to medium-low and simmer, stirring now and then, until apples are fall-apart tender, about 1 hour. Remove from heat. Stir in $\frac{1}{4}$ tsp (1 mL) cinnamon. Transfer to a blender or food processor and purée until smooth.

To Vary the Flavor
Substitute 1 tbsp (15 mL) apple butter with:
- 1 tbsp (15 mL) pear butter
- 1 tbsp (15 mL) pumpkin butter

Apple Cider

Also known as sweet apple cider. Made by crushing several apple varieties into a pomace, then pressing out the juice. Tiny apple solids in the juice darken when exposed to air, giving cider its distinctive caramel color.

If You Don't Have It

Substitute 1 cup (250 mL) non-alcoholic apple cider with:
- 1 cup (250 mL) apple juice

To Vary the Flavor

Substitute 1 cup (250 mL) nonalcoholic apple cider with:
- 1 cup (250 mL) pear cider

Apple Corer

A utensil, often stainless steel, designed to cut and easily remove the core, or center, from apples.

If You Don't Have It

Substitute an apple corer with:
- melon baller (to scoop the core from an apple halved lengthwise)
- paring knife (to cut the core from an apple halved lengthwise)
- countertop peeling-coring-slicing machine

Apple, Dried

Commercially produced, slices of peeled apples are treated with sulfur dioxide and dehydrated. Apple slices may also be dried in home food dehydrators.

> 8 oz (250 g) =
> 4 cups (1 L) cooked

If You Don't Have It

Substitute 1 oz (30 g) dried apples with:
- 1 oz (30 g) dried pears
- 1 oz (30 g) dried Asian pears

Applejack

See APPLE BRANDY.

Apple Juice

Juice pressed from fresh apples that is filtered and heat-treated to be shelf stable. Also available in concentrate that is shelf-stable or frozen.

If You Don't Have It

Substitute 1 cup (250 mL) apple juice with:
- 1 cup (250 mL) apple cider
- 1 cup (250 mL) pear cider
- 1 cup (250 mL) white grape juice (sweeter)

Apple Pear

See ASIAN PEAR.

Apple Pie Spice

A commercial or homemade combination of spices especially suited to enhance apple pie but also a wonderful seasoning for French toast, pancakes, waffles, sugar cookies, and other desserts. The mixture almost always contains cinnamon and nutmeg with a range of optional additions, including allspice, cardamom, cloves, mace, or ginger.

If You Don't Have It

Substitute 1 tbsp (15 mL) apple pie spice with:
- 1 tbsp (15 mL) Homemade Apple Pie Spice: Combine 2 tsp (10 mL) ground cinnamon, 1 tsp (5 mL) ground nutmeg and pinch ground allspice.

To Vary the Flavor

Substitute 1 tbsp (15 mL) apple pie spice with:
- 1 tbsp (15 mL) pumpkin pie spice (adds ginger flavor)
- 2 tsp (10 mL) ground cinnamon + $\frac{1}{2}$ tsp (2 mL) ground nutmeg + $\frac{1}{2}$ tsp (2 mL) ground cardamom (adds pungent aroma)

Applesauce

Apples cooked to a smooth or chunky purée that may be sweetened or flavored with cinnamon or other spices.

If You Don't Have It

Substitute 1 cup (250 mL) applesauce with:
- 1 cup (250 mL) Homemade Applesauce: Peel, core and dice 4 medium-size sauce apples (See Picking Apples, page 564). Place in a saucepan over medium heat with $\frac{1}{4}$ cup (50 mL) water, $\frac{1}{4}$ cup (50 mL) granulated sugar (optional), and $\frac{1}{8}$ tsp (0.5 mL) salt. Simmer until soft, about 15 minutes. For chunky applesauce, smash with the back of a large spoon or a potato masher. For smooth applesauce, pass the mixture through a food mill. Add $\frac{1}{4}$ tsp (1 mL) cinnamon and more sugar, if desired. Makes $1\frac{1}{2}$ cups (375 mL).
- 1 cup (250 mL) pumpkin purée
- 1 cup (250 mL) plum purée
- 1 cup (250 mL) fat-free, fruit-based butter and oil replacement such as Smucker's "Baking Healthy" (for baking only).
- $\frac{1}{2}$ cup (125 mL) fat-free, fruit-based butter and oil replacement such as Sunsweet "Lighter Bake" (for baking only).

Apple Schnapps

Clear liqueur flavored with apples. Also available as sour apple schnapps.

If You Don't Have It

Substitute 2 tbsp (25 mL) apple schnapps with:
- 2 tbsp (25 mL) apple brandy (Calvados or applejack)

Apricot

Highly prized fruit with floral aroma and luscious orange flesh is a member of the rose family. First cultivated in China before 2000 BC. The versatile fruit is eaten out of hand, dried, simmered into preserves, and added to savory dishes.

1 lb (500 g) fresh =
8 to 14 = 2½ cups
(625 mL) sliced or halved

If You Don't Have It

Substitute 1 lb (500 g) apricots with:
- 1 lb (500 g) apriums (a hybrid fruit that's a cross between apricot and plum; very apricot-like)
- 1 lb (500 g) pluots (a hybrid fruit that's a cross between apricot and plum; more plum-like)

To Vary the Flavor

Substitute 1 lb (500 g) apricots with:
- 1 lb (500 g) small peaches
- 1 lb (500 g) small nectarines

See also APRICOT, DRIED.

Apricot Brandy

Dry distilled spirit made from apricot juice. Hungarian Barack Pálinka is renowned.

If You Don't Have It

Substitute 2 tbsp (25 mL) apricot brandy with:
- 2 tbsp (25 mL) apricot schnapps
- 2 tbsp (25 mL) apricot liqueur (sweeter)
- 1 tbsp (15 mL) brandy + 1 tbsp (15 mL) apricot nectar

To Vary the Flavor

Substitute 2 tbsp (25 mL) apricot brandy with:
- 2 tbsp (25 mL) peach schnapps
- 2 tbsp (25 mL) cherry brandy

Apricot, Dried

A preservation method for fully ripe apricots; they are typically treated with sulphur dioxide and dried in the sun.

1 lb (500 g) = 2½ to
3 cups (625 to 750 mL)

If You Don't Have It

Substitute 1 oz (30 g) dried apricots with:
- 1 oz (30 g) dried peaches
- 1 oz (30 g) dried nectarines
- 1 oz (30 g) dried apples

Apricot Liqueur

Alcoholic beverage made from mashed apricots and sweetened brandy.

If You Don't Have It
Substitute 2 tbsp (25 mL) apricot liqueur with:
- 2 tbsp (25 mL) apricot schnapps (less sweet; higher alcohol)
- 2 tbsp (25 mL) apricot brandy (less sweet; higher alcohol)
- 2 tbsp (25 mL) apricot nectar (heavier body; no alcohol)

To Vary the Flavor
Substitute 2 tbsp (25 mL) apricot liqueur with:
- 2 tbsp (25 mL) peach or cherry liqueur

Aprium

A fruit cross between apricot and plum that more strongly resembles the apricot.

1 lb (500 g) fresh =
8 to 14 = 2½ cups
(625 mL) sliced or halved

If You Don't Have It
Substitute 1 lb (500 g) apriums with:
- 1 lb (500 g) apricots
- 1 lb (500 g) pluots
- 1 lb (500 g) plums

Aquavit

Also known as akvavit. A caraway-flavored colorless liquor of Scandinavian origin distilled from grain or potatoes.

If You Don't Have It
Substitute 2 tbsp (25 mL) aquavit with:
- 2 tbsp (25 mL) vodka (lacks the aroma of caraway)
- 2 tbsp (25 mL) vodka + ⅛ tsp (0.5 mL) caraway seeds soaked at room temperature for at least 1 month

Aqua Vitae

See BRANDY.

Arak

See ANISE LIQUEUR.

Arame

A sweet and mild dried Japanese seaweed. The skinny dark brown strips can be rehydrated and added to salads or vegetable stir-fries.

If You Don't Have It
Substitute 1 oz (30 g) arame with:
- 1 oz (30 g) hijiki (stronger brine flavor; black color)
- 1 oz (30 g) wakame (green to dark brown color)
- 1 oz (30 g) dulse (stronger brine flavor; maroon color)
- 1 oz (30 g) kombu or kelp (stronger brine flavor; dark brown to black color)

Arborio Rice

See VARIETIES OF RICE (PAGE 591).

Arctic Char

See CHAR.

Ardennes Ham

Also known as Jambon d'Ardennes. Belgian salt-cured, smoked ham with dark brown exterior. Best served in very thin slices.

If You Don't Have It

Substitute 1 lb (500 g) Ardennes ham with:

- 1 lb (500 g) Bayonne ham
- 1 lb (500 g) Westphalian ham (adds juniper and lighter smoked flavors)
- 1 lb (500 g) prosciutto (lacks smoke flavor)
- 1 lb (500 g) serrano or Iberico ham (lacks smoke flavor)
- 1 lb (500 g) other smoked or country ham

Arepa

Thick, Venezuelan flatbread reminiscent of a cross between polenta and a pancake. Often topped or filled with cheese and herbs.

If You Don't Have It

Substitute 1 arepa with:

- 1 sope
- 1 chalupa
- 1 gordita
- 1 corn tortilla (thinner and stiffer)

Armagnac

Brandy produced in southwestern France that is second only to cognac in stature.

If You Don't Have It

Substitute 2 tbsp (25 mL) Armagnac with:

- 2 tbsp (25 mL) cognac (lighter body)

Armenian Cracker Bread

See LAVASH.

Arracacha

Also known as Peruvian carrot and white carrot. A popular vegetable in South America and the Caribbean with a texture like that of potatoes and flavor similar to a combination of parsnip, celery, and carrot with a whiff of roasted chestnuts.

If You Don't Have It

Substitute 1 lb (500 g) arracacha with:

- 1 lb (500 g) potatoes (similar texture; lacks arracacha flavor)
- 4 oz (125 g) potatoes + 4 oz (125 g) parsnips + 4 oz (125 g) carrots + 4 oz (125 g) celeriac

Arrowhead

Also known as Chinese potato. A root vegetable that tastes like a mix of sunchoke and potato with some bitterness.

If You Don't Have It
Substitute 1 cup (250 mL) chopped arrowhead with:
- ½ cup (125 mL) chopped potato + ½ cup (125 mL) chopped sunchoke

Arrowroot Powder

The roots of a dried, ground tropical tuber used as a thickening agent. Use 2 tsp (10 mL) arrowroot to thicken 1 cup (250 mL) liquid.

If You Don't Have It
Substitute 2 tsp (10 mL) arrowroot powder (for thickening) with:
- 1 tbsp (15 mL) quick-cooking tapioca
- 1 heaping tbsp (15 mL) all-purpose flour
- 1½ tsp (7 mL) cornstarch, potato starch, or rice starch
- 1 tsp (5 mL) instant mashed potato flakes

Artichoke Heart

Also known as artichoke bottom. The cup-shaped meaty base, with interior tender leaves attached, of a globe artichoke. The most tender and desirable part of the otherwise fibrous-leafed vegetable.

If You Don't Have It
Substitute 1 cup (250 mL) freshly cooked artichoke hearts with:
- 1 cup (250 mL) frozen artichoke hearts
- 1 cup (250 mL) canned artichoke hearts (saltier flavor from canning brine)
- 1 cup (250 mL) marinated artichoke hearts (more savory flavor from marinade)

To Vary the Flavor
Substitute 1 cup (250 mL) freshly cooked artichoke hearts with:
- 1 cup (250 mL) freshly cooked hearts of palm
- 1 cup (250 mL) canned hearts of palm

Artificial Sweeteners

See SUCRALOSE.

Arugula

Also known as rocket. A pungent, peppery leafy green similar in shape to radish greens.

1 oz (30 g) =
1 cup (250 mL)

If You Don't Have It
Substitute 1 cup (250 mL) arugula with:
- 1 cup (250 mL) watercress
- 1 cup (250 mL) baby spinach leaves (milder flavor; add pepper for more bite)
- 1 cup (250 mL) Belgian endive, dandelion greens, escarole, or radicchio (for salads)

Asadero

Also known as Chihuahua cheese and Oaxaca cheese. A Mexican white cow's milk cheese fashioned in rounds and braids.

> 4 oz (125 g) = 1 cup
> (250 mL) shredded

If You Don't Have It
Substitute 1 oz (30 g) asadero with:
- 1 oz (30 g) Sonoma or Monterey Jack cheese
- 1 oz (30 g) Teleme cheese
- 1 oz (30 g) mozzarella cheese

Asafetida Powder

Also known as devil's dung, and stinking gum. Powdered gum resin with a pungent garlic and onion flavor. Often used in Indian dishes.

If You Don't Have It
Substitute ¼ tsp (1 mL) asafetida powder with:
- ¼ tsp (1 mL) garlic powder + ¼ tsp (1 mL) onion powder (less pungent)

Asiago

Sharp cow's milk cheese from the Veneto dating from the 1500s. Semisoft young Asiago can be sliced and used like provolone.

> 4 oz (125 g) = 1 cup
> (250 mL) grated

If You Don't Have It
Substitute 1 oz (30 g) aged Asiago with:
- 1 oz (30 g) Parmesan (slightly sharper flavor)
- 1 oz (30 g) Grana Padano (slightly sharper flavor)
- 1 oz (30 g) Pecorino Romano (sharper flavor; less sweet)
- 1 oz (30 g) dry Jack cheese (more nutty flavor)

For Better Health
Substitute 1 oz (30 g) aged Asiago with:
- 1 oz (30 g) Sapsago (more herbal flavor; lower in fat)

Asian Celery

See CHINESE CELERY.

Asian Noodles

See A SNAPSHOT OF ASIAN NOODLES (PAGE 588).

Asian Pear

Also known as apple pear. Ultra-juicy, crisp, sweet fruit that ranges from tiny to very large. The flesh is somewhat translucent and the skin can be yellow green to golden brown.

If You Don't Have It
Substitute 1 Asian pear with:
- 1 Bosc pear (less tart; softer flesh)
- 1 apple (similar texture; apple flavor)
- 1 quince (for cooking only; more tart flavor)

Asparagus

A spear-shaped green vegetable that is a member of the lily family. The cultivated plants take several years to mature and require careful tending and harvesting by hand. Many growers bury the stalks to prevent photosynthesis, resulting in the preferred white asparagus.

1 lb (500 g) fresh = 12 to 20 spears = 3½ cups (875 mL) chopped

If You Don't Have It
Substitute 1 lb (500 g) asparagus with:
- 1 lb (500 g) broccoli
- 1 lb (500 g) canned hearts of palm

Asparagus Varieties
Substitute 1 lb (500 g) green asparagus with:
- 1 lb (500 g) white asparagus (milder flavor; more bitter texture)
- 1 lb (500 g) purple asparagus (sweeter, juicier, and more tender)

Aspic Powder

Commercial gelatin powder flavored with fish, poultry, meat, or vegetable stock.

If You Don't Have It
Substitute ¼ oz (7 g) aspic powder with:
- ¼ oz (7 g) flavored gelatin (meat, fish, or vegetable)

Atemoya

A fruit that's a cross between cherimoya and sweetsop. Native to South America and the West Indies, atemoya's sweet, creamy flesh is studded with black seeds and tastes like mango-scented vanilla custard. The grayish green skin is sturdy and covered with a petal-like pattern.

If You Don't Have It
Substitute 1 lb (500 g) atemoya with:
- 1 lb (500 g) cherimoya
- 1 lb (500 g) sweetsop
- 1 lb (500 g) mango + ¼ tsp (1 mL) vanilla extract

See also CHERIMOYA; SWEETSOP.

Aubergine

See EGGPLANT.

Avocado

A member of the laurel family native to Mexico but now grown in California and Florida, the avocado fruit boasts a 7,000-year history of cultivation. The delicately nutty, pale green buttery flesh is best enjoyed raw, particularly mashed into guacamole.

1 lb (500 g) = 2½ cups (625 mL) chopped = 1½ cups (375 mL) puréed

If You Don't Have It

Substitute 1 cup (250 mL) chopped avocado with:
- 1 cup (250 mL) cooked chayote squash (much lower in fat and less creamy; use cooked in soups and dips or prepare as you would yellow summer squash)

Avocado Varieties

Choose 1 cup (250 mL) chopped avocado from these California varieties:
- 1 cup (250 mL) chopped Hass avocado (rich and creamy; best for guacamole, mashing, sauces, and soups)
- 1 cup (250 mL) chopped Fuerte avocado (slightly less rich and creamy)
- 1 cup (250 mL) chopped Pinkerton avocado (slightly less rich and creamy)
- 1 cup (250 mL) chopped Reed avocado (flesh stays firm when ripe; best for salads)
- 1 cup (250 mL) chopped or sliced avocadito (small Fuerte avocado or cocktail avocado best for salads and garnishing)

For Better Health

Substitute 1 cup (250 mL) chopped California avocado with:
- 1 cup (250 mL) chopped Florida avocado (25 to 50% less fat than California avocados)
- ½ cup (125 mL) chopped California avocado + ½ cup (125 mL) chopped tomatillos (for lower-calorie guacamole)
- ½ cup (125 mL) chopped California avocado + ½ cup (125 mL) puréed raw peas (for lower-calorie guacamole)

Avocado Leaves

Often toasted and used like bay leaves.

If You Don't Have It

Substitute 1 toasted avocado leaf with:
- 1 hoja santa leaf (adds aromas of root beer and fennel)
- 2 bay leaves (adds more resinous pine-like aroma)

Awabi

See ABALONE.

Azuki Bean

See THE WIDE WORLD OF DRIED BEANS (PAGE 566).

Babaco to Byrrh

Babaco

Ecuadorian hybrid of papaya with a mild flavor hinting at banana, pineapple and strawberry.

If You Can't Find It
Substitute 1 lb (500 g) babaco with:
- 1 lb (500 g) casaba melon
- 1 lb (500 g) papaya

Baby Broccoli

See BROCCOLINI.

Bacalao

See SALT COD.

Back Bacon

See CANADIAN BACON.

Bacon

Also known as American bacon and streaky bacon. Pork belly that is brined and smoked, sometimes double smoked. Can be purchased in slabs or slices and must be cooked before eating.

If You Don't Have It
Substitute 1 slice (about ¾ oz /22 g) bacon with:
- 1 thin slice (about ¾ oz /22 g) pancetta (wonderful spice aromas; unsmoked)
- ¾ oz (22 g) salt pork (saltier; fattier; unsmoked; best as flavoring in soups, stews, and sauces)
- ¾ oz (22 g) smoked sausage
- ¾ oz (22 g) smoked ham
- ¾ oz (22 g) fatback (unsalted; fattier; unsmoked; best as flavoring in soups, stews, and sauces; or for barding)
- 2 to 3 tsp (10 to 15 mL) real bacon bits

Bacon (cont'd)

1 lb (500 g) raw =
18 to 22 regular slices =
10 to 14 thick slices

1 lb (500 g) cooked
= 1½ cups (375 mL)
crumbled

For Better Health
Substitute 1 slice (about ¾ oz /22 g) bacon with:
- 1 slice turkey bacon (less fat and fewer calories; retains shape better than sliced bacon)
- 1 slice vegetarian bacon (less fat and fewer calories; made from vegetable protein; flavored like smoked bacon)
- 1 slice Canadian or back bacon (less fat and calories)
- ¾ oz (22 g) smoked ham
- 2 to 3 tsp (10 to 15 mL) imitation bacon-flavored bits (vegetarian)

See also CANADIAN BACON; FATBACK; PANCETTA; SALT PORK.

Bacon Bits

Pieces of cooked bacon that have been preserved and dried. Imitation bacon-flavor bits are made from vegetable protein.

If You Don't Have It
Substitute 1 tbsp (15 mL) bacon bits or chips with:
- 1 to 2 slices bacon, crisply cooked, drained, and crumbled
- 1 tbsp (15 mL) imitation bacon-flavored bits (vegetarian)

Bacon Press

A flat, heavy piece of metal, often cast iron, with a handle for gripping that sits atop bacon to prevent curling as it fries.

If You Don't Have It
Substitute a bacon press with:
- heavy skillet (such as cast-iron)
- foil-wrapped brick or flat rock

Bagaceira

See GRAPPA.

Bagel

A yeast bun with a hole in the center. The dense, texture is achieved by boiling the risen dough before baking. Of Eastern European Jewish origin, the bagel first gained popularity in New York City.

If You Don't Have It
Substitute 1 bagel with:
- 1 bialy (flatter; filled with sautéed onions)
- 1 English muffin (slightly smaller; more light and airy crumb; less chewy)
- 1 soft pretzel (less dense)
- 2 slices dense, chewy bread (such as sourdough)

Bagoong

See SHRIMP PASTE.

Baguette

See FRENCH BREAD.

Bainiku

See UMEBOSHI.

Baker's Ammonia

See AMMONIUM BICARBONATE.

Baker's Caramel

A browning agent made from darkly caramelized sugar and used in baked goods such as pumpernickel bread.

If You Don't Have It

Substitute 1 tsp (5 mL) baker's caramel with:
- 1 tsp (5 mL) gravy browning such as Kitchen Bouquet or Gravy Master
- 1 tsp (5 mL): Homemade Baker's Caramel: Stir together ½ cup (125 mL) granulated sugar and ½ cup (125 mL) water in a small, heavy saucepan. Place over medium-low heat and cook, without stirring, until the sugar dissolves completely. Increase the heat to medium-high and bring to a boil. Reduce heat to medium and attach a candy thermometer to the inside of the pan. Boil gently until the mixture turns from clear to dark amber (about 350°F/180°C on the thermometer), 10 to 15 minutes. Do not stir. Every 5 minutes or so, dip a pastry brush in hot water and brush down the insides of the pan to dissolve any sugar crystals there (this helps prevent the caramel from crystallizing). Immediately remove from heat and let cool slightly but not to the point of hardening. Stand back and stir in 3 tbsp (45 mL) hot water to thin the mixture and prevent it from hardening (stand back because the mixture will sputter; wear oven mitts or heatproof silicone gloves to be perfectly safe). Let cool completely and refrigerate in an airtight glass bottle or other container for up to 6 months. Makes about ⅓ cup (75 mL).

Baker's Wax

See PARAFFIN WAX.

Baking Chocolate

See CHOCOLATE, UNSWEETENED.

Baking Pans

See PAN SIZE EQUIVALENTS (PAGE 606); SPECIFIC TYPES.

Baking Powder

Most baking powder in North American is double-acting, which contains two acids that react as leavening agents at different times in the baking process. For delicate baked goods, use aluminum-free baking powder to avoid a tinny aftertaste.

If You Don't Have It

Substitute 1 tsp (5 mL) double-acting baking powder with:

- ¼ tsp (1 mL) baking soda + ¼ tsp (1 mL) cornstarch + ½ tsp (2 mL) cream of tartar
- 1¼ tsp (6 mL) single-acting baking powder
- 1½ tsp (7 mL) phosphate or tartrate baking powder
- 1 tsp (5 mL) ammonium bicarbonate (creates light, airy cookies; best for small baked goods so ammonia odor can evaporate during baking)

To Vary the Flavor

Substitute 1 tsp (5 mL) double-acting baking powder with:

- ¼ tsp (1 mL) baking soda + ½ cup (125 mL) buttermilk or soured milk (reduce liquid in recipe by ½ cup/125 mL)
- ¼ tsp (1 mL) baking soda + ¼ cup (50 mL) molasses (reduce liquid in recipe by 3 tbsp/45 mL and adjust sweetener)

Baking Sheet

Insulated baking sheets, also known as air-bake cookie sheets, have a layer of air insulation between two sheets of metal to promote more even heating and browning.

If You Don't Have It

Substitute a thin, lightweight baking sheet with:

- insulated baking sheet (heats more slowly and evenly; helps prevent burning and premature browning)
- two lightweight baking sheets nested together (simulates an insulated baking sheet; especially good for cookies; helps prevent spreading, burning and premature browning)
- heavy-gauge aluminum baking sheet (helps prevent burning and premature browning)

Baking Soda

Also known as bicarbonate of soda. An alkali used to leaven baked goods. When combined with acidic ingredients, baking soda creates carbon dioxide gas bubbles that cause batter or dough to rise.

1 tsp (5 mL) = 5 g

If You Don't Have It

Substitute 1 tsp (5 mL) baking soda with:

- 1 tsp (5 mL) potassium bicarbonate

Baking Stone

Also known as a pizza stone. Thick, heavy slab of stone that absorbs moisture and creates crisper, deeper brown crusts on bread and pizza cooked in gas or electric ovens.

If You Don't Have It
Substitute a baking stone with:
- unglazed quarry tiles (preferably, high-fired)
- brick oven
- outdoor ceramic cooker or smoker

Baloney

See BOLOGNA.

Balsamic Vinegar

See CHOOSING VINEGAR (PAGE 600).

Balsam Pear

See BITTER MELON.

Bamboo Leaves

To use as a food wrapper, soak dried bamboo leaves in water until pliable.

If You Don't Have It
Substitute bamboo leaves (as a food wrapper) with:
- lotus leaves
- banana leaves
- aluminum foil
- parchment paper

Bamboo Shoot

The inner white section of certain edible young bamboo plants. A basic ingredient in Chinese, Japanese, and other Asian cooking, the mild flavor is reminiscent of artichokes. Available canned or fresh. Fresh bamboo shoots must be cooked to eliminate their toxic hydrocyanic acid.

> 8 oz (250 g) can
> = 1¼ cups
> (300 mL) sliced

If You Don't Have It
Substitute 1 cup (250 mL) freshly cooked bamboo shoots with:
- 1 cup (250 mL) canned bamboo shoots

To Vary the Flavor
Substitute 1 cup (250 mL) freshly cooked bamboo shoots with:
- 1 cup (250 mL) cooked jicama (sweeter)
- 1 cup (250 mL) peeled raw or canned water chestnuts (more crisp)
- 1 cup (250 mL) cooked taro (more starchy)
- 1 cup (250 mL) cooked artichoke hearts (more tender)

Bamboo Skewer

See SKEWER.

Banana

The sweet, starchy, seedless fruit of a tropical perennial herb that resembles a palm tree. North Americans favor yellow Cavendish bananas, but countless varieties with different characteristics are cultivated around the world.

1 lb (500 g) fresh
= 3 to 4 medium =
2 cups (500 mL) sliced
= 1¾ cups (425 mL)
mashed

If You Don't Have It

Substitute 1 lb (500 g) ripe Cavendish bananas with:
- 1 lb (500 g) very ripe black plantains (larger; less sweet; more starchy; best for baking, mashing, and frying)

Banana Varieties

Choose 1 lb (500 g) ripe bananas from other varieties:
- 1 lb (500 g) burro bananas (shorter; adds slight lemon flavor)
- 1 lb (500 g) blue java or ice cream banana (adds sweet ice cream-like flavor)
- 1 lb (500 g) dwarf or finger bananas (sweeter)
- 1 lb (500 g) red bananas (sweeter; best for baking)
- 1 lb (500 g) manzano bananas (smaller; drier flesh; adds strawberry-apple flavor)
- 1 lb (500 g) Orinoco bananas (adds strawberry flavor)

See also PLANTAIN.

Banana Bud

Also known as banana blossom and banana heart. The interior of the male part of the banana flower is blanched several times to remove the bitterness.

1 lb (500 g) = about 1 bud

If You Don't Have It

Substitute 1 lb (500 g) banana buds with:
- 1 lb (500 g) artichokes

Banana Leaves

Often used for wrapping and flavoring steamed foods such as tamales. According to Mexican cooking authority Rick Bayless "banana leaves impart a very special herby-green flavor that you can't get from any other leaf."

1 lb (500 g) = 10 to 12
12-inch/(30 cm) squares

If You Don't Have It

Substitute banana leaves (as a food wrapper) with:
- corn husks (much smaller; adds mild corn aroma)
- hoja santa leaves (much smaller; adds aromas of root beer and fennel)
- parchment paper (no flavor)
- aluminum foil (no flavor; reduce cooking time slightly)

Banana Pepper

See SWEET PEPPERS; CHOOSING FRESH CHILES (PAGE 582).

Banana Squash

This variety is so large that grocers usually cut it into smaller chunks before displaying it. It's tasty, but the biggest virtue of banana squash is its beautifully golden flesh.

If You Don't Have It

Substitute 1 cup (250 mL) chopped banana squash with:
- 1 cup (250 mL) chopped butternut squash (less fruity flavor)
- 1 cup (250 mL) chopped buttercup squash (less fruity flavor; drier texture)
- 1 cup (250 mL) chopped delicata squash (less fruity flavor)

B&B

Also known as Bénédictine and Brandy. A liqueur that blends Bénédictine — a sweet French cognac-based liqueur flavored with herbs and fruit peels — with brandy.

If You Don't Have It

Substitute 2 tbsp (25 mL) B&B with:
- 1 tbsp (15 mL) Bénédictine + 1 tbsp (15 mL) brandy
- 2 tbsp (25 mL) Bénédictine

Barbados Cherry

See ACEROLA.

Barbados Sugar

See SUGAR, RAW.

Barbecue Sauce

A thick and sweet tomato-based sauce used to baste and/or accompany barbecued meat. Endless variations exist and can include ingredients such as onion, mustard, spices, garlic, beer, wine, and vinegar.

If You Don't Have It

Substitute 1 cup (250 mL) barbecue sauce with:
- 1 cup (250 mL) ketchup + $\frac{1}{2}$ to 1 tsp (2 to 5 mL) liquid smoke seasoning
- 1 cup (250 mL) canned barbecue Sloppy Joe sauce
- 1 cup (250 mL) Homemade Barbecue Sauce: Combine 2 cups (500 mL) ketchup, 3 tbsp (45 mL) dark brown sugar, 3 tbsp (45 mL) cider vinegar, 2 tbsp (25 mL) yellow prepared mustard, 2 tbsp (25 mL) Worcestershire sauce, 2 tsp (10 mL) paprika, $1\frac{1}{2}$ tsp (7 mL) salt, 1 tsp (5 mL) garlic powder, $\frac{1}{2}$ tsp (2 mL) onion powder, and $\frac{1}{2}$ tsp (2 mL) ground black pepper in a saucepan. Bring to a boil over high heat. Reduce heat to medium-low and simmer until thickened, about 20 minutes. Makes 3 cups (750 mL).

Barbecuing

A dry-heat cooking method that uses the indirect, low heat (200° to 230°F/90° to 110°C) of smoldering wood to slowly cook and smoke food.

If You Don't Have It

Substitute barbecuing with:

- gas or charcoal grilling (faster; higher heat; much less smoke flavor)
- gas or charcoal grilling + liquid smoke seasoning brushed onto food or added to marinade or sauce
- stovetop smoking (using a covered stovetop smoker with wood chips in the bottom and food in the top)

See also GRILL.

Barley

A robust grain dating from the Stone Age, barley is a versatile ingredient in cereals, breads, soups, and pilafs. When malted, it is used to make whiskey and beer. Pearl barley is the most common variety but hulled or whole-grain barley is more nutritious because the outer layer of bran is not polished away.

> 1 cup (250 mL) medium pearl barley =
> 3½ to 4 cups
> (875 mL to 1 L) cooked
>
> 1 cup (250 mL) quick-cooking = 3 cups (750 mL) cooked

If You Don't Have It

Substitute 1 cup (250 mL) pearl barley with:

- 1 cup (250 mL) Arborio or Carnaroli rice (less chewy; more starchy)
- 2 cups (500 mL) orzo pasta (less nutritious)
- 1 cup (250 mL) buckwheat groats (more earthy and chewy)
- 1 cup (250 mL) Scotch barley (more chewy and flavorful)
- 1 cup (250 mL) barley grits (more chewy and flavorful)

To Save Time

Substitute 1 cup (250 mL) pearl barley with:

- 1¼ cups (300 mL) quick-cooking barley (takes 10 minutes to cook)

For Better Health

Substitute 1 cup (250 mL) pearl barley with:

- 1 cup (250 mL) hulled or whole-grain barley (chewier; higher in fiber; increase liquid and cooking time)

Barley Flour

See CHOOSING AMONG WHOLE-GRAIN AND ALTERNATIVE FLOURS (PAGE 586).

Barley Grits

Barley grains that have been hulled and cracked into pieces. Available in health food stores.

If You Don't Have It

Substitute 1 cup (250 mL) barley grits with:

- 1 cup (250 mL) buckwheat grits (more earthy, grassy flavor)
- 1 cup (250 mL) hominy grits (more creamy texture)

Barley Malt Syrup

Also known as malted cereal syrup and malt syrup. Similar to molasses, barley malt syrup is used mostly in beer and bread making.

If You Don't Have It
Substitute 1 cup (250 mL) barley malt syrup with:
- ⅔ cup (150 mL) molasses
- ¾ cup (175 mL) rice bran syrup
- ¾ cup (175 mL) maple syrup

See also SUGAR, GRANULATED.

Barracuda

Also known as California or Pacific barracuda. Firm-fleshed, moderate-fat fish similar to mahi-mahi.

If You Don't Have It
Substitute 1 lb (500 g) barracuda with:
- 1 lb (500 g) mahi-mahi
- 1 lb (500 g) swordfish
- 1 lb (500 g) mako shark
- 1 lb (500 g) tuna
- 1 lb (500 g) pompano
- 1 lb (500 g) wahoo or other mackerel

Basil

An annual plant that originated in India, sweet basil — with tender green leaves and a flavor reminiscent of cloves — has become the signature fresh herb of the Italian kitchen. Most renowned as the base of pesto, a paste of pine nuts, garlic, extra virgin olive oil, and Parmesan, and Pecorino cheeses.

If You Don't Have It
Substitute 1 tbsp (15 mL) chopped fresh basil with:
- 1 tsp (5 mL) dried basil
- 1 tsp (5 mL) dried Italian seasoning

To Vary the Flavor
Substitute 1 tbsp (15 mL) chopped fresh basil with:
- 1 tbsp (15 mL) chopped fresh oregano
- 1 tbsp (15 mL) chopped fresh mint (works well in Thai dishes)
- 1 tbsp (15 mL) chopped fresh parsley or cilantro (especially for sauces such as pesto)
- 2 tsp (10 mL) chopped fresh thyme

Basil Varieties
Choose 1 tbsp (15 mL) chopped fresh basil from these varieties:
- 1 tbsp (15 mL) chopped fresh opal or purple basil (purple color; milder flavor than sweet basil; purple ruffle basil has serrated leaves)
- 1 tbsp (15 mL) chopped fresh Thai basil (more anise-like aroma than sweet basil)
- 1 tbsp (15 mL) chopped fresh lemon basil (more lemony aroma than sweet basil)

Basil (cont'd)

- 1 tbsp (15 mL) chopped fresh holy basil (more lemony aroma than sweet basil)
- 1 tbsp (15 mL) chopped fresh cinnamon basil (more cinnamon-like aroma than sweet basil)

Basmati Rice

See VARIETIES OF RICE (PAGE 591).

Bass

See BLACK SEA BASS; GROUPER; STRIPED BASS.

Batata

See BONIATO.

Bauchant

See ORANGE LIQUEUR.

Bavarian Blue Cheese

Mild, creamy German blue cheese.

If You Don't Have It
Substitute 1 oz (30 g) Bavarian blue cheese with:
- 1 oz (30 g) Blue Castello
- 1 oz (30 g) Danish blue (stronger flavor)
- 1 oz (30 g) Gorgonzola (more pungent flavor)

Bay Leaf

Also known as bay laurel and laurel leaf. Aromatic leaf of the Mediterranean evergreen bay laurel tree, used to season soups, stews, vegetables, and meats. Ancient Greeks and Romans revered the leaf as a symbol of triumph. Turkish bay leaves are about half the size yet have more complex flavor than the California variety. Use about two Turkish bay leaves to replace one California bay leaf.

1 whole leaf = ¼ tsp (1 mL) crushed

If You Don't Have It
Substitute 2 dried bay leaves with:
- 1 fresh bay leaf
- ½ tsp (2 mL) crushed dried bay leaf

To Vary the Flavor
Substitute 1 dried bay leaf with:
- ¼ tsp (1 mL) juniper berries (adds characteristic flavor of gin; especially good in a bouquet garni for stews or crushed in a spice rub for grilled meats)

Bayonne Ham

Also known as jambon Bayonne. Mildly smoked boneless French ham that's cured in wine.

If You Don't Have It

Substitute 1 lb (500 g) Bayonne ham with:
- 1 lb (500 g) Ardennes ham
- 1 lb (500 g) York ham
- 1 lb (500 g) Westphalian ham (adds juniper flavor)
- 1 lb (500 g) prosciutto (lacks smoke flavor)
- 1 lb (500 g) serrano or Iberico ham (lacks smoke flavor)
- 1 lb (500 g) any mildly smoked ham

Bean Curd

See TOFU.

Bean Herb

See EPAZOTE.

Bean Sauce

Also known as bean paste. Seasonings prepared from fermented soybeans, popular in many Asian cuisines. Styles vary from thin to thick, smooth to chunky, salty to sweet.

If You Don't Have It

Substitute 1 tbsp (15 mL) Chinese brown bean sauce with:
- 1 tbsp (15 mL) hoisin sauce (milder)
- 1 tbsp (15 mL) Thai bean sauce (more salty)
- 1 tbsp (15 mL) black bean sauce (more salty; stronger flavor)
- 1 tbsp (15 mL) chile bean sauce (more salty and spicy)

See also BLACK BEAN SAUCE; CHILE PASTE; RED BEAN PASTE.

Beans, Dried

See FERMENTED BLACK BEANS; REFRIED BEANS; SWITCHING LENTILS (PAGE 569); THE WIDE WORLD OF DRIED BEANS (PAGE 566).

Bean Sprouts

See MUNG BEAN SPROUTS.

Beans, Shelling

See BLACK-EYED PEAS, FRESH; CRANBERRY BEAN; EDAMAME; FAVA BEAN; LIMA BEAN; PEAS, SHELLING.

Beans, Snap

See GREEN BEAN; YARD-LONG BEAN.

Bean Threads

See A SNAPSHOT OF ASIAN NOODLES (PAGE 588).

Bear

Popular in Germany and Russia, bear meat is high in protein and low in fat and calories. Cook wild bear meat thoroughly to avoid trichinosis.

If You Don't Have It

Substitute 1 lb (500 g) bear meat with:
- 1 lb (500 g) venison such as elk, moose, or caribou
- 1 lb (500 g) buffalo
- 1 lb (500 g) beef (higher fat and calories)

Beaufort Cheese

A fine French cheese similar to Swiss Gruyère with a rich nutty flavor and just a few small holes.

If You Don't Have It

Substitute 1 oz (30 g) Beaufort cheese with:
- 1 oz (30 g) Gruyère
- 1 oz (30 g) Comté

Beau Monde® Seasoning

A commercial spice blend including dried onion, celery seeds, and salt.

If You Don't Have It

Substitute 1 tsp (5 mL) Beau Monde® Seasoning with:
- ½ tsp (2 mL) celery salt + ½ tsp (2 mL) onion powder
- 1 tsp (5 mL) seasoned salt
- ½ tsp (2 mL) table salt
- ½ tsp (2 mL) Mei Yen seasoning

Beaumont Cheese

Also known as Tomme de Beaumont. French cow's milk cheese.

If You Don't Have It

Substitute 1 oz (30 g) Beaumont cheese with:
- 1 oz (30 g) Muenster
- 1 oz (30 g) Reblochon

Beechnut

Also known as beechmast. Nuts of the beech tree widely used as animal food and as food for people during times of famine.

If You Don't Have It

Substitute 1 cup (250 mL) shelled beechnuts with:
- 1 cup (250 mL) hazelnuts
- 1 cup (250 mL) chestnuts

Beef

The best cattle breeds for beef include Angus, Kobe (Wagyu), and Piedmontese.

If You Don't Have It

Substitute 1 lb (500 g) beef with:
- 1 lb (500 g) buffalo (leaner)
- 1 lb (500 g) venison (leaner; if wild-caught, marinate in wine or vinegar to tame the gamey taste)

See also BEEF, GROUND; JERKY.

Beef, Ground

Tough yet flavorful cuts of meat are often ground to reduce their toughness while keeping the flavor. Among popular cuts of ground beef, ground chuck is the most flavorful, followed by ground round and ground sirloin.

If You Don't Have It
Substitute 1 lb (500 g) ground beef with:
- 1 lb (500 g) ground lamb, pork, or veal (a combination of ground beef, pork, and veal is traditional for meat loaf and meatballs)

For Better Health
Substitute 1 lb (500 g) ground beef (30% fat) with:
- 1 lb (500 g) ground chuck (25 to 30% fat)
- 1 lb (500 g) lean ground round (20 to 25% fat)
- 1 lb (500 g) extra-lean ground sirloin (15% fat)
- 1 lb (500 g) ground turkey or ground turkey with dark meat
- 1 lb (500 g) ground pork loin
- 1 lb (500 g) ground chicken
- 1 lb (500 g) vegetarian ground beef or crumbles (less chewy)
- 1 lb (500 g) tofu, frozen, thawed, and crumbled with a few quick pulses in a food processor (less chewy; less flavorful)
- 1 cup (250 mL) textured vegetable protein granules, reconstituted in $1\frac{1}{2}$ to 2 cups (375 to 500 mL) vegetable stock or other liquid (less chewy; much less flavorful)

Beef Jerky

See BILTONG; JERKY.

Beef Stock

See STOCK, BEEF.

Beer

Beverage with a low alcohol content (from 3 to 12%) brewed from water, malted barley or other cereal grains, hops, and yeast. Beers, including lager and Pilsner, are typically bottom-fermented (the yeast sinks in the fermentation tank). Ales, which are top-fermented (the yeast rises in the fermentation tank), are more full-flavored and frequently higher in alcohol.

If You Don't Have It
Substitute 1 cup (250 mL) beer (for soups and stews) with:
- 1 cup (250 mL) chicken or beef stock + 2 dashes Angostura bitters (optional)
- 1 cup (250 mL) red wine
- 1 cup (250 mL) sake (Japanese rice wine; less bitter, slightly sweet flavor; lighter body)

Beer Styles
Choose 1 cup (250 mL) beer from these specific styles:
- 1 cup (250 mL) lager (light color; mild flavor; light body; bubbly)
- 1 cup (250 mL) malt liquor (similar to lager; higher alcohol; fuller body)

Beer (cont'd)

- 1 cup (250 mL) pale ale (slightly bitter; fruity; medium body)
- 1 cup (250 mL) India pale ale (bitter; fruity; higher alcohol; medium to full body)
- 1 cup (250 mL) porter or stout (dark color; bitter flavor; full body)
- 1 cup (250 mL) wheat beer (light color; slightly sweet flavor; light body)
- 1 cup (250 mL) bock beer (dark color; slightly sweet flavor; full body)

For Better Health

Substitute 1 cup (250 mL) beer with:

- 1 cup (250 mL) light beer (fewer calories)
- 1 cup (250 mL) nonalcoholic beer

Beer Bean

See EDAMAME.

Beer Cheese

See BIERKÄSE.

Beet

Also known as beetroot (British). Edible globular root, most commonly scarlet in color, but also yellow and sometimes white. For the best flavor and color, leave the beet's peel and stem on during cooking.

> 1 lb (500 g) =
> 3 to 5 medium =
> 2 cups (500 mL) diced

If You Don't Have It

Substitute 1 cup (250 mL) chopped red beets with:

- 1 cup (250 mL) chopped canned beets
- 1 cup (250 mL) chopped beefsteak tomatoes

Beet Varieties

Choose 1 cup (250 mL) chopped beets from these varieties:

- 1 cup (250 mL) chopped golden beets (slightly sweeter; orange color)
- 1 cup (250 mL) chopped Chioggia beets (concentric red and white rings of color)
- 1 cup (250 mL) chopped baby beets (sweeter; quick-cooking)

Beet Greens

Edible green leafy tops of beets.

> 1 lb (500 g) fresh
> = 1⅓ to 2 cups
> (325 to 500 mL) cooked

If You Don't Have It

Substitute 1 lb (500 g) beet greens with:

- 1 lb (500 g) red or green chard
- 1 lb (500 g) turnip greens
- 1 lb (500 g) mature spinach

Begonia

See PICKING EDIBLE FLOWERS (PAGE 604).

Belacan

See SHRIMP PASTE.

Belgian Endive

A variety of chicory with a long tight head that resembles a small ear of corn. Leaves are white with some yellow, green, or red tips. Pleasantly bitter flavor. Eaten raw in salads or braised as a vegetable.

If You Don't Have It
Substitute 1 cup (250 mL) Belgian endive with:
- 1 cup (250 mL) radicchio (red color; bitter flavor)
- 1 cup (250 mL) arugula (green color; more tender; less bitter; more peppery)
- 1 cup (250 mL) watercress (green color; more tender; less bitter; more peppery)

See also CHICORY.

Bell Pepper

Named for their shape, bell peppers all start out green but some varieties ripen to red, orange, or yellow and become sweeter.

1 lb (500 g) = 2 large
= 2½ cups (625 mL)
chopped = 3 cups
(750 mL) sliced

If You Don't Have It
Substitute 1 cup (250 mL) chopped fresh bell pepper with:
- 1 cup (250 mL) chopped fresh, canned, or bottled pimiento
- 1 cup (250 mL) chopped fresh Cubanelle peppers
- 1 cup (250 mL) chopped fresh banana peppers
- 1 cup (250 mL) chopped fresh bull's horn peppers
- 1 cup (250 mL) chopped fresh Anaheim peppers (spicier)
- 1 cup (250 mL) chopped fresh poblano peppers (spicier)
- ½ cup (125 mL) dried bell peppers

See also SWEET PEPPER; CHOOSING FRESH CHILES (PAGE 582).

Bell Pepper, Roasted Red

Whole peppers charred quickly over an open flame, such as an oven broiler, barbecue, or open gas flame, then peeled. The partially cooked flesh develops a sweet, caramelized flavor.

If You Don't Have It
Substitute 1 cup (250 mL) chopped roasted red peppers with:
- 1 cup (250 mL) chopped jarred pimientos (drained)

Bellyfish

See MONKFISH.

Bel Paese

A versatile, semisoft cheese of Italian origin with a mild flavor and buttery texture. It melts smoothly for pizza or casseroles and is also delicious with fruit.

If You Don't Have It

Substitute 1 oz (30 g) Bel Paese with:
- 1 oz (30 g) Monterey Jack
- 1 oz (30 g) mozzarella
- 1 oz (30 g) Muenster
- 1 oz (30 g) Gouda
- 1 oz (30 g) Fontina

Beluga

See CHANGING ROE (PAGE 594).

Bénédictine

A sweet cognac-based liqueur flavored with herbs and fruit peels, Bénédictine is named after the monks of the Abbey at Fecamp in Normandy, who developed it in the early 1500s.

If You Don't Have It

Substitute 2 tbsp (25 mL) Bénédictine with:
- 2 tbsp (25 mL) B&B (less sweet)
- 2 tbsp (25 mL) Chartreuse (green or yellow color)
- 2 tbsp (25 mL) Drambuie (mild licorice flavor)

See also B&B.

Berbere

Ethiopian blend of spices used to season soups and stews. May be a dry spice mix or a wet paste including cardamom, coriander, fenugreek, garlic, red pepper, and other spices.

If You Don't Have It

Substitute 1 tbsp (15 mL) berbere with:
- 1 tbsp (15 mL) harissa (spicier; less aromatic)
- 1 tbsp (15 mL) Homemade Berbere Paste: Toast 1 tsp (5 mL) coriander seeds, 1 tsp (5 mL) black peppercorns, 1 tsp (5 mL) cardamom seeds, 1 tsp (5 mL) fenugreek seeds, $\frac{1}{2}$ tsp (2 mL) cumin seeds, $\frac{1}{4}$ tsp (1 mL) allspice berries, and $\frac{1}{4}$ tsp (1 mL) whole cloves in a dry skillet over medium heat until fragrant, about 2 minutes. Remove spices from pan. Let cool, then coarsely grind in a spice grinder or with a mortar and pestle. Heat 1 tbsp (15 mL) vegetable oil in the same pan over medium-low heat and add $\frac{1}{2}$ cup (125 mL) minced fresh onion. Cook until onion is soft, about 5 minutes. Add 2 minced garlic cloves and 2 tsp (10 mL) minced fresh ginger. Cook for 1 minute. Remove from heat and stir in 2 tbsp (25 mL) mild paprika, ground spice blend, 2 tbsp (25 mL) vegetable oil, 1 tbsp (15 mL) kosher salt, $\frac{1}{2}$ to 1 tsp (2 to 5 mL) ground cayenne pepper and $\frac{1}{4}$ tsp (1 mL) grated nutmeg. Let cool. Refrigerate for up to 3 weeks in an airtight container. Makes about $\frac{3}{4}$ cup (175 mL).

Bergamot

An herb in the mint family used in the cooking of Mexico and the Southwest United States.

If You Don't Have It

- Substitute 1 tbsp (15 mL) chopped fresh bergamot with:
- 1 tbsp (15 mL) chopped fresh oregano, basil, or mint

See also ORANGE, SOUR.

Bergamot Orange

See ORANGE, SOUR.

Berry

See SPECIFIC TYPES.

Beurre Manié

Also known as kneaded butter. A paste of softened butter and flour that is used to thicken and enrich sauces.

If You Don't Have It

Substitute 2 tbsp (25 mL) beurre manié with:
- 2 tbsp (25 mL) roux
- 2 tbsp (25 mL) Homemade Beurre Manié: Combine 1 tbsp (15 mL) softened butter and 1 tbsp (15 mL) all-purpose flour. Knead together.
- 1½ tbsp (22 mL) tapioca starch whisked with 2 tbsp (25 mL) cold water
- 1½ tsp (7 mL) cornstarch whisked with 2 tsp (10 mL) cold water

Bialy

Jewish-American yeast roll that's a first cousin to bagels. Instead of a center hole, bialys have a center depression that's often filled with onions. Named after the Polish city of Bialystok.

If You Don't Have It

Substitute 1 bialy with:
- 1 onion or plain bagel (thicker)
- 1 English muffin (smaller; more light and airy crumb; less chewy; no onion flavor)
- 2 slices dense, chewy bread (such as sourdough; no onion flavor)
- 1 soft pretzel

Bibb Lettuce

See BUTTERHEAD LETTUCE.

Bicarbonate of Soda

See BAKING SODA.

Bierkäse

Also known as beer cheese. Soft ripened German cheese with a sharp taste.

If You Don't Have It
Substitute 1 oz (30 g) Bierkäse with:
- 1 oz (30 g) Limburger

Bierwurst

Garlicky German dark red cooked sausage most frequently sliced and served on sandwiches.

If You Don't Have It
Substitute 1 lb (500 g) Bierwurst with:
- 1 lb (500 g) cervelat
- 1 lb (500 g) Blockwurst
- 1 lb (500 g) bologna
- 1 lb (500 g) cooked salami

Bilberry

Also known as blaeberry, whinberry, and whortleberry. A bluish purple berry related to the blueberry and cranberry. Common in the British Isles and far northern climes of North America.

1 pint = 3 cups (750 mL)

If You Don't Have It
Substitute 1 cup (250 mL) bilberries with:
- 1 cup (250 mL) huckleberries (slightly sweeter)
- 1 cup (250 mL) cranberries (red color; more tart)
- 1 cup (250 mL) blueberries (larger and sweeter)
- 1 cup (250 mL) red currants (red color)

Biltong

Dried and sometimes smoked meat indigenous to southern Africa. One version is prepared by coating a large cut of beef with spice rub and vinegar, then hanging it to air-dry and later smoke. This type is more tender than the type made from drying seasoned strips of zebra or other game meat in the sun.

If You Don't Have It
Substitute 1 oz (30 g) biltong with:
- 1 oz (30 g) beef jerky (less spicy; more neutral flavor)
- 1 oz (30 g) pemmican (more complex flavor)

For Better Health
- 1 oz (30 g) turkey jerky (leaner)
- 1 oz (30 g) vegetarian jerky (leaner)

See also JERKY; PEMMICAN.

Bindenfleisch

See BÜNDNERFLEISCH.

Bing Cherry

See CHERRY.

Biscotti

Crisp Italian cookies that are twice baked. Traditionally eaten by dunking in sweet dessert wine or coffee.

If You Don't Have It
Substitute 1 lb (500 g) biscotti with:
- 1 lb (500 g) mandlebrot (adds almond flavor)
- 1 lb (500 g) amaretti (adds almond flavor)

Biscuit

See CRACKER.

Biscuit Cutter

Circular implement that's typically smooth on the interior and scalloped on the outside. Used for cutting quick-bread biscuit dough.

If You Don't Have It
Substitute a biscuit cutter with:
- cookie cutter of any shape
- clean tuna can or other can with both ends removed
- inverted wine or drinking glass

See also COOKIE CUTTER.

Biscuit Mix

Boxed mixture of flour and leavening that requires only the addition of milk to make biscuit dough. With eggs added, the mix can also be used to prepare pancakes, waffles, and other quick breads.

If You Don't Have It
Substitute 1 cup (250 mL) biscuit mix with:
- 1 cup (250 mL) Homemade Biscuit Mix: Whisk together 3 cups (750 mL) cake or pastry flour, $\frac{1}{3}$ cup (75 mL) powdered buttermilk or whole milk, 1 tbsp (15 mL) baking powder, and 1 tsp (5 mL) salt. When ready to bake, cut in $\frac{1}{2}$ cup (125 mL) cold butter or vegetable shortening. Use immediately or refrigerate in an airtight container for up to 3 months (without butter). Makes about $3\frac{1}{3}$ cups (825 mL) (without butter).

Bishop's Weed

See AJWAIN.

Bison

See BUFFALO.

Bitter Melon

Also known as balsam pear. Sour fruit used in Chinese cooking. Bitter melon resembles a bumpy-skinned cucumber with green to yellow orange color.

If You Don't Have It
Substitute 1 cup (250 mL) chopped bitter melon with:
- 1 cup (250 mL) chopped winter melon (less bitter)

See also LOOFAH, ANGLED.

Bitter Orange

See ORANGE, SOUR.

Bitters

A distilled, high-alcohol blend of barks, flowers, herbs, seeds, roots, and other aromatics. Bitters are used to flavor many cocktails and foods. Also called upon to aid digestion, stimulate the appetite, and cure hangovers.

If You Don't Have It
- Substitute ¼ tsp (1 mL) bitters with:
- ½ tsp (2 mL) Worcestershire sauce (for cooking and savory drinks)

Bitter Varieties
Choose ¼ tsp (1 mL) bitters from these specific types:
- ¼ tsp (1 mL) Angostura bitters
- ¼ tsp (1 mL) Peychaud's bitters
- ¼ tsp (1 mL) orange bitters (adds orange flavor)
- ¼ tsp (1 mL) Pommeranzen bitters (adds orange flavor)

See also AMER PICON; FERNET BRANCA.

Bittersweet Chocolate

See CHOCOLATE, BITTERSWEET.

Blacang

See SHRIMP PASTE.

Blachan

See SHRIMP PASTE.

Black Bean

See THE WIDE WORLD OF DRIED BEANS (PAGE 566).

Black Bean Sauce

A distinctively flavored condiment prepared from fermented black beans and garlic, and sometimes seasoned with star anise. Hot black bean sauce contains chile paste, as well as garlic, toasted sesame oil, and sugar.

If You Don't Have It
Substitute 1 tbsp (15 mL) black bean sauce with:
- 1 tbsp (15 mL) hot black bean sauce (spicier)
- 1 tbsp (15 mL) black bean and garlic sauce (adds garlic flavor)

To Vary the Flavor
Substitute 1 tbsp (15 mL) black bean sauce with:
- 1 tbsp (15 mL) Thai bean sauce (milder)
- 1 tbsp (15 mL) Chinese brown bean sauce (milder; less salty)

See also BEAN SAUCE.

Blackberry

Also known as bramble. A large, deep purple berry that grows wild on thorny bushes. In England, blackberries are often combined with apples to make pie.

> 1 pint fresh =
> 2 cups (500 mL)
>
> 10 oz (300 g) frozen =
> 2 cups (500 mL)

If You Don't Have It

Substitute 1 cup (250 mL) blackberries with:
- 1 cup (250 mL) loganberries (red color)
- 1 cup (250 mL) boysenberries (slightly sweeter)
- 1 cup (250 mL) olallieberries (larger; sweeter)
- 1 cup (250 mL) raspberries (smaller; sweeter)

See also MARIONBERRY.

Black Cod

See SABLEFISH.

Black Corinth

See CHAMPAGNE GRAPES.

Black Currant

See CURRANT, FRESH.

Black Currant Jelly

See CURRANT JELLY.

Black-Eyed Peas, Fresh

Also known as cowpeas and southernpeas. If you've only ever tried them dried, try to find some black-eyed beauties in the shell. They can be prepared like fresh lima beans but have a more complex, earthy, almost nutty taste.

> 1 lb (500 g) fresh in shell
> = 1¼ cups (300 mL)
> shelled

If You Don't Have It

Substitute 1 lb (500 g) fresh black-eyed peas (weighed in shell) with:
- 1 lb (500 g) fresh cranberry beans (cream and red-speckled color)
- 1 lb (500 g) fresh Dragon Tongue beans (deep reddish brown and cream color)
- 1 lb (500 g) fresh Tongue of Fire beans (green and red color)
- 1 lb (500 g) fresh Romano beans (green color)
- 1 lb (500 g) fresh Kentucky Wonder beans (green color)
- 1 lb (500 g) fresh lima beans (green color)
- 1 lb (500 g) fresh edamame (green color)

See also PEAS, SHELLING; THE WIDE WORLD OF DRIED BEANS (PAGE 566).

Blackfish

Also known as black trout, Chinese Steelhead, and tautog. Northwest Atlantic fish in the wrasse family with delicate flavor, tiny bones, and dark skin.

If You Don't Have It
Substitute 1 lb (500 g) blackfish with:
- 1 lb (500 g) grouper
- 1 lb (500 g) striped bass
- 1 lb (500 g) red snapper (flakier)

Black Forest Ham

A moist German ham that is prepared by salt-curing, air-drying, and smoking over fire or pine wood. The traditional practice of coating the ham in beef blood to produce a dark surface has given way to a spice rub and smoking that create a similar hue.

If You Don't Have It
Substitute 1 lb (500 g) Black Forest ham with:
- 1 lb (500 g) Bradenham ham (similar black exterior)
- 1 lb (500 g) Virginia ham (such as Smithfield ham; milder flavor)
- 1 lb (500 g) Westphalian ham (adds juniper aroma)
- 1 lb (500 g) prosciutto

Black Mustard Seeds

See MUSTARD SEEDS.

Black Onion Seeds

See NIGELLA.

Black Pepper

See PEPPERCORN.

Black Pudding

See BLOOD SAUSAGE.

Black Sea Bass

Caught off the Atlantic coast of the U.S., this popular fish responds well to any style of cooking. The succulent flesh is the result of a diet rich in shrimp, crabs, and mollusks.

If You Don't Have It
Substitute 1 lb (500 g) black sea bass with:
- 1 lb (500 g) rockfish
- 1 lb (500 g) red snapper
- 1 lb (500 g) grouper
- 1 lb (500 g) ocean perch
- 1 lb (500 g) striped bass
- 1 lb (500 g) tilefish
- 1 lb (500 g) catfish

Black Sesame Seeds

See SESAME SEEDS.

Black Sturgeon Roe

See CHANGING ROE (PAGE 594).

Black Trout

See BLACKFISH.

Black Trumpet Mushroom

See SHUFFLING MUSHROOMS (PAGE 572).

Black Walnut

See WALNUT.

Blaeberry

See BILBERRY.

Blender

A small electrical kitchen appliance with a tall cylinder shaped like a pitcher with short rotating blades at the base. Excellent for puréeing and for chopping small amounts of foods.

If You Don't Have It
Substitute a blender with:
- food processor fitted with a metal blade (best for puréeing soups and sauces; avoid overfilling; not recommended for crushing ice)
- immersion blender (for immersing into soups or sauces to purée)

Bleu d'Auvergne

A soft-rind cow's milk blue cheese from France that is designated with the appellation d'origine contrôlée (AOC).

If You Don't Have It
Substitute 1 oz (30 g) Bleu d'Auvergne with:
- 1 oz (30 g) Bleu des Causses
- 1 oz (30 g) Roquefort
- 1 oz (30 g) Fourme d'Ambert
- 1 oz (30 g) Maytag Blue

Bleu de Bresse

Soft-blue, full-fat cow's milk cheese from the Rhone-Alps region of France.

If You Don't Have It
Substitute 1 oz (30 g) Bleu de Bresse with:
- 1 oz (30 g) Blue Castello
- 1 oz (30 g) Cambozola
- 1 oz (30 g) Gorgonzola
- 1 oz (30 g) Brie (less pungent)

Bleu de Gex

French cow's milk appellation d'origine contrôlée (AOC) *blue cheese from Franche-Comté. The word Gex is stamped into the rind.*

If You Don't Have It
Substitute 1 oz (30 g) Bleu de Gex with:
- 1 oz (30 g) Fourme d'Ambert
- 1 oz (30 g) Stilton

Bleu des Causses

Likened to a cow's milk version of Roquefort, this appellation d'origine contrôlée (AOC) *blue cheese is produced in the Midday-Pyrenees.*

If You Don't Have It
Substitute 1 oz (30 g) Bleu des Causses with:
- 1 oz (30 g) Bleu d'Auvergne (milder)
- 1 oz (30 g) Roquefort
- 1 oz (30 g) Fourme d'Ambert
- 1 oz (30 g) Maytag Blue

Blockwurst

Spicy German pork sausage, sold ready-to-eat for sandwiches.

If You Don't Have It
Substitute 1 lb (500 g) Blockwurst with:
- 1 lb (500 g) cervelat
- 1 lb (500 g) Bierwurst
- 1 lb (500 g) bologna
- 1 lb (500 g) cooked salami

Blood Orange

See ORANGE, BLOOD.

Blood Sausage

Also known as black pudding, blood pudding, and boudin noir. A style of sausage dating from ancient times and still produced in the British Isles and many European countries. Typically made with pork blood, cereal grain, and seasonings.

If You Don't Have It
Substitute 1 lb (500 g) blood sausage with these specific types:
- 1 lb (500 g) Blutwurst (German)
- 1 lb (500 g) boudin rouge (Cajun)
- 1 lb (500 g) morcilla (Spanish)
- 1 lb (500 g) Zungenwurst (German; includes tongue)

Blueberry

Sweet-tart, smooth, blue berries with grayish blush. Cultivars of wild blueberries are a great success of commercial berry cultivation, having been introduced in New Jersey in 1920.

> 1 pint fresh
> = 2 cups (500 mL)
>
> 10 oz (300 g) frozen
> = 1½ cups (375 mL)

If You Don't Have It

Substitute 1 cup (250 mL) blueberries with:
- 1 cup (250 mL) huckleberries (more tart)
- 1 cup (250 mL) red currants (red color; more tart)
- 1 cup (250 mL) raspberries or strawberries (for serving fresh)

Blue Castello

Rich triple-crème Danish blue cheese with a relatively mild flavor.

If You Don't Have It

Substitute 1 oz (30 g) Blue Castello with:
- 1 oz (30 g) Bleu de Bresse
- 1 oz (30 g) Cambozola
- 1 oz (30 g) Saga Blue
- 1 oz (30 g) Gorgonzola (more pungent)

Blue Cheese

A large class of cheeses that have been treated with molds that create blue or green veins and mildly to strongly pungent flavors.

If You Don't Have It

Substitute 1 oz (30 g) blue cheese with:
- 1 oz (30 g) feta cheese (much milder)

For Better Health

Substitute 1 oz (30 g) blue cheese with:
- ½ oz (15 g) blue cheese + ½ oz (15 g) reduced-fat cream cheese (for sauces and dressings)

See also SPECIFIC TYPES.

Blue Cheshire

See CHESHIRE.

Blue Crab

See CRAB.

Blue Curaçao

See ORANGE LIQUEUR.

Bluefin

See TUNA, FRESH.

Bluefish

Also known as elft, lüfer, and tailor. Nicknamed Bulldog of the Sea because of its voracious nature. The dark, oily strip that runs down the center of the fish should be removed to prevent the flesh from absorbing a fishy flavor.

If You Don't Have It
Substitute 1 lb (500 g) bluefish with:
- 1 lb (500 g) mackerel
- 1 lb (500 g) butterfish
- 1 lb (500 g) tilefish
- 1 lb (500 g) halibut
- 1 lb (500 g) cod

Boar

Also known as wild boar. Renowned in classical myths and as the centerpiece of annual medieval European feasts.

If You Don't Have It
Substitute 1 lb (500 g) boar meat with:
- 1 lb (500 g) pork (more pale; richer; milder-tasting)

Boboli

See PIZZA CRUST.

Bockwurst

German ground veal sausage seasoned with chives and parsley. A springtime tradition enjoyed with bock beer.

If You Don't Have It
Substitute 1 lb (500 g) Bockwurst with:
- 1 lb (500 g) fresh Bratwurst

Boiling Water

Often called for in recipes to cook rice or pasta or to soak dried mushrooms or sun-dried tomatoes.

To Vary the Flavor
Substitute 1 cup (250 mL) boiling water with:
- 1 cup (250 mL) boiling beef, chicken or vegetable stock
- 1 cup (250 mL) boiling vegetable juice

To Save Time
Substitute 1 cup (250 mL) boiling water with:
- 1 cup (250 mL) hot tap water, brought to a boil if necessary (much faster, especially for pasta; for soaking dried mushrooms and sun-dried tomatoes, very hot tap water is sufficient; may slightly affect flavor if you haven't drawn hot water from the tap in a while)

Bok Choy

Also known as Chinese white cabbage, pak choi, pak choy, and white mustard cabbage. Looks like a bulbous head of white or pale green celery with tender, pale green or dark green leaves.

If You Don't Have It

Substitute 1 lb (500 g) bok choy with:

- 1 lb (500 g) Chinese broccoli (darker green stems; slightly sweeter, less cabbagey flavor)
- 1 lb (500 g) Napa cabbage (paler green yellow color; more tender; less juicy; great for stir-frying)
- 1 lb (500 g) green chard (less cabbagey flavor)
- 1 lb (500 g) collard greens (thinner, greener stems; larger leaves)
- 1 lb (500 g) celery (in place of bok choy stems in stir-fries)

Bok Choy Varieties

Choose 1 lb (500 g) bok choy from these varieties:

- 1 lb (500 g) mature bok choy (the type common in American markets; sweet; juicy; mild cabbage flavor)
- 1 lb (500 g) choy sum or Chinese flowering cabbage (similar to mature bok choy but slightly smaller stems and leaves; often blossoms with clusters of small yellow flowers)
- 1 lb (500 g) Canton bok choy (slightly stronger cabbage flavor)
- 1 lb (500 g) Shanghai bok choy (short, squat, green stems; often sold as baby bok choy; mellow cabbage flavor)
- 1 lb (500 g) Taiwan bok choy (thinner stems; more delicate leaves; very mild cabbage flavor)

See also NAPA CABBAGE; TATSOI; YAU CHOY.

Bologna

Also known as baloney. Spiced sandwich meat that is the mainstay of many a bagged lunch. Named after the Italian city of Bologna.

If You Don't Have It

Substitute 1 lb (500 g) bologna with:

- 1 lb (500 g) mortadella (similar but with cubes of pork fat and garlic flavor)
- 1 lb (500 g) galantina (more chunky)
- 1 lb (500 g) olive loaf (adds olive flavor)

For Better Health

Substitute 1 lb (500 g) bologna with:

- 1 lb (500 g) Gelbwurst (lower in fat and calories)

Bombay Duck

Also known as bummalo. Not a duck but rather a fish (Bommaloay Macchi) that is native to Mumbai (formerly Bombay), India.

If You Don't Have It

Substitute 1 lb (500 g) Bombay duck with:
- 1 lb (500 g) salt cod or another strongly flavored salted dried fish

Boniato

Also known as batata and camote. A sweet potato cultivar with brown or red skin and white flesh. Popular in Caribbean cooking.

If You Don't Have It

Substitute 1 cup (250 mL) chopped boniato with:
- 1 cup (250 mL) chopped white or cushcush yam
- 1 cup (250 mL) chopped russet potato
- 1 cup (250 mL) chopped sweet potato (orange flesh; much sweeter flavor; moister texture)

See also SWEET POTATO.

Bonito

A small variety of tuna often dried and used in Japanese dishes particularly to make dashi, a clear Japanese soup stock.

If You Don't Have It

Substitute 1 cup (250 mL) bonito flakes (katsuobushi or hanakatsuo) with:
- 1 cup (250 mL) dried dulse (a seaweed; adds briny but not fishy flavor)

See also TUNA, FRESH.

Borage

Herb with pretty blue flowers, large hairy leaves, and a cucumber-like flavor. Larger leaves may be cooked as a vegetable.

If You Don't Have It

Substitute 1 tbsp (15 mL) fresh borage with:
- 1 tbsp (15 mL) fresh salad burnet (to replace borage leaves as an herb)
- 2 tsp (10 mL) fresh thyme (to replace borage leaves as an herb)
- 1 tbsp (15 mL) fresh spinach (to replace borage leaves for cooking)
- 1 tbsp (15 mL) fresh nasturtiums (to replace flowers for salads)

See also PICKING EDIBLE FLOWERS (PAGE 604).

Borlotti Bean

See CRANBERRY BEAN, FRESH; THE WIDE WORLD OF DRIED BEANS (PAGE 566).

Bosc Pear

See PICKING PEARS (PAGE 565).

Boston Lettuce

See BUTTERHEAD LETTUCE.

Bottarga

See CHANGING ROE (PAGE 594).

Boudin Blanc

A delicate French white sausage made with pork and chicken. In Louisiana, Cajun boudin blanc is made with pork and has a spicier, more complex flavor.

If You Don't Have It

Substitute 1 lb (500 g) boudin blanc with:
- 1 lb (500 g) German Weisswurst (mild flavor)
- 1 lb (500 g) white Bratwurst (mild flavor)

Boudin Noir

See BLOOD SAUSAGE.

Boudin Rouge

Cajun blood sausage.

If You Don't Have It

Substitute 1 lb (500 g) boudin rouge with:
- 1 lb (500 g) Blutwurst (German)
- 1 lb (500 g) boudin blanc (Cajun; minus the pork blood)
- 1 lb (500 g) morcilla (Spanish)

Bouillon

See STOCK.

Bounceberry

See CRANBERRY.

Bouquet Garni

The classic flavoring trio of the French kitchen: bay leaf, parsley, and thyme.

If You Don't Have It

Substitute 1 bouquet garni with:
- 1 Homemade Classic Bouquet Garni: Combine 3 to 4 sprigs fresh parsley, 1 sprig fresh thyme, and 1 bay leaf. Tie together with string or a clean plastic twist-tie. Or tie shut in a cheesecloth or a clean coffee filter (use cheesecloth or a coffee filter if you want only the aroma of the herbs but not their texture in the dish).

Bourbon

See WHISKEY.

Boursault

Triple-crème cheese with the consistency of thick sour cream. Look for paper-wrapped cylinders with no discoloration.

If You Don't Have It

Substitute 1 oz (30 g) Boursault with:
- 1 oz (30 g) Brillat-Savarin
- 1 oz (30 g) Explorateur
- 1 oz (30 g) Gratte-Paille
- 1 oz (30 g) Brie

Boursin

Triple-crème cheese with a whipped butter texture; seasoned with herbs, garlic, or cracked peppercorns.

If You Don't Have It

Substitute 1 oz (30 g) boursin with:
- 1 oz (30 g) Rondelé
- 1 oz (30 g) Alouette
- 1 oz (30 g) herbed cream cheese + 1½ tsp (7 mL) softened butter

Bowls

Essential kitchen equipment for mixing and serving. Stock a range of sizes, from small to large. For mixing, many cooks prefer sturdy and versatile stainless steel.

If You Don't Have It

Substitute bowls with:
- hollowed-out squash (for hot and cold soups)
- hollowed-out melons (for cold soups)
- hollowed-out citrus fruit (for cold soups)
- large coffee cups or mugs (for soup or creamy desserts)
- wineglasses (for soup or creamy desserts)
- large saucepan or pot (for mixing doughs and batters)

Boysenberry

In 1923, horticulturist Rudolph Boysen crossed a blackberry, loganberry, and raspberry to father his namesake fruit. The size of large raspberries, this sweet berry is purplish red.

1 pint fresh =
2⅔ cups (650 mL)

If You Don't Have It

Substitute 1 cup (250 mL) boysenberries with:
- 1 cup (250 mL) loganberries (redder color)
- 1 cup (250 mL) blackberries (more tart; larger seeds)
- 1 cup (250 mL) olallieberries (larger; sweeter)
- 1 cup (250 mL) raspberries (smaller; sweeter)

Bramble

See BLACKBERRY.

Bran

See OAT BRAN; WHEAT BRAN.

Brandy

Liquor distilled from wine or the juice of other fermented fruits. The word brandy is derived from the Dutch brandewijn (burned wine) because the wine is heated during distillation. The Latin term aqua vitae and the French term eau de vie ("water of life") both refer to colorless brandy such as Kirsch.

If You Don't Have It

Substitute ¼ cup (50 mL) brandy with:
- 2 to 3 tsp (10 to 15 mL) brandy extract + ¼ cup (50 mL) water or liquid in recipe

To Vary the Flavor

Substitute ¼ cup (50 mL) brandy with:
- ¼ cup (50 mL) bourbon or rum (especially with chocolate in baking)
- ¼ cup (50 mL) fruit syrup (to replace fruit brandies)

See also ARMAGNAC; B&B; COGNAC; METAXA; SPECIFIC FLAVORS.

Brandy Extract

Concentrated brandy flavoring.

If You Don't Have It

Substitute ½ tsp (2 mL) brandy extract with:
- 1 to 1½ tbsp (15 to 22 mL) brandy (adds alcohol)
- ½ tsp (2 mL) rum extract (adds rum flavor)
- ½ tsp (2 mL) vanilla extract (adds vanilla flavor)

Bratwurst

German fresh pork and veal sausage seasoned with spices that may include caraway seeds, coriander, ginger, and nutmeg.

If You Don't Have It

Substitute 1 lb (500 g) Bratwurst with:
- 1 lb (500 g) smoked Bratwurst (adds smoke flavor)
- 1 lb (500 g) French boudin blanc (delicate flavor)
- 1 lb (500 g) Cajun boudin blanc (spicier, more complex flavor)
- 1 lb (500 g) German Weisswurst (mild flavor)
- 1 lb (500 g) Bockwurst (mild flavor)

Braunschweiger

Spreadable smoked liverwurst named after the German town of Braunschweig (Brunswick).

If You Don't Have It

Substitute 1 lb (500 g) Braunschweiger with:
- 1 lb (500 g) liverwurst (unsmoked)
- 1 lb (500 g) Mettwurst
- 1 lb (500 g) Teewurst (spicier)
- 1 lb (500 g) pâté

See also CERVELAT; LIVERWURST.

Brazil Nut

Also known as cream nuts and para nuts. Mostly a foraged crop in the Amazonian jungle. The nuts are actually segments similar to orange wedges found inside a round fruit the size of a coconut.

2 lbs (1 kg) in shell =
1 lb (500 g) shelled

If You Don't Have It
Substitute 1 cup (250 mL) Brazil nuts with:
- 1 cup (250 mL) macadamia nuts
- 1 cup (250 mL) almonds
- 1 cup (250 mL) pecans

See also PARADISE NUT.

Bread

See FRENCH BREAD; ITALIAN BREAD; SPECIFIC TYPES.

Bread Crumbs

A thrifty cook's binding agent. Fresh bread crumbs are soft and the size of peas. Dry crumbs are powdered like fine sand.

3 slices fresh bread =
1 cup (250 mL) fresh
bread crumbs

4 slices dry bread =
1 cup (250 mL) dry
bread crumbs

If You Don't Have It
Substitute 1 cup (250 mL) plain dry bread crumbs with:
- 3 to 4 slices oven-dried bread, crushed
- 1¼ cups (300 mL) croutons or stuffing cubes, crushed
- 1 cup (250 mL) panko (Japanese bread crumbs; large crumbs; retains crispness better)
- ¾ cup (175 mL) cracker crumbs
- 1 tbsp (15 mL) quick-cooking oats (for thickening)

To Vary the Flavor
Substitute 1 cup (250 mL) plain dry bread crumbs with:
- 1 cup (250 mL) seasoned dry bread crumbs
- 1 cup (250 mL) crushed melba toasts
- 1 cup (250 mL) matzo meal
- 1 cup (250 mL) crushed tortilla chips
- 1 cup (250 mL) crushed dry-bagged stuffing mix
- 1 cup (250 mL) crushed pretzels
- 1 cup (250 mL) crushed cornflakes
- 1 cup (250 mL) crushed potato chips

See also COOKIE CRUMBS; CORNFLAKE CRUMBS; CRACKER CRUMBS; PANKO.

Bread Flour

See FLOUR, BREAD.

Breadfruit

Rough green-skinned fruit, native to the Pacific. In 1789, Captain William Bligh of the HMS Bounty, was ordered to transport breadfruit plants from Polynesia to the British Caribbean colonies.

If You Don't Have It

Substitute 1 cup (250 mL) chopped breadfruit with:
- 1 cup (250 mL) chopped canned breadfruit
- 1 cup (250 mL) chopped jackfruit
- 1 cup (250 mL) chopped or sliced green or yellow plantains
- 1 cup (250 mL) chopped potatoes

See also JACKFRUIT.

Bream

See PORGY.

Bresaola

The beef equivalent of prosciutto crudo *originated in the Lombardy region of Italy.*

If You Don't Have It

Substitute 1 lb (500 g) bresaola with:
- 1 lb (500 g) Bündnerfleisch
- 1 lb (500 g) Brési (French)
- 1 lb (500 g) biltong (Aftrican)
- 1 lb (500 g) prosciutto (richer; milder flavor)

Brick Cheese

Pale yellow brick-shaped cheese from Wisconsin ranges in flavor from mild to potent as it ages.

4 oz (125 g) = 1 cup (250 mL) shredded

If You Don't Have It

Substitute 1 oz (30 g) brick cheese with:
- 1 oz (30 g) German or Danish Tilsit
- 1 oz (30 g) Havarti
- 1 oz (30 g) Cheddar
- 1 oz (30 g) Limburger (combine with Cheddar for a milder flavor)

Brie

The granddaddy of this most fashionable of French cheeses, Brie de Meaux, dates from the 700s. While it is now a mold-ripened cheese, Brie de Meaux was originally eaten unripened.

If You Don't Have It

Substitute 1 oz (30 g) Brie with:
- 1 oz (30 g) Camembert
- 1 oz (30 g) Explorateur
- 1 oz (30 g) Reblochon

Brill

European flatfish that tastes very much like turbot.

If You Don't Have It

Substitute 1 lb (500 g) brill with:
- 1 lb (500 g) turbot
- 1 lb (500 g) Dover sole

Brillat-Savarin Cheese

Lucious triple-crème cheese named in honor of French food philosopher Jean Anthelme Brillat-Savarin.

If You Don't Have It

Substitute 1 oz (30 g) Brillat-Savarin with:

- 1 oz (30 g) Boursault
- 1 oz (30 g) Explorateur
- 1 oz (30 g) Gratte-Paille
- 1 oz (30 g) Saint-André
- 1 oz (30 g) Brie

Brine

A solution of salt, water and, sometimes, sugar. Used to moisten, flavor, or pickle various vegetables and meats.

If You Don't Have It

Substitute 4 quarts (4 L) brine with:

- 4 quarts (4 L) Homemade Basic Brine: Combine 4 cups (1 L) water, ¾ cup (175 mL) granulated sugar, and ¾ cup (175 mL) kosher salt in a saucepan. Boil over high heat until sugar and salt are dissolved, about 2 minutes. Remove from heat. Add 3 quarts (3 L) cold water, 1 tsp (5 mL) cracked peppercorns, 1 sliced celery rib, 1 sliced carrot, ½ sliced small onion, 6 sprigs fresh parsley and/or thyme, and 3 bay leaves. Place pork or poultry in the brine for 2 to 4 hours per pound (500 g) of meat, depending upon the meat's thickness. Discard the brine and cook the meat (browning it first improves the color).

Brine-Cured Ham

See HAM, WET-CURED.

Brinza Cheese

See BRYNDZA.

Brioche

A sweet French yeast bread enriched with plenty of butter and eggs. The classic baking mold produces a ridged loaf with a domed top.

If You Don't Have It

Substitute 1 lb (500 g) brioche with:

- 1 lb (500 g) challah (less rich)
- 1 lb (500 g) shokupan (rich Japanese white bread)
- 1 lb (500 g) croissants (less eggy, more airy texture)
- 1 lb (500 g) Kugelhopf (filled with dried and candied fruit and nuts)

Broad Bean

See FAVA BEAN.

Broad-Leaved Endive

See ESCAROLE.

Broccoflower™

Also known as Cauli-Broc. Often labeled as a cross between cauliflower and broccoli, the brand named Broccoflower™ is actually a cultivar of Italian green cauliflower.

> 1 lb (500 g) fresh =
> 2½ to 3 cups
> (625 to 750 mL) florets

If You Don't Have It
Substitute 1 lb (500 g) Broccoflower™ with:
- 1 lb (500 g) cauliflower (white color; stronger cabbage flavor)
- 1 lb (500 g) broccoli (darker green color; softer texture; stronger flavor)
- 8 oz (250 g) cauliflower + 8 oz (250 g) broccoli (stronger flavor)

Broccoletti

See BROCCOLI RAAB.

Broccoli

In an 18th century British gardening dictionary, an entry for broccoli described it as Italian asparagus.

> 1 lb (500 g) fresh =
> 2 cups (500 mL) chopped
>
> 10 oz (300 g) frozen =
> 1½ cups (375 mL)
> chopped

If You Don't Have It
Substitute 1 lb (500 g) broccoli with:
- 1 lb (500 g) Broccoflower™ (lighter green color; milder flavor; firmer texture)
- 1 lb (500 g) cauliflower (white color; stronger cabbage flavor; firmer texture)
- 1 lb (500 g) broccoli raab (more bitter flavor; includes leaves; cooks more quickly)

See also BROCCOLI ROMANESCO.

Broccolini

Also known as asparation, baby broccoli, and mini-broccoli. The skinny stalks look like broccoli on a diet. This trademarked hybrid of broccoli and Chinese broccoli is crisp with a delicate broccoli flavor.

> 1 lb (500 g) fresh =
> 2 cups (500 mL)
> chopped

If You Don't Have It
Substitute 1 lb (500 g) Broccolini with:
- 1 lb (500 g) asparagus (straighter stalks; tighter heads)
- 1 lb (500 g) Chinese broccoli (darker green color; thicker stems)
- 1 lb (500 g) broccoli (shorter, thicker stems; more cabbagey flavor)
- 1 lb (500 g) broccoli raab (more bitter flavor; includes leaves)

See also CHINESE BROCCOLI.

Broccoli Raab

Also known as broccoletti, cime di rapa, and rapini. More closely related to the turnip family than the broccoli bunch, this sharp, pungent green resembles a bouquet of radish greens interspersed with small broccoli-like buds.

1 lb (500 g) fresh = 2 cups (500 mL) chopped

If You Don't Have It

Substitute 1 lb (500 g) broccoli raab with:
- 1 lb (500 g) Chinese broccoli (darker green color; milder flavor)
- 1 lb (500 g) bitter greens (such as dandelion, mustard, or turnip)
- 1 lb (500 g) green or red chard (sweeter flavor)
- 1 lb (500 g) broccoli (shorter, thicker stems; less bitter, more cabbagey flavor; takes longer to cook)

Broccoli Romanesco

Similar to Broccoflower™ but with beautiful conical florets in the repeating shape of a fractal. The plant thrives in Italy between Rome and Naples.

1 lb (500 g) fresh = 2½ to 3 cups (625 to 750 mL) florets = 1½ to 2 cups (375 to 500 mL) chopped

If You Don't Have It

Substitute 1 lb (500 g) broccoli Romanesco with:
- 1 lb (500 g) Broccoflower™ (very similar, but with round florets)
- 1 lb (500 g) cauliflower (white color; stronger cabbage flavor)
- 1 lb (500 g) broccoli (darker green color; softer texture; stronger flavor)
- 8 oz (250 g) cauliflower + 8 oz (250 g) broccoli (stronger flavor)

Broiler

A direct source of cooking heat, usually in the oven.

If You Don't Have It

Substitute a broiler with:
- grill (heat will come from below instead of above; otherwise, the cooking methods are very similar; grilling over coals will add smoke flavor)

Broth

See STOCK.

Brown Bean Sauce

See BEAN SAUCE.

Brown Rice

See RICE.

Brown Rice Syrup

A sweetener made from fermented brown rice. Similar in consistency to honey but less sweet.

If You Don't Have It

Substitute 1 cup (250 mL) brown rice syrup with:
- ¾ cup (175 mL) maple syrup or honey + 2 tbsp (25 mL) water or other liquid from the recipe (slightly thinner consistency; adds maple or honey flavor)
- ¾ cup (175 mL) barley malt syrup
- ½ cup (125 mL) molasses

See also SUGAR, GRANULATED.

Brown Sugar

See SUGAR, DARK BROWN; SUGAR, LIGHT BROWN.

Brussels Sprouts

Tiny sprouts are the tastiest of this cabbage family member. In farmer's markets, look for sprouts clustered in tight rows on the thick stalk on which they grew.

If You Don't Have It

Substitute 1 lb (500 g) Brussels sprouts with:
- 1 lb (500 g) broccoli florets (darker green color; milder flavor; cooks more quickly)
- 1 lb (500 g) chopped green cabbage (cooks more quickly)

Bryndza

Also known as brinza cheese. Brine-cured sheep's milk cheese from Romania. Young Bryndza is soft enough to spread and gets increasingly crumbly when aged.

If You Don't Have It

Substitute 1 oz (30 g) Bryndza cheese with:
- 1 oz (30 g) feta
- 1 oz (30 g) aged chèvre
- 1 oz (30 g) ricotta salata
- 1 oz (30 g) cotija
- 1 oz (30 g) myzithra
- 1 oz (30 g) haloumi (adds mint flavor)

Buah Keras

See CANDLENUT.

Bûcheron

See CHÈVRE.

Buckwheat Flour

See CHOOSING AMONG WHOLE-GRAIN AND ALTERNATIVE FLOURS (PAGE 586).

Buckwheat Groats

Although treated as a cereal grain, the buckwheat plant is actually an herb. Groats are the hulled, crushed kernels cooked like rice.

If You Don't Have It
Substitute 1 cup (250 mL) buckwheat groats with:
- 1 cup (250 mL) kasha (roasted buckwheat groats; adds sweeter, toasted flavor)
- 1 cup (250 mL) rice, millet or quinoa (cooks more quickly)
- 1 cup (250 mL) buckwheat grits, barley grits or hominy grits (each cooks more quickly)

Buddha's Hand

See CITRON.

Buffalo

Also known as bison. Lean, tender buffalo meat has more iron and less fat than beef and it doesn't taste gamey.

If You Don't Have It
Substitute 1 lb (500 g) buffalo with:
- 1 lb (500 g) beef (richer)
- 1 lb (500 g) venison (gamier)

Buffalo Fish

Freshwater fish that's similar to carp. Popular as a smoked fish, it can also be prepared in a variety of other ways.

If You Don't Have It
Substitute 1 lb (500 g) buffalo fish with:
- 1 lb (500 g) carp

Buffalo Milk Mozzarella

See MOZZARELLA.

Bulbing Fennel

See FENNEL, FRESH.

Bulgur

Also known as bulgur wheat and burghul. Steamed, dried, crushed wheat kernels that reach their apex in the Middle Eastern salad tabbouleh.

1 cup (250 mL) dry = 3 cups (750 mL) cooked

If You Don't Have It
Substitute 1 cup (250 mL) bulgur with:
- 1 cup (250 mL) cracked wheat (takes longer to cook)
- 1 cup (250 mL) quinoa
- 1 cup (250 mL) rice
- 1 cup (250 mL) whole wheat couscous

See also CRACKED WHEAT.

Bull's Horn

See SWEET PEPPERS.

Bummalo

See BOMBAY DUCK.

Bunching Onion

See ONION, GREEN.

Bündnerfleisch

Also known as Bindenfleisch. Delicate Swiss beef jerky.

If You Don't Have It

Substitute 1 lb (500 g) Bündnerfleisch with:
- 1 lb (500 g) Bresaola (Italian)
- 1 lb (500 g) Brési (French)
- 1 lb (500 g) biltong (African)
- 1 lb (500 g) prosciutto (richer; milder flavor)

Bundt Pan

See PAN SIZE EQUIVALENTS (PAGE 606).

Burdock

Also known as gobo and great burdock. A skinny, long (up to a yard/90 cm long) root most valued in Japanese cooking.

If You Don't Have It

Substitute 1 lb (500 g) burdock with:
- 1 lb (500 g) salsify (white or black)
- 1 lb (500 g) asparagus (to replace wild green burdock)
- 1 lb (500 g) artichoke hearts
- 1 lb (500 g) carrots (orange color; sweeter flavor)

Burghul

See BULGUR.

Burnet

See SALAD BURNET.

Butter

Salt is added to butter as a preservative. Use unsalted butter for baking and for the freshest taste. When substituting butter with lower-fat alternatives in baking, replace no more than half of the total amount of butter for the best results.

1 lb (500 g) = 2 cups
(500 mL) = 4 sticks

1 stick =
4 oz (125 g) =
½ cup (125 mL) =
8 tbsp (120 mL) =
¾ cup (175 mL) whipped

If You Don't Have It

Substitute ½ cup (125 mL) unsalted butter with:

- ½ cup (125 mL) salted butter (decrease salt in recipe by ¼ tsp/1 mL)
- ½ cup (125 mL) European-style butter such as Plugra (lower moisture content; creates flakier pastries, crisper cookies, and creamier sauces)
- ½ cup (125 mL) margarine (less flavorful; makes baked goods softer)
- ¾ cup (175 mL) whipped butter (for spreading only)
- ½ cup (125 mL) margarine spread (for spreading only)

To Vary the Flavor

Substitute ½ cup (125 mL) butter with:

- ½ cup (125 mL) Homemade Flavored Butter: Stir ½ cup (125 mL) softened butter until smooth and mix in flavorings of choice. Reshape by rolling in plastic wrap if necessary. Garlic Butter: 1 minced garlic clove, ¼ tsp (1 mL) salt, and ¼ tsp (1 mL) pepper. Herb Butter: ¼ cup (50 mL) chopped fresh herbs, 1½ tsp (7 mL) orange or lemon juice, ¼ tsp (1 mL) salt, and ¼ tsp (1 mL) pepper. Citrus Butter: 1½ tsp (7 mL) grated lemon, lime or orange zest, 1½ tbsp (22 mL) lemon, lime or orange juice, ¼ tsp (1 mL) salt, and ¼ tsp (1 mL) pepper
- ½ cup (125 mL) Browned Butter: Melt ½ cup (125 mL) butter in a small saucepan over medium heat and cook until golden brown or dark golden brown, 10 to 15 minutes. Use like melted butter or chill until firm and use like butter.
- 7 tbsp (105 mL) bacon or pork fat or ⅓ cup (75 mL) chicken or poultry fat (for sautéing, frying, and sauces)
- 7 tbsp (105 mL) shortening or lard (for pastry and baking; creates flakier pastry and crisper cookies because shortening and lard lack the water content of butter; many cooks use half shortening or lard and half butter for flakiness and flavor)

For Better Health

Substitute ½ cup (125 mL) butter with:

- ½ cup (125 mL) "light" butter (a product with half the calories and fat of butter due mostly to

the addition of water; works best as a spread,
in frostings and toppings, or melted for drizzling;
in pie and pastry doughs, chill light butter and shred
before quickly mixing with dry ingredients; in cookie
dough, omit one egg white per ½ cup (125 mL) light
butter used; in pancake and quick bread batters,
omit ¼ cup (50 mL) milk or other liquid from recipe
per ½ cup (125 mL) light butter used)

- ¼ cup (50 mL) butter or buttermilk + ¼ cup
  (50 mL) well-drained, unsweetened applesauce,
  prune purée or baby food prunes (for baking;
  applesauce works well with lighter-color or spice
  batters; puréed prunes work best with darker
  batters, such as chocolate; creates slightly chewier
  texture; use pastry or cake flour for lighter texture;
  increase sugar for more crispness)
- 3 tbsp (45 mL) butter + 3 tbsp (45 mL) vegetable
  oil (for baking, especially quick breads and some
  cookie doughs; reduce baking time slightly; baked
  goods will be slightly more chewy; use pastry or
  cake flour for lighter texture; increase sugar for
  more crispness)
- ½ cup (125 mL) apple butter (for baking; reduce
  baking time slightly; baked goods will be slightly
  more chewy; use pastry or cake flour for lighter
  texture; adjust sugar if apple butter is sweetened)
- ½ cup (125 mL) fat-free, fruit-based butter and oil
  replacement such as Smucker's "Baking Healthy"
  (for baking)
- ¼ cup (50 mL) fat-free, fruit-based butter and
  oil replacement such as Sunsweet "Lighter Bake"
  (for baking)
- ½ cup (125 mL) marshmallow crème (for fillings
  and frostings)
- ½ cup (125 mL) oil (for sautéing and frying). Or
  use a mixture of butter and oil. Or use a nonstick
  pan coated with cooking oil spray (or 1 to 2 tsp/
  5 to 10 mL oil or butter) and heat the pan thoroughly

See also BUTTER, CLARIFIED; MARGARINE; OIL;
VEGETABLE SHORTENING.

Butter Bean

See FAVA BEAN; LIMA BEAN.

Butter Cake

Standard cake, usually frosted, which can be baked in round, rectangular, or novelty shaped pans.

If You Don't Have It

Substitute 1 lb (500 g) butter cake with:

- 1 lb (500 g) pound cake (denser texture; higher in fat)
- 1 lb (500 g) sponge cake (lighter texture; lower in fat)
- 1 lb (500 g) angel food cake (lighter, more airy texture; lower in fat)

Butter, Clarified

Also known as drawn butter. The clear golden butterfat that is skimmed from the milk solids after unsalted butter is slowly melted. Useful for sautéing because it has a higher smoke point than solid butter. Ghee, a type of clarified butter, has an even higher smoke point (about 375°F/190°C) because it is simmered longer to evaporate excess moisture.

If You Don't Have It

Substitute ½ cup (125 mL) clarified butter with:

- ½ cup (125 mL) Homemade Clarified Butter: Melt ½ cup (125 mL) + 2 tbsp (25 mL) butter in a skillet over low heat, skimming foam from surface. Heat until white milk solids sink to bottom of pan, 10 to 15 minutes. Let cool slightly, then strain and discard white milk solids, leaving golden clarified butter. Clarified butter keeps in an airtight container in the refrigerator for up to 6 months.
- ½ cup (125 mL) ghee (darker color; deeper, nuttier flavor; higher smoke point)
- ½ cup (125 mL) vegetable oil (less flavorful; use olive oil for richer flavor)
- ½ cup (125 mL) unsalted butter (adds rich flavor of milk solids; lower smoke point)

Butter Cookie

Also known as petit beurre. Thin crisp wafer-like cookies.

If You Don't Have It

Substitute 1 lb (500 g) butter cookies with:

- 1 lb (500 g) shortbread cookies (less crisp)

Buttercup Squash

Bulbous green winter squash topped with a small cap. Classic squash flavor with notes of honey, roasted chestnuts, and sweet potatoes.

1 lb (500 g) = 1 cup (250 mL) cooked and mashed

If You Don't Have It

Substitute 1 cup (250 mL) chopped buttercup squash with:

- 1 cup (250 mL) chopped butternut squash (more easily peeled; creamier)
- 1 cup (250 mL) chopped pumpkin (creamier)
- 1 cup (250 mL) chopped delicata squash (moister)
- 1 cup (250 mL) chopped sweet potato (sweeter; moister)

Butterfish

Also known as dollarfish, Pacific pompano, and pomfret. True to its name this high-fat fish has a rich flavor. Don't confuse butterfish with sablefish, which is a different fish altogether.

If You Don't Have It
Substitute 1 lb (500 g) butterfish with:
- 1 lb (500 g) pompano
- 1 lb (500 g) spot
- 1 lb (500 g) yellowfin or skipjack tuna
- 1 lb (500 g) mackerel
- 1 lb (500 g) bluefish
- 1 lb (500 g) striped bass

See also POMPANO; SABLEFISH.

Butterhead Lettuce

Boston (large leaves) and Bibb (smaller leaves) are the two most popular types of this variety of head lettuce.

1 lb (500 g) = 6 cups (1.5 L) pieces

If You Don't Have It
Substitute 1 cup (250 mL) butterhead lettuce with:
- 1 cup (250 mL) mâche
- 1 cup (250 mL) leaf lettuce
- 1 cup (250 mL) crisphead lettuce such as iceberg

Butterhead Varieties
Choose 1 cup (250 mL) butterhead lettuce from these varieties:
- 1 cup (250 mL) Bibb lettuce (smaller leaves; more complex flavor)
- 1 cup (250 mL) Boston lettuce (larger leaves; mild flavor)

Buttermilk

Originally the liquid that was left after churning whole milk into butter. Commercial buttermilk is a tart, thick dairy product created by adding special bacteria to nonfat or low-fat milk.

If You Don't Have It
Substitute 1 cup (250 mL) buttermilk with:
- 1 tbsp (15 mL) lemon juice or vinegar + enough milk to equal 1 cup (250 mL) (for baking; let stand for 5 to 10 minutes before using)
- 1 cup (250 mL) water + $\frac{1}{4}$ cup (50 mL) powdered buttermilk
- $\frac{1}{2}$ cup (125 mL) plain yogurt + $\frac{1}{2}$ cup (125 mL) milk
- 1 cup (250 mL) plain yogurt (thicker)
- 1 cup (250 mL) sour cream
- 1 cup (250 mL) milk + 1 to $1\frac{1}{2}$ tsp (5 to 7 mL) cream of tartar (for baking)

Butter Muslin

See CHEESECLOTH.

Butternut

Also known as white walnut. A New England nut with a high oil content.

1 lb (500 g) shelled = 3½ cups (875 mL) chopped

If You Don't Have It

Substitute 1 cup (250 mL) chopped butternuts with:

- 1 cup (250 mL) chopped walnuts or black walnuts
- 1 cup (250 mL) chopped pecans

Butternut Squash

A long winter squash that can grow up to a foot (30 cm) long and 5 inches (12.5 cm) wide. For easy peeling, prick hard shell several times with a fork; microwave on High for 2 to 3 minutes.

1 lb (500 g) = 1 cup (250 mL) cooked and mashed

If You Don't Have It

Substitute 1 cup (250 mL) chopped butternut squash with:

- 1 cup (250 mL) chopped buttercup squash (less moist)
- 1 cup (250 mL) chopped delicata squash (less fruity flavor)
- 1 cup (250 mL) chopped pumpkin (sweeter; moister)
- 1 cup (250 mL) chopped sweet potato (sweeter; moister)

Byrrh

A tangy, bittersweet French vermouth that's made with quinine and red wine. It's usually mixed with club soda.

If You Don't Have It

Substitute 2 tbsp (25 mL) byrrh with:

- 2 tbsp (25 mL) Dubonnet blanc or Lillet
- 2 tbsp (25 mL) Amer Picon (more bitter)

Cabbage to Cynar

Cabbage

The green cultivar of this crucifer is ubiquitous in coleslaw and sauerkraut, but cooks often prefer the red variety for its gorgeous garnet hue, a result of pigments known as anthocyanins.

> 1 lb (500 g) = 6 cups (1.5 L) shredded
>
> 1 lb (500 g) raw = 12 oz (375 g) cooked

If You Don't Have It
Substitute 1 lb (500 g) green or red cabbage with:
- 1 lb (500 g) Brussels sprouts
- 1 lb (500 g) savoy cabbage (milder; more tender)
- 1 lb (500 g) napa cabbage (milder; more delicate)

See also BOK CHOY; NAPA CABBAGE; SAVOY CABBAGE.

Cabbage Turnip

See KOHLRABI.

Cabrales

Handmade in small amounts, this Spanish cheese is a blue for blue cheese lovers. Often crafted from a blend of cow's milk for acidity, goat's milk for piquancy, and sheep's milk for richness.

If You Don't Have It
Substitute 1 oz (30 g) cabrales with:
- 1 oz (30 g) Picon
- 1 oz (30 g) Gamonedo
- 1 oz (30 g) Roquefort

Cachaça

Also known as pinga. Brazilian sugarcane brandy that forms the bedrock of the country's fashionable caipirinha cocktail.

If You Don't Have It

Substitute 3 tbsp (45 mL) cachaça with:

- 3 tbsp (45 mL) aguardiente de caña (may add anise flavor)
- 3 tbsp (45 mL) white rum
- 3 tbsp (45 mL) vodka

Caciocavallo

This sharp Southern Italian formaggio *literally means "cheese on horseback." The name may be a reference to the method of drying pairs of cheeses tied to opposite ends of a pole, in balance like a saddlebag on a horse.*

4 oz (125 g) = 1 cup (250 mL) shredded

If You Don't Have It

Substitute 1 oz (30 g) Caciocavallo with:

- 1 oz (30 g) provolone
- 1 oz (30 g) scamorza

Cactus Leaf

See NOPALE.

Cactus Pear

See PRICKLY PEAR.

Caerphilly

Tangy cow's milk cheese named after a village in Wales. In times past, Caerphilly was the traditional lunch of Welsh coal miners. The cheese is best eaten fresh.

4 oz (125 g) = 1 cup (250 mL) shredded

If You Don't Have It

Substitute 1 oz (30 g) Caerphilly with:

- 1 oz (30 g) Cheddar, Cheshire, or Lancashire

Cajeta

Luscious Latin condiment of caramelized sugar and goat's or cow's milk.

If You Don't Have It

Substitute 1 cup (250 mL) cajeta with:

- 1 cup (250 mL) dulce de leche
- 1 cup (250 mL) caramel sauce (bottled commercial brands won't be nearly as flavorful as homemade goat's milk cajeta)

Cajun Seasoning

Also known as Cajun spice mix and Cajun spice seasoning. A blend of signature southern Louisiana herbs and spices that's likely to contain black pepper, cayenne pepper, garlic, mustard powder, and thyme. On the heels of widespread interest in Cajun cooking during the 1980s, Paul Prudhomme, Emeril Lagasse, and other celebrity chefs have marketed their own signature blends.

If You Don't Have It

Substitute 1 tbsp (15 mL) Cajun seasoning with:

- 1 tbsp (15 mL) Homemade Cajun seasoning: Combine ¾ tsp (4 mL) paprika, ¾ tsp (4 mL) ground black pepper, ½ tsp (2 mL) garlic powder, ⅛ to ¼ tsp (0.5 to 1 mL) cayenne pepper, ¼ tsp (1 mL) dried thyme, ¼ tsp (1 mL) dried oregano, ¼ tsp (1 mL) onion powder, and a pinch of mustard powder. Add salt to taste. Makes about 1 tablespoon (15 mL). Recipe can be doubled. Store seasoning in an airtight container for up to 6 months.
- 1 tbsp (15 mL) Creole seasoning (very similar)

See also CREOLE SEASONING.

Cake Flour

See FLOUR, CAKE.

Cake Pans

See PAN SIZE EQUIVALENTS (PAGE 606).

Calabaza

Also known as West Indian pumpkin. Sweet, orange-fleshed squash. A staple in the Caribbean and Latin America, it can be substituted in any recipe calling for acorn, butternut, or other hard-shelled winter squash.

1 lb (500 g) = 2 cups (500 mL) cooked

If You Don't Have It

Substitute 1 cup (250 mL) chopped calabaza with:
- 1 cup (250 mL) chopped small sugar or pie pumpkin
- 1 cup (250 mL) chopped butternut squash
- 1 cup (250 mL) chopped buttercup squash
- 1 cup (250 mL) chopped acorn squash
- 1 cup (250 mL) chopped sweet potato

Calabrese Sausage

See SALAMI.

Calamari

See SQUID.

Calamata Olive

See CHOOSING AMONG OLIVES (PAGE 570).

Calamondin

Also known as kalamansi. A hybrid of mandarin orange and kumquat that looks like a mandarin orange but has juicier, more acidic flesh.

If You Don't Have It

Substitute 1 calamondin with:

- 2 to 3 kumquats (for the flesh or zest)
- ¼ mandarin orange + ½ lemon (for the flesh or zest)
- 1 tsp (5 mL) mandarin orange juice + 1 tbsp (15 mL) lemon juice (to replace 1 tbsp/15 mL calamondin juice)

Calendula

See PICKING EDIBLE FLOWERS (PAGE 604).

California Barracuda

See BARRACUDA.

California Jack Cheese

See JACK CHEESE.

Callaloo

The large green leaves of the taro root are enjoyed in the Caribbean as a cooked vegetable. Also the namesake ingredient of callaloo soup, a melange of coconut milk, okra, yams, chiles, lime juice, and pork or seafood.

If You Don't Have It

Substitute 1 lb (500 g) callaloo with:

- 1 lb (500 g) Chinese kale
- 1 lb (500 g) mature spinach
- 1 lb (500 g) green chard
- 1 lb (500 g) mustard greens
- 1 lb (500 g) turnip greens
- 1 lb (500 g) collard greens

Calvados

See APPLE BRANDY.

Calypso Bean

See THE WIDE WORLD OF DRIED BEANS (PAGE 566).

Cambozola

A German cheese with a downy rind and soft, blue-veined paste. Tastes like a cross between Camembert and Gorgonzola.

If You Don't Have It

Substitute 1 oz (30 g) Cambozola with:

- 1 oz (30 g) Blue Castello
- 1 oz (30 g) Bleu de Bresse
- 1 oz (30 g) Saga blue
- ½ oz (15 g) Gorgonzola + ½ oz (15 g) Camembert

Camembert

In the French village of Camembert, a statue honors Marie Harel as "the creator of Camembert cheese."

If You Don't Have It

Substitute 1 oz (30 g) Camembert with:
- 1 oz (30 g) Brie
- 1 oz (30 g) Explorateur
- 1 oz (30 g) Reblochon

Campari

Brand name of a vivid red, bittersweet Italian aperitivo. Milanese café owner Gaspare Campari created the drink in the 1860s and it's still very fashionable.

If You Don't Have It

Substitute 3 tbsp (45 mL) Campari with:
- 3 tbsp (45 mL) Fernet Branca

Canadian Bacon

Also known as back bacon. The Rolls-Royce of bacon is prepared from lean tenderloin of pork that has been cured and smoked. In addition to Canadian bacon, back bacon includes various cuts of British and Irish back bacon, all of which resemble ham more closely than slab bacon. In the United States, Canadian bacon is sold cooked.

If You Don't Have It

Substitute 1 slice (about 1 oz) Canadian bacon with:
- 1 oz (30 g) smoked ham
- 1 oz (30 g) Irish bacon (back bacon prepared from the eye of the loin)
- 1 oz (30 g) pancetta
- 1 oz (30 g) bacon

Candied Fruit

See SPECIFIC FRUITS.

Candlenut

Also known as Indian walnut. The oily nuts were formerly used to make candles. Toxic unless cooked, the roasted nuts are widely used in Javanese and other Southeast Asian kitchens.

If You Don't Have It

Substitute 1 cup (250 mL) candlenuts with:
- 1 cup (250 mL) macadamia nuts
- 1 cup (250 mL) Brazil nuts
- 1 cup (250 mL) cashews

Canela

See CINNAMON.

Canned Heat

See STERNO©.

Cannellini Bean

See THE WIDE WORLD OF DRIED BEANS (PAGE 566).

Canning Wax

See PARAFFIN WAX.

Canola Oil

See OIL; SUBSTITUTING OILS (PAGE 598).

Cantal

Also known as Cantal de Salers and Fourme du Cantal. Popular semifirm cow's milk cheese from the Auvergne region of France.

If You Don't Have It

Substitute 1 oz (30 g) Cantal with:
- 1 oz (30 g) Laguiole (sharper)
- 1 oz (30 g) Cheshire
- 1 oz (30 g) Lancashire
- 1 oz (30 g) Cheddar

Cantaloupe

Also known as musk melon. In the U.S., musk melons covered with raised netted webbing are marketed as cantaloupes. European cantaloupes, named for the town of Cantalupo near Rome, include the French Charentais.

1 medium = 2 lbs (1 kg) = 3 cups (750 mL) diced

If You Don't Have It

Substitute 1 cup (250 mL) chopped cantaloupe with:
- 1 cup (250 mL) chopped Persian melon
- 1 cup (250 mL) chopped Crenshaw melon
- 1 cup (250 mL) chopped Santa Claus melon
- 1 cup (250 mL) chopped honeydew melon
- 1 cup (250 mL) chopped casaba melon

See also CHARENTAIS MELON.

Cape Capensis

Also known as cape hake and cape whiting. Among the best tasting in the hake family, this fish swims in South African waters.

If You Don't Have It

Substitute 1 lb (500 g) cape capensis with:
- 1 lb (500 g) sole
- 1 lb (500 g) flounder
- 1 lb (500 g) cod
- 1 lb (500 g) pollock

Cape Gooseberry

Also known as golden berry, ground cherry, and husk tomato. A tart golden berry covered with a parchment husk that looks like a Chinese lantern.

If You Don't Have It

Substitute 1 lb (500 g) cape gooseberries with:
- 1 lb (500 g) green or yellow tomatillos (adds lemon and apple aromas)
- 1 lb (500 g) gooseberries (more tart)
- 1 lb (500 g) yellow cherry tomatoes (sweeter)

Cape Hake

See CAPE CAPENSIS.

Caper

The unopened flower bud of a Mediterranean shrub that when pickled forms appetizingly bitter capric acid.

If You Don't Have It

Substitute 1 tsp (5 mL) capers with:
- 1 tsp (5 mL) green olives (leave whole to garnish a martini)
- 1 tsp (5 mL) caper berries (large Spanish capers with the stem on; used as a garnish)
- 1 tsp (5 mL) chopped pickles

Capeshark

See DOGFISH.

Cape Whiting

See CAPE CAPENSIS.

Capicola

Also known as capicollo and coppa. Italian pork shoulder that is salted and air-dried to cure. Produced in a "sweet" style coated with ground black pepper and a "hot" style coated with ground red pepper.

If You Don't Have It

Substitute 4 oz (125 g) capicola with:
- 4 oz (125 g) prosciutto
- 4 oz (125 g) bresaola (beef)
- 4 oz (125 g) Bündnerfleisch (beef; drier)
- 4 oz (125 g) Brési (beef; drier)
- 4 oz (125 g) biltong (beef; drier)

Capon

See CHICKEN.

Caprini

Small Italian goat's milk cheeses molded into cylinders. From the Piedmont region. The whimsical name means "little goats."

If You Don't Have It

Substitute 1 oz (30 g) caprini with:
- 1 oz (30 g) Robiola Piemonte
- 1 oz (30 g) Petit Suisse

See also CHÈVRE; GOAT'S MILK.

Carambola

Also known as star fruit. Crosswise slices of this long yellow fruit look like stars. The tart variety, best as a ctirus-like garnish, has ribs that are thinner than the sweet variety, which is wonderful for desserts and fruit salads.

> 1 lb (500 g) =
> 2 to 3 carambolas

If You Don't Have It

Substitute 1 lb (500 g) carambola with:
- 1 lb (500 g) kiwifruit (greener color)
- 1¼ lbs (625 g) navel oranges, peeled (orange color; sweeter)
- 1¼ lbs (625 g) Spanish, Galia or Ogen melon (pale to bright green color)

Caraway Seeds

This herb and its delicate anise flavor are popular in German rye bread, the Arabic spice mix tabil, and the fiery North African harissa.

If You Don't Have It

Substitute 1 tsp (5 mL) caraway seeds with:
- 1 tsp (5 mL) dill seeds
- 1 tsp (5 mL) anise seeds

Carbonated Water

See SODA WATER.

Cardamom

This relative of ginger is the third most expensive flavoring in the world after saffron and vanilla. The tiny, spicy-sweet seeds grow enclosed in green or more aromatic brown/black fibrous pods.

If You Don't Have It

Substitute 10 whole green or white cardamom pods (seeds removed and crushed) with:
- ½ tsp (2 mL) ground cardamom

To Vary the Flavor

Substitute ½ tsp (2 mL) ground cardamom with:
- ½ tsp (2 mL) ground cinnamon
- ¼ tsp (1 mL) ground cinnamon + ¼ tsp (1 mL) ground nutmeg or cloves

Cardoon

Resembling celery on steroids, mild-tasting cardoons are essential for dipping into the Piedmontese bagna caôda (a fondue of olive oil, anchovy, and garlic).

If You Don't Have It

Substitute 1 cup (250 mL) chopped cardoons with:
- 1 cup (250 mL) chopped artichoke hearts
- 1 cup (250 mL) chopped celery
- 1 cup (250 mL) chopped salsify
- ½ cup (125 mL) chopped artichoke hearts + ½ cup (125 mL) chopped celery

Caribou

A large member of the deer family closely related to reindeer. An important food source for Native Americans.

If You Don't Have It

Substitute 1 lb (500 g) caribou with:

- 1 lb (500 g) reindeer
- 1 lb (500 g) red, fallow, or white-tailed deer
- 1 lb (500 g) moose
- 1 lb (500 g) elk
- 1 lb (500 g) antelope
- 1 lb (500 g) gazelle

See also VENISON.

Carissa

Also known as Natal plum. A native South African plum-like fruit with red flesh speckled with white. The flavor is tart and the texture slightly granular.

If You Don't Have It

Substitute 1 lb (500 g) carissa with:

- 1 lb (500 g) karanda
- 1 lb (500 g) gooseberries (especially for jellies and jams)
- 1 lb (500 g) cranberries (especially for jellies and jams)

Carnation

See PICKING EDIBLE FLOWERS (PAGE 604).

Carob

Also known as locust bean and Saint John's bread. A caffeine-free, chocolate-like flavoring made from the pods of the carob tree.

If You Don't Have It

Substitute 1 cup (250 mL) carob with:

- 1 cup (250 mL) minus 3 tbsp (45 mL) cocoa powder (to replace carob powder)
- 1 cup (250 mL) chocolate chips (to replace carob chips)

Carom Seeds

See AJWAIN.

Carp

Originating in the Danube and other central European rivers, carp has conquered the world as a quick-growing aquaculture fish. Perhaps best known as the primary ingredient of Jewish gefilte fish.

If You Don't Have It

Substitute 1 lb (500 g) carp with:

- 1 lb (500 g) buffalofish
- 1 lb (500 g) freshwater bass
- 1 lb (500 g) bluefish (higher in fat; softer flesh)

Carrageen

Also known as Irish moss. An Atlantic seaweed that's the base of carageenan, a common food additive that emulsifies, stabilizes, and thickens countless food products from soup to ice cream.

If You Don't Have It

Substitute 1 oz (30 g) carrageen (for thickening) with:
- 1 tsp (5 mL) agar powder
- 1½ tsp (7 mL) gelatin powder

Carrot

Carrots are available in red, white, and purple colors in addition to the familiar orange variety. The orange "baby-cut" carrots sold in plastic bags are not truly baby carrots but mature carrots machine-cut for convenience.

> 1 large carrot = 1 cup
> (250 mL) grated

If You Don't Have It

Substitute 1 cup (250 mL) chopped carrots with:
- 1 cup (250 mL) chopped parsnips
- 1 cup (250 mL) chopped daikon
- 1 cup (250 mL) chopped turnips
- 1 cup (250 mL) chopped celery

Carrot Juice

An easy-to-ingest source of beta-carotene. To flavor rice, couscous, or other grain pilafs, cook the grain in equal parts carrot juice and water.

If You Don't Have It

Substitute 1 cup (250 mL) fresh carrot juice with:
- 1 cup (250 mL) canned carrot juice
- 1 cup (250 mL) V8® Juice (red color; a commercial blend of tomato, spinach, celery, carrot, beet, lettuce, watercress, and parsley juices)

Casaba Melon

A type of winter melon similar to honeydew but with a rough skin.

> 1 lb (500 g) = 1 to
> 1½ cups (250 to 375 mL)
> cubed

If You Don't Have It

Substitute 1 cup (250 mL) chopped casaba melon with:
- 1 cup (250 mL) chopped Santa Claus melon
- 1 cup (250 mL) chopped Crenshaw melon
- 1 cup (250 mL) chopped Persian melon
- 1 cup (250 mL) chopped honeydew melon
- 1 cup (250 mL) chopped cantaloupe

Cascabel Chile

See CHOOSING DRIED CHILES (PAGE 578).

Cashel Bleu

County Tipperary Irish blue cheese with a creamy texture and a thin pinkish red rind.

If You Don't Have It

Substitute 1 oz (30 g) Cashel Blue with:
- 1 oz (30 g) Gorgonzola
- 1 oz (30 g) Stilton
- 1 oz (30 g) Fourme d'Ambert
- 1 oz (30 g) Roquefort

Cashew

The shell of this buttery nut is highly toxic. Great care is taken in processing commercially sold shelled cashews, which are perfectly safe.

1 lb (500 g) = 3⅓ cups (825 mL)

If You Don't Have It

Substitute 1 cup (250 mL) cashew nuts with:
- 1 cup (250 mL) peanuts
- 1 cup (250 mL) pine nuts
- 1 cup (250 mL) pistachio nuts

Cashew Butter

A paste of ground roasted cashew nuts, oil, and salt.

If You Don't Have It

Substitute 1 cup (250 mL) cashew butter with:
- 1 cup (250 mL) Homemade Cashew Butter: Put 2 cups (500 mL) roasted cashews and ¼ tsp (1 mL) salt in a blender or food processor fitted with metal blade. Process, gradually adding 4 to 6 tbsp (60 to 90 mL) vegetable oil, until the mixture forms a paste. Add sugar to taste. Makes 1½ cups (375 mL).
- 1 cup (250 mL) peanut butter or almond butter
- 1 cup (250 mL) tahini (strong sesame flavor)

Cassava

Also known as mandioca, manioc, and yuca. A starchy root that is popular in Latin America and a staple in many parts of Africa. Tapioca is one by-product.

If You Don't Have It

Substitute 1 lb (500 g) cassava with:
- 1 lb (500 g) mandiba
- 1 lb (500 g) yautía or malanga
- 1 lb (500 g) taro
- 1 lb (500 g) potatoes

See also TAPIOCA.

Casserole

See PAN SIZE EQUIVALENTS (PAGE 606).

Cassia

See CINNAMON.

Cassis Liqueur

Also known as crème de cassis. A sweet liqueur made with black currants and rum.

If You Don't Have It

Substitute 3 tbsp (45 mL) cassis liqueur with:
- 3 tbsp (45 mL) black currant syrup (sweeter; no alcohol)
- 3 tbsp (45 mL) raspberry liqueur

Cast Iron

One of the least expensive and most durable cookware materials. Cast iron conducts and retains heat fairly well.

If You Don't Have It

Substitute cast-iron cookware with:
- enamelware
- heavy-gauge clad cookware (stainless steel with aluminum or copper core)
- hard anodized aluminum cookware

Catfish

Growing to weights of up to 700 pounds (350 kg), the giant catfish of the Mekong River are reputed to be among the finest tasting fishes in the world.

If You Don't Have It

Substitute 1 lb (500 g) catfish with:
- 1 lb (500 g) grouper
- 1 lb (500 g) tilefish
- 1 lb (500 g) monkfish

Catsup

See KETCHUP.

Caul

The lacy, fatty lining of the abdominal cavity of pigs and sheep used to wrap pâtés and charcuterie.

If You Don't Have It

Substitute 4 oz (125 g) caul fat with:
- 4 oz (125 g) thinly sliced bacon (for barding)
- 4 oz (125 g) thinly sliced pancetta (for barding)

Cauliflower

The fleece (or curd) of cauliflower may be green, orange, pinkish, or yellow. Colored types often have a more pronounced flavor.

1 head = 4 cups
(1 L) florets

If You Don't Have It

Substitute 1 lb (500 g) cauliflower with:
- 1 lb (500 g) Broccoflower™ (light green color)
- 1 lb (500 g) broccoli Romanesco (light green color; conical florets)
- 1 lb (500 g) broccoli (dark green color; softer texture; cooks more quickly)

Cavendish Banana

See BANANA.

Caviar

See CHANGING ROE (PAGE 594).

Cayenne Pepper

A thin, pointed, and very hot chile pepper that's usually dried and crushed (crushed red pepper flakes) or ground (ground red pepper).

If You Don't Have It

Substitute ½ tsp (2 mL) ground cayenne pepper with:

- ½ tsp (2 mL) ground chipotle powder (much smokier)
- ½ tsp (2 mL) ground ancho powder (darker; milder)
- ½ tsp (2 mL) paprika (much milder)
- ¾ tsp (4 mL) crushed red pepper flakes
- ½ tsp (2 mL) chili powder (milder; adds flavors of cumin, oregano, and other spices)
- 1 very small whole dried red chile
- dash of hot pepper sauce
- 1 to 3 tsp (5 to 15 mL) chile paste

See also HOT PEPPER SAUCE; CHOOSING DRIED CHILES (PAGE 578); CHOOSING FRESH CHILES (PAGE 582).

Celeriac

Also known as celery root, knob celery and turnip-rooted celery. Gnarly root celery — more full-flavored and herbaceous than celery stalks or leaves — is beloved in France. Céléri en remoulade (celery root in mustard mayonnaise) is a time-honored bistro appetizer.

1½ lbs (750 g) = 4 cups
(1 L) grated = 1¾ cups
(425 mL) cooked
and puréed

If You Don't Have It

Substitute 1 cup (250 mL) chopped celeriac with:

- 1 cup (250 mL) chopped parsley root (stronger flavor)
- 1 cup (250 mL) chopped celery (milder flavor)
- 1 cup (250 mL) chopped turnips + pinch of celery seeds
- 1 cup (250 mL) chopped parsnips + pinch of celery seeds
- 1 cup (250 mL) chopped carrots + pinch of celery seeds

Céleri Bâtard

See LOVAGE.

Celery

Garnishing a Bloody Mary cocktail with a stick of celery is said to have begun in the 1960s at the swanky Ambassador East Hotel in Chicago. A celebrity, who was served his Bloody Mary with no swizzle stick, grabbed a celery rib from the relish tray to stir his drink.

1 rib = ½ cup (125 mL) sliced

If You Don't Have It

Substitute 1 cup (250 mL) chopped fresh celery with:
- ½ cup (125 mL) dehydrated celery flakes (for soups and stews; much less flavorful)
- ⅔ to 1 cup (150 to 250 mL) chopped Chinese celery (for cooking; stronger flavor)
- 1 cup (250 mL) chopped cardoons (adds mild artichoke flavor)
- 1 cup (250 mL) chopped fennel stalks (adds mild anise flavor)

Celery Cabbage

See NAPA CABBAGE.

Celery Root

See CELERIAC.

Celery Salt

A seasoning blend of ground celery seeds and salt.

If You Don't Have It

Substitute 1 tsp (5 mL) celery salt with:
- ¼ to ½ tsp (1 to 2 mL) ground celery seeds + ½ tsp (2 mL) salt
- 1 tsp (5 mL) Beau Monde® Seasoning (adds dried onion flavor)
- 1 tsp (5 mL) Old Bay Seasoning (adds paprika and other spices)

Celery Seeds

The seeds of a wild celery called lovage have a stronger celery flavor than cultivated celery stalks.

If You Don't Have It

Substitute 1 tsp (5 mL) celery seeds with:
- 1 tsp (5 mL) celery salt (reduce salt in recipe by ½ tsp/2 mL)
- 1 tsp (5 mL) dill seeds
- 3 tbsp (45 mL) chopped celery leaves

Cèpe

See SHUFFLING MUSHROOMS (PAGE 572).

Cervelat

A family of smoked German sausages made with pork and, sometimes, beef. Cervelat is typically a semidry sausage that's sliced and served raw like bologna, but spreadable versions are available. Popular varieties of cervelat include Thuringer and Landjäger. Not to be confused with France's cervelas, a related but smaller fresh sausage.

If You Don't Have It
Substitute 1 lb (500 g) cervelat with:
- 1 lb (500 g) bierwurst
- 1 lb (500 g) blockwurst
- 1 lb (500 g) mortadella
- 1 lb (500 g) bologna

See also BRAUNSCHWEIGER; LANDJÄGER; MORTADELLA; SUMMER SAUSAGE; THURINGER.

Chafing Dish

Derived from the French chauffeur, *which means "to heat," chafing dishes evolved to allow for simple, elegant tableside cooking away from the bustle and mess of the main cooking area.*

If You Don't Have It
Substitute a chafing dish with:
- large fondue pot

Challah

Also known as challa and hallah. Jewish egg-rich bread that is often braided and served on the Sabbath and holidays. Traditionally, when challah is prepared, a pinch of dough is burned in the oven as the bread bakes. The word in Biblical Hebrew refers to this bit of dough and means "the priest's share."

If You Don't Have It
Substitute 1 lb (500 g) challah with:
- 1 lb (500 g) brioche (richer)
- 1 lb (500 g) Portuguese sweet bread
- 1 lb (500 g) raisin bread
- 1 lb (500 g) shokupan (rich Japanese white bread)
- 1 lb (500 g) croissants (less eggy, more airy texture)
- 1 lb (500 g) Kugelhopf (filled with dried and candied fruit and nuts)
- 1 lb (500 g) panettone
- 1 lb (500 g) soft white bread

Champagne

Sparkling wine made by the méthode champenoise, *a meticulous production method that includes a second fermentation in the bottle and the removal of sediment.*

If You Don't Have It
Substitute 1 cup (250 mL) champagne with:
- 1 cup (250 mL) sparkling wine, such as Asti Spumante

Champagne Varieties
Choose 1 cup (250 mL) champagne from these varieties:
- 1 cup (250 mL) brut (the driest; contains less than 1.5% sugar)
- 1 cup (250 mL) extra dry or extra sec (slightly sweet; contains 1.2 to 2% sugar)
- 1 cup (250 mL) sec (medium sweet; contains 1.7 to 3.5% sugar)
- 1 cup (250 mL) demi-sec (sweet; contains 3.3 to 5% sugar)
- 1 cup (250 mL) doux (very sweet; contains more than 5% sugar) Asti Spumante

For Better Health
Substitute 1 cup (250 mL) champagne with:
- 1 cup (250 mL) sparkling cider (no alcohol)

Champagne Grape

Also known as Black Corinth and Zante grape. Tiny, sweet, juicy, purple eating grapes that, ironically, are not used to make champagne.

If You Don't Have It
Substitute 1 cup (250 mL) champagne grapes with:
- 1 cup (250 mL) Muscat grapes (adds musky flavor)
- 1 cup (250 mL) Flame seedless grapes (red color)
- 1 cup (250 mL) Thompson seedless grapes (larger; pale green color)

See also CURRANTS, DRIED.

Chana Flour

See CHOOSING AMONG WHOLE-GRAIN AND ALTERNATIVE FLOURS (PAGE 586).

Chanterelle

See SHUFFLING MUSHROOMS (PAGE 572).

Chaource

Named after a town in the Champagne region of France, this soft-rind cow's milk cheese resembles Camembert.

If You Don't Have It
Substitute 1 oz (30 g) Chaource cheese with:
- 1 oz (30 g) Ervy-le-Châtel
- 1 oz (30 g) Camembert
- 1 oz (30 g) Brie

Chapati

Indian flatbread made with whole wheat flour and little or no fat.

If You Don't Have It

Substitute 1 chapati with:
- 1 roti (a generic term for Indian flatbread; similar to chapati; usually made with whole wheat flour)
- 1 paratha (griddle-cooked whole wheat flatbread with fat in the dough; richer; more flaky)
- 1 poori (deep-fried flatbread made with whole wheat flour; crisper)
- 1 naan (more puffy flatbread made from refined wheat flour and cooked on the walls of a tandoor or clay-lined oven; sometimes flavored with garlic, herbs, or other aromatics)
- 1 whole wheat pita bread (similar to naan)
- 1 whole wheat flour tortilla

Chapati Flour

Also known as atta. Finely milled whole wheat flour that is mixed with water to make Indian flatbread.

If You Don't Have It

Substitute 1 cup (250 mL) chapati flour with:
- ⅓ cup (75 mL) whole wheat flour + ⅓ cup (75 mL) all-purpose flour + ⅓ cup (75 mL) cake flour (makes tender breads)
- ⅓ cup (75 mL) whole wheat flour + ⅔ cup (150 mL) all-purpose flour (more firm breads)

Char

Also known as Arctic char. A fish with pink flesh and salmon-trout flavor aquacultured in Iceland.

If You Don't Have It

Substitute 1 lb (500 g) char with:
- 1 lb (500 g) salmon
- 1 lb (500 g) striped bass

Chard

Also known as leaf beet, spinach beet, and Swiss chard. Ranging in stem color from white to magenta, chard's green leafy stalks are related to the common beet. Both the stalks and leaves are beloved in Spain and Italy, where they are often sautéed in olive oil and garlic.

If You Don't Have It

Substitute 1 lb (500 g) chard with:
- 1 lb (500 g) turnip greens
- 1 lb (500 g) mature spinach
- 1 lb (500 g) bok choy
- 1 lb (500 g) mustard greens
- 1 lb (500 g) Tuscan kale

Chard Varieties

Choose 1 lb (500 g) chard from these varieties:
- 1 lb (500 g) red chard (maroon stalks; slightly more tender than green chard)
- 1 lb (500 g) green chard (white stalks)

Charentais Melon

Small French melon with fragrant orange flesh and yellow rind.

> 1 lb (500 g) =
> 1 to 1½ cups
> (250 to 375 mL) cubed

If You Don't Have It

Substitute 1 cup (250 mL) chopped Charentais melon with:
- 1 cup (250 mL) chopped cantaloupe
- 1 cup (250 mL) chopped Persian melon
- 1 cup (250 mL) chopped Crenshaw melon
- 1 cup (250 mL) chopped Santa Claus melon
- 1 cup (250 mL) chopped honeydew melon

Charoli Nuts

Small, dark brown nuts with a flavor reminiscent of nutmeg. Often used in Indian desserts.

If You Don't Have It

Substitute 1 cup (250 mL) charoli nuts with:
- 1 cup (250 mL) unsalted pistachios + pinch of grated nutmeg

Chartreuse

An aromatic liqueur originally bottled by French Carthusian monks. The green variety is minty, spicy, and more intense than the yellow, which is lower in alcohol, sweetened with honey, and tinted with saffron. Chartreuse V.E.P. (in both colors) is aged for 12 years in oak to produce a more complex and mellow spirit.

If You Don't Have It

Substitute 3 tbsp (45 mL) Chartreuse with:
- 3 tbsp (45 mL) Izarra
- 3 tbsp (45 mL) Strega
- 3 tbsp (45 mL) Bénédictine
- 3 tbsp (45 mL) Drambuie (mild licorice flavor)

Chartreuse Varieties

Choose 3 tbsp (45 mL) Chartreuse from these varieties:
- 3 tbsp (45 mL) green Chartreuse (green color; more bracing flavor and heavier body than yellow Chartreuse)
- 3 tbsp (45 mL) yellow Chartreuse (pale golden color; sweeter flavor and lighter body than green Chartreuse)

Chaurice

See CHORIZO.

Chaya

Also known as tree spinach. The extremely nutritious leaves of a Central American shrub are covered with stinging hairs. When picked young, however, they are tender and may be cooked like spinach.

If You Don't Have It

Substitute 1 lb (500 g) chaya with:
- 1 lb (500 g) spinach
- 1 lb (500 g) green chard
- 1 lb (500 g) turnip greens

Chayote

Also known as mirliton and vegetable pear. A mild gourd-like fruit that's shaped like a pear.

If You Don't Have It
Substitute 1 lb (500 g) chayote with:
- 1 lb (500 g) bottle gourd or cucuzza
- 1 lb (500 g) zucchini
- 1 lb (500 g) yellow crookneck squash
- 8 oz (250 g) summer squash + 8 oz (250 g) kohlrabi

Cheddar

In 1840, English dairy farmers in Somerset created a tasty wedding present for Queen Victoria: a Cheddar cheese weighing 1,100 pounds (500 kg). In Wisconsin 120 years later, dairy farmers created a bigger 34,951-pound (16,000 kg) Cheddar.

> 1 lb (500 g) = 4 cups (1 L) shredded

If You Don't Have It
Substitute 1 oz (30 g) Cheddar cheese with:
- 1 oz (30 g) Colby
- 1 oz (30 g) Cheshire
- 1 oz (30 g) Double Gloucester
- 1 oz (30 g) Leicester
- 1 oz (30 g) Lancashire
- 1 oz (30 g) Jack cheese
- 1 oz (30 g) American cheese

For Better Health
Substitute 1 oz (30 g) Cheddar cheese with:
- 1 oz (30 g) reduced-fat Cheddar

See also CHESHIRE; GLOUCESTER; LANCASHIRE; LEICESTER; WENSLEYDALE.

Chee Hou Sauce

Also known as chu hou paste. Popular dark brown Chinese braising sauce made from soybeans, garlic, and ginger.

If You Don't Have It
Substitute ¼ cup (50 mL) chee hou sauce with:
- ¼ cup (50 mL) hoisin sauce (sweeter)

Cheese

Fresh cheeses, such as Italian ricotta, are meant to be enjoyed immediately. Other cheese curds are cooked, pressed, and aged in controlled environments to produce semifirm cheeses, such as Cheddar, and hard cheeses, such as Parmesan.

For Better Health
Substitute 1 oz (30 g) cheese with:
- 1 oz (30 g) reduced-fat cheese (made with partially skimmed milk; avoid fat-free cheeses, which do not melt well and have lost all semblance of cheese due to lack of fat)
- 1 oz (30 g) soy cheese (vegetarian; find a brand you like)

See also SPECIFIC TYPES.

Cheesecloth

Also known as butter muslin. Loosely woven cotton cloth used for culinary functions, such as straining, lining molds, and encasing a bouquet garni.

If You Don't Have It
Substitute cheesecloth with:
- nylon mesh, such as clean nylon stockings (for straining)
- clean kitchen towel (for straining)
- coffee filters (for straining and bouquet garni)

Cheez Whiz

See PROCESSED CHEESE.

Cherimoya

Also known as custard apple. This fruit has petal-patterned jade-green skin filled with granular creamy flesh that has a flavor suggesting mango, papaya, pineapple, and vanilla.

If You Don't Have It
Substitute 1 lb (500 g) cherimoya with:
- 1 lb (500 g) atemoya
- 1 lb (500 g) soursop
- 1 lb (500 g) sweetsop
- 1 lb (500 g) mango or papaya + ¼ tsp (1 mL) vanilla extract

See also ATEMOYA; SOURSOP; SWEETSOP.

Chéri Suisse

See CHERRY LIQUEUR.

Cherry

The name cherry is derived from the ancient Greek word kerasos, *which was also the name of a city in Asia Minor. Historians debate whether this small stone fruit was named for the city, or the city named for the fruit. Cherry varieties are generally classified as sweet or sour.*

> 1 lb (500 g) fresh =
> 2½ to 3 cups
> (625 to 750 mL) pitted
>
> 10 oz (300 g) frozen =
> 1 cup (250 mL)
>
> 16-oz (454 mL) can =
> 1½ cups (375 mL) drained

If You Don't Have It
Substitute 1 lb (500 g) cherries with:
- 1 lb (500 g) acerola
- 1 lb (500 g) chokecherries (to replace sour cherries for cooking)
- 1 lb (500 g) apricots
- 1 lb (500 g) plums
- 1 lb (500 g) peaches
- 1 lb (500 g) nectarines

Cherry Varieties
Choose 1 lb (500 g) cherries from these varieties:
- 1 lb (500 g) sweet cherries such as Bing, Lambert, and Royal Ann (best for snacking, but some varieties taste good cooked; yellow-and-red Royal Anns or Napoleons are often used to make maraschino cherries)
- 1 lb (500 g) sour cherries such as Early Richmond, Montmorency, and Morello (smaller, softer, and more tart than sweet cherries; best for cooking in pies, jams, and sauces)

See also CHERRY, DRIED; CHOKECHERRY.

Cherry, Candied

Also known as glacé cherries. These sugar-soaked cherries are sold in red and green versions. Often used in cakes, breads, and other desserts.

If You Don't Have It

Substitute 1 cup (250 mL) candied cherries with:
- 1 cup (250 mL) dried cherries, dried cranberries, or other dried fruit

---

Cherry, Dried

Both sweet and sour varieties are available commercially dried like raisins. Eat out-of-hand for a snack or use in savory and dessert recipes.

15 oz (426 g) =
2½ cups (625 mL)

If You Don't Have It

Substitute 1 cup (250 mL) dried cherries with:
- 1 cup (250 mL) dried cranberries (more tart)
- 1 cup (250 mL) dried blueberries (dark blue color)
- 1 cup (250 mL) raisins
- 1 cup (250 mL) currants

Cherry Liqueur

Several types of cherry liqueur can be used interchangeably, including Cherry Heering, Cherry Marnier, Cherry Rocher, Kirschenliqueur.

If You Don't Have It

Substitute 3 tbsp (45 mL) cherry liqueur with:
- 3 tbsp (45 mL) Crème de cerise (sweeter)
- 3 tbsp (45 mL) cherry cordial or cherry syrup (sweeter; nonalcoholic)
- 3 tbsp (45 mL) Maraschino liqueur (less sweet)
- 3 tbsp (45 mL) Chéri Suisse (adds chocolate flavor)
- 3 tbsp (45 mL) Kirsch (cherry brandy; less sweet)
- 3 tbsp (45 mL) cherry schnapps (less sweet)
- 3 tbsp (45 mL) cherry vodka (less sweet)
- 3 tbsp (45 mL) cherry whiskey (less sweet)
- 1 to 1½ tsp (5 to 7 mL) cherry extract + 3 tbsp (45 mL) water or liquid in recipe (less sweet)

Cherry Pepper

See CHOOSING FRESH CHILES (PAGE 582).

Cherrystone Clam

See CLAM.

Cherry Tomato

See TOMATO.

Chervil

Also known as cicely, cicily, and sweet cicely. A relative of parsley, chervil's delicate anise note is finest in the fresh leaf form.

If You Don't Have It

Substitute 1 tbsp (15 mL) chopped fresh chervil with:
- 1 tbsp (15 mL) chopped fresh parsley
- 1 tbsp (15 mL) chopped fresh tarragon (stronger anise flavor)
- 1 tbsp (15 mL) chopped fresh fennel leaves
- 1 tbsp (15 mL) chopped fresh fines herbes (usually includes chervil, chives, parsley, and tarragon)
- 1 tbsp (15 mL) cicely (stronger anise flavor)
- 1 tsp (5 mL) dried chervil or parsley

See also CICELY.

Cheshire

Renowned English cow's milk cheese made only in its region of origin near the town of Chester. It's crumbly and tastes similar to Cheddar. The pale cheese is often colored orange with annatto. Blue Cheshire is as rich as Stilton but less robust.

If You Don't Have It

Substitute 1 oz (30 g) Cheshire cheese with:
- 1 oz (30 g) English Cheddar
- 1 oz (30 g) Wensleydale
- 1 oz (30 g) Leicester
- 1 oz (30 g) Colby (less flavorful)
- 1 oz (30 g) Jack, especially aged (pale color; less flavorful)

Chestnut

These sweet nuts generally contain more starch and less oil than other tree nuts and have played an important role as a food staple in rural areas of Europe, Asia, and North America.

1 lb (500 g) in shell =
12 oz (375 g) shelled =
35 to 40 chestnuts
shelled and peeled =
2 cups (500 mL)

3 oz (90 g) dried = 1 cup
(250 mL) fresh

8 oz (250 g) purée =
about 1 cup (250 mL)

If You Don't Have It

Substitute 1 cup (250 mL) fresh shelled chestnuts with:
- 1 cup (250 mL) canned or jarred chestnuts
- 1 cup (250 mL) hazelnuts
- 1 cup (250 mL) pecans
- 1 cup (250 mL) macadamia nuts
- 1 cup (250 mL) chufa nuts

See also NUTS.

Chestnut, Candied

Also known as marrons glacés. Shelled and peeled chestnuts poached in syrup until candied.

If You Don't Have It

Substitute 1 cup (250 mL) candied chestnuts with:
- 1 cup (250 mL) chestnut cream
- 1 cup (250 mL) candied fruit such as cherries

Chestnut Cream

Also known as crème de marron. Puréed chestnuts sweetened with brown sugar and vanilla.

If You Don't Have It

Substitute 1 cup (250 mL) chestnut cream with:
- 1 cup (250 mL) candied chestnuts + dash of vanilla puréed in small food processor (add water or Homemade Simple Syrup, see recipe, page 489, if necessary to thin the purée)

Chestnut Flour

See CHOOSING AMONG WHOLE-GRAIN AND ALTERNATIVE FLOURS (PAGE 586).

Chestnut Purée

Also known as purée de marron. Shelled and peeled chestnuts are cooked in milk and then puréed and passed through a sieve. Employed as a base for soups, stuffings, and desserts.

If You Don't Have It

Substitute 1 cup (250 mL) chestnut purée with:
- 1 cup (250 mL) chestnut cream (omit 1 to 3 tbsp/15 to 45 mL sugar from recipe)
- 1 cup (250 mL) Homemade Chestnut Purée: Put 1 cup (250 mL) shelled and peeled chestnuts (canned or jarred work in a pinch) in a small saucepan and cover with milk or water. Simmer over low heat until very tender, about 1 hour. Add more milk or water as necessary. Purée in a small food processor or blender and press through a sieve.

Chèvre

Also known as goat cheese. The generic French term for cheeses made from goat's milk. The term commonly refers to unaged or fresh goat cheeses that are snowy white, creamy in texture (with a slight chalkiness), and have a mild flavor with a pleasing tang. Aged chèvres have a firmer texture and sharper flavor.

If You Don't Have It

Substitute 1 oz (30 g) chèvre with:
- 1 oz (30 g) cream cheese or mascarpone (to replace fresh chèvre; smoother texture; simpler flavor)

Chèvre Varieties

Choose 1 oz (30 g) chèvre from these specific types:
- 1 oz (30 g) Montrachet (usually ash-covered)
- 1 oz (30 g) Banon (softer texture; wrapped in chestnut leaves)
- 1 oz (30 g) Bûcheron (softer texture; usually covered with black ash or a white rind)
- 1 oz (30 g) Selles-sur-Cher (semifirm texture; sweet, nutty flavor; covered with black ash)

Chèvre (cont'd)

- 1 oz (30 g) Crottin de Chavignol (soft to firm texture and mild to nutty flavor, depending on age)
- 1 oz (30 g) aged chèvre (firmer texture; stronger flavor)

For Better Health
Substitute 1 oz (30 g) chèvre with:
- ½ oz (15 g) chèvre + ½ oz (15 g) reduced-fat cream cheese (less fat and fewer calories)

See also CAPRINI; GOAT'S MILK.

Chicken

Chickens are classified by age and size, which generally dictates their best uses. Tender two- to three-month old broiler-fryers generally weigh 3 to 4 pounds (1.5 to 2 kg) and are best for broiling, roasting, frying, and grilling. Four- to eight-month old roasters weigh 3 to 5 pounds (1.5 to 2.5 kg), have a slightly higher fat content, and taste best roasted. Ten- to eighteen-month old stewing chickens weigh 3 to 6 pounds (1.5 to 3 kg) and have tougher but more flavorful meat that takes best to longer, moist-heat cooking methods such as stewing and braising. Cornish game hens are small hybrid chickens sold at 4 to 6 weeks old and 1 to 2 pounds (500 g to 1 kg).

> 1 lb (500 g) boneless chicken = 3 cups (750 mL) cubed

If You Don't Have It
Substitute 1 lb (500 g) chicken with:
- 1 lb (500 g) turkey
- 1 lb (500 g) rabbit

To Vary the Flavor
Substitute 1 lb (500 g) Cornish hen with:
- 1 lb (500 g) quail (leaner)
- 1 lb (500 g) squab (more tender)
- 1 lb (500 g) grouse (leaner)
- 1 lb (500 g) young pheasant (leaner)

For Better Health
Substitute 1 lb (500 g) chicken with:
- 1 lb (500 g) kosher chicken (raised more humanely with tighter bacterial controls; brined, which makes the meat slightly more salty)
- 1 lb (500 g) free-range chicken (raised more humanely; often fed a vegetarian diet; meat may be slightly less tender but more flavorful)
- 1 lb (500 g) pasture-raised chicken (raised outdoors on a diet with a high percentage of natural forage; meat may be slightly less tender but more flavorful)
- 1 lb (500 g) organic chicken (fed an organic diet)
- 1 lb (500 g) vegetarian chicken products (made with soy protein)
- 1 lb (500 g) extra-firm tofu (more tender; less flavorful)

Chicken, Ground

Skinless, boneless chicken parts run through a meat grinder. Sold packaged in supermarket meat sections. Chunks of raw chicken meat may also be finely chopped in a food processor fitted with a metal blade.

If You Don't Have It
Substitute 1 lb (500 g) ground chicken with:
- 1 lb (500 g) ground turkey (often includes dark meat)
- 1 lb (500 g) ground veal

For Better Health
Substitute 1 lb (500 g) ground chicken with:
- 1 lb (500 g) ground turkey breast

Chickpea

See THE WIDE WORLD OF DRIED BEANS (PAGE 566).

Chickpea Flour

See CHOOSING AMONG WHOLE-GRAIN AND ALTERNATIVE FLOURS (PAGE 586).

Chicory

Leafy perennial plants often served as salads. Types of chicory include broad/narrow leaves, curly/noncurly leaves, heading/nonheading plants. Both red-leaf radicchio and green leafy Sugarloaf are types of chicory.

If You Don't Have It
Substitute 1 cup (250 mL) chicory with:
- 1 cup (250 mL) curly endive
- 1 cup (250 mL) escarole
- 1 cup (250 mL) radicchio (red color)

See also BELGIAN ENDIVE; CURLY ENDIVE; RADICCHIO.

Chicory Root, Roasted

The large roots of some chicory are roasted and ground as a coffee substitute.

If You Don't Have It
Substitute 1 cup (250 mL) brewed roasted chicory root with:
- 1 cup (250 mL) brewed coffee

Chihuahua Cheese

See ASADERO.

Chile

See BELL PEPPER; CAYENNE PEPPER; CHILE OIL; CHILE POWDER; HOT PEPPER SAUCE; PAPRIKA; CHOOSING DRIED CHILES (PAGE 578); CHOOSING FRESH CHILES (PAGE 582).

Chile Bean Paste

See CHILE PASTE.

Chile Garlic Sauce

See CHILE PASTE.

Chile Oil

A mainstay of the Chinese kitchen, this condiment is prepared by steeping hot chiles in vegetable oil. Use sparingly. It's often very spicy.

If You Don't Have It

Substitute ½ tsp (2 mL) chile oil with:

- ½ tsp (2 mL) hot chili sesame oil (less spicy; adds sesame flavor)
- ½ tsp (2 mL) vegetable oil + pinch of cayenne pepper or dash of hot pepper sauce
- ½ tsp (2 mL) Homemade Chile Oil: Heat 1 cup (250 mL) vegetable oil (or toasted sesame oil for hot chile sesame oil) over medium-high heat until hot. Remove from heat and add 1 to 3 tbsp (15 to 45 mL) crushed red pepper flakes. Cover and set aside for 8 to 24 hours. Strain into a clean jar or bottle and discard pepper flakes. Add whole dried chiles (such as cayenne) to oil for decoration. Store oil in a cool place for up to 6 months. Makes 1 cup (250 mL).

Chile Paste

Also known as chili sauce, chile garlic sauce, chile bean paste (when made with fermented beans), and curry paste (when including several spices for curries). Usually refers to one of several Asian chile pastes, condiments made from crushed chiles that are widely used to flavor stir-fries, sauces, marinades, and dressings. May also refer to a Southwestern American chile paste that's used as the basis for chili and other regional Southwestern dishes.

If You Don't Have It

Substitute 1 tbsp (15 mL) chile paste with:

- 1 to 3 tsp (5 to 15 mL) hot sauce
- 2 to 3 tsp (10 to 15 mL) harissa
- 1 tbsp (15 mL) berbere
- 1 tsp (5 mL) red pepper flakes
- ½ tsp (2 mL) ground cayenne pepper
- 1½ tsp (7 mL) bean sauce + 1½ tsp (7 mL) chile paste (adds fermented bean flavor)
- 2 small whole chiles + 1 small clove garlic

Chile Paste Varieties

Choose 1 tbsp (15 mL) chile paste from these specific types:

- 1 tbsp (15 mL) Szechuan chile paste (Chinese chile bean paste; medium-hot; made with chiles, garlic, vinegar, and fermented soybeans)
- 1 tbsp (15 mL) kochu chang (Korean chile bean paste; hot and sweet; made with chiles, sugar, fermented soybeans, and salt)
- 1 tbsp (15 mL) tuong ot toi (Vietnamese chile sauce; hot; one of the simplest; usually includes chiles, garlic, vinegar, and salt)
- 1 tbsp (15 mL) sambal oelek (Southeast Asian chile

paste; hot; one of the simplest; usually includes chiles, sugar, and salt)

- 1 tbsp (15 mL) sambal bajak (Southeast Asian chile paste; hot; usually includes chiles, sugar, salt, garlic, onion, shrimp paste, nuts, and tamarind)
- 1 tbsp (15 mL) nam prik (Thai chile sauce; hot; usually includes chiles, garlic, lime, fish sauce, shrimp paste, tamarind, and sugar; known as nam prik pao when some of the ingredients are cooked)
- 1 tbsp (15 mL) nam prik kaeng khiao wan (thick, green Thai curry paste or sauce; very hot; usually includes chiles, garlic, lime, lemongrass, shrimp paste, coriander, galangal, sugar, and salt)
- 1 tbsp (15 mL) nam prik kaeng phet (thick red Thai curry paste or sauce; hot; usually includes chiles, garlic, lime, lemongrass, shrimp paste, coriander, galangal, and turmeric)
- 1 tbsp (15 mL) nam prik gaeng kari (thick yellow Thai curry paste or sauce; medium-hot; usually includes chiles, garlic, lime, lemongrass, shrimp paste, coriander, galangal, and turmeric)

Chile Pepper

See CHOOSING DRIED CHILES (PAGE 578); CHOOSING FRESH CHILES (PAGE 582).

Chile Powder

Also known as pure chile powder. Red chile powder is usually made from dried and ground red New Mexican chiles. Other pure chile powders often include the name of the dried chile, such as ancho powder and chipotle powder.

If You Don't Have It

Substitute 1 tsp (5 mL) pure chile powder with:
- ½ to 1 tsp (2 to 5 mL) cayenne pepper (most likely hotter)
- 1 to 2 tsp (5 to 10 mL) paprika (milder)
- 1 tsp (5 mL) chile oil
- 1 tsp (5 mL) chili powder (adds cumin, oregano, and salt)

See also CHILI POWDER.

Chile Sauce

A spicier version of ketchup that may be seasoned with chiles or chile powder, green bell peppers, and onions.

If You Don't Have It

Substitute 1 cup (250 mL) chile sauce with:
- 1 cup (250 mL) ketchup
- 1 cup (250 mL) Homemade Chili Sauce: Mix together 1 cup (250 mL) tomato sauce, ¼ cup (50 mL) brown sugar, 3 tbsp (45 mL) apple cider vinegar, 1 tbsp (15 mL) minced mild green chiles, and ¼ tsp (1 mL) ground allspice. Makes about 1¼ cups (300 mL).

Chili

See BELL PEPPER; CAYENNE PEPPER; CHILE OIL; CHILE POWDER; HOT PEPPER SAUCE; PAPRIKA; CHOOSING DRIED CHILES (PAGE 578); CHOOSING FRESH CHILES (PAGE 582).

Chili Bean Paste

See CHILE PASTE.

Chili Garlic Sauce

See CHILE PASTE.

Chili Oil

See CHILE OIL.

Chili Powder

A spice blend used for making chili. Usually includes ground New Mexican chiles, dried oregano, other seasonings, and salt.

If You Don't Have It

Substitute 1 tsp (5 mL) chili powder with:

- 1 tsp (5 mL) Homemade Chili Powder: Mix together 1 tbsp (15 mL) paprika, 2 tsp (10 mL) cumin, 2 tsp (10 mL) dried oregano, 1 tsp (5 mL) garlic powder, 1 tsp (5 mL) onion powder, ½ tsp (2 mL) cayenne pepper, and ¼ tsp (1 mL) allspice. Makes about 3 tablespoons (45 mL).
- ½ to 1 tsp (2 to 5 mL) cayenne pepper (hotter)
- 1 to 2 tsp (5 to 10 mL) paprika (milder)
- 1 tsp (5 mL) chile oil (hotter)

Chiltepín

See CHOOSING DRIED CHILES (PAGE 578); CHOOSING FRESH CHILES (PAGE 582).

Chimichurri

Argentina's answer to pesto. A thick and slightly spicy parsley-garlic sauce often served with grilled meat.

If You Don't Have It

Substitute 1 cup (250 mL) chimichurri with

- 1 cup (250 mL) Homemade Chimichurri: Put 1½ cups (375 mL) packed fresh parsley leaves and 4 garlic cloves in a small food processor and pulse until finely chopped (or finely chop by hand). Add ¼ cup (50 mL) white or red wine vinegar, 3 tbsp (45 mL) minced onion, 2 tsp (10 mL) chopped fresh oregano (or ¼ tsp/1 mL dried), ½ tsp (2 mL) salt, ⅛ to ¼ tsp (0.5 to 1 mL) cayenne pepper, and ⅛ to ¼ tsp (0.5 to 1 mL) ground black pepper. With machine running, gradually add ½ cup (125 mL) olive oil through the feed tube and process to a coarse purée. Makes about 1 cup (250 mL).

- 1 cup (250 mL) pebre (a similar Chilean sauce made with cilantro instead of parsley)
- 1 cup (250 mL) parsley pesto + ½ tsp (2 mL) hot pepper sauce

Chinese Artichoke

Also known as chorogi, Japanese artichoke, and knot-root. A small Asian tuber with a flavor reminiscent of sunchokes (Jerusalem artichokes).

If You Don't Have It
Substitute 1 lb (500 g) Chinese artichokes with:
- 1 lb (500 g) sunchokes
- 1 lb (500 g) salsify

Chinese Black Beans

See FERMENTED BLACK BEANS.

Chinese Broccoli

Also known as Chinese kale, gai lan, kaii laan, and jie lan. This favored Chinese vegetable, probably a native of the Mediterranean, has narrow green stalks with kohlrabi-like sweetness, topped by fairly large collard-like leaves.

If You Don't Have It
Substitute 1 lb (500 g) Chinese broccoli with:
- 1 lb (500 g) broccoli raab (lighter green color; more bitter)
- 1 lb (500 g) broccoli (shorter, thicker stems; much fuller florets)
- 1 lb (500 g) Broccolini™ (lighter green color; skinnier stems)
- 1 lb (500 g) yau choy (paler green stems and leaves; more cabbagey flavor)
- 1 lb (500 g) choy sum or other bok choy (white stems and green leaves; more cabbagey flavor)
- 1 lb (500 g) red chard (sweeter flavor)

See also BROCCOLINI.

Chinese Cabbage

See BOK CHOY; NAPA CABBAGE.

Chinese Celery

Also known as Asian celery, cutting celery, leaf celery, soup celery, kan tsai, and qin cai. Cooking celery valued for its aromatic green leaves, although the skinny stalks are also cooked as a vegetable and aromatic seasoning.

If You Don't Have It
Substitute 1 cup (250 mL) chopped Chinese celery with:
- 1 cup (250 mL) celery (milder flavor)
- 1 cup (250 mL) chopped cardoons (adds mild artichoke flavor)
- 1 cup (250 mL) chopped fennel stalks (adds mild anise flavor)
- 1 cup (250 mL) chopped celery leaves (to replace Chinese celery leaves)
- 1 cup (250 mL) chopped parsley (to replace Chinese celery leaves)
- ½ cup (125 mL) dehydrated celery flakes (for soups and stews; much less flavorful)

Chinese Chives

See GARLIC CHIVES.

Chinese Date, Dried

When dried, apple-like Chinese dates taste similar to the more familiar medjool dates but less sweet.

If You Don't Have It
Substitute 1 cup (250 mL) dried Chinese dates with:
- 1 cup (250 mL) medjool dates (sweeter)
- 1 cup (250 mL) prunes
- 1 cup (250 mL) raisins

Chinese Date, Fresh

Also known as Chinese jujube and red date. Pale green fruit with crisp white flesh similar to apples. Chinese dates are more common dried.

If You Don't Have It
Substitute 1 cup (250 mL) chopped fresh Chinese dates with:
- 1 cup (250 mL) chopped fresh apples

Chinese Duck Sauce

See PLUM SAUCE.

Chinese Five-Spice Powder

An exciting, aromatic seasoning blend of cinnamon, cloves, fennel seed, star anise, and Szechuan pepper.

If You Don't Have It

Substitute 1 tsp (5 mL) Chinese five-spice powder with:

- 1 tsp (5 mL) Homemade Chinese Five-Spice Powder: Mix together 1½ tbsp (22 mL) ground star anise, 2½ tsp (12 mL) ground fennel seed, 1½ tsp (7 mL) cinnamon, ½ tsp (2 mL) ground Szechuan pepper (or salt-free lemon pepper), and ¼ tsp (1 mL) ground cloves. Makes about 3 tablespoons (45 mL).

Chinese Flowering Cabbage

See BOK CHOY.

Chinese Garlic Stems

Also known as garlic flower stems, green garlic, shen sum, and suan tai. Long, pencil-thin, green garlic stems with crunchy texture and garlic flavor.

If You Don't Have It

Substitute 1 cup (250 mL) chopped Chinese garlic stems with:

- 1 cup (250 mL) chopped garlic chives
- ¾ cup (175 mL) chopped green onions or scallions (green and white parts) + ¼ cup (50 mL) chopped garlic
- 1 cup (250 mL) chopped chives (not crunchy; more onion, less garlic flavor)

Chinese Ginger

See FINGERROOT.

Chinese Gooseberry

See KIWIFRUIT.

Chinese Grapefruit

See PUMMELO.

Chinese Ham

See YUNNAN HAM.

Chinese Jujube

See CHINESE DATE, DRIED; CHINESE DATE, FRESH.

Chinese Kale

See CHINESE BROCCOLI.

Chinese Key

See FINGERROOT.

Chinese Okra	*See* LOOFAH, ANGLED.
Chinese Parsley	*See* CILANTRO.
Chinese Pea Pod	*See* PEAS, EDIBLE POD.
Chinese Pear	*See* ASIAN PEAR.
Chinese Potato	*See* ARROWHEAD.
Chinese Spinach	*See* AMARANTH LEAVES.
Chinese Steelhead	*See* BLACKFISH.
Chinese Strainer	*See* STRAINER.
Chinese Vermicelli	*See* A SNAPSHOT OF ASIAN NOODLES (PAGE 588).
Chinese White Cabbage	*See* BOK CHOY.

Chinois

A cone-shaped metal mesh sieve for straining and puréeing cooked foods. The finest mesh chinois is called a bouillon strainer.

If You Don't Have It
Substitute a chinois with:
- fine or medium mesh-strainer

Chinook Salmon

See SALMON.

Chipolata

Also known as little fingers. Tiny, well-seasoned pork sausages. In French cuisine, à la chipolata is a garnish of chipolata, chestnuts, and glazed vegetables that accompanies roasts.

If You Don't Have It
Substitute 1 lb (500 g) chipolata with:
- 1 lb (500 g) hot links (larger)
- 1 lb (500 g) spicy kielbasa (much larger)
- 1 lb (500 g) highly seasoned sausage
- 1 lb (500 g) Vienna sausage (less flavorful)

Chipotle

See CHOOSING DRIED CHILES (PAGE 578).

Chipped Beef

Also known as dried beef. Razor-thin slices of salted, smoked dried beef. Basis of the infamous American military staple creamed chipped beef on toast.

If You Don't Have It
Substitute 4 oz (125 g) chipped beef with:
- 4 oz (125 g) beef jerky (tougher)
- 4 oz (125 g) biltong (tougher; more complex, spicy flavor)
- 4 oz (125 g) pemmican (tougher; more complex flavor)

For Better Health
Substitute 4 oz (125 g) chipped beef with:
- 4 oz (125 g) turkey jerky (tougher; leaner)
- 4 oz (125 g) vegetarian jerky (leaner)

Chive Blossom

See PICKING EDIBLE FLOWERS (PAGE 604).

Chives

Both the skinny green leaves and violet flowers offer mild onion flavor. To simplify chopping chives, snip them with kitchen scissors.

If You Don't Have It
Substitute 1 tbsp (15 mL) chopped fresh chives with:
- 1 tbsp (15 mL) chopped green onions or scallions (green tops only)
- 1 tbsp (15 mL) chopped garlic chives (adds garlic flavor)
- 1 tbsp (15 mL) Chinese garlic stems (adds crunch and garlic flavor)
- 3 tbsp (45 mL) chopped dried chives (much less flavorful)

See also GARLIC CHIVES; ONIONS, GREEN.

Chocolate, Bittersweet

Intensely flavored chocolate made with slightly less sugar than semisweet chocolate and at least 35% chocolate liquor, which is the brown paste remaining after cocoa butter is extracted from cocoa beans.

If You Don't Have It
Substitute 1 oz (30 g) bittersweet chocolate with:
- 1 oz (30 g) semisweet chocolate (add ¼ tsp to ½ tsp/1 to 2 mL unsweetened cocoa powder for richer chocolate flavor)
- ⅔ oz (20 g) unsweetened chocolate + 2 tsp (10 mL) granulated sugar
- 2 heaping tbsp (25 mL) unsweetened cocoa powder + 1 to 1⅓ tbsp (15 to 20 mL) granulated sugar + 1½ tsp (7 mL) butter, shortening, or vegetable oil

Chocolate, Couverture

Dark "covering" chocolate with at least 32% cocoa butter that is used by pastry chefs to coat candies and glaze cakes.

If You Don't Have It
Substitute 1 oz (30 g) couverture chocolate with:
- 1 oz (30 g) bittersweet or semisweet chocolate + ¼ to ½ tsp (1 to 2 mL) butter, shortening, or vegetable oil
- 1 oz (30 g) chocolate confectionery coating (contains no cocoa butter; less rich taste and mouth-feel; melts at a higher temperature)

See also CONFECTIONERY COATING.

Chocolate Curls

Also known as chocolate shavings. Made by warming a thick chocolate bar or square then shaving curls from it with a vegetable peeler.

If You Don't Have It
Substitute ½ cup (125 mL) chocolate curls (for garnishing desserts) with:
- ⅓ cup (75 mL) grated chocolate
- 1 to 3 tbsp (15 to 45 mL) sifted cocoa powder (for dusting)

Chocolate-Hazelnut Spread

See GIANDUJA.

Chocolate Liqueur

Includes brands such as Godiva, Mozart, and Haagen Daz.

If You Don't Have It
Substitute 3 tbsp (45 mL) chocolate liqueur with:
- 3 tbsp (45 mL) water + ¾ tsp (4 mL) chocolate extract
- 3 tbsp (45 mL) chocolate syrup (thicker; sweeter; nonalcoholic)

To Vary the Flavor
Substitute 3 tbsp (45 mL) chocolate liqueur with:
- 3 tbsp (45 mL) crème de cacao (sweeter)
- 3 tbsp (45 mL) Chéri Suisse (combines chocolate and cherry flavors)
- 3 tbsp (45 mL) Vandermint (combines chocolate and mint flavors)
- 3 tbsp (45 mL) Tiramisù liqueur (combines chocolate, coffee, and almond flavors)
- 3 tbsp (45 mL) coffee liqueur
- 3 tbsp (45 mL) almond liqueur
- 3 tbsp (45 mL) hazelnut liqueur

Chocolate, Mexican

Also known as Ibarra chocolate, a popular brand. A grainy sweetened chocolate flavored with cinnamon, almonds, and vanilla.

1 tablet = 3.1 oz (93 g)

If You Don't Have It
Substitute 1 oz (30 g) Mexican chocolate with:
- 1 oz (30 g) semisweet chocolate, + ½ tsp (2 mL) ground cinnamon + 1 drop almond extract + 1 drop vanilla extract
- 1 tbsp (15 mL) cocoa powder (for mole sauces)

Chocolate, Milk

Similar to semisweet chocolate but with more sugar, a minimum of 10% chocolate liquor, and at least 12% added milk solids.

If You Don't Have It
Substitute 6 oz (175 g) milk chocolate with:
- 6 oz (175 g) semisweet or white chocolate
- 6 oz (175 g) sweet chocolate

Chocolate, Semisweet

Sweetened chocolate made with slightly more sugar than bittersweet chocolate and at least 35% chocolate liquor (the brown paste remaining after cocoa butter is extracted from cocoa beans). If the chocolate is to be melted, chips, squares, and bars are generally interchangeable. However, chips contain stabilizers that help them retain their shape during baking. These stabilizers may create a less velvety texture in delicate chocolate sauces and custards.

6 oz (175 g) = 1 cup (250 mL) chips

If You Don't Have It
Substitute 1 oz (30 g) semisweet chocolate with:
- 1 oz (30 g) bittersweet chocolate (richer chocolate flavor)
- ½ oz (15 g) unsweetened chocolate + 1 tbsp (15 mL) granulated sugar
- 3 tbsp (45 mL) unsweetened cocoa powder + 1 to 1½ tbsp (15 to 22 mL) granulated sugar + 1½ tsp (7 mL) butter, shortening, or vegetable oil

To Vary the Flavor
Substitute 6 oz (175 g) or 1 cup (250 mL) semisweet chocolate chips with:
- 6 oz (175 g) chocolate bar or squares, chopped into chunks (chunks from untempered chocolate bars may lose their shape more than chocolate chips)
- 6 oz (175 g) mint-flavored semisweet chocolate chips
- 6 oz (175 g) milk chocolate chips
- 6 oz (175 g) M&Ms
- 6 oz (175 g) peanut butter chips
- 6 oz (175 g) butterscotch chips
- 6 oz (175 g) cinnamon chips
- 6 oz (175 g) white chocolate chips
- 1 cup (250 mL) chopped nuts

Chocolate Semisweet (cont'd)

For Better Health

Substitute 6 oz (175 g) or 1 cup (250 mL) semisweet chocolate chips with:

- 3 oz (90 g) or ½ cup (125 mL) semisweet mini chocolate chips (for better distribution throughout baked goods)
- 6 oz (175 g) or 1 cup (250 mL) carob chips
- 1 cup (250 mL) raisins
- 1 cup (250 mL) chocolate-covered raisins
- 9 tbsp (135 mL) unsweetened cocoa powder + 7 tbsp (105 mL) sugar + 1 tbsp (15 mL) butter, shortening, or vegetable oil (when needed to replace melted semisweet chocolate chips; for same fat content as semisweet chips, use 3 tbsp/45 mL butter, shortening, or oil)

Chocolate Shavings

See CHOCOLATE CURLS.

Chocolate, Sweet

Also known by some brands as sweet German chocolate. Similar to semisweet chocolate but containing more sugar and a minimum of 15% chocolate liquor.

If You Don't Have It

Substitute 1 oz (30 g) sweet chocolate with:

- 1 oz (30 g) semisweet or bittersweet chocolate (richer chocolate and less sweet flavor)
- ½ oz (15 g) unsweetened chocolate + 4 tsp (20 mL) granulated sugar
- 3 tbsp (45 mL) unsweetened cocoa powder + 4 tsp (20 mL) granulated sugar + 1 tbsp (15 mL) butter, shortening, or vegetable oil

Chocolate Syrup

A sweet syrup made from cocoa powder, corn syrup, and other flavorings and thickeners. Available in cans and jars in thin or thick versions. Often used on desserts or to make chocolate milk.

If You Don't Have It

Substitute 1 cup (250 mL) chocolate syrup with:

- 1 cup (250 mL) Homemade Chocolate Syrup: Whisk together ½ cup (125 mL) light corn syrup and ½ cup (125 mL) unsweetened cocoa powder (preferably Dutch-process) in a medium saucepan. (Mixture will be very thick.) Whisk in 1 cup (250 mL) milk, 1⅓ cups (325 mL) granulated sugar, and ⅛ to ¼ tsp (0.5 to 1 mL) salt. Bring to a gentle boil over medium-high heat. Reduce heat to medium-low and simmer until thickened to thin syrup, 5 to 10 minutes. Mixture will thicken further as it cools. Remove from heat and stir in 3 tbsp (45 mL) butter and

½ tsp (2 mL) vanilla extract. Let cool and refrigerate in a glass jar for up to 1 week. Makes about 1½ cups (375 mL).
- ½ to 1 cup (125 to 250 mL) crème de cacao (adds alcohol)

Chocolate, Unsweetened

Also known as baking chocolate or bitter chocolate. Pure solidified chocolate liquor containing 50 to 58% cocoa butter (the natural fat in cocoa beans).

If You Don't Have It

Substitute 1 oz (30 g) or 1 square unsweetened chocolate with:
- 3 tbsp (45 mL) unsweetened cocoa powder + 1 tbsp (15 mL) butter, shortening, or vegetable oil (dissolve cocoa in liquid that is in recipe)
- 1½ to 2 oz (45 to 60 g) bittersweet or semisweet chocolate (decrease sugar in recipe by 3 tbsp/45 mL and butter by ½ tsp/2 mL)

For Better Health

- 3 tbsp (45 mL) unsweetened cocoa powder + 3 tbsp (45 mL) water
- 3 tbsp (45 mL) carob powder + 3 tbsp (45 mL) water

See also COCOA POWDER, UNSWEETENED.

Chocolate, White

Look for white chocolate that contains cocoa butter as the only type of fat. Cheap imitations are made with palm kernel oil or other vegetable fats and little or no cocoa butter.

If You Don't Have It

Substitute 1 oz (30 g) white chocolate with:
- 1 oz (30 g) milk chocolate (adds chocolate color and flavor)

Chokecherry

These North American wild cherries are far too sour (hence the name) to eat out-of-hand but are terrific simmered into jams and jellies.

If You Don't Have It

Substitute 1 lb (500 g) chokecherries (for jams and jellies) with:
- 1 lb (500 g) sour cherries
- 1 lb (500 g) cranberries

Chop Suey Vegetable

See CHRYSANTHEMUM GREENS.

Chop Suey Yam

See JICAMA.

Chopsui Potato

See JICAMA.

Chorizo

Very flavorful, usually red, and often spicy-hot coarse-ground pork sausage. There are dozens of variations on the theme, two most common of which are Mexican chorizo, a fresh pork sausage, and Spanish chorizo, a dry-cured pork sausage that can be sliced and eaten cold like salami and pepperoni.

If You Don't Have It
Substitute 1 lb (500 g) chorizo with:
- 1 lb (500 g) andouille
- 1 lb (500 g) merguez
- 1 lb (500 g) spicy kielbasa
- 1 lb (500 g) hot Italian sausage
- 1 lb (500 g) hot links

Chorizo Varieties
Choose 1 lb (500 g) chorizo from these varieties:
- 1 lb (500 g) fresh Mexican chorizo (spicy; must be cooked)
- 1 lb (500 g) fresh Creole/Cajun chaurice (spicy; must be cooked)
- 1 lb (500 g) cured Spanish chorizo (less spicy; smoked; can be eaten cold)
- 1 lb (500 g) cured Portuguese chouriço or linguiça (less spicy; less paprika than Spanish chorizo; smoked; can be eaten cold)

Chorogi

See CHINESE ARTICHOKE.

Chowder Clam

See SWAPPING CLAMS (PAGE 596).

Choy Sum

See BOK CHOY; YAU CHOY.

Christian IX

See DANBO.

Christmas Melon

See SANTA CLAUS MELON.

Chrysanthemum Greens

Also known as chop suey vegetable and cooking chrysanthemum. The edible, yet bitter, species of the common decorative flower is a popular leafy green in Asian cooking.

If You Don't Have It
Substitute 1 lb (500 g) chrysanthemum greens with:
- 1 lb (500 g) arugula
- 1 lb (500 g) watercress
- 1 lb (500 g) spinach (mature spinach will approximate bitterness better; add pepper for more bite)
- 1 lb (500 g) Belgian endive, dandelion greens, escarole, or radicchio (for salads)

Chufa

Also known as chufa nuts, earth almonds, earthnuts, and tiger nuts. Small tuberous roots of an African sedge plant, chufa "nuts" are popular in Spain and Mexico.

If You Don't Have It
Substitute 1 cup (250 mL) chufa with:
- 1 cup (250 mL) chestnuts
- 1 cup (250 mL) almonds (for horchata)

Chu Hou Paste

See CHEE HOU SAUCE.

Chutney

In Indian cooking, a spicy relish made from a myriad of fruits or vegetables, spices, and aromatics. Types vary greatly by region. British colonials embraced chutney with enthusiasm and popularized a jam-like sweet-and-sour version, the most well-known of which is made with mango.

If You Don't Have It
Substitute 1 cup (250 mL) chutney with:
- 1 cup (250 mL) fruit salsa (may be chunkier; mash or chop to coarse purée if you like; add sugar or lime juice to sweeten or sour the salsa to taste)
- 1 cup (250 mL) dried fruit compote (may be chunkier; mash or chop to coarse purée if you like; may be sweeter; add vinegar, lemon or lime juice to sour it)
- 1 cup (250 mL) marmalade (add lime juice, salt, and red pepper flakes to taste)
- 1 cup (250 mL) Asian sweet chili sauce (add coarsely puréed mango or other fruit if you like)

Ciabatta

The name of this Italian bread means "slipper." The loaf is about 8 inches (20 cm) long with a light, crispy crust.

If You Don't Have It
Substitute 1 lb (500 g) ciabatta with:
- 1 lb (500 g) other Italian bread
- 1 lb (500 g) French bread

See also ITALIAN BREAD.

Cicely

Also known as Spanish chervil, sweet chervil, and sweet cicely. A ferny-leaf herb with an anise flavor more assertive than chervil. Flavors desserts in Scandinavia.

If You Don't Have It

Substitute 1 tbsp (15 mL) chopped fresh cicely with:

- 1 tbsp (15 mL) chopped fresh chervil (milder anise flavor)
- 1 tbsp (15 mL) chopped fresh tarragon (stronger anise flavor)
- 1 tbsp (15 mL) chopped fresh fennel leaves
- 1 tbsp (15 mL) chopped fresh fines herbes (usually includes chervil, chives, parsley, and tarragon)
- 1 tbsp (15 mL) chopped fresh parsley

See also CHERVIL.

Cider

See APPLE CIDER.

Cider Brandy

See APPLE BRANDY.

Cider Spirits

See APPLE BRANDY.

Cider Vinegar

See CHOOSING VINEGAR (PAGE 600).

Cider Whiskey

See APPLE BRANDY.

Cilantro

Also known as fresh coriander and Chinese parsley. The distinctively flavored leaves of the coriander plant are said by supporters to taste of citrus and spice. Detractors compare the flavor to bug-infested linens and soap. The herb is essential in many Asian and South American cuisines, and alone among European kitchens, in Portugal.

If You Don't Have It

Substitute 1 tbsp (15 mL) chopped fresh cilantro with:

- 1 tbsp (15 mL) chopped fresh culantro or culentro (more bitter flavor)
- 1 tbsp (15 mL) chopped fresh parsley
- 1 tbsp (15 mL) chopped fresh mint + dash of lemon juice
- 1 tbsp (15 mL) chopped fresh basil or lemon basil

See also CORIANDER SEEDS.

Cime di Rapa

See BROCCOLI RAAB.

Cinnamon

What is labeled as "cinnamon" in many North American markets is actually cassia, a very similar spice. True cinnamon (also known as Ceylon cinnamon, Seychelles Islands cinnamon and canela) has a lighter brown color compared with the darker, more reddish cassia. True cinnamon also has a more delicate yet more complex aroma. Curiously, in a sensory study conducted by Alan R. Hirsch, MD of the Smell & Taste Treatment and Research Foundation, the aroma of cinnamon buns ranked number one as a sexual turn-on for male subjects.

> 1 3-inch (7.5 cm) stick =
> ½ tsp (2 mL) ground

If You Don't Have It

Substitute 1 cinnamon stick (3 inches/7.5 cm) with:
- ½ tsp (2 mL) ground cinnamon (for mulling, wrap ground cinnamon in cheesecloth or coffee filter and tie with kitchen string or clean twist-tie)
- ⅛ tsp (0.5 mL) cinnamon extract

To Vary the Flavor

Substitute ½ tsp (2 mL) ground cinnamon with:
- ¼ to ½ tsp (1 to 2 mL) ground cardamom (more musky aroma)
- ¼ to ½ tsp (1 to 2 mL) ground allspice
- ¼ to ½ tsp (1 to 2 mL) ground nutmeg
- ½ tsp (2 mL) apple pie spice (adds nutmeg and allspice)
- ½ tsp (2 mL) pumpkin pie spice (adds nutmeg and ginger)

Cinnamon Varieties

Substitute ½ tsp (2 mL) ground cinnamon with:
- ½ tsp (2 mL) Ceylon cinnamon, canela, or Seychelles Islands cinnamon (lighter color than the more common cassia; more delicate yet more complex aroma)
- ½ tsp (2 mL) cassia (darker, redder color than Ceylon cinnamon or canela; slightly more aggressive, almost bitter flavor)

Cinnamon Extract

A concentrated cinnamon flavoring.

If You Don't Have It

Substitute ½ tsp (2 mL) cinnamon extract with:
- 1/16 to ⅛ tsp (0.25 to 0.5 mL) cinnamon oil
- 1½ to 2 tsp (7 to 10 mL) ground cinnamon (adds color of ground spice to recipe)

Cinnamon Oil

A flavoring derived from the pods of the cinnamon tree.

If You Don't Have It

Substitute ⅛ tsp (0.5 mL) cinnamon oil with:
- ½ tsp (2 mL) cinnamon extract

Cinnamon Sugar

See SUGAR, GRANULATED.

Cipollini

See ONION, LITTLE.

Citron

A large citrus fruit that looks like a green-tinged bumpy lemon. The Buddha's hand, or fingered, citron is ribbed and more elongated.

If You Don't Have It

Substitute 1 tbsp (15 mL) citron peel with:
- 1 tbsp (15 mL) lemon peel

Citrónge

See ORANGE LIQUEUR.

Citrus Zester

See ZESTER.

Clam

Edible bivalves that are most appreciated in North America, a legacy that Native Americans passed on to European settlers.

3 dozen medium in shell = 4 cups (1 L) shucked

If You Don't Have It

Substitute 1 lb (500 g) clams with:
- 1 lb (500 g) mussels (more delicate)
- 1 lb (500 g) cockles
- 1 lb (500 g) oysters
- 1 lb (500 g) scallops
- 1 lb (500 g) abalone (tougher)

See also SWAPPING CLAMS (PAGE 596).

Clam Juice

To reduce the saltiness of bottled clam juice, replace the amount called for with half clam juice and half water.

If You Don't Have It

Substitute 1 cup (250 mL) clam juice with:
- 1 cup (250 mL) fish stock
- 1 cup (250 mL) dashi
- ½ cup (125 mL) chicken broth + ½ cup (125 mL) water

Clam Knife

A specially designed cutting implement for prying open clam shells.

If You Don't Have It

Substitute a clam knife with:
- another thick, dull knife such as small spreading knife or spackling knife
- microwaving the clams until they open (about 20 seconds)
- steaming the clams until they open (about 4 minutes)

Clay Pot

A cooking container fashioned from unglazed earthenware. Because it is porous, it must be soaked in water before each use.

If You Don't Have It

Substitute a clay pot with:
- a deep casserole dish (reduce oven temperature by about 100°F/50°C and cooking time by about 30 minutes)
- a Dutch oven (reduce oven temperature by about 100°F/50°C and cooking time by about 30 minutes)

Cleaver

The blade of this ax-like knife can be used to chop everything from vegetables to bone-in poultry. The flat side can be a tenderizer or a crushing tool for garlic.

If You Don't Have It

Substitute a cleaver with:
- a sturdy chef's knife
- a small, clean, hand-held ax

Clementine

See MANDARIN ORANGE.

Cloudberry

Also known as bake-apple berry, mountain berry, and yellow berry. A deliciously tart golden berry related to the raspberry. It grows wild in upper North America and Europe.

If You Don't Have It

Substitute 1 cup (250 mL) cloudberries with:
- 1 cup (250 mL) yellow raspberries (sweeter)
- 1 cup (250 mL) red raspberries (red color; sweeter)
- 1 cup (250 mL) loganberries (red color; slightly sweeter)
- 1 cup (250 mL) blackberries (purple color; large seeds)

Cloud Ear

See SHUFFLING MUSHROOMS (PAGE 572).

Clove

Named after the Latin word for nail, clavus, which it resembles, this brown spice is the dried, flower bud of a tropical evergreen.

35 to 40 whole cloves = 1 tsp (5 mL) ground

If You Don't Have It

Substitute ½ tsp (2 mL) ground cloves with:
- ½ tsp (2 mL) ground allspice

Club Soda

See SODA WATER.

Cockle

These gritty bivalves must be well washed to rid them of sand.

If You Don't Have It

Substitute 1 lb (500 g) cockles with:
- 1 lb (500 g) clams
- 1 lb (500 g) mussels
- 1 lb (500 g) oysters
- 1 lb (500 g) scallops
- 1 lb (500 g) abalone (tougher)

Cocktail Sauce

The classic condiment to accompany chilled shrimp is a mixture of ketchup or chili sauce, prepared horseradish, lemon juice, and Tabasco sauce.

If You Don't Have It

Substitute 1 cup (250 mL) cocktail sauce with:
- 1 cup (250 mL) Homemade Cocktail Sauce: Mix together 1 cup (250 mL) ketchup (or, for better flavor, $\frac{1}{2}$ cup/125 mL ketchup and $\frac{1}{2}$ cup/125 mL chili sauce), $\frac{1}{4}$ cup (50 mL) prepared horseradish, 1 tbsp (15 mL) lemon juice and dash of hot pepper sauce. Makes about $1\frac{1}{4}$ cups (300 mL).

Cocoa Mix

Also known as instant cocoa. A mixture of unsweetened cocoa powder, confectioner's (icing) sugar, and powdered milk for making hot cocoa.

If You Don't Have It

Substitute $\frac{1}{4}$ cup (50 mL) cocoa mix with:
- 3 tbsp (45 mL) powdered milk + $1\frac{1}{2}$ tbsp (22 mL) confectioner's (icing) sugar + $1\frac{1}{2}$ tsp (7 mL) unsweetened cocoa powder + $1\frac{1}{2}$ tsp (7 mL) powdered nondairy creamer
- 4 oz (125 g) Mexican chocolate

Cocoa Powder, Unsweetened

Dried, powdered chocolate liquor with 10 to 22% cocoa butter. Natural (nonalkalized) cocoa includes the natural acidity of cocoa beans. Dutch-process cocoa has an alkali added to neutralize the acidity, mellowing the flavor.

If You Don't Have It

Substitute 3 tbsp (45 mL) unsweetened natural cocoa powder with:
- 1 oz (30 g) unsweetened chocolate (decrease fat in recipe by 1 tbsp/15 mL)
- 2 oz (60 g) semisweet chocolate (decrease fat in recipe by 1 tbsp/15 mL and sugar in recipe by 3 tbsp/45 mL)
- 3 heaping tbsp (45 mL) carob powder
- 3 tbsp (45 mL) Dutch-process cocoa powder + $\frac{1}{8}$ tsp (0.5 mL) cream of tartar (or in lieu of adding cream of tartar, omit baking soda from recipe)

1 oz (30 g) =
$\frac{1}{4}$ cup (50 mL)

Coconut Cream

Flavoring liquid made by simmering and straining 4 parts coconut meat and 1 part water or milk.

If You Don't Have It
Substitute 1 cup (250 mL) coconut cream with:
- 1 cup (250 mL) coconut milk (especially the thicker cream that rises to the top of coconut milk)
- 1 cup (250 mL) light whipping cream or heavy whipping cream (35% butterfat) + ½ tsp (2 mL) coconut extract

For Better Health
Substitute 1 cup (250 mL) coconut cream with:
- 1 cup (250 mL) reduced-fat coconut milk (less rich; thinner consistency)

See also CREAM OF COCONUT.

Coconut, Fresh

The shaggy brown coconut sold in markets is actually only the hard stone center of the fruit of the coconut palm. The outer husk is removed to be used for other purposes.

1 medium coconut =
4 to 5 cups (1 to 1.25 L) shredded

6 cups (1.5 L) shredded = 1 lb (500 g)

If You Don't Have It
Substitute 1 cup (250 mL) fresh shredded coconut with:
- 1 cup (250 mL) packaged unsweetened shredded coconut

Coconut Milk

Flavoring liquid made by simmering, and then straining, equal parts coconut meat and water.

If You Don't Have It
Substitute 1 cup (250 mL) fresh coconut milk with:
- 1 cup (250 mL) canned coconut milk
- 1 cup (250 mL) coconut cream (richer)
- ¼ cup (50 mL) powdered coconut cream + ¾ cup (175 mL) boiling water or milk
- 1 cup (250 mL) Homemade Coconut Milk: Pour 1 cup (250 mL) boiling water or milk over 1 packed cup (250 mL) fresh grated coconut. Let stand for 30 minutes. Then pour the mixture into cheesecloth or a clean damp cloth and squeeze the liquid into a bowl. Discard the grated coconut. Makes about 1 cup (250 mL).

Coconut Milk (cont'd)

For Better Health

Substitute 1 cup (250 mL) coconut milk with:

- 1 cup (250 mL) reduced-fat canned coconut milk
- ½ cup (125 mL) coconut milk + ½ cup (125 mL) coconut water
- 1 cup (250 mL) milk or half-and-half cream + ½ tsp (2 mL) coconut extract

Coconut, Shredded

Also known as flaked coconut.

7 oz (210 g) shredded or flaked = 3 cups (750 mL)

3.5 oz (99 g) =
1⅓ cups (325 mL)

If You Don't Have It

Substitute 1 cup (250 mL) packaged shredded coconut with:

- 1 cup (250 mL) fresh shredded coconut

To Vary the Flavor

Substitute 1 cup (250 mL) packaged shredded coconut with:

- 1 cup (250 mL) finely chopped macadamia nuts

For Better Health

Substitute 1 cup (250 mL) packaged shredded coconut with:

- 1 tsp (5 mL) coconut extract (fewer calories)

Coconut Sugar

See SUGAR, PALM.

Cod

The title of a book by food historian Mark Kurlansky, Cod: A Biography of the Fish That Changed the World, *sums up the global impact of this sea creature that has been fished heavily since medieval times. Before modern refrigeration, cod was preserved by drying it into stockfish, or salting and drying into salt cod.*

If You Don't Have It

Substitute 1 lb (500 g) cod with:

- 1 lb (500 g) pollock
- 1 lb (500 g) haddock
- 1 lb (500 g) hake
- 1 lb (500 g) scrod (young cod)
- 1 lb (500 g) Cape capensis
- 1 lb (500 g) orange roughy
- 1 lb (500 g) tilapia
- 1 lb (500 g) sole
- 1 lb (500 g) flounder
- 1 lb (500 g) tilefish
- 1 lb (500 g) grouper
- 1 lb (500 g) halibut
- 1 lb (500 g) red snapper
- 1 lb (500 g) striped bass

See also SALT COD.

Coffee

Coffee is the world's second largest traded commodity. Oil is the first. Of the two widely cultivated species, high-altitude coffea arabica beans are more complex in flavor than the harsher low altitude coffea robusta.

> 1 lb (500 g) = 5 cups (1.25 L) grounds = 40 brewed cups (6 oz/175 g each)

If You Don't Have It
Substitute 1 cup (250 mL) strong brewed coffee with:
- 1 cup (250 mL) hot water + 2 tsp (10 mL) instant coffee powder or espresso powder

For Better Health
Substitute 1 cup (250 mL) strong brewed coffee with:
- 1 cup (250 mL) brewed decaffeinated coffee
- 1 cup (250 mL) brewed roasted chicory (caffeine-free)

See also ESPRESSO.

Coffee Filter

Paper liners used to hold ground coffee, and prevent grounds from entering the brewed coffee, in automatic drip coffee machines.

If You Don't Have It
Substitute coffee filters with:
- thick paper towels
- triple layer of cheesecloth or folded three times
- nylon mesh, such as clean nylon stockings
- clean kitchen towel

Coffee Liqueur

Neutral spirit or sweetened rum beverage flavored with natural or artificial coffee flavoring.

If You Don't Have It
Substitute 3 tbsp (45 mL) coffee liqueur with:
- 3 tbsp (45 mL) water + ¾ tsp (4 mL) instant coffee granules
- 3 tbsp (45 mL) chocolate liqueur, hazelnut liqueur, or almond liqueur
- 3 tbsp (45 mL) cognac
- 3 tbsp (45 mL) rum

Coffee Liqueur Varieties
Choose 3 tbsp (45 mL) coffee liqueur from these varieties:
- 3 tbsp (45 mL) Kahlúa
- 3 tbsp (45 mL) Crème de café (sweeter; heavier body)
- 3 tbsp (45 mL) Tía Maria (lighter body; adds rum flavor)
- 3 tbsp (45 mL) Tiramisù liqueur (combines chocolate, coffee, and almond flavors)

Cognac

This king of brandies is double distilled and aged a minimum of three years in Limousin oak. The label term X.O. (extra and reserve) means that the cognac is the oldest a producer distributes. Older cognacs are ranked on the label with the following terms: V.S. = very superior; V.S.O.P = very superior old pale; V.V.S.O.P. = very, very, superior old pale.

If You Don't Have It
Substitute 3 tbsp (45 mL) cognac with:
- 3 tbsp (45 mL) Armagnac (drier; more complex flavor)
- 3 tbsp (45 mL) top-shelf brandy
- 3 tbsp (45 mL) top-shelf bourbon

Coho Salmon

See SALMON.

Cointreau

See ORANGE LIQUEUR.

Colander

A bowl-shaped strainer used to wash produce or drain noodles or vegetables after boiling. Large metal ones are best.

If You Don't Have It
Substitute a colander with:
- a medium-mesh strainer
- tongs, pasta spoon, or slotted spoon (for plucking or scooping foods out of hot liquid)

See also STRAINER.

Colby

A soft, springy cheese with mild sweet taste. Because of its high moisture content, Colby cheese should be eaten soon after purchase.

If You Don't Have It
Substitute 1 oz (30 g) Colby cheese with:
- 1 oz (30 g) Cheddar (sharper)
- 1 oz (30 g) Cheshire (sharper)
- 1 oz (30 g) Jack (pale color; milder flavor)
- 1 oz (30 g) American cheese (milder flavor)

For Better Health
Substitute 1 oz (30 g) Colby cheese with:
- 1 oz (30 g) reduced-fat Colby, Cheddar, or Jack

Cold Cuts

See SPECIFIC TYPES.

Collards

Also known as collard greens. A type of dark green cabbage with tall, dense stalks. Frozen collards can be substituted for fresh with a tolerable loss of flavor.

> 1 lb (500 g) fresh =
> 1⅓ to 2 cups (325 to
> 500 mL) cooked

If You Don't Have It
Substitute 1 lb (500 g) collards with:
- 1 lb (500 g) kale
- 1 lb (500 g) mature spinach
- 1 lb (500 g) green chard leaves
- 1 lb (500 g) mustard greens
- 1 lb (500 g) turnip greens
- 1 lb (500 g) callaloo
- 1 lb (500 g) Chinese kale
- 1 lb (500 g) bok choy

Comal

Flat, round griddle for cooking tortillas.

If You Don't Have It
Substitute a comal with:
- a small, thin metal skillet such as a crêpe pan

Comice Pear

See PICKING PEARS (PAGE 565).

Comté

Also known as Gruyère de Comté. Nutty, buttery cheese produced for many centuries in the French Jura Mountains adjacent to Switzerland.

If You Don't Have It
Substitute 1 oz (30 g) Comté with:
- 1 oz (30 g) Gruyère
- 1 oz (30 g) Beaufort
- 1 oz (30 g) Emmental

Conch

Pronounced "konk," this beautiful mollusk is a snail-like creature housed in a shell. The tough flesh must be tenderized before eating.

If You Don't Have It
Substitute 4 oz (125 g) conch meat with:
- 4 oz (125 g) abalone
- 4 oz (125 g) clams
- 4 oz (125 g) whelk

Condensed Milk

See SWEETENED CONDENSED MILK.

Confectioner's Sugar

See SUGAR, CONFECTIONER'S.

Confectionery Coating

Also known as compound chocolate (when flavored with chocolate). A variously flavored and colored dip for candies and confections that contains sugar, powdered milk, and solid fat but no cocoa butter.

If You Don't Have It
Substitute 1 oz (30 g) confectionery coating with:
- 1 oz (30 g) couverture chocolate (contains cocoa butter; richer taste and mouth-feel; melts at a lower temperature)

See also CHOCOLATE, COUVERTURE.

Conger

See EEL.

Convection Oven

Gas or electric oven equipped with a fan to circulate the hot air evenly around the food.

If You Don't Have It
Substitute a convection oven with:
- a gas or electric oven (does not provide circulation of hot air to speed cooking; increase oven temperature by about 25°F/14°C; increase cooking time by about 25%)

Cookie Crumbs

To make crumbs from stale cookies, grind them in a food processor fitted with a metal blade or place in a plastic bag and crush with a rolling pin. Use the crumbs to top fresh-cut fruits, pudding, yogurt, or ice cream. Or, use to "flour" greased cake pans.

---

22 vanilla wafers =
1½ cups (375 mL)
crumbs

18 to 20 chocolate
waters = 1 cup (250 mL)
crumbs

To Vary the Flavor
Substitute 1½ cups (375 mL) cookie crumbs with:
- 1½ cups (375 mL) crushed graham crackers (about 21 squares)
- 1½ cups (375 mL) crushed gingersnaps (about 22)
- 1½ cups (375 mL) crushed vanilla wafer cookies (about 33)
- 1½ cups (375 mL) crushed chocolate wafer cookies (about 32)
- 1½ cups (375 mL) crushed Oreo cookies (about 21, including cookie filling); omit sugar from crust
- 1½ cups (375 mL) crushed wheat, bran or corn flakes (about 4½ cups/1.125 L)
- 1½ cups (375 mL) crushed saltine crackers (about 42); omit sugar from crust and adjust salt in filling (for savory fillings)

For Better Health
Substitute 1 crumb crust with:
- half of cookie crumbs in recipe plus equal amount of crushed saltine or other table crackers (omit salt from recipe)

See also BREAD CRUMBS; PIE CRUST, CRUMB.

Cookie Cutter

A metal implement to cut rolled cookie dough into circles. Cutters also are manufactured in hundreds of novelty shapes. To prevent sticking to soft doughs, dip the cutter in flour or granulated sugar.

If You Don't Have It

Substitute a cookie cutter with:
- biscuit cutter
- clean tuna can or other can with both ends removed
- inverted wine or drinking glass

See also BISCUIT CUTTER; CRUMPET RING.

Cookie Sheet

See BAKING SHEET.

Cooking Spray

See VEGETABLE OIL SPRAY.

Cookware and Bakeware

See SPECIFIC TYPES.

Cooling Rack

Raised racks of sturdy parallel or woven wires that allow air to circulate. Used for cooling cookies, cakes, breads, and pastries so the bottoms won't get soggy.

If You Don't Have It

Substitute a cooling rack with:
- oven rack or toaster oven rack (remove from cool oven)
- flat roasting or broiling rack

Coon

A hybrid Cheddar cheese rarely produced outside of the Midwest United States.

If You Don't Have It

Substitute 1 oz (30 g) coon cheese with:
- 1 oz (30 g) Cheddar
- 1 oz (30 g) Colby
- 1 oz (30 g) Cheshire
- 1 oz (30 g) Jack

Copha

Australians are wild about this highly saturated solid coconut oil, using it in the preparation of candies and pastries.

If You Don't Have It

Substitute 1 cup (250 mL) copha with:
- 1 cup (250 mL) vegetable shortening or lard + 1/8 to 1/4 tsp (0.5 to 1 mL) coconut extract

Coppa

See CAPICOLA.

Copper Bowl

Properly executed, beating egg whites by hand with a balloon whisk in an unlined copper bowl produces one-third more volume of foam.

If You Don't Have It

Substitute a copper bowl for stabilizing whipped egg whites with:
- glass bowl + pinch of powdered copper supplement (available in health food stores)
- silver-plated bowl

Corer

See APPLE CORER.

Coriander Seeds

The dried seeds of the herb coriander are pleasantly spicy. They are a standard item in garam masala and are also called upon to season savory dishes, breads, and cakes.

If You Don't Have It

Substitute 1 tsp (5 mL) coriander seeds with:
- 1 tsp (5 mL) caraway seeds
- 1 tsp (5 mL) fennel seeds
- ¾ tsp (4 mL) cumin seeds
- ½ to ¾ tsp (2 to 4 mL) cardamom seeds

See also CILANTRO; GARAM MASALA.

Corkscrew

The oenophile's best friend, this implement uncorks one of humanity's finest gastronomic achievements.

If You Don't Have It

Substitute a corkscrew with:
- using the blunt end of a table knife or another blunt narrow object, push the cork into the bottle. If the cork breaks into pieces, strain the wine into a decanter, glass pitcher or other spouted container

Corn

Also known as sweet corn. To easily remove the silk from corn-on-the-cob, husk the corn then rub the ears with a damp paper towel. The silk will stick to the towel and the whole lot can be tossed into the trash.

2 medium ears = 1 to 1¼ cups (250 to 300 mL) kernels

10 oz (300 g) frozen kernels = 1¾ cups (425 mL)

If You Don't Have It

Substitute 1 cup (250 mL) fresh corn with:
- 1 cup (250 mL) frozen and thawed corn
- 1 cup (250 mL) canned corn (not as good as frozen and thawed)
- 1 cup (250 mL) other cooked grain such as barley
- 1 cup (250 mL) peas

Cornbread Crumbs

Cornbread dries out quickly but, fortunately, the crumbs make tasty stuffings, when moistened and seasoned, for vegetables or poultry.

> 1 3-inch (7.5 cm) square (1-inch/2.5 cm deep) piece of cornbread = 1 cup (250 mL) crumbs

If You Don't Have It

Substitute 1 cup (250 mL) fresh cornbread crumbs with:
- 1 cup (250 mL) crumbled corn muffin
- 1 cup (250 mL) fresh bread crumbs

Corn Chips

January 29 is designated as National Corn Chip Day in the United States.

If You Don't Have It

Substitute 1 cup (250 mL) corn chips with:
- 1 cup (250 mL) tortilla chips
- 1 cup (250 mL) potato chips

Corned Beef

Beef brisket that is cured in a seasoned brine. The term "corned" refers in old English to the "corns," or small particles of salt, in the brine.

If You Don't Have It

Substitute 1 lb (500 g) corned beef with:
- 1 lb (500 g) pastrami (more tender)

Cornflake Crumbs

Since 1884, when surgeon and health food zealot John Harvey Kellogg applied for a patent for his toasted flaked corn cereal, the crumbs — useful in many recipes — have been the bonus at the bottom of the box.

> 3 cups (750 mL) cornflakes = 1 cup (250 mL) crushed

If You Don't Have It

Substitute 1 cup (250 mL) cornflake crumbs with:
- 1 cup (250 mL) cornmeal
- 1 cup (250 mL) dry bread crumbs
- 1 cup (250 mL) crushed wheat flakes or other cereal flakes
- 1 cup (250 mL) panko (Japanese bread crumbs; large crumbs; retains crispness better)
- 1 cup (250 mL) cracker crumbs
- 1 cup (250 mL) crushed tortilla chips or corn chips
- 1 cup (250 mL) crushed melba toast
- 1 cup (250 mL) matzo meal
- 1 cup (250 mL) crushed dry-bagged stuffing cubes
- 1 cup (250 mL) crushed potato chips
- 1 cup (250 mL) crushed pretzels

See also BREAD CRUMBS; CRACKER CRUMBS; PANKO.

Corn Flour

Finely ground yellow or white cornmeal. In Great Britain, corn flour is the term for cornstarch.

If You Don't Have It

Substitute 1 cup (250 mL) corn flour with:

- 1 cup (250 mL) cornmeal ground in a blender or small food processor until finely textured

See also MASA HARINA; CHOOSING AMONG WHOLE-GRAIN AND ALTERNATIVE FLOURS (PAGE 586).

Corn Grits

Also known as plain grits. Dried, ground, corn that is coarser than corn flour and available in fine, medium, and coarse grinds. Not to be confused with hominy grits, a similar product made from ground hominy.

1 cup (250 mL) = 4½ cups (1.125 L) cooked

If You Don't Have It

Substitute 1 cup (250 mL) corn grits with:

- 1 cup (250 mL) hominy grits
- 1 cup (250 mL) coarse polenta meal (preferably stone-ground)
- 1 cup (250 mL) barley grits
- 1 cup (250 mL) buckwheat grits

See also BARLEY GRITS; HOMINY GRITS.

Corn Husk

When used as a food wrapper, as in tamales, corn husks add a mild corn flavor to the food.

If You Don't Have It

Substitute corn husks (for wrapping foods) with:

- hoja santa leaves (adds aromas of root beer and fennel)
- banana leaves (adds herby-green flavor)
- parchment paper (adds no flavor)
- aluminum foil (adds no flavor)

Cornichon

The French word for "gherkins," cornichons are tiny, crisp, tart pickles.

If You Don't Have It

Substitute 1 cup (250 mL) cornichons with:

- 1 cup (250 mL) sweet gherkins (sweeter)
- 1 cup (250 mL) small whole or sliced dill pickles

See also CUCUMBER.

Cornish Game Hen

See CHICKEN.

Cornmeal

For the most nutrients and a whiff of nuttiness, choose old-fashioned water-ground (also called stone-ground) cornmeal. It retains some of the hull and germ. Store in the refrigerator for up to 4 months.

> 1 lb (500 g) = 3¼ cups (800 mL)

If You Don't Have It

Substitute 1 cup (250 mL) yellow cornmeal with:
- 1 cup (250 mL) blue cornmeal
- 1 cup (250 mL) corn grits (heavier texture)
- 1 cup (250 mL) polenta
- 1 cup (250 mL) corn flour (lighter texture)
- 1 cup (250 mL) crushed tortilla chips or corn chips (for breading; crush chips in a food processor or blender until fine)
- 1 cup (250 mL) self-rising cornmeal (for quick breads; omit 1½ tbsp/22 mL baking powder and ½ tsp/2 mL salt from recipe)

Cornmeal, Self-Rising

For making cornmeal bread, muffins, and other baked goods, this variety of cornmeal is conveniently packaged with baking powder.

If You Don't Have It

Substitute 1 cup (250 mL) self-rising cornmeal with:
- 1 cup (250 mL) minus 3 tbsp (45 mL) cornmeal + 1½ tbsp (22 mL) baking powder + ½ tsp (2 mL) salt
- ¾ cup (175 mL) cornmeal + ¼ cup (50 mL) all-purpose flour + ½ tsp (2 mL) salt + ½ tsp (2 mL) baking powder + ¼ tsp (1 mL) baking soda (to replace cornmeal "mix" made with cornmeal and wheat flour)

Corn Oil

See SUBSTITUTING OILS (PAGE 598).

Corn Salad

See MÂCHE.

Cornstarch

To avoid lumps, dissolve cornstarch (and all other starches or flours used for thickening) in twice the amount of cold liquid before stirring into the hot liquid. One tablespoon (15 mL) cornstarch will thicken 1 cup (250 mL) of liquid.

> 1 lb (500 g) = 3 cups (750 mL))

If You Don't Have It

Substitute 1 tbsp (15 mL) cornstarch (for thickening) with:
- 3 tbsp (45 mL) all-purpose flour (cook a few minutes after thickening to cook out raw flour taste)
- 1 to 1½ tbsp (15 to 22 mL) arrowroot (a better choice if thickened food will be cooked for a long time; also makes sauces more glossy)
- 1½ to 2 tbsp (22 to 25 mL) quick-cooking tapioca
- 2 tsp (10 mL) potato starch, rice starch, or instant mashed potato flakes

Corn Syrup, Dark

Similar to light corn syrup but with added caramel coloring and flavoring.

16 oz (500 mL) = 2 cups (500 mL)

If You Don't Have It
Substitute 1 cup (250 mL) dark corn syrup with:
- ¾ cup (175 mL) light corn syrup + ¼ cup (50 mL) light molasses
- 1 cup (250 mL) light corn syrup (no caramel flavoring; lighter color)
- 1 cup (250 mL) golden syrup (thicker; sweeter)
- 1 cup (250 mL) honey (sweeter; lighter color)
- 1¼ cups (300 mL) packed brown sugar dissolved in ¼ cup (50 mL) hot water or liquid used in recipe

Corn Syrup, Light

Thick, sweet, clear syrup derived from cornstarch.

16 oz (500 mL)= 2 cups (500 mL)

If You Don't Have It
Substitute 1 cup (250 mL) light corn syrup with:
- 1¼ cups (300 mL) granulated sugar dissolved in ¼ cup (50 mL) hot water or liquid used in recipe
- 1 cup (250 mL) golden syrup (thicker; sweeter)
- 1 cup (250 mL) liquid glucose

To Vary the Flavor
Substitute 1 cup (250 mL) light corn syrup with:
- 1 cup (250 mL) dark corn syrup (adds caramel flavor and color)
- 1 cup (250 mL) honey (sweeter; adds amber color)
- 1 cup (250 mL) molasses (deepens flavor and adds darker brown color)

Cotechino

A fresh pork sausage from the Italian city of Modena.

If You Don't Have It
Substitute 4 oz (125 g) cotechino with:
- 4 oz (125 g) mild Italian sausage

Cotija

See QUESO AÑEJO.

Cottage Cheese

Strict lacto-ovo vegetarians can enjoy cottage cheese because it contains no rennet. It's an acid curd cheese, meaning the curds are formed by the natural tendency of warmed milk to curdle on its own.

If You Don't Have It
Substitute 1 cup (250 mL) cottage cheese with:
- 1 cup (250 mL) ricotta
- 1 cup (250 mL) pot cheese

Coulommiers

A French cheese that's a stand-in for Brie except that the round is thicker and smaller.

If You Don't Have It
Substitute 1 oz (30 g) Coulommiers with:
- 1 oz (30 g) Brie
- 1 oz (30 g) Camembert
- 1 oz (30 g) Chaource

Country Ham

See HAM, DRY-CURED.

Courgette

See ZUCCHINI.

Couscous

North African granular semolina steamed and served as a grain side dish. Also the name of a spicy stew that it accompanies.

1 cup (250 mL) = 2½ cups (625 mL) cooked

If You Don't Have It
Substitute 1 cup (250 mL) instant couscous with:
- 1 cup (250 mL) couscous (takes longer to cook)
- 1 cup (250 mL) white rice (takes longer to cook)

For Better Health
Substitute 1 cup (250 mL) instant couscous with:
- 1 cup (250 mL) whole wheat couscous
- 1 cup (250 mL) quinoa
- 1 cup (250 mL) bulgur (takes longer to cook)
- 1 cup (250 mL) brown rice (takes longer to cook)

See also COUSCOUSSIÈRE.

Couscoussière

A North African cooking pot in two parts. The bottom pot is used to simmer a spicy stew and the perforated top part is used to steam the accompanying couscous.

If You Don't Have It
Substitute a couscoussièrre with:
- colander lined with cheesecloth or thick paper towels and set over a pot
- steamer pot with an insert basket lined with cheesecloth or thick paper towels

See also COUSCOUS.

Couverture

See CHOCOLATE, COUVERTURE.

Cowberry

See LINGONBERRY.

Cowpea

See BLACK-EYED PEAS, FRESH.

Crab

Refrigerated pasteurized premium crabmeat in a tub or can makes a suitable substitute for fresh lump crabmeat.

If You Don't Have It

Substitute 1 lb (500 g) crabmeat with:
- 1 lb (500 g) shrimp (firmer texture)
- 1 lb (500 g) lobster (more expensive; firmer)
- 1 lb (500 g) scallops
- 1 lb (500 g) surimi (imitation crabmeat; less flavorful)
- 1 lb (500 g) monkfish
- 1 lb (500 g) cod

See also SURIMI; CHOOSING AMONG CRABS (PAGE 597).

Crab Boil

Also known as fish boil and shrimp boil. A zesty mixture of herbs and spices added to water in which seafood is simmered. May include allspice, bay leaves, red chiles, cloves, dried ginger, mustard seeds, and peppercorns.

If You Don't Have It

Substitute 1 tbsp (15 mL) crab boil with:
- 1 tbsp (15 mL) Homemade Crab Boil: Combine 2 bay leaves, $\frac{1}{2}$ tsp (2 mL) black peppercorns or ground pepper, $\frac{1}{2}$ tsp (2 mL) mustard seeds, $\frac{1}{2}$ tsp (2 mL) dill seeds, $\frac{1}{2}$ tsp (2 mL) coriander seeds, $\frac{1}{4}$ tsp (1 mL) whole cloves, $\frac{1}{4}$ tsp (1 mL) allspice berries, and $\frac{1}{8}$ tsp (0.5 mL) ground ginger in a piece of cheesecloth or coffee filter. Tie with kitchen string or a clean twist-tie. Makes about 1 tablespoon (15 mL).
- 1 tbsp (15 mL) Old Bay seasoning (adds salt, paprika, celery seed, and other flavors)
- 1 tbsp (15 mL) pickling spice

See also OLD BAY SEASONING.

Cracked Wheat

Wheat berries that are broken into fine, medium, and coarse bits. Can be prepared as cereal, in pilafs, or mixed into whole-grain bread doughs.

If You Don't Have It

Substitute 1 cup (250 mL) cracked wheat with:
- 1 cup (250 mL) wheat berries (takes longer to cook)
- 1 cup (250 mL) bulgur (takes less time to cook)
- 1 cup (250 mL) whole wheat couscous (takes less time to cook)
- 1 cup (250 mL) quinoa (takes less time to cook)
- 1 cup (250 mL) brown rice

See also BULGUR.

Cracker

Also known as biscuits (in England). In North America, crackers refer to thin, unsweetened, unleavened wafers. Centuries ago, the term "cracker" referred to a liar or boaster.

If You Don't Have It

Substitute 1 lb (500 g) crackers with:
- 1 lb (500 g) melba toast
- 1 lb (500 g) crisp lavash
- 1 lb (500 g) tortilla chips

Cracker Varieties

Choose 1 lb (500 g) crackers from these common varieties:
- 1 lb (500 g) water crackers (very crisp, dry, and relatively low in salt)
- 1 lb (500 g) soda crackers (crisp, dry, and relatively low in salt)
- 1 lb (500 g) oyster crackers (usually small, round or hexagonal, somewhat crisp, and relatively low in salt)
- 1 lb (500 g) saltines (crisp, dry, and salty)
- 1 lb (500 g) Triscuits (crisp, dry and relatively low in salt; made with whole-grain flour)
- 1 lb (500 g) Ritz crackers (buttery-soft and salty)

See also CRACKER CRUMBS; GRAHAM CRACKER.

Cracker Bread

See LAVASH.

Cracker Crumbs

To re-crisp soggy crackers to make crumbs, spread on a baking sheet and place in a 350°F (180°C) oven for 5 to 10 minutes. Let cool before crumbling.

20 soda/saltine crackers = 1 cup (250 mL) crumbs

If You Don't Have It

Substitute 1 cup (250 mL) cracker crumbs with:
- 1¼ cups (300 mL) dry bread crumbs
- 1½ cups (375 mL) croutons or stuffing cubes, crushed
- 1 cup (250 mL) panko (Japanese bread crumbs; large crumbs; retains crispness better)
- 1 tbsp (15 mL) quick-cooking oats (for thickening)

Cracker Crumb Varieties

Choose 1 cup (250 mL) cracker crumbs from these varieties:
- 1 cup (250 mL) water cracker crumbs (very crisp, dry, and relatively low in salt)
- 1 cup (250 mL) soda cracker crumbs (crisp, dry, and relatively low in salt)
- 1 cup (250 mL) saltine cracker crumbs (crisp, dry, and salty)
- 1 cup (250 mL) Ritz cracker crumbs (buttery-soft and salty)
- 1 cup (250 mL) seasoned dry bread crumbs

Cracker Crumbs (cont'd)

- 1 cup (250 mL) finely crushed melba toasts
- 1 cup (250 mL) matzo meal
- 1 cup (250 mL) finely crushed tortilla chips
- 1 cup (250 mL) crushed dry-bagged stuffing mix
- 1 cup (250 mL) finely crushed pretzels
- 1 cup (250 mL) finely crushed cornflakes
- 1 cup (250 mL) finely crushed potato chips

See also BREAD CRUMBS.

Craisins®

See CRANBERRY, DRIED.

Cranberry

Also known as bearberries, bounceberries and craneberries. Frozen and thawed cranberries make a fair substitute for fresh cranberries, especially in sauces, compotes or dishes including liquid.

12 oz (375 g) fresh or frozen = 3 cups (750 mL) = 4 cups (1 L) sauce

If You Don't Have It

Substitute 1 cup (250 mL) cranberries with:
- 1 cup (250 mL) lingonberries (smaller; more complex flavor)
- 1 cup (250 mL) carissa
- 1 cup (250 mL) blueberries (sweeter)
- 1 cup (250 mL) red currants

Cranberry Bean, Fresh

Also known as borlotti bean and horticultural bean. A cream and red-speckled shell bean that's often harvested when the beans are mature then shelled and enjoyed fresh. Also available dried.

1 lb (500 g) fresh in shell = 1¼ cups (300 mL) shelled

If You Don't Have It

Substitute 1 lb (500 g) fresh cranberry beans (weighed in shell) with:
- 1 lb (500 g) fresh Dragon Tongue beans (deep reddish brown and cream color)
- 1 lb (500 g) fresh Tongue of Fire beans (green and red color)
- 1 lb (500 g) fresh Romano beans (green color)
- 1 lb (500 g) fresh Kentucky Wonder beans (green color)
- 1 lb (500 g) fresh black-eyed peas or other cowpeas (southernpeas; pale green and cream or pink color with black "eye" at center)
- 1 lb (500 g) fresh lima beans (green color)
- 1 lb (500 g) fresh edamame (green color)
- 1 lb (500 g) fresh garden peas (green color)

See also PEAS, SHELLING; THE WIDE WORLD OF DRIED BEANS (PAGE 566).

Cranberry, Dried

Also known as Craisins®. Drying fresh cranberries allows producers to maximize sales of the harvest.

If You Don't Have It

Substitute 1 cup (250 mL) dried cranberries with:
- 1 cup (250 mL) raisins
- 1 cup (250 mL) dried cherries
- 1 cup (250 mL) dried blueberries
- 1 cup (250 mL) currants (smaller, drier)

Cranberry Juice

High in vitamin C, cranberry juice is reputed to promote urinary tract health. It also lends a lovely pink hue to Cosmopolitan cocktails and pink lemonade.

If You Don't Have It

Substitute 1 cup (250 mL) cranberry juice with:
- 1 cup (250 mL) cranberry juice cocktail (up to 27% cranberry juice; may include added water, sweeteners, flavors, and colors)
- 1 cup (250 mL) red grape juice + 1 tsp (5 mL) lemon juice

Cranshaw Melon

See CRENSHAW MELON.

Crawdad

See CRAYFISH.

Crayfish

Also known as crawdads, crawfish, écrevisses, mudbugs, and yabbies. Freshwater crustaceans that look exactly like miniature lobsters, from 3 to 6 inches (7.5 to 15 cm) long and weighing from 2 to 8 ounces (60 to 250 g). Breaux Bridge, Louisiana is known as "The Crawfish Capital of the World."

1 lb (500 g) = 15 large crayfish = 3 oz (90 g) peeled tails

If You Don't Have It

Substitute 1 lb (500 g) crayfish with:
- 1 lb (500 g) shrimp (especially rock shrimp)
- 1 lb (500 g) lobster (especially spiny or rock lobster for the tails)
- 1 lb (500 g) crab

Cream

The luscious milk fat that rises to the top of standing milk that hasn't been homogenized. Ultra-pasteurized creams don't whip as easily and have a detectable cooked milk flavor.

If You Don't Have It

Substitute 1 cup (250 mL) cream with:

- 1 cup (250 mL) yogurt (for uncooked or gently heated sauces, cold soups, and other mixtures; adds slight tanginess)

For Better Health

Substitute 1 cup (250 mL) cream with:

- 1 cup (250 mL) evaporated milk (fewer calories; thinner consistency; whips less easily; adds slight cooked milk flavor)

See also CREAM, CLABBER; CREAM, CLOTTED; CREAM, DOUBLE; CREAM, HALF-AND-HALF; CREAM, LIGHT; CREAM, LIGHT WHIPPING; CREAM, WHIPPING; CRÈME FRAÎCHE; KAYMAK; SOUR CREAM; WHIPPED CREAM.

Cream Cheese

In 1872, New York State dairyman William A. Lawrence developed a method for making cream cheese while attempting to duplicate French Neufchâtel. In 1880, New York cheese distributor A. L. Reynolds packaged the cheese in tin-foil wrappers and called it Philadelphia Brand Cream Cheese because the public equated the City of Brotherly Love with high-quality food products.

1 lb (500 g) = 2 cups (500 mL)

If You Don't Have It

Substitute 1 lb (500 g) cream cheese with:

- 1 lb (500 g) mascarpone cheese
- 1 lb (500 g) boursin cheese (adds herb flavors)

For Better Health

Substitute 1 lb (500 g) cream cheese with:

- 1 lb (500 g) reduced-fat (Neufchâtel) or fat-free cream cheese (block or tub-style; lower in fat and moisture)
- 8 oz (250 g) reduced-fat cream cheese + 8 oz (250 g) fat-free cream cheese
- 1 lb (500 g) reduced-fat ricotta cheese (for cooking)
- 1 lb (500 g) dry-curd cottage cheese (for cooking)
- 1 lb (500 g) puréed silken or soft tofu
- 1 lb (500 g) tofu cream cheese

Cream, Clabber

Cream that has soured and thickened naturally.

If You Don't Have It

Substitute 1 cup (250 mL) clabber cream with:

- 1 cup (250 mL) crème fraîche (thinner consistency)

Cream, Clotted

Also known as Devon cream or Devonshire cream. The heavy cream that is skimmed from gently heated unpasteurized milk.

If You Don't Have It
Substitute 1 cup (250 mL) clotted cream with:
- 1 cup (250 mL) crème fraîche
- ½ cup (125 mL) whipped cream

Cream, Double

Cream that contains 42% butterfat. Not widely available to consumers in the United States.

If You Don't Have It
Substitute 1 cup (250 mL) double cream with:
- 1 cup (250 mL) heavy or whipping cream (35% butterfat)
- 1 cup (250 mL) crème fraîche

Cream, Half-and-Half

A mixture of equal parts milk and cream that contains 10 to 12% butterfat.

If You Don't Have It
Substitute 1 cup (250 mL) half-and-half with:
- ½ cup (125 mL) light or table cream + ½ cup (125 mL) whole milk
- 1 tbsp (15 mL) melted unsalted butter + enough whole milk to equal 1 cup (250 mL)
- ¾ cup (175 mL) whole milk + ¼ cup (50 mL) heavy or whipping cream (35% butterfat)
- 1 cup (250 mL) evaporated milk (for baking)

For Better Health
Substitute 1 cup (250 mL) half-and-half with:
- 1 cup (250 mL) fat-free half-and-half
- 1 cup (250 mL) fat-free evaporated milk (for baking)

Cream, Light

Also known as coffee cream and table cream. Can contain anywhere from 18 to 30% fat; most common content is 20%. In Canada, this cream is known as table cream, while light cream refers to a lighter cream with 5% fat.

If You Don't Have It
Substitute 1 cup (250 mL) light or table cream with:
- 3 tbsp (45 mL) melted unsalted butter + whole milk to equal 1 cup (250 mL)
- ½ cup (125 mL) heavy or whipping cream (35% butterfat) + ½ cup (125 mL) whole milk
- ½ cup (125 mL) evaporated milk + ½ cup (125 mL) whole milk

For Better Health
Substitute 1 cup (250 mL) light or table cream with:
- 1 cup (250 mL) half-and-half
- 1 cup (250 mL) fat-free half-and-half
- ½ cup (125 mL) fat-free evaporated milk + ½ cup (125 mL) whole or 2% milk

Cream, Light Whipping

The most common type of cream sold commercially in the U.S., it contains 30 to 36% fat and frequently stabilizers and emulsifiers.

If You Don't Have It
Substitute 1 cup (250 mL) light whipping cream when not for whipping with:
- ¾ cup (175 mL) whole milk + ¼ cup (50 mL) melted unsalted butter
- 1 cup (250 mL) heavy or whipping cream (35% butterfat; heavier body)

For Better Health
Substitute 1 cup (250 mL) light whipping cream when not for whipping with:
- 1 cup (250 mL) half-and-half

Cream Nut

See BRAZIL NUT.

Cream of Coconut

Ultra-sweet, thick blend of coconut paste, water, and sugar that forms the basis of the tropical piña colada cocktail. Not to be confused with coconut cream, a thick type of coconut milk.

If You Don't Have It
Substitute 1 cup (250 mL) cream of coconut with:
- 1 cup (250 mL) sweetened condensed milk + ¼ to ½ tsp (1 to 2 mL) coconut extract
- 1 cup (250 mL) coconut cream + ¼ to ½ cup (50 to 125 mL) confectioner's (icing) sugar blended together
- 1 cup (250 mL) coconut milk + ¼ to ½ cup (50 to 125 mL) confectioner's (icing) sugar blended together

For Better Health
Substitute 1 cup (250 mL) cream of coconut with:
- 1 cup (250 mL) reduced-fat coconut milk + ¼ to ½ cup (50 to 125 mL) confectioner's (icing) sugar blended together (less rich; thinner consistency)

See also COCONUT CREAM.

Cream of Tartar

An acidic white powder scraped from the inside of wine barrels, it's added to candy and frosting for creaminess and to egg whites before beating to achieve higher volume and stability. Also added to some baking powders.

If You Don't Have It
Substitute 1 tsp (5 mL) cream of tartar with:
- 1 tbsp (15 mL) distilled white vinegar or lemon juice (to add acidity to liquids)

Cream, Whipping

Also known as heavy cream. Cream that contains 35 to 40% butterfat. There is also a light whipping cream with 30 to 35% butterfat available in the U.S. When substituting lower-fat creams for whipping cream in sauces, prevent curdling by heating the sauce over low heat only.

1 cup (250 mL) = 2 cups (500 mL) whipped

If You Don't Have It

Substitute 1 cup (250 mL) heavy or whipping cream (35% butterfat) when not for whipping with:
- 1 cup (250 mL) double cream
- 1 cup (250 mL) crème fraîche
- ²⁄₃ cup (150 mL) whole milk + ⅓ cup (75 mL) melted unsalted butter
- ²⁄₃ cup (150 mL) evaporated milk

For Better Health

Substitute 1 cup (250 mL) heavy or whipping cream (35% butterfat) when not for whipping with:
- 1 cup (250 mL) light or table cream
- 1 cup (250 mL) half-and-half
- 1 cup (250 mL) fat-free half-and-half
- 1 cup (250 mL) 2% or 1% milk + 1 tbsp (15 mL) cornstarch
- ²⁄₃ cup (150 mL) fat-free evaporated milk

See also CREAM, LIGHT WHIPPING; WHIPPED CREAM.

Crema Danica

Also known as Crema Dania. From Denmark, small rectangular 72% butterfat cheese cloaked in a downy white rind.

If You Don't Have It

Substitute 1 oz (30 g) Crema Danica with:
- 1 oz (30 g) Brie
- 1 oz (30 g) Camembert

Crème d'Abricots

Sweet apricot liqueur.

If You Don't Have It

Substitute 3 tbsp (45 mL) crème d'abricots with:
- 3 tbsp (45 mL) apricot liqueur (less sweet)

Crème d'Amande

See ALMOND LIQUEUR.

Crème d'Ananas

Pineapple liqueur.

If You Don't Have It

Substitute 3 tbsp (45 mL) crème d'ananas with:
- 3 tbsp (45 mL) crème de banane (banana flavor)

Crème de Banane

Sweet liqueur with the flavor of ripe bananas.

If You Don't Have It

Substitute 3 tbsp (45 mL) crème de banane with:
- 3 tbsp (45 mL) crème d'ananas (pineapple flavor)

| **Crème de Cacao** | *See* CHOCOLATE LIQUEUR. |

| **Crème de Café** | *See* COFFEE LIQUEUR. |

| **Crème de Cassis** | *See* CASSIS LIQUEUR. |

| **Crème de Cerise** | *See* CHERRY LIQUEUR. |

Crème de Fraise

Sweet, thick strawberry liqueur.

If You Don't Have It

Substitute 3 tbsp (45 mL) crème de fraise with:
- 3 tbsp (45 mL) crème de framboise (raspberry flavor)
- 3 tbsp (45 mL) strawberry liqueur (less sweet; lighter body)
- 3 tbsp (45 mL) strawberry schnapps (less sweet; lighter body)
- 3 tbsp (45 mL) crème de cassis (black currant flavor)

Crème de Framboise

Raspberry liqueur.

If You Don't Have It

Substitute 3 tbsp (45 mL) crème de framboise with:
- 3 tbsp (45 mL) crème de fraise (strawberry flavor)
- 3 tbsp (45 mL) raspberry liqueur (less sweet; lighter body)
- 3 tbsp (45 mL) raspberry schnapps (less sweet; lighter body)
- 3 tbsp (45 mL) crème de cassis (black currant flavor)

| **Crème de Mandarin** | *See* MANDARIN LIQUEUR. |

| **Crème de Marron** | *See* CHESTNUT CREAM. |

Crème de Menthe

Mint liqueur comes in clear (also called "white") and green.

If You Don't Have It

Substitute 3 tbsp (45 mL) crème de menthe with:
- 3 tbsp (45 mL) peppermint schnapps (less sweet; lighter body)
- 3 tbsp (45 mL) Jägermeister (much more bitter and complex)
- ¼ to ½ tsp (1 to 2 mL) peppermint extract + 3 tbsp (45 mL) water or other liquid
- 2 drops peppermint oil + 3 tbsp (45 mL) water or other liquid

Crème de Noix

See WALNUT LIQUEUR.

Crème de Noyaux

See ALMOND LIQUEUR.

Crème de Rose

This liqueur by any other name would still taste of rose petals scented with vanilla and spices.

If You Don't Have It

Substitute 3 tbsp (45 mL) crème de rose with:
- 3 tbsp (45 mL) crème de vanille + 2 to 3 drops rose water

Crème de Vanille

Vanilla-scented liqueur.

If You Don't Have It

Substitute 3 tbsp (45 mL) crème de vanille with:
- ½ tsp (2 mL) vanilla extract + 3 tbsp (45 mL) water or other liquid

Crème de Violette

Liqueur flavored with violets.

If You Don't Have It

Substitute 3 tbsp (45 mL) crème de violette with:
- 3 tbsp (45 mL) Parfait d'Amour (adds citrus flavor)
- 3 tbsp (45 mL) crème de rose (lighter color; adds vanilla flavor)

Crème Fraîche

Matured thickened cream, a specialty of France. Unlike sour cream, crème fraîche won't curdle if boiled.

If You Don't Have It

Substitute 1 cup (250 mL) crème fraîche with:
- 1 cup (250 mL) sour cream or yogurt (for cold or gently heated sauces and cold soups)
- ½ cup (125 mL) sour cream + ½ cup (125 mL) heavy or whipping cream (35% butterfat)
- 1 cup (250 mL) clabber cream (thicker)

Crème Fraîche (cont'd)

- 1 cup (250 mL) Homemade Crème Fraîche: Mix together 1 cup (250 mL) heavy or whipping cream (35% butterfat) and 3 tbsp (45 mL) buttermilk (for a tangy flavor) or ½ cup (125 mL) sour cream (for less tangy flavor). Cover and let stand at room temperature (68° to 72°F/20° to 22°C) overnight or for up to 24 hours. Stir, recover and chill for at least 8 hours before using. Keeps refrigerated for about 10 days.

To Vary the Flavor
Substitute 1 cup (250 mL) crème fraîche with:
- 1 cup (250 mL) Homemade Crème Fraîche (see recipe above) mixed with 1 tbsp (15 mL) chopped fresh herbs, crystallized ginger, or honey before chilling.

Crenshaw Melon

Also known as cranshaw melon. Sweet oval melon with golden-green, lightly ribbed rind and salmon-color flesh. The aroma is spicy. Can weigh up to 9 pounds (4.5 kg).

> 1 lb (500 g) = 1 to 1½ cups (250 to 375 mL) cubed

If You Don't Have It
Substitute 1 cup (250 mL) chopped Crenshaw melon with:
- 1 cup (250 mL) chopped Persian melon
- 1 cup (250 mL) chopped casaba melon
- 1 cup (250 mL) chopped Santa Claus melon
- 1 cup (250 mL) chopped cantaloupe
- 1 cup (250 mL) chopped honeydew melon

Creole Seasoning

The New Orleans city cousin of country Cajun Seasoning.

If You Don't Have It
Substitute 1 tbsp (15 mL) Creole seasoning with:
- 1 tbsp (15 mL) Homemade Creole seasoning: Combine ¾ tsp (4 mL) paprika, ½ tsp (2 mL) ground black pepper, ½ tsp (2 mL) cayenne pepper, ½ tsp (2 mL) garlic powder, ½ tsp (2 mL) onion powder, ½ tsp (2 mL) dried oregano, ½ tsp (2 mL) dried thyme, and ¼ tsp (1 mL) celery seeds (optional). Add salt to taste. Makes about 1 tablespoon (15 mL). To make more, multiply recipe and store in an airtight container for up to 6 months.
- 1 tbsp (15 mL) Cajun seasoning (very similar)

See also CAJUN SEASONING.

Crescenza

See STRACCHINO.

Cress

Derived from the Greek word "to creep." Low-growing plants with small leaves, commonly used on salads but can also be cooked. Includes watercress, upland cress, curly cress, and land cress. Cress is highly perishable, so try to use it as soon as possible after you buy it.

If You Don't Have It
Substitute 1 cup (250 mL) cress with:
- 1 cup (250 mL) arugula
- 1 cup (250 mL) nasturtium leaves
- 1 cup (250 mL) baby spinach leaves + pinch of pepper
- 1 cup (250 mL) radish sprouts
- 1 cup (250 mL) tender dandelion greens

Cress Varieties
Choose 1 cup (250 mL) cress from these varieties:
- 1 cup (250 mL) watercress (peppery; small tender leaves; crunchy stems; use fresh or gently cooked)
- 1 cup (250 mL) upland cress or land cress (elegantly peppery with a bite that comes on slow; often sold as small, micro-cress; tender, round or oval pale green leaves and stems; use fresh)
- 1 cup (250 mL) garden cress or pepper cress (sweetly peppery; often sold as sprouts; tiny, tender leaves and stems; use fresh)
- 1 cup (250 mL) winter cress (bitterly peppery; green leaves similar to arugula in size and shape; use gently cooked to tame the bitterness or mix young winter cress with milder greens to use fresh)

See also NASTURTIUM.

Crisco

See VEGETABLE SHORTENING.

Crisphead Lettuce

One of the "cabbage" lettuces, with crisp leaves that form compacted heads or long-leaved without heads.

If You Don't Have It
Substitute 1 lb (500 g) crisphead lettuce with:
- 1 lb (500 g) romaine lettuce (crunchy; more flavorful)
- 8 oz (250 g) leaf lettuce (less crunchy; less watery)

Crisphead Varieties
Choose 1 lb (500 g) crisphead lettuce from these varieties:
- 1 lb (500 g) Iceberg, Great Lakes, Imperial, Vanguard, or Western lettuce (similar varieties of crisphead lettuce)

See also BUTTERHEAD LETTUCE.

Croaker

Also known as drum. A category of fish that make a deep croaking or drumming noise, especially during breeding season.

If You Don't Have It
Substitute 1 lb (500 g) croaker with:
- 1 lb (500 g) porgy
- 1 lb (500 g) hake

Croaker Varieties
Choose 1 lb (500 g) croaker from these varieties:
- 1 lb (500 g) Atlantic croaker
- 1 lb (500 g) black drum
- 1 lb (500 g) red drum or redfish
- 1 lb (500 g) spot
- 1 lb (500 g) kingfish
- 1 lb (500 g) weakfish

Crocodile

Farm-raised crocodile are an established commodity in Australia, where it is illegal to sell the wild meat.

If You Don't Have It
Substitute 1 lb (500 g) crocodile tail meat with:
- 1 lb (500 g) alligator tail meat
- 1 lb (500 g) turtle meat
- 1 lb (500 g) chicken breast
- 1 lb (500 g) swordfish

Croissant

From the French word meaning "crescent." A breakfast roll that is traditionally made with butter.

If You Don't Have It
Substitute 1 lb (500 g) croissants with:
- 1 lb (500 g) crescent rolls from refrigerated dough (less flavorful)
- 1 lb (500 g) brioche (more eggy; denser texture)
- 1 lb (500 g) challah (more eggy; denser texture)

Crostini

A toasted Italian bread similar to bruschetta but often smaller, thinner, and sometimes with the crust removed. Usually topped and served as an appetizer or canapé.

If You Don't Have It
Substitute 16 crostini with:
- 16 Homemade Crostini: Cut a baguette into ¼-inch (1 cm) thick slices (remove crust if you like). Bake slices at 400°F (200°C), turning once, until just crisp, about 5 minutes. Rub with a cut garlic clove and brush, drizzle, or spray with olive oil. Makes about 16 crostini.
- 16 slices bruschetta (usually larger, thicker, with crust, and typically charcoal-grilled)
- 16 melba toasts
- 16 bagel chips
- 16 crackers

Croustade

An edible container used for stew, creamed meats, or vegetable mixtures. It can be made from pastry, a hollowed bread loaf, or puréed potatoes. Before filling, it is deep-fried or toasted until golden and crisp.

If You Don't Have It

Substitute 16 croustades with:
- 16 frozen prepared phyllo mini-shells (before filling, bake phyllo shells at 350°F/180°C on a baking sheet for 3 to 5 minutes)
- 8 small dinner rolls, each cut in half and hollowed out to leave the crust; brush with melted butter or olive oil and bake at 375°F (190°C) on a baking sheet until crisp, 8 to 12 minutes
- 16 small barquettes (boat-shaped pastry shells)
- 16 crostini (for hors d'oeuvres)
- 16 water crackers (for hors d'oeuvres)
- 16 rounds from slices of white bread (cut rounds with a cookie cutter) pressed into greased regular or mini-muffin cups and baked at 350°F (180°C) until crisp, 8 to 12 minutes
- 6 frozen prepared puff pastry shells (larger and more tender; bake pastry shells at 400°F/200°C on a baking sheet until puffed and golden, about 20 minutes. Remove tops and bake shells for 5 minutes more)

Croutons

Small browned pieces of bread. Usually served with salad. Smaller, commercially prepared croutons or "stuffing cubes" are turned into dressings and stuffings.

If You Don't Have It

Substitute 1 cup (250 mL) croutons with:
- 1 cup (250 mL) Homemade Croutons: Cut your favorite bread (dense, flavorful bread works best) into 1 cup (250 mL) of cubes (up to ½-inch/1 cm thick cubes for stuffing; up to 1½-inch/4 cm cubes for salad croutons) or other shapes. Toss with 2 to 3 tsp (10 to 15 mL) melted butter or oil and, if you like, salt, pepper, herbs, garlic, and/or Parmesan cheese, or other seasonings. Bake on a baking sheet at 350°F (180°C), tossing or turning once or twice to brown evenly, until crisp, about 15 minutes. Makes 1 cup (250 mL).
- 1 cup (250 mL) coarse bread crumbs (to top casseroles)
- 1 cup (250 mL) broken bagel chips (to top salads and casseroles)
- 1 cup (250 mL) broken crostini (to top salads and casseroles)

Crumbs

See BREAD CRUMBS; COOKIE CRUMBS; CORNFLAKE CRUMBS; CRACKER CRUMBS; MATZO MEAL; PANKO; PIE CRUST, CRUMB.

Crumpet

In Britain, a thick, perforated pancake made from batter containing yeast and milk. Cooked on a griddle until the underside is pale gold and smooth.

If You Don't Have It
Substitute 1 crumpet with:
- 1 English muffin (American)
- 1 American biscuit (less airy)
- 1 scone (sweeter; less airy)

Crumpet Ring

Also known as English muffin rings. Stainless-steel rings that are 4 inches (10 cm) in diameter and 1 inch (2.5 cm) deep. Used to form crumpets.

If You Don't Have It
Substitute a crumpet ring with:
- biscuit cutter or cookie cutter
- clean 6-oz (170 g) tuna can with both ends removed

Crust

See PIE CRUST, CRUMB; PIE CRUST, PASTRY.

Crystallized Ginger

See GINGER, CRYSTALLIZED.

Cucumber

At about 4,000 years old, the cucumber is one of the oldest cultivated vegetables. It is 96% water. Used commonly for salads, garnishes, soups and sandwiches, and dressed with yogurt or vinegar.

1 lb (500 g) = 2 cups (500 mL) sliced

If You Don't Have It
Substitute 1 lb (500 g) cucumber with:
- 1 lb (500 g) small zucchini (for cooking; less sweet)

Cucumber Varieties
Choose 1 lb (500 g) cucumber from these varieties:
- 1 lb (500 g) American slicing or garden cucumber (often sold waxed to extend shelf-life; thick, heavy body; bumpy dark green, thick and sometimes bitter-tasting skin; flesh is very mild in flavor; crunchy texture; best peeled and seeded for soups or when mixed with other ingredients)
- 1 lb (500 g) English or European or hothouse cucumber (often sold shrink-wrapped; longer and more slender than American slicing cucumbers; smooth or slightly ridged dark green thin skin; nearly seedless; mildly sweet flavor; less bitter

than American slicing cucumbers; needs no peeling or seeding)

- 1 lb (500 g) Asian or Korean or Japanese cucumber (longer and more narrow than American slicing cucumbers; bumpy pale green to dark green thin skin; nearly seedless; complex, earthy flavor ranging from mild to bitter; juicy, crunchy texture; needs no peeling or seeding; best for sushi)
- 1 lb (500 g) Armenian cucumber or snake melon (long, slender, curved body; ridged, light yellow to pale green razor-thin skin; sweet, mild citrus flavor; extra-crisp texture; needs no peeling or seeding)
- 1 lb (500 g) American pickling or so-called "Kirby" cucumber (short, thick, blunt or slightly curved and pointed body; bumpy, pale-striped yellow to dark green somewhat-thin skin; crunchy, juicy texture; mildly sweet flavor; small seeds; good for slicing, cooking, and pickling)
- 1 lb (500 g) gherkins (often pickled and sold by the French name *cornichon*; small, short, relatively narrow body; bumpy, somewhat thin dark green skin; crunchy texture; sweet flavor; small seeds; good for slicing, cooking, and pickling)

See also CORNICHON; SWEET GHERKIN.

Cucuzza

Sicilian term for squash that looks like an elongated and curved bottle gourd.

If You Don't Have It

Substitute 1 lb (500 g) cucuzza with:
- 1 lb (500 g) bottle gourd
- 1 lb (500 g) winter melon
- 1 lb (500 g) chayote
- 1 lb (500 g) zucchini
- 1 lb (500 g) yellow squash

Culantro

See CILANTRO.

Culatello

"Little backside." An Italian product made from pork hindquarters pressed like ham. The lean meat is salted, soaked in wine, and, traditionally, packed in the pig's bladder. It is moist, delicate, pink, and eaten raw. Originated in Parma.

If You Don't Have It
Substitute 4 oz (125 g) culatello with:
- 4 oz (125 g) prosciutto (fattier; not soaked in wine during aging)

To Vary the Flavor
Substitute 4 oz (125 g) culatello with:
- 4 oz (125 g) Serrano or Iberico ham
- 4 oz (125 g) Ardennes ham (adds smoke flavor)
- 4 oz (125 g) Bayonne ham (adds mild smoke flavor)
- 4 oz (125 g) Westphalian ham (adds juniper and mild smoke flavors)

Cumberland Sausage

Traditional British spicy sausage made of coarse-cut pork. Sometimes sold by length from a long coil.

If You Don't Have It
Substitute 4 oz (125 g) Cumberland sausage with:
- 4 oz (125 g) Cambridge, Oxford, or other British sausage
- 4 oz (125 g) relatively mild pork sausage

Cumin

Also known as cumin seeds. Spice made from dried tiny seedlike fruits of an herb in the parsley family. Cumin is mentioned in the Bible and was probably used by the Romans. It is used in the Netherlands to flavor certain cheeses, in India in garam masala, and in Mexican and Tex-Mex dishes of North America.

1 oz (30 g) = 4½ tbsp (67 mL) whole seed = 4 tbsp (60 mL) ground

If You Don't Have It
Substitute 1 tsp (5 mL) amber cumin seeds (ground) with:
- 1 tsp (5 mL) chili powder (most commercial chili powder blends contain a high percentage of amber cumin; adds oregano, mild chile pepper, salt, and pepper flavors)
- 1 tsp (5 mL) ground coriander (adds musky, lemony aroma)
- ½ tsp (2 mL) caraway (adds mild licorice aroma)

Cumin Varieties
Choose 1 tsp (5 mL) amber cumin seeds (whole or ground) from these varieties:
- 1 tsp (5 mL) white cumin (similar to the common amber cumin; available in Asian markets)
- 1 tsp (5 mL) black cumin (sweeter; more peppery; often used in curries; available in Asian markets)

Curaçao

See ORANGE LIQUEUR.

Curly Endive

A green that grows in loose heads of lacy leaves with prickly texture and slightly bitter taste. Frisée is blanched curly endive. It has paler yellow or light green leaves and is slightly sweet and less bitter. It can be used interchangeably with curly endive.

If You Don't Have It

Substitute 1 cup (250 mL) curly endive with:
- 1 cup (250 mL) chicory
- 1 cup (250 mL) escarole (less bitter; softer leaves)
- 1 cup (250 mL) radicchio (red color)

See also BELGIAN ENDIVE; CHICORY; ESCAROLE; FRISÉE.

Currant, Dried

The dried fruit of the seedless Zante grape. Not to be confused with fresh currants.

If You Don't Have It

Substitute 1 cup (250 mL) dried currants with:
- 1 cup (250 mL) raisins (dark or golden; larger than currants)
- 1 cup (250 mL) finely chopped soft prunes
- 1 cup (250 mL) finely chopped soft dates
- 1 cup (250 mL) dried blueberries, cherries, or cranberries

See also CHAMPAGNE GRAPES; CURRANT, FRESH; RAISIN.

Currant, Fresh

Small round red, white, or black berries that grow in northern temperate regions. Red currants were domesticated in Europe in the 16th century. White currants are an uncommon variant of red currants. Black currants were cultivated a century later than red currants and thought inferior; they were used in Britain to treat sore throats and have an abundance of vitamin C. Frozen currants can be substituted for fresh, especially in jams.

If You Don't Have It

Substitute 1 cup (250 mL) fresh currants with:
- 1 cup (250 mL) elderberries (purple black color; bitter flavor)
- 1 cup (250 mL) gooseberries (light yellow to pale green color; tart flavor)
- 1 cup (250 mL) bilberries (purple color; sharp, sweet flavor)
- 1 cup (250 mL) blueberries (purple color; sweet flavor)

Currant Varieties

Choose 1 cup (250 mL) fresh currants from these varieties:
- 1 cup (250 mL) black currants or cassis (dark color; tart)
- 1 cup (250 mL) red currants (red color; slightly sweet; slightly tart)
- 1 cup (250 mL) white currants (white color; slightly sweet; less tart)

Currant Jelly

The two main types are red currant jelly and less common black currant jelly. Red currant jelly is often used to accompany lamb and other meats.

If You Don't Have It
Substitute 1 cup (250 mL) currant jelly with:
- 1 cup (250 mL) grape jelly
- 1 cup (250 mL) scuppernong or muscadine jelly

Curry Leaf

Also known as kari leaf. Green shiny leaf of a small tree that grows wild in South Asia. The leaves are aromatic and used for flavor in cooking. The curry leaf's function corresponds to the Western use of bay leaf, often fried, and removed before the dish is served.

If You Don't Have It
Substitute 10 fresh curry leaves with:
- 10 good-quality dried curry leaves

To Vary the Flavor
Substitute 10 fresh curry leaves with:
- 5 to 10 makrut (kaffir) lime leaves (adds lime, mandarin orange, and lemon aromas)
- 5 fresh bay leaves (adds piney, resinous, woodsy aromas)
- 1 tbsp (15 mL) chopped fresh cilantro (adds grassy, lemony aromas)

Curry Paste

See CHILE PASTE.

Curry Powder

Originally, this powder was an attempt to produce a ready-made spice mix similar to homemade spice blends in India. Likely to include coriander, cumin, mustard seeds, pepper, fenugreek, and turmeric. Commercial "Madras" curry powder is usually spicier than curry powder without the Madras label.

If You Don't Have It
Substitute 1 tsp (5 mL) curry powder with:
- 1 tsp (5 mL) Homemade Curry Powder: Combine $3\frac{1}{2}$ tsp (17 mL) ground coriander, $2\frac{1}{2}$ tsp (12 mL) ground turmeric, 1 tsp (5 mL) ground cumin, 1 tsp (5 mL) crushed fenugreek seeds, $\frac{1}{2}$ tsp (2 mL) ground black pepper, $\frac{1}{2}$ tsp (2 mL) mustard powder, $\frac{1}{2}$ tsp (2 mL) ground allspice, $\frac{1}{4}$ tsp (1 mL) ground ginger, and $\frac{1}{8}$ to $\frac{1}{4}$ tsp (0.5 to 1 mL) cayenne pepper. Add salt to taste. Makes about 3 tablespoons (45 mL).
- $\frac{1}{2}$ tsp (2 mL) turmeric (just for yellow color; adds much less flavor)

Cusk

Also known as torsk or tusk. A saltwater fish similar to cod that's found in Arctic waters. The flesh is firm and moderately oily. Best for grilling or baking.

If You Don't Have It
Substitute 1 lb (500 g) cusk with:
- 1 lb (500 g) cod
- 1 lb (500 g) pollock
- 1 lb (500 g) haddock
- 1 lb (500 g) hake
- 1 lb (500 g) scrod (young cod)
- 1 lb (500 g) Cape capensis
- 1 lb (500 g) tilapia
- 1 lb (500 g) sole
- 1 lb (500 g) flounder
- 1 lb (500 g) tilefish
- 1 lb (500 g) turbot
- 1 lb (500 g) grouper
- 1 lb (500 g) halibut
- 1 lb (500 g) red snapper
- 1 lb (500 g) striped bass

Custard Apple

See CHERIMOYA.

Custard Squash

See PATTYPAN SQUASH.

Cuttlefish

Also known as inkfish. An edible cephalopod with ink sacs and ten appendages, it resembles a large squid. Japan is the largest market. Available both fresh and dried.

If You Don't Have It
Substitute 1 lb (500 g) cuttlefish with:
- 1 lb (500 g) squid (smaller; firmer; tenderize by simmering salted water or by pounding)
- 1 lb (500 g) octopus, preferably young (firmer; tenderize by simmering in salted water or by pounding)

Cynar

An Italian aperitivo or digestivo made from artichokes and various herbs. Served plain or with a splash of soda water over ice.

If You Don't Have It
Substitute 3 tbsp (45 mL) Cynar with:
- 3 tbsp (45 mL) Byrrh

Daikon to
Dutch-Process Cocoa

Daikon

See RADISH.

Daisy

See PICKING EDIBLE FLOWERS (PAGE 604).

Dal

See PEAS, SPLIT; SWITCHING LENTILS (PAGE 569);
THE WIDE WORLD OF DRIED BEANS (PAGE 566).

Danbo

*Also known as Christian IX.
Mildly sweet, pale yellow
cheese from Denmark with
red or yellow wax cover.*

If You Don't Have It

Substitute 1 oz (30 g) Danbo with:
- 1 oz (30 g) Tybo or Samsoe + small pinch of
  caraway seeds
- 1 oz (30 g) mild Cheddar or American cheese
  + small pinch of caraway seeds

Dandelion

*Young, tender dandelion
greens work well in salads
or gently cooked. Older,
more bitter dandelion
greens taste best when
mellowed by cooking.*

If You Don't Have It

Substitute 1 cup (250 mL) dandelion greens with:
- 1 cup (250 mL) arugula
- 1 cup (250 mL) watercress or upland cress
- 1 cup (250 mL) nasturtium leaves
- 1 cup (250 mL) curly endive
- 1 cup (250 mL) baby spinach leaves + pinch
  of pepper

See also PICKING EDIBLE FLOWERS (PAGE 604).

Danish Blue

*Also known as Danablu.
A widely distributed cow's
milk blue cheese from
Denmark that's delicious
paired with fruit, dark
breads, and red wines.*

If You Don't Have It
Substitute 1 oz (30 g) Danish blue with:
- 1 oz (30 g) aged Gorgonzola
- 1 oz (30 g) Roquefort
- 1 oz (30 g) Stilton
- 1 oz (30 g) Saga blue
- 1 oz (30 g) Blue Castello

Danish Port Salut

See ESROM.

Dasheen

See TARO.

Dashi

*Japanese broth made with
dried bonito tuna flakes.
Dashi-no-moto is the
instant form, sold as
concentrate, granulated,
or powdered.*

If You Don't Have It
Substitute 1 cup (250 mL) dashi with:
- 1 cup (250 mL) Homemade Dashi: Put one 2-inch (5 cm) square piece of kombu (kelp) and 2¼ cups (550 mL) fresh water in a small pot. Bring to a boil over high heat. Remove from heat and stir in 3 tbsp (45 mL) bonito flakes. Let stand for a few minutes until bonito flakes sink. Remove and discard kombu. Strain stock into an airtight container. Cool, seal, and refrigerate for up to 5 days. Makes about 2 cups (500 mL).
- 1 cup (250 mL) reconstituted instant dashi (dashi-no-moto)
- 1 cup (250 mL) chicken stock + 3 tbsp (45 mL) dulse (seaweed) flakes or a 1-inch (2.5 cm) square of kombu, brought to a boil, removed from heat and cooled for 5 minutes, then strained (not as flavorful)

Date

*Multiple varieties of fresh
and dried dates are enjoyed
in the Middle East and
North Africa. Westerners
are generally more familiar
with dried medjool or deglet
noor varieties. When
dried, dates become softer
and sweeter.*

If You Don't Have It
Substitute 1 cup (250 mL) dried dates with:
- 1 cup (250 mL) dried figs
- 1 cup (250 mL) raisins

Date Sugar

Dehydrated and ground date pieces.

If You Don't Have It
Substitute 1 cup (250 mL) date sugar with:
- 1 cup (250 mL) light brown or granulated sugar (fewer nutrients)

Daylily

See PICKING EDIBLE FLOWERS (PAGE 604).

Decanter

A glass or crystal container with a bulbous bottom and a stopper that fits in the narrow neck. Used to serve or display wines and other spirits.

If You Don't Have It
Substitute a decanter with:
- tall decorative glass jar with a cork, as used for flavored oils and vinegars
- decorative glass pitcher

Decorating Sugar

See SUGAR, DECORATING.

Deep-Frying

See FRYING.

Deer

The main species eaten by humans are fallow deer, red deer, roe deer, and white-tailed deer. Since prehistoric times, deer meat has provided protein to people around the world.

If You Don't Have It
Substitute 1 lb (500 g) deer with:
- 1 lb (500 g) reindeer (technically a species of deer; eaten mostly in northern Europe and Asia, particularly in Sweden, Finland, and Russia)
- 1 lb (500 g) caribou
- 1 lb (500 g) elk
- 1 lb (500 g) antelope
- 1 lb (500 g) gazelle

Deer Subspecies
Choose 1 lb (500 g) deer from these subspecies:
- 1 lb (500 g) white-tailed deer (the most common deer in North America)
- 1 lb (500 g) red deer (among the largest deer; found mostly in the Scottish Highlands)
- 1 lb (500 g) fallow deer (found near the Mediterranean and other parts of Europe)
- 1 lb (500 g) roe deer (among the smallest; considered the best-tasting by many cooks)

See also VENISON.

Degreasing Pitcher

See FAT SEPARATOR.

Delicata Squash

Also known as sweet potato squash. The yellow flesh tastes like a combination of butternut squash and sweet potatoes.

If You Don't Have It
Substitute 1 cup (250 mL) chopped delicata squash with:
- 1 cup (250 mL) chopped sweet dumpling squash
- 1 cup (250 mL) chopped butternut squash
- 1 cup (250 mL) chopped buttercup squash
- 1 cup (250 mL) chopped pumpkin
- 1 cup (250 mL) chopped sweet potato

Demerara Sugar

See SUGAR, RAW.

Demi-Glace

The classic French mother sauce, prepared by reducing equal measures of sauce espagnole *(brown sauce) and brown veal stock.*

For Better Health
Substitute 1 cup (250 mL) veal demi-glace with:
- 1 cup (250 mL) veggie glace (commercially available roasted vegetable demi-glace)

See also GLACE DE VIANDE.

Derby

Sage Derby (strongly flavored with sage) is a popular variety of this mild, semifirm cow's milk cheese.

If You Don't Have It
Substitute 1 oz (30 g) Derby cheese with:
- 1 oz (30 g) mild Cheddar
- 1 oz (30 g) Colby
- 1 oz (30 g) Cheshire
- 1 oz (30 g) Vermont Sage (to replace Sage Derby)

Dessert Wine

See WINE, DESSERT.

Devon Cream

See CREAM, CLOTTED.

Dewberry

A close relative of the blackberry that produces smaller berries.

If You Don't Have It
Substitute 1 cup (250 mL) dewberries with:
- 1 cup (250 mL) blackberries (larger)
- 1 cup (250 mL) tayberries (larger; red color)
- 1 cup (250 mL) youngberries (larger; red color)
- 1 cup (250 mL) loganberries (dark red color)
- 1 cup (250 mL) raspberries (sweeter; red color)

Dextrose

See GLUCOSE, LIQUID.

Dianthus

See PICKING EDIBLE FLOWERS (PAGE 604).

Digestive Biscuit

Also known as sweetmeal biscuit and wheatmeal biscuit. The commercial name of a British favorite: slightly sweet whole wheat biscuits that are eaten with cheese.

If You Don't Have It
Substitute 1 lb (500 g) digestive biscuits with:
- 1 lb (500 g) graham crackers (sweeter)
- 1 lb (500 g) teething biscuits

Dijon Mustard

See MUSTARD.

Dill

A member of the parsley family, dill is related to fennel but exudes aromas of caraway and lemon rather than anise.

If You Don't Have It
Substitute 1 tbsp (15 mL) fresh dill with:
- 1 tbsp (15 mL) fresh tarragon (particularly with eggs, fish, and chicken)
- 1 tbsp (15 mL) fresh fennel leaves (for garnishing)

Dill Seeds

Along with the leaves of this annual herb, dill seeds have a special affinity with Scandinavian and eastern European cooking.

If You Don't Have It
Substitute 1 tsp (5 mL) dill seeds with:
- 1 tsp (5 mL) caraway seeds (stronger aroma)
- 1 tsp (5 mL) celery seeds (adds celery aroma)

Dogfish

Also known as capeshark and sand shark. The name of these various small sharks is reference to the small size and shape.

If You Don't Have It
Substitute 1 lb (500 g) dogfish with:
- 1 lb (500 g) shark
- 1 lb (500 g) swordfish
- 1 lb (500 g) mahi-mahi (sweeter)

Dollarfish

See BUTTERFISH.

Dolphin Fish

See MAHI-MAHI.

Dorado

See MAHI-MAHI.

Dory

See JOHN DORY.

Double Boiler

Two nesting pots in which the bottom holds simmering water to gently heat or melt the ingredient — perhaps, custard, chocolate, or sauce — in the top pot.

If You Don't Have It

Substitute a double boiler with:

- stainless-steel or heatproof bowl set over a saucepan of simmering water (make sure that the bowl does not touch the water)
- microwave oven (for melting chocolate; put small, similar-size pieces of chocolate into a bone-dry microwave-safe bowl and microwave on Medium power in 30-second increments, stopping to stir after every increment; microwave only until chocolate can be stirred smooth)
- 250°F (120°C) oven (for melting chocolate; place small, similar-size pieces of chocolate into a bone-dry heatproof bowl; place in a preheated 250°F/120°C oven for 8 to 10 minutes, or just until chocolate can be stirred smooth)
- heating pad set to high (for melting chocolate; place small, similar-size pieces of chocolate into a bone-dry glass bowl; set the bowl on the heating pad for 10 minutes, or just until chocolate can be stirred smooth; keep the chocolate melted for several hours by setting the heating pad to low and putting the bowl on the pad)
- warming tray set to low (for melting chocolate; place small, similar-size pieces of chocolate into a bone-dry heatproof bowl; set the bowl on the warming tray for 5 to 10 minutes, or just until chocolate is almost melted; stir smooth off the heat)

Double Gloucester

See GLOUCESTER.

Doughnut

Also known as donut. Although leavened fried balls of dough have a long and festive history in Europe, the ring-shaped pastry seems particularly American.

If You Don't Have It

Substitute 1 lb (500 g) doughnuts with:
- 1 lb (500 g) zeppoli (Italian doughnuts; chewier, fluffier, greasier)
- 1 lb (500 g) funnel cakes (German-American deep-fried dough; fluffier; greasier)
- 1 lb (500 g) génoise, sponge cake, or pound cake

Dove

See SQUAB.

Dover Sole

See SOLE.

Dragées

Tiny hard round candies, in silver and other colors, used to decorate confections.

If You Don't Have It

Substitute 1 tbsp (15 mL) dragées with:
- 1 tbsp (15 mL) jimmies
- 1 tbsp (15 mL) nonpareils
- 1 tbsp (15 mL) M&Ms
- 1 tbsp (15 mL) colored sugar sprinkles

Dragon's Eye

See LONGAN.

Drambuie

A liqueur of Scotch blended with heather honey and herbs.

If You Don't Have It

Substitute 3 tbsp (45 mL) Drambuie with:
- 3 tbsp (45 mL) Grandtully
- 3 tbsp (45 mL) Lochan Ora
- 3 tbsp (45 mL) Glayva

Drawn Butter

See BUTTER, CLARIFIED.

Dried Bonito

See BONITO.

Dried Crayfish

In Louisiana, crayfish season runs from late October to early July. The rest of the year, dried crayfish remains an option.

If You Don't Have It

Substitute 1 oz (30 g) dried crayfish with:
- 1 oz (30 g) dried shrimp

Dried Fruit

See SPECIFIC TYPES.

Dried Shrimp

A pungent flavoring in Asian and Latin American cooking. To reconstitute dried shrimp, soak them in warm water. The soaking water is used in some preparations as additional flavoring.

If You Don't Have It
Substitute 1 oz (30 g) dried shrimp with:
- 1 oz (30 g) dried crayfish

Drum

See CROAKER.

Dry-Cured ham

See HAM, DRY-CURED.

Dry Milk

Also known as powdered milk. Long a staple of thrifty homemakers, dehydrated milk is available in full-fat and fat-free versions. Although the flavor of the reconstituted powder doesn't duplicate fresh fluid milk, the powder is a convenient ingredient in baked goods, pancakes, and waffles.

1 lb (500 g) = 3⅔ cups (900 mL) = 14 cups (3.5 L) reconstituted

1⅓ cups (325 mL) = 4 cups (1 L) reconstituted

⅓ cup (75 mL) = 1 cup (250 mL) reconstituted

If You Don't Have It
Substitute 1 cup (250 mL) dry milk (reconstituted) with:
- 1 cup (250 mL) whole milk (3.5% fat)

For Better Health
Substitute 1 cup (250 mL) nonfat dry milk (reconstituted) with:
- 1 cup (250 mL) fat-free milk (less than 0.5% fat)

See also BUTTERMILK.

Dry Mustard

See MUSTARD, POWDERED.

Dublin Bay Prawn

Also known as langoustine, lobsterette, and scampi. Small salt-water crustaceans resembling 6- to 8-inch (15 to 20 cm) lobsters.

If You Don't Have It
Substitute 1 lb (500 g) Dublin Bay prawns with:
- 1 lb (500 g) crayfish
- 1 lb (500 g) spiny or rock lobster (larger)
- 1 lb (500 g) Maine lobster (larger)
- 1 lb (500 g) jumbo shrimp or prawns

Dubonnet

A bittersweet, herbal apéritif. Dubonnet rouge (red) is based on red wine, flavored with quinine. Dubonnet blanc (blond) resembles dry vermouth.

If You Don't Have It
Substitute 3 tbsp (45 mL) Dubonnet with:
- 3 tbsp (45 mL) Lillet
- 3 tbsp (45 mL) Byrrh
- 3 tbsp (45 mL) Raphael
- 3 tbsp (45 mL) Punt e Mes

Duck

Also known as duckling. Most duck is sold frozen although fresh duck is available in some markets. Broilers and fryers are less than 8 weeks of age; roosters no more than 16 weeks. Ducks generally weigh between 3 and 5 pounds (1.5 to 2.5 kg). The USDA classifications for duck quality are A, B, and C. The highest grade, A, is usually what is found in markets. Look for the grade stamp on the wrapping or on a tag attached to the wing.

If You Don't Have It
Substitute 1 lb (500 g) duck with:
- 1 lb (500 g) squab
- 1 lb (500 g) goose (less fatty)
- 1 lb (500 g) turkey
- 1 lb (500 g) rabbit
- 1 lb (500 g) chicken

Duck Egg

Prepared with almost ritualistic precision, the preparation of 17-day-old fertilized duck egg, called balut, is a Filipino delicacy.

If You Don't Have It
Substitute 1 duck egg with:
- 1 extra-large chicken egg, especially from a pasture-raised hen (less rich; less flavorful)
- 5 quail eggs (smaller; less rich; less flavorful)

Duck Fat

Most renowned in the cooking of Gascony in southwestern France, where it is utilized as a cooking medium and a preservative. Confit de canard *is duck that is cooked and stored in its own fat.*

If You Don't Have It

Substitute 1 tbsp (15 mL) duck fat with:
- 1 tbsp (15 mL) goose fat
- 1 tbsp (15 mL) lard or pork fat
- 1 tbsp (15 mL) chicken fat

Duckling

See DUCK.

Duck Sauce

See PLUM SAUCE.

Dukka

Also known as dukkah. Coarsely ground Egyptian seasoning mix often based on almonds, chickpeas, or hazelnuts with spicy additions such as coriander, cumin, pepper, and sesame seeds.

If You Don't Have It

Substitute 1 tbsp (15 mL) dukka with:
- 1 tbsp (15 mL) Homemade Dukka: Toast 1 cup (250 mL) hazelnuts or almonds in a dry frying pan over medium heat until fragrant, about 3 minutes. Remove and let cool slightly. Then rub off skins in a kitchen towel if you like (skins may be slightly bitter). Toast ½ cup (125 mL) sesame seeds and ¼ cup (50 mL) coriander seeds in same pan. Transfer to a plate to cool. Combine cooled nuts and seeds in a food processor, in a mortar with a pestle or in a large electric spice grinder. Add 1 tbsp (15 mL) cumin seeds, ½ tsp (2 mL) salt, and ½ tsp (2 mL) ground black pepper. Process or pound to a coarse powder. Makes about 1¼ cups (300 mL).

Dulse

Maroon-color sea vegetable. Rich in iron. Often powdered and used as a salt substitute.

If You Don't Have It

Substitute 1 oz (30 g) dulse with:
- 1 oz (30 g) arame (milder brine flavor; dark brown color)
- 1 oz (30 g) wakame (similar brine flavor; dark green to brown color)
- 1 oz (30 g) hijiki (stronger brine flavor; black color)
- 1 oz (30 g) kombu (stronger brine flavor; dark brown to black color)

Dumpling Wrappers

See WON TON SKINS.

Dungeness Crab

See CHOOSING AMONG CRABS (PAGE 597).

Durum Flour

See FLOUR, DURUM.

Dutch Oven

A large cast-iron pot with a tight-fitting lid traditionally used for Pennsylvania Dutch stews and braises.

If You Don't Have It

Substitute a Dutch oven with:
- any large, heavy, ovenproof pot with a tight-fitting lid

Dutch-Process Cocoa

See COCOA POWDER, UNSWEETENED.

Early Richmond Cherry to Extracts

Early Richmond Cherry

See CHERRY.

Earthenware

High-fired earthenware cooking pots are sturdier than those fired at low temperatures.

If You Don't Have It
Substitute earthenware with:
- stoneware
- porcelain
- heatproof glass

Eau de Vie

See BRANDY.

Edam

Next to Gouda, this mild yellow cheese is the second most popular cheese export from the Netherlands.

1 lb (500 g) = 4 cups (1 L) grated or shredded

If You Don't Have It
Substitute 1 oz (30 g) Edam with:
- 1 oz (30 g) Gouda (richer; less tangy)
- 1 oz (30 g) Leyden (spicier; may be flavored with caraway or cumin)
- 1 oz (30 g) Fontina (richer; less tangy)

Edamame

Also known as green soybean. In Japan, young soybean pods are picked at the start of summer then boiled and salted for snacking like peanuts.

1 lb (500 g) in shell =
1 cup (250 mL) shelled

If You Don't Have It
Substitute 1 lb (500 g) shelled and cooked edamame with:
- 1 lb (500 g) cooked green peas
- 1 lb (500 g) cooked fresh lima beans
- 1 lb (500 g) cooked fresh fava beans
- 1 lb (500 g) cooked beans such as cannellini, kidney, or black-eyed peas

Eel

A notorious burglar in 18th century Japan claimed that he could see in the dark because he ate so much eel, which are rich in vision-enhancing vitamin A.

If You Don't Have It
Substitute 1 lb (500 g) eel with:
- 1 lb (500 g) lamprey (milder flavor)
- 1 lb (500 g) monkfish (more tender)
- 1 lb (500 g) mullet (more flaky)

Eel Types
Choose 1 lb (500 g) eel from these types:
- 1 lb (500 g) freshwater eel (mostly farmed or seasonal; slightly fishier taste than saltwater eels)
- 1 lb (500 g) elver or baby eel (tender; sweet)
- 1 lb (500 g) conger eel (tougher)
- 1 lb (500 g) smoked eel (less rich; adds smoke flavor)

Egg

See EGG, WHOLE.

Egg Beater

See ROTARY BEATER.

Eggnog

In early American cookbooks, this luscious combination of eggs, cream, and spices was recommended for invalids.

If You Don't Have It
Substitute 1 cup (250 mL) eggnog with:
- 1 cup (250 mL) heavy or whipping cream (35% butterfat), light or table cream, or whole milk (less rich; thinner consistency)
- ½ tsp (2 mL) to 1 cup (250 mL) advocaat (Dutch liqueur made with egg yolks and brandy)

For Better Health
Substitute 1 cup (250 mL) eggnog with:
- 1 cup (250 mL) reduced-fat eggnog (less fat; fewer calories)

Egg Noodle

Although some Asian noodles contain egg, the term egg noodles generally refers to Eastern European flat pasta strips.

1 lb (500 g) dried =
5 cups (1.25 L) cooked

If You Don't Have It
Substitute 1 lb (500 g) dried egg noodles with:
● 8 oz (250 g) dried strand pasta such as linguine, fettuccine, or pappardelle

See also PASTA, DRIED RIBBONS; PASTA, DRIED SHAPES; PASTA, DRIED STRANDS; PASTA, FRESH.

Eggplant

Also known as aubergine. To remove bitterness (especially in older or larger eggplants), sprinkle the cut eggplant with salt and let drain briefly in a colander. Rinse off the salt if necessary.

1 lb (500 g) globe eggplant = 1 medium = 4½ cups (1.125 L) peeled and cubed = 1¾ cups (425 mL) roasted

1 medium globe eggplant = about 3 Asian eggplants

If You Don't Have It
Substitute 1 lb (500 g) eggplant with:
● 1 lb (500 g) portobello mushrooms (particularly the caps to replace eggplant slices)
● 1 lb (500 g) zucchini or yellow squash

Eggplant Varieties
Choose 1 lb (500 g) eggplant from these varieties:
● 1 lb (500 g) American, Italian-American, or globe eggplant (bell shape; dark purple skin; relatively tough flesh with mild to bitter flavor)
● 1 lb (500 g) baby or Italian purple eggplant (round or bell shape; thin to thick purple skin; relatively tender to tough flesh with mild to bitter flavor)
● 1 lb (500 g) Japanese or Asian eggplant (usually long, slender shape; tender, light violet to medium purple skin with sweet flavor; creamy flesh; cooks faster than globe eggplant)
● 1 lb (500 g) Chinese eggplant (usually long, slender shape; tender, white to lavender or violet skin; sweet, delicate, creamy flesh with few seeds; cooks faster than globe eggplant)
● 1 lb (500 g) elongated green-skinned eggplant (long, slender shape; tender, pale green skin; sweet, meaty flesh; cooks faster than globe eggplant)
● 1 lb (500 g) round green-skinned or Thai eggplant (size and shape of limes; thick green skin, flecked with yellow or white; mild, sweet, meaty, and seedy flesh)
● 1 lb (500 g) white-skinned eggplant (round or elongated shape; thick white skin; mild flesh)
● 1 lb (500 g) striped Spanish or European eggplant (large round or bell shape; relatively tough skin with white to purple color and purple or pink stripes; mild, creamy flesh with few seeds)

Egg Replacer, Powdered

Eggs were first commercially dried and processed into powder in St. Louis, Missouri, around 1880. A vegetarian version of powdered eggs known as "egg replacer" combines various starches, such as potato starch, and leavening agents. Egg replacer is popular among vegans and available in most health food stores.

If You Don't Have It

Substitute 1½ tsp (7 mL) egg replacer powder mixed with 3 tbsp (45 mL) cold water with:
- 3 tbsp (45 mL) liquid egg substitute
- 2 egg whites (zero fat and cholesterol)
- 1 large egg (adds fat and cholesterol; makes richer baked goods)

See also EGG WHITE.

Egg Ring

A round metal form, with or without a handle, to hold and shape an egg as it's fried.

If You Don't Have It

Substitute an egg ring with:
- biscuit cutter
- cookie cutter
- clean tuna can or other short can with both ends removed

Egg Roll Wrappers

Also known as egg roll skins. A simple dough made from flour and water. When stuffing egg roll skins, keep the stack moist by covering with a damp towel.

If You Don't Have It

Substitute 1 lb (500 g) egg roll wrappers with:
- 1 lb (500 g) empanada wrappers (round)
- 1 lb (500 g) rolled pasta (cut to desired shape)
- 1 lb (500 g) won ton skins (thinner; square or rectangular)
- 1 lb (500 g) dumpling wrappers (thinner; round)
- 1 lb (500 g) rice paper (thinner, large; cut to desired shape; makes extra-crispy rolls)

See also WON TON SKINS.

Eggs

See EGG WHITE; EGG, WHOLE; EGG YOLK.

Egg Scissors

A gadget with a scissors-like handle used to snip the top of the shell from soft-cooked eggs.

If You Don't Have It

Substitute egg scissors with:
- sharp knife and a steady hand
- kitchen scissors

Egg Separator

A small cup centered in a round frame made of plastic, metal, or ceramic. The cup catches the yolk while slots around the frame let the white slip through to a container beneath.

If You Don't Have It

Substitute an egg separator with:

- small, clean funnel (pour cracked egg into funnel; gently shake white through funnel spout; yolk remains in funnel)
- clean hands (pour cracked egg into palm; part fingers slightly to let whites slip through)

Egg Slicer

A device that cuts a hard-cooked egg into neat slices with one swift stroke. Its cutting mechanism of parallel wires is drawn down over the egg, which rests in an indented tray.

If You Don't Have It

Substitute an egg slicer with:

- sharp knife for slicing

Egg Substitute

Liquid egg products formulated as substitutes for whole eggs. Such products contain mostly egg white. The yolk is replaced with other ingredients such as nonfat milk, tofu, vegetable oils, emulsifiers, stabilizers, antioxidants, gum, artificial color, minerals, and vitamins.

If You Don't Have It

Substitute 3 tbsp (45 mL) egg substitute with:

- 2 egg whites (zero fat and cholesterol)
- 3 tbsp (45 mL) liquid pasteurized eggs (reduces risk of bacterial contamination; especially for uncooked or gently cooked preparations)
- 1 large egg (adds fat and cholesterol; makes richer baked goods)
- 1½ tsp (7 mL) powdered egg replacer + 3 tbsp (45 mL) cold water (for baking and thickening)

See also EGG REPLACER, POWDERED.

Egg Wash

Egg yolk or white, beaten with some water or milk, that is brushed on breads and other baked goods to promote a golden, shiny crust.

If You Don't Have It

Substitute ¼ cup (50 mL) egg wash with:

- 1 tbsp (15 mL) milk or cream + 1 to 2 tsp (5 to 10 mL) granulated sugar: brush milk over pastry, sprinkle with sugar (produces a more homestyle country glaze)

Egg White

The albumen content of an egg, which accounts for nearly 70% of the liquid weight. It contains more than half the egg's protein and many other nutrients.

1 dozen large eggs = 1½ cups (375 mL) egg whites

1 egg = 3 tbsp (45 mL) egg whites

1 cup (250 mL) = 7 egg whites

If You Don't Have It

Substitute 1 large egg white with:
- 3 tbsp (45 mL) frozen and thawed egg white
- 1 tbsp (15 mL) powdered egg white + 3 tbsp (45 mL) water (reduces risk of bacterial contamination)
- 2 tsp (10 mL) meringue powder + 3 tbsp (45 mL) water (reduces risk of bacterial contamination; adds small amount of sugar)

See also EGG, WHOLE.

Egg, Whole

Egg shell and yolk color may vary, but color has nothing to do with egg quality or flavor. The color comes from pigments in the outer layer of the shell and ranges in breeds from white to deep brown. The breed of hen determines the color of the shell. Breeds with white feathers and ear lobes lay white eggs; breeds with red feathers and ear lobes lay brown eggs. To measure half an egg, beat 1 whole egg, then measure out 1½ tbsp (22 mL).

1 large egg = 3 tbsp (45 mL) yolks and whites

4 jumbo eggs = 5 large eggs = 6 medium eggs = 7 small eggs = 1 cup (250 mL) yolks and whites

1 dozen large eggs = 2⅓ cups (575 mL) yolks and whites

If You Don't Have It

Substitute 1 large whole egg (2 oz/60 g) with:
- 2 large egg yolks + 1 tbsp (15 mL) cold water, optional (for cooking and baking; makes richer baked goods)
- 2 large egg yolks (for thickening sauces and custards)
- 3 tbsp (45 mL) vegetable oil + 1 tbsp (15 mL) water (for baking)
- 2 to 3 tbsp (25 to 45 mL) mayonnaise (for cakes)
- 3½ tbsp (52 mL) frozen and thawed egg
- 2½ tbsp (32 mL) powdered whole egg + 2½ tbsp (32 mL) water
- 1 tsp (5 mL) cornstarch + 3 tbsp (45 mL) additional liquid in recipe (for thickening)
- 3 tbsp (45 mL) water, milk, or other liquid + 3 tbsp (45 mL) flour + 1½ tsp (7 mL) shortening, + ½ tsp (2 mL) baking powder (for baking)
- 1 tsp (5 mL) baking powder + 1 tsp (5 mL) vinegar (if using to replace 1 additional egg when at least 1 egg is already in recipe)

To Vary the Flavor

Substitute 1 large egg with:
- 1 duck egg (larger; richer; more flavorful)
- 3 to 4 quail eggs (smaller)

For Better Health

Substitute 1 large whole egg (2 oz/60 g) with:

- 2 egg whites (zero fat and cholesterol; makes baked goods less tender; add 1 tbsp/15 mL oil to improve texture)
- 3 tbsp (45 mL) egg white (for precise measurement in baking recipes; to make measuring easier, whisk egg white with a pinch of salt to loosen texture)
- 3 tbsp to ¼ cup (45 to 50 mL) liquid egg substitute (zero cholesterol; results in more gummy baked goods; add 1 tbsp/15 mL oil to improve texture)
- 3 tbsp (45 mL) liquid pasteurized eggs (to reduce risk of bacterial contamination; especially for uncooked or gently cooked preparations)
- 3 tbsp (45 mL) ground flaxseed + ⅛ tsp (0.5 mL) baking powder + 3 tbsp (45 mL) water (for baking, especially quick breads)
- half a ripe banana, mashed + ¼ tsp (1 mL) baking powder (for baking, especially quick breads)
- ¼ cup (50 mL) firm tofu, crumbled and sautéed with aromatics (vegan substitute for scrambled eggs; add turmeric or saffron for yellow color)

See also DUCK EGG; EGG SUBSTITUTE; EGG WHITE; EGG YOLK; QUAIL EGG

Egg Yolk

With the exception of riboflavin and niacin, the yolk contains a higher proportion of the egg's vitamins than the white. Egg yolks are one of the few foods naturally containing vitamin D.

1 dozen large eggs = ⅞ cup (220 mL) egg yolks

1 egg = 1 tbsp (15 mL) egg yolk

1 cup (250 mL) = 14 egg yolks

If You Don't Have It

Substitute 2 egg yolks with:

- 1 large whole egg (for thickening sauces)
- 3 tbsp (45 mL) frozen and thawed egg yolk
- ¼ cup (50 mL) powdered egg yolk + 4 tsp (20 mL) water (for baking)

For Better Health

Substitute 2 egg yolks with:

- 1 egg white (for baking and cooking; zero fat and cholesterol; may result in less tender baked goods)

See also EGG, WHOLE.

Elbow Macaroni

See PASTA, DRIED SHAPES.

Elderberry

Both elderberries and elderflowers must be cooked before eating to destroy the tiny amount of poisonous alkaloid they contain. The tart-tasting, purple-black berries make excellent jelly. The elderflowers are wonderful in teas (employed by Native Americans as an antidote to colds) or cooked into fritters, muffins, or pancakes.

If You Don't Have It
Substitute 1 cup (250 mL) elderberries with:
- 1 cup (250 mL) fresh black currants or cassis (dark color; tart)
- 1 cup (250 mL) fresh red currants (red color; slightly sweet; slightly tart)
- 1 cup (250 mL) fresh white currants (white color; slightly sweet; less tart)
- 1 cup (250 mL) gooseberries (light yellow to pale green color; tart)
- 1 cup (250 mL) cranberries (red color; tart)
- 1 cup (250 mL) lingonberries (red color; tart)

Elk

The North American game animal, which can stand 5 feet (1.5 m) at the shoulder, is larger than the European elk. American president and renowned sportsman Theodore Roosevelt was partial to elk tongue, pronouncing it, "excellent to take out as a lunch on a long hunting trip."

If You Don't Have It
Substitute 1 lb (500 g) elk with:
- 1 lb (500 g) reindeer
- 1 lb (500 g) caribou
- 1 lb (500 g) red, fallow, or white-tailed deer
- 1 lb (500 g) moose
- 1 lb (500 g) antelope
- 1 lb (500 g) gazelle

See also VENISON.

Elver

See EEL.

Emmental

Also known as Emmentaler and Emmenthaler. Named for Switzerland's Emmental Valley, versions of this buttery, nutty cheese are produced in Austria, France, Germany, and the United States.

If You Don't Have It
Substitute 1 oz (30 g) Emmental with:
- 1 oz (30 g) Jarlsberg
- 1 oz (30 g) Gruyère
- 1 oz (30 g) Swiss
- 1 oz (30 g) French Comté
- 1 oz (30 g) Beaufort

Empanada Wrappers

Dough rounds that are stuffed with savory or sweet fillings before they are baked or fried. Sold frozen in some supermarkets.

If You Don't Have It
Substitute 1 lb (500 g) empanada wrappers with:
- 1 lb (500 g) egg roll wrappers (square)
- 1 lb (500 g) won ton skins (thinner; round)
- 1 lb (500 g) dumpling wrappers (thinner; round)
- 1 lb (500 g) rolled pasta (cut to desired shape)
- 1 lb (500 g) rice paper (thinner, large; cut to desired shape; makes crispy empanadas)

Emu

A nonflying game bird. Emu is now farm-raised in its native Australia and in North America. It tastes like beef but is softer in texture.

If You Don't Have It
Substitute 1 lb (500 g) emu with:
- 1 lb (500 g) ostrich
- 1 lb (500 g) beef (firmer texture; richer)
- 1 lb (500 g) turkey
- 1 lb (500 g) chicken

Enamelware

For best heat conduction, choose enamelware cooking pans with a cast-iron core.

If You Don't Have It
Substitute enamelware with:
- cast-iron cookware (may react with acidic foods, altering their flavor and color)

Endive

See BELGIAN ENDIVE; CURLY ENDIVE; ESCAROLE.

English Bean

See FAVA BEAN.

English Muffin

Round yeast buns that are "baked" on a griddle. The preferred method for cutting the muffin in half before toasting is to split it with a fork and gently pull it apart. This creates a textured surface that catches plenty of butter and jam.

If You Don't Have It
Substitute 1 English muffin with:
- 1 crumpet
- 1 biscuit (less airy)
- 1 bagel (denser; chewier)
- 1 scone (sweeter; less airy)
- 1 croissant (richer; flakier)
- 2 slices sturdy bread (especially toasted)

English Muffin Ring

See CRUMPET RING.

Enoki

See SHUFFLING MUSHROOMS (PAGE 572).

Epazote

Also known as bean herb, Mexican tea, pigweed, wormseed, and worm weed. A strongly flavored wild herb called for in many Mexican bean dishes because it counters flatulence.

If You Don't Have It

Substitute 1 tbsp (15 mL) chopped fresh epazote with:
- 1 tsp (5 mL) dried epazote
- 1 tbsp (15 mL) chopped fresh savory
- 1 tbsp (15 mL) chopped fresh parsley

Épices Fines

See SPICE PARISIENNE.

Epoisses de Bourgogne

A pungent soft paste cheese from the French region of Burgundy. The rind is washed with marc, a clear eau de vie.

If You Don't Have It

Substitute 1 oz (30 g) Epoisses de Bourgogne with:
- 1 oz (30 g) Ami du Chambertin
- 1 oz (30 g) Langres
- 1 oz (30 g) Pont-l'Évêque
- 1 oz (30 g) French-Alsatian Meunster

Escarole

Also known as Batavian endive, broad-leaved endive, and endive. A type of endive that forms flat-leaf, relatively compact heads with dark green outer leaves and pale hearts. The chewy leaves are pleasantly bittersweet.

If You Don't Have It

Substitute 1 cup (250 mL) escarole with:
- 1 cup (250 mL) curly endive
- 1 cup (250 mL) chicory
- 1 cup (250 mL) radicchio (red color)
- 1 cup (250 mL) arugula (more tender)

Espresso

The standard cuppa coffee in Italy is prepared by forcing steam through finely ground, packed coffee to make a robust brew. A properly executed espresso is crowned with foam called crema or schiuma.

If You Don't Have It

Substitute ¼ cup (50 mL) brewed espresso with:
- ¼ cup (50 mL) strong brewed coffee
- ¼ cup (50 mL) hot water + 1 to 2 tsp (5 to 10 mL) instant espresso powder

For Better Health

Substitute ¼ cup (50 mL) brewed espresso with:
- ¼ cup (50 mL) brewed decaffeinated espresso
- ¼ cup (50 mL) brewed roasted chicory (caffeine-free)

See also COFFEE.

Esrom

Also known as Danish Port Salut. Pleasantly pungent when young, this pale yellow Danish cheese, named for Esrom, Denmark, intensifies in flavor as it ages.

If You Don't Have It
Substitute 1 oz (30 g) Esrom with:
- 1 oz (30 g) Tilsit
- 1 oz (30 g) Havarti
- 1 oz (30 g) Fontina
- 1 oz (30 g) French Port Salut or Saint Paulin

Essences

See FLAVORING OILS.

Ethyl Alcohol

See NEUTRAL SPIRITS.

Evaporated Milk

Homogenized milk that is cooked (to reduce the water content by 60%) and then canned. It has a slightly caramelized flavor.

If You Don't Have It
Substitute 1 cup (250 mL) evaporated whole milk (8% to 10% fat) with:
- 1 cup (250 mL) Milnot, a brand of evaporated milk that whips better than others
- $2\frac{1}{4}$ cups (550 mL) whole milk, gently simmered in a saucepan until reduced to 1 cup (250 mL)
- 1 cup (250 mL) whole milk (3.5% to 4% fat; not for whipping)
- 1 cup (250 mL) half-and-half (10 to 12% fat; not for whipping)
- 1 cup (250 mL) light or table cream (20% fat; not for whipping)
- 1 cup (250 mL) light whipping cream (30% fat) or heavy whipping cream (35% fat)

For Better Health
Substitute 1 cup (250 mL) evaporated whole milk with:
- 1 cup (250 mL) fat-free evaporated milk (0.5% fat)

See also SWEETENED CONDENSED MILK.

Explorateur

Luscious white rind cylinders of triple-crème cheese.

If You Don't Have It
Substitute 1 oz (30 g) Explorateur with:
- 1 oz (30 g) Boursault
- 1 oz (30 g) Brillat-Savarin
- 1 oz (30 g) Gratte-Paille
- 1 oz (30 g) Brie
- 1 oz (30 g) Camembert

Extracts

Various concentrated flavorings derived from foods through evaporation or distillation. Because of their intensity, a tiny amount of extract can greatly impact the flavor of a dish without changing its consistency.

If You Don't Have It
Substitute 1 tsp (5 mL) flavoring extract with:
- ⅛ tsp (0.5 mL) flavoring oil

See also SPECIFIC TYPES.

Falernum to Fuzzy Gourd

Falernum

A West Indian flavoring syrup that tastes of almonds, ginger, and lime.

If You Don't Have It

Substitute 3 tbsp (45 mL) falernum with:

- 5 tsp (25 mL) orgeat syrup (preferably, add 1 tsp/ 5 mL lime juice and $\frac{1}{2}$ tsp/2 mL ginger juice)
- 5 tsp Homemade Simple Syrup (see recipe, page 489; preferably, add 1 tsp/5 mL lime juice, $\frac{1}{2}$ tsp/2 mL ginger juice, and $\frac{1}{8}$ tsp/0.5 mL almond extract)
- 3 tbsp (45 mL) grenadine (adds red color and pomegranate flavor; preferably, add 1 tsp/5 mL lime juice, $\frac{1}{2}$ tsp/2 mL ginger juice, and $\frac{1}{8}$ tsp/0.5 mL almond extract)

Farfel

Matzo or dried noodles broken into small pieces. Often used in Jewish cookery.

If You Don't Have It

Substitute 1 cup (250 mL) farfel with:

- 1 cup (250 mL) broken crackers
- 1 cup (250 mL) broken fried (crisp) chow mein noodles
- 1 cup (250 mL) broken tortilla chips
- 1 cup (250 mL) broken cornflakes
- 1 cup (250 mL) broken potato chips

Farina

Derived from the Latin, the word means "flour" in English and Italian.

If You Don't Have It

Substitute 1 cup (250 mL) farina with:
- 1 cup (250 mL) semolina
- 1 cup (250 mL) durum wheat flour
- 1 cup (250 mL) cornmeal (preferably coarsely ground)
- 1 cup (250 mL) corn grits

Farmer Cheese

Also known as farmer's cheese. A drier version of cottage cheese usually pressed into a loaf.

If You Don't Have It

Substitute 1 oz (30 g) farmer cheese with:
- 1 oz (30 g) Homemade Farmer Cheese: Wrap 1 cup (250 mL) cottage cheese in a piece of cheesecloth or a coffee filter and put in a strainer or colander. Set the colander over a bowl and refrigerate until the liquid drains into the bowl and the cheese firms up. Makes about ¾ cup (175 mL).
- 1 oz (30 g) ricotta cheese, drained in cheesecloth (may add more liquid)
- 1 oz (30 g) dry-curd cottage cheese
- 1 oz (30 g) cream cheese (especially for dips; may add more liquid)
- 1 oz (30 g) sour cream (especially for dips; may add more liquid)
- 1 oz (30 g) Monterey Jack cheese

Fat

See BUTTER; LARD; VEGETABLE SHORTENING; SPECIFIC TYPES.

Fatback

The layer of fresh fat that runs down a pig's back. It is typically unsalted and used to make cracklings or rendered into lard. In Italy, a delicate type of fatback called lardo is salt-cured, seasoned, and eaten like prosciutto.

If You Don't Have It

Substitute 4 oz (125 g) fatback with:
- 4 oz (125 g) salt pork (drop into boiling water for 30 seconds to extract excess salt)
- 4 oz (125 g) caul fat
- 4 oz (125 g) bacon (adds smoke flavor; drop into boiling water for 30 seconds to extract excess salt)

Fat Mop

See GREASE MOP.

Fat Separator

Also known as a degreasing pitcher. Ingenious heatproof pitcher with a spout that reaches to the bottom of the cup. You pour in fatty liquid, such as sauce, stock or pan drippings, let the fat rise to the top, then pour out the defatted liquid.

If You Don't Have It
Substitute a fat separator with:
- grease mop or fat mop
- chilling pan of soup, stock or other liquid until fat congeals on top, then spooning off fat
- skimming fat from surface with a ladle, large spoon, or bulb baster
- dragging folded paper towels across surface of liquid until fat is removed (for small amounts of fat)
- placing ice cubes in a slotted spoon and dragging across surface of liquid, then discarding ice as it becomes covered with fat (for small amounts of fat)

Fat Substitutes

See BUTTER; LARD; VEGETABLE SHORTENING.

Fava Bean

Also known as broad bean, butter bean, English bean, and Windsor bean.
Beloved in Mediterranean France and in Italy, fresh young favas need only be shelled before eating. More mature beans may also need to be peeled. Favas are also available dried.

> 1 lb (500 g) in shell =
> 1 to 1½ cups
> (250 to 375 mL) shelled
>
> 1 lb (500 g) dried =
> 2 cups (500 mL) =
> 4½ cups (1.125 L) cooked

If You Don't Have It
Substitute 1 cup (250 mL) shelled and peeled fresh fava beans with:
- 1 cup (250 mL) fresh edamame (shelled green soybeans)
- 1 cup (250 mL) fresh baby lima beans (sweeter)
- 1 cup (250 mL) sugar snap peas (in the shell)
- 1 cup (250 mL) chickpeas, red kidney beans, or cannellini beans (to replace dried favas in soups and stews)

See also THE WIDE WORLD OF DRIED BEANS (PAGE 566).

Feijoa

Also known as pineapple guava. A green-skinned tropical fruit that's the size and shape of an egg with cream-color granular flesh that tastes of Concord grapes, lemon pineapple, and quince.

If You Don't Have It
Substitute 1 lb (500 g) feijoa with:
- 1 lb (500 g) guava
- 1 lb (500 g) kiwifruit
- 1 lb (500 g) pineapple
- 1 lb (500 g) blueberries or strawberries

Fennel, Fresh

Also known as bulbing fennel and finocchio. Often mislabeled as anise, both the bulb and copious aromatic greens of this crisp, sweet vegetable are extremely versatile. To replace fresh fennel leaves, use hoja santa leaves, dill, or parsley.

1 lb (500 g) = 3 cups (750 mL) sliced

If You Don't Have It

Substitute 1 lb (500 g) fresh fennel bulb with:
- 1 lb (500 g) celery (cooks faster; preferably, add 1 tsp/5 mL crushed fennel seeds or 1 tbsp/15 mL anise liqueur, such as Pernod or Ricard, to add anise flavor)
- 1 lb (500 g) bok choy stems (preferably, add 1 tsp/5 mL crushed fennel seeds or 1 tbsp/15 mL anise liqueur, such as Pernod or Ricard, to add anise flavor)
- 1 lb (500 g) udo

Fennel Seeds

The seeds of the common fennel plant add delicate licorice flavor to a variety of preparations from liqueurs to sausages.

If You Don't Have It

Substitute 1 tsp (5 mL) fennel seeds with:
- 1 tsp (5 mL) anise seeds
- 1 tsp (5 mL) caraway seeds (less sweet)
- 1 tsp (5 mL) dill seeds (milder)
- 1 tsp (5 mL) cumin seeds (more earthy aroma)
- 1 tsp (5 mL) yellow mustard seeds (less complex aroma)

Fenugreek Leaves

Also known as fenugreek greens and methi leaves. These bitter greens are common in Indian and Pakistani cooking. They are typically added to breads or chickpea fritters.

If You Don't Have It

Substitute 1 tbsp (15 mL) chopped fresh fenugreek leaves with:
- 1 tsp (5 mL) dried fenugreek leaves
- 1 tbsp (15 mL) chopped fresh Chinese celery leaves
- 1 tbsp (15 mL) chopped fresh celery leaves
- 1 tbsp (15 mL) packed watercress

Fenugreek Seeds

Yellowish brown seeds used to flavor Indian curries. The aroma is similar to celery. Slow toasting brings out the full flavor, but too much heat can turn the seeds bitter.

If You Don't Have It

Substitute 1 tsp (5 mL) fenugreek seeds with:
- 1 tsp (5 mL) yellow mustard seeds

Fermented Black Bean

Also known as Chinese or salty black bean. Small black soybeans preserved in salt. The flavor is pungent and complex.

If You Don't Have It

Substitute ½ cup (125 mL) fermented black beans with:

- ½ cup (125 mL) black bean sauce (may add garlic and anise flavors)
- ½ cup (125 mL) cooked soybeans + 1 tbsp (15 mL) soy sauce

Fernet Branca

An astringent Italian bitters concocted from 40-some ingredients that include chamomile and rhubarb. Reputed to soothe upset tummies and tame a hangover.

If You Don't Have It

Substitute 3 tbsp (45 mL) Fernet Branca with:

- 3 tbsp (45 mL) Branca Menta (adds mint flavor)
- 3 tbsp (45 mL) Amer Picon
- 3 tbsp (45 mL) Campari
- 3 tbsp (45 mL) Unicum
- 3 tbsp (45 mL) Punt e Mes

Feta Cheese

The salty cheese most closely associated with Greek cooking, feta is traditionally made from sheep's or goat's milk. It's often referred to as a pickled cheese because it is cured and stored in its own salty whey.

4 oz (125 g) =
1 cup (250 mL) crumbled

If You Don't Have It

Substitute 1 oz (30 g) feta cheese with:

- 1 oz (30 g) aged chèvre
- 1 oz (30 g) Brinza
- 1 oz (30 g) ricotta salata
- 1 oz (30 g) cotija
- 1 oz (30 g) myzithra
- 1 oz (30 g) haloumi (may add mint flavor)
- 1 oz (30 g) crumbly blue cheese (less salty; more pungent)

For Better Health

Substitute 1 oz (30 g) feta cheese with:

- ½ oz (15 g) feta cheese + ½ oz (15 g) reduced-fat or fat-free cream cheese (for blending with other ingredients

Fiddlehead Fern

Also known as ostrich fern and pohole. The coiled head of an unopened wild fern. Savored as a gourmet vegetable, fiddleheads must be cooked.

If You Don't Have It

Substitute 1 cup (250 mL) fiddlehead ferns with:

- 1 cup (250 mL) pencil-thin asparagus
- 1 cup (250 mL) haricot verts (slender French green beans)

Field Lettuce

See MÂCHE.

Field Peas

See PEAS, SPLIT.

Fig, Dried

Stored in a low-humidity location at about 55°F (13°C), figs keep well for up to 6 months.

1 lb (500 g) =
40 medium = 3 cups
(750 mL) chopped

If You Don't Have It
Substitute 1 lb (500 g) dried figs with:
- 1 lb (500 g) pitted dried dates
- 1 lb (500 g) pitted prunes
- 1 lb (500 g) raisins
- 1 lb (500 g) dried apricots

Fig, Fresh

Eaten as a luscious fruit, a fig is actually the flower of the fig tree inverted into itself. The fig is a sweet treat composed of 55% sugar.

1 lb (500 g) = 9 medium
= 2½ cups (625 mL)
chopped

If You Don't Have It
Substitute 1 lb (500 g) fresh figs with:
- 1 lb (500 g) pears, nectarines, apricots or other ripe, soft-fleshed fruit

Filbert

See HAZELNUT.

Filé Powder

The ground dried leaves of the sassafras tree. Often used to flavor and thicken Creole gumbo.

If You Don't Have It
Substitute 1 tbsp (15 mL) filé powder (for thickening) with:
- 2 cups (500 mL) okra (especially in gumbo and African stews; cook gradually to release okra's viscous, thickening "slime")
- 2 tsp (10 mL) cornstarch mixed with 1 tbsp (15 mL) cold water

Filo

See PHYLLO.

Fines Herbes

A seasoning blend of delicate minced fresh chervil, chives, parsley, and tarragon.

If You Don't Have It
Substitute 1 tbsp (15 mL) fines herbes with:
- 1 tbsp (15 mL) Homemade Classic Fines Herbes: Combine ¾ tsp (4 mL) chopped fresh chervil, ¾ tsp (4 mL) chopped fresh chives, ¾ tsp (4 mL) chopped fresh tarragon, and ¾ tsp (4 mL) chopped fresh parsley.

Fingered Citron

See CITRON.

Fingerroot

Also known as Chinese ginger. This long, finger-shaped relative of gingerroot is popular in Thai cooking.

If You Don't Have It
Substitute 1 tbsp (15 mL) chopped fresh fingerroot with:
- 1 tbsp (15 mL) chopped fresh galangal
- 1 tbsp (15 mL) chopped fresh ginger

Finnan Haddie

Also known as finnan haddock. Salted, smoked Scottish haddock was originally smoked over peat fires.

If You Don't Have It
Substitute 1 lb (500 g) finnan haddie with:
- 1 lb (500 g) smoked mackerel
- 1 lb (500 g) smoked sturgeon
- 1 lb (500 g) smoked bluefish
- 1 lb (500 g) smoked salmon

Finocchio

See FENNEL, FRESH.

Fish

See SPECIFIC TYPES.

Fish Boil

See CRAB BOIL.

Fish Sauce

Also known as nam pla, nuoc nam, patis, and shottsuru. A common seasoning in Southeast Asian cooking made from the liquid of salted fermented anchovies.

If You Don't Have It
Substitute 1 tbsp (15 mL) fish sauce with:
- 1 tbsp (15 mL) Homemade Fish Sauce Substitute: Combine ¼ cup (50 mL) soy sauce, 3 tbsp (45 mL) anchovy paste or 18 whole anchovy fillets, 3 tbsp (45 mL) water, 1 smashed garlic clove, and a pinch of brown sugar in a saucepan. Simmer over medium heat for 10 minutes. Then strain, pressing gently through a small sieve. Makes about ½ cup (125 mL).

Fish Sauce (cont'd)

- 1 tbsp (15 mL) soy sauce (preferably, add 1/2 tsp/ 2 mL powdered dulse seaweed for briny flavor)
- 1 tbsp (15 mL) fermented tofu
- 1 tbsp (15 mL) Homemade Vegetarian Fish Sauce Substitute: Combine 1/4 cup (50 mL) soy sauce and 1 tsp (5 mL) rice vinegar in a small bowl. Press 3 tbsp (45 mL) fermented black beans through small sieve or garlic press into bowl. Mix in 1 tbsp (15 mL) yellow miso. Let stand for 15 to 20 minutes. Stir and strain through small sieve. Makes about 1/3 cup (75 mL).
- 1 tsp (5 mL) shrimp sauce (more pungent)

Fish Sauce Varieties

Choose 1 tbsp (15 mL) fish sauce from these varieties:
- 1 tbsp (15 mL) Thai fish sauce (nam pla)
- 1 tbsp (15 mL) Vietnamese fish sauce (nuoc nam)
- 1 tbsp (15 mL) Vietnamese vegetarian fish sauce (nuoc mam an chay)
- 1 tbsp (15 mL) Japanese fish sauce (shottsuru)
- 1 tbsp (15 mL) Filipino fish sauce (patis)

Five-Spice Powder

See CHINESE FIVE-SPICE POWDER.

Flageolet

See THE WIDE WORLD OF DRIED BEANS (PAGE 566).

Flatfish

See BRILL; FLOUNDER; HALIBUT; PLAICE; SOLE; TURBOT.

Flavored Syrup

Manufactured in dozens of varieties that include fruits, nuts, and other aromatics. Often added to complement Italian coffee or specialty drinks.

If You Don't Have It

Substitute 3 tbsp (45 mL) flavored syrup with:
- 3 tbsp (45 mL) Homemade Flavored Syrup: Combine 1/2 cup (125 mL) granulated sugar and 1/2 cup (125 mL) water in a medium saucepan. Bring to a boil over high heat. Reduce heat to medium-low and simmer for 5 minutes. Let cool, then stir in 1/4 to 3/4 tsp (1 to 4 mL) flavored extract, such as vanilla, almond, or hazelnut. Makes about 1/2 cup (125 mL).
- 3 tbsp (45 mL) nut, fruit, or other flavored liqueur (adds alcohol)
- 3 tbsp (45 mL) syrup from canned fruit packed in syrup (to replace fruit-flavored syrup)

Flavoring Extracts

See EXTRACTS.

Flavoring Oils

Also known as essences. Concentrated oil extracted from plants and other foods. Used in small amounts to flavor recipes.

If You Don't Have It

Substitute $\frac{1}{8}$ tsp (0.5 mL) flavoring oil with:
- $\frac{1}{2}$ to 1 tsp (2 to 5 mL) flavoring extract

Flounder

A tasty, fine-textured flatfish that is at home in kitchens from Australia to Spain. Types include winter flounder, summer flounder, yellowtailed flounder, and greenback flounder.

If You Don't Have It

Substitute 1 lb (500 g) flounder with:
- 1 lb (500 g) plaice or dab
- 1 lb (500 g) sole
- 1 lb (500 g) brill
- 1 lb (500 g) turbot

See also SOLE.

Flour, All-Purpose

Bleached all-purpose flour is whiter and lower in vitamin E than unbleached flour. Otherwise, the two can be used interchangeably. Most flour is sold pre-sifted, so sifting is generally unnecessary unless a recipe specifically calls for sifted flour.

> 1 lb (500 g) = $3\frac{1}{3}$ cup (825 mL)

If You Don't Have It

Substitute 1 tbsp (15 mL) unsifted all-purpose flour (for thickening) with:
- 1 tbsp (15 mL) instant flour (such as Wondra; reduces lumps)
- $1\frac{1}{2}$ tsp (7 mL) cornstarch, potato starch, or rice starch mixed with 1 tbsp (15 mL) cold water
- 1 tsp (5 mL) instant mashed potato flakes
- 2 tsp (10 mL) arrowroot
- 1 tbsp (15 mL) quick-cooking tapioca
- 1 tbsp (15 mL) cornmeal
- 2 egg yolks

Substitute 1 cup (250 mL) unsifted all-purpose flour (for baking) with:
- 1 cup (250 mL) + 3 tbsp (45 mL) sifted all-purpose flour
- 1 cup (250 mL) + 3 tbsp (45 mL) cake flour (creates much lighter texture; not recommended for cookies and quick breads)

Flour, All-Purpose (cont'd)

- 1 cup (250 mL) unsifted self-rising flour (omit baking powder and salt from recipe)
- 1 cup (250 mL) pastry flour (creates lighter texture; not recommended for cookies)
- 1½ cups (375 mL) dry bread crumbs
- 1 cup (250 mL) rolled oats

For Better Health

Substitute 1 cup (250 mL) unsifted all-purpose flour with:

- ½ cup (125 mL) whole wheat flour + ½ cup (125 mL) all-purpose flour (adds fiber; add 1 tbsp/15 mL liquid to recipe)
- 1 cup (250 mL) unsifted whole wheat pastry flour (omit 3 tbsp/45 mL liquid from recipe; for quick breads and desserts; has lower gluten content than whole wheat flour)
- ½ cup (125 mL) unsifted whole wheat pastry flour + ½ cup (125 mL) unsifted oat flour (omit 3 tbsp/45 mL) liquid from recipe; for delicate baked goods such as cakes; oat flour creates a lighter texture; sift the flours to lighten the texture further)
- ½ cup (125 mL) unsifted cake flour + ½ cup (125 mL) unsifted whole wheat flour (mix gently; wheat flour contains additional gluten which can make baked goods tough if batter is overmixed)
- ¼ cup (50 mL) wheat germ + ¾ cup (175 mL) unsifted all-purpose flour (adds fiber)
- 1 cup (250 mL) minus 3 tbsp (45 mL) sifted oat flour
- 1 cup (250 mL) minus 3 tbsp (45 mL) rice flour (use to replace up to half of all-purpose flour in recipe)

See also BISCUIT MIX; SEMOLINA; CHOOSING AMONG WHEAT FLOURS (PAGE 585); CHOOSING AMONG WHOLE-GRAIN AND ALTERNATIVE FLOURS (PAGE 586).

Flour, Bread

Unbleached, high-gluten hard-wheat flour blended with a small amount of malted barley (to boost yeast activity) and vitamin C or potassium bromate (to make gluten more elastic and retain air bubbles in the dough).

> 1 lb (500 g) = 3 cups (750 mL) sifted

If You Don't Have It
Substitute 1 cup (250 mL) unsifted bread flour with:
- 1 cup (250 mL) all-purpose flour (preferably, add 2 tsp/10 mL gluten flour to improve structure)

For Better Health
Substitute 1 cup (250 mL) unsifted bread flour with:
- 1 cup (250 mL) whole wheat flour (adds fiber; preferably, add 2 tsp/10 mL gluten flour to improve structure)

See also CHOOSING AMONG WHEAT FLOURS (PAGE 585).

Flour, Cake

A soft-wheat flour with a high starch content that produces tender cakes and baked goods.

> 1 lb (500 g) = 4½ cups (1.125 L)

If You Don't Have It
Substitute 1 cup (250 mL) sifted cake flour with:
- 1 cup (250 mL) pastry flour (to improve texture, mix batter gently and separate the eggs, beating the whites to soft peaks then folding them into batter; cakes will be less delicate than with cake flour)
- 1 cup (250 mL) minus 3 tbsp (45 mL) sifted all-purpose flour + 3 tbsp (45 mL) cornstarch (to improve texture, mix batter gently and separate the eggs, beating the whites to soft peaks then folding them into batter; cakes will be less delicate than with cake flour)

See also CHOOSING AMONG WHEAT FLOURS (PAGE 585).

Flour, Durum

Finely ground durum (high-gluten) wheat.

If You Don't Have It
Substitute 1 cup (250 mL) durum wheat flour with:
- 1 cup (250 mL) semolina (more coarse)

See also CHOOSING AMONG WHEAT FLOURS (PAGE 585).

Flour, Graham

Coarsely ground whole wheat flour developed by the Reverend Sylvester Graham, an early health food advocate.

> 1 lb (500 g) = 3¾ cups (925 mL)

If You Don't Have It
Substitute 1 cup (250 mL) unsifted graham flour with:
- 1 cup (250 mL) whole wheat flour
- ½ cup (125 mL) unsifted whole wheat flour + ½ cup (125 mL) unsifted all-purpose flour
- 1 cup (250 mL) minus 3 tbsp (45 mL) unsifted all-purpose flour + 3 tbsp (45 mL) wheat germ

See also FLOUR, WHOLE WHEAT; GRAHAM CRACKER; CHOOSING AMONG WHEAT FLOURS (PAGE 585).

Flour, Instant

A granular flour that dissolves quickly to thicken gravies, sauces, and other dishes.

If You Don't Have It
Substitute 1 tbsp (15 mL) instant flour (for thickening) with:
- 1 tbsp (15 mL) all-purpose flour mixed with 3 tbsp (45 mL) cold water
- 1½ tsp (7 mL) cornstarch, potato starch, or rice starch mixed with 1 tbsp (15 mL) cold water
- 1 tsp (5 mL) instant mashed potato flakes
- 2 tsp (10 mL) arrowroot mixed with 1 tbsp (15 mL) cold water
- 1 tbsp (15 mL) quick-cooking tapioca
- 1 tbsp (15 mL) cornmeal

Flour, Pastry

Contains slightly more protein than cake flour. Particularly good for biscuits, cookies, and pie crusts.

> 1 lb (500 g) = 4¼ cups (1.05 L)

If You Don't Have It
Substitute 1 cup (250 mL) unsifted pastry flour with:
- ⅔ cup (150 mL) unsifted all-purpose flour + ⅓ cup (75 mL) cake flour (to improve texture, handle dough gently, use very cold fat, and only as little liquid as necessary)

For Better Health
Substitute 1 cup (250 mL) unsifted pastry flour with:
- 1 cup (250 mL) unsifted whole wheat pastry flour (adds fiber)

See also CHOOSING AMONG WHEAT FLOURS (PAGE 585).

Flour, Self-Rising

All-purpose flour with baking powder and salt added.

> 1 lb (500 g) = 3 cups (750 mL) sifted

If You Don't Have It
Substitute 1 cup (250 mL) unsifted self-rising flour with:
- 1 cup (250 mL) unsifted all-purpose flour + 1½ tsp (7 mL) baking powder + ½ tsp (2 mL) salt

See also BISCUIT MIX; CHOOSING AMONG WHEAT FLOURS (PAGE 585).

Flour, Semolina

Durum (high-gluten) wheat flour that is more coarsely ground than most flours.

If You Don't Have It
Substitute 1 cup (250 mL) semolina flour with:
- 1 cup (250 mL) durum wheat flour (finer grind)

For Better Health
Substitute 1 cup (250 mL) semolina flour with:
- 1 cup (250 mL) spelt flour (low-gluten content; for those with wheat allergies)
- 1 cup (250 mL) Kamut© flour (medium-low gluten content; for those with wheat allergies)

See also CHOOSING AMONG WHEAT FLOURS (PAGE 585).

Flour Sifter

See SIFTER.

Flour, Whole Wheat

Because it contains the wheat germ, this hearty flour has more fiber, nutrients, and oil than white flour. Best stored in the refrigerator or freezer to prevent rancidity.

> 1 lb (500 g) = 3⅓ cups (825 mL)

If You Don't Have It
Substitute 1 cup (250 mL) unsifted whole wheat flour with:
- 1 cup (250 mL) minus 3 tbsp (45 mL) unsifted all-purpose flour + 3 tbsp (45 mL) wheat germ
- ½ cup (125 mL) unsifted whole wheat flour + ½ cup (125 mL) unsifted all-purpose flour
- 1 cup (250 mL) graham flour

See also FLOUR, GRAHAM; CHOOSING AMONG WHEAT FLOURS (PAGE 585).

Flowering Chives

See GARLIC CHIVES.

Flower Pepper

See SZECHUAN PEPPER.

Flowers, Edible

See PICKING EDIBLE FLOWERS (PAGE 604).

Focaccia

A dimpled, flat Italian bread often garnished with savory toppings or ingredients worked into the dough. From the Latin focus *for hearth.*

If You Don't Have It

Substitute 1 lb (500 g) focaccia with:
- 1 lb (500 g) fougasse (French focaccia)
- 1 lb (500 g) prebaked pizza crust (such as Boboli)
- 1 lb (500 g) bread dough (roll flat before baking)
- 1 lb (500 g) sliced sourdough or other chewy bread (to replace sliced focaccia used to make sandwiches)

Fondue Pot

A communal pot set over a low flame to hold molten cheese, oil, or chocolate into which diners dip breads, vegetables, meats, or foods. The classic cheese fondue was originally a Swiss family-style meal.

If You Don't Have It

Substitute a fondue pot with:
- heavy earthenware or stoneware pot set over a low flame, on a warming tray, or a on a heating pad set to high
- heavy-bottomed saucepan (enameled cast iron works particularly well) set over a low flame, on a warming tray, or on a heating pad set to high
- chafing dish set over a low flame

Fontina

This beautiful melting cheese is the base for fonduta, *the Valle d'Aosta fondue.*

If You Don't Have It

Substitute 1 oz (30 g) fontina with:
- 1 oz (30 g) raclette
- 1 oz (30 g) Gruyère or Emmental
- 1 oz (30 g) Appenzeller
- 1 oz (30 g) Morbier
- 1 oz (30 g) Beaufort
- 1 oz (30 g) Bel Paese
- 1 oz (30 g) provolone

Food Mill

An old-fashioned kitchen utensil used to strain skins, seeds, and other solids from foods. The mill looks like a perforated saucepan but with a hand-cranked strainer plate at the bottom.

If You Don't Have It

Substitute a food mill with:
- pressing food through a medium-mesh sieve
- blender or food processor (for puréeing foods; will not separate out skins or seeds)

Food Processor

The ubiquitous home food processor was introduced in 1973 by Carl G. Sontheimer under the brand name Cuisinart®. He modeled it after an industrial blender he had seen at a food trade show.

If You Don't Have It
Substitute a food processor with:
- blender (not recommended for blending doughs and batters)

To Save Time
Substitute a food processor with:
- hand-blender (especially for soups and sauces)

Fourme d'Ambert

French blue-veined cheese that dates from Roman times. Easily recognized by its tall cylindrical shape.

If You Don't Have It
Substitute 1 oz (30 g) Fourme d'Ambert with:
- 1 oz (30 g) Bleu de Gex
- 1 oz (30 g) Bleu d'Auvergne
- 1 oz (30 g) Cambozola
- 1 oz (30 g) Stilton

Foxberry

See LINGONBERRY.

Fraise des Bois

Also known as wild or alpine strawberries. Tiny, wild strawberries from France with a sweet, musky flavor.

If You Don't Have It
Substitute 1 cup (250 mL) cup fraise des bois with:
- 1 cup (250 mL) strawberries (larger)

See also STRAWBERRY.

Framboise

Also known as raspberry brandy. A clear, powerful eau de vie made from raspberries.

If You Don't Have It
Substitute 3 tbsp (45 mL) framboise with:
- 3 tbsp (45 mL) raspberry liqueur (sweeter)
- 3 tbsp (45 mL) raspberry syrup (sweeter; no alcohol)
- 1 tsp (5 mL) raspberry extract (add 5 tsp/25 mL liquid to recipe if necessary)

To Vary the Flavor
Substitute 3 tbsp (45 mL) framboise with:
- 3 tbsp (45 mL) kirsch (cherry flavor)

See also RASPBERRY LIQUEUR.

Frangelico

See HAZELNUT LIQUEUR.

Frankfurter

Also known as frank, wiener, and hot dog (when served in a bun). A mildly seasoned smoked sausage, probably of German origin, that became a star in the United States. Kosher and all-beef frankfurters enjoy the best reputation.

If You Don't Have It
Substitute 1 lb (500 g) frankfurters with:
- 1 lb (500 g) Knackwurst
- 1 lb (500 g) kielbasa (larger)
- 1 lb (500 g) Bockwurst (made with veal)
- 1 lb (500 g) Bratwurst
- 1 lb (500 g) cocktail wieners (smaller)
- 1 lb (500 g) Vienna sausages (smaller)
- 1 lb (500 g) chipolata (spicier)

For Better Health
Substitute 1 lb (500 g) frankfurters with:
- 1 lb (500 g) reduced-fat frankfurters
- 1 lb (500 g) vegetarian hot dogs

French Bread

"True French bread contains neither sugar nor milk," writes French chef Madeleine Kamman. "It is a white bread with a long-baked crispy and crackling crust, which makes the best sandwiches with butter, salami, boiled ham, or country pâté."

If You Don't Have It
Substitute 1 lb (500 g) French bread with these types:
- 1 lb (500 g) baguette (narrow loaf about 2 feet/61 cm long)
- 1 lb (500 g) baton (similar to a baguette but smaller)
- 1 lb (500 g) pain Parisienne (wider than baguette)
- 1 lb (500 g) ficelle (narrower than baguette)
- 1 lb (500 g) bâtarde (wider than baguette)
- 1 lb (500 g) boule (round loaf)

To Vary the Flavor
Substitute 1 lb (500 g) French bread with:
- 1 lb (500 g) Italian bread (usually shorter and rounder than French bread)

Freshwater Eel

See EEL.

Frisée

Blanched curly endive with pale yellow or light green leaves and a slightly sweet, less bitter flavor than curly endive.

If You Don't Have It
Substitute 1 cup (250 mL) frisée with:
- 1 cup (250 mL) curly endive or curly chicory (more bitter)
- 1 cup (250 mL) escarole (softer leaves)
- 1 cup (250 mL) radicchio (red color)

See also BELGIAN ENDIVE; CHICORY; ESCAROLE.

Frog

The hind legs are the edible part with a flavor akin to tender young chicken.

1 lb (500 g) = 8 legs

If You Don't Have It

Substitute 1 lb (500 g) frog's legs with:
- 1 lb (500 g) chicken breast or tenders
- 1 lb (500 g) scallops

Frogfish

See MONKFISH.

Fromage Blanc

This soft fresh cream cheese is delightful when sweetened and served with fresh fruit. For the French dessert coeur à la crème, it's folded with meringue and chilled in a heart-shaped mold.

If You Don't Have It

Substitute 1 oz (30 g) fromage blanc with:
- 1 oz (30 g) yogurt cheese
- 1 oz (30 g) quark
- ½ oz (15 g) cream cheese + ½ oz (15 g) cream, blended
- ½ oz (15 g) cottage cheese + ½ oz (15 g) yogurt, blended

Frozen Nondairy Whipped Topping

See WHIPPED TOPPING.

Fructose

Also known as fruit sugar and levulose. This by-product of fruits and honey is sweeter than sucrose but contains only half the calories.

If You Don't Have It

Substitute 1 cup (250 mL) fructose with:
- 1⅓ cups (325 mL) granulated sugar (baked goods will be drier)
- 1⅓ cups (325 mL) Sucanat (powdered organic sugarcane juice, which retains all its vitamins and minerals; baked goods will be drier)
- 1 cup (250 mL) + 2 tbsp (25 mL) honey (for baking, reduce liquid in recipe by ⅓ cup/75 mL; add heaping ¼ tsp/1 mL baking soda to neutralize acidity of honey)
- ⅔ cup (150 mL) granulated sugar + ⅔ cup (150 mL) sugar-free sugar substitute such as Splenda or DiabetiSweet

Fruit Brandy

See SPECIFIC TYPES.

Fruit, Fresh

For the finest fruit, you don't have to look far. Locally grown fruit harvested at the peak of its season will taste better and be more nutritious than fruits that are picked before they ripen to be shipped thousands of miles to market. Choose plump, healthy looking fruits that are fragrant, a prime indicator of flavor.

If You Don't Have It
Substitute 1½ cups (375 mL) fresh chopped fruit with:
- 1 (16 oz/454 g) can, drained

See also SPECIFIC TYPES.

Fruit Liqueur

Alcoholic beverage flavored with fruit and composed of spirits, sweeteners, and water. Usually enjoyed in small glasses as an after-dinner drink.

If You Don't Have It
Substitute 3 tbsp (45 mL) fruit liqueur with:
- 3 tbsp (45 mL) fruit syrup (sweeter)
- 3 tbsp (45 mL) fruit wine (thinner consistency)
- 1 tsp (5 mL) fruit extract

See also SPECIFIC TYPES.

Fruit Sugar

See FRUCTOSE.

Fruta Bomba

See PAPAYA.

Frying

Cooking food in a shallow layer or deep layer of hot fat (deep-fat frying).

For Better Health
Substitute frying with:
- oven-frying. Mimic the technique of deep-fat frying by using a very hot oven and a thin coating of fat on the surface of the food. Preheat oven to 475°F (240°C). Preheat a rimmed baking sheet in oven for 10 minutes. Dip food in batter, if using, then spray or brush generously with cooking oil spray or another fat. Put food on hot baking sheet and bake, turning once, until brown and crisp. Works well for oven-fried French fries, tortilla chips, vegetable chips (such as plantain chips or potato chips), turnovers, and breaded meats, poultry, seafood, and vegetables.

Frying Pan

Also known as a skillet. A long-handled and usually round heavy pan with sides that slope so steam (the enemy of crisping) doesn't accumulate inside.

If You Don't Have It
Substitute a frying pan with:
- wok (for frying, stir-frying, and sautéing)
- sauté pan (for frying and sautéing)
- griddle (for light sautéing; has lower rims or none at all)

Funnel

Pennsylvania cooks used their funnels to create a deep-fried pastry that has become a popular concession treat. Made by pouring batter through a funnel held over a pot of hot fat, the resulting freeform pastry, dusted with confectioner's sugar or honey, looks like the abstract painting of the doughnut world.

If You Don't Have It
Substitute a funnel with:
- paper, wax paper, or aluminum foil rolled into a cone shape

Fuzzy Gourd

Also known as fuzzy melon, hairy melon (or squash or gourd), and little winter melon. A green cylindrical Chinese squash that sports a five o'clock shadow. Peel before using. The flesh tastes like a combination of zucchini and cucumber with a tinge of lemon.

If You Don't Have It
Substitute 1 lb (500 g) fuzzy gourd with:
- 1 lb (500 g) zucchini
- 8 oz (250 g) zucchini + 8 oz (250 g) cucumber
- 1 lb (500 g) cucuzza
- 1 lb (500 g) yellow squash
- 1 lb (500 g) pattypan squash
- 1 lb (500 g) Armenian cucumber or snake melon (long, slender, curved body; ridged, light yellow to pale green razor-thin skin; sweet, mild citrus flavor; extra-crisp texture; needs no peeling or seeding)

See also WINTER MELON.

Gai Choy to Gyoza Wrappers

Gai Choy

See MUSTARD GREENS.

Gai Lan

See CHINESE BROCCOLI.

Galangal

A rhizome that exists in two forms: white-flesh greater galangal (Thai ginger), and the stronger orange-flesh lesser galangal.

> 1 tbsp (15 mL) chopped fresh = 1½ tsp (7 mL) powdered

If You Don't Have It

Substitute 1 tbsp (15 mL) chopped fresh galangal (greater galangal) with:
- 1 tbsp (15 mL) chopped fresh ginger + ⅛ to ¼ tsp (0.5 to 1 mL) lemon juice (less pungent)
- 1 tbsp (15 mL) chopped fresh lesser galangal (more pungent; orange flesh)
- 1 tbsp (15 mL) chopped fresh fingerroot

Galantina

An Italian cooked salami that contains pancetta, pistachios, spices, and veal.

If You Don't Have It

Substitute 1 lb (500 g) galantina with:
- 1 lb (500 g) mortadella (less chunky; has cubes of pork fat and garlic flavor)
- 1 lb (500 g) bologna (less complex flavor)
- 1 lb (500 g) olive loaf (adds olive flavor)

For Better Health

Substitute 1 lb (500 g) galantina with:
- 1 lb (500 g) Gelbwurst (lower in fat and calories)

Galia Melon

A hybrid melon developed in Israel to thrive in desert growing conditions. Tastes like a sweeter version of cantaloupe.

> 1 lb (500 g) =
> 1 to 1½ cups
> (250 to 375 mL) cubed

If You Don't Have It

Substitute 1 cup (250 mL) chopped Galia melon with:
- 1 cup (250 mL) chopped honeydew
- 1 cup (250 mL) chopped Santa Claus melon
- 1 cup (250 mL) chopped cantaloupe
- 1 cup (250 mL) chopped Persian melon

Galliano

Also known as Liquore Galliano. Spicy, herbal proprietary Italian liqueur. A mixer in the Harvey Wallbanger, Golden Cadillac, and other cocktails.

If You Don't Have It

Substitute 3 tbsp (45 mL) Galliano with:
- 3 tbsp (45 mL) Roiano (sweeter)
- 3 tbsp (45 mL) Neopolitan liqueur or other less expensive imitation Galliano
- 3 tbsp (45 mL) sambuca (stronger licorice flavor; fewer herbal flavors)
- 3 tbsp (45 mL) anesone, anisette, or other anise-flavored liqueur (more anise flavor; fewer herbal flavors)

Game

See SPECIFIC TYPES.

Game Hen

See CHICKEN.

Gammel Dansk®

Danish bitters made from dozens of spices, roots, and wild rowanberries from the island of Zealand, steeped in neutral spirits for 3 months.

If You Don't Have It

Substitute 3 tbsp (45 mL) Gammel Dansk® with:
- 3 tbsp (45 mL) Fernet Branca

Gamonedo

Lightly smoked cave-aged cheese from northeast Spain made with set proportions of cow's, sheep's, and goat's milk.

If You Don't Have It

Substitute 1 oz (30 g) Gamonedo with:
- 1 oz (30 g) Cabrales
- 1 oz (30 g) Picón
- 1 oz (30 g) Roquefort
- 1 oz (30 g) Gorgonzola

Garam Masala

Scintillating blend of toasted ground spices that originated in northern India. Many variations exist. Garam masala is added to a dish toward the end of the cooking or sprinkled on top just before serving.

If You Don't Have It

Substitute 1 tbsp (15 mL) garam masala with:

- 1 tbsp (15 mL) Homemade Basic Garam Masala: Combine 1 tsp (5 mL) cumin seeds, 1 tsp (5 mL) coriander seeds, 1 tsp (5 mL) black peppercorns, 1 tsp (5 mL) cardamom seeds (scraped from pods), ½ tsp (2 mL) whole cloves, and two 3-inch (7.5 cm) cinnamon sticks (broken into pieces) in a skillet. Toast over medium heat, shaking often, until fragrant, about 3 minutes. Let cool then grind in a spice grinder. Makes about ¼ cup (50 mL).

To Save Time

Substitute 1 tbsp (15 mL) garam masala with:

- 1 tbsp (15 mL) Homemade Quick Garam Masala: Combine ½ tsp (2 mL) ground cumin, ½ tsp (2 mL) ground coriander, ½ tsp (2 mL) ground black pepper, ½ tsp (2 mL) ground cardamom, ½ tsp (2 mL) ground cinnamon, and ¼ tsp (1 mL) ground cloves. Toast spices just before using. Makes about 1 tablespoon (15 mL).

Garbanzo Bean

See THE WIDE WORLD OF DRIED BEANS (PAGE 566).

Garbanzo Bean Flour

See CHOOSING AMONG WHOLE-GRAIN AND ALTERNATIVE FLOURS (PAGE 586).

Garden Pea

See PEAS, SHELLING.

Gari

Nigerian flour made from fermented, roasted, and ground cassava.

If You Don't Have It

Substitute 1 cup (250 mL) gari with:

- 1 cup (250 mL) tapioca or cassava flour (lacks fermented flavor)
- 1 cup (250 mL) cream of wheat (lacks fermented flavor)

See also CASSAVA.

Garlic

Hundreds of varieties of "the stinking rose" are grown worldwide, including hardneck types, such as rocambole, porcelain, and purple stripe, as well as softneck varieties, such as artichoke and silverskin. To remove garlicky aromas from your fingers, rub them on stainless steel (such as the bowl of a stainless-steel spoon) under cool running water.

---

1 head = 8 to 12 cloves

1 clove =
½ tsp (2 mL) minced

If You Don't Have It

Substitute 1 clove fresh garlic (minced or pressed) with:
- ½ tsp (2 mL) jarred minced garlic or liquid garlic seasoning
- ½ to 1 tsp (2 to 5 mL) roasted garlic (mellower, sweeter flavor)
- ½ tsp (2 mL) garlic chives (less pungent; adds green color)
- ½ to 1 tsp (2 to 5 mL) minced shallots (less pungent)
- ⅛ tsp (0.5 mL) garlic powder
- ¼ tsp (1 mL) granulated garlic
- ½ tsp (2 mL) garlic flakes or instant garlic
- ½ tsp (2 mL) garlic salt (omit ½ tsp/2 mL salt from recipe)
- ½ tsp (2 mL) garlic juice (less pungent)
- ⅛ tsp (0.5 mL) asafetida powder (more pungent; combines onion and garlic flavors)

Garlic Varieties

Choose 1 clove fresh garlic from these varieties:
- 1 clove white-skinned American or California garlic (very pungent)
- 1 clove purple-skinned Italian or Mexican garlic (less pungent)
- ½ tsp (2 mL) clove elephant garlic (actually a type of leek; mild)
- ½ tsp (2 mL) minced fresh green or immature garlic (very mild)

Garlic Blossom

See PICKING EDIBLE FLOWERS (PAGE 604).

Garlic Butter

See BUTTER.

Garlic Chives

Also known as Chinese chives and ku chai. An herb that looks like chives but tastes of garlic instead of onion. Snip garlic chives with kitchen scissors for quick cutting.

If You Don't Have It

Substitute 1 cup (250 mL) chopped garlic chives with:
- 1 cup (250 mL) chopped chives (less garlicky, more oniony flavor)
- 1 cup (250 mL) chopped green onions or scallions (green tops only; less garlicky, more oniony flavor; add 2 to 3 tsp/10 to 15 mL chopped fresh garlic for more garlic flavor)
- 1 cup (250 mL) chopped Chinese garlic stems (more pungent garlic flavor; adds crunch)

Garlic Chives (cont'd)

Garlic Chive Varieties

Choose 1 cup (250 mL) chopped garlic chives from these varieties:

- 1 cup (250 mL) chopped green garlic chives (flat green leaves; mellow garlic flavor when cooked)
- 1 cup (250 mL) chopped yellow garlic chives (green garlic chives grown under wraps to prevent photosynthesis; flat yellow, tender leaves; mellow garlic flavor when cooked)
- 1 cup (250 mL) chopped flowering garlic chives (round green leaves; mellow garlic flavor when cooked; works best in soups, stews, or with moist-heat cooking methods)

Garlic Mayonnaise

See MAYONNAISE.

Garlic Oil

Commercially available gourmet oil — often extra virgin olive oil — in which garlic has been macerated. A convenient ingredient for dipping, salad dressings, or sautéing vegetables.

If You Don't Have It

Substitute ¼ cup (50 mL) garlic oil with:

- ¼ cup (50 mL) roasted garlic oil (mellower, sweeter flavor)
- ¼ cup (50 mL) Homemade Garlic Oil: Combine 1 small garlic clove and ¼ cup (50 mL) olive oil in small saucepan over low heat. Heat until garlic is mildly fragrant, about 10 minutes. Discard garlic and use oil immediately. Or let cool, refrigerate in an airtight glass jar, and use within 1 day.

Garlic Press

When buying a garlic press, look for the easy-cleaning type, which has prongs to push bits of garlic back out through the holes.

If You Don't Have It

Substitute a garlic press with:

- finely mincing the food with a chef's knife, then pressing the mound of minced food with the flat side of the knife

Garlic Salt

A seasoning of ground dried garlic and salt sold on the supermarket spice shelf.

If You Don't Have It

Substitute 1 tsp (5 mL) garlic salt with:

- ¼ tsp (1 mL) garlic powder + ¾ tsp (4 mL) salt

Gelatin

Before the introduction of commercial gelatin in the late 1800s, cooks who wanted jelled dishes had to boil calves' feet or knuckles to extract the gelatin. Use 1 tbsp (15 mL) unflavored powdered gelatin to gel 2 cups (500 mL) of liquid.

If You Don't Have It

Substitute ¼ oz (8 g) pkg (1 tbsp/15 mL) unflavored gelatin with:

- 4 sheets (9-by 4-inches/23 by 10 cm) leaf gelatin
- 1 tbsp (15 mL) kosher or vegetarian powdered gelatin (for those eating kosher and vegetarians who prefer gelling agents from non-animal sources)
- 2 tsp (10 mL) agar powder (a sea vegetable; suitable for vegetarians)
- 1 oz (30 g) carrageen (a sea vegetable; suitable for vegetarians; reconstitute the dried carrageen in cool water; cook the reconstituted carrageen with the liquid to be gelled; then strain out the carrageen)

Gelatin, Flavored

Also known as gelatin dessert mix and Jell-O®. The Jell-O Museum in LeRoy, New York, houses exhibits dedicated to "America's Favorite Dessert."

If You Don't Have It

Substitute 3 oz (90 g) pkg powdered flavored gelatin, prepared, with:

- 1 tbsp (15 mL) unflavored gelatin + 2 cups (500 mL) fruit juice

Gelato

See ICE CREAM.

Gelbwurst

Mild pork and veal sausage dubbed "diet bologna" in Germany because of its relatively low-fat content.

If You Don't Have It

Substitute 1 lb (500 g) Gelbwurst with:

- 1 lb (500 g) bologna (higher in fat and calories)
- 1 lb (500 g) mortadella (has cubes of pork fat and garlic flavor)
- 1 lb (500 g) galantina (chunkier; more complex flavor)
- 1 lb (500 g) olive loaf (adds olive flavor)

Génoise

This versatile sponge cake is named génoise by the French, reputedly after its origin in Genoa, Italy. However, the Italian word for the same sponge cake is pan di Spagna, *which means "Spanish bread."*

If You Don't Have It

Substitute 1 lb (500 g) génoise with:

- 1 lb (500 g) sponge cake (less moist)
- 1 lb (500 g) ladyfingers (especially for tiramisù)
- 1 lb (500 g) pound cake (moister, denser texture)

Geoduck

See SWAPPING CLAMS (PAGE 596).

Gervais

See PETIT SUISSE.

Ghee

See BUTTER, CLARIFIED.

Gherkin

See CUCUMBER; SWEET GHERKIN.

Gianduja

Also known as chocolate-hazelnut spread or paste. The most widely distributed brand is Nutella©.

If You Don't Have It

Substitute 1 cup (250 mL) gianduja with:

- 1 cup (250 mL) creamy peanut butter (omits chocolate and hazelnut flavors)
- 3 oz (90 g) or ½ cup (125 mL) milk chocolate + ½ cup (125 mL) creamy peanut butter, cashew butter, or almond butter; melt in a double boiler and stir until smooth

Gin

Juniper berries give gin its distinctive bouquet. Essential in the dry martini and countless classic cocktails. Not to be confused with sloe gin, which is a sweetened liqueur.

If You Don't Have It

Substitute 3 tbsp (45 mL) gin with:

- 3 tbsp (45 mL) vodka
- 3 tbsp (45 mL) white rum
- 3 tbsp (45 mL) brandy

Gin Varieties

Choose 3 tbsp (45 mL) gin from these varieties:

- 3 tbsp (45 mL) London gin (dry; complex flavor)
- 3 tbsp (45 mL) American gin (less dry; slightly less complex flavor)
- 3 tbsp (45 mL) Dutch or Hollands gin (sweeter; more complex flavor than dry gin)
- 3 tbsp (45 mL) golden gin (golden color; aged in wood)

See also SLOE GIN.

Ginger Ale

James Vernor created ginger ale in 1866 and sold it in his Detroit, Michigan drug store for 30 years before opening a factory to produce and bottle it.

If You Don't Have It

Substitute 1 cup (250 mL) ginger ale with:

- 1 cup (250 mL) ginger beer (stronger ginger flavor)
- 1 cup (250 mL) lemon and lime flavored soda such as 7-Up© (no ginger flavor)
- 1 cup (250 mL) soda water (adds no flavor)

Ginger Beer

Ginger ale with attitude. Ginger beer comes in alcoholic and nonalcoholic versions.

If You Don't Have It

Substitute 1 cup (250 mL) ginger beer with:
- 1 cup (250 mL) ginger ale (milder ginger flavor)
- 1 cup (250 mL) lemon and lime flavored soda, such as 7-Up© (no ginger flavor)
- 1 cup (250 mL) soda water (adds no flavor)

Ginger, Crystallized

Also known as candied ginger. Fresh ginger pieces simmered in syrup until tender and then drained and coated with granulated sugar.

If You Don't Have It

Substitute 3 tbsp (45 mL) minced crystallized ginger with:
- 3 tbsp (45 mL) Homemade Crystallized Ginger: Mix together $\frac{2}{3}$ cup (150 mL) granulated sugar and $\frac{1}{2}$ cup (125 mL) water in a small saucepan. Bring to a boil over high heat. Then add $\frac{1}{2}$ cup (125 mL) peeled, sliced ginger. Reduce heat and simmer for 20 to 30 minutes. Strain ginger pieces, then dry on a rack and sprinkle with sugar. When completely cool, store in an airtight container for up to 1 month. Mince as needed. Makes about $\frac{1}{2}$ cup (125 mL).
- 2 tsp (10 mL) minced fresh ginger + $\frac{1}{8}$ to $\frac{1}{2}$ tsp (0.5 to 2 mL) granulated sugar (stronger ginger flavor)
- $\frac{1}{8}$ tsp (0.5 mL) ground ginger

Ginger, Fresh

Also known as gingerroot. Young ginger (spring ginger) is relatively mild, tender and doesn't need peeling. The more common mature ginger should be peeled. Unpeeled ginger may be refrigerated for up to 3 weeks or frozen for up to 6 months.

1 oz (30 g) =
$\frac{1}{4}$ cup (50 mL) sliced

1 tbsp (15 mL)
minced fresh =
$\frac{1}{8}$ tsp (0.5 mL) ground

If You Don't Have It

Substitute 1 tbsp (15 mL) fresh ginger (minced or grated) with:
- 1 tbsp (15 mL) fresh galangal (minced or grated)
- 3 tbsp (45 mL) rinsed crystallized ginger, minced (for baking or where a little sugar is acceptable in recipe)
- $\frac{1}{8}$ tsp (0.5 mL) ground ginger (for baking)

Ginger, Ground

The dried, ground form of fresh ginger is a distinctive spice in its own right lending its name and zing to gingerbread, gingersnaps, and other gingery treats.

If You Don't Have It

Substitute 1 tsp (5 mL) ground ginger (for baking) with:

- ⅓ cup (75 mL) minced crystallized ginger, rinsed to remove sugar
- 1 tbsp (15 mL) grated or minced fresh ginger (preferably add ½ tsp/2 mL ground ginger to help better distribute the flavor)
- 1 to 2 tsp (5 to 10 mL) ginger juice (add to wet ingredients)

To Vary the Flavor

Substitute 1 tsp (5 mL) ground ginger with:

- 1 tsp (5 mL) pumpkin pie spice (adds cinnamon, clove, and nutmeg aromas)
- 1 tsp (5 mL) allspice (adds cinnamon, clove, and nutmeg aromas)
- 1 tsp (5 mL) ground cardamom (adds musky citrus aroma)

Ginger Juice

Look for the juice squeezed from fresh ginger in specialty markets or natural food stores.

1 oz (30 g)
(about ¼ cup/50 mL)
fresh ginger =
2 tsp (10 mL) juice

If You Don't Have It

Substitute 1 tbsp (15 mL) ginger juice with:

- 1 tbsp (15 mL) Homemade Ginger Juice: Press 1½ oz (45 g), about ⅓ cup (75 mL) minced fresh ginger, in a garlic press and squeeze out juice. Makes about 1 tablespoon (15 mL).

Gingerroot

See GINGER, FRESH.

Gingersnap Crumbs

Also known as ginger biscuit or ginger nut (British). Crisp and spicy cookie often sweetened with molasses. Closely related to German pfeffernüesse *and Scandinavian* peppernott.

If You Don't Have It

Substitute 1½ cups (375 mL) crushed gingersnaps with:

- 1½ cups (375 mL) crushed graham crackers (about 21 squares)
- 1½ cups (375 mL) crushed vanilla wafer cookies (about 33)
- 1½ cups (375 mL) crushed chocolate wafer cookies (about 32)

- 1½ cups (375 mL) crushed Oreo cookies (about 21, including cookie filling); omit sugar from crust
- 1½ cups (375 mL) crushed wheat, bran or corn flakes (about 4½ cups/1.125 L)
- 1½ cups (375 mL) crushed saltine crackers (about 42); omit sugar from crust and adjust salt in filling (for savory fillings)

Ginkgo Nut

An American petrified ginkgo forest in Washington state is estimated to be 15 million years old.

If You Don't Have It

Substitute 1 oz (30 g) ginkgo nuts with:
- 1 oz (30 g) cashew nuts
- 1 oz (30 g) blanched almonds
- 1 oz (30 g) blanched hazelnuts
- 1 oz (30 g) pine nuts

Gjetost

A Norwegian cheese made from goat's and cow's milk whey that is cooked until caramelized. The texture may be spreadable or semifirm.

If You Don't Have It

Substitute 1 oz (30 g) gjetost with:
- 1 oz (30 g) mysost

See also MYSOST.

Glacé Cherry

See CHERRY, CANDIED.

Glace de Viande

Brown stock (usually beef, veal, or poultry) reduced to a syrup that gels when chilled. Often used to glaze meats or gloss up and flavor sauces at the last minute. Commercial versions are available.

If You Don't Have It

Substitute 1 tbsp (15 mL) glace de viande with:
- 1 tbsp (15 mL) Homemade Glace de Viande: Strain and degrease 4 cups (1 L) brown beef, veal, or chicken stock. Then bring to a boil in a medium saucepan over medium-high heat. Reduce heat and boil gently until reduced by about half (about 2 cups/500 mL), skimming foam from surface. Strain into a smaller saucepan and simmer vigorously until reduced by half again, reducing the heat as necessary to avoid burning (this will take 2 to 4 hours). When reduced to 1 cup (250 mL) and lightly coating the back of a spoon, strain into a jar or other airtight container and refrigerate up to 2 months or freeze for up to 6 months (glaze will gel when chilled). Makes about 1 cup (250 mL).

Glacé Fruits

See SPECIFIC FRUITS.

Glass Noodles

See A SNAPSHOT OF ASIAN NOODLES (PAGE 588).

Glasswort

See SALICORNIA.

Glayva™

Scottish whiskey liqueur flavored with almonds, Seville oranges, herbs, and spices.

If You Don't Have It
Substitute 3 tbsp (45 mL) Glayva™ with:
- 3 tbsp (45 mL) Drambuie
- 3 tbsp (45 mL) Grandtully
- 3 tbsp (45 mL) Lochan Ora

Gloucester

Also known as double Gloucester. A fine mellow English cheese originally made only with the milk from Gloucester cows, which are now nearly extinct. The harder-to-find single Gloucester is made with skimmed milk instead of the whole milk and cream used to make double Gloucester.

1 lb (500 g) = 4 cups
(1 L) shredded

If You Don't Have It
Substitute 1 oz (30 g) Gloucester with:
- 1 oz (30 g) Cheshire (more complex flavor)
- 1 oz (30 g) Cheddar

Gloucester Varieties
Choose 1 oz (30 g) Gloucester from these varieties:
- 1 oz (30 g) double Gloucester (creamier, milder, more complex flavor)
- 1 oz (30 g) Huntsman cheese (a layer of Stilton sandwiched between two layers of double Gloucester)

For Better Health
Substitute 1 oz (30 g) Gloucester with:
- 1 oz (30 g) single Gloucester (lower in fat; drier and crumblier than double Gloucester)

Glucose, Liquid

Also known as dextroglucose and dextrose. Common sweetener used in the production of soft drinks. It doesn't crystallize easily, so it is also used in candies, frostings, and baked goods.

If You Don't Have It
Substitute ½ cup (125 mL) liquid glucose with:
- ½ cup (125 mL) light corn syrup

Glutinous Rice

See VARIETIES OF RICE (PAGE 591).

Goat

Because they thrive in mountainous habitats on thorny scrub, the meat of goats has been an important protein source for many cultures around the world.

If You Don't Have It

Substitute 1 lb (500 g) baby goat with:
- 1 lb (500 g) lamb

Goat Cheese

See CHÈVRE.

Goatfish

See RED MULLET.

Goat's Milk

Liquid goat's milk is a good source of calcium for people who are allergic to cow's milk. Goat's milk is also typically transformed into a wide variety of fresh local cheeses. Goat's milk cheese is chalk white because it contains no carotene pigments like cow's or sheep's milk.

If You Don't Have It

Substitute 1 cup (250 mL) goat's milk with:
- 1 cup (250 mL) sheep's milk (for cheese making)
- 1 cup (250 mL) cow's milk (for drinking and baking; milder)
- 1 cup (250 mL) soy milk (for drinking and baking; milder, slightly beany tasting; may be sweetened or unsweetened)
- 1 cup (250 mL) almond milk (for drinking and baking; sweeter)
- 1 cup (250 mL) rice milk (for drinking and baking; sweeter)

See also CHÈVRE.

Gobo

See BURDOCK.

Godiva Liqueur

See CHOCOLATE LIQUEUR.

Goetta

The pride of Cincinnati, Ohio, goetta is a rustic pâté of simmered pork, oats, and spices. The city hosts two annual festivals dedicated to the local specialty.

If You Don't Have It

Substitute 1 lb (500 g) goetta with:
- 1 lb (500 g) scrapple (sausage and cornmeal)
- 1 lb (500 g) loose breakfast sausage

Golden Nugget Squash

It may sound like a Las Vegas casino but this sweet winter squash is named for its bright orange skin and flesh.

If You Don't Have It

Substitute 1 cup (250 mL) chopped golden nugget squash with:
- 1 cup (250 mL) chopped buttercup squash
- 1 cup (250 mL) chopped butternut squash
- 1 cup (250 mL) chopped Baby blue hubbard squash
- 1 cup (250 mL) chopped acorn squash
- 1 cup (250 mL) chopped kabocha squash

Golden Raspberry

See RASPBERRY.

Golden Syrup

Also known as light treacle (British). Made by cooking the water from sugarcane juice, golden syrup has a rich, toasty flavor. It can be used as a topping or ingredient in cooking or baking.

If You Don't Have It

Substitute 1 cup (250 mL) golden syrup with:
- ¾ cup (175 mL) light corn syrup + ¼ cup (50 mL) light molasses (slightly thinner; less sweet)
- ½ cup (125 mL) dark corn syrup + ½ cup (125 mL) honey (slightly thinner; less sweet)
- 1 cup (250 mL) pure maple syrup (thinner; less sweet; adds maple flavor)

Goldschläger®

A Swiss brand of cinnamon schnapps glamorized with particles of 24-karat gold leaf flakes.

If You Don't Have It

Substitute 3 tbsp (45 mL) Goldschläger with:
- 3 tbsp (45 mL) cinnamon schnapps

Goldwasser

Generic name for an herbal Swiss or German liqueur in which particles of gold leaf flakes are suspended. Danziger® is a well-known producer.

If You Don't Have It

Substitute 3 tbsp (45 mL) Goldwasser with:
- 3 tbsp (45 mL) Silverwasser (has silver flakes)
- 3 tbsp (45 mL) Liqueur d'Or
- 3 tbsp (45 mL) Strega
- 3 tbsp (45 mL) Kümmel
- 3 tbsp (45 mL) aquavit

Goliath Grouper

In 2001, the common name of this fish, jewfish, was replaced by the more politically correct goliath grouper.

If You Don't Have It

Substitute 1 lb (500 g) goliath grouper with:
- 1 lb (500 g) striped bass
- 1 lb (500 g) cod
- 1 lb (500 g) catfish
- 1 lb (500 g) red snapper

Gomashio

Japanese seasoning mixture of toasted sesame seeds and sea salt.

If You Don't Have It

Substitute 1 tsp (5 mL) gomashio with:
- 1 tsp (5 mL) Homemade Gomashio: Toast 1½ tbsp (22 mL) sea salt in a heavy skillet over medium heat until fragrant and gray in color, 5 to 7 minutes. Remove and let cool. Toast 1 cup (250 mL) unhulled brown sesame seeds in same skillet until fragrant, 4 to 6 minutes. Remove and let cool. Coarsely grind toasted salt and sesame seeds in a mortar and pestle or spice grinder until sandy in texture. Store in an airtight container in a cool dry place for up to 4 months. Makes about 1 cup (250 mL).
- 1 tsp (5 mL) sesame seeds + pinch of salt

Goose

Foie gras (rich goose liver) and confit (goose cooked and preserved in its own rendered fat) are specialties of southwestern France.

If You Don't Have It

Substitute 1 lb (500 g) goose with:
- 1 lb (500 g) duck (smaller; fattier)
- 1 lb (500 g) squab (smaller; less fatty)
- 1 lb (500 g) turkey dark meat (less fatty; more tender)
- 1 lb (500 g) rabbit (less fatty)
- 1 lb (500 g) chicken dark meat (less fatty; more tender)

Gooseberry

Wild and domesticated bush berries that thrive in northern European climes. Canned gooseberries make a good substitute when the berries will be cooked.

If You Don't Have It

Substitute 1 cup (250 mL) gooseberries with:
- 1 cup (250 mL) fresh red or white currants (smaller)
- 1 cup (250 mL) kiwifruit (larger; sweeter)

See also CAPE GOOSEBERRY.

Goose Fat

The fat rendered from these large plump birds is prized as a flavorful cooking medium in many European kitchens.

If You Don't Have It
Substitute 1 tbsp (15 mL) goose fat with:
- 1 tbsp (15 mL) duck fat
- 1 tbsp (15 mL) lard or pork fat
- 1 tbsp (15 mL) chicken fat

Gordita

A plump corn tortilla that's first cooked on a griddle and then fried in oil before being filled with ground pork, chorizo, or other savory stuffings.

If You Don't Have It
Substitute 1 gordita with:
- 1 arepa (split, for stuffing)
- 1 chalupa (split, for stuffing; elongated shape)
- 1 corn tortilla (thinner and stiffer)
- 1 flour tortilla (thinner)
- 1 small pita bread (split, for stuffing)

Gorgonzola

One of the world's greatest blue-veined cheeses made from cow's milk in the region of Lombardy. Mild, creamy Gorgonzola dolce is aged for 3 months. More pungent, aged types are variously labeled di monte, naturale, piccante, and stagionata.

If You Don't Have It
Substitute 1 oz (30 g) Gorgonzola with:
- 1 oz (30 g) Roquefort (less creamy)
- 1 oz (30 g) Stilton (less creamy)
- 1 oz (30 g) Gorgonzola dolce or Dolcelatte (young gorgonzola; milder)
- 1 oz (30 g) Cambozola (less complex flavor)
- 1 oz (30 g) Saga (less complex flavor)

Gouda

Young Gouda melts well in cooking. Aged Gouda, often encased in black wax, has a sharper, more pronounced flavor.

If You Don't Have It
Substitute 1 oz (30 g) Gouda with:
- 1 oz (30 g) farmer's Gouda or Boerenkaas
- 1 oz (30 g) Edam (less rich)
- 1 oz (30 g) Leyden (adds caraway or cumin flavors)
- 1 oz (30 g) Samsoe

Graham Cracker

The Reverend Sylvester Graham concocted the sweet, crisp whole wheat cracker in the 1830s and proclaimed it a health food.

If You Don't Have It
Substitute 1 lb (500 g) graham crackers with:
- 1 lb (500 g) digestive biscuits (sweeter)
- 1 lb (500 g) teething biscuits
- 1 lb (500 g) wheatmeal biscuits (Australian graham crackers)

To Vary the Flavor

Substitute 1½ cups (375 mL) crushed graham crackers for pie crust (about 21 squares) with:

- 1½ cups (375 mL) crushed gingersnaps (about 22)
- 1½ cups (375 mL) crushed vanilla wafer cookies (about 33)
- 1½ cups (375 mL) crushed chocolate wafer cookies (about 32)
- 1½ cups (375 mL) crushed Oreo cookies (about 21, including cookie filling); omit sugar from crust
- 1½ cups (375 mL) crushed wheat, bran or corn flakes (about 4½ cups/1.125 L)
- 1½ cups (375 mL) crushed saltine crackers (about 42); omit sugar from crust and adjust salt in filling (for savory fillings)

See also CRACKER; FLOUR, GRAHAM.

Graham Flour

See FLOUR, GRAHAM.

Grain Alcohol

See NEUTRAL SPIRITS.

Grains of Paradise

Also known as alligator pepper, Guinea pepper, and melegueta pepper. Pungent aromatic seeds of a West African reed-like herb.

If You Don't Have It

Substitute 1 tsp (5 mL) ground grains of paradise with:

- ½ tsp (2 mL) ground cardamom + ½ tsp (2 mL) ground black peppercorns

Gram Flour

See CHOOSING AMONG WHOLE-GRAIN AND ALTERNATIVE FLOURS (PAGE 586).

Granadilla

See PASSION FRUIT.

Grana Padano

A Parmesan-style, hard grating cheese produced in the Italian regions of Lombardy and Piedmont.

If You Don't Have It

Substitute 1 oz (30 g) Grana Padano with:

- 1 oz (30 g) Parmesan
- 1 oz (30 g) Pecorino Romano (sharper flavor; less sweet)
- 1 oz (30 g) aged Asiago (slightly milder)
- 1 oz (30 g) dry Jack cheese (more nutty flavor)

For Better Health

Substitute 1 oz (30 g) Grana Padano (for grating) with:

- 1 oz (30 g) Sapsago (more herbal flavor; lower in fat)

Grand Marnier

See ORANGE LIQUEUR.

Granola

Embraced by back-to-nature types in the 1960s and '70s, this breakfast/snack food typically combines oats and other grains, nuts, and dried fruits.

If You Don't Have It
Substitute 1 cup (250 mL) granola with:
- 1 cup (250 mL) muesli (the original Swiss granola)

Gran Torres

See ORANGE LIQUEUR.

Grapefruit

The only citrus fruit to originate in the New World, grapefruit is likely a natural mutation between a pummelo and another citrus fruit. It takes its name from its habit of growing in clusters like grapes.

If You Don't Have It
Substitute 1 cup (250 mL) grapefruit segments with:
- $\frac{1}{2}$ cup (125 mL) pummelo segments + $\frac{1}{2}$ cup (125 mL) orange segments
- 1 cup (250 mL) Ugli fruit™ segments
- 1 cup (250 mL) tangelo segments

Grapefruit Juice

Grapefruit juice decreases the production of a certain enzyme in the intestines that are involved in the metabolizing of many prescription and nonprescription drugs. Always consult your physician or pharmacist before taking medication with grapefruit juice.

If You Don't Have It
Substitute 1 cup (250 mL) grapefruit juice with:
- $\frac{1}{2}$ cup (125 mL) pummelo juice + $\frac{1}{2}$ cup (125 mL) orange juice

To Vary the Flavor
Substitute 1 cup (250 mL) grapefruit juice with:
- 1 cup (250 mL) pummelo juice
- 1 cup (250 mL) orange juice
- 1 cup (250 mL) pineapple juice

Grapefruit Knife

A flexible knife, serrated on both sides of the blade, that makes quick work of sectioning grapefruit.

If You Don't Have It
Substitute a grapefruit knife with:
- small serrated knife

Grape Jelly

Comedian Adam Sandler speaks for the six-year-old in all of us with the line "I Love Grape Jelly" from his silly song Grape Jelly.

If You Don't Have It
Substitute 1 cup (250 mL) grape jelly with:
- 1 cup (250 mL) scuppernong or muscadine jelly
- 1 cup (250 mL) red currant jelly

Grape Juice

More than 85% of the content of grapes is juice.

If You Don't Have It
Substitute 1 cup (250 mL) grape juice with:
- 1 cup (250 mL) de-alcoholized wine (less sweet)
- 1 cup (250 mL) apple juice (less sweet; apple flavor)

Grape Juice Varieties
Choose 1 cup (250 mL) grape juice from these varieties:
- 1 cup (250 mL) white grape juice
- 1 cup (250 mL) red grape juice
- 1 cup (250 mL) sparkling grape juice (carbonated)
- 1 cup (250 mL) juice blend (many juice blends are based on grape juice; flavors will vary)

Grape Leaves

Also known as vine leaves. Edible food wrappers associated with Greek and Middle Eastern cookery. Packed commercially in brine. Rinse under cool running water to remove excess salt before using.

If You Don't Have It
Substitute 10 brined grape leaves with:
- 10 Homemade Prepared Grape Leaves: Bring 4 cups (1 L) water to a boil in a deep, wide sauté pan over high heat. Add 1½ tsp (7 mL) salt and 10 fresh, unsprayed grape leaves. Reduce heat to medium and simmer until soft, 5 to 10 minutes. Drain. Makes 10.
- 10 green cabbage leaves, simmered in salted water until tender (as food wrappers)
- 10 small green chard leaves, thick ribs removed, simmered in salted water until tender (as food wrappers)

Grapeseed Oil

See SUBSTITUTING OILS (PAGE 598).

Grape, Table

The bestselling grape in the U.S. is the Thompson Seedless. The average American eats about 8 pounds (4 kg) of grapes each year.

If You Don't Have It
Substitute 1 cup (250 mL) green table grapes with:
- 1 cup (250 mL) blueberries (purple color; blueberry flavor)

Table Grape Varieties
Choose 1 cup (250 mL) green table grapes from:
- 1 cup (250 mL) red table grapes (red color)
- 1 cup (250 mL) Flame Tokay grapes (red color; thick skin; mild flavor)
- 1 cup (250 mL) Muscat grapes (more complex, musky flavor)
- 1 cup (250 mL) Muscadine or scuppernong grapes (strong, musky flavor; often made into jelly or wine)
- 1 cup (250 mL) champagne grapes (smaller)

Grappa

A distilled spirit produced in northern Italy from fermented grape pomace. The last several decades have seen producers using finer grapes to make more elegant grappas.

If You Don't Have It
Substitute 3 tbsp (45 mL) grappa with:
- 3 tbsp (45 mL) cognac
- 3 tbsp (45 mL) Armagnac

Grappa Varieties
Choose 3 tbsp (45 mL) grappa from these varieties:
- 3 tbsp (45 mL) marc (French)
- 3 tbsp (45 mL) aguardiente (Spanish)
- 3 tbsp (45 mL) testerbranntwein (German)
- 3 tbsp (45 mL) bagaceira (Portuguese)

Grater

Plastic or metal kitchen tool perforated with sharp holes or slits. When cheeses, vegetables, or other foods are drawn over the perforations, they are cut into fine bits or strips.

If You Don't Have It
Substitute a grater with these different types:
- box grater (for shredding, grating, and slicing)
- food processor fitted with a shredding or slicing disc (for shredding or slicing)
- food processor fitted with a metal blade (for grinding foods such as nuts into small pieces)
- flat grater (for shredding or grating)
- Microplane® or rasp (for finely grating cheese, chocolate, nuts, or nutmeg)
- mouli or rotary grater (for grating small amounts of cheese, chocolate, nuts, or nutmeg)
- nutmeg grater (for finely grating small amounts of nutmeg)

Gratin Dish

Shallow ovenproof dish for baking gratins, casserole-type dishes topped with cheese or buttered crumbs.

If You Don't Have It

Substitute a gratin dish with:
- any shallow, wide, heatproof dish such as a quiche dish or pie plate

Gravlax

A Swedish delicacy. Salmon cured in a mixture of salt, sugar, and fresh dill. Should be sliced and served in transparently thin slices.

If You Don't Have It

Substitute 1 lb (500 g) gravlax with:
- 1 lb (500 g) lox or other smoked salmon, especially brined and hot-smoked salmon such as "kippered salmon" or "squaw candy" (preferably, add fresh or dried dill; adds mild smoke flavor)
- 1 lb (500 g) cured or smoked arctic char (preferably, add fresh or dried dill)

See also SMOKED SALMON.

Gravy Browning

Commercial condiment designed to boost the dark color and rich flavor of homemade gravy and sauces. Includes Kitchen Bouquet© and Gravy Master©.

If You Don't Have It

Substitute 1 tsp (5 mL) gravy browning (for brown color) with:
- $\frac{1}{2}$ to 1 tsp (2 to 5 mL) baker's caramel (less salty)
- 2 drops red food coloring + 1 drop green food coloring (adds only brown color, no flavor; will darken 1 cup/250 mL liquid a light brown)
- 1 tsp (5 mL) Worcestershire sauce (adds other flavors)
- 1 tsp (5 mL) steak sauce (adds other flavors)

Grease Mop

Also known as fat mop. A mini-mop with absorbent strips for sopping up oil floating on the surface of soups or stews.

If You Don't Have It

Substitute a grease mop with:
- fat separator
- dragging folded paper towels across surface of liquid until fat is removed (for small amounts of fat)
- skimming fat from surface with a ladle, large spoon, or bulb baster
- placing ice cubes in a slotted spoon and dragging across surface of liquid, then discarding ice as it becomes covered with fat (for small amounts of fat)
- chilling pan of soup, stock or other liquid until fat congeals on top, then spooning off fat

Greek Seasoning

A bottled herb blend of characteristic Greek flavorings.

If You Don't Have It

Substitute 1 tsp (5 mL) Greek seasoning with
- 1 tsp (5 mL) Homemade Greek Seasoning: Combine 1 tsp (5 mL) dried oregano, ¾ tsp (4 mL) onion powder, ¾ tsp (4 mL) garlic powder, ½ tsp (2 mL) ground black pepper, ¼ tsp (1 mL) dried mint, small pinch of cinnamon, and small pinch of nutmeg. Add salt to taste. Makes about 1 tablespoon (15 mL).

Green Bean

Also known as snap beans or string beans. Long ago, there really was a fibrous string that ran down the seam of the string bean pod but it has been bred out of the species. Cooks no longer have to de-string their beans.

> 1 lb (500 g) =
> 3 cups (750 mL)

If You Don't Have It

Substitute 1 lb (500 g) green beans with:
- 1 lb (500 g) yard-long beans (longer; starchier and less sweet)
- 1 lb (500 g) thin asparagus
- 1 lb (500 g) nopales, sliced
- 1 lb (500 g) okra
- 1 lb (500 g) broccoli

Green Bean Varieties

Choose 1 lb (500 g) green beans from these varieties:
- 1 lb (500 g) green snap beans (crisp; mildly sweet)
- 1 lb (500 g) purple snap beans (similar to green snap beans; green when cooked)
- 1 lb (500 g) yellow wax beans (pale yellow color; mild flavor)
- 1 lb (500 g) haricot verts, filet beans, or French beans (green, yellow, or purple color; slender; tender; more complex flavor)
- 1 lb (500 g) Romano or Italian flat beans (green or yellow color; flatter than green snap beans; juicy and meaty; mild flavor)
- 1 lb (500 g) Tongue of Fire beans (green with flecks of pink or purple; flatter than green snap beans; green when cooked)
- 1 lb (500 g) Dragon Tongue beans (pale yellow or cream with maroon or dark purple splotches; similar to yellow wax beans; yellow when cooked)

Green Cabbage

See BOK CHOY; CABBAGE; NAPA CABBAGE; RED CABBAGE; SAVOY CABBAGE.

Green Leaf Lettuce

See LEAF LETTUCE.

Green Onion

See ONION, GREEN.

Green Pepper

See BELL PEPPER.

Green Peppercorn

See PEPPERCORN.

Greens

See SPECIFIC TYPES.

Gremolata

A savory Italian blend of minced fresh garlic, lemon zest, and parsley that garnishes osso buco.

If You Don't Have It
Substitute 1 tbsp (15 mL) gremolata with:
- 1 tbsp (15 mL) Homemade Gremolata: Combine 3 tbsp (45 mL) finely chopped flat-leaf parsley, 1 minced garlic clove, and 1 tsp (5 mL) grated lemon zest. Season to taste with salt and ground black pepper to taste. Makes about 3 tablespoons (45 mL).

Grenadine

Garnet-color, pomegranate-flavored syrup used to flavor beverages and sweets. At one time, made only with pomegranates grown on the island of Grenada.

If You Don't Have It
Substitute 1 tsp (5 mL) grenadine with:
- ¼ to ½ tsp (1 to 2 mL) pomegranate concentrate
- 2 to 3 tsp (10 to 15 mL) pomegranate juice (reduce liquid in recipe by 1 to 2 tsp/5 to 10 mL and add sugar if necessary)
- 1 tsp (5 mL) red currant syrup
- 1 tsp (5 mL) raspberry syrup

Griddle

Cast-iron or cast-aluminum rimless cooking pan or surface that can be a portable unit to sit atop heating elements or a unit built into a stovetop cooking surface. Commonly used to cook pancakes, bacon, French toast, and hot sandwiches.

If You Don't Have It
Substitute a griddle with:
- large frying pan or skillet
- large sauté pan

Grill

A sturdy metal grate that holds foods set over hot charcoal or other heat source. Both indoor and outdoor units are available.

If You Don't Have It

Substitute a grill with:

- broiler (heat comes from above instead of below; to add smoke flavor that would have been achieved by grilling over coals, add 1 to 2 drops liquid smoke to marinade or sauce; or include a smoked food such as chipotle chiles)
- ridged grill pan (gives good grill marks; can steam foods; to add smoke flavor that would have been achieved by grilling over coals, add 1 to 2 drops liquid smoke to marinade or sauce; or include a smoked food such as chipotle chiles)
- electric tabletop grill (gives good grill marks; can steam foods; best for sandwiches; to add smoke flavor that would have been achieved by grilling over coals, add 1 to 2 drops liquid smoke to marinade or sauce; or include a smoked food such as chipotle chiles)

Grits

See BARLEY GRITS; CORN GRITS; HOMINY GRITS.

Groats

See BUCKWHEAT GROATS; OAT GROATS.

Ground Cherry

See CAPE GOOSEBERRY.

Ground Ginger

See GINGER, GROUND.

Ground Red Pepper

See CAYENNE PEPPER.

Grouper

A lean, firm-fleshed fish of the bass family. The strongly flavored skin is often removed before cooking.

If You Don't Have It

Substitute 1 lb (500 g) grouper with:

- 1 lb (500 g) striped bass
- 1 lb (500 g) cod
- 1 lb (500 g) catfish
- 1 lb (500 g) red snapper

See also GOLIATH GROUPER.

Grouse

A distinctively flavored dark-meat game bird widely enjoyed in Great Britain. Young grouse are excellent roasted or braised.

If You Don't Have It

Substitute 1 lb (500 g) grouse with:
- 1 lb (500 g) quail
- 1 lb (500 g) squab
- 1 lb (500 g) young pheasant
- 1 lb (500 g) Cornish game hen (fattier)

Gruyère

One of the finest cheeses in the world, Gruyère has been produced in Switzerland since the 12th century.

If You Don't Have It

Substitute 1 oz (30 g) Gruyère with:
- 1 oz (30 g) Comté
- 1 oz (30 g) Beaufort
- 1 oz (30 g) Emmental

Guanabana

See SOURSOP.

Guanciale

Salt-cured, air-dried pig's jowl and cheek. In Italian cooking, guanciale is used much like pancetta.

If You Don't Have It

Substitute 4 oz (125 g) guanciale with:
- 4 oz (125 g) pancetta
- 4 oz (125 g) hog jowl (adds smoke flavor)
- 4 oz (125 g) bacon (adds smoke flavor)
- 2 to 4 oz (60 to 125 g) salt pork (drop in boiling water for a few minutes to reduce saltiness or reduce salt in recipe if necessary)
- 4 oz (125 g) bacon

See also HOG JOWL.

Guava

Also known as goyave and guayaba. Guava may be one of 140-odd species with sweet or sour aromatic flesh tasting of strawberries, pineapple, banana, or all three.

> 1 medium =
> ½ cup (125 mL) pulp

If You Don't Have It

Substitute ½ cup (125 mL) guava pulp with:
- ½ cup (125 mL) chopped pineapple
- ½ cup (125 mL) strawberries

See also GUAVA PASTE.

Guava Paste

Like a bar of firm jelly, guava paste is prepared by slowly simmering guava, sugar, pectin, and citric acid. Sold in Latin American and some specialty markets.

If You Don't Have It
Substitute ¼ cup (50 mL) guava paste with:
- ¼ cup (50 mL) strawberry preserves
- ¼ cup (50 mL) other tropical fruit preserves

See also GUAVA.

Guayaba

See GUAVA.

Guinea Fowl

Small bird related to chicken and partridge, said to have originated in Guinea, Africa. The meat is dark and pleasingly gamey.

If You Don't Have It
Substitute 1 lb (500 g) guinea fowl with:
- 1 lb (500 g) pheasant
- 1 lb (500 g) Cornish game hen (moister)
- 1 lb (500 g) chicken
  (preferably pasture-raised; moister)

Guinea Pepper

See GRAINS OF PARADISE.

Gur

See JAGGERY.

Gyoza Wrappers

See WON TON SKINS.

Habanero Chile
to Hyssop

Habanero Chile

See CHOOSING FRESH CHILES (PAGE 582).

Haddock

This saltwater fish is a smaller relative of cod. It is low in fat, mild in flavor, and has a firm texture.

If You Don't Have It
Substitute 1 lb (500 g) haddock with:
- 1 lb (500 g) cod
- 1 lb (500 g) pollock
- 1 lb (500 g) blackfish
- 1 lb (500 g) grouper
- 1 lb (500 g) red snapper
- 1 lb (500 g) sea bass
- 1 lb (500 g) tilefish
- 1 lb (500 g) turbot

To Vary the Flavor
Substitute 1 lb (500 g) haddock with:
- 1 lb (500 g) finnan haddie (smoked haddock)

Hairy Melon

See FUZZY GOURD.

Hake

A relative of cod that swims in both the Atlantic and Pacific Oceans. The delicate white flesh is low in fat.

If You Don't Have It

Substitute 1 lb (500 g) hake with:
- 1 lb (500 g) cod
- 1 lb (500 g) pollock
- 1 lb (500 g) red snapper
- 1 lb (500 g) whiting
- 1 lb (500 g) dogfish
- 1 lb (500 g) rockfish
- 1 lb (500 g) sea bass
- 1 lb (500 g) tilefish
- 1 lb (500 g) weakfish

Half-and-Half

See CREAM, HALF-AND-HALF.

Halibut

This very large flatfish can weigh up to 1,000 pounds (500 kg) but typically ranges from 50 to 100 pounds (25 to 50 kg).

If You Don't Have It

- Substitute 1 lb (500 g) halibut with:
- 1 lb (500 g) cod
- 1 lb (500 g) turbot
- 1 lb (500 g) dogfish
- 1 lb (500 g) haddock
- 1 lb (500 g) turbot
- 1 lb (500 g) striped bass

Haloumi

A firm, salty sheep's milk cheese eaten widely in Cyprus, Egypt, and other Middle Eastern countries.

If You Don't Have It

Substitute 1 oz (30 g) haloumi with:
- 1 oz (30 g) feta
- ½ oz (15 g) feta + ½ oz (15 g) mozzarella

Ham

Ham may be a first-rate cured pork product, but it is also synonymous with a second-rate actor.

1 lb (500 g) boneless =
1½ to 3 cups
(375 to 750 mL) chopped
= 1 to 2 cups
(250 to 500 mL) ground

If You Don't Have It

Substitute 1 lb (500 g) ham with:
- 1 lb (500 g) Canadian bacon (usually leaner than ham)
- 1 lb (500 g) canned ham (moister; saltier than wet-cured or dry-cured ham; may be a whole boneless portion or pieces formed into a single shape)
- 1 lb (500 g) picnic ham or picnic shoulder (cured like ham; tougher and fattier)

See also HAM, DRY-CURED; HAM, WET-CURED.

Hamburger

See BEEF, GROUND.

Ham, Dry-Cured

Also known as country ham. Firmer texture and more complex flavor than wet-cured ham.

If You Don't Have It

Substitute 1 lb (500 g) dry-cured ham with:
- 1 lb (500 g) well-aged wet-cured ham (moister; generally milder, less complex flavor)

See also ARDENNES HAM; BAYONNE HAM; BLACK FOREST HAM; CULATELLO; IBERICO HAM; KENTUCKY HAM; PROSCIUTTO; SERRANO HAM; VIRGINIA HAM; WESTPHALIAN HAM; YORK HAM; YUNNAN HAM.

Ham Hock

The lower hind leg of a hog, usually cured, smoked, or both. Contributes hearty campfire flavor to beans, soups, and stews.

If You Don't Have It

Substitute 1 smoked ham hock with:
- 4 oz (125 g) chopped smoked ham
- 4 oz (125 g) cured, smoked hog jowl or guanciale
- 4 to 6 oz (125 to 175 g) smoked turkey drumsticks
- 4 oz (125 g) smoked sausage
- 4 oz (125 g) chopped smoked bacon
- 4 oz (125 g) pancetta (no smoke flavor)
- 2 to 4 oz (60 to 125 g) chopped salt pork (no smoke flavor; reduce salt in recipe if necessary)
- 1 ham bone (no smoke flavor)

Ham, Wet-Cured

Also known as brine-cured ham and city ham. Fully cooked hams sold bone-in, boneless, spiral-sliced, and as ham steak.

If You Don't Have It

Substitute 1 lb (500 g) wet-cured ham with:
- 1 lb (500 g) dry-cured ham (saltier; firmer; more complex flavor)
- 1 lb (500 g) picnic ham or picnic shoulder (cured like ham; tougher and fattier)

Hanakatsuo

See BONITO.

Handkäse

German for "hand cheese" because it's manually molded into irregular shapes. Made from sour milk, the pungent taste and aroma pleases some more than others.

If You Don't Have It

Substitute 1 oz (30 g) Handkäse with:
- 1 oz (30 g) Liederkranz
- 1 oz (30 g) Limburger

Hard-Shell Clam

See SWAPPING CLAMS (PAGE 596).

Hardtack

Also known as sea bread and ship biscuit. Flat, hard biscuit that helped to keep sailors alive on long sea voyages.

If You Don't Have It

Substitute 1 lb (500 g) hardtack with:

- 1 lb (500 g) zweiback

Hare

A well-liked game animal in Europe, this larger relative of the rabbit has never been domesticated. The dark, full-flavored meat is enjoyed in English civet, *French* daube, *German* hansenpfeffer, *and Italian* lepre in agrodolce.

If You Don't Have It

Substitute 1 lb (500 g) hare with:

- 1 lb (500 g) rabbit
- 1 lb (500 g) chicken

See also RABBIT.

Haricot Vert

See GREEN BEAN.

Harissa

A blistering red chile paste that ignites North African palates. One common brand features a picture of an erupting volcano on the can.

If You Don't Have It

Substitute 1 tbsp (15 mL) harissa with:

- 1 tbsp (15 mL) Homemade Harissa: Toast 1 tsp (5 mL) caraway seeds, 1 tsp (5 mL) coriander seeds and ½ tsp (2 mL) cumin seeds in a dry skillet over medium heat until fragrant, about 2 minutes. Grind to a powder in a spice grinder, blender, or with a mortar and pestle. If using a spice grinder, transfer to a blender or small food processor and add 2 chopped garlic cloves, 3 tbsp (45 mL) paprika, 1 tbsp (15 mL) vegetable oil and 1 to 1½ tsp (5 to 7 mL) cayenne pepper. Grind to a paste and add salt to taste. Makes about ⅓ cup (75 mL).
- 1 tbsp (15 mL) tabil (a similar spice paste from Tunisia)
- 1 tbsp (15 mL) chile paste
- 1 tbsp (15 mL) berbere
- 1 to 3 tsp (5 to 15 mL) hot sauce (less aromatic)

Harusame

See A SNAPSHOT OF ASIAN NOODLES (PAGE 588).

Havarti

Often referred to as the Danish version of Tilsit, this tangy cheese is named after the experimental farm on which it was developed.

If You Don't Have It

Substitute 1 oz (30 g) Havarti with:
- 1 oz (30 g) Tilsit
- 1 oz (30 g) Esrom
- 1 oz (30 g) Monterey Jack

Hazelnut

Also known as cobnut, filbert, nocciola, and noisette. To easily peel the dark, bitter skin from hazelnuts, scatter them on a baking sheet and bake in a 350°F (180°C) oven for 12 to 15 minutes, or until the skins begin to part from the nuts. Remove and rub the nuts, a few at a time, between the folds of a dish towel to completely loosen the skins.

1 lb (500 g) shelled =
3½ cups (875 mL) nuts =
4 cups (1 L) ground

If You Don't Have It

Substitute 1 cup (250 mL) shelled hazelnuts with:
- 2 to 4 tbsp (25 to 60 mL) hazelnut oil (for baking and cooking; will add nut flavor but not texture of whole nuts; reduce fat in recipe by 2 to 4 tbsp/25 to 60 mL)
- 1 cup (250 mL) beechnuts
- 1 cup (250 mL) cashews
- 1 cup (250 mL) macadamia nuts
- 1 cup (250 mL) almonds
- 1 cup (250 mL) walnuts

See also NUTS.

Hazelnut Butter

Sweetened paste of ground roasted hazelnuts, oil, and salt.

If You Don't Have It

Substitute 1 cup (250 mL) hazelnut butter with:
- 1 cup (250 mL) Homemade Hazelnut Butter: Put 2 cups (500 mL) roasted hazelnuts (skins removed) and ¼ tsp (1 mL) salt in a blender or food processor fitted with metal blade. Process, gradually adding 4 to 6 tbsp (60 to 90 mL) vegetable oil (and/or hazelnut oil), until the mixture forms a paste. Add sugar to taste. Makes 1½ cups (375 mL).
- 1 cup (250 mL) cashew butter, almond butter, or peanut butter
- 1 cup (250 mL) gianduja (chocolate-hazelnut paste)

See also HAZELNUT PASTE.

Hazelnut Liqueur

Also known as noisette. Frangelico is a widely known brand.

If You Don't Have It
Substitute 3 tbsp (45 mL) hazelnut liqueur with:
- ½ to ¾ tsp (2 to 4 mL) hazelnut extract (add 3 tbsp/45 mL water or other liquid if necessary to replace lost volume in recipe)
- ½ to ¾ tsp (2 to 4 mL) hazelnut extract and reduce liquid in recipe by a scant 3 tbsp (45 mL)

To Vary the Flavor
Substitute 3 tbsp (45 mL) hazelnut liqueur with:
- 3 tbsp (45 mL) almond liqueur, walnut liqueur, coffee liqueur, or chocolate liqueur

Hazelnut Oil

See SUBSTITUTING OILS (PAGE 598).

Hazelnut Paste

Also known as pasta nocciola. A sensuous filling for pastries and confections prepared with ground roasted hazelnuts, egg whites, confectioner's sugar, and hazelnut liqueur.

If You Don't Have It
Substitute 1 cup (250 mL) hazelnut paste with:
- 1 cup (250 mL) Homemade Hazelnut Paste: Grind 2 cups (500 mL) roasted hazelnuts in a food processor or blender until the texture of cornmeal. Add 2 large egg whites, 1 cup (250 mL) confectioner's (icing) sugar, and 1 tsp (5 mL) hazelnut liqueur and blend until smooth. Makes about 1½ cups (375 mL).
- 1 cup (250 mL) gianduja (chocolate-hazelnut paste)

Head Lettuce

See BUTTERHEAD LETTUCE; CRISPHEAD LETTUCE.

Hearts of Palm

This delicacy is the center portion of the stems of Florida's state tree, the cabbage palm. The hearts look like white asparagus and taste faintly of artichoke. Canned versions make a good substitute for fresh.

If You Don't Have It
Substitute 1 cup (250 mL) hearts of palm with:
- 1 cup (250 mL) canned or marinated artichoke hearts
- 1 cup (250 mL) cooked asparagus (for salads)

Heavy Cream

See CREAM, WHIPPING.

Herbal Salt Substitute

Commercial seasoning condiment, such as Mrs. Dash® Original Blend, for those who wish to reduce sodium intake. Proprietary mixtures can contain various spices, herbs, seeds, and dehydrated aromatic vegetables.

If You Don't Have It
Substitute 1 tsp (5 mL) herbal salt substitute with:
- 1 tsp (5 mL) Italian seasoning (salt-free)
- 1 tsp (5 mL) Spike® (a blend of 39 seasonings; salt-free)
- 1 tsp (5 mL) Beau Monde® Seasoning (adds salt)
- ½ tsp (2 mL) table salt

Herbes de Provence

Not quite like a trip to the Riviera, this seasoning blend does, however, evoke the warm, vibrant flavors of the South of France.

If You Don't Have It
Substitute 1 tsp (5 mL) herbes de Provence with:
- 1 tsp (5 mL) Homemade Herbes de Provence: Combine 2 tsp (10 mL) dried thyme, 2 tsp (10 mL) dried savory, 1 tsp (5 mL) dried marjoram, 1 tsp (5 mL) dried lavender, ½ tsp (2 mL) dried rosemary, ½ tsp (2 mL) fennel seeds, and 1 crushed bay leaf. Makes about 3 tablespoons (45 mL).

Herbs

From alexanders (a wild European herb that tastes like bitter celery) to za'atar (Arabic wild thyme) there flourishes a wide world of culinary seasonings derived from the aromatic leaves and stems of tender green plants.

If You Don't Have It
Substitute 1 tbsp (15 mL) chopped fresh herbs with:
- 1 tsp (5 mL) dried herbs
- ¼ to ½ tsp (1 to 2 mL) ground or powdered

See also SPECIFIC TYPES.

Herbsaint

See ANISE LIQUEUR.

Herring

This large family of mostly small fish has more than 100 varieties. American shad is a type of herring, as is the alewife.

If You Don't Have It
Substitute 1 lb (500 g) herring with:
- 1 lb (500 g) sardines (smaller)
- 1 lb (500 g) shad (larger)
- 1 lb (500 g) smelt
- 1 lb (500 g) mackerel

Herring (cont'd)

Herring is particularly beloved in northern and eastern Europe, where it is transformed by pickling, salting, and smoking into Bismarck herring, rollmops, kippered herring, schmaltz herring, and many other cured tidbits.

Herring Varieties

Choose 1 lb (500 g) cured herring from these varieties:
- 1 lb (500 g) red herring (brined and heavily smoked)
- 1 lb (500 g) kippers (split, salted, and lightly smoked)
- 1 lb (500 g) bloaters (split, salted, and lightly smoked; larger than kippers)
- 1 lb (500 g) Bismarck herring (unskinned double fillets marinated in spiced vinegar with onions)
- 1 lb (500 g) rollmops (unskinned double fillets wrapped around pickled cucumber or onion and marinated in spiced vinegar)
- 1 lb (500 g) pickled herring (cured and marinated in sauce of sour cream, mustard, or wine)

See also SHAD; SPRAT.

Herve

Cheese, similar to Limburger that is soft and pungent with a reddish-brown natural coating sometimes flavored with herbs.

If You Don't Have It

Substitute 1 oz (30 g) Herve with:
- 1 oz (30 g) Limburger
- 1 oz (30 g) Liederkranz

Hibachi

"Fire bowl" in Japanese, these compact portable grills are easy to use and versatile.

If You Don't Have It

Substitute a hibachi with:
- grill, especially a portable grill (usually larger and with a lid)
- broiler (heat comes from above instead of below; to add smoke flavor that would have been achieved by grilling over coals in a hibachi, add 1 to 2 drops liquid smoke to marinade or sauce; or include a smoked food such as chipotle chiles)
- ridged grill pan (gives good grill marks; can steam foods; to add smoke flavor that would have been achieved by grilling over coals in a hibachi, add 1 to 2 drops liquid smoke to marinade or sauce; or include a smoked food such as chipotle chiles)
- electric tabletop grill (gives good grill marks; can steam foods; best for sandwiches; to add smoke flavor that would have been achieved by grilling over coals in a hibachi, add 1 to 2 drops liquid smoke to marinade or sauce; or include a smoked food such as chipotle chiles)

Hickory Nut

This family of nuts includes the superb pecan. The common hickory nut is hard to find and tough to crack.

If You Don't Have It
Substitute 1 cup (250 mL) shelled hickory nuts with:
- 1 cup (250 mL) pecans
- 1 cup (250 mL) walnuts

See also PECAN.

Hierba Santa

See HOJA SANTA.

High-Altitude Baking and Cooking

See BAKING AT HIGH ALTITUDE (PAGE 612); COOKING AT HIGH ALTITUDE (PAGE 612).

Hijiki

Also known as hiziki. A Japanese seaweed that is sun-dried before and after boiling. Rich in minerals, it offers a salty, light anise taste. Food safety agencies in Canada, Britain, New Zealand and other countries have cautioned against excessive consumption of hijiki due to high levels of inorganic arsenic, a carcinogen. Other types of seaweed such as kelp (kombu), dulse, and nori do not contain inorganic arsenic and are safe to eat.

If You Don't Have It
Substitute 1 oz (30 g) hijiki with:
- 1 oz (30 g) arame (milder flavor; dark brown color)
- 1 oz (30 g) dulse (stronger flavor; maroon color)
- 1 oz (30 g) wakame (stronger flavor; dark green to brown color)
- 1 oz (30 g) kombu (stronger flavor; dark brown to black color)

Hog Jowl

Cured and smoked hog cheek is a country cooking legacy in the Southern U.S. Fattier than bacon, it's called upon to flavor beans, stews, greens, and other long-simmered dishes.

If You Don't Have It
Substitute 4 oz (125 g) cured, smoked hog jowl with:
- 4 oz (125 g) chopped smoked bacon
- 4 oz (125 g) chopped smoked ham
- 4 oz (125 g) guanciale (no smoke flavor)
- 4 oz (125 g) pancetta (no smoke flavor)
- 4 oz (125 g) prosciutto (no smoke flavor)
- 2 to 4 oz (60 to 125 g) salt pork (no smoke flavor; reduce salt in recipe if necessary)

See also GUANCIALE.

Hoisin Sauce

A dark and complex variety of sweet bean sauce made from fermented beans, salt, sugar, and garlic. This thick, rich paste often seasons sauces and marinades for roasted and barbecued meats.

If You Don't Have It
Substitute 1 tbsp (15 mL) hoisin sauce with:
- 1 tbsp (15 mL) Homemade Hoisin Sauce Substitute: Combine 1 cup (250 mL) minus 3 tbsp (45 mL) thick barbecue sauce (preferably without smoke flavor), 3 tbsp (45 mL) molasses, 4 tsp (20 mL) soy sauce, 4 tsp (20 mL) yeast extract and 2½ tsp (12 mL) Chinese five-spice powder. Makes about 1 cup (250 mL).
- 1 tbsp (15 mL) Chee hou sauce (spicier)
- 1 tbsp (15 mL) Chinese brown bean sauce (spicier)

Hoja Santa

Also known as hierba santa and yerba santa. The large leaves, which taste of anise or sassafras, flavor soups or wrap whole fish in Latin American preparations.

If You Don't Have It
Substitute ½ cup (125 mL) chopped hoja santa leaves (for sauces and stews) with:
- ½ cup (125 mL) chopped Mexican avocado leaves
- ½ cup (125 mL) chopped Mexican or French tarragon
- ½ cup (125 mL) chopped green fennel tops + ⅛ to ¼ tsp (0.5 to 1 mL) ground black pepper

If You Don't Have It
Substitute hoja santa leaves (as a food wrapper) with:
- corn husks (adds mild corn aroma)
- banana leaves (adds herby-green flavor)
- parchment paper (adds no flavor)
- aluminum foil (adds no flavor)

Hollandaise Sauce

In classic French service, hollandaise is set on the plate beside the food it accompanies, never ladled over it.

To Vary the Flavor
Substitute 1 cup (250 mL) hollandaise sauce with:
- 1 cup (250 mL) Bearnaise sauce (adds tarragon flavor)
- 1 cup (250 mL) choron sauce (adds tarragon and tomato flavors)

To Save Time
- 1 cup (250 mL) Homemade Quick Hollandaise Sauce: Put 3 egg yolks, juice of small lemon, ½ tsp (2 mL) salt, and a pinch of mustard powder into a blender or small food processor. Blend ingredients and drizzle in ½ cup (125 mL) melted butter until thickened. Makes about 1 cup (250 mL).

For Better Health

Substitute 1 cup (250 mL) hollandaise sauce with:

- 1 cup (250 mL) Homemade Avgolemono Sauce (fewer calories): Whisk together 3 egg yolks, juice of ½ small lemon, ½ tsp (2 mL) salt, and 1 tsp (5 mL) arrowroot powder or ¾ tsp (4 mL) cornstarch in a small saucepan. Put pan over medium heat. Gradually whisk in 1 cup (250 mL) chicken stock, stirring until thickened. Stir in 1 tbsp (15 mL) chopped fresh herbs if you like. Makes about 1 cup (250 mL).

Holy Basil

See BASIL.

Hom Ha

See SHRIMP SAUCE.

Hominy

A beloved staple of the American South, hominy is dried white or yellow corn kernels that are treated with an alkali, such as lye, to remove the hull. Hominy also features prominently in the hearty Mexican soup known as posole. It is available canned (ready to eat) or dried.

1 lb (500 g) whole = 2½ cups (625 mL)
1 cup (250 mL) whole = 6⅔ cups (1.65 L) cooked

If You Don't Have It

Substitute 1 cup (250 mL) dried or canned hominy with:

- 1 cup (250 mL) samp (broken hominy)
- 1 cup (250 mL) dried or canned beans (for soups and stews)

See also HOMINY GRITS.

Hominy Grits

Hominy that is ground fine, medium, or coarse. Cooked in milk or water until thick, the resulting mush is served hot, or chilled, then sliced and fried.

1 cup (250 mL) = 4½ cups (1.125 L) cooked

If You Don't Have It

Substitute 1 cup (250 mL) hominy grits with:

- 1 cup (250 mL) polenta meal (preferably stone-ground)

To Vary the Flavor

Substitute 1 cup (250 mL) hominy grits with:

- 1 cup (250 mL) barley grits
- 1 cup (250 mL) buckwheat grits

See also BARLEY GRITS; CORN GRITS; HOMINY.

Honey

To produce one pound (500 g) of honey, the bees must visit flowers about 2 million times to extract the nectar.

1 lb (500 g) =
1⅓ cups (325 mL)

If You Don't Have It

Substitute 1 cup (250 mL) honey with:
- 1¼ cups (300 mL) granulated sugar + ¼ cup (50 mL) liquid called for in recipe
- ½ cup (125 mL) granulated sugar + ¾ cup (175 mL) maple syrup, light or dark corn syrup, or light molasses

Honeydew Melon

Choose honeydew that feel heavy in relation to size. Perfectly ripe specimens will subtly wrinkle on the surface of the rind.

1 medium = 3 lbs
(1.5 kg) = 4 to 5 cups
(1 to 1.25 L) cubed

If You Don't Have It

Substitute 1 cup (250 mL) chopped honeydew melon with:
- 1 cup (250 mL) chopped Ogen melon
- 1 cup (250 mL) chopped Galia melon
- 1 cup (250 mL) chopped Santa Claus melon
- 1 cup (250 mL) chopped cantaloupe
- 1 cup (250 mL) chopped Persian melon

Hon-Shimeji

See SHUFFLING MUSHROOMS (PAGE 572).

Hoop Cheese

An almost archaic cheese that is very similar to farmer cheese. In the 1800s, special cutting devices were manufactured to cut precise portions of hoop cheese.

If You Don't Have It

Substitute 1 oz (30 g) hoop cheese with:
- 1 oz (30 g) farmer cheese or pot cheese
- 1 oz (30 g) dry-curd cottage cheese
- 1 oz (30 g) ricotta cheese, drained in cheesecloth (may add more liquid)

Horned Melon

See KIWANO.

Horseradish

An ancient herb that is cultivated mostly for its white pungent roots. The roots can be purchased fresh or grated, processed, and jarred as a condiment.

If You Don't Have It

Substitute 1 tbsp (15 mL) grated fresh horseradish with:
- 1 tbsp (15 mL) prepared white horseradish (less pungent; adds vinegar flavor, reduce vinegar in recipe 1½ tsp/7 mL if necessary)

1 tbsp (15 mL) bottled = 2 tsp (10 mL) freshly grated

- 1 tbsp (15 mL) prepared red horseradish (red color from beet juice; adds vinegar flavor, reduce vinegar in recipe 1½ tsp/7 mL if necessary)
- 1 to 3 tbsp (15 to 45 mL) creamed horseradish (adds sour cream or mayonnaise flavors)
- 1 to 3 tbsp (15 to 45 mL) grated fresh wasabi
- 1 to 3 tbsp (15 to 45 mL) peeled and grated fresh black radish

Hot Chocolate Mix

See COCOA MIX.

Hot Dog

See FRANKFURTER.

Hot Pepper Sauce

At its most basic, the procedure for making hot sauce goes something like this: Hot chiles are chopped or crushed, mixed with salt, and allowed to ferment, often for years. The mash is blended with vinegar and allowed to age again before straining and bottling. The type of chile, the type of aging barrel, and whether solids are retained in the final mix are just three of the variables that affect the characteristics of the final sauce.

If You Don't Have It
Substitute a dash of hot pepper sauce with:
- 1 to 3 tsp (5 to 15 mL) chile paste
- ¼ to ½ tsp (1 to 2 mL) ground cayenne pepper
- ¾ tsp (4 mL) crushed red pepper flakes
- ½ tsp (2 mL) ground chipotle powder (much smokier)
- ½ tsp (2 mL) ground ancho powder (darker; milder)
- ½ tsp (2 mL) paprika (much milder)
- ½ tsp (2 mL) chili powder (milder; adds flavors of cumin, oregano, and other spices)
- 1 very small whole dried red chile

See also CHOOSING DRIED CHILES (PAGE 578); CHOOSING FRESH CHILES (PAGE 582).

Hubbard Squash

A large winter squash with a lumpy dark green or orange shell and slightly grainy, orange flesh. It can be stored whole, unwrapped, at 50°F (10°C) or cooler, for as long as six months.

If You Don't Have It
Substitute 1 lb (500 g) hubbard squash with:
- 1 lb (500 g) Jarrahdale
- 1 lb (500 g) Queensland Blue
- 1 lb (500 g) pumpkin
- 1 lb (500 g) butternut squash
- 1 lb (500 g) buttercup squash

Huckleberry

A wild berry that's often mistaken for the blueberry. But upon closer inspection, the huckleberry has thicker skin, is more tart, and has 10 small, hard seeds in the center.

If You Don't Have It

Substitute 1 cup (250 mL) huckleberries with:
- 1 cup (250 mL) blueberries (sweeter)
- 1 cup (250 mL) bilberries (more tart)
- 1 cup (250 mL) juneberries (apple-like flavor)
- 1 cup (250 mL) red currants (red color; more tart)

Hungarian Pepper

See PAPRIKA.

Husk Tomato

See CAPE GOOSEBERRY; TOMATILLO.

Hyssop

Originating in the eastern Mediterranean, the leaves of this aromatic plant have been used since pre-Christian times. Reminiscent of mint, the leaves are reputed to aid in digesting fat. Used to season a wide variety of dishes including fruits, salads, sausages, and meats.

If You Don't Have It

Substitute 1 tbsp (15 mL) chopped fresh hyssop with:
- 1½ tsp (7 mL) chopped fresh sage + 1½ tsp (7 mL) chopped fresh mint

Ibarra to Izarra

Ibarra

See CHOCOLATE, MEXICAN.

Iberico Ham

Also known as jamón iberico. An artisanal ham that is salted and naturally dried and aged. Produced from the Iberian pig that is native to southwestern Spain.

If You Don't Have It

Substitute 1 oz (30 g) Iberico ham with:
- 1 oz (30 g) serrano ham
- 1 oz (30 g) prosciutto (di Parma or di San Daniele)
- 1 oz (30 g) Ardennes ham (adds smoked flavor)
- 1 oz (30 g) Bayonne ham (adds smoked flavor)

Iceberg Lettuce

See CRISPHEAD LETTUCE.

Ice Cream

This frozen dairy treat has universal appeal — from the intensely flavored gelato of Italy to the lighter kulfi of India to the helado of the Philippines flavored with corn or purple yams.

If You Don't Have It

Substitute 1 cup (250 mL) ice cream with:
- 1 cup (250 mL) soy ice cream
- 1 cup (250 mL) frozen yogurt

For Better Health

Substitute 1 cup (250 mL) ice cream with:
- 1 cup (250 mL) reduced-fat ice cream or frozen yogurt (less fat and fewer calories)

Icing Sugar

See SUGAR, CONFECTIONER'S.

Immersion Blender

See BLENDER.

Indian Date

See TAMARIND CONCENTRATE.

Indian Flatbread

See CHAPATI.

Irish Bacon

See CANADIAN BACON.

Irish Cream Liqueur

A category of commercial liqueurs that blend Irish whiskey, cream, spices, and sweeteners.

If You Don't Have It
Substitute 3 tbsp (45 mL) Irish cream liqueur with:
- 3 tbsp (45 mL) advocaat
- 3 tbsp (45 mL) nonalcoholic eggnog + ⅛ to ¼ tsp (0.5 to 1 mL) brandy

Irish Mist

A liqueur that kisses Irish whiskey with a touch of heather honey.

If You Don't Have It
Substitute 3 tbsp (45 mL) Irish Mist with:
- 3 tbsp (45 mL) Drambuie
- 3 tbsp (45 mL) Grandtully
- 3 tbsp (45 mL) Glayva
- 3 tbsp (45 mL) Lochan Ora

Irish Whiskey

See WHISKEY.

Italian Bread

"In a country where the family is the primary source of physical and emotional sustenance, bread celebrates the richest and simplest pleasure of daily living," writes Carol Field in The Italian Baker. *"It is the single inevitable presence at the table during all three meals of the day, for no Italian would contemplate a meal without bread."*

If You Don't Have It
Substitute 1 lb (500 g) Italian bread with:
- 1 lb (500 g) French bread (usually longer and narrower than Italian bread)

Italian Bread Types
Choose 1 lb (500 g) Italian bread from these types:
- 1 lb (500 g) ciabatta (chewy crust; crumb has large holes)
- 1 lb (500 g) Pugliese (thin chewy-crunchy crust; pillowy crumb)

Italian Herb Seasoning

A packaged herbal blend with a pan-Italian flavor profile.

If You Don't Have It
Substitute 2 tsp (10 mL) Italian herb seasoning with:
- 1 tsp (5 mL) dried oregano + ½ tsp (2 mL) dried basil + ½ tsp (2 mL) dried thyme

Italian Parsley

See PARSLEY.

Italian Sausage

Spiced ground pork mixture piped into casings, generally composed of 60% lean meat and 40% fat. Seasoned with salt, garlic, and fennel seeds. Peperoncini (hot chiles) are added to produce a hot version.

If You Don't Have It
Substitute 1 lb (500 g) Italian sausage with:
- 1 lb (500 g) pork sausage (sweet or hot)

Izarra

An Armagnac-based herbal liqueur that comes in mild yellow and stronger green colors.

If You Don't Have It
Substitute 3 tbsp (45 mL) Izarra with:
- 3 tbsp (45 mL) Chartreuse
- 3 tbsp (45 mL) Strega
- 3 tbsp (45 mL) Bénédictine

Izarra Varieties
Choose 3 tbsp (45 mL) Izarra from these varieties:
- 3 tbsp (45 mL) green Izarra (green color; more bracing flavor and heavier body than yellow Chartreuse)
- 3 tbsp (45 mL) yellow Izarra (pale golden color; sweeter flavor and lighter body than green Chartreuse)

Jack to **Juniper Berry**

Jack

See BUTTERFISH; POMPANO.

Jack cheese

Also known as California Jack, Monterey Jack, and Sonoma Jack. Delightful buttery semisoft cheese named for David Jacks, a 19th century California cheesemaker. Both unaged and aged (dry) are produced.

> 1 lb (500 g) = 4 cups
> (1 L) grated or shredded

If You Don't Have It
Substitute 1 oz (30 g) Jack cheese with:
- 1 oz (30 g) Muenster
- 1 oz (30 g) Gouda
- 1 oz (30 g) Havarti
- 1 oz (30 g) Samsoe
- 1 oz (30 g) Tybo
- 1 oz (30 g) Teleme (softer)

Jack Cheese Varieties
Choose 1 oz (30 g) Jack cheese from these varieties:
- 1 oz (30 g) Monterey or Sonoma Jack (soft, white and mild with an acidic tanginess; tiny flattened holes throughout)
- 1 oz (30 g) Wisconsin Jack (slightly firmer and with fewer or no holes as in Monterey Jack)
- 1 oz (30 g) Pepper Jack or Jalapeño Jack (Monterey Jack with chopped jalapeño peppers)
- 1 oz (30 g) aged or dry Jack (Monterey Jack aged for 7 to 10 months; hard, sharp, and excellent for grating)

Jackfruit

Also known as jak. Related to the breadfruit, southeast Asian specimens can grow up to 90 pounds (45 kg), making it the largest tree-borne fruit. The unripe flesh is cooked as a starchy vegetable, dried, or pickled. The ripe fruit smells terrible but tastes wonderful — like pineapple and banana. The prolific seeds can be candied or dried and ground for flour.

If You Don't Have It

Substitute 1 cup (250 mL) chopped jackfruit with:

- 1 cup (250 mL) chopped breadfruit (smaller)
- 1 cup (250 mL) green or yellow plantains (to replace green jackfruit)
- 1 cup (250 mL) potatoes (to replace green jackfruit)
- 1 cup (250 mL) winter melon (to replace green jackfruit)
- 1 cup (250 mL) fuzzy gourd (to replace green jackfruit)
- 1 cup (250 mL) summer squash (to replace green jackfruit)
- 1 cup (250 mL) canned jackfruit (to replace fresh ripe jackfruit)
- 1 cup (250 mL) papaya (to replace ripe jackfruit)

See also BREADFRUIT.

Jägermeister

Forceful, bitter German liqueur — concocted from a combination of 56 herbs, spices, barks, resins, and seeds — lives up to its name of "hunt master."

If You Don't Have It

Substitute 3 tbsp (45 mL) Jägermeister with:

- 3 tbsp (45 mL) Bénédictine
- 3 tbsp (45 mL) green Chartreuse
- 3 tbsp (45 mL) Fernet Branca

Jaggery

Also known as gur (when made from palm tree sap) and palm sugar. Dark coarse sugar extract from palm trees or sugarcane juice that is favored in India. The soft type is spreadable, while the solid cake is crushed to use as a topping or a confectionery ingredient.

If You Don't Have It

Substitute 1 cup (250 mL) jaggery with:

- 1 cup (250 mL) piloncillo
- 1 cup (250 mL) dark brown sugar + 2 tsp (10 mL) molasses
- 1 cup (250 mL) light brown sugar + 5 tsp (25 mL) molasses
- 1 cup (250 mL) granulated sugar + 4 to 5 tbsp (60 to 75 mL) molasses
- 1 cup (250 mL) palm sugar

Jalapeño Pepper

See CHOOSING DRIED CHILES (PAGE 578); CHOOSING FRESH CHILES (PAGE 582).

Jam

U.S. Department of Agriculture regulations stipulate that these chunky conserves must contain at least 45% fruit.

If You Don't Have It

Substitute 1 cup (250 mL) jam with:
- 1 cup (250 mL) preserves (larger chunks)
- 1 cup (250 mL) jelly (thinner consistency)

Jamaican Jerk

Also known as Jamaican jerk seasoning. Traditionally a seasoning paste slathered on grilled chicken, pork, and other meats. Now also sold as a dry seasoning typically combining hot chiles with allspice, cinnamon, cloves, garlic, ginger, onion, and thyme.

If You Don't have It

Substitute 1 tbsp (15 mL) dry Jamaican jerk seasoning with:
- 1 tbsp (15 mL) Homemade Jamaican Jerk Dry Rub: Combine 1 tbsp (15 mL) dried thyme, 1 tbsp (15 mL) dark brown sugar, 2 tsp (10 mL) ground allspice, 1 tsp (5 mL) ground cinnamon, 1 tsp (5 mL) ground nutmeg, 1 tsp (5 mL) ground coriander, 1 tsp (5 mL) ground black pepper, 1 tsp (5 mL) salt, ½ tsp (2 mL) onion powder, ½ tsp (2 mL) garlic powder, ½ to 1 tsp (2 to 5 mL) cayenne pepper, and ¼ tsp (1 mL) ground ginger. To make a marinade, add ¼ cup (50 mL) vegetable oil, 3 tbsp (45 mL) soy sauce, 3 tbsp (45 mL) lime juice, and 1 tbsp (15 mL) dark rum. Makes about ⅓ cup (75 mL) dry rub.

Japanese Cucumber

See CUCUMBER.

Japanese Eggplant

See EGGPLANT.

Japanese Horseradish

See WASABI.

Japanese Plum

See LOQUAT.

Japanese Sweet Rice Wine

See MIRIN.

Japanese Vermicelli

See A SNAPSHOT OF ASIAN NOODLES (PAGE 588).

Jarlsberg

The Norwegian version of Swiss-style cheese is a fine all-purpose cheese for melting and snacking.

If You Don't Have It

Substitute 1 oz (30 g) Jarlsberg with:

- 1 oz (30 g) Emmental
- 1 oz (30 g) Gruyère
- 1 oz (30 g) Swiss
- 1 oz (30 g) French Comté

Jasmine Rice

See VARIETIES OF RICE (PAGE 591).

Jelly

A conserve made from fruit juice, sugar, and often pectin for gelling. Delicious spread on morning toast and to top cakes, cookies, or doughnuts.

If You Don't Have It

Substitute 1 cup (250 mL) jelly with:

- 1 cup (250 mL) jam (thicker)
- 1 cup (250 mL) preserves (larger chunks)

Jelly Melon

See KIWANO.

Jelly Roll Pan

See PAN SIZE EQUIVALENTS (PAGE 606).

Jerky

Native Americans educated the European colonists on how to preserve meat by drying strips in the sun or at a fire. The name is derived from a Spanish adaptation of the native Peruvian word charqui *for dried meat. The most common variety is beef.*

If You Don't Have It

Substitute 1 oz (30 g) beef jerky with:

- 1 oz (30 g) biltong (spicier; more complex flavor)
- 1 oz (30 g) pemmican (more complex flavor)

For Better Health

Substitute 1 oz (30 g) beef jerky with:

- 1 oz (30 g) turkey jerky (leaner)
- 1 oz (30 g) vegetarian jerky (leaner)

See also BILTONG; PEMMICAN.

Jerusalem Artichoke

See SUNCHOKE.

Jewfish

See GOLIATH GROUPER.

Jicama

A crisp, sweet and juicy tuber with white flesh akin to water chestnut. It can be eaten raw or cooked.

1 lb (500 g) = 4 cups
(1 L) shredded

If You Don't Have It

Substitute 1 cup (250 mL) chopped jicama with:
- 1 cup (250 mL) chopped water chestnuts
- 1 cup (250 mL) chopped sunchokes
- 1 cup (250 mL) chopped Asian radishes such as daikon (add a pinch of sugar to balance the peppery flavor if you like)
- 1 cup (250 mL) chopped turnips

John Dory

Also known as Saint-Pierre. A long, slender body enables this fish to sneak up on prey and snatch them with a huge retractable jaw.

If You Don't Have It

Substitute 1 lb (500 g) John Dory with:
- 1 lb (500 g) porgy
- 1 lb (500 g) grouper
- 1 lb (500 g) monkfish
- 1 lb (500 g) halibut

Johnny Jump-Up

See PICKING EDIBLE FLOWERS (PAGE 604).

Jujube

See CHINESE DATE, FRESH.

Juneberry

Also known as Saskatoon, shadberry, and western serviceberry. Dark purple mild-flavored berry with a bloom on the skin; similar to blueberry. Foraged for centuries by Native Americans in northern U.S. states and Canada. Now mostly cultivated in home gardens.

If You Don't Have It

Substitute 1 cup (250 mL) juneberries with:
- 1 cup (250 mL) blueberries
- 1 cup (250 mL) huckleberries

Juniper Berry

The aromatic berry of a coniferous shrub is usually dried before use as an herb to flavor meats, game, pâtés, sauerkraut, and, most famously, gin.

If You Don't Have It

Substitute 6 juniper berries with:
- 1 tbsp (15 mL) gin (for marinades and sauces; adds alcohol)

Kabocha Squash to **Kumquat**

Kabocha Squash

The generic term for winter squash in Japan, kabocha is the North American marketing term for a variety of cultivars that range from rough-skinned/drum shaped to smoother/globe shaped. These different squash have in common a honey-sweet flesh that's almost as smooth as custard.

> 1 lb (500 g) =
> 1 cup (250 mL)
> cooked and mashed

If You Don't Have It

Substitute 1 cup (250 mL) chopped kabocha squash with:

- 1 cup (250 mL) chopped buttercup squash
- 1 cup (250 mL) chopped butternut squash
- 1 cup (250 mL) chopped Baby Blue Hubbard squash
- 1 cup (250 mL) chopped calabaza
- 1 cup (250 mL) chopped acorn squash
- 1 cup (250 mL) chopped sweet dumpling squash

Kaffir Lime

See MAKRUT LIME.

Kahlúa

See COFFEE LIQUEUR.

Kalamansi

See CALAMONDIN.

Kalamata Olive

See CHOOSING AMONG OLIVES (PAGE 570).

Kale

Members of the cabbage family that grow in loose bunches of leaves rather than heads. Types include curly kale, Russian red kale, and Tuscan black kale. Sweetest if harvested after the frost, these deep green leaves are nutritional superstars bursting with nutrients and phytochemicals. Kale is an excellent source of calcium, folic acid, vitamin C, and potassium.

> 1 lb (500 g) =
> 1½ to 2 cups
> (375 to 500 mL) cooked

If You Don't Have It
Substitute 1 lb (500 g) kale with:
- 1 lb (500 g) collard greens
- 1 lb (500 g) callaloo
- 1 lb (500 g) Chinese kale
- 1 lb (500 g) green chard
- 1 lb (500 g) turnip greens
- 1 lb (500 g) mustard greens
- 1 lb (500 g) spinach

Kale Varieties
Choose 1 lb (500 g) kale from these varieties:
- 1 lb (500 g) curly kale (green to light blue green leaves; mildly sweet flavor; resilient texture)
- 1 lb (500 g) Tuscan kale (dark green to dark purple black leaves that are curled under and have a nubbly surface; deep, complex, mildly sweet flavor; softer texture than curly kale)
- 1 lb (500 g) flowering or ornamental kale (pretty, frilly, light green leaves with cream-color or pinkish purple stems; firm texture; used mostly as a garnish; leaves can be steamed or simmered in salted water.
- 1 lb (500 g) Russian Red kale (light green, oak-leaf-shaped leaves with cream-color to magenta stems; firm texture; deep, mildly sweet flavor)

Kamut© Flour

See CHOOSING AMONG WHOLE-GRAIN AND ALTERNATIVE FLOURS (PAGE 586).

Kangaroo

A staple food of Aboriginal Australians, European colonists took to the kangaroo as game. After a downturn in interest for much of the 20th century, the meat is enjoying a resurgence on tables down under.

If You Don't Have It
Substitute 1 lb (500 g) kangaroo with:
- 1 lb (500 g) antelope
- 1 lb (500 g) gazelle
- 1 lb (500 g) deer
- 1 lb (500 g) elk
- 1 lb (500 g) caribou
- 1 lb (500 g) moose
- 1 lb (500 g) reindeer

Kanten

See AGAR.

Kapi

See SHRIMP PASTE.

Kasha

See BUCKWHEAT GROATS.

Kashkaval

Sheep's milk cheese of Bulgarian origin is a pasta filata type, meaning the curds are stretched into strands before they are molded.

1 lb (500 g) = 4 cups (1 L) shredded

If You Don't Have It

Substitute 1 oz (30 g) young Kashkaval with:
- 1 oz (30 g) Caciocavallo
- 1 oz (30 g) Scamorza
- 1 oz (30 g) provolone

If You Don't Have It

Substitute 1 oz (30 g) aged Kashkaval with:
- 1 oz (30 g) Kefalotyri
- 1 oz (30 g) Pecorino Romano
- 1 oz (30 g) Parmesan
- 1 oz (30 g) Asiago

Kasseri

Greek semihard cheese made from sheep's milk sometimes combined with goat's milk. Salty and pungent with an underlying sweetness.

1 lb (500 g) = 4 cups (1 L) grated or shredded

If You Don't Have It

Substitute 1 oz (30 g) Kasseri with:
- 1 oz (30 g) Kefalotyri
- 1 oz (30 g) Pecorino Romano
- 1 oz (30 g) Parmesan
- 1 oz (30 g) Asiago

See also KEFALOTYRI.

Katsuobushi

See BONITO.

Kaymak

Also known as kaimaki. Middle Eastern clotted cream traditionally prepared from goat's milk or water buffalo milk.

8 oz (250 g) = 1 cup (250 mL)

If You Don't Have It

Substitute 1 cup (250 mL) kaymak with:
- 1 cup (250 mL) clotted cream
- 1 cup (250 mL) crème fraîche

See also CREAM, CLOTTED.

Kecap

Also known as ketjap manis. A dark, syrupy Indonesian condiment made from soybeans. It is sweeter, thicker, and more complexly flavored than soy sauce. Pronounced "ketchap," the word passed into English usage as ketchup, the name for an entirely difference sauce.

If You Don't Have It

Substitute 1 cup (250 mL) kecap with:
- 1 cup (250 mL) Homemade Kecap: Combine ¾ cup (175 mL) tamari or soy sauce, ⅓ cup (75 mL) brown sugar, 3 tbsp (45 mL) molasses, ¼ tsp (1 mL) crushed garlic, and ⅛ tsp (0.5 mL) ground star anise or 1 whole star anise in a saucepan over medium-low heat. Stir until smooth and heated through; if using whole star anise, remove before using. Makes 1⅓ cup (325 mL).
- 1 cup (250 mL) minus 3 tbsp (45 mL) Maggi seasoning + 3 tbsp (45 mL) molasses

Kefalotyri

Made from sheep's milk, sometimes mixed with goat's milk, younger kefalotyri is served as table cheese and in the fried appetizer saganaki. Aged longer, it is an excellent grating cheese.

> 1 lb (500 g) = 4 cups
> (1 L) grated or shredded

If You Don't Have It

Substitute 1 oz (30 g) Kefalotyri with:
- 1 oz (30 g) Pecorino Romano
- 1 oz (30 g) Parmesan
- 1 oz (30 g) Grana Padano
- 1 oz (30 g) Asiago

See also KASSERI.

Kefir

A cultured milk beverage that originated in the Caucasus Mountains.

> 8 oz (250 g) =
> 1 cup (250 mL)

If You Don't Have It

Substitute 1 cup (250 mL) kefir with:
- ¾ cup (175 mL) yogurt + 4 to 5 tbsp (60 to 75 mL) milk
- 1 cup (250 mL) kumiss

See also KEFIR CHEESE; KUMISS.

Kefir Cheese

Soft white cheese made by draining the kefir curds from the whey.

If You Don't Have It

Substitute 1 cup (250 mL) kefir cheese with:
- 1 cup (250 mL) yogurt cheese
- 1 cup (250 mL) cream cheese

See also KEFIR.

Kelp

See KOMBU.

Kentucky Ham

A dry-cured country ham smoked with hickory and apple wood.

> 1 lb (500 g) boneless =
> 1½ to 3 cups
> (375 to 750 mL)
> chopped = 2 cups
> (500 mL) ground

If You Don't Have It

Substitute 1 lb (500 g) Kentucky Ham with:
- 1 lb (500 g) Virginia ham, especially Smithfield ham
- 1 lb (500 g) York ham
- 1 lb (500 g) Yunnan ham

Ketchup

Also known as catsup and catchup. Sweet tomato ketchup is the sole survivor of a broad category of thin salty sauces with a long shelf life. Ketchups of yore included those made from mushrooms, oysters, mussels, and walnuts.

If You Don't Have It

Substitute 1 cup (250 mL) ketchup with:
- 1 cup (250 mL) tomato sauce + ¼ cup (50 mL) granulated sugar + 3 tbsp (45 mL) apple cider vinegar + ½ tsp (2 mL) salt + pinch of ground cloves
- 1 cup (250 mL) chili sauce (adds chopped pickles)
- 1 cup (250 mL) barbecue sauce (darker; more complex flavor)

Kewra

See SCREWPINE LEAF.

Key Lime

See LIME.

Kidney Bean

See THE WIDE WORLD OF DRIED BEANS (PAGE 566).

Kielbasa

Also known as kielbasy and Polish sausage. Fresh or smoked robust garlicky sausage commonly made of pork.

If You Don't Have It

Substitute 1 lb (500 g) kielbasa with:
- 1 lb (500 g) Kolbasz
- 1 lb (500 g) Cajun andouille (spicier)
- 1 lb (500 g) Spanish chorizo
- 1 lb (500 g) linguiça

Kingfish

See CROAKER.

King Mackerel

See MACKEREL.

King Salmon

See SALMON.

Kippered Herring

See HERRING.

Kirby Cucumber

See CUCUMBER.

Kirsch

Also known as Kirschwasser. Clear German brandy named "cherry water" is at home in recipes for fondue, cherries jubilee, and cherry tart.

If You Don't Have It

Substitute 3 tbsp (45 mL) Kirsch with:
- 1 to 1½ tsp (5 to 7 mL) cherry extract + 3 tbsp (45 mL) brandy
- 3 tbsp (45 mL) cherry liqueur (sweeter)
- 3 tbsp (45 mL) cherry syrup (sweeter; nonalcoholic)
- 3 tbsp (45 mL) Maraschino liqueur
- 3 tbsp (45 mL) cherry vodka

To Vary the Flavor

Substitute 3 tbsp (45 mL) Kirsch with:
- 3 tbsp (45 mL) framboise (raspberry flavor)
- 3 tbsp (45 mL) plum brandy (plum flavor)

Kitchen Bouquet

See GRAVY BROWNING.

Kitchen Shears

See POULTRY SHEARS.

Kiwano

Also known as African horned cucumber, horned melon, and jelly melon. More of a curiosity than a cause for gustatory celebration, the flesh of this spiked fruit tastes like the odd offspring of cucumber and banana.

If You Don't Have It

Substitute 1 cup (250 mL) kiwano flesh with:
- 1 cup (250 mL) cucumber flesh, gel, and seeds, especially Armenian cucumber or snake melon + dash of lime juice (paler green color)

Kiwifruit

Also known as Chinese gooseberry. Kiwifruit has ten times the vitamin C of lemons.

2 whole fruit = ¾ cup (175 mL) chopped or sliced

If You Don't Have It

Substitute 1 cup (250 mL) peeled kiwifruit with:
- ½ cup (125 mL) strawberries + ½ cup (125 mL) gooseberries (especially when kiwifruit will be puréed)
- 1 cup (250 mL) pitaya

Knackwurst

Also known as knoblauch and knockwurst. Garlicky smoked beef sausages that look much like hot dogs. Often grilled or served with sauerkraut.

If You Don't Have It

Substitute 1 lb (500 g) Knackwurst with:
- 1 lb (500 g) frankfurters
- 1 lb (500 g) Bockwurst (made with veal)
- 1 lb (500 g) kielbasa (larger)
- 1 lb (500 g) Bratwurst

Knafa

See PHYLLO.

Knob Celery

See CELERIAC.

Kobe Beef

See BEEF.

Kochu Chang

See CHILE PASTE.

Kohlrabi

Also known as cabbage turnip. A type of common cabbage in which the base of the stem grows above ground into a globe from which other skinny, leaf-topped stems emerge. Delicious and crisp served raw. Sweet and satisfying when cooked.

4 medium bulbs = 2 lbs (1 kg) = 3½ cups (875 mL) cubed and cooked

If You Don't Have It

Substitute 1 lb (500 g) kohlrabi bulb with:
- 1 lb (500 g) turnip (more bitter)
- 1 lb (500 g) broccoli stems
- 1 lb (500 g) celeriac

See also KOHLRABI GREENS.

Kohlrabi Greens

The leaves of the kohlrabi bulb taste like collards and can be cooked like them.

> 1 lb (500 g) =
> 1½ to 2 cups
> (375 to 500 mL) cooked

If You Don't Have It

Substitute 1 lb (500 g) kohlrabi greens with:
- 1 lb (500 g) turnip greens
- 1 lb (500 g) collards
- 1 lb (500 g) green chard
- 1 lb (500 g) mature spinach
- 1 lb (500 g) bok choy
- 1 lb (500 g) mustard greens
- 1 lb (500 g) kale

See also KOHLRABI.

Kolbasz

See KIELBASA.

Kombu

Also known as kelp and konbu. A large, diverse, and significant group of Japanese brown seaweeds harvested primarily off the shores of Hokkaido. It is preserved by sun drying. Essential in many dishes, including dashi (soup stock).

If You Don't Have It

Substitute 1 oz (30 g) kombu with:
- 1 oz (30 g) hijiki (stronger brine flavor; black color)
- 1 oz (30 g) wakame (milder brine flavor; dark green to brown color)
- 1 oz (30 g) dulse (milder brine flavor; maroon color)
- ½ tsp (2 mL) salt

Kosher Salt

See SALT.

Koumiss

See KUMISS.

Kudzu Powder

Also known as gok fun (China) and ko fen (Japan). A starch used for thickening. Extract from the roots of kudzu, an Asian forage crop that has become an aggressive weed in the American South. Use 1½ tbsp (22 mL) to thicken 1 cup (250 mL) liquid.

If You Don't Have It

Substitute 1½ tbsp (22 mL) kudzu powder (for thickening) with:
- 2 tsp (10 mL) arrowroot powder
- 1½ tsp (7 mL) cornstarch, potato starch, or rice starch
- 1 tbsp (15 mL) quick-cooking tapioca
- 1 heaping tbsp (15 mL) all-purpose flour
- 1 tsp (5 mL) instant mashed potato flakes

Kugelhopf

Also known as gugelhupf. A decoratively swirled, ring-shaped yeast cake renowned in Central Europe from Eastern France to Austria.

If You Don't Have It
Substitute 1 lb (500 g) kugelhopf with:
- 1 lb (500 g) panettone (Italian sweet yeast bread; tall, cylindrical shape)
- 1 lb (500 g) kulich (Russian sweet yeast bread; usually has icing; tall, cylindrical shape)
- 1 lb (500 g) brioche (French yeast bread; richer; less sweet or not sweet;)

Kulich

A light yeast bread that's prepared to celebrate Russian Easter. The dough is flavored with candied fruit, raisins, and saffron, then baked in a tall cylindrical loaf. It is iced and garnished with almonds and more candied fruit.

If You Don't Have It
Substitute 1 lb (500 g) kulich with:
- 1 lb (500 g) panettone (Italian sweet yeast bread)
- 1 lb (500 g) Kugelhopf (central European sweet yeast bread; tall, ring shape)
- 1 lb (500 g) brioche (French yeast bread; richer; less sweet or not sweet)

Kuminost

See NÖKKELOST.

Kumiss

Also known as koumiss. Of Mongol origin, a slightly alcoholic beverage traditionally fermented from camel's or mare's milk. Cow's milk is now used to make kumiss.

> 8 oz (250 g) =
> 1 cup (250 mL)

If You Don't Have It
Substitute 1 cup (250 mL) kumiss with:
- 1 cup (250 mL) kefir
- ¾ cup (175 mL) yogurt + 4 to 5 tbsp (60 to 75 mL) milk

See also KEFIR.

Kümmel

The name refers to the cumin seeds — among a list of other herbs — that flavor this clear liqueur of Dutch lineage.

If You Don't Have It

Substitute 3 tbsp (45 mL) Kümmel with:

- 3 tbsp (45 mL) aquavit
- 3 tbsp (45 mL) vodka + pinch of caraway seeds + small pinch of cumin seeds + small pinch of fennel seeds, soaked at room temperature for at least 1 month
- 3 tbsp (45 mL) Goldwasser (includes gold flakes)
- 3 tbsp (45 mL) Silverwasser (includes silver flakes)
- 3 tbsp (45 mL) Liqueur d'Or
- 3 tbsp (45 mL) Strega

Kumquat

Although they look like Lilliputian oranges, kumquats are categorized in the Fortunella *genus, not Citrus. Both the sweet skin and tart flesh are completely edible, served raw occasionally in salads but most often candied or preserved in marmalade.*

> 1 lb (500 g) = 1 to 1½ cups (250 to 375 mL) chopped

If You Don't Have It

Substitute 2 to 3 kumquats with:

- 1 calamondin (hybrid of mandarin orange and kumquat; for flesh or zest)
- ¼ mandarin orange + ½ tsp (2 mL) lemon (for flesh or zest)
- 2 to 3 limequats (hybrid of lime and kumquat; for flesh or zest)
- 2 to 3 lemonquats (hybrid of lemon and kumquat; for flesh or zest)

Ladyfingers to Lychee

Ladyfingers

Also known as biscotti di Savoia, savoiardi (both Italian) and sponge fingers. Strips of sponge cake used in the preparation of charlottes, tiramisu, and many other desserts. American ladyfingers are moister than Italian ones.

1 lb (500 g) =
60 to 65 ladyfingers

If You Don't Have It

Substitute 1 lb (500 g) ladyfingers with:
- 1 lb (500 g) sponge cake, cut into small pieces and baked for 10 minutes if necessary to crisp (best for desserts such as tiramisù in which the cake will be soaked in espresso, syrups, or other flavored liquids)
- 1 lb (500 g) génoise, baked for 10 minutes if necessary to crisp
- 1 lb (500 g) pound cake, baked for 10 minutes if necessary to crisp

Lager

See BEER.

Lahvosh

See LAVASH.

Laksa Leaf

See VIETNAMESE MINT.

Laksa Paste

A tantalizing seasoning prepared by grinding candlenuts, lemongrass, hot chiles, galangal, shrimp paste, fresh ginger, garlic, cilantro, turmeric, tamarind, and other spices. Used to spike the broth in the famous Malaysian noodle soup.

If You Don't Have It

Substitute 1 tbsp (15 mL) laksa paste with:

- 1 tbsp (15 mL) Homemade Laksa Paste: Combine ½ cup (125 mL) red curry paste, 2 to 3 tbsp (25 to 45 mL) macadamia nuts or candlenuts, 3 tbsp (45 mL) chopped Vietnamese mint (or 1 tbsp/15 mL chopped mint and 1 tbsp/15 mL chopped cilantro), 3 tbsp (45 mL) vegetable oil, and 1 tbsp (15 mL) shrimp paste in a small food processor or blender. Purée until smooth. Makes about ¾ cup (175 mL).
- 1 tbsp (15 mL) vegetarian laksa paste (has no shrimp paste)

Lamb

The meat of sheep younger than 1 year includes suckling lamb fed only its mother's milk.

If You Don't Have It

Substitute 1 lb (500 g) lamb with:

- 1 lb (500 g) beef
- 1 lb (500 g) pork
- 1 lb (500 g) veal
- 1 lb (500 g) mutton (sheep over 2 years old; tougher, fattier texture; stronger flavor)

Lambert Cherry

See CHERRY.

Lamb's Lettuce

See MÂCHE.

Lamprey

Often erroneously referred to as eel, this primitive, rather grotesque fish survives as an ocean parasite, sucking blood from larger fish.

If You Don't Have It

Substitute 1 lb (500 g) lamprey with:

- 1 lb (500 g) eel (stronger flavor)
- 1 lb (500 g) monkfish (more tender)
- 1 lb (500 g) mullet (more flaky)

Lancashire

Because of its melting quality, this British cheese is often selected for Welsh Rabbit.

1 lb (500 g) = 4 cups (1 L) shredded

If You Don't Have It

Substitute 1 oz (30 g) Lancashire cheese with:

- 1 oz (30 g) Cheshire
- 1 oz (30 g) Cheddar
- 1 oz (30 g) Caerphilly
- 1 oz (30 g) Leicester

Landjäger

Semidry, smoked beef and pork sausage sold in slightly flattened links. Landjäger originated in Switzerland and the name means "hunter."

If You Don't Have It

Substitute 1 lb (500 g) landjäger with:
- 1 lb (500 g) Thuringer
- 1 lb (500 g) Lebanon bologna
- 1 lb (500 g) other semidry or summer sausage
- 1 lb (500 g) salami or other dry sausage
- 1 lb (500 g) pepperoni

See also CERVELAT; SUMMER SAUSAGE.

Langouste

See SPINY LOBSTER.

Langoustine

See DUBLIN BAY PRAWN.

Lap Cheong

Also known as lap cheung and lop chong. Dry-cured, smoked, sweet Chinese sausages made with pork, pork fat, soy sauce, paprika, grains, and alcohol.

If You Don't Have It

Substitute 1 lb (500 g) lap cheong with:
- 1 lb (500 g) Spanish chorizo
- 1 lb (500 g) pepperoni
- 1 lb (500 g) salami

Lappi

Finnish cheese from Lapland is semisoft, semisweet, slices beautifully and melts delightfully.

> 1 lb (500 g) = 4 cups
> (1 L) shredded

If You Don't Have It

Substitute 1 oz (30 g) Lappi with:
- 1 oz (30 g) Emmental
- 1 oz (30 g) Jarlsberg
- 1 oz (30 g) Gruyère
- 1 oz (30 g) Swiss

Lard

Also known as manteca (Spanish) and strutto (Italian). Rendered, filtered pork fat used for frying and in baked goods. The finest quality lard is called leaf lard, which comes from fat encasing hog's

If You Don't Have It

Substitute 1 cup (250 mL) lard with:
- 1 cup (250 mL) vegetable shortening

Lard (cont'd)

kidneys. Not to be confused with lardo, an Italian delicacy of pig's rump fat cured with salt, pepper, herbs, and spices.

---

1 lb (500 g) =
2 cups (500 mL)

To Vary the Flavor

Substitute 1 cup (250 mL) lard with:

- ½ cup (125 mL) lard + ½ cup (125 mL) unsalted butter (for both flakiness and flavor in biscuits, pie crust and pastries)
- 1 cup (250 mL) + 3 tbsp (45 mL) unsalted butter
- 1 cup (250 mL) bacon fat (especially for sautéing)

For Better Health

Substitute 1 cup (250 mL) lard with:

- ½ cup (125 mL) lard + ½ cup (125 mL) vegetable oil (especially in Mexican cooking to retain lard's flavor while lowering saturated fat)

Lardo

See FATBACK; LARD.

Lardons

Also known as lardoons. Narrow strips of fat that are larded, or inserted, into large cuts of meat to season and baste them internally as they roast.

If You Don't Have It

Substitute 1 lb (500 g) lardons with:

- 1 lb (500 g) sliced fatback (for larding or barding)
- 1 lb (500 g) fatty bacon (for barding)

Lasagna

See PASTA, DRIED RIBBONS; PASTA, FRESH.

Lavash

Also known as Armenian cracker bread. Middle Eastern flatbread that can be as wide as 14 inches (35 cm).

If You Don't Have It

Substitute 1 lb (500 g) lavash with:

- 1 lb (500 g) large pita bread or naan (thicker)
- 1 lb (500 g) flour tortillas (especially for making wrap sandwiches)
- 1 lb (500 g) matzo (to replace crisp lavash)

Lavender

Fragrant flowers often candied or used to flavor beverages, salads, and ice creams.

---

1 oz (30 g) fresh =
⅓ cup (75 mL)

1 oz (30 g) dried =
9 tbsp (135 mL)

If You Don't Have It

Substitute 1 tbsp (15 mL) fresh lavender with:

- 1 tsp (5 mL) dried lavender
- 1 drop lavender essential oil

See also PICKING EDIBLE FLOWERS (PAGE 604).

Laver

Also known as jee choy and purple laver. Nutritious dried seaweed that must be soaked in cold water before using in a recipe.

If You Don't Have It
Substitute 1 oz (30 g) laver with:
- 1 oz (30 g) dulse (mild brine flavor; maroon color)
- 1 oz (30 g) nori (mild brine flavor; deep green color)
- 1 oz (30 g) arame (mild brine flavor; dark brown color)
- ½ tsp (2 mL) salt

See also NORI.

Leaf Lettuce

Also known as looseleaf lettuce and Simpson lettuce. Popular types are green leaf, oak leaf, red leaf, and salad bowl. When shopping, choose leaves that look vibrant and evenly colored with no signs of wilting or yellowing.

1 lb (500 g) =
6 cups (1.5 L) pieces

If You Don't Have It
Substitute 1 lb (500 g) leaf lettuce with:
- 1 lb (500 g) butterhead lettuce such as Bibb or Boston (generally larger, slightly thicker leaves)
- 1 lb (500 g) crisphead lettuce such as Great Lakes, Iceberg, Imperial, Vanguard, or Western lettuce (crunchy; less flavorful)
- 1 lb (500 g) romaine lettuce (crunchy; more flavorful than crisphead lettuce)
- 1 lb (500 g) mâche (tender leaves; bittersweet, slightly nutty flavor)

Leaf Lettuce Varieties
Choose 1 lb (500 g) leaf lettuce from these varieties:
- 1 lb (500 g) oak leaf lettuce (tender, oak-leaf shaped leaves with green or red color; mild flavor)
- 1 lb (500 g) lollo rosso (pale green stems; beautiful purplish red, frilly leaves; very mild flavor)
- 1 lb (500 g) lollo biondo (similar to lollo rosso but pale green in color)

Leaveners

See SPECIFIC TYPES.

Lebanon Bologna

Smoked, semidry or summer sausage made of coarsely chopped beef. It was created by German immigrants in Lebanon, Pennsylvania.

If You Don't Have It
Substitute 1 lb (500 g) Lebanon bologna with:
- 1 lb (500 g) Thuringer
- 1 lb (500 g) Landjäger
- 1 lb (500 g) other semidry or summer sausage
- 1 lb (500 g) salami or other dry sausage
- 1 lb (500 g) pepperoni

See also CERVELAT; SUMMER SAUSAGE.

Leberkäse

German for "liver cheese," this pâté is made with pork, eggs, garlic, and onion.

If You Don't Have It

Substitute 1 lb (500 g) Leberkäse with:
- 1 lb (500 g) mortadella (has cubes of pork fat and garlic flavor)
- 1 lb (500 g) bologna (less complex flavor)
- 1 lb (500 g) olive loaf (adds olive flavor)
- 1 lb (500 g) galantina (more chunky; more complex flavor)

For Better Health

Substitute 1 lb (500 g) Leberkäse with:
- 1 lb (500 g) Gelbwurst (lower in fat and calories)

Lecithin

An emulsifier that is found naturally in eggs and many other foods. Also, commercially extracted from soybeans.

If You Don't Have It

Substitute 1 cup (250 mL) lecithin with:
- 1 cup (250 mL) vegetable oil (for baking; adds fat)

Leek

On March 1, St. David's Day, many Welshmen wear leeks in their hats to celebrate a famous battle victory in which the Welsh soldiers wore leeks in their hats.

1 lb (500 g) = 2 large leeks = 2 cups (500 mL) trimmed and chopped = 1 cup (250 mL) cooked

If You Don't Have It

Substitute 1 cup (250 mL) chopped leeks with:
- 1 cup (250 mL) chopped green onions or scallions (white and light green parts only)
- 1 cup (250 mL) chopped shallots (sweeter, more complex flavor)
- 1 cup (250 mL) chopped sweet or storage onions (stronger, less complex flavor)
- 1 cup (250 mL) chopped ramps or wild leeks (lights parts only; but consider leaving ramps whole or cutting into just two pieces to show off their beautiful bulbs and leaves; best as a substitute for leeks that will be served as a side dish; stronger, more complex flavor than cultivated leeks)

See also RAMP.

Lefse

Norwegian flatbread made from mashed potatoes. To rehydrate dried lefse, moisten it and heat briefly in a microwave oven.

If You Don't Have It

Substitute 1 lefse with:
- 1 chapati
- 1 soft lavash
- 1 flour tortilla

Legume

See CRANBERRY BEAN; EDAMAME; FAVA BEAN; GREEN BEAN; LIMA BEAN; PEANUT; PEAS; YARD-LONG BEAN; SWITCHING LENTILS (PAGE 569); THE WIDE WORLD OF DRIED BEANS (PAGE 566).

Leicester

Orange cheese that tastes like Cheddar but is moister. Great for snacking or dishes that call for melted cheese.

1 lb (500 g) = 4 cups (1 L) shredded

If You Don't Have It
Substitute 1 oz (30 g) Leicester cheese with:
- 1 oz (30 g) Cheshire
- 1 oz (30 g) Lancashire
- 1 oz (30 g) Caerphilly
- 1 oz (30 g) Cheddar

Lekvar

See PRUNE PURÉE.

Lemon

Eureka and Lisbon lemons are the familiar variety found in most markets. Meyer lemons are about twice the size and have an almost floral aroma and sweeter juice.

1 medium Eureka or Lisbon lemon = 2 to 3 tbsp (25 to 45 mL) juice = 1 to 2 tsp (5 to 10 mL) zest

1 medium Meyer lemon = ¼ to ⅓ cup (50 to 75 mL) juice = 1 to 3 tbsp (15 to 45 mL) zest

If You Don't Have It
Substitute 1 fresh lemon with:
- ½ tsp (2 mL) Meyer lemon (larger; sweeter)
- 1 lime (slightly smaller; sweeter)
- 1 calamondin (hybrid of kumquat and mandarin orange)
- ½ tsp (2 mL) orange (larger; sweeter)
- ¼ grapefruit (larger; sweeter)
- ¼ pummelo (larger; sweeter)

To Vary the Flavor
Substitute 1 fresh lemon with:
- 1 tbsp (15 mL) chopped fresh lemon basil, lemon balm, or lemon thyme (for hint of lemon flavor)
- 2 to 3 leaves chopped fresh lemon verbena (stronger lemon flavor)

See also LEMON EXTRACT; LEMON JUICE; LEMON ZEST; MEYER LEMON; PRESERVED LEMON.

Lemon Balm

Also known as balm. In Europe, this minty lemon herb seasons salads, poultry, and meats. Also brewed into soothing tea.

---

1 oz (30 g) = 2 cups (500 mL) chopped

1 cup (250 mL) fresh = ¼ cup (50 mL) dried

If You Don't Have It

Substitute 1 tbsp (15 mL) chopped fresh lemon balm with:

- 2½ tsp (12 mL) chopped fresh mint + ½ tsp (2 mL) chopped fresh lemon verbena
- 2 tsp (10 mL) chopped fresh mint + 1 tsp (5 mL) chopped fresh lemon basil or holy basil
- 1 to 2 tsp (5 to 10 mL) lemon zest

To Vary the Flavor

Substitute 1 tbsp (15 mL) chopped fresh lemon balm with:

- 1 tbsp (15 mL) chopped fresh basil
- 1 tbsp (15 mL) chopped fresh mint
- 1 tbsp (15 mL) chopped fresh bergamot (aromas of orange, thyme, sage, and rosemary)

Lemon Extract

For finest flavor, select "pure" lemon extract, which is derived from the fresh fruit.

If You Don't Have It

Substitute ½ tsp (2 mL) lemon extract with:

- 1 to 2 drops lemon oil + ¼ tsp (1 mL) vodka (optional)
- 1 tbsp (15 mL) limoncello (reduce liquid in recipe by 2½ tsp/12 mL and sugar by ¾ tsp/4 mL)
- 1 tsp (5 mL) lemon zest

To Vary the Flavor

Substitute ½ tsp (2 mL) lemon extract with:

- ½ tsp (2 mL) orange extract
- ¾ tsp (4 mL) vanilla extract

Lemongrass

Also known as citronella and sereh (especially when powdered). A perennial tropical grass with delightful lemon scent and flavor. Widely utilized in Thai and other Southeast Asian cuisines.

---

1 trimmed stalk = 1 tbsp (15 mL) dried = 1 tsp (5 mL) powder (sereh powder)

If You Don't Have It

Substitute 1 lemongrass stalk with:

- 1½ tsp (7 mL) lemon zest + ⅛ tsp (0.5 mL) minced fresh ginger
- 1 tsp (5 mL) lemon balm
- 2 lemon leaves
- 2 lemon verbena leaves

Lemon Juice

If you don't own a citrus reamer, cut the lemon in half, stick a fork into the cut side and twist to release the juice.

> 1 medium Eureka
> or Lisbon lemon =
> 2 to 3 tbsp
> (25 to 45 mL) juice
>
> 1 medium Meyer lemon
> = ¼ to ⅓ cup
> (50 to 75 mL) juice

If You Don't Have It

Substitute 1 tbsp (15 mL) fresh lemon juice with:
- 1 tbsp (15 mL) bottled or frozen lemon juice (much weaker flavor)
- 3 tbsp (45 mL) brewed lemon herbal tea (adds other flavors)

To Vary the Flavor

Substitute 1 tbsp (15 mL) fresh lemon juice with:
- 2¼ tsp (11 mL) fresh lime juice
- 1½ tsp (7 mL) white wine vinegar, sherry vinegar, or champagne vinegar

Lemon Liqueur

A sweetened spirit flavored with lemon.

If You Don't Have It

Substitute 3 tbsp (45 mL) lemon liqueur with:
- 3 tbsp (45 mL) limoncello
- 1 tbsp (15 mL) lemon vodka + 1 tbsp (15 mL) sugar syrup
- 3 tbsp (45 mL) lemon vodka (less sweet)
- 5 tsp (25 mL) vodka + 1 tsp (5 mL) lemon juice (less sweet)
- 3 tbsp (45 mL) lemon schnapps

See also LIMONCELLO.

Lemon Oil

Concentrated oil of lemon peels often used in candies.

If You Don't Have It

Substitute 1 drop lemon oil with:
- ½ tsp (2 mL) lemon extract (less concentrated; evaporates at high temperatures; reduce liquid in recipe by ½ tsp/2 mL if necessary)
- 1 tbsp (15 mL) limoncello (reduce liquid in recipe by 1 tbsp/15 mL and sugar by ¾ tsp/4 mL if necessary)
- 1 tsp (5 mL) lemon zest

To Vary the Flavor

Substitute 1 drop lemon oil with:
- 1 drop orange oil
- ¾ tsp (4 mL) vanilla extract (evaporates at high temperatures; reduce liquid in recipe by ¾ tsp/4 mL if necessary)

Lemon Pepper Seasoning

Commercial seasoning blend of ground black peppercorns and lemon zest. Tasty on chicken and vegetables.

1 oz (30 g) =
3 tbsp (45 mL)

If You Don't Have It

Substitute 1 tsp (5 mL) lemon pepper seasoning with:

- ½ tsp (2 mL) grated fresh lemon zest + ¼ tsp (1 mL) salt + ⅛ tsp (0.5 mL) ground black pepper
- ½ tsp (2 mL) ground sumac berries + ½ tsp (2 mL) ground black pepper

For Better Health

Substitute 1 tsp (5 mL) lemon pepper seasoning with:

- 1 tsp (5 mL) salt-free lemon pepper seasoning
- 1 tsp (5 mL) herbal salt substitute

Lemon Verbena

Introduced to Great Britain from Chile in the 1700s, the leaves of this small deciduous shrub are lemon scented. Popular in Europe for lemon tea, the leaves also flavor salads, sauces, and desserts.

1 oz (30 g) = 2 cups (500 mL) chopped

1 cup (250 mL) fresh = ¼ cup (50 mL) dried

If You Don't Have It

Substitute 2 leaves lemon verbena with:

- 1 stalk lemongrass
- 2 tsp (10 mL) lemon balm (adds minty flavor)
- 1½ tsp (7 mL) lemon zest

Lemon Zest

The yellow outer layer of lemon peel contains the essential flavoring oils. When grating or slicing the zest, take care to only remove the yellow skin, not the underlying bitter white membrane.

1 medium Eureka or Lisbon lemon = 1 to 2 tsp (5 to 10 mL) zest

1 medium Meyer lemon = 1 to 3 tbsp (15 to 45 mL) zest

If You Don't Have It

Substitute 1 tsp (5 mL) grated lemon zest with:

- ½ to 1 tsp (2 to 5 mL) dried lemon peel
- ½ tsp (2 mL) lemon extract

To Vary the Flavor

Substitute 1 tsp (5 mL) grated lemon zest with:

- 1 tsp (5 mL) grated lime zest
- 1 tsp (5 mL) grated citron zest
- 1 tsp (5 mL) grated orange zest
- 1 tsp (5 mL) grated kumquat zest
- 1 small stalk lemongrass
- 1 tbsp (15 mL) chopped fresh lemon basil, lemon balm, or lemon thyme (for hint of lemon flavor)
- 2 lemon verbena leaves (stronger lemon flavor)

Lentil

See SWITCHING LENTILS (PAGE 569).

Lettuce

See BUTTERHEAD LETTUCE; CRISPHEAD LETTUCE; LEAF LETTUCE; ROMAINE LETTUCE.

Leyden

Distinctive Dutch cheese fashioned from part-skim cow's milk and buttermilk that's seasoned with caraway or cumin seeds.

1 lb (500 g) = 4 cups (1 L) shredded

If You Don't Have It
Substitute 1 oz (30 g) young Leyden with:
- 1 oz (30 g) Gouda (no caraway or cumin flavors)
- 1 oz (30 g) Edam (less rich; no caraway or cumin flavors)
- 1 oz (30 g) Fontina (less tangy)

Lichi

See LITCHI.

Licor 43®

Sweet, yellow Spanish liqueur formulated from "cuarenta y tres"; ingredients include citrus, fruits, herbs, and vanilla.

If You Don't Have It
Substitute 3 tbsp (45 mL) Licor 43® with:
- 3 tbsp (45 mL) Tuaca
- 3 tbsp (45 mL) crème de vanille or other vanilla liqueur
- 3 tbsp (45 mL) vanilla vodka (less sweet)

Licorice Liqueur

See ANISE LIQUEUR.

Liederkranz

An American cheese that's mildly pungent when young and full-bodied when aged. Created in the late 19th century by New York cheesemaker Emil Frey. Named after a singing society whose members loved the cheese.

1 lb (500 g) = 4 cups (1 L) shredded

If You Don't Have It
Substitute 1 oz (30 g) Liederkranz with:
- 1 oz (30 g) Limburger
- 1 oz (30 g) Handkäse

Lilac

See PICKING EDIBLE FLOWERS (PAGE 604).

Lillet

An apéritif that originated in the French village of Podensac. Blended from white or red wine, brandy, herbs, and fruits.

If You Don't Have It
Substitute 3 tbsp (45 mL) Lillet with:
- 3 tbsp (45 mL) Dubonnet
- 3 tbsp (45 mL) sweet vermouth or sherry (to replace Lillet blanc)
- 3 tbsp (45 mL) Byrrh (to replace sweet Lillet rouge)
- 3 tbsp (45 mL) port (to replace sweet Lillet rouge)

Lima Bean

Also known as butter beans (dried) and Madagascar beans. Plump, kidney-shaped beans come in two distinct types: smaller baby lima beans and the larger, more flavorful Fordhooks. Lima beans can be purchased in season in their pods, also dried or frozen.

1 lb (500 g) in shell = 1 cup (250 mL) shelled

1 lb (500 g) dried = 2⅓ cups (575 mL) = 5½ cups (1.375 L) cooked

If You Don't Have It
Substitute 1 cup (250 mL) lima beans with:
- 1 cup (250 mL) fresh green peas
- 1 cup (250 mL) fresh edamame (shelled green soybeans)
- 1 cup (250 mL) shelled and peeled fresh fava beans
- 1 cup (250 mL) fresh sugar snap peas (in shell)
- 1 cup (250 mL) chickpeas, red kidney beans, black-eyed peas, or cannellini beans (to replace dried limas in soups and stews)

See also THE WIDE WORLD OF DRIED BEANS (PAGE 566).

Limburger

Considered by some people to be the embodiment of stinky cheese, this aromatic dairy product originated in Belgium, took hold in Germany, and is also produced by one American dairy cooperative in Wisconsin.

1 lb (500 g) = 4 cups (1 L) shredded

If You Don't Have It
Substitute 1 oz (30 g) Limburger with:
- 1 oz (30 g) Liederkranz
- 1 oz (30 g) Handkäse
- 1 oz (30 g) Bierkäse

Lime

Persian or Tahiti limes are the familiar variety found in most markets. Mexican or Key limes are smaller and have a more concentrated lime flavor than Persians.

> 1 lb (500 g) = 6 to 8 medium Persian limes = ½ to ⅔ cup (125 to 150 mL) juice
>
> 1 medium Persian lime = 1 to 3 tbsp (15 to 45 mL) juice = 1 to 2 tsp (5 to 10 mL) zest
>
> 1 lb (500 g) = 12 to 16 medium Key limes = ½ to ⅔ cup (125 to 150 mL) juice
>
> 1 medium Key lime = 2 to 3 tsp (10 to 15 mL) juice = ¾ to 1 tsp (4 to 5 mL) zest

If You Don't Have It

Substitute 1 Persian lime with:

- 1 to 2 Key limes (smaller; more intense lime flavor)
- 1 lemon (slightly larger; lemon flavor)
- ½ tsp (2 mL) Meyer lemon (larger; sweeter than familiar Eureka or Lisbon lemon)
- 1 calamondin (hybrid of kumquat and mandarin orange)
- ½ tsp (2 mL) orange (larger; sweeter)
- ¼ grapefruit (larger; sweeter)
- ¼ pummelo (larger; sweeter)

See also LIME JUICE; LIME ZEST; MAKRUT LIME.

Lime Juice

Freshly squeezed lime juice perks up everything from margaritas to seviche. The commercial Rose's lime juice is Key lime juice.

> 1 medium Persian lime = 1 to 3 tbsp (15 to 45 mL) juice
>
> 1 lb (500 g) = 12 to 16 medium Key limes = ½ to ⅔ cup (125 to 150 mL) juice
>
> 1 medium Key lime = 2 to 3 tsp (10 to 15 mL) juice

If You Don't Have It

Substitute 1 tbsp (15 mL) fresh Persian lime juice with:

- 1 tbsp (15 mL) bottled or frozen lime juice (less intense lime flavor)
- 1 tbsp (15 mL) Rose's lime juice (bottled sweetened Key lime juice; less intense lime flavor)

Substitute 1 tbsp (15 mL) fresh Key lime juice with:

- 1½ tsp (7 mL) Persian lime juice + 1½ tsp (7 mL) lemon juice
- 1½ tbsp (22 mL) Persian lime juice (less intense lime flavor)
- 1 tbsp (15 mL) Rose's lime juice (bottled sweetened Key lime juice; less intense lime flavor)

To Vary the Flavor

Substitute 1 tbsp (15 mL) fresh Persian lime juice with:

- 3 to 4 tsp (15 to 20 mL) fresh lemon juice
- 1 tbsp (15 mL) calamondin juice
- 1 to 3 tbsp (15 to 45 mL) orange juice (sweeter)

Lime Zest

The colored outer layer of the lime rind is rich in flavonoids, bioflavonoids, and limonoids.

1 medium Persian lime =
1 to 2 tsp
(5 to 10 mL) zest

1 medium Key lime =
¾ to 1 tsp (4 to 5 mL)
zest

If You Don't Have It

Substitute 1 tsp (5 mL) grated Persian lime zest with:
- ½ to 1 tsp (2 to 5 mL) dried lime peel
- ½ tsp (2 mL) lime extract

To Vary the Flavor

Substitute 1 tsp (5 mL) grated Persian lime zest with:
- 1 tsp (5 mL) grated Key lime zest (more intense lime flavor)
- 1 tsp (5 mL) grated lemon zest
- 1 tsp (5 mL) grated citron zest
- 1 tsp (5 mL) grated orange zest
- 1 tsp (5 mL) grated kumquat zest
- 1 tsp (5 mL) grated calamondin zest

Limoncello

A stylish liqueur produced on Italy's Amalfi coast and in Sicily. It's made by steeping lemon zest in alcohol and then adding sugar syrup. Better brands use real lemon while cheaper versions rely on lemon extract.

If You Don't Have It

Substitute 3 tbsp (45 mL) Limoncello with:
- 3 tbsp (45 mL) Homemade Limoncello: Place the zest (no bitter white membrane) of 6 to 8 clean lemons and 1½ cups (375 mL) of pure grain alcohol or good-quality 100-proof vodka (half of a 750 mL bottle) into a 2-quart (2 L) glass bottle or jar with a cap or lid. Cover and keep in a dark spot for 3 to 5 weeks. Combine 2 cups (500 mL) water and 1 cup (250 mL) granulated sugar. Bring to a boil and simmer over medium-high heat until slightly thickened, about 5 minutes. Let cool then add to the steeping vodka along with another 1½ cups (375 mL) pure grain alcohol or 100-proof vodka. Cover and return to the dark spot for 3 to 5 more weeks. Strain the limoncello into bottles, discarding lemon zest. Seal and store limoncello in the freezer or at room temperature for up to 6 to 8 months. Serve icy cold or toss with fruit or use in a frozen dessert. Makes about 5 cups (1.25 L).
- 1 tbsp (15 mL) lemon vodka + 1 tbsp (15 mL) sugar syrup

Limpa Bread

Also known as Swedish limpa. A moist and fragrant rye bread seasoned with cumin, fennel or anise, and orange zest.

If You Don't Have It
Substitute 1 lb (500 g) limpa bread with:
- 1 lb (500 g) rye bread with caraway seeds (much less aromatic)
- 1 lb (500 g) pumpernickel bread (much less aromatic)

Lingcod

Not a cod, but a type of greenling with sweet and firm white flesh. Sold whole, also cut into fillets or steaks.

If You Don't Have It
Substitute 1 lb (500 g) lingcod with:
- 1 lb (500 g) cod (flakier texture)
- 1 lb (500 g) sablefish or black cod (fuller flavor)

Lingonberry

Also known as cowberry, foxberry, and mountain cranberry. A wild relative of the cranberry that flourishes in Canada, Maine, and Scandinavia. Processed into preserves and sauces. Available fresh only near local growing areas.

1 pint fresh =
2 cups (500 mL)

If You Don't Have It
Substitute 1 cup (250 mL) lingonberries with:
- 1 cup (250 mL) cranberries (larger, more tart; less complex flavor)
- 1 cup (250 mL) red currants
- 1 cup (250 mL) black currants or cassis
- 1 cup (250 mL) elderberries
- 1 cup (250 mL) carissa
- 1 cup (250 mL) bilberries
- 1 cup (250 mL) blueberries (sweeter)

Linguiça

See CHORIZO.

Liqueur

If you only need a small amount of a liqueur for a recipe, buy a miniature bottle at the liquor store checkout.

If You Don't Have It
Substitute 3 tbsp (45 mL) liqueur with:
- 2 tsp (10 mL) liqueur extract
- 1 tbsp (15 mL) fruit syrup (to replace fruit liqueurs)

To Vary the Flavor
- 2 tsp (10 mL) vanilla extract

See also BITTERS; SPECIFIC TYPES.

Liquid Smoke

A natural product made by dissolving real wood smoke (usually hickory) in water. Liquid smoke is often used in barbecue sauces and other food products that have "grilled" or "barbecued" flavor. Look for it in the spice aisle or near the barbecue sauce in well-stocked grocery stores.

If You Don't Have It
Substitute 2 drops liquid smoke (for smoke flavor) with:
- 1 smoked ham hock (adds fat and ham flavor)
- 2 slices bacon (adds fat and bacon flavor)
- 1 tsp (5 mL) canning liquid from canned chipotle peppers (adds spices and considerable heat)
- ½ tsp (2 mL) ground chipotle peppers (adds considerable heat)
- grilling or smoking the food using hickory or other wood

Liquor

See LIQUEUR; SPECIFIC TYPES.

Litchi

Also known as lychee. The fruit of a grand ornamental tree beloved in China. The fruit grows in clusters of burr-like pods that are about the size of ping pong balls.

1 lb (500 g) fresh = 2½ cups (625 mL) sliced

If You Don't Have It
Substitute 1 cup (250 mL) peeled and seeded fresh litchis with:
- 1 cup (250 mL) canned litchis (less aromatic)
- 1 cup (250 mL) peeled and seeded pulasans
- 1 cup (250 mL) peeled and seeded rambutans (less sweet)
- 1 cup (250 mL) peeled and seeded longans (sweeter; less aromatic)

See also LONGAN.

Livarot

From the Calvados region of Normandy, this cheese is related to Camembert but is more pungent and larger in size.

If You Don't Have It
Substitute 1 oz (30 g) Livarot with:
- 1 oz (30 g) Limburger
- 1 oz (30 g) Maroilles
- 1 oz (30 g) Liederkranz
- 1 oz (30 g) Handkäse

Liverwurst

A broad category of liver-based sausages, sometimes smoked, that can range in texture from spreadable to sliceable.

If You Don't Have It
Substitute 1 lb (500 g) liverwurst with:
- 1 lb (500 g) Braunschweiger (smoked liverwurst)
- 1 lb (500 g) pâté
- 1 lb (500 g) Mettwurst
- 1 lb (500 g) Teewurst (spicier)

Loaf Pan

A deep rectangular baking pan most commonly sized 9-by 5-inches (2 L) and 3 inches (7.5 cm) deep.

If You Don't Have It
Substitute a loaf pan with:
- large, clean coffee can with one end removed

See also PAN SIZE EQUIVALENTS (PAGE 606).

Lobster

Also known as American lobster and Maine lobster. Maine lobsters have large claws, while spiny lobsters have no claws.

1 to 1½ lbs (500 to 750 g)
= 2½ to 3 cups
(625 to 750 mL) meat

If You Don't Have It
Substitute 1 lb (500 g) Maine lobster with:
- 1 lb (500 g) Dublin Bay prawns
- 1 lb (500 g) crayfish
- 1 lb (500 g) jumbo shrimp
- 1 lb (500 g) crab
- 1 lb (500 g) scallops

Lobster Variety
Choose 1 lb (500 g) Maine lobster from this variety:
- 1 lb (500 g) spiny or rock lobster (especially for tails)

See also SPINY LOBSTER; CHANGING ROE (PAGE 594).

Lochan Ora®

The only liqueur from Chivas Brothers, this blend includes Scotch whiskey tamed by heather honey, herbs, and spices.

If You Don't Have It
Substitute 3 tbsp (45 mL) Lochan Ora with:
- 3 tbsp (45 mL) Drambuie
- 3 tbsp (45 mL) Grandtully
- 3 tbsp (45 mL) Glayva

Locust Bean

See CAROB.

Loganberry

Large reddish purple fruit is reputed to be a hybrid of blackberry and red raspberry produced in the backyard of California Judge J.H. Logan in the summer of 1880.

1 pint fresh =
2 cups (500 mL)

If You Don't Have It
Substitute 1 cup (250 mL) loganberries with:
- 1 cup (250 mL) boysenberries (hybrid of blackberries, raspberries, and loganberries; reddish purple color)
- 1 cup (250 mL) blackberries (dark purple; more tart; larger seeds)
- 1 cup (250 mL) raspberries (red; sweeter)
- 1 cup (250 mL) tayberries (hybrid of blackberries and raspberries)
- 1 cup (250 mL) olallieberries (larger; sweeter)

Longan

These fruits can be as tiny as an olive or as large as a plum with an easy-to-peel skin. The gray flesh is sweet with overtones of perfumed flowers and pine.

1 lb (500 g) fresh =
2½ cups (625 mL) sliced

If You Don't Have It
Substitute 1 cup (250 mL) peeled and seeded fresh longans with:
- 1 cup (250 mL) peeled and seeded rambutans (less sweet)
- 1 cup (250 mL) peeled and seeded fresh or canned litchis
- 1 cup (250 mL) peeled and seeded pulasans

See also LITCHI.

Loofah, Angled

Also known as angled loofa and Chinese okra. A type of Asian bitter melon with ridged skin.

1 lb (500 g) = 3 cups
(750 mL) sliced

If You Don't Have It
Substitute ½ cup (125 mL) chopped angled loofah with:
- ¼ cup (50 mL) chopped zucchini + ¼ cup (50 mL) chopped English cucumber
- ½ cup (125 mL) chopped zucchini

See also BITTER MELON.

Looseleaf Lettuce

See LEAF LETTUCE.

Lop Chong

See LAP CHEONG.

Loquat

Also known as Japanese plum and Japanese medlar. The earliest of spring fruits to ripen, the loquat is popular in almost all corners of the world except the U.S. It looks like a pear-shaped apricot but contains several very large seeds. The flesh is crisp-tender and juicy, tasting like a blend of cherry, grape, litchi, and plum.

1 lb (500 g) fresh =
2½ cups (625 mL)
sliced or halved

If You Don't Have It
Substitute 1 lb (500 g) loquats with:
- 1 lb (500 g) sour cherries
- 1 lb (500 g) acerola
- 1 lb (500 g) apricots
- 1 lb (500 g) plums

Lotus Leaves

When young and tender, the leaves of the Asian flower are used as herbs. More mature leaves are large enough to use as wrappers for foods to be steamed.

If You Don't Have It

Substitute lotus leaves (as a food wrapper) with:
- softened bamboo leaves
- banana leaves
- parchment paper

Lotus Root

Also known as renkon (Japan). The underwater rhizome of an Asian flower that is torpedo-shape and aerated with a series of round tunnels.

> 1 lb (500 g) = 3 cups (750 mL) sliced

If You Don't Have It

Substitute 1 cup (250 mL) chopped lotus root with:
- 1 cup (250 mL) chopped water chestnuts
- 1 cup (250 mL) chopped jicama
- 1 cup (250 mL) chopped sunchokes
- 1 cup (250 mL) chopped Asian radishes such as daikon (add a pinch of sugar to balance the peppery flavor)

Loukanika

This fresh Greek link sausage, made with lamb or pork, is flavored with orange zest.

If You Don't Have It

Substitute 1 lb (500 g) loukanika with:
- 1 lb (500 g) pork sausage + 1 to 2 tsp (5 to 10 mL) grated fresh orange zest

Lovage

Also known as céleri bâtard, smallage, and smellage. An extremely tall, leafy stalk that tastes like very strong celery. The stalks can be cooked as a vegetable; the leaves can season savory dishes. The dried seeds are known as celery seeds.

> 1 lb (500 g) stalk untrimmed = 2 cups (500 mL) sliced or diced

If You Don't Have It

Substitute 1 tbsp (15 mL) chopped fresh lovage leaves with:
- 1 to 3 tbsp (15 to 45 mL) chopped fresh celery leaves
- ½ tbsp (7 mL) chopped fresh celery leaves + ½ tbsp (7 mL) chopped fresh parsley or chervil

If You Don't Have It

Substitute 1 cup (250 mL) chopped fresh lovage stalks with:
- 1 cup (250 mL) chopped fresh Chinese celery
- 1 cup (250 mL) chopped fresh celery stalks (milder flavor)

Lox

See SMOKED SALMON.

Luganega

*Also known as lucanica.
Thin Italian pork sausage
reputed to be most delicious
when made in Lombardy;
often added to risotto. The
ancient Romans named
certain sausages lucani
after a tribe of that name
in the area that is now
southern Italy.*

If You Don't Have It
Substitute 1 lb (500 g) luganega with:
- 1 lb (500 g) mild Italian sausage

Lumpfish Roe

See CHANGING ROE (PAGE 594).

Lumpia Wrapper

*Thin pastry skin made of
flour or cornstarch, eggs,
and water. Encases savory
fillings for the Filipino
and Indonesian versions
of egg rolls.*

If You Don't Have It
Substitute 1 lb (500 g) lumpia wrappers with:
- 1 lb (500 g) lettuce leaves
- 1 lb (500 g) rice paper
- 1 lb (500 g) dumpling wrappers
- 1 lb (500 g) won ton skins (thicker)
- 1 lb (500 g) empanada wrappers (thicker)
- 1 lb (500 g) egg roll wrappers (thicker)
- 1 lb (500 g) rolled pasta

Lychee

See LITCHI.

Macadamia Nut
to Myzithra

Macadamia Nut

A smooth, buttery nut that is indigenous to Australia but rose to prominence in Hawaii, where 90% of the world's crop is now harvested.

> 5 oz (150 g) can =
> 1 cup (250 mL) whole
>
> 7 oz (210 g) jar =
> 1½ cups (375 mL) whole

If You Don't Have It

Substitute 1 cup (250 mL) macadamia nuts with:
- 2 to 4 tbsp (25 to 60 mL) macadamia nut oil (for baking and cooking; will add nut flavor but not texture of whole nuts; reduce fat in recipe by 2 to 4 tbsp/25 to 60 mL)
- 1 cup (250 mL) candlenuts
- 1 cup (250 mL) Brazil nuts
- 1 cup (250 mL) chestnuts
- 1 cup (250 mL) cashews
- 1 cup (250 mL) almonds
- 1 cup (250 mL) pecans
- 1 cup (250 mL) walnuts

Macaroni

See PASTA, DRIED SHAPES.

Macaroon

Thought to have originated in Venice around 1400, these cookies were traditionally prepared with ground almonds, sugar, and egg whites.

If You Don't Have It

Substitute 1 lb (500 g) macaroons with:
- 1 lb (500 g) amaretti (crisper; heavier)
- 1 lb (500 g) mandelbrot (crisper; heavier)
- 1 lb (500 g) almond or coconut biscotti (crisper; heavier)

Mace

A spunkier version of nutmeg, this spice is the dried, ground reddish skin that covers the nutmeg seed. Generally sold ground but sometimes the whole "blade" is available.

1 oz (30 g) =
4½ tbsp (67 mL)

If You Don't Have It
Substitute 1 tsp (5 mL) ground mace with:
- 1 tsp (5 mL) ground nutmeg (milder aroma)
- 1 tsp (5 mL) ground allspice
- 1 tsp (5 mL) apple pie spice (combination of cinnamon, nutmeg, and allspice)
- 1 tsp (5 mL) ground cinnamon

Mâche

Also known as corn salad, fetticus, field lettuce, field salad, and lamb's lettuce. This tender, sweet salad green, which forms multi-leafed sprigs, has nothing to do with corn or lambs. Highly regarded in Europe, mâche has become a chic lettuce in the United States.

1 lb (500 g) =
6 cups (1.5 L) leaves

If You Don't Have It
Substitute 1 lb (500 g) mâche with:
- 1 lb (500 g) leaf lettuce such as oak leaf or lollo rosso
- 1 lb (500 g) butterhead lettuce such as Bibb or Boston (generally larger, slightly thicker leaves)
- 1 lb (500 g) baby spinach leaves (adds slight bitterness)
- 1 lb (500 g) mild arugula (adds pepperiness)
- 1 lb (500 g) crisphead lettuce such as Great Lakes, Iceberg, Imperial, Vanguard, or Western (much larger leaves; crunchy; less flavorful)
- 1 lb (500 g) romaine lettuce (crunchy; more flavorful than crisphead lettuce)

Mackerel

A high-fat fish with firm texture and pronounced flavor. Includes Atlantic mackerel, chub (Pacific) mackerel, king mackerel (kingfish), Spanish mackerel, cero (painted mackerel), and wahoo (ono).

If You Don't Have It
Substitute 1 lb (500 g) fresh mackerel with:
- 1 lb (500 g) bluefish
- 1 lb (500 g) butterfish
- 1 lb (500 g) shad
- 1 lb (500 g) mahi-mahi
- 1 lb (500 g) pompano
- 1 lb (500 g) striped bass
- 1 lb (500 g) tuna

Madagascar Beans

See LIMA BEAN.

Madeira

Fortified wine produced on the Portuguese island of the same name. Distinctive and versatile, Madeira styles range in color from pale to tawny, in taste from dry to sweet, and in application from sipping to cooking.

If You Don't Have It
Substitute 3 tbsp (45 mL) Madeira with:
- 3 tbsp (45 mL) dry port
- 3 tbsp (45 mL) Marsala
- 3 tbsp (45 mL) dry vermouth
- 3 tbsp (45 mL) dry sherry

Madeira Varieties
Choose 3 tbsp (45 mL) Madeira from these varieties:
- 3 tbsp (45 mL) Sercial (light and dry)
- 3 tbsp (45 mL) Verdelho (medium-dry to medium-sweet)
- 3 tbsp (45 mL) Boal or Bual (medium-sweet)
- 3 tbsp (45 mL) Malmsey or Malvasia (dark, sweet, rich)

Maggi Seasoning

A bottled condiment made from vegetable extract. It is used to enhance sauces, soups, and stews.

If You Don't Have It
Substitute 1 tbsp (15 mL) Maggi Seasoning with:
- 1 tbsp (15 mL) tamari (dark soy sauce)
- 1 tbsp (15 mL) soy sauce

Mahi-Mahi

Also known as dolphinfish and dorado. The Hawaiian name for a type of dolphin (not the familiar mammal!), this medium-fat, firm-fleshed fish is delicious grilled or broiled.

If You Don't Have It
Substitute 1 lb (500 g) mahi-mahi with:
- 1 lb (500 g) swordfish
- 1 lb (500 g) mako shark
- 1 lb (500 g) tuna
- 1 lb (500 g) pompano

Mahón

Unpasteurized cow's milk cheese from the Spanish island of Minorca. It has a hard orange rind with a cheesecloth mesh imprint and traditional cushion shape. Young mahón is sweet and fruity.

1 lb (500 g) = 4 cups (1 L) shredded

If You Don't Have It
Substitute 1 oz (30 g) Mahón cheese with:
- 1 oz (30 g) Gouda
- 1 oz (30 g) Edam
- 1 oz (30 g) Boerenkaas

Makrut Lime

Also known as kaffir lime. The term "makrut lime" is preferred over "kaffir lime" because kaffir has a pejorative connotation. The leaves of this bitter citrus are irreplaceable in Southeast Asian cookery, but some passable alternatives are offered here. The distinctive figure-eight shape looks like two leaves joined at the stem end. The grated zest is also used in cooking.

1 oz (30 g) fresh or frozen = about 75 leaves

If You Don't Have It
Substitute 1 tbsp (15 mL) makrut (kaffir) lime zest with:
- 1 tbsp (15 mL) citron zest
- 1 tbsp (15 mL) lime zest
- 5 to 6 makrut (kaffir) lime leaves + 1 tbsp (15 mL) lime zest

If You Don't Have It
Substitute 6 fresh or frozen makrut (kaffir) lime leaves with:
- 12 dried makrut (kaffir) lime leaves
- 1 tbsp (15 mL) makrut (kaffir) lime zest
- 1 tbsp (15 mL) citron zest
- 1 tbsp (15 mL) lime zest
- 1 tbsp (15 mL) lemon zest
- 1 to 3 tbsp (15 to 45 mL) fresh lemon verbena or lemon thyme

Malanga

See YAUTÍA.

Mallet

A sturdy handle attached to a heavy metal plate that is sometimes ridged. Used to crush, grind, flatten, or tenderize foods.

If You Don't Have It
Substitute a mallet with:
- clean hammer
- rolling pin
- heavy skillet

Malt Liquor

See BEER.

Malt Syrup

See BARLEY MALT SYRUP.

Malt Vinegar

See CHOOSING VINEGAR (PAGE 600).

Malt Whiskey

See WHISKEY.

Mamey Sapote

Also known as mamee, mamey apple, and South American apricot. A Caribbean soft fruit with a rough brown rind. The firm smooth flesh is reddish gold and tastes like a cross between apricots and almonds.

1 medium = 12 oz (375 g) = ⅔ cup (150 mL) pulp

If You Don't Have It

Substitute 1 cup (250 mL) chopped fresh mamey sapote with:
- 1 cup (250 mL) chopped white sapote

See also SAPOTE, WHITE.

Manchego

The cheese of La Mancha. Originally made only from the milk of the Manchego breed of sheep that grazed on the Spanish plains of La Mancha. Smooth, rich, and mellow, it is enjoyed as a table cheese when young (curado). The much longer-aged viejo is excellent for grating.

1 lb (500 g) curado = 4 cups (1 L) shredded

4 oz (125 g) viejo = 1 cup (250 mL) grated

If You Don't Have It

Substitute 1 oz (30 g) Manchego with:
- 1 oz (30 g) Roncal
- 1 oz (30 g) Zamorano
- 1 oz (30 g) Castellano
- 1 oz (30 g) Monterey Jack
- 1 oz (30 g) Cheddar
- 1 oz (30 g) Pecorino Romano (for grating)
- 1 oz (30 g) Parmigiano-Reggiano (for grating)
- 1 oz (30 g) Asiago (for grating)

Mandarin Lime

See RANGPUR.

Mandarin Liqueur

Also known as crème de mandarin. Mandarin orange-flavored, sweetened spirits, or sometimes brandy, such as Belgian Mandarin Napolèon and South African Van der Hum.

If You Don't Have It

Substitute 3 tbsp (45 mL) with:
- 3 tbsp (45 mL) orange liqueur such as Grand Marnier, Cointreau, curaçao, or Triple Sec

Mandarin Orange

Also known as tangerine. Canned mandarin oranges are typically made with sweet, tropical-tasting satsuma mandarins.

If You Don't Have It
Substitute 1 mandarin orange with:
- ½ to 1 navel orange (orange flesh)
- ½ to 1 Moro or blood orange (red flesh; more tart; complex flavor)
- ½ to 1 Minneola tangelo (orange flesh; sweet-tart flavor with honey aromas)
- 1 Rangpur or mandarin lime (sweet-tart; complex mandarin and lime aromas)
- 1 calamondin (orange flesh; acidic)

Mandarin Orange Varieties
Choose 1 mandarin orange from these varieties:
- 1 clementine (sweet; apricot aromas)
- 1 Dancy tangerine (sweet-tart; plum aromas)
- 1 honey tangerine (sweet and juicy; floral aromas)
- 1 satsuma (sweet; tropical aromas)
- 1 temple orange (most likely a hybrid of orange and mandarin; somewhat tart, orange-like aromas)

See also CALAMONDIN; TANGELO; UGLI FRUIT.

Mandarin Pancake

Chinese style wheat-flour crêpe used as a wrapper for Peking duck and other dishes.

If You Don't Have It
Substitute 1 lb (500 g) mandarin pancakes with:
- 1 lb (500 g) crêpes
- 1 lb (500 g) thin dumpling wrappers
- 1 lb (500 g) flour tortillas (thicker)

Mandelbrot

Sometimes dubbed "Jewish biscotti," these dry, crisp pastries are named for the German words mandel *(almond) and* brot *(bread).*

If You Don't Have It
Substitute 1 lb (500 g) mandelbrot with:
- 1 lb (500 g) amaretti (crisper)
- 1 lb (500 g) almond biscotti (crisper)
- 1 lb (500 g) almond macaroons (softer; lighter)

Mangetout

See PEAS, EDIBLE POD.

Mango

The American cooking teacher James Beard wrote, "... to most enjoy a mango one should probably eat it in a bathtub, or at the very least in private."

1 mango = ¾ to 1 cup (175 to 250 mL) purée

If You Don't Have It
Substitute 1 cup (250 mL) chopped fresh mango with:
- 1 cup (250 mL) chopped frozen mango

To Vary the Flavor
Substitute 1 cup (250 mL) chopped fresh mango with:
- 1 cup (250 mL) chopped papaya
- 1 cup (250 mL) chopped peaches
- 1 cup (250 mL) chopped nectarines

Mango Powder

Also called amchur. Ground flesh of unripe sun-dried mango from northern India. Used as a souring agent.

If You Don't Have It
Substitute 1 tsp (5 mL) mango powder with:
- 1 tsp (5 mL) lemon juice or lime juice (for acidity)
- ½ to ¾ tsp (2 to 4 mL) tamarind concentrate or paste (for acidity)

Mangosteen

This small fruit has a tough reddish purple rind that encloses white-skinned segments with the texture of ripened plums.

If You Don't Have It
Substitute 1 cup (250 mL) mangosteen segments with:
- 1 cup (250 mL) bacurí or bacuripari segments

Manioc

See CASSAVA.

Manouri

Also known as manoypi. A rindless Greek cheese made either from sheep's or goat's milk. The cheese is white and creamy and has a fresh, dairy flavor with a hint of citrus.

8 oz (250 g) = 1 cup (250 mL)

If You Don't Have It
Substitute 1 oz (30 g) Manouri cheese with:
- 1 oz (30 g) feta (less creamy; rinse to reduce saltiness if you like)
- 1 oz (30 g) haloumi (may add mint flavor)
- 1 oz (30 g) ricotta salata (less creamy)

Manzanilla

See SHERRY.

Maple Sugar

Nearly twice as sweet as granulated sugar.

If You Don't Have It

Substitute 1 cup (250 mL) finely grated maple sugar with:

- 1 cup (250 mL) minus 3 tbsp (45 mL) granulated or light brown sugar + ⅓ cup (75 mL) maple syrup (reduce liquid in recipe by 3 to 4 tbsp/45 to 60 mL)
- 1 cup (250 mL) minus 3 tbsp (45 mL) granulated or light brown sugar + ¼ cup (50 mL) corn syrup + ¼ to ½ tsp (1 to 2 mL) pure maple extract (reduce liquid in recipe by 3 to 4 tbsp/45 to 60 mL)

See also MAPLE SYRUP.

Maple Syrup

The reduced sap of dormant sugar maple or black maple trees is North America's sweet gift to the world. It requires a remarkable 40 gallons (182 L) of sap to produce a single gallon (4.54 L) of the amber syrup. Quebec, Vermont, New York, and Ontario are the leading processors.

16 fluid oz (454 mL) = 2 cups (500 mL)

If You Don't Have It

Substitute 1 cup (250 mL) pure maple syrup with:

- 1¼ cups (300 mL) granulated sugar (for baking, increase liquid in recipe by ¼ cup/50 mL; add ¼ to ½ tsp/1 to 2 mL pure maple extract to add maple flavor if you like; reduce baking soda in recipe by heaping ¼ tsp/1 mL to balance acidity)
- 1 cup (250 mL) pancake syrup (corn syrup flavored with artificial maple flavor)
- ¾ cup (175 mL) corn syrup + ¼ to ½ tsp (1 to 2 mL) maple extract (for pancakes, also add 3 tbsp/45 mL melted butter)
- 1 cup (250 mL) minus 3 tbsp (45 mL) light molasses
- 1 cup (250 mL) honey
- 1 cup (250 mL) brown rice syrup
- 1¼ cups (300 mL) barley malt syrup

Maple Syrup Varieties

Choose 1 cup (250 mL) maple syrup from these grades:

- 1 cup (250 mL) Grade AA (light amber color; mild flavor)
- 1 cup (250 mL) Grade A (medium to dark amber color; gentle flavor)
- 1 cup (250 mL) Grade B (dark amber color; rich flavor)
- 1 cup (250 mL) Grade C (darkest amber color; strong flavor)

Mapuey

See YAM.

Maraschino Cherry

See CHERRY.

Maraschino Liqueur

See CHERRY LIQUEUR.

Marc

See GRAPPA.

Margarine

Also known as oleo and oleomargarine. It is a culinary irony that a cheap fake butter was invented in France, the country whose classic cuisine is unimaginable without real butter. The developer named his solidified white mixture of beef fat, skimmed milk, and water after margarites, *the Greek word for pearl. Most margarines are now made with vegetable oil, such as "soy margarine" made from soybean oil.*

---

1 lb (500 g) = 2 cups
(500 mL) = 4 sticks

1 stick = ¼ lb (125 g) =
½ cup (125 mL) =
8 tbsp (120 mL) =
¾ cup (175 mL) whipped

If You Don't Have It

Substitute ½ cup (125 mL) unsalted margarine with:
- ½ cup (125 mL) salted margarine (decrease salt in recipe by ¼ tsp/1 mL)
- ½ cup (125 mL) butter (more flavorful; makes baked goods crisper)
- ½ cup (125 mL) European-style butter (lower moisture content; creates flakier pastries, crisper cookies, and creamier sauces)
- ¾ cup (175 mL) whipped butter (for spreading)

To Vary the Flavor

Substitute ½ cup (125 mL) margarine with:
- ½ cup (125 mL) Homemade Flavored Butter: Stir ½ cup (125 mL) softened butter or margarine until smooth and mix in flavorings of choice. Reshape by rolling in plastic wrap if necessary. Garlic Butter: Mix together 1 minced garlic clove, ¼ tsp (1 mL) salt, and ¼ tsp (1 mL) ground black pepper. Herb Butter: Mix together ¼ cup (50 mL) chopped fresh herbs, 1½ tsp (7 mL) orange or lemon juice, ¼ tsp (1 mL) salt, and ¼ tsp (1 mL) ground black pepper. Citrus Butter: Mix together 1½ tsp (7 mL) grated lemon, lime or orange zest, 1½ tbsp (22 mL) lemon, lime or orange juice, ¼ tsp (1 mL) salt, and ¼ tsp (1 mL) ground black pepper.
- ½ cup (125 mL) Browned Butter: Melt ½ cup (125 mL) butter in small saucepan over medium heat and cook until golden brown or dark golden brown. Use like melted margarine or chill until firm and use like margarine

Margarine (cont'd)

- 7 tbsp (105 mL) bacon or pork fat or ⅓ cup (75 mL) chicken or poultry fat (for sautéing, frying, and sauces)
- 7 tbsp (105 mL) shortening or lard (for pastry and baking; creates flakier pastry and crisper cookies because shortening and lard lack water; consider using half shortening or lard and half margarine or butter for flakiness and flavor)

For Better Health

Substitute ½ cup (125 mL) margarine with:

- ½ cup (125 mL) reduced-fat margarine (fewer calories; more water; for spreading only; not for baking)
- ½ cup (125 mL) whipped margarine or margarine spread (fewer calories; more air; for spreading only; not for baking)
- ¼ cup (50 mL) margarine or buttermilk + ¼ cup (50 mL) well-drained, unsweetened applesauce or baby food prunes (for baking; applesauce works well with lighter-color or spice batters; puréed prunes work best with darker batters, such as chocolate; creates slightly chewier texture; use pastry or cake flour for lighter texture; increase sugar for more crispness)
- 3 tbsp (45 mL) margarine + 3 tbsp (45 mL) oil (for baking, especially cookie doughs; reduce baking time slightly; product will be slightly more chewy; use pastry or cake flour for lighter texture; increase sugar for more crispness)
- ½ cup (125 mL) apple butter (for baking; reduce baking time slightly; product will be slightly more chewy; use pastry or cake flour for lighter texture; adjust sugar if apple butter is sweetened)
- ½ cup (125 mL) fat-free, fruit-based butter and oil replacement such as Smucker's "Baking Healthy" (for baking only)
- ¼ cup (50 mL) fat-free, fruit-based butter and oil replacement such as Sunsweet "Lighter Bake" (for baking only)
- ½ cup (125 mL) marshmallow crème (for fillings and frostings)
- ½ cup (125 mL) oil (for sautéing and frying). Or use a mixture of margarine and oil. Or use a nonstick pan coated with cooking oil spray (or 1 to 2 tsp/5 to 10 mL oil or margarine) and heat the pan thoroughly

See also BUTTER; OIL; VEGETABLE SHORTENING.

Marigold

See PICKING EDIBLE FLOWERS (PAGE 604).

Marinade

A seasoned liquid in which various foods are soaked to absorb flavor or to tenderize them prior to cooking. Typical ingredients are oil, wine, citrus juice, vinegar, aromatics, herbs, and spices.

If You Don't Have It
Substitute 1 cup (250 mL) marinade with:
- 1 cup (250 mL) salad dressing or vinaigrette with similar flavors
- ½ cup (125 mL) spice rub with similar flavors (for flavoring meats; pat over entire surface)

Marionberry

Also known as Marion blackberry. Named after Marion County, Oregon, where it was developed, this blackberry variety is a cross between the Chehalem blackberry and olallieberry.

> 1 pint fresh =
> 2 cups (500 mL)

If You Don't Have It
Substitute 1 cup (250 mL) marionberries with:
- 1 cup (250 mL) blackberries (smaller)
- 1 cup (250 mL) loganberries (red color)
- 1 cup (250 mL) boysenberries (slightly sweeter)
- 1 cup (250 mL) olallieberries (sweeter)
- 1 cup (250 mL) raspberries (smaller; sweeter)

Marjoram

A distinctive, widely used culinary herb from the genus Origanum, of which four main species exist. One species, Origanum majorana, tastes similar to thyme, while the others have varying shades of oregano flavor.

> 1 oz (30 g) = 6 tbsp
> (90 mL) chopped

If You Don't Have It
Substitute 1 tbsp (15 mL) chopped fresh marjoram with:
- 1 tsp (5 mL) dried marjoram

To Vary the Flavor
Substitute 1 tbsp (15 mL) chopped fresh marjoram with:
- 2 to 3 tsp (10 to 15 mL) chopped fresh oregano
- 1 tbsp (15 mL) chopped fresh sweet basil
- 2 to 3 tsp (10 to 15 mL) chopped fresh thyme
- 1 tbsp (15 mL) chopped fresh summer savory
- 1 to 2 tsp (5 to 10 mL) chopped fresh sage
- 1 tsp (5 mL) dried Italian seasoning (adds oregano, thyme, and basil flavors)
- 1 tsp (5 mL) Herbes de Provence (adds other flavors such as thyme, savory, lavender, fennel, and bay leaf)

Marlin

Also known as spearfish. The name for several large firm-flesh billfish pursued around the globe as a prized game catch.

If You Don't Have It
Substitute 1 lb (500 g) marlin with:
- 1 lb (500 g) swordfish
- 1 lb (500 g) mako shark
- 1 lb (500 g) tuna
- 1 lb (500 g) mahi-mahi

Marmalade

Citrus fruit preserve that includes strips of zest along with the fruit. Seville, or bitter, orange is the most common.

If You Don't Have It
Substitute 1 tbsp (15 mL) marmalade with:
- 1 tbsp (15 mL) chutney (more complex flavor; add sugar or honey to taste)
- 1 tbsp (15 mL) preserves or jam

Maroilles

Named after an abbey in northern France, this square, semisoft cheese has a piercing surface aroma that belies the rich, yellow cheese inside.

If You Don't Have It
Substitute 1 oz (30 g) Maroilles with:
- 1 oz (30 g) Gris de Lille
- 1 oz (30 g) Livarot
- 1 oz (30 g) Limburger
- 1 oz (30 g) Pont-l'Évêque
- 1 oz (30 g) Herve
- 1 oz (30 g) Liederkranz

Marsala

A Denominazione di Origine Controllata (DOC) fortified wine from Sicily enjoyed both for sipping and cooking. Marsala Fine and Superiore *are made with* sifone *(sweet wine and alcohol) and/or vino cotto (reduced grape must) in varying percentages and a blend of red and white wines. Marsala Vergine or Solera is formulated like Spanish sherry, with a blend of aged wines from different barrels. Stravecchio is a Marsala Vergine aged for a decade in wooden barrels.*

If You Don't Have It
Substitute 3 tbsp (45 mL) Marsala with:
- 3 tbsp (45 mL) Madeira
- 1 tbsp (15 mL) dry sherry + 1 tbsp (15 mL) sweet vermouth
- 3 tbsp (45 mL) dry sherry

Marshmallow

Originally a confection made by boiling the pulpy roots of the marsh mallow plant with sugar. Today's marshmallows are a combination of sugar, corn syrup, and gelatin.

> 1 lb (500 g) =
> 4 cups (1 L) =
> 100 miniature marshmallows
>
> 1 large = 10 miniature

If You Don't Have It
Substitute 8 to 10 regular marshmallows with:
- 1 cup (250 mL) mini-marshmallows
- ¾ cup (175 mL) marshmallow creme (sweeter; spreadable)

Marshmallow Crème

Also known as marshmallow cream. A convenient topping of whipped melted marshmallows, such as Marshmallow Fluff®.

> 7.5 oz (225 g) jar =
> 2½ cups (625 mL)

If You Don't Have It
Substitute 1 cup (250 mL) marshmallow crème with:
- 16 large or 160 miniature marshmallows + 2 tsp (10 mL) corn syrup, stirred until smooth in a double boiler or stainless steel bowl over simmering water

Marzipan

A paste of ground almonds and sugar that has myriad confectionery uses in Europe, North Africa, the Middle East, India, and Mexico. It is a filling for yeast breads, cakes, petits fours, macaroons, and sweet meats. It is also an edible sculpting medium for pastry artists.

> 7 oz (210 g) =
> ⅞ cup (220 mL)

If You Don't Have It
Substitute 2½ cups (625 mL) marzipan with:
- 2 cups (500 mL) almond paste + 1 cup (250 mL) confectioner's (icing) sugar + 3 tbsp (45 mL) light corn syrup, combined with a pastry blender or kneaded together by hand until pliable

Masa

Traditional Mexican dough for corn tortillas. It is prepared from dried corn kernels that are cooked and soaked overnight in limewater. The corn is then drained and ground.

1 lb (500 g) = 2 cups (500 mL)

If You Don't Have It

Substitute 1 cup (250 mL) fresh masa with:
- 1 cup (250 mL) masa harina + 1 cup (250 mL) plus 3 tbsp (45 mL) hot water

See also MASA HARINA.

Masa Harina

"Dough flour" made from dried masa is a convenient ingredient for preparing corn tortillas and other dishes.

1 lb (500 g) = 3 cups (750 mL)

If You Don't Have It

Substitute 1 cup (250 mL) masa harina with:
- 1 cup (250 mL) prepared fresh masa
- 1 cup (250 mL) harinilla (masa harina made from blue corn)
- 1 cup (250 mL) corn flour (texture will be less appealing)

See also MASA.

Mascarpone

Luscious Italian fresh, soft cow's milk cheese with only slightly less fat than butter. The finest is said to come from Lombardy and Emilia-Romagna.

8 oz (250 g) = 1 cup (250 mL)

If You Don't Have It

Substitute 1 cup (250 mL) mascarpone cheese with:
- 1 cup (250 mL) crème fraîche
- ½ cup (125 mL) cream cheese + ½ cup (125 mL) sour cream, blended by hand or in a small food processor until smooth
- ¾ cup (175 mL) cream cheese + ¼ cup (50 mL) heavy or whipping cream (35% butterfat), blended by hand or in a small food processor until smooth
- ½ cup (125 mL) ricotta cheese + ½ cup (125 mL) heavy or whipping cream (35% butterfat), blended by hand or in a food processor until smooth

For Better Health

Substitute 1 cup (250 mL) mascarpone cheese with:
- ½ cup (125 mL) mascarpone cheese + ½ cup (125 mL) Neufchâtel cheese

Masticha

Greek brandy-based liqueur flavored with gum mastic, an amber-color plant resin that tastes of licorice. The island of Chios is the main producer of Greek mastic.

If You Don't Have It
Substitute 3 tbsp (45 mL) Masticha with:
- 3 tbsp (45 mL) ouzo
- 3 tbsp (45 mL) Metaxa
- 3 tbsp (45 mL) arak, sambuca, or other anise liqueur

Matar Dal

See PEAS, SPLIT; SWITCHING LENTILS (PAGE 569).

Matsutake Mushroom

See SHUFFLING MUSHROOMS (PAGE 572).

Matzo

Also known as matzoh. Cracker-like unleavened Jewish bread is traditionally eaten for Passover.

If You Don't Have It
Substitute 1 lb (500 g) matzo with:
- 1 lb (500 g) crisp lavash

See also MATZO MEAL.

Matzo Meal

Fine or medium-consistency crumbs made from crushing matzo. Matzo meal is a thickener, a breading agent, and an ingredient in many Jewish dishes, such as gefilte fish and matzo balls.

> 1 cup (250 mL) =
> 3 crushed matzos

If You Don't Have It
Substitute 1 cup (250 mL) matzo meal with:
- 3 matzos, crushed (in a food processor or using a bag and a rolling pin) to the texture of fine or medium-fine crumbs
- 1 cup (250 mL) cracker crumbs

To Vary the Flavor
Substitute 1 cup (250 mL) matzo meal with:
- 1 cup (250 mL) plain dry bread crumbs
- 1 cup (250 mL) crushed melba toasts
- 1 cup (250 mL) crushed tortilla chips
- 1 cup (250 mL) crushed dry-bagged stuffing mix
- 1 cup (250 mL) crushed pretzels
- 1 cup (250 mL) crushed cornflakes
- 1 cup (250 mL) crushed potato chips

See also MATZO.

Maui Onion

See ONION, SWEET.

Mayonnaise

New York delicatessen owner Richard Hellmann began mass-producing mayonnaise in 1912 from his wife, Nina's, recipe. The condiment was an immediate hit and was said to boost the popularity of coleslaw.

32 oz (1 kg) jar =
4 cups (1 L)

If You Don't Have It

Substitute 1 cup (250 mL) mayonnaise with:

- 1 cup (250 mL) Homemade Mayonnaise: Whisk together 1 egg yolk, 1 tbsp (15 mL) lemon juice, and ½ tsp (2 mL) salt using a whisk or in a food processor. While whisking or with the machine running, blend in ½ cup (125 mL) olive oil or vegetable oil in a thin steady stream until mixture is blended and thick. Makes about 1 cup (250 mL).
- 1 cup (250 mL) sour cream
- 1 cup (250 mL) yogurt
- 1 cup (250 mL) cottage cheese, puréed in a blender or small food processor
- ½ cup (125 mL) mayonnaise + ½ cup (125 mL) yogurt or sour cream

To Vary the Flavor

Substitute 1 cup (250 mL) mayonnaise with:

- 1 cup (250 mL) Homemade Aïoli: Make 1 cup (250 mL) Homemade Mayonnaise (above) or use store-bought, adding 2 minced garlic cloves or 2 to 4 tsp (10 to 20 mL) mashed roasted garlic along with the egg yolk and reducing lemon juice to 1 tsp (5 mL). Add salt to taste. Makes about 1 cup (250 mL).
- 1 cup (250 mL) Homemade Tartar Sauce: Make 1 cup (250 mL) Homemade Mayonnaise (above) or use store-bought, stirring in 3 tbsp (45 mL) minced cornichons, gherkins, or pickle relish, 1 tbsp (15 mL) minced scallions or shallots, and 1 tsp (5 mL) drained capers. Add salt to taste. Makes about 1 cup (250 mL).
- 1 cup (250 mL) Homemade Rouille: Make 1 cup (250 mL) Homemade Mayonnaise (above) or use store-bought, adding ⅓ to ½ cup (75 to 125 mL) roasted red bell peppers, 1 large garlic clove, and a pinch of cayenne pepper. Add salt to taste. Makes about 1 cup (250 mL).
- 1 cup (250 mL) Homemade Rémoulade: Make 1 cup (250 mL) Homemade Mayonnaise (above) or use store-bought, stirring in 1 tbsp (15 mL) minced cornichons, 1 tbsp (15 mL) drained capers, 1 tbsp (15 mL) chopped fresh parsley, 1½ tsp (7 mL) chopped fresh tarragon, 1 tsp (5 mL) Dijon mustard, 1 minced garlic clove, and 1 finely chopped hard-boiled egg. Add salt to taste. Makes about 1 cup (250 mL).

- 1 cup (250 mL) Homemade Chipotle Mayonnaise:
Make 1 cup (250 mL) Homemade Mayonnaise (left)
or use store-bought, stirring in 2 to 3 tsp (10 to
15 mL) finely chopped canned chipotle peppers in
adobo sauce. If you like, also stir in 1 tbsp (15 mL)
lime juice, 1 tbsp (15 mL) chopped fresh cilantro,
1 to 2 tsp (5 to 10 mL) tomato purée, and $\frac{1}{2}$ tsp
(2 mL) minced garlic. Add salt to taste. Makes about
1 cup (250 mL).

For Better Health
Substitute 1 cup (250 mL) mayonnaise with:
- 1 cup (250 mL) Homemade Mayonnaise Substitute:
Whisk together 1 tbsp (15 mL) cornstarch, $1\frac{1}{4}$ tsp
(6 mL) mustard powder, 1 tsp (5 mL) honey, and
$\frac{1}{2}$ tsp (2 mL) salt in a small saucepan. Gradually
whisk in $\frac{3}{4}$ cup (175 mL) buttermilk and 1 egg.
Cook over medium heat, whisking constantly, until
thickened and bubbly, 3 to 5 minutes. Remove from
heat and whisk in 3 tbsp (45 mL) lemon juice and
1 tbsp (15 mL) olive oil. Makes about 1 cup (250 mL).
- 1 cup (250 mL) reduced-fat mayonnaise
- $\frac{1}{2}$ cup (125 mL) reduced-fat mayonnaise + $\frac{1}{2}$ cup
(125 mL) low-fat yogurt

Maytag Blue

*An esteemed American
cheese produced by heirs
to the appliance company
in Newton, Iowa.*

4 oz (125 g) = 1 cup
(250 mL) crumbled

If You Don't Have It
Substitute 1 oz (30 g) Maytag Blue cheese with:
- 1 oz (30 g) Roquefort
- 1 oz (30 g) Fourme d'Ambert
- 1 oz (30 g) Bleu d'Auvergne
- 1 oz (30 g) Bleu des Causses

Measuring Cups

See VOLUME EQUIVALENTS (PAGE 610).

Meat

*Originally, the edible
portion of something. In
the 1300s, meat began to
refer only to the edible
portion of animals.*

For Better Health
Substitute 1 lb (500 g) meat with:
- 1 lb (500 g) tofu or vegetarian beef, pork, or poultry
products (these generally have fewer calories)

See also BEEF; LAMB; PORK; VEAL.

Meat Tenderizer, Powdered

Sold in supermarkets, this white powder contains papain — an enzyme found in papaya that breaks down the fibers of meat — as well as salt, sweetener, and anti-caking agents.

If You Don't Have It
Substitute 1 cup (250 mL) powdered meat tenderizer with:
- 2 cups (500 mL) papaya or kiwi purée or juice (add to marinade or spread over surface of meat; marinate in refrigerator 30 minutes to 1 hour)

Meat Thermometer

See THERMOMETER.

Mei Yen Seasoning

See MONOSODIUM GLUTAMATE.

Melba Toast

The great French chef Auguste Escoffier created this thin, dry toast to honor opera star Dame Nellie Melba.

If You Don't Have It
Substitute 16 Melba toasts with:
- 16 thinly cut crostini or bruschetta
- 16 bagel chips
- 16 crackers
- 16 zwieback

Melegueta Pepper

See GRAINS OF PARADISE.

Mellowfruit

See PEPINO.

Melon

See SPECIFIC TYPES.

Melon Pear

See PEPINO.

Menudo Mix

Also known as menudo spices. The typical seasoning blend that flavors Mexican tripe stew.

If You Don't Have It
Substitute 1 tbsp (15 mL) menudo mix with:
- 1 tsp (5 mL) dried Mexican oregano + ½ tsp (2 mL) onion flakes + ¼ to ½ tsp (1 to 2 mL) garlic flakes + ½ tsp (2 mL) cumin seeds + ¼ to ½ tsp (1 to 2 mL) crushed red pepper flakes

Merguez

North African beef sausage spiced and colored red with fiery harissa. Often grilled or served as an accompaniment to couscous.

If You Don't Have It

Substitute 1 lb (500 g) merguez sausage with:
- 1 lb (500 g) chorizo
- 1 lb (500 g) andouille
- 1 lb (500 g) spicy kielbasa
- 1 lb (500 g) hot Italian sausage
- 1 lb (500 g) hot links

See also HARISSA.

Meringue Powder

Convenient, shelf-stable product made of dried egg whites, cornstarch, sugar, and cream of tartar. Can be used as an egg white substitute for meringues or other baked goods or to make confectionery icings.

If You Don't Have It

Substitute 1 tbsp (15 mL) meringue powder with:
- 1 tbsp (15 mL) powdered egg white
- 3 tbsp (45 mL) frozen and thawed egg white
- 1 large egg white (to replace reconstituted meringue powder when making meringue)

Mescal

See TEQUILA.

Mesclun

Also known as gourmet salad mix and salad mix. The French word for an assortment of young salad greens.

> 1 lb (500 g) =
> 6 cups (1.5 L)

If You Don't Have It

Substitute 1 lb (500 g) mesclun with:
- 1 lb (500 g) Homemade Mesclun: Combine 4 oz (125 g) oak leaf lettuce, 2 oz (60 g) arugula, 2 oz (60 g) tatsoi, 2 oz (60 g) frisée, 2 oz (60 g) mizuna, 2 oz (60 g) radicchio, and 2 oz (60 g) mâche or dandelion greens. Makes about 1 pound (500 g).

Metaxa

A proprietary Greek spirit blended from aged brandy and sweet wine, and flavored with herbs and spices. The finest type, Metaxa Grande Fine, resembles Spanish Sherry.

If You Don't Have It

Substitute 3 tbsp (45 mL) Metaxa with:
- 3 tbsp (45 mL) cognac
- 3 tbsp (45 mL) Armagnac
- 3 tbsp (45 mL) sherry

Metric Conversion

See METRIC CONVERSIONS (PAGE 609).

Mettwurst

Also known as Schmierwurst. A spreadable smoked German sausage seasoned with coriander and white pepper.

If You Don't Have It

Substitute 1 lb (500 g) Mettwurst with:
- 1 lb (500 g) Teewurst (spicier)
- 1 lb (500 g) liverwurst
- 1 lb (500 g) Braunschweiger (smoked liverwurst)
- 1 lb (500 g) pâté

Mexican Chocolate

See CHOCOLATE, MEXICAN.

Mexican Custard Apple

See SAPOTE, WHITE.

Mexican Green Tomato

See TOMATILLO.

Mexican Lime

See LIME.

Mexican Potato

See JICAMA.

Meyer Lemon

Not a true lemon, but believed to be a cross between a lemon and a mandarin orange. Meyer lemons have sweeter and more orange flesh and juice than the common Eureka and Lisbon lemons.

> 1 medium Meyer lemon
> = ¼ to ⅓ cup
> (50 to 75 mL) juice =
> 1 to 3 tbsp
> (15 to 45 mL) zest

If You Don't Have It

Substitute 1 Meyer lemon with:
- 1 large Eureka or Lisbon lemon (smaller; more acidic; add ¼ to ½ tsp/1 to 2 mL sugar if you like)
- ½ tsp (2 mL) orange (larger; sweeter)
- ¾ Eureka or Lisbon lemon + ¼ orange (to replace Meyer lemon juice)
- 1 lime (slightly smaller)
- 1 calamondin (hybrid of kumquat and mandarin orange)
- ¼ grapefruit (larger; sweeter)
- ¼ pummelo (larger; sweeter)

See also LEMON.

Mezcal

See TEQUILA.

Mezzaluna

Also known as lunetta. Italian "half moon" shaped knife with handles at either end for rocking back and forth over food to chop it.

If You Don't Have It
Substitute a mezzaluna with:
- sharp chef's knife used with a rocking motion

Microplane®

See GRATER.

Microwave Oven

About the size of a small refrigerator, the first microwave ovens for home use went on sale in 1947. Price: about $3,000.

If You Don't Have It
Substitute a microwave oven with:
- steamer (for steaming fish, vegetables, and other foods)
- saucepan and a gas or electric burner (for heating and reheating soups, sauces, and most other foods; add 30 to 50% more cooking time)
- double boiler (for melting chocolate)
- gas or electric oven (for melting chocolate and for cooking and reheating casseroles and other foods that may be cooked in a microwave oven; add 30 to 50% more cooking time)

Midori

Glowing green Japanese liqueur that tastes like very sweet honeydew melon.

If You Don't Have It
Substitute 3 tbsp (45 mL) midori with:
- 3 tbsp (45 mL) honeydew melon schnapps (less sweet)

To Vary the Flavor
Substitute 3 tbsp (45 mL) midori with:
- 3 tbsp (45 mL) watermelon liqueur
- 3 tbsp (45 mL) orange liqueur
- 3 tbsp (45 mL) strawberry liqueur
- 3 tbsp (45 mL) raspberry liqueur

Milk, Dry

See DRY MILK.

Milk, Fat-Free

Also known as skim milk and nonfat milk. Fat-free cow's milk can legally contain no more than 0.5% fat. One cup (250 mL) of fat-free milk contains 86 calories and 301 milligrams of calcium.

If You Don't Have It

Substitute 1 cup (250 mL) fat-free milk (less than 0.5% fat) with:

- ⅓ cup (75 mL) nonfat dry milk + ¾ cup (175 mL) water
- ¼ cup (50 mL) nonfat skim milk + 1 cup (250 mL) minus 3 tbsp (45 mL) water
- ½ cup (125 mL) evaporated skim milk + ½ cup (125 mL) water (adds slight caramelized flavor)

Milk, Sour

See SOUR MILK.

Milk, Whole

Whole cow's milk contains about 3½% fat. Prior to the uniform practice of commercial homogenization that disperses and suspends the fat through the liquid milk, it was possible for the naked eye to see the milkfat rise to the top of a jar and form luscious, thick cream.

1 quart = 4 cups (1 L)

If You Don't Have It

Substitute 1 cup (250 mL) whole milk (3.5% fat) with:

- 1 cup (250 mL) minus 3 tbsp (45 mL) fat-free milk + 3 tbsp (45 mL) melted butter or margarine
- 10 tbsp (150 mL) fat-free milk + 6 tbsp (90 mL) half-and-half
- ¾ cup (175 mL) 2% milk + ¼ cup (50 mL) half-and-half
- 1 cup (250 mL) minus 1 tbsp (15 mL) half-and-half + 3 tbsp (45 mL) water (omit 1 tbsp/15 mL butter, shortening, or oil from recipe)
- ½ cup (125 mL) evaporated whole milk + ½ cup (125 mL) water (adds slight caramelized flavor)
- 1 cup (250 mL) minus 3 tbsp (45 mL) water + ¼ cup (50 mL) dry milk
- 1 cup (250 mL) minus 3 tbsp (45 mL) water + ¼ cup (50 mL) nonfat dry milk + 1 tbsp (15 mL) melted butter or margarine

To Vary the Flavor

Substitute 1 cup (250 mL) whole milk (3.5% fat) with:

- 1 cup (250 mL) raw milk (more complex flavor; unpasteurized; adds beneficial enzymes)
- 1 cup (250 mL) buttermilk (more tangy; for baking, reduce baking powder in recipe by 2 tsp/10 mL and add ½ tsp/2 mL baking soda)
- 1 cup (250 mL) sour cream (more tangy; for baking, creates moister, more tender baked goods; reduce baking powder in recipe by 1 tsp/5 mL, reduce fat by 2 to 3 tbsp/25 to 45 mL, and add ½ tsp/2 mL baking soda)
- 1 cup (250 mL) fruit juice or potato water (for baking)

For Better Health

Substitute 1 cup (250 mL) whole milk (3.5% fat) with:

- 1 cup (250 mL) acidophilus milk (cow's milk with added beneficial enzymes)
- 1 cup (250 mL) reduced-fat, low-fat, or fat-free milk (2%, 1%, or less than 0.5% fat; thinner consistency; yields less rich results)
- 1 cup (250 mL) lactose-free milk (for the lactose intolerant)
- 1 cup (250 mL) goat's milk (for the lactose intolerant; more tangy taste)
- 1 cup (250 mL) soy milk, rice milk, or almond milk (for the lactose intolerant or vegetarians; may be sweetened)
- 1 cup (250 mL) oat milk (for the lactose intolerant or vegetarians; may be sweetened)

See also BUTTERMILK; CREAM; EVAPORATED MILK; MILK, FAT-FREE; SOUR MILK; SWEETENED CONDENSED MILK.

Millet

A protein-rich grain that is a staple to nearly one-third of the people on Earth. The whole grains are boiled into hot cereals, simmered in pilafs and ground into flour.

1 cup (250 mL) =
3½ cups (875 mL) cooked

If You Don't Have It

Substitute 1 cup (250 mL) millet with:

- 1 cup (250 mL) quinoa
- 1 cup (250 mL) couscous (cooks more quickly)
- 1 cup (250 mL) bulgur
- 1 cup (250 mL) rice
- 1 cup (250 mL) kasha (roasted buckwheat groats; takes more time to cook)

See also CHOOSING AMONG WHOLE-GRAIN AND ALTERNATIVE FLOURS (PAGE 586).

Mimolette

From the Lille region of France, a semihard golden unpasteurized cow's milk cheese with intense nutty flavor.

1 lb (500 g) = 4 cups
(1 L) shredded

If You Don't Have It

Substitute 1 oz (30 g) Mimolette cheese with:

- 1 oz (30 g) Edam
- 1 oz (30 g) Gouda
- 1 oz (30 g) mild Cheddar (to replace aged Mimolette)

Mint

Also known as herbia buena or yerba buena (in Spanish). Peppermint and spearmint may be the most commercially popular varieties, but more than 500 varieties of mint are believed to exist, including apple mint, chocolate mint, ginger mint, horsemint, lamb mint, lemon mint, orange mint, and pineapple mint.

2 oz (60 g) = 1½ cups (375 mL) chopped

If You Don't Have It

Substitute 1 tbsp (15 mL) chopped fresh mint with:
- 1 tsp (5 mL) dried mint
- 1 tsp (5 mL) mint from herbal mint tea bag (will often be peppermint)
- ¼ to ½ tsp (1 to 2 mL) mint extract
- 1 drop oil of peppermint
- 1 to 3 tbsp (15 to 45 mL) crème de menthe (reduce liquid in recipe by 1 to 3 tbsp/15 to 45 mL if necessary; reduce sugar by 1 tsp/5 mL)
- 3 to 4 tbsp (45 to 60 mL) peppermint schnapps (reduce liquid in recipe by 3 to 4 tbsp/45 to 60 mL if necessary)
- 1 tbsp (15 mL) chopped fresh parsley (preferably, add a pinch of dried mint)
- 1 tbsp (15 mL) chopped fresh basil (works well in savory and sweet dishes)

Mint Varieties

Choose 1 tbsp (15 mL) chopped fresh mint from these varieties:
- 1 tbsp (15 mL) chopped fresh spearmint (gentle mint aroma)
- 1 tbsp (15 mL) chopped fresh peppermint (more assertive, peppery mint aroma)
- 1 tbsp (15 mL) chopped fresh pineapple or apple mint (gentle mint and green apple aromas)
- 1 tbsp (15 mL) chopped fresh lemon mint (gentle mint and citrus aromas)

See also OIL OF PEPPERMINT; VIETNAMESE MINT.

Mint Chutney

Just one of a kaleidoscope of Indian fresh piquant relishes, refreshing mint chutney goes well with biriani, dosas, and samosas.

If You Don't Have It

Substitute ½ cup (125 mL) mint chutney with:
- ½ cup (125 mL) Homemade Mint-Cilantro Chutney: Combine ¼ cup (50 mL) fresh mint leaves, ¼ cup (50 mL) fresh cilantro leaves, 3 tbsp (45 mL) coarsely chopped onion, 3 tbsp (45 mL) water, 1 tbsp (15 mL) lime juice, 1 tsp (5 mL) granulated sugar, ⅛ tsp (0.5 mL) salt, and a pinch of cayenne pepper in a small food processor or blender. Makes about ½ cup (125 mL).

Mint Extract

A blend of oil of peppermint, oil of spearmint, alcohol, and water, used to flavor candies, frostings, cakes, and cookies.

If You Don't Have It

Substitute ½ tsp (2 mL) mint extract with:
- ⅛ tsp (0.5 mL) oil of peppermint

Mint Oil

See OIL OF PEPPERMINT.

Mint Sauce

The classic British accompaniment to roast lamb. The properties in mint that aid digestion help to counteract the fatty meat.

If You Don't Have It

Substitute 1 cup (250 mL) mint sauce with:
- ½ cup (125 mL) Homemade Mint Sauce: Mix together 1¼ cups (300 mL) apple cider vinegar (or white wine vinegar), ¼ cup (50 mL) water, and 3 tbsp (45 mL) light brown sugar in a saucepan. Bring just to a simmer over medium heat. Remove from heat and stir in ¼ cup (50 mL) minced fresh mint. Let cool to room temperature. Cover and refrigerate for up to 2 days. Makes about 1½ cups (375 mL).

Mirabelle

See PLUM; PLUM BRANDY.

Mirin

Also known as Japanese sweet rice wine. Used in Japanese cooking to flavor sauces, glazes, and other dishes. Sold in many supermarkets.

If You Don't Have It

Substitute ½ cup (125 mL) mirin with:
- 1½ to 2 tbsp (22 to 25 mL) sugar dissolved in ½ cup (125 mL) dry sherry, vermouth, white wine, or sake
- ½ cup (125 mL) amontillado sherry

Mirliton

See CHAYOTE.

Miso

Fermented soybean paste with the addition of barley, rice, or rye. Created in China, miso is now mostly associated with Japanese cuisine,

If You Don't Have It

Substitute 1 tbsp (15 mL) miso with:
- 1 tbsp (15 mL) Chinese sweet bean paste
- 1 tsp (5 mL) soy sauce
- 2 tsp (10 mL) anchovy paste + ⅛ to ¼ tsp (0.5 to 1 mL) sugar (adds fish flavor)
- ¼ to ½ tsp (1 to 2 mL) salt (less complex flavor)

Miso (cont'd)

in which it is used to make broths, soups, salad dressings, sauces, pickles, and more.

> 5 oz (150 g) =
> ½ cup (125 mL)

- 1 tbsp (15 mL) Hoisin sauce (much sweeter; more complex flavors)
- 1 tbsp (15 mL) umeboshi paste (more sour and pungent)

Miso Varieties

Choose 1 tbsp (15 mL) miso from these varieties:
- 1 tbsp (15 mL) white or shiro miso (pale yellow color; very mild, salty-sweet flavor)
- 1 tbsp (15 mL) yellow or shinshu miso (golden yellow color; mellow salty flavor)
- 1 tbsp (15 mL) barley or mugi miso (reddish brown color; pronounced salty-sweet flavor)
- 2 to 3 tsp (10 to 15 mL) red or sendai miso (reddish yellow color; pronounced salty and pungent flavor)
- 2 to 3 tsp (10 to 15 mL) dark or hatcho miso (reddish brown color; thicker; very strong salty and pungent flavor)

Mixed Spice

Also known as British mixed spice and pudding spice. An English baking standard used to season a variety of desserts and baked goods.

If You Don't Have It

Substitute 1 tsp (5 mL) mixed spice with:
- 1 tsp (5 mL) Homemade Mixed Spice: Combine 4 tsp (20 mL) ground cinnamon, 2 tsp (10 mL) ground coriander, 1 tsp (5 mL) ground allspice, ½ tsp (2 mL) ground nutmeg, ½ tsp (2 mL) ground ginger, and ¼ tsp (1 mL) ground cloves. Makes about 2½ tablespoons (32 mL).
- 1 tsp (5 mL) apple pie spice
- 1 tsp (5 mL) pumpkin pie spice

Mixer, Electric

Tools that beat, mix, or whip foods. Stationary mixers are powerful and come with attachments, such as dough hooks, meat grinders, or ice crushers that expand their utility. Portable mixers are smaller, lighter, and easier to store.

If You Don't Have It

Substitute an electric mixer with:
- rotary beater
- whisk

Mizithra

See MYZITHRA.

Mizuna

Also known as kyona. Of Chinese origin, this mustardy-cabbagey incised-leaf green is beloved in Japan. Use younger leaves in salads and mature leaves for cooking.

If You Don't Have It
Substitute 1 cup (250 mL) mizuna with:
- 1 cup (250 mL) tender mustard greens
- 1 cup (250 mL) tatsoi
- 1 cup (250 mL) tender arugula
- 1 cup (250 mL) mibuna (longer, smooth, slender leaves; more mild flavor)
- 1 cup (250 mL) komatsuna or tendergreen (longer, broader leaves; milder flavor similar to young spinach)

Mochi

See VARIETIES OF RICE (PAGE 591).

Mochiko

See RICE FLOUR, SWEET.

Molasses

Most supermarkets sell unsulfured molasses, which has a lighter, cleaner taste than sulfured molasses, which is processed with sulfur dioxide as a preservative.

8 oz (250 g) = 1 cup (250 mL)

If You Don't Have It
Substitute 1 cup (250 mL) molasses with:
- 1 cup (250 mL) honey, dark corn syrup, or maple syrup
- ¾ cup (175 mL) light or dark brown sugar dissolved in ¼ cup (50 mL) hot water or liquid in recipe
- ¾ cup (175 mL) granulated sugar dissolved in ¼ cup (50 mL) hot water or liquid in recipe + 1¼ tsp (6 mL) cream of tartar (for baking; cream of tartar adds acidity present in molasses)
- 1 cup (250 mL) golden syrup (much lighter in flavor)
- 2 cups (500 mL) brown rice syrup (reduce liquid in recipe by 1 cup/250 mL if necessary)
- 1¾ cups (425 mL) barley malt syrup (reduce liquid in recipe by ¾ cup/175 mL if necessary)

Molasses Varieties
Choose 1 cup (250 mL) molasses from these varieties:
- 1 cup (250 mL) dark molasses (often used in American baked goods; dark brown, thick, mildly sweet)
- 1 cup (250 mL) light or Barbardos molasses (often used like pancake syrup; lighter brown color and milder, sweeter flavor than dark molasses)
- 1 cup (250 mL) blackstrap molasses (used less often in cooking; slightly higher in nutrients; very dark brown to black; thicker; more bitter flavor)

Molcajete y Tejolote

See MORTAR AND PESTLE

Monkfish

Also known as anglerfish, bellyfish, frogfish, goosefish, lotte, and sea devil. A firm-fleshed, low-fat fish with a sweet, mild flavor that is, optimistically, compared to lobster.

If You Don't Have It

Substitute 1 lb (500 g) monkfish with:
- 1 lb (500 g) blackfish
- 1 lb (500 g) lobster
- 1 lb (500 g) carp
- 1 lb (500 g) grouper
- 1 lb (500 g) red snapper
- 1 lb (500 g) tilefish
- 1 lb (500 g) wolffish

Monosodium Glutamate

Also known as MSG. Commercially available as Accent, Mei Yen Seasoning, aji-no-moto, Ve-Tsin, and other products. Identified by Japanese scientists in the 1920s, MSG is a white powder derived from glutamic acid found in seaweed, certain vegetables, and other plants. It is flavorless in itself but acts to intensify the flavor of other foods.

If You Don't Have It

Substitute 1 tsp (5 mL) monosodium glutamate with:
- 1 to 2 tsp (5 to 10 mL) powdered dulse (a sea vegetable)

Montasio

Cow's milk cheese from northeastern Italy's Friuli-Venezia Giulia region is used to make frico, *the regional specialty fried cheese.*

1 lb (500 g) = 4 cups (1 L) shredded

If You Don't Have It

Substitute 1 oz (30 g) Montasio cheese with:
- 1 oz (30 g) Carnia
- 1 oz (30 g) medium-ripe Asiago (less complex flavor)

Monterey Jack

See JACK CHEESE.

Montrachet

*Ash-coated logs of tangy
chèvre from French
Burgundy. At its best
when young and fresh.*

| 8 oz (250 g) =
1 cup (250 mL) |
|---|

If You Don't Have It

Substitute 1 oz (30 g) Montrachet with:
- 1 oz (30 g) Crottin de Chavignol (soft to firm texture and mild to nutty flavor, depending on age)
- 1 oz (30 g) Selles-sur-Cher (semifirm texture; sweet, nutty flavor; covered with black ash)
- 1 oz (30 g) Bûcheron (softer texture; usually covered with black ash or a white rind)
- 1 oz (30 g) Banon (softer texture; wrapped in chestnut leaves)
- 1 oz (30 g) aged chèvre (firmer texture; stronger flavor)

To Vary the Flavor

Substitute 1 oz (30 g) Montrachet with:
- 1 oz (30 g) mascarpone (smoother; less complex flavor)
- 1 oz (30 g) cream cheese (smoother; less complex flavor)

See also CHÈVRE.

Moose

*A large North American
member of the deer family
— the counterpart of the
European elk — that can
weigh up to 1,300 pounds
(650 kg). Moose is valued
for its meat, and, according
to one Inuit chronicler, the
nose is the tastiest morsel.*

If You Don't Have It

Substitute 1 lb (500 g) moose with:
- 1 lb (500 g) elk
- 1 lb (500 g) caribou
- 1 lb (500 g) red, fallow, or white-tailed deer
- 1 lb (500 g) reindeer
- 1 lb (500 g) antelope
- 1 lb (500 g) gazelle

See also VENISON.

Morbier

*A French semisoft, raw
unpasteurized cow's milk
cheese. The pale yellow
paste is divided into two
layers by a thin flavorless
layer of ash. One layer is
the cheese from the morning
milking and the other from
the evening milking.*

If You Don't Have It

Substitute 1 oz (30 g) Morbier with:
- 1 oz (30 g) Fontina
- 1 oz (30 g) Vacherin Fribourgeois
- 1 oz (30 g) Raclette

Morcilla

This blood sausage is a required ingredient in Fabada Asturiana, the famous bean stew of northwest Spain.

If You Don't Have It
Substitute 1 lb (500 g) Morcilla with:
- 1 lb (500 g) Blutwurst (German blood sausage)
- 1 lb (500 g) boudin rouge (Cajun blood sausage)
- 1 lb (500 g) Zungenwurst (German blood sausage; includes tongue)

Morel

See SHUFFLING MUSHROOMS (PAGE 572).

Moro

See ORANGE, BLOOD.

Mortadella

This signature sausage from Bologna is composed of finely ground pork, studded with bits of fat, peppercorns, and pistachios. Some mortadella sausages can weigh as much as 180 pounds (90 kg).

If You Don't Have It
Substitute 1 lb (500 g) mortadella with:
- 1 lb (500 g) bologna (less complex flavor)
- 1 lb (500 g) galantina (chunkier; more complex flavor)
- 1 lb (500 g) olive loaf (adds olive flavor)
- 1 lb (500 g) semidry or summer sausage such as Thuringer, Landjäger, or Lebanon bologna

For Better Health
Substitute 1 lb (500 g) mortadella with:
- 1 lb (500 g) Gelbwurst (lower in fat and calories)

Mortar and Pestle

A combination tool used to grind and mix various foods. The mortar is shaped like a bowl, the pestle fashioned like a thick stick with a rounded end that conforms to the bowl. Can be made of porcelain, wood, stone, marble, or other hard materials. In Mexico, the term for mortar and pestle is molcajete y tejolote.

If You Don't Have It
Substitute a mortar and pestle with:
- coffee or spice grinder (for finely grinding small amounts of dry ingredients such as spices)
- rolling pin or heavy skillet (for coarsely crushing)
- food processor (for crushing larger amounts or wet ingredients such as in pesto)

Mountain Cranberry

See LINGONBERRY.

Mozzarella

Low-moisture mozzarella cheese is typically used in Italian-American cooking. High-moisture mozzarella is often served fresh or used in traditional Italian cooking. Bocconcini are "little mouthfuls" of high-moisture mozzarella (the size of ping-pong balls) floating in whey.

1 lb (500 g) low-moisture mozzarella = 4 cups (1 L) shredded

If You Don't Have It
Substitute 1 oz (30 g) mozzarella with:
- 1 oz (30 g) Scamorza
- 1 oz (30 g) Caciocavallo
- 1 oz (30 g) provolone
- 1 oz (30 g) string cheese
- 1 oz (30 g) queso blanco
- 1 oz (30 g) Bel Paese
- 1 oz (30 g) Muenster
- 1 oz (30 g) Gouda
- 1 oz (30 g) Fontina

Mozzarella Varieties
Choose 1 oz (30 g) mozzarella from these varieties:
- 1 oz (30 g) mozzarella di buffalo (sweeter, moister, more complex taste than cow's milk mozzarella)
- 1 oz (30 g) smoked mozzarella (adds smoke flavor)

Muenster

Also known as Munster. True French Muenster is a soft, yellow pungent cow's milk cheese with an orange rind. It is one of only a few cheeses to ripen from the inside out. American and other versions are white and mild.

1 lb (500 g) = 4 cups (1 L) shredded

If You Don't Have It
Substitute 1 oz (30 g) Muenster cheese with:
- 1 oz (30 g) Beaumont
- 1 oz (30 g) Reblochon
- 1 oz (30 g) Monterey Jack
- 1 oz (30 g) mozzarella
- 1 oz (30 g) Gouda
- 1 oz (30 g) Havarti
- 1 oz (30 g) Bel Paese
- 1 oz (30 g) Fontina

Muesli

Swiss nutritionist Dr. Bircher-Benner created this healthful "mixture" in the late 1800s. Typical ingredients include raw or toasted grains, such as oats, wheat, millet, and barley, mixed with various dried fruits, nuts, bran, wheat germ, and honey or sugar.

If You Don't Have It
Substitute 1 cup (250 mL) muesli with:
- 1 cup (250 mL) granola (very similar)

Mulberry

The black mulberry is the species most often grown for its fruit. Although to the casual eye it looks like a blackberry, it is actually a sorosis like the pineapple. The fruit forms a cluster of small berries, each with surface lobes that are formed from one of a cluster of flowers.

1 pint fresh =
2 cups (500 mL)

If You Don't Have It

Substitute 1 cup (250 mL) mulberries with:
- 1 cup (250 mL) blackberries (smaller; firmer)
- 1 cup (250 mL) loganberries (smaller; red color)
- 1 cup (250 mL) boysenberries (smaller; slightly sweeter)
- 1 cup (250 mL) olallieberries (sweeter)
- 1 cup (250 mL) raspberries (smaller; red color; sweeter)

Mullet

Also known as silver mullet and striped mullet. Members of the gray mullet family are fairly fat, with firm flesh, and pleasantly nutty taste.

If You Don't Have It

Substitute 1 lb (500 g) mullet with:
- 1 lb (500 g) sea bass
- 1 lb (500 g) ocean perch
- 1 lb (500 g) grouper
- 1 lb (500 g) orange roughy

See also RED MULLET.

Mulling Spice Mix

A combination of various flavorings, such as herbs, spices, dried fruit, and sugar, which impart a warm and complex flavor when heated with beer, cider, wine, or other beverages.

If You Don't Have It

Substitute 1 tsp (5 mL) ground mulling spice mix with:
- 1 tsp (5 mL) Homemade Mulling Spice Mix: Combine 1 to 2 three-inch (7.5 cm) cinnamon sticks (or ½ to 1 tsp/2 to 5 mL ground cinnamon) + 2 to 4 whole cloves (or a big pinch of ground cloves) + 2 to 4 whole allspice berries (or a big pinch of ground allspice) + 1 sliced orange. If using ground spices, tie them in cheesecloth or a coffee filter with kitchen string or a clean twist-tie. Makes enough to mull 3 cups (750 mL) cider or red wine.

Mung Bean

See THE WIDE WORLD OF DRIED BEANS (PAGE 566).

Mung Bean Noodles

See A SNAPSHOT OF ASIAN NOODLES (PAGE 588).

Mung Bean Sprouts

Germinated mung beans are widely used in the Chinese kitchen for salads and stir-fried dishes. Crisp fresh bean sprouts may be refrigerated in a plastic bag for up to a week.

1 lb (500 g) = 1 quart = 4 cups (1 L)

If You Don't Have It
Substitute 1 cup (250 mL) mung bean sprouts with:
- 1 cup (250 mL) sunflower sprouts
- 1 cup (250 mL) julienned snow peas
- 1 cup (250 mL) soybean sprouts

Munster

See MUENSTER.

Muscadine Grape

See GRAPE, TABLE; MUSCADINE JELLY.

Muscadine Jelly

A preserve made from a grape native to the southeastern United States. The musky-tasting purple grapes are also used to make scuppernong wine.

If You Don't Have It
Substitute 1 cup (250 mL) scuppernong or muscadine jelly with:
- 1 cup (250 mL) red currant jelly
- 1 cup (250 mL) grape jelly

Mushrooms, Dried

Drying is an excellent method of keeping many mushrooms. Most dried mushrooms have a much more intense flavor than their fresh counterparts.

2 to 3 oz (60 to 90 g) dried and reconstituted = 1 lb (500 g) fresh

If You Don't Have It
Substitute 1½ oz (45 g) dried mushrooms with:
- 8 oz (250 g) sliced fresh mushrooms
- 4 oz (125 g) drained canned sliced mushrooms

See also SHUFFLING MUSHROOMS (PAGE 572).

Mushrooms, Fresh

Cooks often say to clean mushrooms by dry wiping because they soak up water during rinsing. Scientist Harold McGee refuted that theory and recommends rinsing.

1 lb (500 g) fresh =
5 cups (1.25 L) sliced =
6 cups (1.5 L) chopped =
2 cups (500 mL) cooked

If You Don't Have It

Substitute 8 oz (250 g) sliced fresh mushrooms with:
- 4 oz (125 g) drained canned sliced mushrooms
- 1½ oz (45 g) dried mushrooms + ¾ cup (175 mL) boiling water

See also TRUFFLE; SHUFFLING MUSHROOMS (PAGE 572).

Mushrooms, Powdered

Often used to enhance the flavor of sauces, soups, stews, and flour coatings, this powder is made from ground dried mushrooms.

If You Don't Have It

Substitute 1 tbsp (15 mL) powdered mushrooms
- 3 tbsp (45 mL) whole dried mushrooms (pulverized in spice grinder if powder is needed)
- 4 oz (125 g) fresh mushrooms
- 2 oz (60 g) canned mushrooms

Muskmelon

See CANTALOUPE; CASABA; CHARENTAIS MELON; CRENSHAW MELON; GALIA MELON; HONEYDEW MELON; OGEN MELON; PERSIAN MELON; SANTA CLAUS MELON.

Mussels

Smaller mussels are more tender than large ones. Choose live mussels with shells that are intact and closed, or if open, that snap shut when tapped.

1 lb (500 g) medium =
9 to 12 mussels =
¾ to 1 cup
(175 to 250 mL) meat

If You Don't Have It

Substitute 1 lb (500 g) mussels with:
- 1 lb (500 g) oysters
- 1 lb (500 g) soft-shelled or littleneck clams
- 1 lb (500 g) cockles
- 1 lb (500 g) scallops

Mussel Varieties

Choose 1 lb (500 g) mussels from these varieties:
- 1 lb (500 g) blue mussels (shell is 2 to 3 inches/ 5 to 7.5 cm long and dark blue or black)
- 1 lb (500 g) New Zealand green mussels (shell is 3 to 4 inches/7.5 to 10 cm and green)
- 1 lb (500 g) Prince Edward Island mussels (farm-raised; beardless shell is 2 inches/5 cm long and dark blue or black)

Mustard Greens

The plant species Brassica juncea *has as many as 17 subspecies that produce leafy greens that vary greatly in appearance and pungency. From the American soul food classic southern mustard — which is also known as curled mustard and southern curled mustard — to Asian wrapped heart mustard — which is also known as dai gai choy, swatow mustard/cabbage, and heading mustard — these greens feature prominently in the cooking of Asia, India, and Africa.*

---

1 lb (500 g) fresh =
6 to 7 cups
(1.5 to 1.75 L) leaves

1 lb (500 g) fresh =
1⅓ to 2 cups
(325 to 500 mL) cooked

10 oz (300 g) frozen =
1¼ cups (300 mL)
cooked

If You Don't Have It

Substitute 1 lb (500 g) mustard greens with:
- 1 lb (500 g) escarole
- 1 lb (500 g) broccoli raab
- 1 lb (500 g) arugula
- 1 lb (500 g) turnip greens
- 1 lb (500 g) collards
- 1 lb (500 g) kale
- 1 lb (500 g) Chinese kale
- 1 lb (500 g) mature spinach
- 1 lb (500 g) green chard

Mustard Green Varieties

Choose 1 lb (500 g) mustard greens from these varieties:
- 1 lb (500 g) curled or American mustard (long, slender, pale green stems; large, bright green rippled leaves with frilly edges; sharp, hot flavor)
- 1 lb (500 g) wrapped heart mustard or dai gai choy (wide, curved, pale green stems, branching toward wide, bright green leaves; extremely sharp, hot flavor)
- 1 lb (500 g) leaf (bamboo) mustard or juk gai choy (smaller than dai gai choi; straight narrow or slightly wide pale green stems; flat, bright green leaves; mild to slightly strong sharp flavor)
- 1 lb (500 g) red-in-snow mustard (long, slender, pale green stems; large tear-drop shaped leaves with jagged edges; slightly sweet and mildly peppery flavor)
- 1 lb (500 g) Japanese (purple or giant-leaf) mustard (miniature purple greens often sold for salad mixes; mature greens have long, slender, pale green stems; broad, rippled leaves are green on one side and purple on the other; extremely sharp flavor when mature)

Mustard, Powdered

Also known as dry mustard. The vivid yellow-and-red Colman's Mustard tin is one of the most recognizable product packages in the world.

---

1 oz (30 g) =
5 tbsp (75 mL)

If You Don't Have It

Substitute 1 tsp (5 mL) powdered mustard with:
- 1 tbsp (15 mL) prepared mustard minus 1 tsp (5 mL) liquid from recipe
- 1¼ to 1½ tsp (6 to 7 mL) mustard seeds (pulverized in spice grinder if powder is needed)

Mustard, Prepared

An internationally varied condiment prepared from ground mustard seeds, liquid (water, vinegar, wine, beer, or grape must), and other seasonings. More than 700 million pounds (325 million kg) of mustard are consumed annually around the world. Canada takes the title for mustard cultivation champion, growing about 90% of the world's supply.

1 oz (30 g) =
3 tbsp (45 mL)

If You Don't Have It

Substitute 1 tbsp (15 mL) prepared mustard with:

- 1 tsp (5 mL) powdered mustard + 1 to 2 tsp (5 to 10 mL) vinegar or water
- 1 tsp (5 mL) mustard seeds
- 1 tsp (5 mL) caraway seeds
- 1 tsp (5 mL) prepared horseradish
- 1 tsp (5 mL) mayonnaise

Prepared Mustard Varieties

Choose 1 tbsp (15 mL) prepared mustard from these varieties:

- 1 tbsp (15 mL) Dijon mustard (smooth or grainy texture; mild to sharp flavor)
- 1 tbsp (15 mL) Chinese mustard (smooth texture; sharp flavor)
- 1 tbsp (15 mL) Creole mustard (grainy texture; very sharp flavor)
- 1 tbsp (15 mL) hot mustard (smooth or grainy texture; very sharp flavor)
- 1 tbsp (15 mL) German mustard (smooth or grainy texture; mild to sharp flavor)

Mustard Seeds

White (yellow) and brown (Asian) are the two major commercial types. White seeds are mild; the brown more assertive. Whole seeds are used for pickling and seasoning. Ground seeds are the basis for prepared mustards.

If You Don't Have It

Substitute 1 tsp (5 mL) mustard seeds with:

- ¾ to 1 tsp (4 to 5 mL) powdered mustard
- 1 tbsp (15 mL) prepared mustard minus 1 tsp (5 mL) liquid from recipe

Mustard Seed Varieties

Choose 1 tsp (5 mL) mustard seeds from these varieties:

- 1 tsp (5 mL) yellow (white) mustard seeds (sharp flavor; often used to make prepared yellow mustard)
- 1 tsp (5 mL) brown mustard seeds (very sharp flavor; often used in Indian cooking)
- 1 tsp (5 mL) black mustard seeds (very sharp flavor; often used in Indian cooking)

Mutton

See LAMB.

Mysost

Also known as primost. Scandinavian cheese created by caramelizing cow's milk whey.

If You Don't Have It

Substitute 1 oz (30 g) mysost with:
- 1 oz (30 g) gjetost

See also GJETOST.

Myzithra

Also known as Mizithra. A Greek sheep's milk cheese made from the whey of feta and kefalotyri, available both fresh and aged. The fresh resembles cottage cheese. The aged is pungent, somewhat like Italian ricotta salata, and makes an excellent grating cheese.

> 1 lb (500 g) fresh =
> 4 cups (1 L) crumbled
>
> 1 lb (500 g) aged =
> 4 cups (1 L) grated

If You Don't Have It

Substitute 1 oz (30 g) Myzithra cheese with:
- 1 oz (30 g) feta (to replace fresh Myzithra)
- 1 oz (30 g) manouri (to replace fresh Myzithra)
- 1 oz (30 g) cotija (fresh or aged; to replace fresh or aged Myzithra)
- 1 oz (30 g) aged ricotta salata (to replace aged Myzithra for grating)
- 1 oz (30 g) Pecorino Romano (to replace aged Myzithra for grating)
- 1 oz (30 g) Parmesan (to replace aged Myzithra for grating)

Naan to Nuts

Naan

Also known as nan. Indian white-flour flatbread. The traditional preparation uses dough that is lightly leavened by airborne yeast starter. A pleasant smoky note is added when baked in a tandoor oven.

If You Don't Have It

Substitute 1 naan with:
- 1 roti (a generic term for Indian flatbread; similar to chapati; usually made with whole wheat flour)
- 1 chapati (wheat-flour flatbread with little or no fat; less puffy)
- 1 paratha (griddle-cooked whole wheat flatbread with fat in the dough; richer; more flaky)
- 1 poori (deep-fried flatbread made with whole wheat flour; crisper)
- 1 whole wheat pita bread (similar to naan)
- 1 whole wheat flour tortilla

Nameko

See SHUFFLING MUSHROOMS (PAGE 572).

Nam Pla

See FISH SAUCE.

Nam Prik

See CHILE PASTE.

Nan

See NAAN.

Napa Cabbage

Also known as celery cabbage, Chinese cabbage, da bai cai, hakusai, and wong bok. Growing in tightly clustered heads of ivory stalks rimmed with pale green ruffled leaves, this indigenous Chinese cabbage is sweeter and less assertive than European cabbages. It's enjoyed as much for its texture as its flavor and appears raw or cooked in many dishes.

> 1 lb (500 g) =
> 3½ to 4½ cups
> (875 mL to 1.125 L)
> sliced = 1½ to 2 cups
> (375 to 500 mL) cooked

If You Don't Have It

Substitute 1 lb (500 g) napa cabbage with:
- 1 lb (500 g) bok choy (larger, darker green leaves; firmer, juicier stems)
- 1 lb (500 g) savoy cabbage (stronger flavor)
- 1 lb (500 g) green chard (less cabbagey flavor)
- 1 lb (500 g) green or red cabbage (sturdier leaves; stronger flavor)
- 1 lb (500 g) collard greens (thinner, firmer, deeper green stems; larger, darker green leaves)

Napa Cabbage Variety

Choose 1 lb (500 g) napa cabbage from this variety:
- 1 lb (500 g) Michihli (similar, but more elongated with firmer, crunchier stems)

See also BOK CHOY.

Nasturtium

A flower with ruffled blooms in vivid shades of yellow, red, and orange, nasturtiums taste as good as they look. The flowers, along with the leaves and stems, have a pleasant peppery appeal as part of salads, sandwiches, and spreads. Often, nasturtiums are used simply to accessorize a dish.

If You Don't Have It

Substitute 1 cup (250 mL) nasturtium with
- 1 cup (250 mL) marigolds (to replace nasturtium flowers)
- 1 cup (250 mL) pansies (to replace nasturtium flowers)
- 1 cup (250 mL) watercress or other cress (to replace nasturtium leaves)

See also CRESS; PICKING EDIBLE FLOWERS (PAGE 604).

Natal Plum

See CARISSA.

Natural Cocoa

See COCOA POWDER, UNSWEETENED.

Navel Orange

See ORANGE, SWEET.

Navy Bean

See THE WIDE WORLD OF DRIED BEANS (PAGE 566).

Nectarine

A variety of peach without the fuzz.

> 1 lb (500 g) =
> 3 to 4 medium = 2 cups
> (500 mL) chopped =
> 2½ cups (625 mL) sliced
> = 1½ cups (375 mL)
> puréed

If You Don't Have It

Substitute 1 lb (500 g) nectarines with:
- 1 lb (500 g) peaches
- 1 lb (500 g) plums
- 1 lb (500 g) apricots
- 1 lb (500 g) cherries

Nettles

Also known as stinging nettles. Only the young shoots and leaf tops of this defensive plant are eaten. They must be cooked to get rid of formic acid, which can irritate the skin, found in the fibers on the leaves.

> 1 lb (500 g) fresh =
> 1⅓ to 2 cups
> (325 to 500 mL) cooked

If You Don't Have It

Substitute 1 lb (500 g) nettles with:
- 1 lb (500 g) curly endive or frisée
- 1 lb (500 g) escarole
- 1 lb (500 g) kale
- 1 lb (500 g) spinach

Neufchâtel

A French soft white unripened cow's milk cheese that is mild when young and more pungent with age.

> 8 oz (250 g) =
> 1 cup (250 mL)

If You Don't Have It

Substitute 1 lb (500 g) Neufchâtel with:
- 1 lb (500 g) cream cheese (higher in fat)
- 1 lb (500 g) mascarpone (higher in fat)
- 1 lb (500 g) Boursin cheese (adds herb flavors)

See also CREAM CHEESE.

Neutral Spirits

Also known as ethanol, ethyl alcohol, and grain alcohol. Neutral spirits are 190 proof, clear, and tasteless. Aging in wood creates grain spirits with flavor nuances.

If You Don't Have It

Substitute 3 tbsp (45 mL) neutral spirits with:
- ¼ cup (50 mL) 100-proof vodka (reduce liquid in recipe by 3 tbsp/45 mL)
- 3 tbsp (45 mL) grain spirits (wood-aged; mellower flavor)

See also VODKA.

New Zealand Spinach

Also known as Botany Bay greens and tetragonia. A relative of the ice plant, this Pacific Rim native is not related to spinach apart from its vivid green leaves. A cooking vegetable, the flavor is mild and the texture creamy.

1 lb (500 g) fresh =
10 cups (2.5 L) =
6 to 8 cups
(1.5 to 2 L) cooked

If You Don't Have It
Substitute 1 lb (500 g) New Zealand Spinach with:
- 1 lb (500 g) amaranth leaves
- 1 lb (500 g) callaloo
- 1 lb (500 g) chard leaves
- 1 lb (500 g) Chinese kale
- 1 lb (500 g) spinach

Nigella

Mistakenly called black onion seeds, these tiny black seeds have nothing to do with onion seeds. Nutty and peppery, the seeds are much used in the Middle East and India.

If You Don't Have It
Substitute 1 tsp (5 mL) nigella seeds with:
- 1 tsp (5 mL) cumin seeds, especially black cumin seeds
- 1 tsp (5 mL) ajwain
- 1 tsp (5 mL) caraway seeds

Nixtamal

Also known as maiz nixtamalado. These lime-treated, partially cooked, dried starchy corn kernels are sold refrigerated or frozen in Mexican groceries. An essential for the Mexican pork stew posole and other special dishes.

1 lb (500 g) whole =
1¼ cups (300 mL)

If You Don't Have It
Substitute 1 cup (250 mL) nixtamal with:
- 1 cup (250 mL) hominy (fully cooked; softer)

Nökkelost

Also known as kuminost. Danish semifirm cheese enhanced with caraway seeds, cloves, and cumin.

1 lb (500 g) = 4 cups (1 L) shredded

If You Don't Have It
Substitute 1 oz (30 g) Nökkelost with:
- 1 oz (30 g) Leyden (firmer)
- 1 oz (30 g) Gouda (no cumin or caraway flavors)
- 1 oz (30 g) Edam (less rich; no cumin or caraway flavors)

Nonfat Milk

See MILK, FAT-FREE.

Nonpareils

From the French term meaning "without equal," these colored sugar dots are the size of a pinhead and used to decorate cakes, candies, and cookies.

If You Don't Have It
Substitute 1 tbsp (15 mL) nonpareils with:
- 1 tbsp (15 mL) dragées
- 1 tbsp (15 mL) jimmies
- 1 tbsp (15 mL) colored sugar sprinkles (decorating sugar)
- 1 tbsp (15 mL) mini M&Ms

Nonreactive Cookware

See EARTHENWARE; ENAMELWARE; STAINLESS-STEEL COOKWARE.

Nonstick Cookware

Chemist Roy J. Plunkett is the patron saint of dishwashers everywhere. Researching chlorofluorocarbon refrigerants in a DuPont laboratory in 1938, Plunkett accidentally discovered the polymer that came to be Teflon®. An awards luncheon for Plunkett in 1960 also served to introduce Teflon® bakeware to the public. Each guest left the luncheon with a Teflon®-coated muffin pan.

If You Don't Have It
Substitute nonstick cookware with:
- well-seasoned cast-iron cookware + little or no fat, oil, or oil spray (after years of use most cast-iron pans are virtually nonstick)
- anodized aluminum cookware + a small amount of fat, oil, or oil spray (anodized aluminum is relatively low-stick)
- enameled cast-iron cookware + a small amount of fat, oil, or oil spray
- copper, stainless-steel, or clad metal stainless cookware + a fair amount of fat, oil, or oil spray (first heat the fat for the best prevention against sticking)

Noodles

See EGG NOODLE; PASTA; A SNAPSHOT OF
ASIAN NOODLES (PAGE 588).

Nopale

*Also known as cactus leaf.
After removing the thorns
with a vegetable peeler, the
fleshy pads of the prickly
pear cactus taste like green
beans touched with lemon.*

| 1 lb (500 g) fresh =
3 cups (750 mL) cut
into strips |

If You Don't Have It
Substitute 1 lb (500 g) fresh nopales with:
- 1 lb (500 g) okra
- 1 lb (500 g) green beans
- 1 lb (500 g) asparagus

Nopale Varieties
Choose 1 lb (500 g) nopales from these varieties:
- 1 lb (500 g) nopalitos or chopped nopales
  (often sold canned)
- 1 lb (500 g) acitróns (candied nopales)

Nori

*Also known as sushi nori
and yaki-nori (when
toasted). Japanese seaweed
that is dried and pressed
into beautiful sheets that
range in color from dark
green to purple black.
Used most commonly to
wrap sushi and rice balls.*

If You Don't Have It
Substitute 1 oz (30 g) nori with:
- 1 oz (30 g) sea lettuce
- 1 oz (30 g) rice paper
- 1 oz (30 g) dumpling wrappers
- plastic wrap or a silicone mat (for making maki
  rolls without nori or any wrapper)

See also LAVER.

Norway Haddock

See OCEAN PERCH.

Nova

See SMOKED SALMON.

Nuoc Cham

*In the Vietnamese kitchen,
this dipping condiment
adds vibrancy to many
dishes. To prepare it,
nuoc nam (fish sauce)
is seasoned with red
chilies, garlic, lime
juice, ginger, and sugar.*

If You Don't Have It
Substitute 1 cup (250 mL) nuoc cham with:
- 1 cup (250 mL) Homemade Nuoc Cham: Dissolve
  ¼ to ⅓ cup (50 to 75 mL) granulated sugar in
  3 tbsp (45 mL) hot water. Stir in ⅓ cup (75 mL)
  fresh lime juice, ⅓ cup (75 mL) nuoc nam or
  other fish sauce, 1 to 2 minced garlic cloves, and
  1 seeded and minced Thai, cayenne, or serrano
  chile. Let stand for 15 to 20 minutes to blend
  flavors. Makes about 1 cup (250 mL).

Nuoc Nam

See FISH SAUCE.

Nutella

See GIANDUJA.

Nut Flour

See CHOOSING AMONG WHOLE-GRAIN AND ALTERNATIVE FLOURS (PAGE 586).

Nut Meal

Also known as ground nuts. Nuts ground just before using are bound to be fresher than packaged ground nuts. Nut meal has more oil and is coarser than commercial nut flours, which are finely ground from nuts that have already been pressed for their oil.

If You Don't Have It

Substitute 1 cup (250 mL) nut meal with:

- 1 cup (250 mL) Homemade Nut Meal: Grind about 2 cups (500 mL) chilled whole nuts, such as almonds, hazelnuts, pecans, or walnuts, in a nut mill or food processor. If using a food processor, add 1 to 3 tbsp (15 to 45 mL) granulated sugar and use short pulses just until the nuts resemble cornmeal (the sugar and pulsing help to prevent the nut meal from turning to nut butter; reduce sugar in recipe if necessary). Makes about ½ cup (125 mL).
- 1 cup (250 mL) nut flour (finer texture)

See also CHOOSING AMONG WHOLE-GRAIN AND ALTERNATIVE FLOURS ON PAGE 586).

Nutmeg

Oval brown nutmeg seeds keep their flavor for months, or even years, when stored in a cool, dry, dark cupboard. For finest aroma and flavor, grate the seed on a specially designed nutmeg grater or on a fine rasp-style grater.

If You Don't Have It

Substitute 1 tsp (5 mL) ground or grated nutmeg with:

- 1 tsp (5 mL) ground mace
- 1 tsp (5 mL) ground allspice
- 1 to 1½ tsp (5 to 7 mL) ground cinnamon
- 1 tsp (5 mL) apple pie spice (adds cinnamon and allspice flavors)
- 1 tsp (5 mL) pumpkin pie spice (adds cinnamon, allspice, and ginger flavors)

Nutmeg Grater

See GRATER.

Nutritional Yeast

See YEAST, NUTRITIONAL.

Nuts

In botanical terms, a nut is a dry single-seeded fruit that doesn't split open along a seam when mature. Acorns, chestnuts, and hazelnuts are true nuts. In culinary terms, a nut is any of various seeds and fruits with an edible kernel surrounded by a hard covering. The almond is part of a fruit called a drupe, the Brazil nut is a seed enclosed with other seeds in a capsule, and the peanut is a legume. Other non-nut nuts are cashews, pistachios, and walnuts.

---

1 lb (500 g) in shell =
1⅔ cups (400 mL) shelled

1 lb (500 g) shelled =
3 to 4 cups
(750 mL to 1 L) whole =
2¾ to 3¾ cups
(675 to 925 mL) chopped

4 oz (125 g) = ¾ to 1 cup
(175 to 250 mL) chopped

If You Don't Have It
Substitute 1 cup (250 mL) nuts with:
- 2 to 4 tbsp (25 to 60 mL) nut oil, such as almond, hazelnut, macadamia, pecan, pistachio, or walnut (for baking and cooking; will add nut flavor but not texture of whole nuts; reduce fat in recipe by 2 to 4 tbsp/25 to 60 mL)
- 1 cup (250 mL) chocolate chips (for baking)

To Vary the Flavor
Substitute 1 cup (250 mL) nuts with:
- 1 cup (250 mL) toasted nuts (more aromatic; toast nuts in dry pan until fragrant)

For Better Health
Substitute 1 cup (250 mL) nuts with:
- ½ cup (125 mL) toasted nuts, finely chopped (toasting intensifies flavor of nuts so you can use less; finely chopping them better distributes the flavor)
- 1 cup (250 mL) toasted rolled oats (for baking, especially to top baked goods)
- 1 cup (250 mL) Grape-Nuts cereal (for baking; crunchier and less rich)

See also ALMOND; ALMOND PASTE; BRAZIL NUT; BUTTERNUT; CASHEW; CHESTNUT; HAZELNUT; MACADAMIA NUT; PEANUT; PECAN; PINE NUT; PISTACHIO; WALNUT.

Oak Leaf Lettuce to Oyster Sauce

Oak Leaf Lettuce

See LEAF LETTUCE.

Oat Bran

The outer casing of the oat groat is very high in heart-healthy soluble fiber.

If You Don't Have It

Substitute 1 cup (250 mL) oat bran with:

- 1 cup (250 mL) wheat bran
- 1 cup (250 mL) rice bran
- 1 cup (250 mL) wheat germ

Oat Flour

There is no gluten in oat flour, so for baked goods that need gluten's protein structure to rise and trap air bubbles, a flour with gluten must be added to the mix. Generally, oat flour can replace up to one-third of wheat flour in a recipe.

> 1 lb (500 g) =
> 3 cups (750 mL)

If You Don't Have It

Substitute 1 cup (250 mL) oat flour with:

- 1¼ cups (300 mL) old-fashioned oatmeal, ground in blender or food processor to the consistency of flour

See also CHOOSING AMONG WHOLE-GRAIN AND ALTERNATIVE FLOURS (PAGE 586).

Oat Groats

Whole oat grains that are cleaned, toasted, hulled, and cleaned a second time. They are prepared as a cereal or a cooked grain for pilafs, salads, or stuffings.

> 1 cup (250 mL) =
> 2 to 2½ cups
> (500 to 625 mL) cooked

If You Don't Have It

Substitute 1 cup (250 mL) oat groats with:
- 1 cup (250 mL) rye berries
- 1 cup (250 mL) wheat berries (takes longer to cook)
- 1 cup (250 mL) hulled or whole-grain barley (takes longer to cook)
- 1 cup (250 mL) triticale berries or groats (takes longer to cook)
- 1 cup (250 mL) spelt berries or groats (takes longer to cook)
- 1 cup (250 mL) Kamut© berries or groats (takes longer to cook)
- 1 cup (250 mL) kasha (cooks faster)
- 1 cup (250 mL) brown rice (cooks faster)

Oat Milk

Fortified substitute for those who can't or don't want to drink cow's milk. Produced by straining cooked and flavored oats.

If You Don't Have It

Substitute 1 cup (250 mL) oat milk with
- 1 cup (250 mL) Homemade Oat Milk: Put 5 cups (1.25 L) water in a large saucepan and bring to a boil over high heat. Add a pinch of salt and 1 cup (250 mL) old-fashioned rolled oats. Reduce heat to medium-low and simmer gently until oats are very soft and liquid is reduced to level of oats, 30 to 40 minutes. If you like, add ½ to ¾ tsp (2 to 4 mL) vanilla extract. Sweeten to taste with ¼ to ½ cup (50 to 125 mL) brown rice syrup, maple syrup, honey, or sugar. Purée with an immersion blender or in a food processor or blender. Strain through cheesecloth or a fine-mesh sieve set over a large bowl or pitcher. Refrigerate up to 5 days and shake before using. Makes about 3 cups (750 mL).
- 1 cup (250 mL) soy, rice, or almond milk
- 1 cup (250 mL) cow's or goat's milk

Oats, Old-Fashioned

Also known as rolled oats. According to British food authority Alan Davidson, "… it is commonly held that the disproportionately large measure of success and fame achieved by Scottish people on the world stage is partly or even primarily the result of a diet including oatmeal, especially porridge."

> 1 cup (250 mL) =
> 1¾ cups (425 mL) cooked
> 1 lb (500 g) =
> 5 cups (1.25 L) uncooked

If You Don't Have It

Substitute 1 cup (250 mL) old-fashioned rolled oats with:

- 1 cup (250 mL) steel-cut, Irish or Scotch oats (cut oat groats; smaller pieces; takes more time to cook; chewier and more flavorful)
- 1 cup (250 mL) oat groats (larger pieces; takes much longer to cook; much chewier)

To Vary the Flavor

Substitute 1 cup (250 mL) old-fashioned rolled oats with:

- 1 cup (250 mL) nuts (for baking, especially to top baked goods)

To Save Time

Substitute 1 cup (250 mL) old-fashioned rolled oats with:

- 1 cup (250 mL) quick-cooking rolled oats (cooks faster; smaller pieces; less chewy)

Oaxaca Cheese

See ASADERO.

Oca

A tuber from the Andes with a knobby shape resembling fingerling potatoes. The thin skin may be pink, red, or yellow, and the flesh is moist, crisp, waxy, sweet, and sour.

> 1 lb (500 g) = 3½ to
> 4 cups (875 mL to 1 L)
> chopped or sliced

If You Don't Have It

Substitute 1 lb (500 g) oca with:

- 1 lb (500 g) sunchokes
- 1 lb (500 g) arrowhead
- 1 lb (500 g) arracacha
- 1 lb (500 g) boniato
- 1 lb (500 g) artichoke hearts (softer texture; similar flavor)
- 1 lb (500 g) potatoes (drier texture; less complex flavor)

Ocean Perch

Also known as, Norway haddock and redfish. In the 1930s, a shortage of freshwater yellow perch inspired marketers to substitute a similar,

If You Don't Have It

Substitute 1 lb (500 g) ocean perch with:

- 1 lb (500 g) porgy
- 1 lb (500 g) red snapper
- 1 lb (500 g) weakfish
- 1 lb (500 g) whiting
- 1 lb (500 g) mullet

cheaper creature, the redfish, and dub it ocean perch. A member of the rockfish family, ocean perch is not a true perch. Redfish fillets have a firm flake, white flesh, and a taste just slightly more assertive than cod.

Ocean Perch Varieties

Choose 1 lb (500 g) Pacific ocean perch from these varieties:

- 1 lb (500 g) Pacific rockfish
- 1 lb (500 g) bocaccio
- 1 lb (500 g) yelloweye rockfish
- 1 lb (500 g) yellowtail rockfish
- 1 lb (500 g) widow rockfish

See also PERCH.

Octopus

The Japanese catch about half of the world's octopus. It is often blanched briefly, then is thinly sliced and served with a dip. Octopus is also frequently prepared nimono *style, in a long-simmered stew to tenderize it.*

If You Don't Have It

Substitute 1 lb (500 g) octopus with:

- 1 lb (500 g) squid
- 1 lb (500 g) cuttlefish (more tender)

Ogen Melon

An Israeli melon that is similar to honeydew.

2 lbs (1 kg) = 3 cups (750 mL) diced

If You Don't Have It

Substitute 1 cup (250 mL) chopped Ogen melon with:

- 1 cup (250 mL) chopped honeydew melon
- 1 cup (250 mL) chopped Galia melon
- 1 cup (250 mL) chopped Santa Claus melon
- 1 cup (250 mL) chopped cantaloupe
- 1 cup (250 mL) chopped Persian melon

Oil

Oils are liquid at room temperature, while fats (such as butter and vegetable shortening) are solid at room temperature. Recipes that refer to unspecified "oil" generally mean vegetable oil, which includes a wide variety of oils made from nuts, seeds, or other plant sources. The most common vegetable

If You Don't Have It

Substitute ¼ cup (50 mL) vegetable oil with:

- ¼ cup (50 mL) melted butter, margarine, bacon drippings, shortening, or lard (for sautéing and frying)
- 2 tbsp (25 mL) vegetable oil + 2 tbsp (25 mL) butter (for sautéing and frying; combines flavor of butter with higher smoke point of oil)
- cooking oil spray (or 1 tbsp/15 mL oil) and a nonstick pan (for sautéing; reduces total calories and fat; heat the pan thoroughly before cooking to help prevent sticking)

Oil (cont'd)

oils are canola oil and soybean oil, which are interchangeable. Olive oil can also replace canola oil and soybean oil for salad dressings, sautéing, and even baking if using a light-flavored olive oil.

To Vary the Flavor

Substitute ½ cup (125 mL) vegetable oil with:

- ½ cup (125 mL) "light" butter (adds butter flavor with fewer calories and less fat than butter due mostly to the addition of water; works best as a spread, in frostings and toppings, or melted for drizzling; in pie and pastry doughs, chill light butter and shred before quickly mixing with dry ingredients; in pancake and quick bread batters, omit 2 tbsp/25 mL milk or other liquid from recipe per ½ cup/125 mL light butter used)
- ¼ cup (50 mL) oil + ¼ cup (50 mL) butter (for baking; especially quick breads; increase baking time slightly; baked goods will be slightly more tender)
- ½ cup (125 mL) vegetable oil + 2 tsp (10 mL) toasted sesame oil (best for dressings and uncooked or gently cooked sauces)
- ⅓ cup (75 mL) vegetable oil + 2½ tsp (12 mL) highly flavored nut or seed oil such as walnut, pecan, almond, hazelnut, macadamia, pistachio, or pumpkin oil (best for dressings and uncooked or gently cooked sauces)

For Better Health

Substitute ½ cup (125 mL) vegetable oil with:

- ¼ cup (50 mL) buttermilk + ¼ cup (50 mL) well-drained, unsweetened applesauce or baby food prunes (for baking; puréed prunes work best with darker batters and doughs, such as chocolate or spice batters)
- ½ cup (125 mL) fat-free, fruit-based butter and oil replacement such as Smucker's "Baking Healthy" (for baking only)
- ¼ cup (50 mL) fat-free, fruit-based butter and oil replacement such as Sunsweet "Lighter Bake" (for baking only)
- ½ cup (125 mL) flaxseed oil (for dressings and uncooked sauces; flaxseed oil is rich in the same heart-healthy omega-3 fatty acids found in fish; avoid heating flaxseed oil, which destroys its omega-3's)

See also BUTTER; CHILE OIL; OLIVE OIL; SESAME OIL; SUBSTITUTING OILS (PAGE 598).

Oil of Bitter Almonds

The essential flavoring oil extracted from bitter almonds, which need to be heated to destroy the poisonous prussic acid that they contain.

If You Don't Have It
Substitute 1 drop oil of bitter almonds with:
- ¼ to ½ tsp (1 to 2 mL) almond extract

Oil of Lemon

See LEMON OIL.

Oil of Orange

See ORANGE OIL.

Oil of Peppermint

Although it's used for countless flavorings and fragrances, perhaps the most beloved use is to give candy canes that aroma of Christmas.

If You Don't Have It
Substitute 1 drop oil of peppermint with:
- 1 drop oil of spearmint (slightly milder)
- ⅛ to ¼ tsp (0.5 to 1 mL) mint extract
- 1 tbsp (15 mL) chopped fresh mint
- 1 tsp (5 mL) dried mint

Oka

A semisoft cheese made by Trappist monks in Quebec, Canada. It has wonderful melting properties and a nutty taste.

> 1 lb (500 g) = 4 cups
> (1 L) shredded

If You Don't Have It
Substitute 1 oz (30 g) oka cheese with:
- 1 oz (30 g) Port Salut
- 1 oz (30 g) Raclette
- 1 oz (30 g) Morbier

Okara

The white, flaky by-product of tofu production is high in fiber and protein. Look for it in Asian markets where fresh tofu is stocked.

If You Don't Have It
Substitute 1 lb (500 g) okara with:
- 1 lb (500 g) firm tofu (moister; slice into slabs and put a heavy skillet on top to press out excess liquid)

Okra

African slaves introduced this green pod vegetable to the American South, where it gained great interest, particularly as a thickener for the wonderful Louisiana gumbo.

---

1 lb (500 g) fresh =
2¼ cups (550 mL)
chopped and cooked

10 oz (300 g) frozen =
1¼ cups (300 mL)
chopped

15½ oz (440 mL) can
= 1¾ cups (425 mL)
chopped

If You Don't Have It
Substitute 2 cups (500 mL) okra (for thickening) with:
- 1 tbsp (15 mL) filé powder
- 1 cup (250 mL) nopales, sliced
- 2 tsp (10 mL) cornstarch mixed with 1 tbsp (15 mL) cold water

To Vary the Flavor
Substitute 2 cups (500 mL) okra with:
- 2 cups (500 mL) green beans
- 2 cups (500 mL) asparagus
- 2 cups (500 mL) broccoli

Olallieberry

This cross between a youngberry and a loganberry resembles blackberry. Delightful snatched from the bramble to the mouth.

---

1 pint fresh =
2 cups (500 mL)

If You Don't Have It
Substitute 1 cup (250 mL) olallieberries with:
- 1 cup (250 mL) Marionberries (slightly more tart)
- 1 cup (250 mL) loganberries (red color)
- 1 cup (250 mL) youngberries (dark red color)
- 1 cup (250 mL) boysenberries (slightly more tart)
- 1 cup (250 mL) raspberries (sweeter)
- 1 cup (250 mL) blackberries (slightly more tart)

See also BLACKBERRY; MARIONBERRY.

Old Bay Seasoning

In 1939, German-American immigrant Gustav Brunn settled in Baltimore and developed a blend of more than a dozen herbs and spices that would become Old Bay Seasoning. Synonymous with the Chesapeake Bay and

If You Don't Have It
Substitute 1 tbsp (15 mL) Old Bay Seasoning with:
- 1 tbsp (15 mL) Homemade Old Bay Seasoning:
  In a spice grinder or with a mortar and pestle, combine 1 tbsp (15 mL) celery salt or 1 tsp (5 mL) celery seeds, 2 tsp (10 mL) salt, 3 whole bay leaves, ¾ tsp (4 mL) brown mustard seeds or ½ tsp (2 mL) mustard powder, ½ tsp (2 mL) black peppercorns or ½ tsp (2 mL) ground black pepper, 10 allspice berries or ¼ tsp (1 mL) ground allspice, 10 whole cloves or ¼ tsp (1 mL) ground cloves, ½ tsp (2 mL) sweet paprika,

crabs, Old Bay is also used to flavor many other dishes.

$\frac{1}{8}$ tsp (0.5 mL) cayenne pepper, $\frac{1}{8}$ tsp (0.5 mL) ground ginger, $\frac{1}{8}$ tsp (0.5 mL) ground mace, $\frac{1}{8}$ tsp (0.5 mL) cardamom seeds (removed from pods or $\frac{1}{8}$ tsp/0.5 mL ground cardamom), and a pinch of ground cinnamon. Grind to a coarse powder and store in an airtight container. Makes about 2 tablespoons (25 mL).

- 1 tbsp (15 mL) crab boil
- 1 tbsp (15 mL) pickling spice

Oleomargarine

See MARGARINE.

Olive Loaf

This cold cut is bologna studded with green olives.

If You Don't Have It
Substitute 1 lb (500 g) olive loaf with:

- 1 lb (500 g) mortadella (includes cubes of pork fat and garlic flavor)
- 1 lb (500 g) bologna
- 1 lb (500 g) galantina (more chunky)

For Better Health
Substitute 1 lb (500 g) olive loaf with:

- 1 lb (500 g) Gelbwurst (less fat and fewer calories)

Olive Oil

The primary table oil of the Mediterranean basin is now recognized internationally for its health-giving properties and its distinctive flavor. Numerous varieties of olives, which are adapted to the growing conditions of different regions, are grown for oil. After the ripe olives are gathered, stems and leaves are removed and the olives are washed in preparation for the first cold-pressing, which yields oil of the highest quality and finest flavor. Keeping the

If You Don't Have It
Substitute $\frac{1}{2}$ cup (125 mL) olive oil (for cooking) with these other cooking oils:

- $\frac{1}{2}$ cup (125 mL) corn oil (similar smoke point of 410°F/210°C; mild flavor; yellow color; fat content is 13% saturated, 62% polyunsaturated, and 25% monounsaturated)
- $\frac{1}{2}$ cup (125 mL) untoasted sesame seed oil (415°F/213°C smoke point; mild nutty flavor; light yellow color; fat content is 18% saturated, 41% polyunsaturated, and 41% monounsaturated)
- $\frac{1}{2}$ cup (125 mL) canola or rapeseed oil (435°F/224°C smoke point; flavorless; light yellow color; fat content is 6% saturated, 32% polyunsaturated, and 62% monounsaturated)
- $\frac{1}{2}$ cup (125 mL) grapeseed oil (445°F/229°C smoke point; mild flavor; fat content is 13% saturated, 70% polyunsaturated, and 17% monounsaturated)

Olive Oil (cont'd)

temperature of the oil below 86°F (30°C) is critical to maintain the distinct characteristics of the oil. If the temperature climbs higher, the oil cannot be considered cold-pressed. Up to 90% of the oil is obtained from the olives during the first cold pressing. The remaining 10% is extracted in refineries that use heat and/or chemical processes to remove the oil remaining in the paste. Although it may appear that darker green oil is more intensely flavored, the color is not a reliable indicator of flavor. Greener oils may simply be pressed from greener olives earlier in the season. Different varieties of olives produce oil in varying shades of green and gold. Plus, most oils (unless they are a boutique bottling from a single olive grove) are blends of several olive varieties, perhaps from various growing areas. The various olive oil grades, from extra virgin to extra light, are defined here.

- ½ cup (125 mL) peanut oil (450°F/230°C smoke point; neutral yet rich flavor; golden color; fat content is 17% saturated, 35% polyunsaturated, and 48% monounsaturated)
- ½ cup (125 mL) safflower oil (450°F/230°C smoke point; flavorless; light texture; fat content is 9% saturated, 76% polyunsaturated, and 15% monounsaturated)
- ½ cup (125 mL) soybean oil (450°F/230°C smoke point; light color; fat content is 14% saturated, 61% polyunsaturated, and 25% monounsaturated)

Olive Oil Varieties

Choose ½ cup (125 mL) olive oil from these varieties:

- ½ cup (125 mL) extra virgin olive oil (made from first cold-pressing; acid content of 1% or less; golden to deep green color; very full, rich flavor; best for uncooked or gently heated dishes)
- ½ cup (125 mL) virgin olive oil (made from first cold-pressing; acid content of 1 to 3%; slightly less rich flavor than extra virgin oil; good for sautéing)
- ½ cup (125 mL) fine or fino olive oil (a blend of virgin and extra virgin oils; acid content of 1 to 3%; slightly less rich flavor than extra virgin oil; good for sautéing)
- ½ cup (125 mL) olive oil or pure olive oil (extracted with chemical solvents and refined; may be a blend of refined and virgin oils; acid content higher than 3%; generally, a lower quality oil; good for frying)
- ½ cup (125 mL) pumace olive oil (extracted with chemical solvents and refined; acid content higher than 3%; the lowest quality oil available; good for frying due to a relatively high smoke point of 460° to 470°F/238° to 243°C)
- ½ cup (125 mL) light or extra light olive oil (highly refined and filtered oil that's lighter in color and flavor than other olive oils; same fat and calorie content as other olive oils; good for baking when you don't want a noticeable olive flavor; good for frying due to a relatively high smoke point of 460° to 470°F/238° to 243°C)

See also BUTTER; SUBSTITUTING OILS (PAGE 598).

Olives

The Roman Cato's manual On Farming (circa 175 BC) devotes more space to olive growing and oil making than to any other single topic. Today, olives are grown in Spain, Italy, Turkey, Greece, Tunisia, Morocco, California, France, Syria, Australia, and South Africa.

15 large or 36 small ripe pitted olives =
1 cup (250 mL) chopped

$4\frac{1}{2}$ oz (140 g) can =
$\frac{2}{3}$ cup (150 mL) chopped

If You Don't Have It

Substitute $\frac{1}{2}$ cup (125 mL) olives with:

- 2 to 3 tbsp (25 to 45 mL) capers (for salty, pickled flavor)
- $\frac{1}{2}$ cup (125 mL) caper berries (as a cocktail garnish)
- $\frac{1}{2}$ cup (125 mL) cocktail onions (as a cocktail garnish)

See also CHOOSING AMONG OLIVES (PAGE 570).

Omelet Pan

The French take their omelet making so seriously that they designed a special skillet with a flat bottom, shallow sloping sides, and a long handle to facilitate the preparation.

If You Don't Have It

Substitute an omelet pan with:

- crêpe pan (for small omelets)
- 6-inch (15 cm) to 10-inch (25 cm) sauté pan or skillet (for small and large omelets)

Onion Flakes

For all those cooks who tear up at the very thought of peeling an onion, dehydrated chopped onions exist.

$\frac{1}{4}$ cup (50 mL) = 1 cup (250 mL) raw, chopped

1 tbsp (15 mL) onion flakes = 1 tsp (5 mL) onion powder =
1 small onion
($\frac{1}{2}$ cup/125 mL chopped)

If You Don't Have It

Substitute 1 tbsp (15 mL) onion flakes with:

- 2 to 3 tbsp (25 to 45 mL) jarred minced onion
- $\frac{3}{4}$ to 1 tsp (4 to 5 mL) onion powder
- $\frac{3}{4}$ to 1 tsp (4 to 5 mL) onion salt (reduce salt by $\frac{1}{2}$ to 1 tsp/2 to 5 mL)
- $\frac{3}{4}$ tsp (4 mL) liquid onion seasoning
- $\frac{1}{2}$ cup (125 mL) chopped fresh or frozen onion
- $\frac{2}{3}$ cup (150 mL) chopped leeks, green onions, or scallions (white and light green parts only)

Onion, Green

Also known as bunching. Immature onions with long, slender green tops and small, rounded white bulbs. Scallions look very similar but have straight rather than rounded "bulbs" and a slightly milder flavor.

> 1 bunch = 5 oz (150 g) = 10 green onions = 1 cup (250 mL) chopped (white part only) = 3½ cups (875 mL) chopped (white and green parts)

If You Don't Have It

Substitute 1 bunch green onions (white and green parts) with:
- 1 bunch scallions (slightly milder flavor)
- 1 bunch ramps (wild leeks; milder flavor)
- 3 to 4 cups (750 mL to 1 L) chopped leeks (milder flavor)
- 3 cups (750 mL) chopped shallots (more complex flavor)
- 3 to 4 cups (750 mL to 1 L) chopped chives (milder flavor; best raw or lightly cooked)

To Vary the Flavor

Substitute 1 bunch green onions with:
- 3 cups (750 mL) chopped garlic chives (adds garlic flavor)
- 3 cups (750 mL) chopped Chinese garlic stems (adds pungent garlic flavor and crunch)

See also SCALLIONS.

Onion, Instant Minced

Dehydrated chopped onions that are slightly larger than onion flakes.

> 1 tbsp (15 mL) instant minced onion = 1¾ tsp (9 mL) onion flakes = ½ to ¾ tsp (4 mL) onion powder = ½ tsp (2 mL) small onion (¼ cup/50 mL chopped)

If You Don't Have It

Substitute 1 tbsp (15 mL) instant minced onion with:
- 1¾ tsp (9 mL) onion flakes
- ½ to ¾ tsp (2 to 4 mL) onion powder
- ½ to ¾ tsp (2 to 4 mL) onion salt (reduce salt by ½ tsp/2 mL)
- ½ tsp (2 mL) liquid onion seasoning
- ¼ cup (50 mL) chopped fresh or frozen onion
- ⅓ cup (75 mL) chopped leeks, green onions, or scallions (white and light green parts only)

Onion, Little

These diminutive onions are as appealing for their shape as for their mild allium flavor. When pickled, little pearl onions embellish the Gibson cocktail. Other varieties of little onions are discussed right.

> 4 oz (125 g) =
> 15 to 30 little onions

If You Don't Have It
Substitute 1 lb (500 g) any little onions with:
- 1 lb (500 g) green onion bulbs, trimmed
- 1 lb (500 g) shallots (more complex flavor)
- 1 lb (500 g) small storage onions (best for cooking, rather than pickling or creaming)

Little Onion Varieties
Choose 1 lb (500 g) any little onions from these varieties:
- 1 lb (500 g) pearl onions (tiny, white, oval or round bulbs; mildly sweet; best for pickling or creaming whole)
- 1 lb (500 g) boiling onions (small, oval or round bulbs that are white, yellow, or red; best for cooking whole)
- 1 lb (500 g) cipollini or Italian pearl onions (small, round bulbs with a flattened shape and yellow or red color; sweeter than boiling onions; best for cooking whole)

Onion Powder

Dehydrated onions ground into convenient powder form.

> 1 tsp (5 mL) onion powder = 1 tbsp (15 mL) onion flakes = 1 small onion (½ cup/125 mL chopped)

If You Don't Have It
Substitute 1 tsp (5 mL) onion powder with:
- 1 tbsp (15 mL) onion flakes
- 2 to 3 tbsp (25 to 45 mL) jarred minced onion
- ¾ to 1 tsp (4 to 5 mL) onion salt (reduce salt by ½ to 1 tsp/2 to 5 mL)
- ¾ tsp (4 mL) liquid onion seasoning
- ½ cup (125 mL) chopped fresh or frozen onion
- ⅔ cup (150 mL) chopped leeks, green onions, or scallions (white and light green parts only)

To Vary the Flavor
Substitute 1 tsp (5 mL) onion powder with:
- ¼ to ½ tsp (1 to 2 mL) asafetida powder (more pungent; more complex garlic and onion flavor)
- ½ to 1 tsp (2 to 5 mL) garlic powder (adds garlic flavor)

Onion Salt

A condiment of onion powder mixed with salt.

If You Don't Have It
Substitute 1 tsp (5 mL) onion salt with:
- ½ tsp (2 mL) onion powder + ½ tsp (2 mL) salt
- 1 tbsp (15 mL) onion flakes (add salt to taste)
- 2 to 3 tbsp (25 to 45 mL) jarred minced onion (add salt to taste)
- ¾ tsp (4 mL) liquid onion seasoning (add salt to taste)
- ½ cup (125 mL) chopped fresh or frozen onion (add salt to taste)
- ⅔ cup (150 mL) chopped leeks, green onions, or scallions (white and light green parts only; add salt to taste)

To Vary the Flavor
Substitute 1 tsp (5 mL) onion salt with:
- 1 tsp (5 mL) Beau Monde® Seasoning (adds celery seeds)
- 1 tsp (5 mL) seasoned salt (adds paprika and other flavors)
- ½ tsp (2 mL) table salt (no onion flavor)

Onion Soup Mix

When Lipton's introduced dry Onion Soup Mix in 1952, the course of party dips was forever altered.

1⅜ oz (40 g) pkg =
¼ cup (50 mL)

If You Don't Have It
Substitute ¼ cup (50 mL) onion soup mix with:
- ¼ cup (50 mL) Homemade Onion Soup Mix: Combine 3 tbsp (45 mL) instant minced onion, 2 tbsp (25 mL) beef bouillon (crushed or granules), ½ tsp (2 mL) onion powder, ¼ tsp (1 mL) parsley flakes (optional), ⅛ tsp (0.5 mL) ground celery seeds, a pinch of ground black pepper, a pinch of sweet paprika, and salt to taste. Makes about ¼ cup (50 mL). To make soup, dissolve mix in 4 cups (1 L) boiling water. To make dips, combine with 2 cups (500 mL) sour cream or plain yogurt.

Onion, Storage

True to their name, storage onions are long keeping because they are high in sulfur and low in water. These pungent onions are available year-round; best cooked to temper the sharp flavor. Onions should be firm and heavy for their size. Avoid onions that have sprouted, have an odor, or have green or moldy blemishes. Store onions in a cool dark spot in a container that allows air to circulate.

> 1 lb (500 g) =
> 4 to 5 medium =
> 4 cups (1 L) chopped
>
> 1 medium =
> ¾ to 1 cup
> (175 to 250 mL) chopped

If You Don't Have It

Substitute 1 medium storage onion (1 cup/250 mL chopped) with:

- 1 cup (250 mL) chopped sweet onion (sweeter; moister; works well cooked or uncooked; reduce sugar if necessary to balance sweetness)
- 1 cup (250 mL) frozen chopped onion
- 1 cup (250 mL) chopped shallots (mellower, more complex flavor)
- 1¼ cups (300 mL) chopped leeks, green onions, or scallions (white and light green parts only)
- ⅓ cup (75 mL) jarred minced onion
- 2 tbsp (25 mL) dried onion flakes
- 1½ to 2 tsp (7 to 10 mL) onion powder
- 1½ to 2 tsp (7 to 10 mL) onion salt (reduce salt by ½ to 1 tsp/2 to 5 mL)
- 1½ tsp (7 mL) liquid onion seasoning

Storage Onion Varieties

Choose 1 medium storage onion (1 cup/250 mL chopped) from these varieties:

- 1 cup (250 mL) chopped yellow globe onions (widely used among home cooks; relatively pungent, complex flavor; best for cooking)
- 1 cup (250 mL) chopped white globe onions (white color; less pungent, less complex flavor than yellow onions; good for cooking; can be used raw if pieces are rinsed)
- 1 cup (250 mL) chopped Spanish onions (larger and slightly sweeter but otherwise very similar to yellow or white globe onions; good for cooking; can be used raw if pieces are rinsed)
- 1 cup (250 mL) chopped red or Italian red onions (purplish red and white color; slightly sweeter and less pungent than yellow globe onions; good for cooking; can be used raw if pieces are rinsed)
- 1 cup (250 mL) chopped Bermuda onions (white or yellow color; slightly sweeter and less pungent than yellow globe onions; good for cooking; can be used raw if pieces are rinsed)

See also ONION, SWEET.

Onion, Sweet

Sweet onions are seasonal, usually available from April to August, depending upon the growing region. They are crisp and juicy, served raw or lightly cooked. Vidalia from Georgia, Walla Walla from Washington, Maui from Hawaii, and other sweet onions have flavor characteristics particular to their growing area.

> 1 medium = 1½ to 2 cups (375 to 500 mL) chopped

If You Don't Have It

Substitute 1 cup (250 mL) chopped sweet onion with:
- 1 cup (250 mL) chopped storage onion (less sweet; less moist; best for cooking; if using raw, rinse to soften pungency; add sugar if necessary to balance sweetness)
- 1 cup (250 mL) frozen chopped onion
- 1 cup (250 mL) chopped shallots (more complex flavor)
- 1¼ cups (300 mL) chopped leeks, green onions, or scallions (white and light green parts only)
- ⅓ cup (75 mL) instant minced onion
- 2 tbsp (25 mL) onion flakes
- 1½ to 2 tsp (7 to 10 mL) onion powder
- 1½ to 2 tsp (7 to 10 mL) onion salt (reduce salt by ½ to 1 tsp/2 to 5 mL)
- 1½ tsp (7 mL) liquid onion seasoning

Sweet Onion Varieties

Choose 1 cup (250 mL) chopped sweet onion from these varieties:
- 1 cup (250 mL) chopped Vidalia onions (pale yellow color; crunchy, juicy texture; sweet, mild, and pleasantly pungent flavor; best raw or lightly cooked)
- 1 cup (250 mL) chopped Maui onions (pale yellow color; crunchy, juicy texture; sweet, mild, and pleasantly pungent flavor; best raw or lightly cooked)
- 1 cup (250 mL) chopped Walla Walla onions (pale yellow color; crunchy, juicy texture; sweet, mild, and pleasantly pungent flavor; best raw or lightly cooked)
- 1 cup (250 mL) chopped Texas Supersweet or other Texas sweet onions (white, pale yellow, or red color; crunchy, juicy; sweet, mild, and slightly more pungent than Vidalia onions; best raw or lightly cooked)
- 1 cup (250 mL) chopped Sweet Imperial or other California sweet onions (pale yellow or red; crunchy, juicy; sweet, mild, and slightly more pungent than Vidalia onions; best raw or lightly cooked)
- 1 cup (250 mL) chopped Grand Canyon, NuMex, Mayan, or OSO Sweet onions (pale yellow or red; crunchy, juicy; sweet, mild, and slightly less complex flavor than Vidalia onions; best raw or lightly cooked)

See also ONION, STORAGE.

Ono

See MACKEREL; WAHOO.

Opal Basil

See BASIL.

Orange, Blood

Mediterranean citrus with garnet-flecked orange flesh or completely garnet flesh. The juice can be light or dark burgundy. Full-bodied orange flavor with a hint of plum or raspberry.

1 lb (500 g) = 3 medium
= 1 to 1¼ cups
(250 to 300 mL) juice

If You Don't Have It
Substitute 1 blood orange with:
- 1 navel orange (orange flesh)
- 1 to 2 Mandarin oranges (such as tangerines; sweeter)

Blood Orange Varieties
Choose 1 blood orange from these varieties:
- 1 Moro orange (deep burgundy flesh and juice; sweet-tart flavor with hint of raspberries)
- 1 Sanguinelli orange (garnet-flecked flesh and juice; sweet-tart flavor with a hint of plum)

Orange Extract

Like all flavoring extracts, store this flavoring in a cool, dark place, and keep the lid on tightly. Properly stored, it will maintain its flavor for a long time, only gradually losing potency.

If You Don't Have It
Substitute ½ tsp (2 mL) orange extract with:
- 1 to 2 drops orange oil + ¼ tsp (1 mL) vodka (optional)
- 2 to 3 tsp (10 to 15 mL) orange liqueur (reduce liquid in recipe by 2½ tsp/12 mL if necessary)
- 1 tsp (5 mL) orange zest
- ½ to ¾ tsp (2 to 4 mL) orange flower water

To Vary the Flavor
Substitute ½ tsp (2 mL) orange extract with:
- ½ tsp (2 mL) lemon extract
- ¾ tsp (4 mL) vanilla extract
- ¾ tsp (4 mL) rum extract

Orange Flower Water

The orange flower water of Provence is renowned. The "water" is a distillate produced like cognac or whisky. It takes about 4 pounds (2 kg) of flower petals to make 1 quart (1 L).

If You Don't Have It

Substitute ½ tsp (2 mL) orange flower water with:

- ¼ to ½ tsp (1 to 2 mL) orange extract
- 1 to 2 drops orange oil + ¼ tsp (1 mL) vodka (optional)
- 2 to 3 tsp (10 to 15 mL) orange liqueur (reduce liquid in recipe by 2½ tsp/12 mL if necessary)
- 1 tsp (5 mL) orange zest

To Vary the Flavor

Substitute ½ tsp (2 mL) orange flower water with:

- ½ tsp (2 mL) rose water
- ¼ to ½ tsp (1 to 2 mL) lemon extract
- ¾ tsp (4 mL) vanilla extract
- ¾ tsp (4 mL) rum extract

Orange Juice

The Florida Department of Citrus developed the process for making frozen concentrated orange juice in 1945. The patent on the technology was given to the U.S. government to advance the nation's frozen food industry.

1 medium sweet orange = 6 to 8 tbsp (90 to 120 mL) juice

If You Don't Have It

Substitute 1 cup (250 mL) fresh orange juice with:

- ¼ cup (50 mL) frozen orange juice concentrate + ¾ cup (175 mL) water
- 2 cups (500 mL) brewed orange herbal tea (may add other flavors; reduce liquid in recipe by 1 cup/250 mL if necessary)
- 1 cup (250 mL) blood orange juice (sweeter)
- 1 cup (250 mL) sour orange juice (much more bitter; excellent for marinades)

To Vary the Flavor

Substitute 1 cup (250 mL) fresh orange juice with:

- 1 cup (250 mL) pineapple juice (sweeter)
- 1 cup (250 mL) grapefruit juice (more tart)
- 1 cup (250 mL) fruit nectar such as mango or peach (thicker; sweeter)

Orange Liqueur

What do the Alfonso special, elephant's kick, margarita, morning glory, Park Avenue and Santa Cruz rum daisy have in common? None of these cocktails would exist without a splash of orange liqueur.

If You Don't Have It

Substitute 2 tbsp (25 mL) orange liqueur with:

- 2 tsp (10 mL) orange extract (reduce liquid in recipe by 4 tsp/20 mL if necessary)
- 2 to 4 drops orange oil + ½ tsp (2 mL) vodka (optional; reduce liquid in recipe by 2 tbsp/25 mL if necessary)
- 2 tsp (10 mL) orange zest
- 1 to 1½ tsp (5 to 7 mL) orange flower water

- 1 tbsp (15 mL) orange juice concentrate (add 1 tbsp/15 mL liquid to recipe if necessary)
- 3 tbsp (45 mL) orange juice (reduce liquid in recipe by 1 tbsp/15 mL if necessary)
- 2 tbsp (25 mL) Midori (honeydew melon liqueur)

Orange Liqueur Varieties

Choose 2 tbsp (25 mL) orange liqueur from these varieties:

- 2 tbsp (25 mL) Cointreau (colorless; relatively dry but slightly sweeter than Grand Marnier; complex, balanced flavor; made from curaçao sour orange and sweet orange peels)
- 2 tbsp (25 mL) Citrónge (similar to Cointreau; colorless; relatively dry but slightly sweeter than Grand Marnier; complex flavor; made from Haitian sour orange and Jamaican sweet orange peels)
- 2 tbsp (25 mL) curaçao (sweeter than Cointreau; less complex flavor; amber, clear, orange, or blue color; made from curaçao sour orange and sweet orange peels)
- 2 tbsp (25 mL) Triple Sec (colorless; sweeter than curaçao; less complex flavor; made from curaçao sour orange and sweet orange peels)
- 2 tbsp (25 mL) Grand Marnier (amber color; relatively dry; complex, balanced flavor; made from Haitian sour orange and sweet orange peels)
- 2 tbsp (25 mL) Bauchant (similar to Grand Marnier; amber color; relatively dry; complex flavor; made from curaçao sour orange and sweet orange peels)
- 2 tbsp (25 mL) Gran Torres (amber color; medium-dry; mild orange flavor; made from sweet orange peels)
- 2 tbsp (25 mL) mandarin liqueur (sweeter than most orange liqueurs)
- 2 tbsp (25 mL) kumquat liqueur (more sweet-tart flavor than most orange liqueurs)
- 2 tbsp (25 mL) Sabra (chocolate-flavored orange liqueur)

Orange Oil

Also known as oil of orange. An essential oil extracted from the zest of oranges; used in flavorings. Two other essential oils from oranges are used mainly in perfumery. Oil of petitgrain is taken from the leaves and twigs. Oil of neroli is derived from the blossoms.

If You Don't Have It
Substitute 1 drop orange oil with:
- ¼ to ½ tsp (1 to 2 mL) orange extract (less concentrated; evaporates at high temperatures; reduce liquid in recipe by ½ tsp/2 mL if necessary)
- 1 to 1½ tsp (5 to 7 mL) orange zest

To Vary the Flavor
Substitute 1 drop orange oil with:
- 1 drop lemon oil
- ¾ tsp (4 mL) vanilla extract (evaporates at high temperatures; reduce liquid in recipe by ¾ tsp/4 mL if necessary)

Orange Roughy

This mild, white-fleshed fish was christened by Australians and New Zealanders because its skin is orange and rough. The same fish swims in waters off South Africa, where it is known by the less fortunate moniker slimehead.

If You Don't Have It
Substitute 1 lb (500 g) orange roughy with:
- 1 lb (500 g) ocean perch
- 1 lb (500 g) blackfish
- 1 lb (500 g) flounder
- 1 lb (500 g) sole
- 1 lb (500 g) haddock
- 1 lb (500 g) red snapper
- 1 lb (500 g) tilapia

Orange, Sour

Also known as bitter orange. The juice of sour oranges was a popular flavoring in medieval Europe. In fact, the sour orange arrived in Europe some 500 years prior to the sweet (both types of citrus originated in China.) Today, sour oranges have limited commercial use. The Seville is raised mostly in Spain for the production of British orange marmalade. The peel of another sour orange, the diminutive

If You Don't Have It
Substitute 1 medium sour orange with:
- 1 calamondin (hybrid of mandarin orange and kumquat; sweeter)
- 2 to 3 kumquats (smaller; acidic flesh; sweet peel)
- ½ to 1 sweet orange (larger; much sweeter)
- 1 mandarin orange (much sweeter)
- 1 lime (for candying the peel)
- 1 to 2 tbsp (15 to 25 mL) sweet orange juice + 3 to 4 tsp (15 to 20 mL) lime or lemon juice (to replace 3 tbsp/45 mL sour orange juice)

Bergamot, is an ingredient in Earl Grey tea and is also candied. An essential oil, called essence of bergamot, is extracted from the peel for use in perfumes and confections.

---

1 medium sour orange = 2 to 3 tbsp (25 to 45 mL) juice = ⅓ to ½ cup (75 to 125 mL) chopped = 1 to 2 tbsp (15 to 25 mL) grated zest

---

Sour Orange Varieties

Choose 1 sour orange from these varieties:

- 1 Spanish Bittersweet or Daidai orange (oblong; used for juice, peel, and essential oil)
- 1 Bergamot orange (often candied or used to make Earl Grey tea)
- 1 Seville orange (often used for juice, marmalade, and to make orange liqueurs)
- 1 to 2 Chinotto oranges (often candied)

See also ORANGE, SWEET.

Orange, Sweet

Numerous varieties of sweet oranges are cultivated for their juice and for eating out-of-hand. Many agree that the seedless navel orange may be the best eating orange. Kept in a high humidity atmosphere at about 35°F (2°C), oranges will maintain their appetizing qualities for nearly 2 months.

---

1 medium = ⅓ to ½ cup (75 to 125 mL) juice = ¾ cup (175 mL) chopped = 2 to 3 tbsp (25 to 45 mL) grated zest

---

If You Don't Have It

Substitute 1 sweet orange with:

- 1 large blood orange (sweeter; garnet or garnet-flecked flesh)
- 2 mandarin oranges (smaller; sweet-tart)
- 1 to 2 sour oranges (smaller; much more bitter)
- 2 calamondin (hybrid of kumquat and mandarin orange; smaller; more tart)
- 1 Meyer lemon (more tart and lemony)
- 4 to 6 kumquats (more tart; best for eating out of hand)
- ¼ to ½ tsp (1 to 2 mL) pummelo (larger; more tart)
- ½ tsp (2 mL) grapefruit (larger; more tart)
- 1 to 2 limes (smaller; more tart)
- 1 large lemon (smaller; more tart)

Sweet Orange Varieties

Choose 1 fresh sweet orange from these varieties:

- 1 navel-type orange such as Dream Navel, Cara Cara, or California Navel (often seedless; peels and segments easily; best for eating out-of-hand)
- 1 Valencia-type orange such as Valencia, Rhode Red, Kona, or Hamlin (often seeded; extremely juicy; sweet-tart flavor; best for juicing)

See also ORANGE, BLOOD; ORANGE FLOWER WATER; ORANGE JUICE; ORANGE LIQUEUR; ORANGE OIL; ORANGE, SOUR; ORANGE ZEST.

Orange Zest

No doubt the term "zest" was chosen for the skin of oranges and other citrus because of the excitement it brings to so many foods. When grated, the thin, colored outer skin releases aromatic essential oils that enhance preparations from appetizers to desserts.

> 1 medium sweet orange
> = 2 to 3 tbsp
> (25 to 45 mL) grated zest

If You Don't Have It

Substitute 1 tbsp (15 mL) grated orange zest with:
- 1 tbsp (15 mL) dried orange peel
- 1½ tsp (7 mL) orange extract

To Vary the Flavor

Substitute 1 tsp (5 mL) grated orange zest with:
- 1 tsp (5 mL) mandarin orange zest
- 1 tsp (5 mL) calamondin zest
- 1 tsp (5 mL) kumquat zest
- 1 tsp (5 mL) lemon or lime zest
- 1 tsp (5 mL) finely chopped candied orange peel (reduce sugar in recipe by ¼ tsp/1 mL if necessary)

Oregano

The "pizza herb" is not one specific plant but rather various species of marjoram that carry the characteristic oregano flavor — a combination of sweet/pungent mint and thyme. Many culinary experts say that oregano's full flavoring potential is realized when the leaves are dried rather than fresh.

> ½ oz (15 g) fresh =
> ½ cup (125 mL) chopped

If You Don't Have It

Substitute 1 tbsp (15 mL) fresh oregano leaves with:
- 1 tsp (5 mL) dried oregano leaves

To Vary the Flavor

Substitute 1 tbsp (15 mL) fresh oregano leaves with:
- 1 tbsp (15 mL) fresh marjoram
- 1 tbsp (15 mL) fresh thyme
- 1 tbsp (15 mL) fresh sweet basil
- 1 tbsp (15 mL) fresh summer savory
- 1 to 2 tsp (5 to 10 mL) fresh sage
- 1 tbsp (15 mL) fresh parsley
- 1 tsp (5 mL) dried Italian seasoning (adds thyme and basil flavors)
- 1 tsp (5 mL) dried Greek seasoning (adds onion, garlic, black pepper, mint and cinnamon flavors)
- 1 tsp (5 mL) Herbes de Provence (adds flavors such as thyme, savory, lavender, fennel, and bay leaf)

Orgeat Syrup

This sweet almond beverage flavoring — enhanced with rose water or orange-flower water — appears in the mai tai, scorpion, and other cocktails.

If You Don't Have It
Substitute 2 tbsp (25 mL) orgeat syrup with:
- 2 tbsp (25 mL) Homemade Simple Syrup (see recipe, page 489) + $\frac{1}{8}$ to $\frac{1}{4}$ tsp (0.5 to 1 mL) almond extract + 1 to 2 drops rose water or orange flower water
- 2 tbsp (25 mL) almond liqueur such as Amaretto + 1 to 2 drops rose water or orange flower water (less sweet; add 1 to 3 tsp/5 to 15 mL sugar to recipe if necessary to balance sweetness)
- 2 tbsp (25 mL) crème d'amande or crème de noyaux + 1 to 2 drops rose water or orange flower water (thicker texture, pink color)

To Vary the Flavor
Substitute 2 tbsp (25 mL) orgeat syrup with:
- 2 tbsp (25 mL) falernum (adds lime and ginger flavors)

Ossau-Iraty Brebis Pyrenees

A traditional, unpasteurized, semisoft cheese from the French Western Pyrenees, which takes its name from two regions, Ossau and Iraty. Made exclusively from the milk of Manech ewes, the cheese is usually shaped in a wheel with a natural rind.

1 lb (500 g) = 4 cups (1 L) shredded

If You Don't Have It
Substitute 1 oz (30 g) Ossau-Iraty cheese with:
- 1 oz (30 g) Etorki
- 1 oz (30 g) Prince de Claverolle
- 1 oz (30 g) Comté

Ostrich

It doesn't taste like chicken! This big African bird, now raised as game on specialty ranches, tastes like beef.

If You Don't Have It
Substitute 1 lb (500 g) ostrich with:
- 1 lb (500 g) rhea
- 1 lb (500 g) emu
- 1 lb (500 g) beef (fattier)
- 1 lb (500 g) turkey

Ouzo

See ANISE LIQUEUR.

Oven

According to culinary etymologist Mark Morton, the word oven *sprang from an Indo-European word that meant "fire-pot" and morphed into the Old English word* ofn *near the 10th century. By the 1300s, the term was spelled* oven *as it is today.*

To Vary the Flavor

Substitute a conventional gas or electric oven with:

- brick oven (excellent for baking; absorbs moisture and creates a crisp crust)
- tandoor oven (made of brick and clay; excellent for breads and meats; absorbs moisture and creates a crisp crust)

To Save Time

- convection oven (an oven with forced hot air to speed cooking; not recommended for delicate mixtures such as soufflés and meringues)
- microwave oven (speeds heating; best for reheating casseroles or other foods that would be reheated in an oven; not recommended for reheating bread and baked goods)

Ovenproof Pan

Skillets with handles fashioned from the same heatproof material as the pan — cast iron, stainless clad aluminum or steel, and others — are convenient for searing foods on the stovetop and finishing the cooking in the oven.

If You Don't Have It

Substitute an ovenproof pan with:

- plastic- or rubber-handled pan (wrap the handle in several layers of heavy-duty foil to protect it from heat)

Oyster

"Unique in a group of foods that includes truffles, lobster, artichokes, mangoes, passion fruit, and a score of other 'love' foods, oysters are food for the initiated few," write Joan Reardon and Ruth Ebling in Oysters: A Culinary Celebration. *"Often compared to a seductive woman, there is a mystery, a subtlety, a quality that defies explanation about them.*

If You Don't Have It

Substitute 1 lb (500 g) oysters with:

- 1 lb (500 g) smoked oysters
- 1 lb (500 g) mussels (more delicate)
- 1 lb (500 g) cockles
- 1 lb (500 g) soft-shell clams (for frying)
- 1 lb (500 g) littleneck or cherrystone clams (for serving on the half-shell)
- 1 lb (500 g) scallops
- 1 lb (500 g) abalone (tougher)

No other food evokes such strong feelings of utter bliss or revulsion; no other food has been written about more eloquently or more trivially."

| 1 cup (250 mL) shucked = 13 to 19 medium |
| 3.66 oz (175 g) can smoked = 14 to 16 oysters |

Oyster Varieties
Choose 1 lb (500 g) oysters from these varieties:
- 1 lb (500 g) Eastern, Atlantic or bluepoint oysters (native to North American Atlantic Coast from Canada to the Gulf of Mexico; elongated, layered, gray to brown shell; 2 to 4 inches/5 to 10 cm long; often eaten on the half-shell)
- 1 lb (500 g) Pacific Japanese oysters (usually farmed and harvested at 6 inches/15 cm long; gray to brown shell)
- 1 lb (500 g) Olympia (native to the U.S. Pacific Coast; 1 to $1\frac{1}{2}$-inch/2.5 to 4 cm shell)
- 1 lb (500 g) European or belon oyster (native to France; farmed in the United States; $1\frac{1}{2}$ to 3-inch/4 to 7.5 cm, rounded, and slightly flattened shell; often eaten on the half-shell)

Oyster Knife

A sturdy knife with a stubby handle is essential for opening oysters safely. To use, insert the tip into the hinge of the scrubbed oyster shell to pry open. After opening, use the blade to cut under the oyster to release it from the shell.

If You Don't Have It
Substitute an oyster knife with:
- another thick, dull knife such as a small spreading knife or spackling knife
- microwaving the oysters until they open (about 20 seconds) or steaming them until they open (about 4 minutes)

Oyster Mushroom

See SHUFFLING MUSHROOMS (PAGE 572).

Oyster Sauce

A classic Chinese sauce that is a powerful concentration of oysters, soy sauce, salt, and other seasonings. Thai oyster sauces tend to have richer oyster flavor than Chinese oyster sauces.

If You Don't Have It
Substitute 1 tbsp (15 mL) oyster sauce with:
- 1 tbsp (15 mL) vegetarian oyster sauce (made with mushrooms and vegetable protein instead of oysters)
- 2 tsp (10 mL) soy sauce or teriyaki sauce + 1 tsp (5 mL) canning liquid from canned oysters + pinch of sugar (if using soy sauce)

Pale Ale to Purslane

Pale Ale	*See* BEER.
Palm Sugar	*See* JAGGERY.
Pancake Syrup	*See* MAPLE SYRUP.
Pancake Turner	*See* TURNER.

Pancetta

Cured Italian pork belly, the same cut as American bacon, although generally not smoked like American bacon, except in some Alpine provinces. In Spain, a related unsmoked bacon is known as tocino. A similar French bacon called ventrèche is often used to make lardons.

1 lb (500 g) = 16 slices

If You Don't Have It

Substitute 1 slice (about 1 oz/30 g) pancetta with:
- 1 slice (about 1 oz/30 g) guanciale (cured hog jowl)
- 1 thick slice (about 1 oz/30 g) American slab bacon (adds smoke flavor; drop in boiling water for 2 minutes to reduce smoke flavor)
- 1 oz (30 g) Canadian bacon (adds smoke flavor)
- 1 oz (30 g) salt pork (saltier; fattier; best as flavoring in soups, stews, and sauces)
- 1 oz (30 g) prosciutto
- 1 oz (30 g) smoked ham (adds smoke flavor)
- 1 oz (30 g) smoked sausage (adds smoke flavor)

Panch Phoran

A Bengali spice mix that typically includes the seeds of cumin, fennel, fenugreek, mustard, and nigella.

If You Don't Have It

Substitute 1 tbsp (15 mL) panch phoran with:
- 1 tbsp (15 mL) Homemade Panch Phoran: Combine 1½ tsp (7 mL) brown mustard seeds, 1¼ tsp (6 mL) nigella seeds, 1 tsp (5 mL) cumin seeds, ¾ tsp (4 mL) fenugreek seeds, ½ tsp (2 mL) fennel seeds. Makes about 1½ tablespoons (22 mL).
- 1 tbsp (15 mL) garam masala

Pandanus

See SCREWPINE LEAF.

Panela Cheese

Fresh, crumbly white cheese of Mexican origin.

| 8 oz (250 g) = 1 cup (250 mL) |

If You Don't Have It

Substitute 1 oz (30 g) panela with:
- 1 oz (30 g) dry-cured cottage cheese

See also PILONCILLO.

Panettone

A fixture of Italian Christmas celebrations, this cupola-shaped, brioche-like cake is typically studded with raisins and candied fruits.

If You Don't Have It

Substitute 1 lb (500 g) panettone with:
- 1 lb (500 g) ciambellone (unyeasted Italian coffee cake)
- 1 lb (500 g) kulich (Russian sweet yeast bread; usually has icing; tall, cylindrical shape)
- 1 lb (500 g) Kugelhopf (central European sweet yeast bread; tall, ring shape)
- 1 lb (500 g) brioche (French yeast bread; richer; less sweet or not sweet)
- 1 lb (500 g) fruitcake

Panir

Also known as paneer. Indian fresh pressed cheese produced from cow's or water buffalo's milk. It is pressed to remove excess moisture. Often served diced and sautéed, it also appears in many vegetarian dishes.

| 8 oz (250 g) = 1 cup (250 mL) |

If You Don't Have It

Substitute 1 oz (30 g) panir with:
- 1 oz (30 g) farmer cheese
- 1 oz (30 g) pot cheese
- 1 oz (30 g) firm tofu, cubed
- 1 oz (30 g) feta cheese, cubed and rinsed to remove excess salt
- 1 oz (30 g) dry-curd cottage cheese

Panko

Also known as panko bread crumbs and Japanese bread crumbs. Coarser than fine dry bread crumbs, panko make light and crispy gratin toppings and coatings for deep-fried foods.

8 oz (250 g) =
2⅓ cups (575 mL)

If You Don't Have It
Substitute 1 cup (250 mL) panko with:
- 3 to 4 slices or large chunks bread, shredded (preferably with a food processor shredding disc) and baked on a baking sheet at 300°F/150°C until dry, about 5 minutes
- 1 cup (250 mL) bread crumbs
- ¾ cup (175 mL) cracker crumbs
- 1 cup (250 mL) crushed melba toasts
- 1 cup (250 mL) matzo meal
- 1 cup (250 mL) crushed tortilla chips
- 1 cup (250 mL) crushed dry-bagged stuffing mix
- 1 cup (250 mL) crushed pretzels
- 1 cup (250 mL) crushed cornflakes
- 1 cup (250 mL) crushed potato chips

Pans

See SPECIFIC TYPES; PAN SIZE EQUIVALENTS (PAGE 606).

Pansy

See PICKING EDIBLE FLOWERS (PAGE 604).

Papalo

Also known as papaloquelite. Mexican herb with grass-like leaves tastes like a more potent cilantro. Said to be an acquired taste, papalo is almost always used raw.

If You Don't Have It
Substitute 1 tbsp (15 mL) chopped fresh papalo with:
- 3 to 4 tsp (15 to 20 mL) chopped fresh cilantro
- 1 tbsp (15 mL) chopped fresh culantro or culentro (more bitter flavor)
- 1 tbsp (15 mL) chopped fresh parsley

Papaw

Also known as pawpaw. A custard apple fruit of a small North American tree that is related to tropical cherimoya. The smooth, sweet yellow pulp tastes like creamy banana and pear. When referred to as "pawpaw," it is confused with the totally unrelated papaya.

If You Don't Have It
Substitute 1 lb (500 g) papaws with:
- 1 lb (500 g) blue java or ice cream bananas (sweet ice cream–like flavor)
- 1 lb (500 g) Orinoco bananas (strawberry flavor)
- 1 lb (500 g) burro bananas (slight lemon flavor)
- 1 lb (500 g) dwarf or finger bananas
- 1 lb (500 g) red bananas (best for baking)
- 1 lb (500 g) manzano bananas (drier flesh; strawberry-apple flavor)
- 1 lb (500 g) yellow Cavendish bananas

See also CHERIMOYA.

Papaya

Also known as fruta bomba. A wonderful fruit that grows in tropics spanning the globe. In appearance, papaya resembles a large pear-shaped melon. When ripe, the skin is blotchy yellow orange over green and the flesh yields to the touch. The sweet orange flesh is smooth, compact, and delicately scented.

1 medium = 10 to 12 oz
(300 to 375 g) =
1½ to 2 cups
(375 to 500 mL)
chopped or sliced

If You Don't Have It

Substitute 1 lb (500 g) papaya with:
- 1 lb (500 g) babaco
- 1 lb (500 g) pepino
- 1 lb (500 g) mango
- 1 lb (500 g) peaches
- 1 lb (500 g) nectarines

See also PAPAYA, GREEN.

Papaya, Green

Also known as unripe papaya. Larger unripe fruits are cooked as a vegetable or made into pickles. In Thai kitchens, long strands of peeled green papaya are used to make refreshing salads.

2 lbs (1 kg) = 4½ to 6 cups
(1.125 to 1.5 L)

If You Don't Have It

Substitute 1 lb (500 g) green papaya with:
- 1 lb (500 g) chayote

See also PAPAYA.

Pappadam

Also known as papad, papadam, and poppadum. Wafer-thin Indian flatbreads made from lentil flour may be plain or seasoned with peppers, garlic, and other flavorings.

If You Don't Have It

Substitute 1 lb (500 g) pappadam with:
- 1 lb (500 g) crisp lavash
- 1 lb (500 g) water crackers

To Vary the Flavor

Substitute 1 lb (500 g) pappadam with:
- 1 lb (500 g) shrimp chips

Paprika

Also known as Hungarian pepper and Spanish pepper. Dried and ground sweet pimentos achieve their glory in Hungarian cuisine, particularly to flavor and color paprikás, *which the rest of the world calls goulash. Depending upon the peppers used, paprika can vary from sweetly mild to very hot.*

If You Don't Have It
Substitute 1 tbsp (15 mL) paprika with:
- 1 tbsp (15 mL) ancho chile powder (darker reddish brown color; earthier, fruitier aromas)
- pinch of cayenne pepper (much hotter)
- pinch of ground chipotle powder (adds smokiness and heat)
- 1 tbsp (15 mL) chili powder (slightly more pungent; adds flavors of cumin, oregano, and other spices)

Paprika Varieties
Choose 1 tbsp (15 mL) paprika from these varieties:
- 1 tbsp (15 mL) Spanish paprika (somewhat pungent)
- 1 tbsp (15 mL) sweet Hungarian paprika (milder, more complex flavor than Spanish paprika)
- 1 tbsp (15 mL) hot Hungarian paprika (somewhat pungent, more complex flavor than Spanish paprika)

Paradise Nut

Also known as monkey pot nut and sapucaya nut. This wild specimen grows in Brazil and Guyana and is said to have a superb, distinctive flavor. Like its relative the Brazil nut, the paradise nut grows inside a big, woody container.

> 1 lb (500 g) =
> 3⅓ cups (825 mL)

If You Don't Have It
Substitute 1 cup (250 mL) paradise nuts with:
- 1 cup (250 mL) Brazil nuts
- 1 cup (250 mL) macadamia nuts

See also BRAZIL NUT.

Paraffin Wax

Also known as baker's wax and canning wax. A small amount of melted wax can be mixed into chocolates to forestall melting.

If You Don't Have It
Substitute 1 tbsp (15 mL) paraffin wax with:
- 2 to 3 tsp (10 to 15 mL) vegetable shortening (for chocolate confections; less firm)

Paratha

Also known as parata, Indian flaky bread — often stuffed with spicy vegetable or meat mixtures — that is fried or cooked on a griddle.

If You Don't Have It

Substitute 1 paratha with:
- 1 naan (puffy flatbread made from refined wheat flour and cooked on the walls of a tandoor or clay-lined oven; less rich; sometimes flavored with garlic, herbs, or other aromatics)
- 1 poori (deep-fried flatbread made with whole wheat flour; crisper)
- 1 chapati (flatbread made with whole wheat flour and little or no fat)
- 1 roti (a generic term for Indian flatbread; similar to chapati; usually made with whole wheat flour)
- 1 whole wheat pita bread (similar to naan)
- 1 whole wheat flour tortilla

Parchment Paper

Also known as baking paper or cooking parchment. If you don't have a nonstick baking pan, make it nonstick by lining the pan with parchment paper. The paper saves cleanup time, too, because you just throw it away when finished.

If You Don't Have It

Substitute parchment paper with:
- aluminum foil (for lining baking pans; for cooking "en papillote" or steaming food in a parchment paper package, use pieces of aluminum foil or foil cooking bags)
- silicone baking mat (for lining baking pans)
- nonstick baking sheet
- plastic resealable bag (to replace a parchment paper cone for piping icings or fillings)

Parfait d'Amour

A liqueur fashionable in the 19th century — redolent of spices, vanilla, orange, and flowers — that's making something of a comeback.

If You Don't Have It

Substitute 1 oz (30 g) Parfait d'Amour with:
- 1 oz (30 g) crème de rose (lighter color; adds vanilla aroma)
- 1 oz (30 g) crème de violette (purple color; violet flower aroma)
- 1 oz (30 g) curaçao + 1 drop rose water + 1 small drop vanilla extract + 1 small drop almond extract (use colored curaçao)

Parma Ham

See PROSCIUTTO.

Parmesan

True Parmesan is an Italian cow's milk grana (grating cheese) made only in the legally designated Parmigiano-Reggiano zone encompassing Parma, Reggio nell'Emilia, Bologna, Modena, and Mantua.

4 oz (125 g) =
1 cup (250 mL) grated

If You Don't Have It

Substitute 1 oz (30 g) Parmesan with:
- 1 oz (30 g) Grana Padano
- 1 oz (30 g) Pecorino Romano (sharper)
- 1 oz (30 g) aged Asiago (milder)
- 1 oz (30 g) aged Manchego (milder)
- 1 oz (30 g) dry Jack cheese (more nutty flavor)

For Better Health

Substitute 1 oz (30 g) Parmesan cheese with:
- 1 oz (30 g) Sapsago (more herbal flavor; lower in fat)

Parrot Fish

Also known as uhu. Parrot Fish are named for their beak-like teeth, which are designed to chomp on coral. They filter out the nutritious algae and excrete the sand.

If You Don't Have It

Substitute 1 lb (500 g) parrot fish with:
- 1 lb (500 g) blue-striped snapper or taape

Parsley

The leaves of this agreeable herb come two ways: flat (Italian) and curly.

1 oz (30 g) =
1 cup (250 mL) chopped

If You Don't Have It

Substitute 1 tbsp (15 mL) chopped fresh parsley with:
- 1 tbsp (15 mL) chopped fresh chervil
- 1 tsp (5 mL) dried parsley or chervil (much less flavorful)
- 1 tbsp (15 mL) chopped fresh cilantro (adds grassy, citrusy aromas)
- 1 tbsp (15 mL) chopped fresh tarragon (adds anise aroma)

Parsley Root

A root-vegetable subspecies of parsley is favored in parts of Europe as an ingredient in soups, stews, or vegetable side dishes.

1 lb (500 g) = 3 cups (750 mL) chopped = 2 cups (500 mL) cooked

If You Don't Have It

Substitute 1 cup (250 mL) chopped parsley root with:
- ½ cup (125 mL) chopped celeriac + ½ cup (125 mL) chopped carrots (milder)
- 1 cup (250 mL) chopped celeriac (milder)
- 1 cup (250 mL) chopped carrots + pinch of celery seeds
- 1 cup (250 mL) chopped turnips + pinch of celery seeds
- 1 cup (250 mL) chopped parsnips + pinch of celery seeds

Parsnip

Underutilized roots related to carrot, celeriac and parsley root.

> 1 lb (500 g) = 3 cups (750 mL) chopped = 2 cups (500 mL) cooked

If You Don't Have It

Substitute 1 cup (250 mL) chopped parsnips with:
- 1 cup (250 mL) chopped carrots
- 1 cup (250 mL) chopped arracacha
- 1 cup (250 mL) chopped turnips
- 1 cup (250 mL) chopped salsify
- 1 cup (250 mL) chopped celeriac
- 1 cup (250 mL) chopped parsley root
- 1 cup (250 mL) chopped taro
- 1 cup (250 mL) chopped burdock

Partridge

An important game bird in Europe and central Asia. The bird has a small chicken-like shape and is plump and tasty.

If You Don't Have It

Substitute 1 lb (500 g) partridge with:
- 1 lb (500 g) grouse
- 1 lb (500 g) quail
- 1 lb (500 g) pheasant
- 1 lb (500 g) squab
- 1 lb (500 g) Cornish game hen

Partridge Varieties

Choose 1 lb (500 g) partridge from these varieties:
- 1 lb (500 g) grey or English partridge
- 1 lb (500 g) red-legged or French partridge

Passion Fruit

The exquisite aroma and taste of this exotic fruit is unique. The name is a reference to the fruit's blossom resembling various details of the Passion of Christ.

> 12 to 14 passion fruits = about 1 cup (250 mL) juice, pulp, or purée

If You Don't Have It

Substitute 1 cup (250 mL) passion fruit pulp or juice with:
- 1 cup (250 mL) canned passion fruit nectar (to replace fresh passion fruit juice)
- ½ cup (125 mL) pineapple juice + ½ cup (125 mL) Key lime juice (to replace fresh passion fruit juice)
- 1 cup (250 mL) guava pulp (to replace passion fruit pulp)

Passion Fruit Varieties

Choose 1 cup (250 mL) passion fruit pulp from:
- 1 cup (250 mL) maracuja or purple passion fruit pulp (the true passion fruit; reddish purple-brown skin, often wrinkled, or pale yellow skin; intensely aromatic greenish orange, sweet-tart pulp)
- 1 cup (250 mL) granadilla pulp (slightly larger than maracuja; orange skin with specks of white; milder, pale gray, sweet-tart pulp)

Passion Fruit Liqueur

Tasting of honey, jasmine, and lemon, the intense essence of passion fruit flavors this liqueur.

If You Don't Have It
Substitute 2 tbsp (25 mL) passion fruit liqueur with:
- 2 tbsp (25 mL) passion fruit syrup (nonalcoholic)
- 1 tbsp (15 mL) passion fruit nectar + 1 tbsp (15 mL) brandy (less sweet)

To Vary the Flavor
Substitute 2 tbsp (25 mL) passion fruit liqueur with:
- 2 tbsp (25 mL) fruit brandy such as apricot brandy (less sweet)

Pasta, Dried Ribbons

Thin pasta ribbons, such as linguine, marry well with thin, smooth sauces. Wide ribbons, such as pappardelle, go best with thick, smooth sauces or sauces with small chunks. To substitute regular dried lasagna with no-boil or oven-ready lasagna, add 25% more sauce or liquid, which will be absorbed by the no-boil lasagna.

> 1 lb (500 g) = 8 cups (2 L) cooked

If You Don't Have It
Substitute 1 lb (500 g) dried pasta ribbons with these varieties:
- 1 lb (500 g) dried fettuccine, lasagna, linguine, pappardelle, or tagliatelle
- 8 oz (250 g) dried wide egg noodles
- 1 lb (500 g) dried wide Asian wheat noodles

For Better Health
Substitute 1 lb (500 g) dried pasta ribbons with:
- 1 lb (500 g) dried whole wheat pasta ribbons (higher fiber)
- 1 lb (500 g) dried Jerusalem artichoke pasta ribbons (higher fiber)
- 1 lb (500 g) dried quinoa pasta ribbons (gluten-free)
- 1 lb (500 g) dried spelt pasta ribbons (low-gluten)
- 1 lb (500 g) dried Kamut® pasta ribbons (low-gluten)
- 1 lb (500 g) dried rice pasta ribbons (gluten-free)
- 1 lb (500 g) dried wide Asian rice noodles (gluten-free)

Pasta, Dried Shapes

When cooking various shaped pastas together, choose similar sizes so they cook at the same rate. Large shapes and tubes, such as rigatoni, go best with sauces that have large chunks. Small shapes and

If You Don't Have It
Substitute 1 lb (500 g) dried pasta shapes with these varieties:
- 1 lb (500 g) dried elbow macaroni, medium shells, rotini, twists, spirals, wagon wheels, bow ties, mostaccioli, penne, radiatore, rigatoni, or ziti

For Better Health
Substitute 1 lb (500 g) dried pasta shapes with:
- 1 lb (500 g) dried whole wheat pasta shapes (higher fiber)

tubes, such as macaroni, go best with smooth sauces or sauces that have small chunks.

1 lb (500 g) dried =
8 cups (2 L) cooked

- 1 lb (500 g) dried Jerusalem artichoke pasta shapes (higher fiber)
- 1 lb (500 g) dried quinoa pasta shapes (gluten-free)
- 1 lb (500 g) dried spelt pasta shapes (low-gluten)
- 1 lb (500 g) dried Kamut® pasta shapes (low-gluten)
- 1 lb (500 g) dried rice pasta shapes (gluten-free)

See also EGG NOODLE; A SNAPSHOT OF ASIAN NOODLES (PAGE 588).

Pasta, Dried Soup

"A vegetable soup can tell you where you are in Italy almost as precisely as a map," writes Italian cooking authority Marcella Hazan. For instance, she says, the soups of the south are "founded on tomato, garlic, and olive oil, often filled out with pasta."

1 lb (500 g) =
8 cups (2 L) cooked

If You Don't Have It
Substitute 1 lb (500 g) dried soup pasta with these varieties:
- 1 lb (500 g) acini de pepe, ditalini, elbow macaroni, orzo, pastina, rizo, or rosamarina

Pasta, Dried Strands

Thin strands, such as angel hair, go best with thin sauces. Thick strands, such as perciatelli, go well with thick sauces or sauces with small chunks.

1 lb (500 g) dried =
7 to 8 cups
(1.75 to 2 L) cooked

If You Don't Have It
Substitute 1 lb (500 g) dried pasta strands with these varieties:
- 1 lb (500 g) dried angel hair, capellini, bucatini, perciatelli, spaghetti, or vermicelli
- 1 lb (500 g) dried Asian wheat noodles
- 8 oz (250 g) dried egg noodles

For Better Health
Substitute 1 lb (500 g) dried pasta strands with:
- 1 lb (500 g) dried whole wheat pasta strands (higher fiber)
- 1 lb (500 g) dried Jerusalem artichoke pasta strands (higher fiber)
- 1 lb (500 g) dried buckwheat pasta or soba noodles (higher fiber)
- 1 lb (500 g) dried quinoa pasta strands (gluten-free)
- 1 lb (500 g) dried spelt pasta strands (low-gluten)
- 1 lb (500 g) dried Kamut® pasta strands (low-gluten)

Pasta, Dried Strands (cont'd)

- 1 lb (500 g) dried rice pasta strands (gluten-free)
- 1 lb (500 g) dried Asian rice noodles (gluten-free)
- 1 medium-large (6 lb/3 kg) spaghetti squash, cooked (7 to 8 cups/1.75 to 2 L cooked strands; adds squash flavor but makes a novel and more nutritious alternative to pasta and can be served just like spaghetti; pierce a whole spaghetti squash once or twice then bake at 375°F/190°C until tender, about 40 minutes; cool slightly and cut lengthwise, pouring spaghetti-like strands into a bowl or onto plates)

See also EGG NOODLE; A SNAPSHOT OF ASIAN NOODLES (PAGE 588).

Pasta, Filled

Ingredients for pasta fillings are seemingly limitless. The morsels are classified according to the various ways of folding and sealing the pasta.

1 lb (500 g) = 5⅓ cups (1.325 L) cooked

If You Don't Have It
Substitute 1 lb (500 g) frozen filled pasta with these varieties:
- 1 lb (500 g) frozen filled agnolotti, capelletti, ravioli, tortellini, or tortelloni

Pasta, Fresh

Also known as pasta fresca. Created from soft wheat flour and eggs, fresh pasta is more akin to egg noodles than to macaroni-style factory pasta made with semolina flour.

1½ lbs (750 g) = 8 cups (2 L) cooked

If You Don't Have It
Substitute 1 lb (500 g) fresh pasta with:
- 1 lb (500 g) egg roll wrappers (especially for filled pasta)
- 1 lb (500 g) won ton skins (especially for filled pasta; smaller than egg roll wrappers)
- 1 lb (500 g) dumpling wrappers (especially for filled pasta; thinner than egg roll wrappers; round instead of square corners)
- 1 lb (500 g) empanada wrappers (especially for filled pasta; round)

Pasta Machine

This chrome tool for rolling and cutting pasta dough clamps to the counter.

If You Don't Have It
Substitute a roller-type pasta machine with:
- heavy rolling pin, sharp knife, and plenty of time

Pastis

See ANISE LIQUEUR.

Pastrami

Highly seasoned beef brisket or round that is dry-cured, smoked, and cooked.

If You Don't Have It
Substitute 1 lb (500 g) pastrami with:
- 1 lb (500 g) corned beef (less tender)

Pastry

See PIE CRUST, PASTRY.

Pastry Bag

A simple but ingenious cone-shaped bag, usually made of plastic or canvas. Frosting, whipped cream, soft cookie dough, and mashed potatoes are just some of the foods that pass through pastry bags.

If You Don't Have It
Substitute a pastry bag (for piping frostings and fillings) with:
- plastic resealable bag (fill bag and cut off one corner)
- parchment paper (roll into a cone and fill)

Pastry Blender

A series of U-shaped sturdy metal wires attached to a handle. Used to cut butter or other fat into a flour mixture for making pie crusts, biscuits, and other baked goods.

If You Don't Have It
Substitute a pastry blender with:
- food processor (for cutting fat into dry ingredients and making pastry dough)
- knife and hands (chop fat into small pieces and mix quickly into dry ingredients with fingers; if your hands are warm, run them under cold water to help prevent them from melting the fat)
- fork tines (for cutting fat into dry ingredients)
- table knives (use two knives to cut fat into dry ingredients)

Pastry Brush

Useful tool for applying glazes and marinades, these brushes are made in many sizes and materials.

If You Don't Have It
Substitute a pastry brush with:
- clean, unused paint brush of similar size

Pastry Cloth

A large canvas cloth makes rolling and transferring pie dough an easy task. Rubbing flour into the fibers makes the cloth an excellent nonstick surface. After each use, the cloth should be brushed well to remove all fat residue before storing.

If You Don't Have It
Substitute a pastry brush with:
- large silicone baking mat

Pastry Flour

See FLOUR, PASTRY

Pastry Shell

See PATTY SHELL.

Pastry Wheel

Fluted-edge pastry wheels that cut decorative designs in doughs are called jagging wheels or pastry jaggers.

If You Don't Have It
Substitute a pastry wheel with:
- pizza wheel
- sharp knife

Pâté

In classic French cuisine, a seasoned finely ground meat mixture (terrine) baked in pastry. In modern parlance, the term has come to refer to the forcemeat mixture with or without a crust.

If You Don't Have It
Substitute 1 lb (500 g) pâté with:
- 1 lb (500 g) liverwurst
- 1 lb (500 g) Braunschweiger (smoked liverwurst)

Pâté Varieties
Choose 1 lb (500 g) pâté from these varieties:
- 1 lb (500 g) goose pâté (milder)
- 1 lb (500 g) duck pâté (stronger)
- 1 lb (500 g) pâté de foie gras (more complex flavor; primarily goose liver; may also include pork liver, eggs, and truffles)

Pâte Brisée

See PIE CRUST, PASTRY.

Patis

See FISH SAUCE; SHRIMP SAUCE.

Pattypan Squash

Also known as scallopini (when young). Pale green or bright yellow summer squash with a fetching scalloped border, often delivers more in looks than taste.

1 lb (500 g) = 3 cups (750 mL) chopped

If You Don't Have It
Substitute 1 lb (500 g) pattypan squash with:
- 1 lb (500 g) yellow squash
- 1 lb (500 g) zucchini
- 1 lb (500 g) cucuzza
- 1 lb (500 g) fuzzy gourd

Patty Shell

A cup-shaped puff pastry shell that can be filled with various creamed dishes. Fresh ones are sold in some bakeries. Frozen unbaked shells are stocked in supermarkets.

If You Don't Have It
Substitute 1 lb (500 g) patty shells with:
- 1 lb (500 g) barquettes (boat-shaped pastry shells)
- 1 lb (500 g) phyllo shells or knafa (less rich; more crisp; shape knafa into shells in ramekins or muffin cups)

See also PUFF PASTRY.

Pawpaw

See PAPAW.

Pea

See PEAS, EDIBLE PODS; PEA SHOOTS; PEAS, SHELLING; PEAS, SPLIT.

Pea Bean

See THE WIDE WORLD OF DRIED BEANS (PAGE 566).

Peach

China gave the world one of its most prized pleasures in this fruit. Of the two basic categories, freestone peaches are eaten as fresh fruit, while clingstones (with flesh that sticks to the stone) are most often commercially canned.

1 lb (500 g) fresh =
4 medium =
2½ cups (625 mL)
chopped or sliced =
1½ cups (375 mL) purée

If You Don't Have It
Substitute 1 lb (500 g) peaches with:
- 1 lb (500 g) nectarines
- 1 lb (500 g) apricots
- 1 lb (500 g) plums
- 1 lb (500 g) apriums (cross between an apricot and plum)
- 1 lb (500 g) pluots (cross between a plum and an apricot)
- 1 lb (500 g) cherries
- 1 lb (500 g) mango
- 1 lb (500 g) papaya

Peach, Dried

Sulfur dioxide is often added to commercially dried fruit to improve shelf life and color.

1 lb (500 g) =
3 cups (750 mL)

If You Don't Have It
Substitute 1 lb (500 g) dried peaches with:
- 1 lb (500 g) dried apricots
- 1 lb (500 g) dried nectarines
- 1 lb (500 g) dried cherries

Peanut

Also known as goobers and ground nuts. Spaniards and Portuguese slave traders transported these legumes from South America to Europe and Africa. African slaves introduced them to the American South.

1 lb (500 g) =
3½ to 4 cups
(875 mL to 1 L) chopped
= 4 cups (1 L)
ground meal

If You Don't Have It
Substitute 1 cup (250 mL) peanuts with:
- 1 cup (250 mL) cashews
- 1 cup (250 mL) almonds
- 1 cup (250 mL) pistachios
- 1 cup (250 mL) pine nuts
- 1 cup (250 mL) walnuts
- 1 cup (250 mL) pecans

See also NUTS.

Peanut Butter

In the late 1800s, a physician in St. Louis ground peanuts into a spread for his patients with bad teeth. At the 1904 Louisiana Purchase Exposition in St. Louis, it was promoted as a health food, but the oil separated from the grainy solids. In 1933, a California packer homogenized the peanuts into a stable butter marketed as Skippy Churned Peanut Butter.

If You Don't Have It
Substitute 1 cup (250 mL) peanut butter with:
- 1 cup (250 mL) Homemade Peanut Butter: Put 2 cups (500 mL) roasted peanuts (skins removed) and ¼ tsp (1 mL) salt in a blender or food processor fitted with metal blade. Process, gradually adding 4 to 6 tbsp (60 to 90 mL) vegetable oil and/or peanut oil, until the mixture forms a paste. Add sugar to taste. Makes 1½ cups (375 mL).
- 1 cup (250 mL) almond butter
- 1 cup (250 mL) cashew butter
- 1 cup (250 mL) gianduja (chocolate-hazelnut spread)
- 1 cup (250 mL) tahini (pronounced sesame flavor)

Peanut Butter Chips

Also known as peanut butter morsels. Sweetened peanut butter candies shaped like chocolate morsels used for baking and snacks.

> 6 oz (175 g) =
> 1 cup (250 mL)

If You Don't Have It
Substitute 1 cup (250 mL) peanut butter chips with:
- 1 cup (250 mL) butterscotch chips
- 1 cup (250 mL) cinnamon chips
- 1 cup (250 mL) chocolate chips
- 1 cup (250 mL) chopped nuts

Pea Pods

See PEAS, EDIBLE POD.

Pear

An atypical fruit that ripens well off the tree, pear varieties number in the thousands.

> 1 lb (500 g) fresh =
> 3 medium =
> 2 cups (500 mL) sliced

If You Don't Have It
Substitute 1 lb (500 g) pears with:
- 1 lb (500 g) apples
- 1 lb (500 g) Asian pears (more crisp)
- 1 lb (500 g) quinces

See also PICKING PEARS (PAGE 565).

Pear Brandy

Clear pear-flavored eau de vie from France and Switzerland. The finest brands encapsulate a whole Williams pear (the European name for Bartlett) inside each bottle. The painstaking process involves placing an individual bottle over a budding fruit and allowing the fruit to ripen in the bottle before it is filled with brandy.

If You Don't Have It
Substitute 2 tbsp (25 mL) pear brandy with:
- 2 tbsp (25 mL) apple brandy such as Calvados or applejack
- 1 tbsp (15 mL) cognac or brandy + 1 tbsp (15 mL) pear nectar
- 2 tbsp (25 mL) other fruit brandy such as cherry brandy

Pear, Dried

High concentrations of sugar in dried pears ward off bacteria and help the fruit remain supple.

> 1 lb (500 g) dried =
> 2¾ cups (675 mL) =
> 5½ cups (1.375 L) cooked

If You Don't Have It

Substitute 1 oz (30 g) dried pears with:
- 1 oz (30 g) dried Asian pears
- 1 oz (30 g) dried apples

Peas, Edible Pod

Also known as mangetout (England and France), snow pea, and sugar snap pea. Truly a no-waste vegetable, snow peas and sugar snap peas require little, if any, cooking to enjoy.

> 1 lb (500 g) =
> 3 cups (750 mL)

If You Don't Have It

Substitute 1 lb (500 g) edible pod peas with:
- 1 lb (500 g) mung bean sprouts
- 1 lb (500 g) fresh edamame or fava beans
- 1 lb (500 g) asparagus
- 1 lb (500 g) broccoli

Edible Pod Pea Varieties

Choose 1 oz (30 g) edible pod peas from these varieties:
- 1 lb (500 g) sugar snap peas (sweet, crisp, rounded pods with medium-size peas)
- 1 lb (500 g) snow peas (medium-sweet, crisp-tender, flattened pods with small peas)

Peas, Shelling

The most glamorous incarnation of the common fresh garden pea is the French petits pois harvested when young and sweet. The sugar in shelled peas starts to turn to starch the moment they are picked. If you can't grow your own or buy from a farmer, the best choice may be frozen baby peas.

> 1 lb (500 g) fresh in pod
> = 1 cup (250 mL) shelled

If You Don't Have It

Substitute 1 lb (500 g) fresh shelling peas (weighed in shell) with:
- 1 lb (500 g) fresh black-eyed peas or other cowpeas (southernpeas; pale green and cream or pink color with black "eye" at center)
- 1 lb (500 g) fresh lima beans (green color)
- 1 lb (500 g) fresh edamame (green color)
- 1 lb (500 g) fresh cranberry beans (cream and red-speckled color)
- 1 lb (500 g) fresh Dragon Tongue beans (deep reddish brown and cream color)
- 1 lb (500 g) fresh Tongue of Fire beans (green and red color)
- 1 lb (500 g) fresh Romano beans (green color)
- 1 lb (500 g) fresh Kentucky Wonder or runner beans (green color)

See also BEANS, SHELLING; BLACK-EYED PEA, FRESH.

Pea Shoots

Also known as pea leaves and pea tendrils. Imbued with whimsical curlicues, the green leaves of fresh peas are delicious added to salads.

> 1 lb (500 g) fresh =
> 10 cups (2.5 L)

If You Don't Have It

Substitute 1 cup (250 mL) pea shoots with:
- 1 cup (250 mL) baby spinach leaves (less sweet)
- 1 cup (250 mL) garden or upland cress (more peppery)

Peas, Split

Also known as field peas. A variety of green or yellow peas cultivated to be dried. After drying, they split along a natural seam. In India, peas are stewed into a variety of dals. In the west, green split pea soup with ham is a classic.

> 1 lb (500 g) =
> 2⅓ cups (575 mL) dried
> = 5 cups (1.25 L) cooked

If You Don't Have It

Substitute 1 lb (500 g) green or yellow split peas with:
- 1 lb (500 g) lentils
- 1 lb (500 g) dried black-eyed peas

See also SWITCHING LENTILS (PAGE 569).

Pecan

This luminary of the hickory family is synonymous with the American South. The name comes from the Algonquin word paccan which refers to hickories.

> 1 lb (500 g) in shell =
> 2 cups (500 mL) shelled
>
> 1 lb (500 g) shelled =
> 4 cups (1 L) halves =
> 3¾ cups (925 mL) chopped

If You Don't Have It

Substitute 1 cup (250 mL) shelled pecans with:
- 2 to 4 tbsp (25 to 60 mL) pecan oil (for baking and cooking; will add nut flavor but not texture of whole nuts; reduce fat in recipe by 2 to 4 tbsp/ 25 to 60 mL)
- 1 cup (250 mL) walnuts
- 1 cup (250 mL) hazelnuts
- 1 cup (250 mL) hickory nuts
- 1 cup (250 mL) pistachios
- 1 cup (250 mL) macadamia nuts
- 1 cup (250 mL) Brazil nuts

For Better Health

Substitute 1 cup (250 mL) pecans with:
- 1 cup (250 mL) rolled oats, toasted (for baking)

See also NUTS.

Pecorino

A sharp, sheep's milk cheese, pecorino romano is produced in the regions of Lazio and Sardinia, as well as Grosseto province in Tuscany. Pecorino toscano is made only from milk drawn between September and June. Pecorino siciliano is studded with whole black peppercorns. Pecorino sardo, (fiore di sardo), is made on the island of Sardinia.

1 lb (500 g) young =
4 cups (1 L) shredded

4 oz (125 g) aged =
1 cup (250 mL) grated

If You Don't Have It
Substitute 1 oz (30 g) pecorino cheese (for grating) with:
- 1 oz (30 g) Parmesan (slightly milder and less salty)
- 1 oz (30 g) Grana Padano
- 1 oz (30 g) aged Asiago
- 1 oz (30 g) aged Manchego
- 1 oz (30 g) dry Jack cheese (more nutty flavor)

For Better Health
Substitute 1 oz (30 g) pecorino cheese (for grating) with:
- sapsago (more herbal flavor; lower in fat)

See also ROMANO.

Peeler

See VEGETABLE PEELER.

Pemmican

Loaves or small cakes composed of a paste of pulverized ground meat or fish, hot fat, and dried berries or other fruits. Of Native American origin.

If You Don't Have It
Substitute 1 oz (30 g) pemmican with:
- 1 oz (30 g) beef jerky (less complex flavor)
- 1 oz (30 g) biltong (spicier; more complex flavor)

For Better Health
Substitute 1 oz (30 g) pemmican with:
- 1 oz (30 g) turkey jerky (leaner)
- 1 oz (30 g) vegetarian jerky (leaner)

See also BILTONG; JERKY.

Pepino

Also known as melon pear and treemelon. A glossy gold and violet skinned fruit related to eggplant with a mild taste and melon-like texture.

1 lb (500 g) =
3 cups (750 mL)

If You Don't Have It
Substitute 1 lb (500 g) pepinos with:
- 1 lb (500 g) babacos
- 1 lb (500 g) tamarillos
- 1 lb (500 g) papaya
- 1 lb (500 g) pears
- 1 lb (500 g) Charentais melon or cantaloupe
- 1 lb (500 g) prickly pears

Pepitas

See PUMPKIN SEEDS.

Peppadew™ Piquanté Pepper

Peppadews, the vivid red sweet-hot South African peppers, are available jarred or in the delicatessen section of some supermarkets.

> 8 oz (250 g) drained = 1 cup (250 mL)

If You Don't Have It
Substitute 1 cup (250 mL) Peppadew™ Piquanté peppers with:
- 1 cup (250 mL) peperoncini
- 1 cup (250 mL) pickled cherry peppers
- 1 cup (250 mL) pimentos
- 1 cup (250 mL) red Anaheim chiles
- 1 cup (250 mL) red New Mexico chiles
- 1 cup (250 mL) sun-dried tomatoes

Pepper

See BELL PEPPER; PEPPERCORN; CHOOSING DRIED CHILES (PAGE 578); CHOOSING FRESH CHILES (PAGE 582).

Peppercorn

The berry of the climbing vine pepper plant native to India and Indonesia is the most popular spice in the world. Green peppercorns are immature berries usually packed in brine. White peppercorns are mature, skinned, dried berries. Black peppercorns are the most popular type. They are slightly underripe berries that turn dark after they dry. Tellicherry and Lampong are considered the finest types of black pepper.

> 1 tsp (5 mL) peppercorns = 1½ tsp (7 mL) ground pepper

If You Don't Have It
Substitute 1 tsp (5 mL) peppercorns with:
- 1½ tsp (7 mL) ground pepper
- 1 tsp (5 mL) pink peppercorns (milder; not a true peppercorn)
- 1 tsp (5 mL) Szechuan pepper (milder; adds citrus aromas; not a true peppercorn)
- ¼ to ½ tsp (1 to 2 mL) cayenne pepper (spicier)
- ½ to 1 tsp (2 to 5 mL) black or yellow mustard seeds (sharper)

Peppercorn Varieties
Choose 1 tsp (5 mL) peppercorns from these varieties:
- 1 tsp (5 mL) black peppercorns (strong, almost hot flavor)
- 1 tsp (5 mL) white peppercorns (smaller and hotter but less aromatic than black peppercorns)
- 1 tsp (5 mL) green peppercorns (milder than black peppercorns; usually pickled)
- 1 tsp (5 mL) true pink peppercorns (milder than black peppercorns with berry-like aromas; usually pickled)

See also PINK PEPPERCORN; SZECHUAN PEPPER.

Pepper Mill

Former New York Times *restaurant critic Bryan Miller once wrote, "The disparity between a restaurant's price and food quality rises in direct proportion to the size of the pepper mill.*

If You Don't Have It
Substitute a pepper mill with:
- mortar and pestle
- spice grinder or clean coffee grinder

Peppermint

See MINT.

Peppermint Extract

See MINT EXTRACT.

Peppermint Oil

See OIL OF PEPPERMINT.

Peppermint Schnapps

Created in the 1930s, this is the first popular single-flavored liqueur bearing the schnapps name. It generally has a higher proof than other fruit schnapps liqueurs.

If You Don't Have It
Substitute 2 tbsp (25 mL) peppermint schnapps with:
- 1 to 2 tbsp (15 to 25 mL) crème de menthe (thicker; sweeter)
- ¼ to ½ tsp (1 to 2 mL) peppermint extract
- 1 drop oil of peppermint

Pepperoncini

Italian-style pickled sweet-hot chiles similar in taste and appearance to small Anaheim chiles.

8 oz (250 g) drained = 1 cup (250 mL)

If You Don't Have It
Substitute 1 cup (250 mL) pepperoncini with:
- 1 cup (250 mL) pickled cherry peppers
- 1 cup (250 mL) pickled Anaheim chiles
- 1 cup (250 mL) cup Peppadew™ Piquanté peppers
- 1 cup (250 mL) pickled pimientos
- 1 cup (250 mL) other pickled peppers

Pepperoni

Firm, dry, ready-to-eat Italian sausage prepared from beef and pork. Generally sliced very thin, it's most popular on pizza but also makes a good appetizer or addition to pasta.

If You Don't Have It

Substitute 1 oz (30 g) pepperoni with:
- 1 oz (30 g) Calabrese sausage
- 1 oz (30 g) soppressata
- 1 oz (30 g) other dry Italian salami

See also SALAMI.

Pequín Chile

See CHOOSING DRIED CHILES (PAGE 578).

Perch

True perch is a moderate-size freshwater fish with two dorsal fins that originated in Eurasia and was introduced in other waters as a prize for anglers. The term perch has been widely misapplied to a number of similar-seeming marine life. The Eastern European fish called pike-perch (zander) is also unrelated.

If You Don't Have It

Substitute 1 lb (500 g) with:
- 1 lb (500 g) pike
- 1 lb (500 g) porgy
- 1 lb (500 g) rockfish
- 1 lb (500 g) red snapper
- 1 lb (500 g) grouper

See also OCEAN PERCH; PIKE.

Periwinkle

Also known as bigaro, sea snail, or winkle. A univalve mollusk that looks like a big snail. The most common edible specimen grows in the north Atlantic attached to rocks, wharves, and pilings.

If You Don't Have It

Substitute 1 lb (500 g) periwinkles with:
- 1 lb (500 g) whelks
- 1 lb (500 g) limpets
- 1 lb (500 g) snails
- 1 lb (500 g) scallops
- 1 lb (500 g) cockles
- 1 lb (500 g) clams
- 1 lb (500 g) oysters

Pernod

See ANISE LIQUEUR.

Persian Lime

See LIME.

Persian Melon

Large sweet muskmelon with salmon-color flesh. Late summer is the peak season.

1 medium = 5 lbs (2.5 kg)
= 7½ cups (1.875 L) diced

If You Don't Have It

Substitute 1 cup (250 mL) chopped Persian melon with:
- 1 cup (250 mL) chopped Crenshaw melon
- 1 cup (250 mL) chopped cantaloupe
- 1 cup (250 mL) chopped Santa Claus melon
- 1 cup (250 mL) chopped honeydew melon
- 1 cup (250 mL) chopped casaba melon

Persimmon

Also known as kaki. A flame orange astringent fruit of both Chinese and North American origin, persimmons must be extremely ripe to be palatable. An outstanding source of vitamin A, the fruit is also high in fiber and a good source of potassium.

9 oz (270 g) =
¾ cup (175 mL) pulp

If You Don't Have It

Substitute 1 lb (500 g) persimmons with:
- 1 lb (500 g) plums
- 1 lb (500 g) pumpkin purée (to replace puréed persimmons)
- 1 lb (500 g) applesauce (to replace puréed persimmons)

Persimmon Varieties

Choose 1 lb (500 g) persimmons from these varieties:
- 1 lb (500 g) Hachiya persimmons (teardrop-shaped; flame orange skin and very soft flesh when ripe; reminiscent of plums with a tangy edge when ripe; tannic and bitter-tasting when unripe)
- 1 lb (500 g) Fuyu persimmons (smaller and rounder than Hachiya persimmons; slightly milder flavor than Hachiyas; flesh is firm when ripe)

Persimmon, Dried

Native Americans dried ripe wild persimmons and formed the paste into bricks to eat during the winter months.

If You Don't Have It

Substitute 1 cup (250 mL) dried persimmons with:
- 1 cup (250 mL) dried plums (prunes)
- 1 cup (250 mL) dried apricots
- 1 cup (250 mL) dried peaches

Pesto

The word translates from Italian as "pounded." Undoubtedly the most famous type is the basil pesto from Genoa, which traditionally is ground into a paste with a pestle in a mortar.

If You Don't Have It

Substitute 1 cup (250 mL) pesto with:
- 1 cup (250 mL) Homemade Pesto: Put 2 chopped garlic cloves, 10 cups (2.5 L) loosely packed fresh basil, 2 cups (500 mL) grated Parmigiano-Reggiano cheese, ¾ cup (175 mL) pine nuts, ¾ tsp (4 mL) salt, and ⅛ tsp (0.5 mL) ground black pepper in a food processor or blender. Blend until finely chopped, about 30 seconds. Scrape down sides of bowl then turn on machine and gradually add ¾ cup (175 mL) extra virgin olive oil, blending to a loose paste, about 20 seconds. For thinner pesto, add more oil. Taste and add more salt and pepper if necessary. Spoon into airtight containers and refrigerate for up to 1 week or freeze for up to 1 year. Replace the basil with cilantro, parsley, or other leafy herbs if you like. Makes about 2¼ cups (550 mL).

To Vary the Flavor

Substitute 1 cup (250 mL) pesto with:
- 1 cup (250 mL) tapenade (saltier; strong olive flavor)

Peter Heering

See CHERRY LIQUEUR.

Petit Suisse

Also known as the popular brand name Gervais. A rich, French cheese with tangy sweet flavor and the consistency of very soft cream cheese.

8 oz (250 g) =
1 cup (250 mL)

If You Don't Have It

Substitute 1 oz (30 g) Petit Suisse with:
- 1 oz (30 g) Robiola Piemonte
- 1 oz (30 g) Caprini
- 1 oz (30 g) fromage blanc
- 1 oz (30 g) cream cheese

Pheasant

The flesh of female pheasants is plumper, juicier, and more tender than that of the males. Very young hens are delicious roasted.

1 average = 3 lbs (1.5 kg)

If You Don't Have It

Substitute 1 lb (500 g) pheasant with:
- 1 lb (500 g) guinea fowl
- 1 lb (500 g) grouse
- 1 lb (500 g) quail
- 1 lb (500 g) partridge
- 1 lb (500 g) squab
- 1 lb (500 g) Cornish hen (fattier)

Phyllo

Also known as filo. Fresh phyllo dough may be found in Greek or Middle Eastern food stores. Most supermarkets carry packaged frozen phyllo dough.

If You Don't Have It
Substitute 1 lb (500 g) phyllo dough with:
- 1 lb (500 g) strudel dough
- 1 lb (500 g) puff pastry (less crisp)

To Save Time
Substitute 1 lb (500 g) phyllo dough with:
- 1 lb (500 g) kadaif or knafa preshredded phyllo dough (best for top and bottom crusts; does not roll into turnovers like phyllo sheets; toss the thawed dough with butter instead of brushing with butter)

Pickerel

See PIKE.

Pickling Spice

This spice blend was a much more common cupboard staple in the days when fruits and vegetables were canned in home kitchens. Contemporary usage calls for pickling spice in a variety of dishes from chutney to sauerbraten.

If You Don't Have It
Substitute 1 tbsp (15 mL) pickling spice with:
- 1 tbsp (15 mL) Homemade Pickling Spice: Combine 1 broken 3-inch (7.5 cm) cinnamon stick, 4 to 5 crushed bay leaves, 1 to 2 broken small dried chile peppers (or 1 to 2 tsp/5 to 10 mL crushed red pepper flakes), 2 tbsp (25 mL) mustard seeds, 1 tbsp (15 mL) whole allspice, 1 tbsp (15 mL) coriander seeds, 1 tbsp (15 mL) black or white peppercorns, 1 tbsp (15 mL) ground ginger, 1 tbsp (15 mL) dill seeds, 2 tsp (10 mL) cardamom seeds (scraped from pods; optional), and 1 tsp (5 mL) whole cloves. Store in an airtight container. Makes about ½ cup (125 mL).
- 1 tbsp (15 mL) crab boil
- 1 tbsp (15 mL) Old Bay seasoning

Picon

Spanish raw cow's milk cheese (sometimes with added sheep and goat's milk) that is naturally blued from mold spores circulating in the aging caves.

4 oz (125 g) =
1 cup (250 mL) crumbled

If You Don't Have It
Substitute 1 oz (30 g) Picon with:
- 1 oz (30 g) Cabrales
- 1 oz (30 g) Gamonedo
- 1 oz (30 g) Roquefort

Pie Cherry

See CHERRY.

Pie Crust, Crumb

For those with pastry phobia, a crumb crust is easy to execute. Simply combine cookie crumbs with butter or other fat, perhaps some spices, and press into the pie pan before baking.

If You Don't Have It
Substitute 1 crumb crust with:
- 1 Homemade Graham Cracker Crumb Crust: Mix together 1½ cups (375 mL) crushed graham crackers (about 21 squares), 3 tbsp (45 mL) packed brown sugar, 3 tbsp (45 mL) melted butter, and ½ to 1 tsp (2 to 5 mL) cinnamon (optional). Press into greased 9-inch (23 cm) pie pan and bake at 350°F (180°C) until light brown, about 8 minutes. Let cool and fill.

To Vary the Flavor
Substitute 1½ tsp (7 mL) crumbs for crust with:
- 1½ cups (375 mL) crushed gingersnaps (about 22)
- 1½ cups (375 mL) crushed vanilla wafer cookies (about 33)
- 1½ cups (375 mL) crushed chocolate wafer cookies (about 32)
- 1½ cups (375 mL) crushed Oreo cookies (about 21, including cookie filling); omit sugar from crust
- 1½ cups (375 mL) crushed wheat, bran or corn flakes (about 4½ cups/1.125 L)
- 1½ cups (375 mL) crushed saltine crackers (about 42); omit sugar from crust and adjust salt in filling (for savory fillings)

For Better Health
Substitute 1 crumb crust with:
- ½ tsp (2 mL) of cookie crumbs in recipe plus equal amount of crushed saltine or other table crackers (omit salt from recipe)

See also PIE CRUST, PASTRY.

Pie Crust, Pastry

Also known as pâte brisée (France). "I was taught to make tender, flaky pastry as if it were one word, tenderflaky," writes cooking authority Shirley Corriher.

If You Don't Have It
Substitute one 9-inch (23 cm) pie crust with:
- 1 sheet from half a 15-oz (450 g) package refrigerated pie crust sheets (not in a tin)

Pie Crust, Pastry (cont'd)

"Nothing could be further from the truth — tenderness is one characteristic, flakiness a totally different characteristic."

To Vary the Flavor

Substitute one 9-inch (23 cm) pie crust with:
● 1 sheet puff pastry, rolled into a 9-inch (23 cm) circle (richer)

For Better Health

Replace one 9-inch (23 cm) pie crust with:
● 3 sheets (6 half-sheets) phyllo dough layered with cooking spray, oil, or melted butter

See also PIE CRUST, CRUMB.

Pie Pan

See PAN SIZE EQUIVALENTS (PAGE 606).

Pie Weights

Heavy metal pellets used to weigh down a pie crust while blind baking (baking the crust without a filling).

If You Don't Have It

Substitute pie weights with:
● dried beans

Pigeon

See SQUAB.

Pigeon Pea

See THE WIDE WORLD OF DRIED BEANS (PAGE 566).

Pike

A freshwater family of game fish with long bodies and formidable teeth that includes small pickerels and large muskellunge (muskie). The walleyed pike is not a pike but rather a perch. The Eastern European fish called pike-perch (zander) is unrelated.

If You Don't Have It

Substitute 1 lb (500 g) pike with:
● 1 lb (500 g) walleye

See also PERCH.

Pilchard

A small, oily European Atlantic fish that's a shelf staple either canned in oil or tomato sauce.

If You Don't Have It

Substitute 1 lb (500 g) pilchards with:
● 1 lb (500 g) sardines
● 1 lb (500 g) shad
● 1 lb (500 g) herring
● 1 lb (500 g) mackerel
● 1 lb (500 g) bluefish

Piloncillo

*Also known as panela
and panocha. Mexican
unrefined brown sugar
shaped into a hard
truncated cone. Sometimes
available in lighter* (blanco
or claro) *or darker* (oscuro
or prieto), *the flavor is like
molassesy brown sugar.*

```
1-inch (2.5 cm) tall cone
    = 1 oz (30 g) =
    2 tbsp (25 mL)
```

If You Don't Have It
Substitute 1 cup (250 mL) (about 7 oz/210 g)
piloncillo with:
- 1 cup (250 mL) dark brown sugar + 1 to 2 tbsp
  (15 to 25 mL) molasses
- 1 cup (250 mL) jaggery

Pimento

See ALLSPICE.

Pimiento

*Also known as pimento.
A red, heart-shaped
pepper that is dried to
be ground into paprika.
Also famous as the
stuffing for green olives.*

```
1 lb (500 g) = 2 large =
    2½ cups (625 mL)
    chopped = 3 cups
    (750 mL) sliced
```

If You Don't Have It
Substitute 2 tbsp (25 mL) chopped pimiento with:
- 2 to 3 tbsp (25 to 45 mL) chopped fresh red
  bell pepper
- 1 tbsp (15 mL) dried red bell pepper + 2 tbsp
  (25 mL) hot water

Pimm's

*Summer in England for a
certain segment of society
is impossible without a
refreshing Pimm's Cup, a
cocktail made with Pimm's
#1, soda, and a twist. The
gin-based quinine and
herbal liqueur was created
in the 1800s by London
oyster bar owner James
Pimm.*

If You Don't Have It
Substitute 2 tbsp (25 mL) Pimm's Cup #1 with:
- 2 tbsp (25 mL) gin + ½ tsp (2 mL) granulated
  sugar dissolved in ½ tsp (2 mL) water + dash of
  Angostura bitters

Pineapple

The introduction of plastic-wrapped peeled and cored pineapples in supermarkets was a joyful innovation for fanciers of fresh pineapple.

> 1 medium pineapple = 5 cups (1.25 L) cubes

If You Don't Have It
Substitute 1 cup (250 mL) chopped fresh pineapple with:
- 1 cup (250 mL) chopped canned pineapple
- 1 cup (250 mL) papaya
- 1 cup (250 mL) guava
- 1 cup (250 mL) mango
- 1 cup (250 mL) feijoa

Pineapple Variety
Choose 1 cup (250 mL) chopped fresh pineapple from this variety:
- 1 cup (250 mL) chopped golden pineapple (sweeter; juicier)

Pineapple, Candied

Also known as crystallized pineapple and glacé pineapple. Choose candied pineapple that has good color and some pliability.

If You Don't Have It
Substitute 1 oz (30 g) candied pineapple with:
- 1 oz (30 g) candied papaya

Pineapple Guava

See FEIJOA.

Pineapple Juice

Available either natural or sweetened in cans, bottles, or as frozen concentrate, this tropical juice graces many cocktails and punches.

If You Don't Have It
Substitute 1 cup (250 mL) pineapple juice with:
- 1 cup (250 mL) orange juice
- 1 cup (250 mL) grapefruit juice
- 1 cup (250 mL) fruit nectar such as mango or peach (thicker; sweeter)

Pine Nut

Also known as pignoli and piñon. Oily, distinctively flavored seeds extracted from the inside of pinecones.

> 8 oz (250 g) = 1½ cups (375 mL)

If You Don't Have It
Substitute 1 cup (250 mL) shelled pine nuts with:
- 1 cup (250 mL) walnuts
- 1 cup (250 mL) almonds
- 1 cup (250 mL) pecans
- 1 cup (250 mL) cashews
- 1 cup (250 mL) pistachios
- 1 cup (250 mL) peanuts

See also NUTS.

Pinga

See CACHAÇA.

Pink Bean

See THE WIDE WORLD OF DRIED BEANS (PAGE 566).

Pink Peppercorn

Pink or red berries of schinus trees that are sold as pink peppercorns. Not true pink peppercorns, which come from the same Piper nigrum vines that produce black, white, and green peppercorns.

If You Don't Have It

Substitute 1 tsp (5 mL) pink peppercorns with:
- 1 tsp (5 mL) freeze-dried green peppercorns
- 1 tsp (5 mL) white peppercorns (smaller, stronger)
- 1 tsp (5 mL) black peppercorns (stronger)
- 1 tsp (5 mL) Szechuan pepper (adds citrus aromas)
- ½ tsp (2 mL) ground pepper

See also PEPPERCORN.

Pinto Bean

See THE WIDE WORLD OF DRIED BEANS (PAGE 566).

Pisco

A typical Chilean or Peruvian grape brandy that is not wood aged. The Pisco Sour is the signature cocktail of Peru.

If You Don't Have It

Substitute 2 tbsp (25 mL) pisco with:
- 2 tbsp (25 mL) grappa
- 2 tbsp (25 mL) cognac
- 2 tbsp (25 mL) Armagnac

Pistachio

A rich and subtle-tasting nut with a beige shell and lovely pale green fruit. Convenient for nibblers because the shell of mature pistachios is partially split open. Some commercial suppliers color pistachios red with vegetable dyes, a practice which has its detractors and its advocates.

1 lb (500 g) in shell = 2 cups (500 mL) shelled
1 lb (500 g) shelled = 3½ to 4 cups (875 mL to 1 L)

If You Don't Have It

Substitute 1 cup (250 mL) unsalted pistachio nuts with:
- 1 cup (250 mL) salted pistachios, rinsed under cool water
- 2 to 4 tbsp (25 to 60 mL) pistachio oil (for baking and cooking; will add nut flavor but not texture of whole nuts; reduce fat in recipe by 2 to 4 tbsp/ 25 to 60 mL)

To Vary the Flavor

Substitute 1 cup (250 mL) unsalted pistachio nuts with:
- 1 cup (250 mL) pine nuts
- 1 cup (250 mL) almonds
- 1 cup (250 mL) hazelnuts
- 1 cup (250 mL) cashews

See also NUTS.

Pita Bread

Also known as pocket bread. Circular Middle Eastern flatbread that splits horizontally to create two pouches that can be filled with meats, vegetables, or other stuffings.

If You Don't Have It

Substitute 1 pita bread with:
- 1 arepa
- 1 gordita
- 1 naan
- 1 lavash
- 1 flour tortilla
- 1 small baked pizza crust

See also PIZZA CRUST.

Pitaya

Also known as apple cactus. A Latin American cactus fruit ranging in color from pink to yellow. The grainy flesh is studded with seeds.

If You Don't Have It

Substitute 1 cup (250 mL) pitaya with:
- 1 cup (250 mL) kiwifruit

Pizza Crust

"It is generally assumed by all relevant historians, including the typically chauvinistic Neapolitan ones, that no date can be put on the beginnings of the bread part of the pizza. Flatbreads like it go back forever. The word 'pizza' is obviously related to the word 'pita,'" writes Arthur Schwartz in Naples at Table.

If You Don't Have It

Substitute 1 (18-inch/45 cm) pizza crust with:
- 1 (18-inch/45 cm) focaccia
- 1 (18-inch/45 cm) refrigerated or frozen pizza shell
- 1 tube (10 oz/300 g) refrigerated pizza dough, rolled into an 18-inch (45 cm) round
- 1 piece fresh, refrigerated, or frozen bread dough rolled into an 18-inch (45 cm) round
- 1 (18-inch/45 cm) prebaked pizza crust (such as Boboli)
- 2 wide loaves baked French or Italian bread, halved lengthwise
- 3 to 4 (6-inch/15 cm) rounds pita bread

See also PITA BREAD.

Pizza Wheel

Also known as a pizza cutter. Designed to cut pizzas into wedges, this rolling round cutter can also mince herbs and cut rolled fresh pasta into various shapes.

If You Don't Have It

Substitute a pizza wheel with:
- sharp knife

Plaice

Also known as Canadian plaice and sand dab (North America). A saltwater flatfish of the flounder family. It has a fine-textured flesh and mild flavor.

If You Don't Have It

Substitute 1 lb (500 g) plaice with:
- 1 lb (500 g) sole
- 1 lb (500 g) flounder
- 1 lb (500 g) brill
- 1 lb (500 g) turbot
- 1 lb (500 g) haddock

Plain Flour

See FLOUR, ALL-PURPOSE.

Plantain

Also known as cooking banana, plátano, and plátano macho. Best used when still green, plantain has a squash-like flavor and is often used as a potato substitute in Latin America and some African countries.

> 2 medium =
> 1¼ lbs (625 g) = 2 cups
> (500 mL) cooked slices

If You Don't Have It

Substitute 1 lb (500 g) plantains with:
- 1 lb (500 g) potatoes (to replace unripe green or yellow plantains)
- 1 lb (500 g) yams (to replace unripe green or yellow plantains)
- 1 lb (500 g) sweet potatoes (to replace unripe green or yellow plantains)
- 1 lb (500 g) breadfruit (to replace green or yellow plantains)
- 1 lb (500 g) jackfruit (to replace green or yellow plantains)
- 1 lb (500 g) underripe bananas (to replace ripe black plantains)

Plastic Wrap

Various clinging clear sheets used to wrap and cover foods; can be made from polyethylene, polyvinylidene chloride and polyvinyl chloride.

If You Don't Have It

Substitute plastic wrap with:
- plastic bags (for storing food; or cut bags to use as plastic wrap)
- wax paper (for wrapping food and covering food to be microwaved)
- aluminum foil (for wrapping food)

Pleurotus

See SHUFFLING MUSHROOMS (PAGE 572).

Plugra

See BUTTER.

Plum

Also known as fresh prune. A drupe related to apricot, peach, and particularly cherry, modern commercial plums are either of Japanese or European origin. Japanese plums, such as Santa Rosa, are originally from China and are the clingstone type. Most have crimson to dark red skin with juicy, yellow or reddish flesh. European freestone plums are smaller, denser, and less juicy, with blue or purple skin and golden flesh. These are the plums that are dried into prunes. Varieties include Italian and Empress. The small, tart Damson plums are typically made into preserves.

1 lb (500 g) fresh =
2½ cups (625 mL) sliced;
2 cups (500 mL) cooked

If You Don't Have It
Substitute 1 lb (500 g) plums with:
- 1 lb (500 g) plumcots (a hybrid of equal parts plum and apricot)
- 1 lb (500 g) pluots (hybrid of plum and apricot that's closer to a plum)
- 1 lb (500 g) apriums (hybrid of apricot and plum that's closer to an apricot)
- 1 lb (500 g) apricots
- 1 lb (500 g) nectarines
- 1 lb (500 g) peaches
- 1 lb (500 g) cherries
- 1 lb (500 g) loquats
- 1 lb (500 g) mangoes

Plum Varieties
Choose 1 lb (500 g) plums from these varieties:
- 1 lb (500 g) Friar plums (popular Japanese variety; large, round; purple black skin; pale, juicy, sweet flesh)
- 1 lb (500 g) Santa Rosa plums (popular Japanese variety; medium-size, round; red skin speckled with tiny yellow spots; sweet-tart flesh)
- 1 lb (500 g) Red Beaut plums (Japanese variety; small, round; bright red skin; yellow, mildly sweet flesh)
- 1 lb (500 g) greengage plums (Japanese variety; small, round; green to yellow skin; sweet-tart flesh)
- 1 lb (500 g) Kelsey plums (Japanese variety; small, oval; green to yellow skin; sweet flesh)
- 1 lb (500 g) Damson plums (small, oval European variety; deep purple skin; sweet-tart flesh)
- 1 lb (500 g) Mirabelle plums (small, oval European variety; yellow to red skin; sweet-tart flesh)
- 1 lb (500 g) Italian prune plums (small, oval European variety; green to purple skin; sweet flesh)

See also PRUNE; SLOE.

Plum Brandy

A European eau de vie that's much appreciated in France, Germany, and Eastern European countries.

If You Don't Have It
Substitute 2 tbsp (25 mL) plum brandy with:
- 2 tbsp (25 mL) other fruit brandy such as apricot brandy
- 2 tbsp (25 mL) grappa
- 2 tbsp (25 mL) sloe gin

Plum Brandy Varieties

Choose 2 tbsp (25 mL) plum brandy from
these varieties:

- 2 tbsp (25 mL) slivovitz (colorless; bittersweet;
  may be made from different plum varieties)
- 2 tbsp (25 mL) quetsch (colorless; bittersweet;
  made with Alsatian quetch plums)
- 2 tbsp (25 mL) mirabelle (colorless; sweet; made
  with golden Mirabelle plums)
- 2 tbsp (25 mL) prunelle (pale green to dark amber;
  sweet and thick liqueur; made with sloes)

Plumcot

See PLUM.

Plum, Dried

See PRUNE.

Plum Sauce

*Also known as Chinese
duck sauce. A thick,
sweet-tart Chinese sauce
made from plums, apricots,
vinegar, and sugar. In
traditional Cantonese
cooking, used as a dipping
sauce for rich duck
or goose.*

If You Don't Have It

Substitute 1 cup (250 mL) plum sauce with:

- 1 cup (250 mL) Homemade Plum Sauce: Combine
  1 cup (250 mL) apricot or plum jam, 2 to 3 tbsp
  (25 to 45 mL) rice vinegar or cider vinegar, 2 to
  3 tsp (10 to 15 mL) grated fresh ginger, 1 tsp
  (5 mL) sugar, 1 finely minced small garlic clove,
  ¼ tsp (1 mL) crushed red pepper flakes, and ¼ tsp
  (1 mL) salt in a small saucepan. Bring to a boil
  over high heat. Reduce heat to medium-low and
  simmer gently for 5 minutes. Taste and add more
  vinegar, salt, or sugar if necessary. Cool and
  refrigerate in an airtight container for up to
  2 weeks. Makes about 1 cup (250 mL).
- 1 cup (250 mL) mango chutney (chunkier; spicier)

Pluot

See PLUM.

Poblano

See CHOOSING DRIED CHILES (PAGE 578); CHOOSING
FRESH CHILES (PAGE 582).

Pocket Bread

See PITA BREAD.

Pod Pea

See PEAS, EDIBLE POD.

Poha

See CAPE GOOSEBERRY.

Poire Williams

See PEAR BRANDY.

Polenta

The Italian version of cornmeal mush was once a staple in parts of northern Italy.

> 1 lb (500 g) = 3 cups (750 mL) uncooked
>
> 1 cup (250 mL) = 4 cups (1 L) cooked

To Save Time
Substitute 1 lb (500 g) homemade chilled polenta with:
- 1 lb (500 g) prepared polenta (available in the produce aisle of many grocery stores)

See also POLENTA MEAL.

Polenta Meal

Ground dried white or yellow corn used to make polenta.

If You Don't Have It
Substitute 1 cup (250 mL) polenta meal with:
- 1 cup (250 mL) cornmeal (preferably stone-ground)
- 1 cup (250 mL) corn grits (preferably stone-ground)

See also POLENTA.

Pollock

Also known as pollack. A member of the cod family found in the North Atlantic. The flesh is white and firm with a mild flavor.

If You Don't Have It
Substitute 1 lb (500 g) pollock with:
- 1 lb (500 g) cod
- 1 lb (500 g) plaice
- 1 lb (500 g) flounder
- 1 lb (500 g) sole
- 1 lb (500 g) brill
- 1 lb (500 g) turbot
- 1 lb (500 g) haddock
- 1 lb (500 g) blackfish

Pomegranate Juice

To easily juice a pomegranate, roll the whole fruit back and forth on a hard surface with your palms until all the juice sacs have popped. Insert a straw

If You Don't Have It
Substitute 1 cup (250 mL) fresh pomegranate juice with:
- 1 cup (250 mL) bottled pomegranate juice (less flavorful; may be from concentrate)
- 3 tbsp (45 mL) pomegranate concentrate, pomegranate syrup, or pomegranate molasses (much more concentrated flavor; add 13 tbsp (195 mL) liquid to recipe if necessary to dilute and add volume)

*into the pomegranate
and tilt to extract the
juice into a cup.*

> 3 to 4 large =
> 1 quart (1 L) juice

To Vary the Flavor

Substitute 1 cup (250 mL) fresh pomegranate juice with:
- ⅓ cup (75 mL) grenadine (may add alcohol and other flavors; add ⅔ cup/150 mL liquid to recipe if necessary)
- 1 cup (250 mL) cranberry juice (more tart; lighter red color)
- ⅓ cup (75 mL) red currant syrup (thicker; sweeter; add ⅔ cup/150 mL liquid to recipe if necessary)
- ⅓ cup (75 mL) raspberry syrup (thicker; sweeter; add ⅔ cup/150 mL liquid to recipe if necessary)

Pomegranate Seeds, Dried

Also known as anardana. In Indian and Middle Eastern cooking, used as a souring agent or condiment.

If You Don't Have It

Substitute 1 tbsp (15 mL) dried pomegranate seeds with:
- 1 tbsp (15 mL) lemon or lime juice (as a souring agent)

Pomelo

See PUMMELO.

Pomfret

See BUTTERFISH.

Pompano

Also known as yellowtail (from the Pacific) and jack (worldwide). Considered to be one of the finest-eating saltwater fish, this small blue green and silver firm-fleshed fish belongs to the Jack family.

If You Don't Have It

Substitute 1 lb (500 g) pompano with:
- 1 lb (500 g) butterfish
- 1 lb (500 g) mahi-mahi
- 1 lb (500 g) tuna

See also BUTTERFISH.

Pont-l'Évêque

Also known as Moyaux cheese. Savory and piquant French cow's milk cheese with a hint of tangy sweetness. The ridged brown crust (from the straw mats on which it is cured) is edible and the cheese itself is yellow and supple.

If You Don't Have It

Substitute 1 oz (30 g) Pont-l'Évêque with:
- 1 oz (30 g) Reblochon
- 1 oz (30 g) Camembert (milder)
- 1 oz (30 g) Livarot (stronger)
- 1 oz (30 g) Maroilles (stronger)

Ponzu

A Japanese dipping sauce often served with sashimi and chirinabe, *a one-pot dish of fish, tofu and vegetables.*

If You Don't Have It
Substitute 1 cup (250 mL) ponzu with:
- 1 cup (250 mL) Homemade Ponzu Sauce: Combine ½ cup (125 mL) tamari or soy sauce, ¼ cup (50 mL) lemon juice, 2 tbsp (25 mL) lime juice, 3 tbsp (45 mL) rice vinegar, 3 tbsp (45 mL) dried bonito flakes (optional), 1 tbsp (15 mL) mirin, and a 1 to 2-inch (2.5 to 5 cm) square of kombu (optional). Let stand for 24 hours at room temperature (or overnight if not using bonito flakes and kombu). Strain before using (don't bother straining if not using bonito flakes and kombu). Makes about 1 cup (250 mL).

Poppadum

See PAPPADAM.

Poppy Seeds

While narcotic prior to ripening, poppy seeds yield wonderful benign cooking seeds when ripened. The dark bluish black poppy seeds are favored for pastries and breads in Eastern Europe. In India, a smaller, off-white poppy seed thickens curries and sauces. When roasted, the seeds contribute a nutty note to spice mixtures.

> 5 oz (150 g) =
> 1 cup (250 mL)

If You Don't Have It
Substitute 1 cup (250 mL) poppy seeds with:
- 1 cup (250 mL) canned prepared poppy seeds (to replace 1 cup/250 mL ground poppy seeds for fillings)

To Vary the Flavor
Substitute 1 cup (250 mL) poppy seeds with:
- 1 cup (250 mL) sesame seeds (to replace whole seeds as a topping)

Porgy

Also known as scup, sea bream, and sheepshead. This low-fat and delectably flavored fish inhabits oceans around the world.

If You Don't Have It
Substitute 1 lb (500 g) porgy with:
- 1 lb (500 g) croaker
- 1 lb (500 g) spot
- 1 lb (500 g) pompano
- 1 lb (500 g) rockfish
- 1 lb (500 g) ocean perch
- 1 lb (500 g) bluefish

Pork

Select raw pork that is moist and firm to the touch. Loin cuts should be a pale pink with pure white fat. Shoulder and leg cuts will be darker with a slightly coarser texture. Avoid cuts that are dry, gray, red, or otherwise discolored. Because of consumer demand, pork is now bred to be lean, which means it can easily dry out if overcooked. Use an instant-read thermometer to gauge the exact moment when pork is safe to eat but still succulent. The internal temperature should read 160°F (71°C). Remove a roast from the heat when it reads 155°F (68°C) because the temperature will rise to 160°F (71°C) as it rests.

If You Don't Have It
Substitute 1 lb (500 g) pork with:
- 1 lb (500 g) boar (darker; leaner; stronger-tasting)
- 1 lb (500 g) lamb
- 1 lb (500 g) veal
- 1 lb (500 g) beef
- 1 lb (500 g) turkey
- 1 lb (500 g) chicken

Port

Also known as porto. A sweet fortified wine named for the Portuguese shipping city of Oporto. Vintage ports can be long-lived, often developing character for 50 or more years.

If You Don't Have It
Substitute 2 tbsp (25 mL) port with:
- 2 tbsp (25 mL) Madeira
- 2 tbsp (25 mL) dry vermouth
- 2 tbsp (25 mL) Lillet Rouge
- 2 tbsp (25 mL) beef stock (for sauces)

Port Varieties
Choose 2 tbsp (25 mL) port from these general varieties:
- 2 tbsp (25 mL) vintage port (made from a single vintage; aged the longest)
- 2 tbsp (25 mL) tawny port (light amber color; made from a blend of vintages; ages less than vintage port)
- 2 tbsp (25 mL) ruby port (bright red color; made from a blend of lesser-quality vintages; aged only 2 years or less)

Port Salut

A mild semisoft cow's milk cheese that originated in a monastery in Brittany. The cylinders have an orange rind that covers a pale yellow interior.

1 lb (500 g) = 4 cups (1 L) grated or shredded

If You Don't Have It
Substitute 1 oz (30 g) Port Salut with:
- 1 oz (30 g) Saint Paulin
- 1 oz (30 g) Esrom
- 1 oz (30 g) Tilsit
- 1 oz (30 g) Havarti
- 1 oz (30 g) Oka
- 1 oz (30 g) Muenster

Portuguese Sweet Bread

Also known as pao duce. A domed crown typically tops this sweet, airy loaf.

If You Don't Have It
Substitute 1 lb (500 g) Portuguese sweet bread with:
- 1 lb (500 g) challah
- 1 lb (500 g) brioche

Posole

See HOMINY.

Potassium Bicarbonate

A colorless alkali used in baking powder and antacid medicine.

If You Don't Have It
Substitute 1 tsp (5 mL) potassium bicarbonate with:
- 1 tsp (5 mL) baking soda

Potato

Russet Burbank is the most widely known high-starch baking potato. Other types include low-starch boilers, such as round red, and medium-starch all-purpose potatoes, such as Yukon Gold.

1 lb (500 g) = 4 cups (1 L) chopped = 1¾ cups (425 mL) cooked and mashed

If You Don't Have It
Substitute 1 lb (500 g) potatoes with:
- 1 lb (500 g) cassava
- 1 lb (500 g) yautía or malanga
- 1 lb (500 g) taro
- 1 lb (500 g) sweet potatoes
- 1 lb (500 g) parsnips
- 1 lb (500 g) sunchokes
- 1 lb (500 g) jicama
- 1 lb (500 g) unripe green or yellow plantains

See also CHOOSING AMONG POTATOES (PAGE 575).

Potato Chips

One day in 1853, at Moon's Lake House in Saratoga Springs, New York, a customer kept returning french fries to chef George Crum because they were too thick. Reputedly, Crum sliced the potatoes increasingly thinner and gave birth to potato chips.

If You Don't Have It

Substitute 1 lb (500 g) potato chips with:
- 1 lb (500 g) sweet potato or other vegetable chips
- 1 lb (500 g) bagel chips
- 1 lb (500 g) tortilla chips

For Better Health

Substitute 1 lb (500 g) potato chips with:
- 1 lb (500 g) pretzels

Potato Flour

See CHOOSING AMONG WHOLE-GRAIN AND ALTERNATIVE FLOURS (PAGE 586).

Pot Cheese

A slightly drier version of cottage cheese.

If You Don't Have It

Substitute 1 oz (30 g) pot cheese with:
- 1 oz (30 g) cottage cheese, drained in cheesecloth (may add more liquid)
- 1 oz (30 g) ricotta cheese, drained in cheesecloth (may add more liquid)
- 1 oz (30 g) farmer cheese (firmer)
- 1 oz (30 g) hoop cheese (firmer)
- 1 oz (30 g) panir
- 1 oz (30 g) cream cheese (especially for dips; may add more liquid)
- 1 oz (30 g) sour cream (especially for dips; may add more liquid)

Potsticker Wrappers

See WON TON SKINS.

Poultry

See CHICKEN; DUCK; GOOSE; GUINEA FOWL; PHEASANT; TURKEY.

Poultry Seasoning

The herb sage is often the constant in this flavoring blend designed for fowl.

If You Don't Have It

Substitute 1 tsp (5 mL) poultry seasoning with:
- 1 tsp (5 mL) Homemade Poultry Seasoning: Combine ¾ tsp (4 mL) dried thyme, ½ tsp (2 mL) crushed or rubbed sage, ½ tsp (2 mL) dried marjoram, ¼ tsp (1 mL) ground black pepper, and a pinch of nutmeg (optional). Makes about 2 teaspoons (10 mL).

Poultry Shears

Heavy-duty kitchen shears make quick work of cutting up chicken, duck, and other poultry. Good-quality poultry shears have slip-proof handles and slightly curved blades. One of the blades is typically serrated for gripping and cutting through bones.

If You Don't Have It
Substitute poultry shears with:
- cleaver
- heavy chef's knife

Pound Cake

Said to date from the early 1700s, the traditional recipe for pound cake was easy to recall: 1 pound of butter, 1 pound of sugar, 1 pound of flour, and 1 pound of eggs.

If You Don't Have It
Substitute 1 lb (500 g) pound cake with:
- 1 lb (500 g) butter cake (lighter texture; lower in fat)
- 1 lb (500 g) génoise (lighter texture; less moist)
- 1 lb (500 g) sponge cake (lighter texture; lower in fat)
- 1 lb (500 g) ladyfingers (lighter texture; lower in fat)
- 1 lb (500 g) angel food cake (lighter, more airy texture; lower in fat)

Powdered Egg White

Pasteurized dried egg whites, available in many supermarkets, are an economical, convenient, shelf-stable alternative to fresh egg whites.

If You Don't Have It
Substitute 1 tbsp (15 mL) powdered egg white with:
- 1 tbsp (15 mL) meringue powder
- 2 tbsp (25 mL) frozen and thawed egg white (to replace reconstituted powdered egg white)
- 1 large egg white (to replace reconstituted powdered egg white)

Powdered Ginger

See GINGER, GROUND.

Powdered Milk

See DRY MILK.

Powdered Sugar

See SUGAR, CONFECTIONER'S.

Pozole

See HOMINY.

Praline

A brittle candy made with almonds or hazelnuts and caramelized sugar that can be used as a pastry ingredient or a dessert garnish. To make praline powder, grind cooled praline in a food processor until it resembles the texture of cornmeal.

If You Don't Have It

Substitute 1 cup (250 mL) praline with:

- 1 cup (250 mL) Homemade Praline: Combine 1½ cups (375 mL) granulated sugar and 1 cup (250 mL) almonds or hazelnuts (with skins) in a heavy saucepan over low heat. Stir now and then until the sugar melts. Cook until sugar is deep amber (about 315°F/155°C). Pour mixture onto a greased baking sheet, spreading quickly with a wooden spoon. Let cool completely then crack into small pieces. Makes about 2 cups (500 mL).

See also PRALINE PASTE.

Praline Paste

A creamy confection made from almond or hazelnut butter and sugar.

If You Don't Have It

Substitute 1 cup (250 mL) praline paste with:

- 1 cup (250 mL) Homemade Praline Paste: Grind 2 cups (500 mL) Homemade Praline (see recipe above) in a food processor or blender until the texture of cornmeal. Add 2 large egg whites and 1 tsp (5 mL) almond or hazelnut liqueur; blend until smooth. Makes about 1½ cups (375 mL).
- 1 cup (250 mL) chopped roasted nuts mixed with 1 cup (250 mL) granulated sugar

To Vary the Flavor

Substitute 1 cup (250 mL) praline paste with:

- 1 cup (250 mL) hazelnut paste
- 1 cup (250 mL) walnut paste
- 1 cup (250 mL) pecan paste
- 1 cup (250 mL) pistachio paste
- 1 cup (250 mL) gianduja (adds chocolate flavor)
- 1 cup (250 mL) sweetened chestnut purée

Prawn

In North America, the term prawn refers to freshwater crustaceans, such as Hawaii blue prawns, that resemble shrimp.

1 lb (500 g) in shell = 11 to 15

If You Don't Have It

Substitute 1 lb (500 g) freshwater prawns with:

- 1 lb (500 g) crayfish
- 1 lb (500 g) jumbo shrimp
- 1 lb (500 g) Dublin bay prawns
- 1 lb (500 g) spiny or rock lobster (larger)
- 1 lb (500 g) Maine lobster (larger)

See also DUBLIN BAY PRAWN; SHRIMP.

Prepared Mustard

See MUSTARD, PREPARED.

Preserved Lemon

Also known as salt-cured lemon. Essential in Moroccan cooking, these lemons are cured for several months in salty brine.

If You Don't Have It
Substitute 1 preserved lemon with:
- 1 Homemade Preserved Lemon: Cut 4 small lemons (preferably thin-skinned) lengthwise into quarter sections starting from the flower end and cutting down to within about $\frac{1}{4}$ inch (0.5 cm) of the stem end, keeping quarters attached to each other at the stem end. Open up the almost-quartered lemons like flowers and put them in a large glass bowl or wide-mouthed jar. Sprinkle with $1\frac{3}{4}$ cups (425 mL) Kosher salt and $\frac{1}{4}$ cup (50 mL) granulated sugar and toss to coat, especially the cut sides. Cover and refrigerate for at least 1 month or for up to 6 months, stirring the lemons or inverting jar to redistribute the juices. Makes 4.

To Save Time
Substitute 1 preserved lemon with:
- 1 sliced lemon, 1 tsp (5 mL) salt, and pinch of sugar heated in 2 tsp (10 mL) olive oil over medium-low heat until lemon is very tender, 20 to 30 minutes

To Vary the Flavor
Substitute 1 preserved lemon with:
- $\frac{1}{2}$ cup (125 mL) dry-cured olives

Preserves

Similar to jam, preserves are made from much larger or whole pieces of fruit.

If You Don't Have It
Substitute 1 cup (250 mL) preserves with:
- 1 cup (250 mL) jam (smoother consistency)
- 1 cup (250 mL) jelly (thinner consistency)

Pressure Cooker

Because steam builds up inside this pressurized cooking pot, the foods contained inside cook at a very high temperature, which means they cook in a fraction of the time of traditional methods.

If You Don't Have It
Substitute a pressure cooker with:
- large pot with a tight-fitting lid (generally, you can sauté or bring foods to a boil then reduce heat and simmer as you would in a pressure cooker; triple or quadruple the cooking time; increase liquid by 20 to 40% to compensate for moisture loss)

Pretzel

In the American town of Lititz, Pennsylvania, the first commercial pretzel factory was established in 1861.

If You Don't Have It

Substitute 1 lb (500 g) pretzels with:

- 1 lb (500 g) potato chips (to replace hard pretzels)
- 1 lb (500 g) sweet potato or other vegetable chips (to replace hard pretzels)
- 1 lb (500 g) bagel chips (to replace hard pretzels)
- 1 lb (500 g) tortilla chips (to replace hard pretzels)
- 1 lb (500 g) nuts (to replace hard pretzels)
- 1 lb (500 g) crackers (to replace hard pretzels)
- 1 lb (500 g) Grape-Nuts cereal (to replace crushed hard pretzels)
- 1 lb (500 g) bagels (to replace soft pretzels)
- 1 lb (500 g) bialys (to replace soft pretzels)

Prickly Pear

Also known as cactus pear. Pear-shaped cactus fruit with flesh that varies in color from pale green to magenta.

1 large = ½ cup (125 mL) chopped or puréed

If You Don't Have It

Substitute 1 lb (500 g) prickly pears with:

- 1 lb (500 g) pepinos
- 1 lb (500 g) tamarillos
- 1 lb (500 g) Charentais melon or cantaloupe
- 1 lb (500 g) honeydew or Ogen melon
- 1 lb (500 g) golden or red watermelon
- 1 lb (500 g) pears

Prickly Pear Cactus

See NOPALE.

Primost

See MYSOST.

Processed Cheese

Also known as American cheese. Velveeta is the king of processed cheese, introduced by Kraft in 1928.

1 oz (30 g) = 1 slice

If You Don't Have It

Substitute 1 oz (30 g) processed cheese with:

- 1 oz (30 g) American cheese
- 1 oz (30 g) processed cheese spread such as Cheez Whiz (moister)
- 1 oz (30 g) Bel Paese

See also AMERICAN CHEESE.

Prosciutto

Ham that is salt- and air-cured, produced from pork leg in various styles in different parts of Italy. Its distinction in terms of fragrance and sweetness is attributed to unique climatic conditions. The finest examples are generally acknowledged to be prosciutto di Parma *and* prosciutto di San Daniele.

If You Don't Have It
Substitute 1 lb (500 g) prosciutto with:
- 1 lb (500 g) culatello (less fatty; soaked in wine during aging)
- 1 lb (500 g) Serrano or Iberico ham
- 1 lb (500 g) Ardennes ham (adds smoke flavor)
- 1 lb (500 g) Bayonne ham (adds mild smoke flavor)
- 1 lb (500 g) Westphalian ham (adds juniper and mild smoke flavors)
- 1 lb (500 g) York ham (adds mild smoke flavor)
- 1 lb (500 g) Smithfield ham (add smoke flavor)
- 1 lb (500 g) Yunnan ham (adds smoke flavor)
- 1 lb (500 g) bresaola (less fatty; stronger flavor)

Prosecco

See WINE, SPARKLING.

Provolone

Sharp southern Italian cow's milk cheese. The largest provoloni *can be as long as 6 feet (1.8 m).*

> 1 lb (500 g) = 4 cups (1 L) shredded

If You Don't Have It
Substitute 1 oz (30 g) provolone with:
- 1 oz (30 g) caciocavallo
- 1 oz (30 g) scamorza
- 1 oz (30 g) mozzarella
- 1 oz (30 g) fontina
- 1 oz (30 g) young Asiago

Prune

Also known as dried plums. Southwest France is the best place to be a prune. There, dried plums get to steep in Armagnac, the wonderful brandy of the region.

> 1 lb (500 g) = 2½ cups (625 mL) = 4 to 4½ cups (1 to 1.125 L) cooked

If You Don't Have It
Substitute 1 lb (500 g) prunes with:
- 1 lb (500 g) dried figs
- 1 lb (500 g) Chinese dates
- 1 lb (500 g) medjool dates
- 1 lb (500 g) raisins
- 1 lb (500 g) dried persimmons
- 1 lb (500 g) dried blueberries, cherries, or cranberries
- 1 lb (500 g) dried apricots

See also PLUM.

Prunelle

See PLUM BRANDY.

Prune Purée

Also known as lekvar and prune butter. Sometimes used instead of butter to make lower-fat chocolate or heavily spiced baked goods. Use ⅓ cup (75 mL) prune purée in place of ½ cup (125 mL) butter.

If You Don't Have It
Substitute 1 cup (250 mL) prune purée with:
- 1 cup (250 mL) Homemade Prune Purée: Purée 1 cup (250 mL) pitted prunes and ½ cup (125 mL) water in a blender or food processor until smooth. Makes about 1⅓ cups (325 mL).
- 1 cup (250 mL) baby food prunes

To Vary the Flavor
Substitute 1 cup (250 mL) prune purée with:
- 1 cup (250 mL) apple butter
- 1 cup (250 mL) well-drained applesauce
- 1 cup (250 mL) fat-free, fruit-based butter and oil replacement such as Sunsweet "Lighter Bake"

Puff Pastry

Also known as pâte feuilletée. A triumph of the French pastry kitchen, this flaky pastry is made by placing thin rolled sheets of chilled butter between sheets of flour-water dough then repeatedly folding and rolling the packet. During baking, the water in the butter creates steam that causes the thin dough layers to puff up into hundreds of flaky layers.

If You Don't Have It
Substitute 1 lb (500 g) puff pastry with:
- 1 lb (500 g) phyllo dough (less puffy)
- 1 lb (500 g) pie dough (denser and less puffy; less rich; best for replacing puff pastry crust in pies)

See also PATTY SHELL.

Pulasan

Closely related to rambutans, these popular southeast Asian fruits have short spines on their dark red skins and, inside, a small amount of sweet, delicate pulp surrounding an easily removed seed.

1 lb (500 g) fresh =
2 cups (500 mL)

If You Don't Have It
Substitute 1 cup (250 mL) peeled and seeded fresh pulasans with:
- 1 cup (250 mL) peeled and seeded rambutans (slightly less sweet)
- 1 cup (250 mL) peeled and seeded longans
- 1 cup (250 mL) peeled and seeded fresh or canned litchis

See also LITCHI; RAMBUTAN.

Pulque

Of Aztec origin, this thick white Mexican beverage is fermented from various agave plants.

If You Don't Have It

Substitute 2 tbsp (25 mL) pulque with:
- 2 tbsp (25 mL) tequila (clear or amber color; higher alcohol)
- 2 tbsp (25 mL) mezcal (clear or amber color; higher alcohol)

Pummelo

Also known as Chinese grapefruit and shaddock (England). This Malaysian ancestor of grapefruit can weigh as much as 25 pounds (12.5 kg).

If You Don't Have It

Substitute 1 cup (250 mL) pummelo segments with:
- 1 cup (250 mL) grapefruit segments (more acidic)
- 1 cup (250 mL) Ugli™ fruit segments
- 1 cup (250 mL) sweet orange segments
- 1 cup (250 mL) tangelo segments

Pumpernickel Bread

A dark, slightly sour bread with a high proportion of rye flour to wheat flour.

If You Don't Have It

Substitute 1 lb (500 g) pumpernickel bread with:
- 1 lb (500 g) rye bread (especially marbled or sourdough rye)
- 1 lb (500 g) Russian black bread
- 1 lb (500 g) limpa bread (more aromatic)

See also CHOOSING AMONG WHOLE-GRAIN AND ALTERNATIVE FLOURS (PAGE 586).

Pumpkin

Is pumpkin a fruit or a vegetable? It's actually a large versatile winter squash that may be a stuffing for savory tortelli di zucca *or the spiced sweetened custard for Thanksgiving pie.*

1 lb (500 g) fresh =
1 cup (250 mL)
cooked and mashed

1 15 oz (425 g) can =
1¾ cups (425 mL) mashed

1 29 oz (820 g) can =
3½ cups (875 mL) mashed

If You Don't Have It

Substitute 1 cup (250 mL) chopped fresh pumpkin with:
- 1 cup (250 mL) canned pumpkin purée (to replace mashed pumpkin)
- 1 cup (250 mL) chopped butternut squash
- 1 cup (250 mL) chopped buttercup squash
- 1 cup (250 mL) chopped sweet dumpling squash
- 1 cup (250 mL) chopped Hubbard squash
- 1 cup (250 mL) chopped calabaza
- 1 cup (250 mL) chopped sweet potato

Pumpkin Pie Spice

American pumpkin pie, or pudding, as it was known in Colonial times, was not seasoned with its now-trademark warm spice mix until the 1800s, when clipper ships made spices a more common, affordable commodity.

If You Don't Have It

Substitute 1 tsp (5 mL) pumpkin pie spice with:

- 1 tsp (5 mL) Homemade Pumpkin Pie Spice: Combine ½ tsp (2 mL) ground cinnamon, ¼ tsp (1 mL) ground nutmeg, ¼ tsp (1 mL) ground ginger, and ⅛ tsp (0.5 mL) ground cloves. Makes about 1 teaspoon (5 mL).
- 1 tsp (5 mL) apple pie spice

Pumpkin Seed Oil

See SUBSTITUTING OILS (PAGE 598).

Pumpkin Seeds

Also known as pepitas when shelled. To toast pumpkin seeds, remove the seeds from pumpkin cavity, separating the seeds from the pulp and fiber. Rinse well in a colander under cold water then spread the seeds on a kitchen towel to dry. Spread the dry seeds on a baking sheet in a single layer. Toss with oil to coat and roast at 250°F (120°C) until golden, stirring now and then, for about 1 hour. Sprinkle with salt or other seasonings if desired. The seed shells, which house the seeds, are edible. Store in an airtight container at room temperature for up to 3 months or in the refrigerator for up to 1 year.

If You Don't Have It

Substitute 1 cup (250 mL) pumpkin seeds with:

- 2 to 4 tbsp (25 to 60 mL) pumpkin seed oil (for baking and cooking; will add toasted pumpkin seed flavor but not texture of whole seeds; reduce fat in recipe by 2 to 4 tbsp/25 to 60 mL)
- 1 cup (250 mL) other squash seeds
- 1 cup (250 mL) sunflower seeds

Punt e Mes

Carpano brand sweetened fortified wine served as an aperitivo. It contains quinine, which stimulates production of digestive enzymes and hence appetite.

If You Don't Have It
Substitute 2 tbsp (25 mL) Punt e Mes with:
- 2 tbsp (25 mL) Lillet Rouge
- 2 tbsp (25 mL) Dubonnet Rouge
- 2 tbsp (25 mL) Byrrh
- 2 tbsp (25 mL) Raphael
- 2 tbsp (25 mL) Fernet Branca
- 2 tbsp (25 mL) Campari
- 2 tbsp (25 mL) dry vermouth + dash of Angostura bitters

Pure Grain Alcohol

See NEUTRAL SPIRITS.

Purple Laver

See LAVER.

Purslane

Also known as pursley, pussley, and verdolagas. A green of ancient origin and international usage, now rediscovered by gourmet diners. Wild purslane offers more interesting flavor than cultivated. The juicy pad-like leaves are tart like sorrel. Older leaves respond well to cooking.

4 oz (125 g) = 2 cups (500 mL) chopped

If You Don't Have It
Substitute 1 lb (500 g) purslane with:
- 1 lb (500 g) spinach
- 1 lb (500 g) garden cress or watercress
- 1 to 2 tbsp (15 to 25 mL) file powder (for thickening soups and stews)
- 1½ to 2 cups (375 to 500 mL) okra (for thickening soups and stews)

Quahog to Quinoa Flour

Quahog

See SWAPPING CLAMS (PAGE 596).

Quail

Commercially raised
in Europe, these tiniest
of game birds are related
to partridges. American
quail are birds from a
different family. Types
of quail include blue
quail, bobwhites, brown
quails, bush quails,
California quails,
and mountain quails.

If You Don't Have It
Substitute 1 lb (500 g) quail with:
- 1 lb (500 g) partridge
- 1 lb (500 g) squab
- 1 lb (500 g) young pheasant
- 1 lb (500 g) grouse
- 1 lb (500 g) guinea fowl
- 1 lb (500 g) Cornish hen (fattier)

Quail Egg

Considered a gourmet
delicacy, the tiny speckled
shells vary in color,
including white, blue,
and brown.

If You Don't Have It
Substitute 5 quail eggs with:
- 1 extra-large chicken egg, especially from
  a pasture-raised hen
- 1 small duck egg (richer; more flavorful)

Quark

A fresh-curd skim milk cheese that's a phenomenon in Germany, accounting for about half the total cheese consumed in that country.

8 oz (250 g) =
1 cup (250 mL)

If You Don't Have It

Substitute 1 oz (30 g) quark with:
- 1 oz (30 g) sour cream, fromage blanc, or yogurt cheese
- ½ oz (15 g) ricotta cheese + ½ oz (15 g) sour cream, blended
- ½ oz (15 g) cream cheese or mascarpone + ½ oz (15 g) cream, blended
- ½ oz (15 g) drained cottage cheese + ½ oz (15 g) yogurt, blended

Quatre Épices

In classic French cuisine, "four spices" is used in charcuterie, terrines, and pâtés. Despite its name, the blend often contains more than four spices.

If You Don't Have It

Substitute 1 tsp (5 mL) quatre épices with:
- 1 tsp (5 mL) Homemade Savory Quatre Épices: Combine 1¾ tsp (9 mL) ground white pepper, ¾ tsp (4 mL) ground allspice, ½ tsp (2 mL) ground nutmeg, and ¼ tsp (1 mL) ground cloves. Makes about 1 tablespoon (15 mL).
- 1 tsp (5 mL) Homemade Sweet Quatre Épices: Combine 1 tsp (5 mL) ground cinnamon, 1 tsp (5 mL) ground nutmeg, 1 tsp (5 mL) ground allspice, and ¼ tsp (1 mL) ground cloves. Makes about 1 tablespoon (15 mL).
- 1 tsp (5 mL) Spice Parisienne or épices fines (more complex flavor; may include white pepper and herbs; if so, use to replace savory quatre épices)
- ½ tsp (2 mL) ground white or black pepper + ½ tsp (2 mL) pumpkin pie spice or apple pie spice (to replace savory quatre épices)
- 1 tsp (5 mL) apple pie spice or pumpkin pie spice (to replace sweet quatre épices)

See also SPICE PARISIENNE.

Queso Añejo

Mexican for "aged cheese." Also known as "Cotija" after North America's most widely distributed queso añejo, which is made in Cotija, Michoacan, Mexico.

4 oz (125 g) =
1 cup (250 mL) grated

If You Can't Find It

Substitute 1 oz (30 g) queso añejo or Cotija with:
- 1 oz (30 g) Pecorino Romano
- 1 oz (30 g) Parmesan
- 1 oz (30 g) aged Asiago
- 1 oz (30 g) dry Jack

Queso Asadero

See ASADERO.

Queso Blanco

See QUESO FRESCO.

Queso Fresco

Also known as queso blanco. This Mexican, white, fresh cheese resembles farmer cheese in texture.

4 oz (125 g) =
1 cup (250 mL) crumbled

If You Don't Have It

Substitute 1 oz (30 g) queso fresco with:
- 1 oz (30 g) pressed, salted farmer cheese
- 1 oz (30 g) young goat cheese
- 1 oz (30 g) feta cheese (rinsed to remove some salt)
- 1 oz (30 g) dry cottage cheese + ⅛ tsp (0.5 mL) alt

Queso Gamonedo

See GAMONEDO.

Queso Ibores

See SIERRA IBORES.

Queso Manchego

See MANCHEGO.

Quetsch

See PLUM BRANDY.

Quince

A wonderfully aromatic fruit that can be roughly shaped like a pear or an apple. The flavor also evokes pear and apple, as well as pineapple and guava. Quince requires cooking, and its abundant natural pectin makes it well-suited to jellies and preserves.

1 lb (500 g) = 3 to
4 medium = 1½ cups
(375 mL) chopped

If You Don't Have It

Substitute 1 lb (500 g) quinces with:
- 1 lb (500 g) tart apples such as Granny Smith or pippin (sweeter)
- 1 lb (500 g) Asian pears (sweeter)
- 1 lb (500 g) Bosc pears (sweeter; softer flesh)

Quinine Water

See TONIC WATER.

Quinoa

Pride of the Andes, this ultra-nutritious grain has a pleasantly nutty taste and sprightly texture that belie its healthfulness. Before using quinoa, rinse it in a strainer to remove the naturally bitter saponin that coats the surface of the seeds.

1½ cups (375 mL) =
4 cups (1 L) cooked

If You Don't Have It
Substitute 1 cup (250 mL) quinoa with:
- 1 cup (250 mL) millet
- 1 cup (250 mL) couscous, especially whole wheat (cooks more quickly)
- 1 cup (250 mL) bulgur
- 1 cup (250 mL) cracked wheat (takes longer to cook)
- 1 cup (250 mL) rice
- 1 cup (250 mL) kasha (roasted buckwheat groats; takes more time to cook)

Quinoa Flour

See also CHOOSING AMONG WHOLE-GRAIN AND ALTERNATIVE FLOURS (PAGE 586).

Rabbit to Rye Flour

Rabbit

These domesticated rodents have fine, all-white-fleshed meat. Fresh and frozen rabbits, whole or cut up, are available in some specialty food markets. Rabbit can replace chicken in many recipes.

If You Don't Have It
Substitute 1 lb (500 g) rabbit with:
- 1 lb (500 g) hare
- 1 lb (500 g) turkey
- 1 lb (500 g) chicken
- 1 lb (500 g) duck

Raclette

A mellow, Gruyère-like Swiss cow's milk cheese. The traditional way of serving raclette is to set a hunk of the cheese in front of an open fire and scrape the resulting melted cheese onto dark bread.

1 lb (500 g) = 4 cups (1 L) shredded

If You Don't Have It
Substitute 1 oz (30 g) Raclette with:
- 1 oz (30 g) Gruyère
- 1 oz (30 g) Emmental
- 1 oz (30 g) Jarlsberg
- 1 oz (30 g) Appenzeller
- 1 oz (30 g) Reblochon
- 1 oz (30 g) oka
- 1 oz (30 g) fontina

Radicchio

The Italian word for all chicory, which range in color from cream to garnet. In North America, the word usually refers to the Chioggia variety, which has a round compact head and variegated white and garnet leaves. The bittersweet leaves are enjoyed in salads, braises, and many other ways.

1 medium head =
8 to 10 leaves

If You Don't Have It

Substitute 1 lb (500 g) radicchio with:
- 1 lb (500 g) Belgian endive, especially red-tipped
- 1 lb (500 g) chicory
- 1 lb (500 g) curly endive
- 1 lb (500 g) escarole
- 1 lb (500 g) arugula
- 1 lb (500 g) watercress
- 1 lb (500 g) red oak-leaf lettuce (less bitter)

Radicchio Varieties

Choose 1 lb (500 g) radicchio from these varieties:
- 1 lb (500 g) Chioggia (most popular North American variety; compact, round head; wide white stems and maroon leaves; bitter, slightly sweet flavor; crunchy and chewy texture)
- 1 lb (500 g) Verona (similar to Chioggia but head is looser and slightly more oval in shape; thicker, narrower stems; brighter maroon-color leaves; similar flavor and texture)
- 1 lb (500 g) Early Treviso (elongated, loose head with white stems and maroon leaves; similar in shape to loose-headed mature bok choy; flavor and texture similar to Chioggia)
- 1 lb (500 g) Late Treviso (elongated, semiloose head with slender white stems and maroon leaves that twirl together at the top; flavor and texture slightly more bitter than Chioggia)
- 1 lb (500 g) Castelfranco (round, loose head with delicate out-turned leaves similar to a rose; cream-color stems with pale yellow and maroon-speckled leaves; milder flavor and more tender texture than Chioggia)

See also CHICORY.

Radish

Christmas Eve in Oaxaca, Mexico is called the Night of the Radishes because of the custom of carving big radishes into the shapes of animals.

If You Don't Have It

Substitute 1 lb (500 g) radishes with:
- 1 lb (500 g) jicama (sweeter; add a pinch of pepper or horseradish for more bite)
- 1 lb (500 g) turnips or parsnips (for soups and stews; add a pinch of pepper or horseradish for more bite)

8 oz (250 g) =
10 to 14 radishes =
1½ cups (375 mL) sliced

Radish Varieties
Choose 1 lb (500 g) radishes from these varieties:
- 1 lb (500 g) table radishes (the American favorite; red, pink, or white peel; slightly peppery, crisp, and juicy flesh)
- 1 lb (500 g) Asian radishes (such as white daikon, green-skinned moo, or red-fleshed beauty heart; generally peppery-sweet, crisp, and juicy flesh)
- 1 lb (500 g) black radishes (black peel; firmer, drier, more assertive flesh that's similar to horseradish)

Rainbow Runner

Also known as Hawaiian salmon, kamanu, and runner. A member of the large Jack family found in tropical Atlantic and Pacific waters. Mostly a game fish, it is rarely seen in markets.

If You Don't Have It
Substitute 1 lb (500 g) rainbow runner with:
- 1 lb (500 g) parrot fish
- 1 lb (500 g) amberjack
- 1 lb (500 g) pompano
- 1 lb (500 g) yellowtail
- 1 lb (500 g) mahi-mahi

Rainbow Trout

See TROUT.

Raisin

In 1876, Scottish immigrant William Thompson developed a variety of sweet seedless grapes with thin skin. The variety dried well. Today 95% of California raisins — which comprise 50% of the world's supply — are processed from Thompson seedless grapes.

15 oz (450 g) =
2½ cups (625 mL)

If You Don't Have It
Substitute 1 cup (250 mL) raisins with:
- 1 cup (250 mL) finely chopped dried apricots
- 1 cup (250 mL) finely chopped soft prunes
- 1 cup (250 mL) finely chopped soft dates
- 1 cup (250 mL) dried berries such as blueberries or cranberries
- 1 cup (250 mL) dried cherries

Raisin Varieties
Choose 1 cup (250 mL) raisins from these varieties:
- 1 cup (250 mL) dark raisins (usually sun-dried Thompson seedless grapes)
- 1 cup (250 mL) golden raisins or sultanas (usually dried Thompson seedless grapes treated with sulfur dioxide to retain color; moister and plumper than dark raisins)
- 1 cup (250 mL) currants (dried Zante grapes; firmer and sweeter than dark raisins)
- 1 cup (250 mL) Muscat raisins (dried Muscat grapes; sweeter and more musky aroma than dark raisins)

See also CURRANT, DRIED.

Raki

See ANISE LIQUEUR.

Rambutan

This tropical fruit looks like a small, spiny sea creature. Inside, the sweet translucent flesh tastes like its relative, the litchi, although a little more acidic. The fruit is available canned in syrup.

> 1 lb (500 g) fresh =
> 2 cups (500 mL)

If You Don't Have It

Substitute 1 cup (250 mL) peeled and seeded fresh rambutans with:

- 1 cup (250 mL) peeled and seeded longans (sweeter)
- 1 cup (250 mL) peeled and seeded fresh or canned litchis
- 1 cup (250 mL) peeled and seeded pulasans

See also LITCHI; PULASAN.

Ramekin

Stoneware baking dish that looks like a shrunken straight-sided soufflé dish.

If You Don't Have It

Substitute 3-oz (90 mL) ramekins with:

- 3-oz (90 mL) custard cups

Ramen

See A SNAPSHOT OF ASIAN NOODLES (PAGE 588).

Ramps

Also known as wild leeks. This wild onion grows nearly the length of the Appalachian Chain, but it is in West Virginia that this pungent vegetable comes into its glory at springtime celebrations. The towns of Elkins, Richwood, and Swiss-settled Helvetia are well-known for their ramp festivals.

> 1 lb (500 g) =
> 2 cups (500 mL)
> trimmed and chopped =
> 1 cup (250 mL) cooked

If You Don't Have It

Substitute 1 lb (500 g) ramps with:

- 1 lb (500 g) leeks (white and light green parts only; milder, less complex flavor)
- 1 lb (500 g) green onions (white and light green parts only; less complex flavor)
- 1 lb (500 g) shallots (sweeter)
- 1 lb (500 g) sweet or storage onions (less complex flavor)
- 1 lb (500 g) garlic chives (adds garlic flavor)
- 1 lb (500 g) Chinese garlic stems (sharper garlic flavor; adds crunch)

Rangpur

Also known as mandarin lime. This orange-skinned citrus is similar to mandarin orange but more acidic.

1 rangpur = 2 to 3 tbsp
(25 to 45 mL) juice =
⅓ to ½ cup
(75 to 125 mL) chopped
= 1 to 2 tbsp
(15 to 25 mL) grated zest

If You Don't Have It

Substitute 1 rangpur with
- 1 calamondin
- 1 lemon
- 1 lime
- ½ lime + ¼ mandarin orange, blood orange, or navel orange

Rapeseed Oil

See SUBSTITUTING OILS (PAGE 598).

Rapini

See BROCCOLI RAAB.

Ras el Hanout

An essential spice mixture in Algeria, Morocco, and Tunisia. For the most intense aromas, use whole spices and toast them before grinding to a powder.

If You Don't Have It

Substitute 1 tsp (5 mL) ras el hanout with:
- 1 tsp (5 mL) Homemade Ras el Hanout: Combine 2 tbsp (25 mL) ground ginger, 1 tbsp (15 mL) ground cumin, 2 tsp (10 mL) ground coriander, 2 tsp (10 mL) ground cinnamon, 2 tsp (10 mL) ground nutmeg, 2 tsp (10 mL) ground allspice, 2 tsp (10 mL) ground cardamom, 1½ tsp (7 mL) ground black pepper, 1½ tsp (7 mL) turmeric, 15 saffron threads (crushed), ¼ tsp (1 mL) ground cloves, and ¼ tsp (1 mL) cayenne pepper. Makes about ½ cup (125 mL).
- 1 tsp (5 mL) garam masala

Raspberry

Because they are so fragile, the finest raspberries are picked ripe from the bush. Choose packaged raspberries that are dry with no moisture stains at the bottom of the container. Highly perishable, raspberries should be

If You Don't Have It

Substitute 1 cup (250 mL) raspberries with:
- 1 cup (250 mL) strawberries
- 1 cup (250 mL) loganberries (hybrid of blackberries and raspberries)
- 1 cup (250 mL) boysenberries (hybrid of blackberries, raspberries, and loganberries)

Raspberry (cont'd)

consumed within 2 to 3 days of purchase.

½ pint fresh =
1⅓ cups (325 mL)

1 lb (500 g) loose-pack
frozen = 3⅜ cups (844 mL)

10 oz (300 g) frozen in
syrup = 1¾ cups (425 mL)

- 1 cup (250 mL) olallieberries (hybrid of youngberries and loganberries)
- 1 cup (250 mL) tayberries (hybrid of blackberries and raspberries)
- 1 cup (250 mL) blackberries

Raspberry Varieties

Choose 1 cup (250 mL) raspberries from these varieties:

- 1 cup (250 mL) red raspberries
- 1 cup (250 mL) yellow or golden raspberries
- 1 cup (250 mL) thimbleberries such as black raspberries

Raspberry Brandy

See FRAMBOISE.

Raspberry Liqueur

Sweetened raspberry-flavored spirit, not to be confused with framboise (raspberry) eau de vie.

If You Don't Have It

Substitute 2 tbsp (25 mL) raspberry liqueur with:

- 2 tbsp (25 mL) crème de framboise (sweeter; heavier body)
- 2 tbsp (25 mL) framboise (less sweet; higher alcohol)
- 2 tbsp (25 mL) raspberry schnapps (less sweet; higher alcohol)
- 2 tbsp (25 mL) raspberry syrup (sweeter; no alcohol)
- 1 tsp (5 mL) raspberry extract (add 5 tsp/20 mL liquid to recipe if necessary)

To Vary the Flavor

Substitute 2 tbsp (25 mL) raspberry liqueur with:

- 2 tbsp (25 mL) cherry liqueur
- 2 tbsp (25 mL) orange liqueur
- 2 tbsp (25 mL) cassis liqueur
- 2 tbsp (25 mL) crème de fraise (strawberry flavor; sweeter; heavier body)

See also FRAMBOISE.

Rattlesnake Bean

See THE WIDE WORLD OF DRIED BEANS (PAGE 566).

Ravioli

See PASTA, FILLED.

Raw Milk

See MILK, WHOLE.

Raw Sugar

See SUGAR, RAW.

Razor Clam

See SWAPPING CLAMS (PAGE 596).

Reamer

A hand-held tool with a large, ridged, conical point designed for extracting juice from halved citrus.

If You Don't Have It

Substitute a reamer with:
- handheld, table-top, or electric juicer
- fork

Reblochon Cheese

Purchase this uncooked French cow's milk cheese from a reliable vendor to ensure perfect ripeness. When overripe, the cheese becomes unpleasantly bitter.

If You Don't Have It

Substitute 1 oz (30 g) Reblochon with:
- 1 oz (30 g) Pont-l'Évêque
- 1 oz (30 g) Beaumont
- 1 oz (30 g) Brie
- 1 oz (30 g) Camembert
- 1 oz (30 g) Muenster
- 1 oz (30 g) Esrom
- 1 oz (30 g) Port Salut

Red Banana

See BANANA.

Red Bean

See THE WIDE WORLD OF DRIED BEANS (PAGE 566).

Red Bean Paste

Also known as sweet red bean paste. Used as a filling in many Chinese sweets, this mixture of azuki beans, sugar, lard, and vanilla is sold canned in smooth and chunky versions.

If You Don't Have It

Substitute 1 cup (250 mL) sweet red bean paste with:
- 1 cup (250 mL) Homemade Sweet Red Bean Paste: Soak 8 oz (250 g; 1 generous cup/250 mL) rinsed and picked over azuki or other small red beans in water to cover overnight. Drain and cover with fresh water in a medium pot. Bring to a boil then reduce heat and simmer gently until beans are very tender, 1½ to 2 hours. Remove from heat, drain and let cool. For a chunky paste, return beans to pot and mash until chunky. For a smooth paste, force softened beans through a fine mesh strainer, discarding pulp in the strainer. Return the beans to the pot and stir in 1 cup (250 mL)

Red Bean Paste (cont'd)

granulated sugar, ½ cup (125 mL) vegetable shortening, lard, or vegetable oil, and a pinch of salt. Cook over medium-low heat, stirring now and then, until the mixture forms a thick paste, about 15 minutes. Let cool and refrigerate for up to 1 week. Makes about 2 cups (500 mL).

See also BEAN SAUCE.

Red Bell Pepper

See BELL PEPPER.

Red Cabbage

This crucifer takes it gorgeous garnet hue from anthocyanins, which are water-soluble and turn a dingy gray blue when cooked. But anthocyanins retain their color in the presence of acidity. The moral: add some lemon juice or vinegar to help retain the color of cooked red cabbage.

1 lb (500 g) =
3½ to 4½ cups
(875 mL to 1.125 L)
shredded = 2 cups
(500 mL) cooked

If You Don't Have It

Substitute 1 lb (500 g) red cabbage with:
- 1 lb (500 g) green cabbage
- 1 lb (500 g) Brussels sprouts
- 1 lb (500 g) savoy cabbage (milder)
- 1 lb (500 g) napa cabbage (milder; more delicate)

Red Chile Powder

See CHILE POWDER.

Red Chile Sauce

See CHILE PASTE; CHILE SAUCE.

Red Currant

See CURRANT.

Red Currant Jelly

See CURRANT JELLY.

Red Date

See CHINESE DATE, FRESH.

Red Delicious Apple

See PICKING APPLES (PAGE 564).

Redfish

See CROAKER.

Red Leaf Lettuce

See LEAF LETTUCE.

Red Mullet

This reddish pink sea creature is a Mediterranean member of the goatfish family, not a true mullet. It is enjoyed in Europe for its lean, firm flesh.

If You Don't Have It

Substitute 1 lb (500 g) red mullet with:
- 1 lb (500 g) red snapper
- 1 lb (500 g) black sea bass
- 1 lb (500 g) smelt
- 1 lb (500 g) trout

See also MULLET.

Red Pepper Flakes

See CAYENNE PEPPER.

Red Shiso

See SHISO.

Red Snapper

The winner of the popularity contest in this 200+ species typically comes to market in the 2 to 8-pound (1 to 4 kg) range. Smaller red snapper are often sold whole, while larger fish are cut into steaks and fillets.

If You Don't Have It

Substitute 1 lb (500 g) red snapper with:
- 1 lb (500 g) silk snapper
- 1 lb (500 g) vermilion (generally of lesser quality than red snapper)
- 1 lb (500 g) yellowtail or other snapper (generally of lesser quality than red snapper)
- 1 lb (500 g) blackfish
- 1 lb (500 g) black sea bass
- 1 lb (500 g) striped bass
- 1 lb (500 g) grouper
- 1 lb (500 g) haddock
- 1 lb (500 g) halibut
- 1 lb (500 g) tilefish
- 1 lb (500 g) turbot

See also SNAPPER.

Refried Beans

Also known as frijoles refritos. Mexican cooking authority Diana Kennedy explains why these cooked beans fried only once are called refried. "The Mexicans have a habit of qualifying a word to emphasize the meaning by adding the prefix re-. They will get the oil very hot (requemar), or something will be very good (retebien). Thus refrito means well fried, which they certainly are, since they are fried until they are almost dry."

If You Don't Have It

Substitute 1 cup (250 mL) refried beans with:

- 1 cup (250 mL) Homemade Refried Beans: Heat 2 tbsp (25 mL) lard, bacon drippings, or vegetable oil in a large skillet over medium heat. Add ¾ cup (175 mL) chopped onion and sauté until almost browned, 5 to 8 minutes. Add 2 minced garlic cloves and cook for 2 minutes. Add 4 cups (1 L) cooked or canned black beans and mash to a chunky purée with a potato masher or wooden spoon. Stir in 1 cup (250 mL) cooking or canning liquid and 2 tsp (10 mL) chopped fresh epazote or oregano and cook over medium-low heat until slightly soupy, about 10 minutes, or until almost dry, about 15 minutes. Add salt to taste. Makes about 4 cups (1 L).

For Better Health

Substitute 1 cup (250 mL) refried beans with:

- 1 cup (250 mL) cooked or canned black beans, mashed with ¼ cup (50 mL) canning or cooking liquid
- 1 cup (250 mL) cooked or canned pinto beans, mashed with ¼ cup (50 mL) canning or cooking liquid

Refrigerator

Also known as the fridge. The electric appliance that exiled the icebox was first manufactured successfully for the home kitchen in 1916 by the Kelvinator Company.

If You Don't Have It

Substitute a refrigerator with:

- cooler filled with ice
- putting well-covered food outdoors when the outdoor temperature is between 32° and 40°F (0° and 4°C).

Reindeer

A large deer particularly valued as game meat in Scandinavia and Russia. The flavor is superior to its relative the caribou.

If You Don't Have It

Substitute 1 lb (500 g) reindeer with:

- 1 lb (500 g) caribou
- 1 lb (500 g) red, fallow, or white-tailed deer
- 1 lb (500 g) elk
- 1 lb (500 g) antelope
- 1 lb (500 g) gazelle

See also VENISON.

Rémoulade

See MAYONNAISE.

Rhea

A threatened species of large, flightless, omniverous South American bird. The rhea has a powerful immune system that enables injured birds to heal rapidly.

If You Don't Have It
Substitute 1 lb (500 g) rhea with:
- 1 lb (500 g) ostrich
- 1 lb (500 g) emu
- 1 lb (500 g) beef (fattier)
- 1 lb (500 g) buffalo
- 1 lb (500 g) turkey
- 1 lb (500 g) chicken

Rhubarb

Although rhubarb is botanically a vegetable, it's treated as a tart fruit and typically prepared with plenty of sugar.

> 1 lb (500 g) fresh =
> 2 cups (500 mL)
> chopped and cooked

If You Don't Have It
Substitute 1 lb (500 g) rhubarb with:
- 1 lb (500 g) cranberries
- 1 lb (500 g) gooseberries (for tartness; green color)
- 1 lb (500 g) quinces
- 1 lb (500 g) sorrel (for tartness; green color; much more tender)

Ricard

See ANISE LIQUEUR.

Rice

Rice grains, the seeds of a type of grass, sustain about half of the world's population. Brown rice, with only the hull removed, is closest to the naturally harvested state. The intact bran layers contribute nutty flavor, slightly chewy texture, and a wealth of nutrients and fiber. It requires more liquid and takes longer to cook than white rice, although a quick-cooking brown rice is now marketed. Rice that is

If You Don't Have It
Substitute 1 cup (250 mL) uncooked white rice with:
- 1 cup (250 mL) uncooked converted rice (more fluffy and separate grains when cooked; slightly increase cooking time)
- 2 cups (500 mL) uncooked orzo pasta (cooks faster)
- 1¼ cups (300 mL) uncooked couscous (cooks much faster)
- ¾ cup (175 mL) uncooked pearl barley (chewier; more complex flavor; increase liquid and cooking time)

To Save Time
Substitute 1 cup (250 mL) uncooked white rice with:
- 1 cup (250 mL) uncooked instant or quick white rice (cooks faster; less flavorful than white rice)
- 1 cup (250 mL) uncooked instant or quick brown rice (cooks faster; less flavorful than brown rice)

Rice (cont'd)

milled, or polished, becomes white rice. Depending upon the variety, the grains themselves can be long, medium, or short. Parboiled or converted rice is rough rice soaked in warm water under pressure, steamed, and dried before milling. This procedure gelatinizes the starch and ensures that the grains separate after cooking. It also retains more nutrients than conventionally milled white rice, but it takes a few minutes longer to cook. Instant rice, also known as quick-cooking rice, is milled, completely cooked, enriched, and dehydrated. Preparation takes only a few minutes.

---

1 cup (250 mL)
long-grain white rice =
3 cups (750 mL) cooked

1 cup (250 mL)
medium-grain white rice
= 3 cups (750 mL) cooked

1 cup (250 mL)
short-grain white rice =
3 cups (750 mL) cooked

1 cup (250 mL) brown
or whole-grain rice =
4 cups (1 L) cooked

For Better Health

Substitute 1 cup (250 mL) uncooked white rice with:

- 1 cup (250 mL) uncooked brown rice (higher in fiber; chewier; more complex, nutty flavor; increase liquid and slightly increase cooking time)
- 1 cup (250 mL) uncooked wild rice (higher in fiber; chewier; more complex, nutty flavor; increase liquid and cooking time)
- 1¼ cups (300 mL) uncooked whole wheat couscous (high in fiber)
- 1 cup (250 mL) uncooked quinoa (higher in fiber, protein, and other nutrients)
- ¾ cup (175 mL) uncooked millet (higher in fiber and other nutrients)
- ¾ cup (175 mL) uncooked pearl barley (higher in fiber; increase liquid and cooking time; especially to replace short-grain or medium-grain rice)
- ¾ cup (175 mL) uncooked hulled or whole-grain barley (higher in fiber; chewier; more complex flavor; increase liquid and cooking time)
- 1 cup (250 mL) uncooked bulgur (higher in fiber; chewier; more nutty flavor; increase liquid and cooking time)
- 1⅓ cups (325 mL) uncooked wheat berries (higher in fiber; chewier; more nutty flavor; increase liquid and cooking time)
- 1½ cups (375 mL) uncooked kasha (higher in fiber; chewier; more earthy flavor; increase liquid and cooking time)
- 1¼ cups (300 mL) uncooked rye berries (higher in fiber; chewier; more nutty flavor; increase liquid and cooking time)
- 1 cup (250 mL) uncooked Kamut® berries or groats (higher in fiber; chewier; more nutty flavor; increase liquid and cooking time)
- 1⅓ cups (325 mL) uncooked triticale berries or groats (higher in fiber; chewier; more nutty flavor; increase liquid and cooking time)
- 1⅓ cups (325 mL) uncooked spelt berries or groats (higher in fiber; chewier; more nutty flavor; increase liquid and cooking time)

See also WILD RICE; VARIETIES OF RICE (PAGE 591).

Rice Bran

Bran is the outer cuticle layers and germ directly beneath the hull that remain intact in brown rice but are stripped off when white rice is polished. Rice bran has a sweet, nutty flavor and is rich in vitamins, minerals, and fiber.

12 oz (375 g) =
3 cups (750 mL)

If You Don't Have It

Substitute 1 cup (250 mL) rice bran with:
- 1 cup (250 mL) oat bran
- 1 cup (250 mL) wheat bran
- 1 cup (250 mL) wheat germ

Rice Cake

Packaged snack discs prepared from puffed rice and a variety of flavorings. A favorite among dieters.

If You Don't Have It

Substitute 1 rice cake with:
- ½ cup (125 mL) popcorn

Rice Cooker

Electrical pot specially designed to cook rice and keep it warm until serving time. In general, all ingredients are combined using 10 to 20% less liquid than you would using the top-of-the-range method (use ¼ to ½ cup/50 to 125 mL less per cup/250 mL of rice).

If You Don't Have It

Substitute a rice cooker with:
- saucepan with a tight-fitting lid (use 10 to 20% more liquid or ¼ to ½ cup/50 to 125 mL more per cup/250 mL of rice)
- pressure cooker (reduce liquid by 20% and reduce cooking time by 60 to 70%)

Rice Cracker

Crisp Asian snack crackers prepared from rice flour, often seasoned with soy sauce, seaweed, chilies, or many other flavorings.

If You Don't Have It

Substitute 1 lb (500 g) rice crackers with:
- 1 lb (500 g) crisp lavash
- 1 lb (500 g) water crackers
- 1 lb (500 g) bagel chips
- 1 lb (500 g) tortilla chips
- 1 lb (500 g) potato chips
- 1 lb (500 g) sweet potato or other vegetable chips
- 1 lb (500 g) pretzels

Rice Flour

See RICE FLOUR, SWEET; CHOOSING AMONG WHOLE-GRAIN AND ALTERNATIVE FLOURS (PAGE 586).

Rice Flour, Sweet

Also known as glutinous rice flour, mochi flour, mochiko, and sweet rice powder. Made from highly starchy varieties of glutinous rice, this flour is used in many Asian countries as the base for dumplings and other sweets. Also an excellent thickener that, like tapioca, doesn't separate after freezing and thawing.

If You Don't Have It

Substitute 1 tbsp (15 mL) sweet rice flour (for thickening) with:

- 1½ to 2 tbsp (22 to 25 mL) quick-cooking tapioca (does not separate when frozen)
- 2 tsp (10 mL) arrowroot powder (separates when frozen)
- 2 to 3 tbsp (25 to 45 mL) kudzu powder (separates when frozen)
- 1 tbsp (15 mL) cornstarch (separates when frozen)
- 2 tbsp (25 mL) instant or all-purpose flour (cook a few minutes after thickening to cook out raw flour taste; separates when frozen)
- 2 tsp (10 mL) potato starch or instant mashed potato flakes (separates when frozen)

Rice Milk

Liquid extracted from cooked rice and used as a dairy substitute.

If You Don't Have It

Substitute 1 cup (250 mL) rice milk with:

- 1 cup (250 mL) almond milk
- 1 cup (250 mL) oat milk
- 1 cup (250 mL) sweetened soy milk
- 1 cup (250 mL) cow's milk
- 1 cup (250 mL) acidophilus milk (adds beneficial enzymes)
- 1 cup (250 mL) lactose-free milk (for the lactose intolerant)
- 1 cup (250 mL) goat's milk (for the lactose intolerant; more tangy taste than cow's milk)

Rice Noodles

See A SNAPSHOT OF ASIAN NOODLES (PAGE 588).

Rice Paper

Also known as spring roll wrappers. Southeast Asian circular or triangular shaped sheets made from rice flour and water. They are generally available dried and require soaking before using so they soften enough to allow them to be rolled up. The papers are used to wrap ingredients.

If You Don't Have It
Substitute 1 lb (500 g) rice paper with:
- 1 lb (500 g) phyllo dough
- 1 lb (500 g) dumpling wrappers (thicker; round)
- 1 lb (500 g) thinly rolled fresh pasta (cut to desired shape)
- 1 lb (500 g) egg roll wrappers (thicker)
- 1 lb (500 g) won ton skins (thicker)
- 1 lb (500 g) empanada wrappers (thicker; round)

Ricer

Also known as a potato ricer. Looking like a garlic press on steroids, this lever-operated plunger forces cooked potatoes, carrots, turnips, or other soft foods through a perforated template to purée them.

If You Don't Have It
Substitute a ricer with:
- food mill
- hand-held potato masher
- medium-mesh sieve and back of wooden spoon
- electric mixer
- blender or food processor (not recommended for mashing potatoes and other starchy roots and tubers; results are too gummy)

Rice Sticks

See A SNAPSHOT OF ASIAN NOODLES (PAGE 588).

Rice Wine

See MIRIN; SAKE.

Ricotta

The name means "re-cooked." This fresh Italian cheese is pleasantly granular and lightly sweet. In Italy, most ricottas are made by cooking the whey drained from producing mozzarella, provolone, or other cheeses. In the U.S., skim or whole milk is often added to the whey.

8 oz (250 g) =
1 cup (250 mL)

If You Don't Have It
Substitute 1 oz (30 g) ricotta cheese with:
- 1 oz (30 g) Myzithra
- 1 oz (30 g) cottage cheese, puréed until smooth
- 1 oz (30 g) farmer cheese (firmer)
- 1 oz (30 g) pot cheese (firmer)
- 1 oz (30 g) hoop cheese (firmer)
- 1 oz (30 g) fromage blanc
- 1 oz (30 g) mashed firm tofu (for texture; much less flavorful)

Ricotta Salata

Also known as canestrata.
Ricotta that is allowed to
drain more than the fresh
version to become drier in
texture. It is also salted.

4 oz (125 g) = 1 cup
(250 mL) crumbled

If You Don't Have It

Substitute 1 oz (30 g) ricotta salata with:
- 1 oz (30 g) feta (stronger flavor; rinse to reduce saltiness)
- 1 oz (30 g) Manouri (creamier)
- 1 oz (30 g) Haloumi (may add mint flavor)
- 1 oz (30 g) aged Myzithra (to replace aged ricotta salata)
- 1 oz (30 g) Cotija (may be soft or firm)
- 1 oz (30 g) Pecorino Romano (to replace aged ricotta salata; sharper flavor)
- 1 oz (30 g) Parmesan (to replace aged ricotta salata)

Ring Mold

See PAN SIZE EQUIVALENTS (PAGE 606).

Risotto Rice

See VARIETIES OF RICE (PAGE 591).

Ritz Cracker

See CRACKER.

Roasted Red Pepper

See BELL PEPPER, ROASTED RED.

Roasting Rack

A flat or adjustable
V-shaped metal rack on
which to hold meat or fowl
above the bottom of the
roasting pan. Because
hot air can circulate, the
entire roast browns and
crisps evenly.

If You Don't Have It

Substitute a roasting rack with:
- upper oven rack with pan set on lower oven rack
- cooling rack set in roasting pan or rimmed baking sheet

Robiola Lombardia

A creamy cow's milk
cheese that originated
in the Lombardy town
of Robbio.

If You Don't Have It

Substitute 1 oz (30 g) Robiola Lombardia with:
- 1 oz (30 g) Taleggio
- 1 oz (30 g) Reblochon
- 1 oz (30 g) Pont-l'Évêque

See also ROBIOLA PIEMONTE.

Robiola Piemonte

*Also known as Robiola
di Roccaverano. A well-
known variation of
Robiola Lombardia,
named after a village in
Piedmont, is made from
goat's milk, sheep's milk,
cow's milk or sometimes
a mixture of the trio.*

If You Don't Have It
Substitute 1 oz (30 g) Robiola Piemonte:
- 1 oz (30 g) caprini or creamy young chèvre
- ½ oz (15 g) ricotta + ½ oz (15 g) mascarpone, blended
- 1 oz (30 g) Petit Suisse

See also ROBIOLA LOMBARDIA.

Rocambole

See GARLIC.

Rock and Rye

*This is a citrus liqueur
that's based on rye whiskey.
A piece of rock candy floats
in every bottle.*

If You Don't Have It
Substitute 2 tbsp (25 mL) rock and rye with:
- 2 tbsp (25 mL) Southern Comfort

Rock Cornish Hen

See CHICKEN.

Rocket

See ARUGULA.

Rockfish

See OCEAN PERCH; STRIPED BASS.

Rock Lobster

See SPINY LOBSTER.

Rock Salt

See TRADING SALTS (PAGE 602).

Rock Sugar

See SUGAR, ROCK.

Rocoto Chile

See CHOOSING FRESH CHILES (PAGE 582).

Roe

See CHANGING ROE (PAGE 594).

Rolled Oats

See OATS, OLD-FASHIONED.

Rolling Pin

A solid, heavy cylindrical tool used primarily to roll dough but also to crush crackers, flatten cutlets, and perform other tasks. Pins are fashioned from wood, marble, ceramic, glass, and plastic.

If You Don't Have It

Substitute a rolling pin with:
- wine bottle
- clean, heavy-duty cardboard tube (such as one from a poster or poster mailing tube) wrapped in plastic wrap

Romaine Lettuce

Also known as Cos lettuce. Leaf of choice for the classic Caesar salad.

1 lb (500 g) =
6 cups (1.5 L) pieces

If You Don't Have It

Substitute 1 lb (500 g) Romaine lettuce with:
- 1 lb (500 g) crisphead lettuce such as Iceberg, Great Lakes, or Imperial (rounder, crisper leaves; less flavorful; more watery)
- 1 lb (500 g) butterhead lettuce such as Bibb or Boston (smaller, more tender leaves; less watery)
- 8 oz (250 g) leaf lettuce such as oak or lollo (smaller, more tender leaves; less watery)
- 8 oz (250 g) mâche (tender leaves; bittersweet, slightly nutty flavor)

Romano

Also known as Pecorino Romano. A style of pungent, hard Italian grating cheese produced from sheep's milk.

If You Don't Have It

Substitute 1 oz (30 g) Romano cheese with:
- 1 oz (30 g) Parmesan (slightly milder)
- 1 oz (30 g) Grana Padano
- 1 oz (30 g) aged Asiago (slightly sweeter)
- 1 oz (30 g) aged Manchego (milder)
- 1 oz (30 g) dry Jack cheese (more nutty)

Romano Varieties

Choose 1 oz (30 g) Romano cheese from these varieties:
- 1 oz (30 g) Pecorino Romano (made with sheep's milk; sharp, salty, delicate fruity aromas)
- 1 oz (30 g) Caprino Romano (made with goat's milk; sharper than Pecorino Romano)
- 1 oz (30 g) Vacchino Romano (made with cow's milk; much milder than Pecorino Romano)

For Better Health

Substitute 1 oz (30 g) Romano cheese with:
- 1 oz (30 g) Sapsago (lower in fat and calories; more herbal flavor)

See also PECORINO.

Rondelé

A Wisconsin brand of European-style soft cheeses.

> 8 oz (250 g) =
> 1 cup (250 mL)

If You Don't Have It

Substitute 1 oz (30 g) Rondelé with:
- 1 oz (30 g) boursin
- 1 oz (30 g) Alouette
- 1 oz (30 g) herbed cream cheese + 1½ tsp (7 mL) softened butter

Root Beer

Originally, this foamy beverage was prepared with sassafras. Today it is a blend of anise, cinnamon, cloves, ginger, juniper, licorice, lemon oil, orange oil, sarsaparilla, vanilla, and wintergreen.

If You Don't Have It

Substitute 1 cup (250 mL) root beer with:
- 1 cup (250 mL) birch beer
- 1 cup (250 mL) cola (less aromatic)
- 1 cup (250 mL) ginger beer (sharper flavor)

Roquefort

Genuine French Roquefort takes its blue cheese character from sheep's milk, naturally occurring Peniciullium roqueforti bacteria, and the constant conditions of the aging caves.

> 4 oz (125 g) =
> 1 cup (250 mL) crumbled

If You Don't Have It

Substitute 1 oz (30 g) Roquefort with:
- 1 oz (30 g) Gorgonzola
- 1 oz (30 g) Maytag Blue
- 1 oz (30 g) Stilton
- 1 oz (30 g) Cashel Blue
- 1 oz (30 g) Fourme d'Ambert
- 1 oz (30 g) Bleu d'Auvergne
- 1 oz (30 g) Bleu des Causses
- 1 oz (30 g) Danish Blue

Rose

See PICKING EDIBLE FLOWERS (PAGE 604).

Rose Essence

A far more concentrated form of rose water, which Indian cooks use to flavor beverages and desserts.

If You Don't Have It

Substitute 1 tsp (5 mL) rose essence with:
- 1 tbsp (15 mL) rose water
- 2 tbsp (25 mL) rose syrup (sweeter; reduce liquid in recipe by a scant 2 tbsp/25 mL if necessary)

To Vary the Flavor

Substitute 1 tsp (5 mL) rose essence with:
- 1 tbsp (15 mL) other flower-based water such as orange flower water
- 1 to 1½ tsp (5 to 7 mL) almond or vanilla extract

See also ROSE SYRUP; ROSE WATER.

Rosemary

When you purchase fresh rosemary for a recipe and don't use all of it, you can easily dry or freeze the remainder for future use. Wash the branches and dry thoroughly on a towel. Place in a small paper bag to dry in a cool pantry or place in a resealable bag and store in the freezer.

If You Don't Have It

Substitute 1 tbsp (15 mL) chopped fresh rosemary with:
- 1 to 2 tsp (5 to 10 mL) crushed dried rosemary

To Vary the Flavor

Substitute 1 tbsp (15 mL) chopped fresh rosemary with:
- 2 tsp (10 mL) chopped fresh sage or thyme
- 1 tbsp (15 mL) chopped fresh summer savory
- 1 tbsp (15 mL) chopped fresh basil or oregano

Rose Syrup

Also known as rose-scented syrup. Essence of rose combined with a sugar syrup. This floral sweetener is used in the Middle East, India, and Southeast Asia in desserts and beverages.

If You Don't Have It

Substitute 1 tbsp (15 mL) rose syrup with:
- 1½ tsp (7 mL) rose water (less sweet)
- ½ tsp (2 mL) rose essence (less sweet)

To Vary the Flavor

Substitute 1 tbsp (15 mL) rose syrup with:
- 1 tbsp (15 mL) other flavored syrup, such as almond, hazelnut, orange, or vanilla

See also ROSE ESSENCE; ROSE WATER.

Rose Water

In the Middle East, India, and China, this intense distillation of rose petals is used as a food flavoring.

If You Don't Have It

Substitute 1 tsp (5 mL) rose water with:
- ¼ to ½ tsp (1 to 2 mL) rose essence
- 2 tsp (10 mL) rose syrup (sweeter)

To Vary the Flavor

Substitute 1 tsp (5 mL) rose water with:
- 1 to 2 tbsp (15 to 25 mL) Parfait d'Amour (adds rose, orange, and vanilla aromas, sweetness, and alcohol)
- 1 to 2 tbsp (15 to 25 mL) crème de rose (adds rose and vanilla aromas, sweetness, and alcohol)
- 1 to 2 tbsp (15 to 25 mL) crème de violette (adds violet flower aroma, sweetness, alcohol, and purple color)
- 1 tsp (5 mL) other flower-based water such as orange flower water
- ½ tsp (2 mL) vanilla extract
- ¼ to ½ tsp (1 to 2 mL) almond extract

See also ROSE ESSENCE; ROSE SYRUP.

Rotary Beater

Also known as egg beater. The American classic hand-cranked rotary beater has inspired not one, but two volumes by collectibles author Don Thornton. Beat This: The Eggbeater Chronicles *and* The Eggbeater Chronicles.

If You Don't Have It
Substitute a rotary beater with:
- whisk
- fork
- pastry blender
- electric mixer

Roti

Indian whole wheat flatbread cooked on a griddle. When the roti is held over an open flame for a few seconds to complete cooking, it puffs like a balloon.

If You Don't Have It
Substitute 1 roti with:
- 1 chapati (flatbread made with whole wheat flour and little or no fat)
- 1 paratha (griddle-cooked whole wheat flatbread with fat in the dough; richer; more flaky)
- 1 poori (deep-fried flatbread made with whole wheat flour; crisper)
- 1 naan (more puffy flatbread made from refined wheat flour and cooked on the walls of a tandoor or clay-lined oven; sometimes flavored with garlic, herbs, or other aromatics)
- 1 whole wheat pita bread (similar to naan)
- 1 whole wheat flour tortilla

See also CHAPATI.

Rotisserie

Also known as a spit roaster. A cooking implement that automates one of the most ancient culinary methods: slowly revolving meat or poultry over a heat source to roast and baste simultaneously.

If You Don't Have It
Substitute a rotisserie with:
- stationary roasting rack and very frequent turning (food may be less moist and less evenly browned; save yourself the trouble and get a rotisserie)

Roux

A cooked mixture of flour and fat used for thickening sauces, soups, and stews. White roux and blond roux — cooked until slightly golden — are made with butter and used for delicately colored dishes. Brown roux can be made with butter or the drippings from pork or beef roasts. Cooked to a walnut color, brown roux is used for more robust soups and sauces. In Creole and Cajun roux, lard is often used and the mixture may be cooked for an hour or until very dark and deeply flavored.

If You Don't Have It

Substitute ½ cup (125 mL) roux with:

- ½ cup (125 mL) beurre manié (¼ cup/50 mL softened butter + ¼ cup/50 mL flour, kneaded together; less flavorful)
- ¼ cup (50 mL) instant flour (less flavorful)
- ¼ cup (50 mL) all-purpose flour + ½ cup (125 mL) cold water, whisked together (less flavorful)
- 2 tbsp (25 mL) cornstarch, potato starch, or rice starch + ¼ cup (50 mL) cold water, whisked together (less flavorful)
- 3 tbsp (45 mL) arrowroot + ¼ cup (50 mL) cold water, whisked together (less flavorful)
- 4 tsp (20 mL) instant mashed potato flakes (less flavorful)
- 5 tbsp (75 mL) tapioca starch + ½ cup (125 mL) cold water, whisked together (less flavorful)
- ¼ cup (50 mL) cornmeal (adds mild corn flavor)

Roux Varieties

Choose ½ cup (125 mL) roux from these varieties:

- ½ cup (125 mL) white roux (cooked until beige and not browned; best for light or cream-based sauces and soups)
- ½ cup (125 mL) blond roux (cooked until golden or lightly browned; slightly more flavorful than white roux; best for light or cream-based sauces and soups)
- ½ cup (125 mL) brown roux (cooked until deeply browned and richly toasted or nutty in flavor and aroma; best for dark sauces, soups, and stews)

Royal Ann Cherry

See CHERRY.

Rubber Spatula

See SPATULA.

Ruby Port

See PORT.

Rum

Fermented sugarcane juice that is distilled and aged. May be flavored with spices or tropical fruits.

If You Don't Have It
Substitute 2 tbsp (25 mL) rum with:
- ¾ to 1 tsp (4 to 5 mL) rum extract or brandy extract + 2 tbsp (25 mL) apple cider or water
- 2 tbsp (25 mL) brandy
- 2 tbsp (25 mL) bourbon

Rum Varieties
Choose 2 tbsp (25 mL) rum from these varieties:
- 2 tbsp (25 mL) light, white, or silver rum (colorless; light body; light, dry flavor)
- 2 tbsp (25 mL) flavored rum, such as coconut rum (colorless; light body; lightly sweet flavor infused with tropical aromas such as coconut)
- 2 tbsp (25 mL) gold or amber rum (amber color; medium body; aged longer than light rum; more flavorful and less harsh-tasting than white rum)
- 2 tbsp (25 mL) añejo rum (similar to gold or amber rum but aged longer)
- 2 tbsp (25 mL) spiced rum (colorless or amber color; light to medium body; flavored with spices such as vanilla)
- 2 tbsp (25 mL) dark rum (dark amber color; medium to full body; aged longer than gold or amber rum; more complex, molasses-like flavor than gold or amber rum; Jamaican rum is a dark rum)
- 2 tbsp (25 mL) Demerara rum (dark amber color; medium to full body; more complex flavor than white or amber rum; may be higher in alcohol than other dark rums)

See also RUM EXTRACT.

Rum Extract

Good for adding rum flavor — with only a trace amount of the alcohol found in rum — to cakes, pies, breads, and savory fruit dishes.

If You Don't Have It
Substitute 1 tsp (5 mL) rum extract with:
- 2 to 3 tbsp (25 to 45 mL) rum (omit 2 to 3 tbsp/25 to 45 mL liquid from recipe if necessary)

To Vary the Flavor
Substitute 1 tsp (5 mL) rum extract with:
- 1 tsp (5 mL) brandy extract
- 1 tsp (5 mL) vanilla extract

Runner Bean

See PEAS, SHELLING.

Rusk

See ZWIEBACK.

Russian Easter Bread

See KULICH.

Rutabaga

Also known as Canadian, Russian, Swedish, and yellow turnip. The Rodney Dangerfield of the vegetable world, this golden globe root vegetable deserves far more respect in the kitchen than it gets. Newly harvested sweet rutabagas are delightful tossed into salads and stir-fries. The vegetable may also be steamed, mashed, sautéed, or roasted until caramelized.

> 1 medium = 1½ to 2 lbs
> (750 g to 1 kg) =
> 4 to 5 cups
> (1 to 1.25 L) cubed

If You Don't Have It

Substitute 1 cup (250 mL) chopped rutabaga with:
- 1 cup (250 mL) chopped turnips (sweeter)
- 1 cup (250 mL) chopped broccoli stems (sweeter, milder)
- 1 cup (250 mL) chopped kohlrabi bulb (sweeter, milder)
- 1 cup (250 mL) chopped Asian radishes such as daikon (more peppery)
- 1 cup (250 mL) chopped black radishes (much sharper and hotter flavor)

Rye Bread

Dark, hearty breads made from rye flour (often with some wheat flour) are preferred in northeastern Europe, Scandinavia, and in parts of North America settled by immigrants from these areas. The characteristic acidic flavor comes from the sourdough leavening.

If You Don't Have It

Substitute 1 lb (500 g) rye bread with:
- 1 lb (500 g) pumpernickel bread
- 1 lb (500 g) limpa bread (more aromatic)
- 1 lb (500 g) Russian black bread

Rye Flour

See CHOOSING AMONG WHOLE-GRAIN AND ALTERNATIVE FLOURS (PAGE 586).

Saanen to Szechuan Pepper

Saanen

A Swiss cheese of amazing longevity, sometimes edible for 200 years. Traditionally, a child's birth is commemorated with an individual saanen cheese. Tiny pieces are consumed on special occasions during the person's lifetime. In some cases, the cheese outlives the person.

> 4 oz (125 g) =
> 1 cup (250 mL) grated

If You Don't Have It
Substitute 1 oz (30 g) Saanen with:
- 1 oz (30 g) Sbrinz
- 1 oz (30 g) Spalen or Sparen
- 1 oz (30 g) aged Asiago
- 1 oz (30 g) Parmesan (slightly sharper)
- 1 oz (30 g) Grana Padano (slightly sharper)
- 1 oz (30 g) dry Jack cheese (more nutty flavor)

For Better Health
Substitute 1 oz (30 g) Saanen with:
- 1 oz (30 g) Sapsago (more herbal flavor; lower in fat)

Sablefish

Also known mistakenly as Alaska cod, black cod, and butterfish. Neither butterfish nor cod, this oily Pacific Northwest fish is excellent for smoking. Often sold as smoked black cod.

If You Don't Have It
Substitute 1 lb (500 g) sablefish with:
- 1 lb (500 g) mackerel
- 1 lb (500 g) whitefish
- 1 lb (500 g) salmon
- 1 lb (500 g) blackfish
- 1 lb (500 g) grouper
- 1 lb (500 g) smoked black cod (adds smoke flavor)

See also BUTTERFISH.

Sabra Liqueur

From Israel, a chocolate-orange sweetened spirit.

If You Don't Have It

Substitute 2 tbsp (25 mL) Sabra liqueur with:

- 2 tbsp (25 mL) orange liqueur (omits chocolate flavor)
- 2 tbsp (25 mL) crème de cacao (sweeter)
- 2 tbsp (25 mL) Cheri Suisse (combines chocolate and cherry flavors)
- 2 tbsp (25 mL) Vandermint (combines chocolate and mint flavors)
- 2 tbsp (25 mL) Tiramisu liqueur (combines chocolate, coffee, and almond flavors)

See also ORANGE LIQUEUR.

Safflower

Also known as bastard saffron, false saffron, and kasubha. Related to sunflowers and thistles, the stunning orange flowers of this plant have long been substituted for the much more expensive saffron.

If You Don't Have It

Substitute 1 tsp (5 mL) crushed dried safflower florets with:

- ½ tsp (2 mL) turmeric + ½ tsp (2 mL) mild paprika (for yellow orange color; adds more pungent flavor)
- 1 to 1½ tsp (5 to 7 mL) annatto seeds (for yellow orange color; steep the seeds in hot water or oil liquid until richly colored then drain and use the colored liquid, discarding the seeds)
- 2 drops yellow food coloring + 1 drop red food coloring mixed into water or other liquid in the recipe (for yellow orange color)
- 10 to 15 crushed saffron threads (for yellow orange color; adds earthy, floral aromas; much more expensive)

See also SAFFRON.

Safflower Oil

See SUBSTITUTING OILS (PAGE 598).

Saffron

This most expensive of seasonings is found in the orange red stigmas of the crocus flower. It takes 70,000 flowers — the stigmas of which must be harvested by hand — to yield a pound of saffron. Saffron has a spicy aroma, pleasantly bitter flavor, and a gorgeous red gold hue.

10 to 15 threads = pinch = ⅛ to ¼ tsp (0.5 to 1 mL) powder

If You Don't Have It
Substitute 10 to 15 crushed saffron threads with:
- 1 tsp (5 mL) crushed dried safflower florets (for yellow orange color; much milder, less complex aroma; much less expensive)
- ½ tsp (2 mL) turmeric + ½ tsp (2mL) mild paprika (for yellow orange color; adds more pungent flavor)
- 1 to 1½ tsp (5 to 7 mL) annatto seeds (for yellow orange color; steep the seeds in hot water or oil liquid until richly colored then drain and use the colored liquid, discarding the seeds)
- 2 drops yellow food coloring + 1 drop red food coloring mixed into water or other liquid in the recipe (for yellow orange color)

See also SAFFLOWER; TURMERIC.

Saga Blue

A luxurious Danish double- or triple-crème cheese with subtle blue veining, mellow flavor, and an edible white rind.

If You Don't Have It
Substitute 1 oz (30 g) Saga blue with:
- 1 oz (30 g) Bleu de Bresse
- 1 oz (30 g) Cambozola
- 1 oz (30 g) Blue Castello
- 1 oz (30 g) Danish Blue
- 1 oz (30 g) Gorgonzola (more pungent, complex flavor)

Sage

An evergreen perennial of the mint family, this robustly flavored herb worked its way into European kitchens in the 16th century.

1 oz (30 g) rubbed sage = 1 cup (250 mL)

1 oz (30 g) ground sage = ¼ cup (50 mL)

If You Don't Have It
Substitute 1 tbsp (15 mL) chopped fresh sage with:
- 1 tsp (5 mL) dried sage
- 1 tbsp (15 mL) chopped fresh pineapple sage (adds pineapple aromas)

To Vary the Flavor
Substitute 1 tbsp (15 mL) chopped fresh sage with:
- 3 to 4 tsp (15 to 20 mL) chopped fresh summer savory
- 1 tbsp (15 mL) chopped fresh rosemary
- 3 to 4 tsp (15 to 20 mL) chopped fresh thyme, basil, or oregano
- 1 to 2 tsp (5 to 10 mL) poultry seasoning (sage and other herbs such as thyme and marjoram)

Sage Derby

See DERBY

Sago

A light starch used for thickening, obtained from sago and other palms. It is processed into flour, meal, and pearls similar to tapioca. Most widely used in India, Southeast Asia, Central and South America, the Caribbean, and among native Australians.

If You Don't Have It

Substitute 1 tbsp (15 mL) sago flour or pearls (for thickening) with:

- 1 tbsp (15 mL) tapioca flour or pearls
- 2 tsp (10 mL) arrowroot powder
- 1 heaping tbsp (15 mL) all-purpose flour
- 1½ tsp (7 mL) cornstarch, potato starch, or rice starch

Saint Agur

Creamy, spicy cow's milk blue from Auvergne in south-central France. Delicious spread on raisin bread, with pears, or savored with a glass of Sauternes.

If You Don't Have It

Substitute 1 oz (30 g) Saint Agur with:

- 1 oz (30 g) Bleu d'Auvergne
- 1 oz (30 g) Bleu de Gex
- 1 oz (30 g) Fourme d'Ambert
- 1 oz (30 g) Cambozola
- 1 oz (30 g) Stilton

Saint Albray

This mild and spicy soft cheese made at the base of the French Pyrenees is instantly recognizable by the scalloped shape of its whitish red rind.

If You Don't Have It

Substitute 1 oz (30 g) Saint Albray with:

- 1 oz (30 g) Camembert
- 1 oz (30 g) Brie
- 1 oz (30 g) Explorateur

Saint André

Velvety French triple-crème cheese is delightful paired with ripe pineapple, mangoes, or other tropical fruits.

If You Don't Have It

Substitute 1 oz (30 g) Saint André with:

- 1 oz (30 g) Brillat-Savarin
- 1 oz (30 g) Explorateur
- 1 oz (30 g) Boursault
- 1 oz (30 g) Gratte-Paille

Sainte-Maure de Touraine

Log-shaped goat's cheese from central France that has straw in the center to aerate the cheese.

If You Don't Have It

Substitute 1 oz (30 g) Sainte-Maure de Touraine with:

- 1 oz (30 g) Crottin de Chavignol (soft to firm texture and mild to nutty flavor, depending on age)
- 1 oz (30 g) Selles-sur-Cher (semifirm texture; sweet, nutty flavor; covered with black ash)

Saint-Marcellin

A creamy, unpasteurized, natural-rind cheese made from cow's or goat's milk. Usually round in shape with a wrinkly, whitish rind. The young cheese varies in texture from runny to firm. The flavor is yeasty, nutty, and fruity.

If You Don't Have It
Substitute 1 oz (30 g) Saint-Marcellin with:
- 1 oz (30 g) Banon

Saint-Nectaire

A semisoft French cheese from Auvergne in south-central France. Patches of white, yellow, and red mold grow on the rind during cellar ripening.

If You Don't Have It
Substitute 1 oz (30 g) Saint-Nectaire with:
- 1 oz (30 g) Tomme de Savoie
- 1 oz (30 g) Beaumont
- 1 oz (30 g) Reblochon

Saint Paulin

Originally made by Trappist Monks, this is France's first pasteurized milk cheese. St. Paulin is a pleasant dessert or table cheese. It is creamy in texture but firm enough to slice. Beware of imitation cheeses that are encased in an inedible plastic rind.

1 lb (500 g) = 4 cups
(1 L) shredded

If You Don't Have It
Substitute 1 oz (30 g) Saint Paulin with:
- 1 oz (30 g) Port Salut
- 1 oz (30 g) Esrom
- 1 oz (30 g) Tilsit
- 1 oz (30 g) Havarti
- 1 oz (30 g) Oka
- 1 oz (30 g) Muenster

Sake

Japanese brewed alcoholic rice drink that plays a major role in the country's cuisine. It's ranked with soy sauce, miso, and dashi in terms of essential ingredients.

If You Don't Have It
Substitute ½ cup (125 mL) sake with:
- ½ cup (125 mL) Shaoxing wine
- ½ cup (125 mL) dry vermouth
- ½ cup (125 mL) dry sherry
- ½ cup (125 mL) flat beer (preferably lager)

Salad Burnet

An herb with a cucumber aroma used in salads, to season vegetables, and brewed into tea.

2 oz (60 g)= 1½ cups (375 mL) chopped

If You Don't Have It

Substitute 1 tbsp (15 mL) fresh salad burnet with:
- 1 tbsp (15 mL) fresh borage or country borage

Salad Spinner

A utensil that makes quick, easy work of drying greens, herbs, and other delicate ingredients.

If You Don't Have It

Substitute a salad spinner with:
- clean pillowcase (especially for large amounts of greens; shake or spin washed greens in pillowcase until dry)
- colander or large mesh strainer (wash greens in colander or strainer then cover with kitchen towel and shake over sink until dry)
- kitchen towels (wash greens, put on towel and pat dry with more towels)

Salamander

A tool used for caramelizing or browning the surface of certain dishes. It is a wooden-handled iron rod attached to a heavy iron disc that is heated until red hot. To use, it is passed back and forth above the surface of the dish to be browned. It's named for a mythical lizard said to survive in fire.

If You Don't Have It

Substitute a salamander with:
- broiler
- blowtorch (especially for crème brûlée)

Salami

The term for a variety of seasoned Italian ground meat products, usually pork based, that are packed in casing. The three basic types are fresh, dry-aged, and cooked (cotto). Salt is probably the only

If You Don't Have It

Substitute 1 lb (500 g) salami with:
- 1 lb (500 g) pepperoni
- 1 lb (500 g) Spanish chorizo
- 1 lb (500 g) cured Portuguese chouriço or linguiça
- 1 lb (500 g) prosciutto
- 1 lb (500 g) summer sausage

ingredient common to all salami. Pepper, spices, and other seasonings are added depending upon individual formulas. The fineness of the grind, the amount of added fat, and whether or not the meat is marinated also affect the resulting product. Fresh salami, such as pork sausage (salsiccia), contains raw meat and must be cooked before eating. Dry-aged salami, such as finocchiona, are "cured" by hanging in dry, crisp air. Cotto or cooked salami, such as mortadella, are cooked but still must be refrigerated and eaten shortly after purchase.

Salami Varieties

Choose 1 lb (500 g) salami from these popular varieties:

- 1 lb (500 g) Milanese or Milano salami (made with pork and beef; gently seasoned with garlic and pepper)
- 1 lb (500 g) Genovese or Genoa salami (made with pork and veal; well-seasoned with pepper and garlic)
- 1 lb (500 g) finocchiona salami (made with pork; coarse texture; seasoned with fennel seeds)
- 1 lb (500 g) sopressata (made with pork; slightly flattened shape; dry and well-seasoned with pepper)
- 1 lb (500 g) Neapolitan or Napoli salami (made with pork and beef; long and thin; spicy with red and black pepper)
- 1 lb (500 g) Sardinian or Sardo salami (made with pork; spicy with red pepper)
- 1 lb (500 g) Calabrian or Calabrese sausage or salami (made with pork; short and squat; dry and spicy with red pepper)
- 1 lb (500 g) kosher salami (made only with beef; cooked; moist)

See also MORTADELLA; PEPPERONI.

Salicornia

Also known as glasswort, samphire, sea bean, and sea pickle. A crunchy, juicy, salty-tasting green sea plant, salicornia shouldn't be confused with rock samphire, a different sea plant that grows along the coasts of France and the U.K.

If You Don't Have It

Substitute 1 lb (500 g) salicornia with:

- 1 lb (500 g) haricots verts or young green beans, dipped in boiling water for 10 to 20 seconds and salted (softer)
- 1 lb (500 g) thin asparagus, dipped in boiling water for 10 to 20 seconds and salted (softer)
- 1 lb (500 g) caper berries (for a briny garnish; softer)
- 1 lb (500 g) gherkins or very crisp pickles (for a briny garnish; softer)

Salmon

This delicious and healthful fish swims only in waters of the Northern Hemisphere. Once a prized game catch, it was typically caught in spring as it began its journey from the ocean upriver to the spot where it was born to lay its own eggs. Due to declining fish populations, in large part because of river pollution, salmon are now widely raised in fish farms. Most Atlantic salmon sold in North American markets is farmed. Pacific salmon comes mostly from Alaska, and may be farmed or wild-caught. Pacific includes several varieties such as Chinook, coho, sockeye, pink, and chum salmon.

If You Don't Have It

Substitute 1 lb (500 g) salmon with:
- 1 lb (500 g) trout
- 1 lb (500 g) char
- 1 lb (500 g) striped bass
- 1 lb (500 g) swordfish
- 1 lb (500 g) marlin
- 1 lb (500 g) tuna

Salmon Varieties

Choose 1 lb (500 g) salmon from these varieties:
- 1 lb (500 g) Chinook or king salmon (flesh is pale to deep red, high-fat, soft, and succulent with pronounced flavor)
- 1 lb (500 g) coho or silver salmon (flesh is pink to reddish orange, high-fat, and firm with rich flavor)
- 1 lb (500 g) sockeye, blueback, or red salmon (flesh is dark red, high-fat, and firm with strong flavor; often canned)
- 1 lb (500 g) pink or humpback salmon (flesh is pink, medium-fat, and firm with delicate flavor)
- 1 lb (500 g) chum or dog salmon (flesh is pale to bright orange, relatively low-fat, and firm with mild flavor)

See also SALMON, CANNED; SMOKED SALMON; CHANGING ROE (PAGE 594).

Salmon, Canned

In 1985, the Alaska Seafood Marketing Institute promoted canned salmon by popularizing a salmon burger consisting of the canned fish mixed with mayonnaise, bread crumbs, and Parmesan cheese served on a hamburger bun.

> 6 oz (170 g) can =
> ⅔ to ¾ cup
> (150 to 175 mL) drained

To Vary the Flavor

Substitute 1 (6-oz/170 g) can salmon with:
- 1 (6-oz/170 g) can tuna
- 1 (6-oz/170 g) can mackerel

Salsa

Versatile tomato-based condiment. Mix some with mayonnaise or oil/vinegar for a zesty dressing for cooked meats, seafood, or vegetables. Add some to chunky tomatoes for a spicy pasta sauce. Or pour over fish fillets or chicken breasts before baking.

If You Don't Have It
Substitute 1 cup (250 mL) fresh salsa with:
- 1 cup (250 mL) refrigerated salsa (sold in tubs in the refrigerated produce section of many grocery stores)
- 1 cup (250 mL) jarred salsa + 1 tbsp (15 mL) chopped fresh cilantro + 1 tsp (5 mL) fresh lime juice

Salsiccia

See SALAMI; SAUSAGE.

Salsify

Also known as oyster plant and white salsify. Looking like gnarled, hairy white carrots, this root tastes like delicate cooked artichoke heart. A related root, black salsify (also known as black oyster plant and scorzonera) is a dark brown-skinned, straighter root that tastes of coconut mixed with artichoke.

> 1 lb (500 g) fresh =
> 4 to 5 roots = 3 cups
> (750 mL) chopped =
> 2 cups (500 mL) cooked

If You Don't Have It
Substitute 1 lb (500 g) salsify with:
- 1 lb (500 g) artichoke hearts
- 1 lb (500 g) sunchokes
- 1 lb (500 g) Chinese artichokes
- 1 lb (500 g) cardoons
- 1 lb (500 g) burdock
- 1 lb (500 g) parsnips
- 1 lb (500 g) arracacha

Salsify Varieties
Choose 1 lb (500 g) salsify from these varieties:
- 1 lb (500 g) salsify or white salsify (pale skin; multiple roots and hairy-looking rootlets; mild flavor reminiscent of artichoke hearts and sunchokes)
- 1 lb (500 g) scorzonera or black salsify (brown skin on a single root; slightly thicker and longer than white salsify; mild flavor reminiscent of artichoke hearts, coconut, and sunchokes)

Salt

The most common salt is table salt, a fine-grain refined salt with additives that prevent it from clumping. The trace element iodine is often added to table salt, a practice that began as a preventive

If You Don't Have It
Substitute 1 tsp (5 mL) table salt with:
- 1 to 1½ tsp (5 to 7 mL) seasoned salt (adds other flavors such as paprika, onion, celery, and/or garlic)
- 1½ to 2 tsp (7 to 10 mL) Beau Monde® Seasoning (adds onion and celery flavors)
- 2 tsp (10 mL) soy sauce (adds dark color)
- 3 to 4 tsp (15 to 20 mL) anchovy paste (adds fish flavor)

Salt (cont'd)

measure against
hypothyroidism. Many
cooks use table salt for
baking and salt shakers
but prefer Kosher and
sea salts for cooking.

> 1 tsp (5 mL) table salt =
> 1 tsp (5 mL) fine-grained
> sea salt = 1⅛ to 1½ tsp
> (5.5 to 7 mL) Kosher salt

- 1 tsp (5 mL) powdered dulse or other seaweed (adds briny flavor; for soups and stews)
- 2 tbsp (25 mL) yellow or shinshu miso (for sauces, soups and stews)
- 4 to 6 tsp (20 to 30 mL) dark or hatcho miso (for sauces, soups and stews)

For Better Health

Substitute 1 tsp (5 mL) salt with:

- 2 tsp (10 mL) Italian seasoning (usually salt-free)
- 2 tsp (10 mL) herbal salt substitute such as Mrs. Dash® (salt-free)
- 1 tsp (5 mL) salt substitute such as No Salt® or Lite Salt® (may contain some sodium and taste slightly bitter)
- 1 to 2 tbsp (15 to 25 mL) chopped fresh herbs (for flavor; bay leaf also enhances the savory flavor of low-sodium sauces and soups)
- 1 tsp (5 mL) lemon zest or juice (for flavor; especially good with vegetables)

See also HERBAL SALT SUBSTITUTE; SEASONED SALT; TRADING SALTS (PAGE 602).

Salt Cod

Also known as bacalao
(Spanish), baccalà (Italian),
and morue (French).
Salting and partially
drying cod started as a
prerefrigeration method
of preserving the fish.
Not to be confused with
stockfish, which is dried
but not salted cod.

If You Don't Have It

Substitute 1 lb (500 g) salt cod with:

- 1 lb (500 g) other salted and dried fish such as mackerel

See also COD.

Salt Mill

A device for grinding
coarse salt. Look for types
that have a grinder made
from a substance other
than carbon steel, which
will corrode on contact
with salt.

If You Don't Have It

Substitute a salt mill with:

- pepper mill
- mortar and pestle
- heavy pan or rolling pin for crushing

Salt Pork

Also known as pickled pork. A layer of pork belly fat with some lean streaks that is preserved by salting. Prior to refrigeration, the use of salt pork was much more common than it is now.

4 oz (125 g) =
1 cup (250 mL) cracklings

If You Don't Have It

Substitute 4 oz (125 g) salt pork with:
- 4 oz (125 g) bacon (leaner; adds smoke flavor)
- 4 oz (125 g) ham (leaner)
- 4 oz (125 g) pancetta (leaner)
- 4 oz (125 g) fatback (not salted; add salt as necessary)
- 4 oz (125 g) hog jowls or cheeks (adds smoke flavor)
- 4 oz (125 g) guanciale (leaner)
- 1 ham hock (may add smoke flavor)

Salt Substitute

See SALT.

Sambal Bajak

See CHILE PASTE.

Sambal Oelek

See CHILE PASTE.

Sambuca

See ANISE LIQUEUR.

Samp

See HOMINY.

Samphire

See SALICORNIA.

Samsoe

Foremost Danish cow's milk cheese is Swiss-style with a yellow paste and small random holes. Mild and nutty, it's a good cooking and eating cheese.

1 lb (500 g) = 4 cups
(1 L) shredded

If You Don't Have It

Substitute 1 oz (30 g) Samsoe with:
- 1 oz (30 g) Tybo (slightly milder)
- 1 oz (30 g) Danbo (may add caraway flavor)
- 1 oz (30 g) Emmental (drier; more complex flavor)
- 1 oz (30 g) Gouda

Sand Dab

See PLAICE.

Sanguinelli

See ORANGE, BLOOD.

Sansho

Also known as Japanese pepper. A seasoning made from the prickly ash tree and used in Japanese cooking. The flavor is not hot but rather tangy with lemon aromas.

If You Don't Have It

Substitute 1 tsp (5 mL) sansho with:
- 1 tsp (5 mL) Szechuan pepper
- 1 tsp (5 mL) lemon pepper seasoning
- ½ tsp (2 mL) black pepper + ½ tsp (2 mL) lemon zest

See also SZECHUAN PEPPER.

Santa Claus Melon

Also known as Christmas melon. At peak season in December, the outside of this fruit resembles a watermelon but inside it's more like a honeydew melon.

2 lbs (1 kg) =
3 cups (750 mL) diced

If You Don't Have It

Substitute 1 cup (250 mL) chopped Santa Claus melon with:
- 1 cup (250 mL) chopped honeydew melon
- 1 cup (250 mL) chopped Galia melon
- 1 cup (250 mL) chopped Ogen melon
- 1 cup (250 mL) chopped casaba melon
- 1 cup (250 mL) chopped Crenshaw melon (orange flesh)
- 1 cup (250 mL) chopped Persian melon (orange flesh)
- 1 cup (250 mL) cantaloupe (orange flesh)

Sapodilla

The fruit of a Central American tree that also produces chicle, from which chewing gum is made. The juicy, translucent flesh tastes, surprisingly, a bit like maple syrup.

1 lb (500 g) fresh =
2½ cups (625 mL) sliced

If You Don't Have It

Substitute 1 lb (500 g) sapodillas with:
- 1 lb (500 g) pears
- 1 lb (500 g) mamey sapote
- 1 lb (500 g) white sapote
- 1 lb (500 g) cherimoya
- 1 lb (500 g) mango
- 1 lb (500 g) apricot

Sapote, White

Also known as Mexican custard apple, zapote and zapote blanco. A Latin American fruit with cream-color flesh that's the consistency of custard. Depending upon the variety, white sapote tastes of peach, lemon, mango, caramel, or vanilla. Often mistakenly called sapote and sapota.

> 2 white sapotes = 1 cup
> (250 mL) mashed pulp

If You Don't Have It
Substitute 1 lb (500 g) white sapote with:
- 1 lb (500 g) peaches
- 1 lb (500 g) mango
- 1 lb (500 g) sapodillas
- 1 lb (500 g) cherimoya

Sapote Varieties
Choose 1 lb (500 g) white sapote from these varieties:
- 1 lb (500 g) black sapote (color and texture of chocolate pudding, for which makes a novel substitute)
- 1 lb (500 g) mamey sapote (salmon-color flesh with a flavor reminiscent of apricots)

See also MAMEY SAPOTE.

Sapsago

Also known as Schbzierger. A cone-shaped, low-fat cheese produced in Switzerland. The pale green color and herbal flavor come from a clover called melilot.

> 4 oz (125 g) =
> 1 cup (250 mL) grated

If You Don't Have It
Substitute 1 oz (30 g) Sapsago with:
- 1 oz (30 g) Parmesan (higher in fat; less herbal flavor)
- 1 oz (30 g) Romano (higher in fat; less herbal flavor)
- 1 oz (30 g) dry Jack cheese (higher in fat; more nutty flavor)
- 1 oz (30 g) aged Asiago (higher in fat; less herbal flavor)

Sapucaia Nut

See PARADISE NUT.

Sardines

Not a true variety of fish but rather a generic term applied to various small silvery saltwater fish such as herring, pilchard, and sprats. Said to be a name given to small pilchards — one of the first fish to be packed in oil — caught off the coast of Sardinia.

If You Don't Have It
Substitute 1 lb (500 g) sardines with:
- 1 lb (500 g) anchovies
- 1 lb (500 g) small herring
- 1 lb (500 g) small pilchards
- 1 lb (500 g) sprats
- 1 lb (500 g) shad
- 1 lb (500 g) smelts
- 1 lb (500 g) small mackerel

Sausage

Broadly defined, sausage is a seasoned ground meat mixture stuffed into tubular casings or molded into special shapes.

For Better Health
Substitute 1 lb (500 g) pork sausage with:
- 1 lb (500 g) turkey sausage (less fat and fewer calories)
- 1 lb (500 g) vegetarian sausage (less fat and fewer calories)

See also SPECIFIC TYPES.

Sauté Pan

A wide pan with curved sides designed to brown cutlets, chops, and other foods.

If You Don't Have It
Substitute a sauté pan with:
- frying pan or skillet
- wide saucepan
- wok

Savory

Known in parts of Europe as the bean herb because its pleasant spicy nature benefits beans, peas, and lentils. Summer savory is milder and the spiky leaves are more tender than those of winter savory.

1 oz (30 g) fresh =
⅔ cup (150 mL)

If You Don't Have It
Substitute 1 tbsp (15 mL) chopped fresh savory with:
- 1 tsp (5 mL) dried savory

To Vary the Flavor
Substitute 1 tbsp (15 mL) chopped fresh savory with:
- 2 to 3 tsp (10 to 15 mL) chopped fresh thyme
- 1 to 1½ tsp (5 to 7 mL) chopped fresh thyme + 1 to 1½ tsp (5 to 7 mL) chopped fresh mint
- 1 to 2 tsp (5 to 10 mL) chopped fresh sage
- 2 to 3 tsp (10 to 15 mL) chopped fresh rosemary
- 1 tsp (5 mL) Herbes de Provence (adds other flavors such as thyme, marjoram, lavender, rosemary, fennel, and bay leaf)

Savoy Cabbage

Mellower in flavor than common green cabbage, the leaves of savoy cabbage are also more tender and crinkled.

1 lb (500 g) =
3½ to 4½ cups
(875 mL to 1.125 L)
thinly sliced =
2 cups (500 mL) cooked

If You Don't Have It
Substitute 1 lb (500 g) savoy cabbage with:
- 1 lb (500 g) green cabbage (more crisp; stronger flavor)
- 1 lb (500 g) napa cabbage (wider, white, crunchy stems; more delicate, pale green, mild-tasting leaves)
- 1 lb (500 g) bok choy (wider, white, crunchy stems; larger, darker green leaves)
- 1 lb (500 g) Brussels sprouts

See also CABBAGE.

Sbrinz

A cow's milk grating cheese from Switzerland that is aged for 2 to 3 years. The golden cheese has a brownish rind. Aged for under 2 years, the cheese is called spalen.

> 4 oz (125 g) =
> 1 cup (250 mL) grated

If You Don't Have It

Substitute 1 oz (30 g) Sbrinz with:
- 1 oz (30 g) Saanen
- 1 oz (30 g) Spalen or Sparen (younger)
- 1 oz (30 g) aged Asiago
- 1 oz (30 g) Parmesan (slightly sharper)
- 1 oz (30 g) Grana Padano (slightly sharper)
- 1 oz (30 g) dry Jack cheese (more nutty flavor)

Scallions

Members of the onion family with a white, straight-sided bottom and dark green leaves, both of which are edible. They are slightly milder in flavor than immature green or spring onions.

> 1 bunch = 5 oz (150 g) =
> 10 scallions =
> 1 cup (250 mL) chopped
> (white part only) =
> 3½ cups (875 mL)
> chopped (white and
> green parts)

If You Don't Have It

Substitute 1 bunch scallions (white and green parts) with:
- 1 bunch green onions (slightly stronger flavor)
- 1 bunch ramps (wild leeks; milder flavor)
- 3 to 4 cups (750 mL to 1 L) chopped leeks (milder flavor)
- 3 to 4 cups (750 mL to 1 L) chopped chives (milder flavor; best raw or lightly cooked)

To Vary the Flavor

Substitute 1 bunch scallions with:
- 3 cups (750 mL) chopped garlic chives (adds garlic flavor)
- 3 cups (750 mL) chopped Chinese garlic stems (adds pungent garlic flavor and crunch)

See also ONION, GREEN.

Scallopini

See PATTYPAN SQUASH.

Scallops

The fan-shaped shell, joined by the muscle that is called a scallop, is a beloved artistic motif. Scallops fall into two basic groups by size. Bay scallops are about ½ inch (1 cm) in diameter and sea scallops are about

If You Don't Have It

Substitute 1 lb (500 g) scallops with:
- 1 lb (500 g) shark (less creamy)
- 1 lb (500 g) skate (less creamy)
- 1 lb (500 g) mussels (more delicate)
- 1 lb (500 g) clams (smoother)
- 1 lb (500 g) cockles (smoother)
- 1 lb (500 g) oysters (smoother)
- 1 lb (500 g) whelks (tougher)
- 1 lb (500 g) abalone (tougher)

Scallops (cont'd)

1½ inches (4 cm) in diameter. Fresh scallops should be ivory to pale pink in color. If they are bright white, shiny, and clumping together, they have most likely been soaked in brine, which dilutes the flavor and increases the weight (and price). For the best quality and value, look for unsoaked, or "dry," scallops, which remain separate and retain their ivory or pale pink color.

> 1 lb (500 g) =
> 100 bay scallops
> or 30 sea scallops

- 1 lb (500 g) shrimp (firmer)
- 1 lb (500 g) lobster (firmer)
- 1 lb (500 g) monkfish (firmer)
- 1 lb (500 g) cod (flakier)

Scallop Varieties

Choose 1 lb (500 g) scallops from these varieties:

- 1 lb (500 g) bay scallops (about ½ inch/1 cm in diameter; delicate, moist texture; very sweet flavor; usually available only winter in eastern North America)
- 1 lb (500 g) calico scallops (about ½ inch/1 cm in diameter; less delicate texture than bay scallops; sweet flavor; best when very briefly and gently cooked)
- 1 lb (500 g) sea scallops (about 1½ inch/4 cm in diameter; firmer than bay scallops; mildly sweet flavor)

Scamorza

Also known as scamorze and scamorzo. Fashioned in small ovals or gourd shapes, this mild Italian cheese is like a firm, salty mozzarella. It is sometimes available smoked.

> 1 lb (500 g) = 4 cups
> (1 L) shredded

If You Don't Have It

Substitute 1 oz (30 g) scamorza with:

- 1 oz (30 g) mozzarella (moister)
- 1 oz (30 g) Caciocavallo
- 1 oz (30 g) provolone
- 1 oz (30 g) string cheese
- 1 oz (30 g) queso blanco
- 1 oz (30 g) young kashkaval
- 1 oz (30 g) Bel Paese
- 1 oz (30 g) Muenster
- 1 oz (30 g) Gouda
- 1 oz (30 g) Fontina

Schinkenwurst

Also known as Bierschinken and ham bologna. A German cold cut with chunks of ham suspended in a bologna sausage.

If You Don't Have It

Substitute 1 lb (500 g) Schinkenwurst with:

- 1 lb (500 g) Bierwurst (firmer)
- 1 lb (500 g) cervelat (firmer)
- 1 lb (500 g) Jagdwurst (firmer)
- 1 lb (500 g) Bierschinken (includes pistachios)
- 1 lb (500 g) mortadella (may include pistachios)

Schmaltz

Rendered chicken fat used in Ashkenazi Jewish cooking as a spread and frying fat. It is sometimes flavored with apple, onion, and other seasonings.

If You Don't Have It
Substitute 1 cup (250 mL) schmaltz with:

- 1 cup (250 mL) Homemade Schmaltz: Put skin and fat from 4 medium chickens (4 to 5 packed cups/1 to 1.25 L) in a deep nonstick skillet or sauté pan and cook over low heat until fat melts. Increase heat to medium-low and add 1 sliced medium onion (and ½ cup/125 mL grated apple and/or 1 sliced garlic clove, if you like). Cook until the onions are golden brown. Let cool slightly then strain the fat into a glass jar or other airtight container, discarding solids (or use solids for another purpose). Refrigerate for up to 6 months. Makes about 2 cups (500 mL).
- 1 cup (250 mL) rendered, strained duck fat (preferably rendered with onions in pan)
- 1 cup (250 mL) rendered, strained goose fat (preferably rendered with onions in pan)
- 1 cup (250 mL) margarine or vegetable shortening (preferably heated with onions then strained; much less flavorful)

For Better Health
- 1 cup (250 mL) vegetable oil (preferably heated with onions then strained; much less flavorful)

Schnapps

See SPECIFIC TYPES.

Scone

A Scottish/British quick bread traditionally cooked on a griddle but now most often baked. Similar in texture to American biscuits.

If You Don't Have It
Substitute 1 scone with:

- 1 wedge shortcake
- 1 American biscuit (preferably made with sugar in dough)
- 1 crumpet (less sweet; less crumbly; more airy)
- 1 English muffin (less sweet; less crumbly; more airy)
- 1 croissant (preferably sweetened; richer; flakier)

Scorzonera

See SALSIFY.

Scotch

See WHISKEY.

Scotch Salmon

See SMOKED SALMON.

Scrapple

Enjoyed mostly in northeastern America, this savory Pennsylvania Dutch pudding loaf is made from pork scraps, cornmeal mush, and seasonings. After it firms, scrapple is sliced and fried.

If You Don't Have It

Substitute 1 lb (500 g) scrapple with:
- 1 lb (500 g) goetta (a similar loaf made with sausage and oatmeal)
- 1 lb (500 g) loose breakfast sausage
- 1 lb (500 g) hash
- 1 lb (500 g) bacon

Screwpine Leaf

Also known as pandanus and rampe leaf. The palm-like leaves of the screwpine tree average about 2 feet (61 cm) in length. Their sweet, grassy flavor lends a subtle fragrance and green color to many southeast Asian dishes. Look for screwpine leaves fresh, frozen, or dried in Asian markets. Green pandan paste and essence are also available. Kewra, a floral-scented essence used in sweet and savory dishes, is made from the flowers of a related variety of pandanus.

If You Don't Have It

Substitute 1 fresh screwpine leaf with:
- ½ to 1 tsp (2 to 5 mL) screwpine or pandan powder
- ½ tsp (2 mL) pandan paste
- 1 drop pandan essence + 1 small drop green food coloring
- 1 drop green food coloring (for color only)

Scrod

See COD.

Scungilli

See WHELK.

Scup

See PORGY.

Sea Bass

See BLACK SEA BASS.

Sea Bream

See PORGY.

Sea Devil

See MONKFISH.

Sea Lettuce

An ocean vegetable that spans the globe. The crinkled leaves turn from pale to dark green as the plant matures.

If You Don't Have It
Substitute 1 oz (30 g) sea lettuce with:
- 1 oz (30 g) kelp
- 1 oz (30 g) nori
- 1 oz (30 g) wakame
- 1 oz (30 g) dulse

Sea Pickle

See SALICORNIA.

Sea Salt

See SALT; TRADING SALTS (PAGE 602).

Sea Snail

See PERIWINKLE.

Seasoned Salt

Regular table salt blended and packaged with various seasonings for convenience. Popular types include celery salt, garlic salt, onion salt, and proprietary blends such as Lawry's Seasoned Salt.

If You Don't Have It
Substitute 1 tsp (5 mL) seasoned salt with:
- 1 tsp (5 mL) Homemade Seasoned Salt: Combine 1 tbsp (15 mL) salt, ⅛ tsp (0.5 mL) paprika, ⅛ tsp (0.5 mL) granulated sugar, a pinch of onion powder, and a pinch of garlic powder. Makes 1 generous tablespoon (15 mL).
- 1 tsp (5 mL) Beau Monde® Seasoning
- ½ tsp to ¾ tsp (2 to 4 mL) table salt
- ½ tsp (2 mL) Mei Yen seasoning

For Better Health
Substitute 1 tsp (5 mL) seasoned salt with:
- 1 tsp (5 mL) herbal salt substitute (no sodium)

See also HERBAL SALT SUBSTITUTE; SALT.

Sea Trout

See CROAKER.

Sea Vegetables

See AGAR; ARAME; CARRAGEEN; DULSE; HIJIKI; KOMBU; LAVER; NORI; SALICORNIA; SEA LETTUCE; WAKAME.

Seaweed

See ARAME; CARRAGEEN; DULSE; HIJIKI; KOMBU; LAVER; NORI; WAKAMI.

Seckel Pear

See PICKING PEARS (PAGE 565).

Seitan

Also known as wheat meat. A vegetarian meat replacement produced from wheat gluten. Its bland flavor and chewy texture lend it to a variety of seasonings.

If You Don't Have It

Substitute 1 lb (500 g) seitan with:
- 1 lb (500 g) tempeh (stronger flavor)
- 1 lb (500 g) extra-firm tofu, pressed of excess water (softer texture)
- 1 lb (500 g) extra-firm tofu, frozen then pressed of excess water (more spongy texture)
- 1 lb (500 g) portobello mushroom caps (adds mushroom flavor)
- 1 lb (500 g) prepared vegetarian meat substitute (available refrigerated and frozen in many grocery stores)

Self-Rising Cornmeal

See CORNMEAL, SELF-RISING.

Self-Rising Flour

See FLOUR, SELF-RISING.

Selles-sur-Cher

See CHÈVRE.

Seltzer

See SODA WATER.

Semolina

See FLOUR, SEMOLINA.

Sereh

See LEMONGRASS.

Serrano Chile

See CHOOSING DRIED CHILES (PAGE 578); CHOOSING FRESH CHILES (PAGE 582).

Serrano Ham

Spanish "mountain ham" that is dry-salted and aged for a year or more.

If You Don't Have It

Substitute 1 oz (30 g) Serrano ham with:
- 1 oz (30 g) Iberico ham
- 1 oz (30 g) prosciutto (di Parma or di San Daniele)
- 1 oz (30 g) Ardennes ham (adds smoke flavor)
- 1 oz (30 g) Bayonne ham (adds smoke flavor)
- 1 oz (30 g) Westphalian ham (adds smoke and juniper flavors)
- 1 oz (30 g) York ham (adds smoke flavor)
- 1 oz (30 g) Smithfield or other Virginia ham (adds smoke flavor)

Sesame Butter

A thick paste made from ground toasted unhulled sesame seeds. It's similar to tahini but thicker and darker. Store opened sesame butter in the refrigerator.

If You Don't Have It
Substitute 1 cup (250 mL) sesame butter with:
- 1 cup (250 mL) sesame paste (thinner and slightly sweeter)
- 1 cup (250 mL) minus 2 tbsp (25 mL) almond, cashew or peanut butter + 2 tbsp (25 mL) toasted sesame oil
- 1 cup (250 mL) almond, cashew or peanut butter

See also TAHINI.

Sesame Chili Oil

See CHILE OIL; SESAME OIL.

Sesame Oil, Toasted

Also known as dark sesame oil. Of Chinese origin, the oil extracted from roasted sesame seeds is often used as a pungent flavoring for marinades and sauces.

If You Don't Have It
Substitute 1 tsp (5 mL) toasted sesame oil with:
- 2 tsp (10 mL) sesame seeds, toasted, crushed and mixed with 1 tsp (5 mL) peanut oil (adds texture of crushed seeds to dish)
- 2 tsp (10 mL) tahini (thicker than oil and lacks toasted flavor)
- 1 tsp (5 mL) hot chili sesame oil (adds spicy flavor)

See also SESAME OIL, UNTOASTED; SUBSTITUTING OILS (PAGE 598).

Sesame Oil, Untoasted

Cooking oil pressed from sesame seeds is high in polyunsaturated fatty acids and has good keeping qualities. It is very highly esteemed in Japan.

If You Don't Have It
Substitute 1 tbsp (15 mL) untoasted sesame oil with:
- $\frac{1}{2}$ tsp (2 mL) toasted sesame oil + $2\frac{1}{2}$ tsp (12 mL) vegetable oil

See also SESAME OIL, TOASTED; SUBSTITUTING OILS (PAGE 598).

Sesame Paste

See TAHINI.

Sesame Salt

See GOMASHIO.

Sesame Seeds

Also known as benne seeds. Minuscule seeds of a very tall annual herb of African and Indian origin. Distinctively nutty and sweet, the seeds are widely employed as a flavoring ingredient in Eastern Mediterranean, Middle Eastern, Indian, Chinese, and Japanese cooking. Depending upon the variety, sesame seeds can be white, yellow, brown, or black.

1 oz (30 g) =
3 tbsp (45 mL)

If You Don't Have It

Substitute 1 tbsp (15 mL) sesame seeds with:
- 1 tbsp (15 mL) white or black poppy seeds
- 1 tbsp (15 mL) pumpkin seeds (much larger)
- 1 tbsp (15 mL) finely chopped peanuts
- 1 tbsp (15 mL) finely chopped almonds
- 1 tbsp (15 mL) finely chopped cashews

Sesame Seed Varieties

Choose 1 tbsp (15 mL) sesame seeds from these varieties:
- 1 tbsp (15 mL) muki goma or hulled white sesame seeds (white color; mild sesame flavor)
- 1 tbsp (15 mL) shiro goma or unhulled white sesame seeds (beige color; mild sesame flavor; slightly more bitter)
- 1 tbsp (15 mL) kuro goma or black sesame seeds (stronger sesame flavor)

Seven-Spice Seasoning

See SHICHIMI TOGARASHI.

Seville Orange

See ORANGE, SOUR.

Shad

This large member of the herring family tastes good but challenges cooks (and diners) with its many tiny bones. The American Micmac tribe has a legend that shad was formerly a porcupine that asked the Great Spirit Manitou to change it into another creature. The spirit turned the porcupine inside out and tossed it into a river, where it became a shad. The roe from shad is a springtime delicacy.

If You Don't Have It

Substitute 1 lb (500 g) shad with:
- 1 lb (500 g) herring (smaller)
- 1 lb (500 g) sardines (smaller)
- 1 lb (500 g) pilchards
- 1 lb (500 g) smelt
- 1 lb (500 g) mackerel
- 1 lb (500 g) bluefish
- 1 lb (500 g) blackfish

See also CHANGING ROE (PAGE 594).

Shaddock

See PUMMELO.

Shallot

*An allium that's much
loved in French and
Asian cooking. Smaller
and more delicately
flavored than an ordinary
round onion, a shallot
divides into a cluster of
small bulbs with skins
that are grayish brown,
golden, pale pink, or red.*

1 lb (500 g) = 4 cups (1 L) chopped
1 medium shallot = ½ to 1 oz (15 to 30 g) = 1 tbsp (15 mL) minced

If You Don't Have It
Substitute 1 chopped shallot with:
* 1 tsp (5 mL) freeze-dried shallots (much less flavorful)

To Vary the Flavor
Substitute 1 chopped shallot with:
* ¼ cup (50 mL) chopped ramps or wild leeks (light part only)
* ¼ cup (50 mL) chopped leeks or storage onions + ½ tsp (2 mL) minced garlic (red onions work well)
* ¼ cup (50 mL) chopped green onions or scallions (white and light green parts part only)
* ¼ cup (50 mL) chopped sweet or storage onions (more pungent; red onions work well)

Shao Mai Skins

See WON TON SKINS.

Shaoxing Wine

*Chinese yellow grain
rice wine. Its unique
flavor is essential in
many Chinese dishes.*

If You Don't Have It
Substitute ½ cup (125 mL) Shaoxing wine with:
* ½ cup (125 mL) sake
* ½ cup (125 mL) dry vermouth
* ½ cup (125 mL) dry sherry
* ½ cup (125 mL) flat beer (preferably lager)

Shark

*Edible species include
angel shark, dogfish,
hammer-head shark, and
porbeagle. Despite their
terrifying reputation, the
odds are stacked against
the shark. For each person
a shark attacks, one
million sharks are
captured by fishermen.*

If You Don't Have It
Substitute 1 lb (500 g) shark with:
* 1 lb (500 g) mahi-mahi
* 1 lb (500 g) pompano
* 1 lb (500 g) swordfish
* 1 lb (500 g) marlin
* 1 lb (500 g) tuna

Sharlyn Melon

The netted outer layer covers a greenish orange rind. The sweet white flesh tastes like a blend of cantaloupe and honeydew melon.

2 lbs (1 kg) =
3 cups (750 mL) diced

If You Don't Have It

Substitute 1 cup (250 mL) chopped Sharlyn melon with:

- 1 cup (250 mL) chopped Spanish melon (pale green flesh)
- 1 cup (250 mL) chopped Ogen melon (greener flesh)
- 1 cup (250 mL) chopped Galia melon (greener flesh)
- 1 cup (250 mL) chopped Crenshaw melon (orange flesh)
- 1 cup (250 mL) chopped Persian melon (orange flesh)
- 1 cup (250 mL) chopped Charentais melon (orange flesh)
- 1 cup (250 mL) chopped cantaloupe (orange flesh)
- 1 cup (250 mL) chopped honeydew melon (pale green flesh)

Sharpening Steel

Also known as a butcher's steel. A steel doesn't really sharpen a knife blade; it only keeps the blade honed after it has been sharpened on a stone.

If You Don't Have It

Substitute a sharpening steel with:

- whetstone (to sharpen the blade)
- electric knife-sharpener or honer

Sheepshead

See PORGY.

Shelling Beans

See BLACK-EYED PEAS, FRESH; CRANBERRY BEAN; EDAMAME; FAVA BEAN; LIMA BEAN; PEAS, SHELLING.

Shelling Peas

See PEAS, SHELLING.

Sherry

This fortified wine, developed in the southern Spanish city of Jerez, is now internationally imitated with varying levels of success. The Spanish solera system produces wines of consistent quality year

If You Don't Have It

Substitute 2 tbsp (25 mL) sherry with:

- 2 tbsp (25 mL) dry vermouth (especially for sauces and soups)
- 2 tbsp (25 mL) sake (especially for sauces and soups)
- 2 tbsp (25 mL) dry white wine + pinch of sugar (especially for sauces and soups)
- 2 tbsp (25 mL) Madeira (darker color)

after year by using recently made sherry to top off older wines. Sherries come in a range of colors, flavors, and sweetness. Fino is pale and very dry, best enjoyed young and served chilled. Manzanilla is like a fino but with a hint of saltiness from the seaside town in which it is produced. Amontillado, a medium sherry also known as milk sherry, is aged longer and is typically sweeter, darker, and more mellow than a fino. Oloroso, also known as cream or golden sherry, is darker, sweeter, and the most robust. Best enjoyed at room temperature.

- 2 tbsp (25 mL) Port (redder color)
- 2 tbsp (25 mL) unsweetened orange juice or apple juice + ⅛ tsp (0.5 mL) vanilla extract (to replace sweet sherry)

Sherry Varieties
Choose 2 tbsp (25 mL) sherry from these varieties:
- 2 tbsp (25 mL) fino sherry (very dry, light-bodied, and pale silvery gold in color; delicate flavor; often served chilled)
- 2 tbsp (25 mL) Manzanilla sherry (a type of fino sherry; very dry, light-bodied, and pale silvery gold in color; delicate flavor with a whiff of sea air; often served chilled)
- 2 tbsp (25 mL) Amontillado or milk sherry (an aged fino sherry; medium-dry, medium-bodied, and light gold in color; stronger, more nutty flavor than fino sherries)
- 2 tbsp (25 mL) oloroso sherry (sweet, medium- to full-bodied, and golden in color; stronger, more complex flavor than fino or Amontillado sherries)
- 2 tbsp (25 mL) cream sherry (a type of oloroso sherry; sweet, medium- to full-bodied, and golden in color; fuller flavor than fino or Amontillado sherries)
- 2 tbsp (25 mL) Amoroso sherry (a type of oloroso sherry; sweet, medium- to full-bodied, and golden in color; fuller flavor than fino or Amontillado sherries)

Shichimi Togarashi

Also known as seven-spice powder. "Shichimi togarashi is a popular condiment used to enhance the flavor of noodle, hot-pot, and stir-fried dishes," writes Hiroko Shimbo, author of The Japanese Kitchen. *"At noodle restaurants in Japan, a small glass or wooden jar of seven-spice powder appears on every table."*

If You Don't Have It
Substitute 1 tsp (5 mL) shichimi togarashi with:
- 1 tsp (5 mL) Homemade Shichimi Togarashi: Toast 1 tbsp (15 mL) crushed red pepper flakes, 2 tsp (10 mL) whole Szechuan peppercorns (or use untoasted powdered sansho leaves), and 1 tsp (5 mL) white sesame seeds in a dry skillet over medium heat until fragrant, 2 to 4 minutes. Let cool and mix with 1 tsp (5 mL) dried orange peel (preferably mandarin orange), 1 tsp (5 mL) crushed nori or dark green seaweed, ¼ tsp (1 mL) white poppy seeds, and ¼ tsp (1 mL) hemp seeds (optional). Coarsely grind in a spice grinder, clean coffee grinder, or with a mortar and pestle. Makes about 3 tablespoons (45 mL).
- ¾ tsp (4 mL) cayenne pepper + ¼ tsp (1 mL) sesame seeds (much less flavorful)

Shiitake

See SHUFFLING MUSHROOMS (PAGE 572).

Shimeji

See SHUFFLING MUSHROOMS (PAGE 572).

Shiso

Also known as Japanese basil and perilla. This annual herb has been cultivated in Japan since the 8th century. The jagged-edged green leaf, minty and refreshing, is used in salads, sushi, sashimi, tempura, and other dishes. A reddish purple variety, called akajiso, is used to color pickled plums (umeboshi).

If You Don't Have It

Substitute 1 fresh shiso leaf with:
- 2 to 3 fresh peppermint leaves (to replace green shiso leaves as garnish)
- 2 to 3 fresh lemon basil or cinnamon basil leaves (to replace green shiso leaves as garnish)
- 2 to 3 fresh purple ruffle basil leaves (to replace red shiso leaves; adds clove-like flavors)

Shiso Varieties

Choose 1 fresh shiso leaf from these varieties:
- 1 fresh green shiso leaf (bright green leaf with jagged edges; highly aromatic perfume reminiscent of mint)
- 1 fresh red shiso leaf (ruffled maroon leaf with jagged edges; less aromatic than green shiso leaf; often used for color and flavor in pickled foods such as umeboshi plums and ginger)

Shokupan

In Japanese, the word literally means "eating bread." This white, rectangular loaf — enriched with eggs, butter, and cream — is an adaptation of Western factory bread.

If You Don't Have It

Substitute 1 lb (500 g) shokupan with:
- 1 lb (500 g) brioche
- 1 lb (500 g) challah (less rich)
- 1 lb (500 g) croissants (less eggy, more airy texture)
- 1 lb (500 g) Kugelhopf (filled with dried and candied fruit and nuts)

Shortbread

This crumbly, buttery cookie is traditionally linked with the yule season in Scotland. It is baked in a round decorative earthenware mold, which is notched around the edges to represent beams of sunlight.

If You Don't Have It

Substitute 1 lb (500 g) shortbread cookies with:
- 1 lb (500 g) butter cookies (more crisp)

Shortcake

A rich, sweet, and tender biscuit — either baked as a single large round or individual rounds.

If You Don't Have It
Substitute 1 wedge shortcake with:
- 1 scone
- 1 American biscuit (preferably made with sugar in dough)
- 1 slice pound cake (richer; moister; sweeter)
- 1 crumpet (less sweet; less crumbly; more airy)

Shortening

See VEGETABLE SHORTENING.

Shottsuru

See FISH SAUCE.

Shoyu

See SOY SAUCE.

Shredder

See GRATER.

Shrimp

While marketing names vary shrimp are classified by size indicating the number of shrimp per pound.

If You Don't Have It
Substitute 1 lb (500 g) shrimp with:
- 1 lb (500 g) prawns (especially to replace jumbo shrimp)
- 1 lb (500 g) Dublin Bay prawns (especially to replace jumbo shrimp)
- 1 lb (500 g) crayfish (especially to replace rock shrimp)
- 1 lb (500 g) crab (less firm)
- 1 lb (500 g) lobster (more expensive; firmer)
- 1 lb (500 g) scallops (moister)

Shrimp Varieties
Choose 1 lb (500 g) shrimp from these popular varieties:
- 1 lb (500 g) brown, gray, California or bay shrimp (tiny shrimp that turn brown or gray when briefly cooked)
- 1 lb (500 g) northern or pink shrimp (pink body; small to medium size; found in the Atlantic and Pacific)
- 1 lb (500 g) Gulf pink shrimp (red or light brown shell; relatively large)

Shrimp (cont'd)

1 lb (500 g) in shell =
8 oz (250 g) shelled =
2 cups (500 mL) cooked

1 lb (500 g) colossal =
10 or fewer shrimp

1 lb (500 g) jumbo =
11 to 15 shrimp

1 lb (500 g) extra-large =
16 to 20 shrimp

1 lb (500 g) large =
21 to 30 shrimp

1 lb (500 g) medium =
31 to 35 shrimp

1 lb (500 g) small =
36 to 45 shrimp

1 lb (500 g) miniature =
about 100 shrimp

- 1 lb (500 g) Pacific white shrimp (medium-size with a somewhat clear shell and blue green hues on the legs and tail; among the popular farmed varieties)
- 1 lb (500 g) Gulf brown and white shrimp (brown are medium-size with a brown shell; white are medium-size with a somewhat clear shell and blue green hues on the legs and tail)
- 1 lb (500 g) California or Monterey spot prawns (actually a type of shrimp; white spots on body; medium to relatively large)
- 1 lb (500 g) black tiger shrimp (grayish black strips on a thick shell; relatively large; popular farmed variety)

See also PRAWN; SHRIMP, DRIED.

Shrimp Boil

See CRAB BOIL.

Shrimp Chips

Chinese snack that's popular in Indonesia, these crisp nibblers are made from tapioca flour and shrimp paste. When dropped into hot oil, shrimp chips puff up instantaneously.

If You Don't Have It

Substitute 1 lb (500 g) shrimp chips with:
- 1 lb (500 g) crackling or fried pork rinds (crunchier; adds pork flavor)
- 1 lb (500 g) pappadam (thinner; more brittle; lacks shrimp flavor)
- 1 lb (500 g) crisp lavash (thinner; lacks shrimp flavor)
- 1 lb (500 g) water crackers (thinner; more brittle; lacks shrimp flavor)

Shrimp, Dried

Small dried shrimp are often used in Asian and Latin American kitchens for their concentrated pungent seafood flavor. They are available whole, chopped, or ground into powder.

If You Don't Have It

Substitute 1 oz (30 g) whole dried shrimp with:
- 1 oz (30 g) whole dried crayfish (less fishy aroma)

Shrimp Paste

Also known as bagoong, blacang, kapi, and terasi. Pungent seasoning paste made from fermented shrimp.

If You Don't Have It
Substitute 1 tsp (5 mL) shrimp paste with:
- 1 mashed anchovy fillet (less pungent)
- 1 tsp (5 mL) anchovy paste (less pungent)

See also SHRIMP SAUCE.

Shrimp Powder

See SHRIMP, DRIED.

Shrimp Sauce

Also known as patis (Philippines) and hom ha (Hong Kong). This moist version of shrimp paste is used as a condiment and seasoning in Southeast Asian cookery.

If You Don't Have It
Substitute 1 tbsp (15 mL) shrimp sauce with:
- 1 tbsp (15 mL) fish sauce (less pungent)
- 2 mashed anchovy fillets or 2 tsp (10 mL) anchovy paste + 1 tsp (5 mL) soy sauce (less pungent; thicker)

See also SHRIMP PASTE.

Shropshire Blue

A relatively new blue cheese created in the 1970s by Mrs. Hutchinson Smith in Shropshire, England. Shropshire Blue is similar to Stilton in shape and texture but with a sharper flavor and bright orange color created with annatto.

If You Don't Have It
Substitute 1 oz (30 g) Shropshire Blue with:
- 1 oz (30 g) Blue Cheshire (mellower)
- 1 oz (30 g) Stilton (slightly mellower; lacks orange color)
- 1 oz (30 g) Blue Wensleydale (lacks orange color)
- 1 oz (30 g) Roquefort (lacks orange color)
- 1 oz (30 g) Maytag Blue (lacks orange color)
- 1 oz (30 g) Gorgonzola (creamier; lacks orange color)

Sichuan Pepper

See SZECHUAN PEPPER.

Sierra Ibores

Also known as queso Ibores. Traditional Spanish unpasteurized goat's milk cheese that is now produced commercially in small modern dairies. The rind is rubbed with paprika and olive oil, while the cheese itself is firm, almost crumbly, yet buttery on the tongue.

If You Don't Have It
Substitute 1 oz (30 g) Sierra Ibores with:
- 1 oz (30 g) aged Manchego (made with sheep's milk)
- 1 oz (30 g) Romano (especially Caprino Romano made with goat's milk)
- 1 oz (30 g) Parmesan (made with cow's milk)
- 1 oz (30 g) aged Asiago (made with cow's milk)

Sieve

See STRAINER.

Sifter

Washing a flour sifter is likely to gum up the works. To clean, simply tap the sifter to remove all solid particles then wipe with a clean dry paper towel.

If You Don't Have It
Substitute a sifter with:
- fine-mesh strainer or sieve
- fine-holed shaker (for quickly sifting small amounts of a single ingredient such as confectioner's sugar, flour, or cocoa powder for dusting)

Silken Tofu

See TOFU.

Silverwasser

Also known as Silberwasser. "Silver water" is a European herbal liqueur made glamorous by adding particles of silver.

If You Don't Have It
Substitute 2 tbsp (25 mL) Silverwasser with:
- 2 tbsp (25 mL) Goldwasser (includes gold instead of silver flakes)
- 2 tbsp (25 mL) Kümmel
- 2 tbsp (25 mL) aquavit
- 2 tbsp (25 mL) Liqueur d'Or
- 2 tbsp (25 mL) Strega

Simple Syrup

See SUGAR SYRUP.

Single-Malt Scotch

See WHISKEY.

Single-Malt Whiskey

See WHISKEY.

Skate

Also known as skate wing and ray. The fins (wings) are the edible part of this fish and have a flavor and texture reminiscent of scallops. To remove the characteristic ammonia odor, skate is soaked in acidulated water before cooking.

If You Don't Have It
Substitute 1 lb (500 g) skate with:
- 1 lb (500 g) sea scallops
- 1 lb (500 g) crab

Skewer

From Italian spiedini *to Indonesian* satay, *long thin pointed rod is utilized by cooks around the world as an efficient tool to hold small pieces of food together during cooking.*

If You Don't Have It
Substitute metal skewers with:
- double metal skewers (these have two long prongs to prevent food from spinning around)
- bamboo skewers (soak in liquid for 20 minutes to prevent burning; food cooks slightly more slowly because wood doesn't conduct heat as well as metal)
- stiff rosemary sprigs (remove leaves from sprigs or let the leaves be; adds wonderful rosemary aroma)
- stiff stainless-steel wire (in a pinch)

To Save Time
Substitute metal skewers with:
- no skewers (if chunks of food are large enough to be grilled without falling through the grill rack, just toss them on the grill)

Skillet

See FRYING PAN.

Skim Milk

See MILK, FAT-FREE.

Skipjack

See TUNA, FRESH.

Slivovitz

See PLUM BRANDY.

Sloe

A wild, European purple plum with bitingly tart yellow flesh. Sweetened, they make wonderful jam and jellies.

If You Don't Have It
Substitute 1 lb (500 g) sloes with:
- 1 lb (500 g) Damson, Mirabelle, greengage or other tart plums

See also SLOE GIN.

Sloe Gin

A sweet, gin-based liqueur flavored with sloe plums. It is aged in wood-barrels and has a red color.

If You Don't Have It
Substitute 2 tbsp (25 mL) sloe gin with:
- 2 tbsp (25 mL) Homemade Sloe Gin: Freeze 1 lb (500 g) washed fresh sloes until the skins burst, about 2 to 3 days (or pick fresh sloes after the first frost has burst the skins; alternatively, prick the skins to expose the fruit to the gin). Separate the frozen sloes from one another and put them in a large glass jar or bottle to thaw

Sloe Gin (cont'd)

along with 1½ tsp (7 mL) chopped fresh almonds and 2 whole cloves, if you like. Pour in 2 cups (500 mL) gin and 1 cup (250 mL) brown or granulated sugar. Seal and store in a cupboard or other dark place, shaking the jar several times a week until the sugar dissolves, about 4 to 6 weeks. Then shake about once a week for another 2 to 3 months. Strain the liquid into a glass jar or bottle (discard the sloes or save them to make a tipsy crisp or crumble). Let the sloe gin age in the bottle for at least 3 more months before drinking. Makes about 2 cups (500 mL).

- 2 tbsp (25 mL) prunelle (pale green to dark amber plum brandy; sweeter and thicker; made from sloes)
- 2 tbsp (25 mL) slivovitz (colorless plum brandy; bittersweet; may be made from different plum varieties)
- 2 tbsp (25 mL) quetsch plum brandy (colorless plum brandy; bittersweet; made with Alsatian quetch plums)
- 2 tbsp (25 mL) Mirabelle (colorless plum brandy; sweet; made with golden Mirabelle plums)
- 2 tbsp (25 mL) grappa
- 2 tbsp (25 mL) other fruit brandy such as apricot

See also SLOE.

Slotted Spoon

A large spoon perforated with slots or holes enabling foods to be lifted out of a pot and drained simultaneously.

If You Don't Have It

Substitute a slotted spoon with:
- Chinese spider strainer
- small mesh strainer
- tongs or pasta spoon (for plucking or scooping foods out of hot liquid)
- colander nested in larger heatproof bowl or pot (for draining foods and saving liquid)

Slow Cooker

An electric pot, such as Crock-Pot®, designed to cook foods very slowly over the course of several hours.

If You Don't Have It

- covered casserole or heavy heatproof dish and an oven or burner set to low (for stews and braises; requires more attention from the cook)

Smelt

Also known as sparling. This small silvery fish spawns a cult following each spring when warm days and rainy evenings trigger their annual runs from lakes to tributary streams. Easily caught at night in nets, the fish are tasty when battered, fried, and eaten whole.

If You Don't Have It

Substitute 1 lb (500 g) smelt with:
- 1 lb (500 g) shad
- 1 lb (500 g) pilchards
- 1 lb (500 g) anchovies (smaller; stronger flavor)
- 1 lb (500 g) sardines (smaller; stronger flavor)
- 1 lb (500 g) herring (smaller)
- 1 lb (500 g) mackerel

Smelt Varieties

Choose 1 lb (500 g) smelt from these varieties:
- 1 lb (500 g) rainbow smelt (primarily Atlantic variety)
- 1 lb (500 g) whitebait (Pacific variety)
- 1 lb (500 g) eulachon or candlefish (Pacific variety)

Smithfield Ham

See VIRGINIA HAM.

Smoked Haddock

See FINNAN HADDIE.

Smoked Sablefish

See SABLEFISH.

Smoked Salmon

Many different styles exist but basically fall into one of two categories: cold-smoked or hot-smoked. Cold-smoking, which usually produces a more delicate result, is done in temperatures ranging from 70° to 90°F (21° to 32°C) for as briefly as a day or as long as several weeks. Danish-smoked, Irish-smoked, and Scotch-smoked are all cold-smoked, regional Atlantic salmon. The generic moniker "smoked salmon" typically refers to cold-smoked Pacific varieties. European kippered salmon is a split whole salmon that is brined

If You Don't Have It

Substitute 1 lb (500 g) smoked salmon with:
- 1 lb (500 g) gravlax (unsmoked salmon; adds dill flavor)
- 1 lb (500 g) cured or smoked arctic char
- 1 lb (500 g) smoked trout
- 1 lb (500 g) smoked black cod or sablefish
- 1 lb (500 g) smoked sturgeon
- 1 lb (500 g) smoked bluefish
- 1 lb (500 g) smoked mackerel
- 1 lb (500 g) smoked haddock or finnan haddie

Smoked Salmon (cont'd)

and cold-smoked. Indian-cured salmon, a type of jerky, is brined before cold-smoking for up to 2 weeks. Lox is brined (sometimes with sugar added) before cold-smoking. Often lox is referred to on the Eastern seaboard as Nova or Nova Scotia salmon. Hot-smoking is done in temperatures ranging from 120°F to 180°F (48° to 82°C) for a period from 6 to 12 hours. American style kippered salmon is brined and hot-smoked. "Squaw candy" is strips of salt-sugar brined salmon that are hot-smoked.

Smoked Salmon Varieties

Choose 1 lb (500 g) smoked salmon from these varieties:

- 1 lb (500 g) lox (salt-cured, sometimes with sugar, and cold-smoked)
- 1 lb (500 g) nova or Nova Scotia salmon (cold-smoked Atlantic salmon, often from the eastern coast of North America)
- 1 lb (500 g) Scotch salmon (cold-smoked Atlantic salmon from Scotland; often less salty than lox)
- 1 lb (500 g) Irish salmon (cold-smoked Atlantic salmon from Ireland; often less salty than lox)
- 1 lb (500 g) Danish or Dutch salmon (cold-smoked Atlantic salmon from Denmark; often less salty than lox)
- 1 lb (500 g) "squaw candy" (sweet strips of brine-cured, hot-smoked salmon)
- 1 lb (500 g) kippered salmon (brined, hot-smoked salmon steak, fillet, or chunks)

See also GRAVLAX.

Snapper

There are more than 200 varieties of this medium-size tasty tropical fish with quick-to-snap jaws sporting canine-like teeth. Red snapper is a household name but others are blubberlip snapper, Malabar blood snapper, mutton snapper, schoolmaster, silk snapper, and spotted rose snapper.

If You Don't Have It

Substitute 1 lb (500 g) snapper with:
- 1 lb (500 g) blackfish
- 1 lb (500 g) black sea bass
- 1 lb (500 g) striped bass
- 1 lb (500 g) grouper
- 1 lb (500 g) haddock
- 1 lb (500 g) halibut

Snapper Varieties

Choose 1 lb (500 g) snapper from these varieties:
- 1 lb (500 g) red snapper (medium; pinkish red over entire body; black edge on tail; firm texture; mild flavor; similar to silk snapper and vermilion snapper)
- 1 lb (500 g) vermilion snapper (small; red upper body flecked with yellow and a series of narrow, dotted blue stripes; firm texture; mild flavor; similar to red snapper)
- 1 lb (500 g) silk snapper (small; pinkish upper body with yellow hues; pinkish yellow fins; black edge on tail; firm texture; mild flavor; similar to red snapper)

- 1 lb (500 g) yellowtail snapper (small to medium; wide, yellow stripe from eye to tail; large yellow forked tail; firm texture; mild flavor)
- 1 lb (500 g) mutton snapper (medium; olive green upper body with light blue stripes, especially below eye; lower fins tinged with red; firm texture; mild flavor)
- 1 lb (500 g) school master snapper (small to medium; grayish brown with yellow tinge and reddish tinge near eye; golden yellow fins; dotted or solid blue line beneath eye; firm texture; mild flavor)
- 1 lb (500 g) gray snapper (small to medium; grayish brown upper body with faint reddish vertical rows; darker brown or black near eye; firm texture; mild flavor)

See also RED SNAPPER.

Snow Crab
See CHOOSING AMONG CRABS (PAGE 597).

Snow Peas
See PEAS, EDIBLE POD.

Soba
See A SNAPSHOT OF ASIAN NOODLES (PAGE 588).

Sockeye Salmon
See SALMON.

Soda Cracker
See CRACKER.

Soda Water

Also known as carbonated water, club soda, and seltzer. Bottled bubbly water with a touch of sodium bicarbonate.

If You Don't Have It
Substitute 1 cup (250 mL) soda water with:
- 1 cup (250 mL) sparkling mineral water (may be less fizzy)

Soft-Shell Clam
See SWAPPING CLAMS (PAGE 596).

Soft-Wheat Flour
See FLOUR, CAKE.

Sole

"At the top-tier fish restaurants, you will be served grilled sole correctly. I was served such a sole in a Paris brasserie…," writes Gina Mallet in Last Chance to Eat. *"The fish arrived hot from the grill — a fine fish that filled the plate, for my inspection. Next, the waiter whisked away the plate and boned the fish. He cut all around it, then pulled the spine out in a single movement without disturbing the fish at all. The sole came back to me looking just the same but boneless, with a thick pat of* maître d'butter *melting on top…."*

If You Don't Have It
Substitute 1 lb (500 g) sole with:
- 1 lb (500 g) turbot
- 1 lb (500 g) brill
- 1 lb (500 g) flounder
- 1 lb (500 g) plaice or dab
- 1 lb (500 g) cod
- 1 lb (500 g) haddock
- 1 lb (500 g) pollock
- 1 lb (500 g) whiting

Sole Varieties
Choose 1 lb (500 g) sole from these varieties:
- 1 lb (500 g) Channel or Dover sole (fine, firm texture; mild, superb flavor)
- 1 lb (500 g) sand or French sole (smaller than Dover sole; fine, firm texture; mild flavor)
- 1 lb (500 g) thickback sole (smaller than Dover sole, with a thicker back; fine, firm texture; mild flavor)

See also FLOUNDER.

Somen

See A SNAPSHOT OF ASIAN NOODLES (PAGE 588).

Sope

In Mexican cooking, a small griddle-fried disc of fresh corn tortilla dough, filled with various mixtures.

If You Don't Have It
Substitute 1 sope with:
- 1 chalupa
- 1 arepa
- 1 gordita
- 1 corn tortilla (thinner and stiffer)

Sopressata

See SALAMI.

Sorghum Flour

Ground from the seeds of a cereal grass, this coarse flour lacks gluten and is mostly eaten cooked as porridge or used to make unleavened breads.

If You Don't Have It
Substitute 1 cup (250 mL) sorghum flour with:
- ½ cup (125 mL) yellow cornmeal + ½ cup (125 mL) white cornmeal

Sorghum Molasses

Also known as sorghum or sorghum syrup. Certain cultivars of the cereal grass sorghum are grown for the sweet sap in their thick stems, which is processed into syrup. It is dark brown with a taste close to sugarcane molasses. In America during the 1800s, sorghum molasses provided a cheap alternative to maple syrup.

If You Don't Have It
Substitute 1 cup (250 mL) sorghum molasses with:
- 1 cup (250 mL) golden syrup (thicker)
- 1 cup (250 mL) light or dark corn syrup (less sweet; dark will add darker amber color and caramel flavor)
- 1 cup (250 mL) molasses (darker; less sweet)
- 1 cup (250 mL) honey (sweeter)
- 1 cup (250 mL) pure maple syrup (thinner; adds maple flavor)

Sorrel

Garden sorrel is also known as belleville sorrel, sour dock, and sour grass. Dock sorrel is also called herb patience and spinach dock. A sour green leaf, both wild and cultivated, that becomes more sour with maturity. It can be used raw in salads or cooked into its characteristic sauce-like consistency.

> 1 oz (30 g) fresh =
> 1⅓ cups (325 mL)

If You Don't Have It
Substitute 1 lb (500 g) sorrel with:
- 1 lb (500 g) arugula (more bitter and nutty, less sour flavor)
- 1 lb (500 g) mature spinach + 1 tbsp (15 mL) lemon zest

Sorrel Varieties
Choose 1 lb (500 g) sorrel from these varieties:
- 1 lb (500 g) cultivated or garden sorrel (the most common variety; grass green, elongated, oval, and silken leaves 5 to 9 inches/12.5 to 23 cm long with two points near the stem; tart, citrus-like flavor)
- 1 lb (500 g) sour grass or sheep sorrel (small, grass green, stretched-out oval, silken leaves 2 to 3 inches/5 to 7.5 cm long with two points near the stem; milder than garden sorrel; especially good for salads)
- 1 lb (500 g) sour, yellow or curly dock (deep green, ruffled plume-shaped leaves 4 to 10 inches/10 to 25 cm long, often tinged with red on the stems; more bitter and tough than garden sorrel; becomes more tender and pleasantly sour when cooked)
- 1 lb (500 g) bitter or broadleaf dock (deep green, broad, heart-shaped leaves 3 to 4 inches/7.5 to 10 cm long and tinged with red on the stems; similar to curly dock but more pedestrian, less complex flavor)

Soufflé Dish

The classic round French ceramic baking dish with straight striated sides is designed to promote even heat distribution and ensure a high rise to a soufflé.

If You Don't Have It

Substitute a soufflé dish with:
- ovenproof baking dish + a foil or parchment "collar" wrapped around the lip of the dish to help facilitate rising (soufflé may not rise as high)

Sour Cream

Commercially cultured dairy product that contains from 18 to 20% butterfat. Its creamy tanginess enhances everything from dips to desserts.

8 oz (250 g) =
1 cup (250 mL)

If You Don't Have It

Substitute 1 cup (250 mL) sour cream with:
- 1 cup (250 mL) soy sour cream (adds light beany flavor)
- 1 cup (250 mL) plain yogurt (more tart; baked goods will be slightly less moist)
- 1 cup (250 mL) drained yogurt (for cheesecake or other dishes in which you want the yogurt to set)
- 1 cup (250 mL) crème fraîche
- ⅓ cup (75 mL) melted unsalted butter + ¾ cup (175 mL) buttermilk, soured milk, or plain yogurt (for baking)
- ⅓ cup (75 mL) melted unsalted butter + ¾ cup (175 mL) milk + 1 tsp (5 mL) lemon juice (for baking)
- 1 cup (250 mL) evaporated milk (especially Milnot brand) or whole milk + 1 tbsp (15 mL) vinegar or lemon juice (let stand 5 minutes before using)
- 1 cup (250 mL) cottage cheese (or ½ cup/125 mL cottage cheese + ½ cup/125 mL plain yogurt) blended with 2 tbsp (25 mL) whole milk or buttermilk and 1 to 2 tbsp (15 to 25 mL) lemon juice
- 6 oz (175 g) cream cheese (¾ cup/175 mL) + 3 tbsp (45 mL) whole milk

For Better Health

Substitute 1 cup (250 mL) sour cream with:
- 1 cup (250 mL) reduced-fat or fat-free sour cream
- 1 cup (250 mL) quark (richer texture than reduced-fat sour cream)
- 1 cup (250 mL) reduced-fat or fat-free plain yogurt
- 1 cup (250 mL) fat-free evaporated milk + 1 tbsp (15 mL) lemon juice

Sourdough Bread

Characteristically tangy bread, traditionally associated with San Francisco, takes its special flavor from the starter, or leavening mixture, which is populated with wild strains of yeast.

If You Don't Have It
Substitute 1 lb (500 g) sourdough bread with:
- 1 lb (500 g) relatively tight-crumbed French bread (slightly less tart flavor)
- 1 lb (500 g) relatively tight-crumbed Italian bread (slightly less tart flavor)

Sour Milk

Milk that has been commercially soured with the addition of certain bacteria to produce a tangier, thickened product.

If You Don't Have It
Substitute 1 cup (250 mL) sour milk with:
- 1 tbsp (15 mL) lemon juice or distilled vinegar + enough milk to equal 1 cup (250 mL) (let stand 5 to 10 minutes before using)
- 1 cup (250 mL) buttermilk
- 1 cup (250 mL) plain yogurt

Soursop

Also known as corossol, guanabana, and prickly custard apple. This spiky-skinned tropical American fruit yields acidic, watery flesh. Lives up to its full potential in drinks such as the Puerto Rican carato and Brazilian champola, in which sweetened soursop juice is mixed with milk or water, and colored pink or green.

If You Don't Have It
Substitute 1 lb (500 g) soursop with:
- 1 lb (500 g) cherimoya (smaller)
- 1 lb (500 g) atemoya (smaller; hybrid of sweetsop and cherimoya)
- 1 lb (500 g) sweetsop (smaller)

See also ATEMOYA; CHERIMOYA; SWEETSOP.

Southern Comfort

Potent (100 proof) American liqueur based on bourbon and peaches.

If You Don't Have It
Substitute 2 tbsp (25 mL) Southern Comfort with:
- 2 tbsp (25 mL) rock and rye
- 1 tbsp (15 mL) peach schnapps + 1 tbsp (15 mL) bourbon

For Better Health
Substitute 2 tbsp (25 mL) Southern Comfort with:
- 2 tbsp (25 mL) peach nectar + dash of cider vinegar (no alcohol)

Soybean Curd

See TOFU.

Soybean, Green

See EDAMAME.

Soybean Sprouts

In Chinese cooking, these sprouts are typically cooked in soups and braised dishes. Sprouted soybeans have a yellow tip and more assertive flavor than mung bean sprouts.

If You Don't Have It
Substitute 1 cup (250 mL) soybean sprouts with:
- 1 cup (250 mL) mung bean sprouts
- 1 cup (250 mL) julienned snow peas

See also MUNG BEAN SPROUTS.

Soy Cheese

Imitation cheese made from soy milk may seem like a great alternative for vegans or those with dairy allergies, but many soy cheeses contain the milk protein casein to improve flavor and melting qualities. Check labels if you are concerned.

If You Don't Have It
Substitute 1 oz (30 g) soy cheese with:
- 1 oz (30 g) cow's milk cheese (usually richer; melts better)

Soy Flour

See CHOOSING AMONG WHOLE-GRAIN AND ALTERNATIVE FLOURS (PAGE 586).

Soy Ice Cream

Creamy frozen dessert made from soy milk and either partially hydrogenated soybean oil or palm oil.

If You Don't Have It
Substitute 1 cup (250 mL) soy ice cream with:
- 1 cup (250 mL) cow's milk ice cream (usually richer and creamier)
- 1 cup (250 mL) frozen yogurt

Soy Mayonnaise

Also known as tofu mayonnaise. For those keen on avoiding eggs or saturated fat, tofu replaces the egg in this product.

If You Don't Have It
Substitute 1 cup (250 mL) soy mayonnaise with:
- 1 cup (250 mL) mayonnaise (contains eggs)
- 1 cup (250 mL) soy sour cream
- 1 cup (250 mL) soy yogurt

Soy Milk

The whitish, opaque liquid obtained from pressed ground soybeans is widely marketed as a healthful alternative to dairy milk. It has more protein than cow's milk with less fat and sodium. Calcium is commonly added to make the nutrient content comparable to cow's milk.

If You Don't Have It

Substitute 1 cup (250 mL) soy milk with:

- 1 cup (250 mL) Homemade Soy Milk: Bring 4 cups (1 L) water to a boil. Whisk together 2 cups (500 mL) plain soy flour and 2 cups (500 mL) cold water then whisk the mixture into the boiling water and return to a boil. Reduce the heat to medium-low and gently simmer for 30 minutes, stirring now and then. Strain into a bowl through a sieve or colander lined with cheesecloth, nylon mesh (such as clean nylon stockings), or coffee filters (straining will take longer if using coffee filters). Whisk in ¼ to ½ cup (50 to 125 mL) confectioner's (icing) sugar, ¼ to ½ tsp (1 to 2 mL) vanilla extract, and a pinch of salt, if you like. Makes about 5½ cups (1.375 L).
- 1 cup (250 mL) minus 2 tbsp (25 mL) water + ¼ cup (50 mL) powdered soy milk

To Vary the Flavor

Substitute 1 cup (250 mL) soy milk with:

- 1 cup (250 mL) cow's milk (less sweet; may have more grassy or barnyardy aroma)

For Better Health

Substitute 1 cup (250 mL) soy milk with:

- 1 cup (250 mL) lactose-free cow's milk (for the lactose-intolerant)
- 1 cup (250 mL) acidophilus cow's milk (adds beneficial enzymes)
- 1 cup (250 mL) goat's milk (for the lactose intolerant; more tangy taste)
- 1 cup (250 mL) rice milk (for the lactose intolerant or vegetarians; may be sweetened)
- 1 cup (250 mL) almond milk (for the lactose intolerant or vegetarians; may be sweetened)
- 1 cup (250 mL) oat milk (for the lactose intolerant or vegetarians; may be sweetened)

Soy Nut

Dry roasted soybeans that, like roasted peanuts, make crunchy nibblers.

If You Don't Have It

Substitute 1 cup (250 mL) soy nuts with:

- 1 cup (250 mL) almonds, peanuts, or other nuts (less crunchy)

Soy Sauce

Also known as shoyu (Japanese). A complex, salty brown condiment that's inextricably bound with the cuisines of China, Japan, and other Asian countries. At its most basic, soy sauce is the liquid produced from a long and complex process of fermenting soy beans. Numerous styles exist, just a few of which are described right. One important distinction to note is that Japanese soy sauces (except for tamari) include roasted wheat in the mash, which makes them sweeter than Chinese soy sauces. The Chinese sauces are made primarily from soybeans, sometimes with small amounts of other grains added.

If You Don't Have It

Substitute 1 tbsp (15 mL) soy sauce with:

- 1 tbsp (15 mL) Maggi Seasoning (darker; more complex flavor)
- scant ¾ tsp (4 mL) Kosher salt + ½ tsp (2 mL) granulated sugar dissolved in 1 tbsp (15 mL) hot water (lighter color; less complex flavor)
- 1 tbsp (15 mL) teriyaki sauce (sweeter; thicker)
- 1 tbsp (15 mL) kecap (sweeter, more complex)

Soy Sauce Varieties

Choose 1 tbsp (15 mL) soy sauce from these varieties:

- 1 tbsp (15 mL) light Chinese soy sauce (thin, light-brown, salty sauce; made mostly with soybeans; used often in cooking)
- 1 tbsp (15 mL) dark Chinese soy sauce (dark brown, somewhat salty sauce; thicker and aged longer than light Chinese soy sauce; includes molasses, which enhances sweetness; made mostly with soybeans; used often as a table sauce)
- 1 tbsp (15 mL) Japanese shiro (thin, very light brown, fairly sweet sauce; made mostly with wheat and a relatively low amount of soybeans)
- 1 tbsp (15 mL) Japanese usukuchi (light brown, salty and sweet sauce; sweetness is enhanced through the addition of amasake, a fermented rice drink)
- 1 tbsp (15 mL) Japanese koikuchi (medium brown, gently salty sauce; made with equal parts soybeans and wheat; the most widely used soy sauce in Japan)
- 1 tbsp (15 mL) Japanese saishikomi (dark brown, rich, strong-flavored, gently salty sauce; made with soybeans and wheat)
- 1 tbsp (15 mL) Japanese tamari (dark brown, rich, strong-flavored, gently salty, lightly sweet sauce; made with soybeans and very little or no wheat; similar to dark Chinese soy sauce)
- 1 tbsp (15 mL) Thai sweet black soy sauce (dark brown to black, rich, strong-flavored, gently salty, fairly sweet sauce; made with soybeans; similar to Indonesian kecap)

For Better Health

Substitute 1 tbsp (15 mL) soy sauce with:

- 1 tbsp (15 mL) low-sodium soy sauce

Soy Sour Cream

Soy milk treated with a souring agent to simulate dairy sour cream. It can replace regular sour cream in any recipe.

If You Don't Have It

Substitute 1 cup (250 mL) soy sour cream with:
- 1 cup (250 mL) sour cream (contains cow's milk)
- 1 cup (250 mL) quark (contains cow's milk)
- 1 cup (250 mL) crème fraîche (contains cow's milk)
- 1 cup (250 mL) soy mayonnaise (less tart)
- 1 cup (250 mL) soy yogurt (for dips and soups; more tart)
- 1 cup (250 mL) drained soy yogurt (for cheesecake or other dishes in which you want the yogurt to set)
- 6 oz (175 mL) soy cream cheese (¾ cup/175 mL) + 3 tbsp (45 mL) soy milk

Soy Yogurt

Also known as soygurt. Lactose-free replacement for yogurt is produced by treating soy milk with "good" bacteria. Look for it plain or fruit-flavored in natural food stores.

If You Don't Have It

Substitute 1 cup (250 mL) soy yogurt with:
- 1 cup (250 mL) yogurt (contains cow's milk)
- 1 cup (250 mL) low-lactose yogurt (contains cow's milk; for the lactose intolerant)
- 1 cup (250 mL) goat's milk yogurt (contains goat's milk; for the lactose intolerant)
- 1 cup (250 mL) soy sour cream (thicker; less tart)
- 1 cup (250 mL) cow's milk sour cream (contains cow's milk; thicker; less tart)
- 1 cup (250 mL) silken tofu, blended until smooth (thicker; less tart)
- 1 cup (250 mL) buttermilk (contains cow's milk; thinner; best for baking, dressings, and gently cooked or uncooked sauces)
- 1 cup (250 mL) quark (richer texture)

Spaetzle

Also known as spätzle. German for "little sparrow," this tiny egg dumpling is sometimes made with dough firm enough to be rolled like noodles. But, a more entertaining way to make spaetzle is to push the dough through the holes of a colander into a pot of boiling water.

If You Don't Have It

Substitute 1 lb (500 g) spaetzle with:
- 1 lb (500 g) egg noodles
- 1 lb (500 g) won ton skins

Spaghetti

See PASTA, DRIED STRANDS.

Spaghetti Squash

Also known as vegetable spaghetti. The uncanny resemblance to strands of spaghetti is the calling card of this mild-tasting squash. After the whole squash is cooked, typically by roasting, it is halved and the seeds are removed. The golden flesh is then raked with a fork to separate the filaments. The vegetable can be served as a side dish or sauced and enjoyed like pasta.

1 medium =
5 lbs (2.5 kg) = 6 cups
(1.5 L) cooked strands

If You Don't Have It
Substitute 1 cup (250 mL) cooked spaghetti squash with:
- 1 cup (250 mL) cooked spaghetti or other strand pasta
- 1 cup (250 mL) cooked butternut squash (solid squash instead of strands; creamier)
- 1 cup (250 mL) cooked buttercup squash (solid squash instead of strands; creamier)
- 1 cup (250 mL) cooked banana squash (solid squash instead of strands; creamier; more fruity aromas)
- 1 cup (250 mL) cooked delicata squash (solid squash instead of strands)

Spalen

See SBRINZ.

Spam

Since its creation by the Hormel Company in the 1920s, this canned seasoned pork product has fathered a family of products including Spam® Hickory Smoked Flavored and Spam® Hot & Spicy. As the product promotion says, Spam® is Crazy Tasty!™

If You Don't Have It
Substitute 12 oz (375 g) spam with:
- 12 oz (375 g) canned ham
- 12 oz (375 g) wet-cured ham

For Better Health
Substitute 12 oz (375 g) spam with:
- 12 oz (375 g) "lite" Spam (fewer calories; less fat; less sodium)

Spanish Mackerel

See MACKEREL.

Spanish Melon

*Sweet and succulent
with flavor like Crenshaw
and color like honeydew.
This muskmelon has
a large egg shape with
a ribbed green rind.*

2 lbs (1 kg) =
3 cups (750 mL) diced

If You Don't Have It

Substitute 1 cup (250 mL) chopped Spanish
melon with:
- 1 cup (250 mL) chopped Crenshaw melon
  (orange flesh)
- 1 cup (250 mL) chopped Sharlyn melon
  (pale green flesh)
- 1 cup (250 mL) chopped casaba melon
  (cream-color flesh)
- 1 cup (250 mL) chopped Ogen melon (green flesh)
- 1 cup (250 mL) chopped Galia melon (green flesh)
- 1 cup (250 mL) chopped Persian melon
  (orange flesh)
- 1 cup (250 mL) chopped cantaloupe (orange flesh)
- 1 cup (250 mL) chopped honeydew melon
  (pale green flesh)

Sparkling Mineral Water

*Bottled water taken from a
source such as a spring or
lake. The water contains
natural carbonation and
dissolved minerals.*

If You Don't Have It

Substitute 1 cup (250 mL) sparkling mineral water
with:
- 1 cup (250 mL) soda water, seltzer, club soda,
  or carbonated water (may be more fizzy)
- 1 cup (250 mL) still mineral water (no fizz)

Sparkling Wine

*The strict and precise
méthode champenoise
produces Champagne, the
finest sparkling wine in
the world, only in the
Champagne region of
France. All other French
sparkling wines are known
as* vins mousseux.
*Spanish sparklers
produced by méthode
champenoise are called*
cava. *Italian bubblies are*
spumante *and Germany's
are* seckt. *Natural is drier
than brut. Brut is drier
than extra dry.*

If You Don't Have It

Substitute 1 cup (250 mL) sparkling wine with:
- 1 cup (250 mL) champagne

For Better Health

Substitute 1 cup (250 mL) sparkling wine with:
- 1 cup (250 mL) sparkling cider (no alcohol)

Sparling

See SMELT.

Spatula

Stirring, scraping, and spreading: spatulas perform these tasks and more. These tools come in many sizes and materials including wood, stainless steel, rubber, plastic, acrylic, and silicone.

If You Don't Have It

Substitute a spatula with:
- pancake turner (for turning and gentle scraping or stirring)
- clean flexible spackling knife or dough scraper (for spreading or stirring)

Spätzle

See SPAETZLE.

Spearfish

See MARLIN.

Spelt Flour

See CHOOSING AMONG WHOLE-GRAIN AND ALTERNATIVE FLOURS (PAGE 586).

Spice Parisienne

Also known as épices fines and sel épice. American term for a bottled spice blend based on the French classic sel épice (spiced salt).

If You Don't Have It

Substitute 1 tsp (5 mL) Spice Parisienne with:
- 1 tsp (5 mL) Homemade Spice Parisienne: Combine 1 to 2 crushed bay leaves, 1 tsp (5 mL) ground white pepper, 1 tsp (5 mL) ground black pepper, 1/2 tsp (2 mL) ground nutmeg, 1/2 tsp (2 mL) ground mace, 1/2 tsp (2 mL) ground allspice, 1/2 tsp (2 mL) crushed dried rosemary, 1/2 tsp (2 mL) dried thyme, 1/4 tsp (1 mL) ground cloves, and 1/8 tsp (0.5 mL) ground cinnamon. Add salt to taste. Makes about 2 tablespoons (25 mL).

To Vary the Flavor

Substitute 1 tsp (5 mL) Spice Parisienne with:
- 1 tsp (5 mL) savory quatre épices (for savory dishes)
- 1 tsp (5 mL) sweet quatre épices (for sweet and savory dishes)
- 1/2 tsp (2 mL) ground white or black pepper + 1/2 tsp (2 mL) pumpkin pie spice or apple pie spice

Spices

See SPECIFIC TYPES.

Spider Strainer

See STRAINER.

Spike©

Nutrition guru Gaylord Hauser developed this all-purpose seasoning blend of 39 herbs, vegetables, spices, and salt.

If You Don't Have It
Substitute 1 tsp (5 mL) Spike© seasoning with:
- 1 tsp (5 mL) seasoned salt
- 1 tsp (5 mL) Beau Monde® Seasoning
- ½ tsp (2 mL) table salt

For Better Health
Substitute 1 tsp (5 mL) Spike© seasoning with:
- 1 tsp (5 mL) herbal salt substitute such as Mrs. Dash©
- 1 tbsp (15 mL) chopped fresh herbs

Spinach

"On the subject of spinach: divide into little piles. Rearrange again into new piles. After five or six maneuvers, sit back and say you are full," advises Delia Ephron in How to Eat Like a Child.

1 lb (500 g) fresh =
10 cups (2.5 L) =
1½ cups (375 mL) cooked

10 oz (300 g) frozen =
1½ cups (375 mL) =
1 cup (250 mL) cooked
and drained

If You Don't Have It
Substitute 1 lb (500 g) spinach with:
- 1 lb (500 g) amaranth or Chinese spinach (especially to replace tender baby spinach)
- 1 lb (500 g) New Zealand spinach (flatter, more narrow leaves than spinach)
- 1 lb (500 g) spinach beet (a variety of beet grown for the leaves; larger, broader, slightly tougher leaves)
- 1 lb (500 g) beet greens (these often have reddish-tinged stems)
- 1 lb (500 g) red or green chard (slightly tougher leaves; thicker stems; slightly sweeter)
- 1 lb (500 g) turnip greens (smaller, teardrop-shaped, paler green leaves; more peppery flavor)
- 1 lb (500 g) kale (larger, tougher, ruffled leaves)
- 1 lb (500 g) sorrel, especially the smaller sheep sorrel (more delicate, pale green leaves; more tart flavor)
- 1 lb (500 g) arugula (smaller, more delicate, pale-green leaves; more bitter and nutty flavor)

Spinach Varieties
Choose 1 lb (500 g) spinach from these popular varieties:
- 1 lb (500 g) flat-leaf or garden spinach (small, flat, delicate, pale green leaves, sometimes with two points near the tender stem; mild bittersweet flavor; preferred for salads)
- 1 lb (500 g) curly leaf spinach (large, crinkly, dark green leaves; rather tough stems; mild bitter flavor; often sold in cellophane bags or frozen)

Spiny Lobster

Also known as rock lobster and langouste. Crustaceans of the family Palinuridae *are lobsters with no claws that flourish in waters warmer than North Atlantic lobster.*

If You Don't Have It

Substitute 1 lb (500 g) spiny lobster with:
- 1 lb (500 g) Maine lobster
- 1 lb (500 g) Dublin Bay prawns
- 1 lb (500 g) crayfish
- 1 lb (500 g) jumbo shrimp
- 1 lb (500 g) crab
- 1 lb (500 g) scallops

Spiral-Sliced Ham

See HAM, WET-CURED.

Spit Roaster

See ROTISSERIE.

Splenda©

See SUCRALOSE.

Split Peas

See PEAS, SPLIT; SWITCHING LENTILS (PAGE 569).

Sponge Cake

Also known as sunshine cake. Sponge cake is the fraternal twin of angel food cake. The only major difference is that it is made with egg yolks and egg whites, instead of egg whites only.

If You Don't Have It

Substitute 1 lb (500 g) sponge cake with:
- 1 lb (500 g) angel food cake (lighter, more airy texture; lower in fat)
- 1 lb (500 g) génoise (moister; slightly less sweet; tighter crumb)
- 1 lb (500 g) soft or soaked crisp ladyfingers (especially for tiramisù)
- 1 lb (500 g) butter cake (moister and richer)
- 1 lb (500 g) pound cake (moister, denser texture)

Spot

See CROAKER.

Sprat

A small, oily fish at home in the North Atlantic. Small sprats that are packed in oil are known as brisling or brisling sardines. Sprats also come smoked.

If You Don't Have It

Substitute 1 lb (500 g) sprats with:
- 1 lb (500 g) smelt
- 1 lb (500 g) anchovies (smaller)
- 1 lb (500 g) pilchards (larger)
- 1 lb (500 g) shad (larger)
- 1 lb (500 g) mackerel
- 1 lb (500 g) smoked sprats

Springform Pan

See PAN SIZE EQUIVALENTS (PAGE 606).

Spring Roll Wrapper

See RICE PAPER.

Sprouts

See ALFALFA SPROUTS; MUNG BEAN SPROUTS; SOYBEAN SPROUTS.

Squab

These farm-raised pigeons are members of the dove family. They are generally marketed at about 4 weeks, weighing about 1 pound (500 g). The meat is dark and tender.

If You Don't Have It

Substitute 1 lb (500 g) squab with:
- 1 lb (500 g) pigeon
- 1 lb (500 g) quail
- 1 lb (500 g) grouse
- 1 lb (500 g) pheasant
- 1 lb (500 g) partridge
- 1 lb (500 g) Cornish hen (fattier)

Squash Blossom

See PICKING EDIBLE FLOWERS (PAGE 604).

Squash, Summer

See PATTYPAN SQUASH; YELLOW SQUASH; ZUCCHINI.

Squash, Winter

See ACORN SQUASH; BANANA SQUASH; BUTTERCUP SQUASH; BUTTERNUT SQUASH; CALABAZA; DELICATA SQUASH; HUBBARD SQUASH; KABOCHA SQUASH; PUMPKIN; SPAGHETTI SQUASH; SWEET DUMPLING SQUASH.

Squid

Also known as calamari and ika (Japanese). A cephalopod that is well-loved in Japan and the Mediterranean countries of Europe but underutilized elsewhere. Its mild flesh responds best to either quick cooking or long simmering. Anything in between renders the squid tough. A Japanese specialty is ika-somen, squid cut in thin strands like somen noodles, served with soy-ginger dressing.

If You Don't Have It

Substitute 1 lb (500 g) squid with:
- 1 lb (500 g) cuttlefish (larger; more tender)
- 1 lb (500 g) baby octopus (firmer; tenderize by simmering in salted water or by pounding)

Stainless-Steel Cookware

Stainless steel is often wrapped around an alloy of iron, carbon, and chromium, a core of aluminum or copper to create nonreactive clad metal cookware with improved heat conductivity.

If You Don't Have It

Substitute stainless-steel cookware with:
- glass cookware (nonreactive; poor heat conduction; good heat retention)
- enamelware (nonreactive; good heat conduction and retention if enameled cast iron; poor heat conduction if enameled steel)
- earthenware (nonreactive; poor heat conduction; good heat retention)

Star Anise

Possibly the prettiest spice in the world, this brown pod is shaped like a lacy eight-pointed star with a seed in each segment. In China, it is widely used in cooking and in teas.

> 1 whole star =
> ½ tsp (2 mL) ground

If You Don't Have It

Substitute 1 whole star anise with:
- ½ tsp (2 mL) ground star anise
- ¾ tsp (4 mL) crushed anise seeds + pinch of ground allspice (less complex flavor)
- ½ tsp (2 mL) Chinese five-spice powder (includes mostly star anise plus fennel seed, cinnamon, Szechuan peppercorns, and cloves)
- 1 tbsp (15 mL) anise or licorice liqueur (weaker anise flavor; adds alcohol and liquid)
- ¼ to ½ tsp (1 to 2 mL) anise extract

See also CHINESE FIVE-SPICE POWDER.

Star Fruit

See CARAMBOLA.

Steamer

Any cooking vessel or basket that cooks food by suspending the food on a rack over simmering water. Includes bamboo steamers, perforated metal "insert" types that fit inside larger saucepans, and collapsible metal types.

If You Don't Have It

Substitute a steamer with:
- Makeshift steamer: crumple balls of foil to line the bottom of a wide pot or deep sauté pan that has a tight-fitting lid. Place a small metal colander, strainer, or wire rack (such as a cooling rack or one from a toaster oven) over the foil balls to use as a steaming basket. Add about 1 inch (2.5 cm) of water to the bottom of the pot, cover, and simmer, adding food to the makeshift basket.
- Use a heatproof (ovenproof) plate set over a metal trivet or clean, empty tuna can with both ends removed (to make a ring on which to prop the plate). Set the trivet or can-ring in the pot, add water, and place the food on the plate. Cover and simmer to steam.

To Save Time

Substitute a steamer with:

- Microwave oven: excels at steaming foods. Place vegetables, chicken, or fish in a microwave-safe container. Put the thick ends of the food toward the middle and add a small amount of liquid such as water or stock (or none at all if the food is very liquidy). Cover tightly with plastic wrap and cook on High power until the food is just cooked through.

Steel

See SHARPENING STEEL.

Sterno©

Also known as canned heat. Sterno gel is a canned portable cooking fuel made from denatured alcohol, water, and gel. It is used in a variety of situations from tabletop to campsite.

If You Don't Have It

Substitute Sterno© with:

- tea candles
- warming tray
- gas burner set on lowest possible setting

Stevia

A plant of South American origin, extracts of which are up to 300 times sweeter than ordinary table sugar. Since 1977, stevia has grown to capture more than 40% of the sweetener market in Japan. In the U.S., the Food and Drug Administration categorizes it as an unsafe food additive and approves its sale only as a "dietary supplement." One European study of stevia's effect on rats found a decrease in male fertility.

If You Don't Have It

Substitute 1/4 tsp (1 mL) liquid stevia with:

- 1 cup (250 mL) granulated sugar
- 1 3/4 cups (425 mL) unsifted confectioner's (icing) sugar
- 1 cup (250 mL) packed light or dark brown sugar
- 1 cup (250 mL) superfine (castor) sugar
- 1 cup (250 mL) turbinado sugar
- 1 cup (250 mL) date sugar
- 2/3 cup (150 mL) granulated fructose or fruit sugar (fructose tends to make baked goods moister, darker, and chewier)
- 1 cup (250 mL) minus 2 tbsp (25 mL) honey (for baking, reduce liquid in recipe by 3 tbsp/45 mL; add 1/4 tsp/1 mL baking soda to neutralize acidity of honey)
- 3/4 cup (175 mL) maple syrup (for baking, reduce liquid in recipe by 3 to 4 tbsp/45 to 60 mL; add scant 1/4 tsp/1 mL baking soda to neutralize acidity of maple syrup)

Stevia (cont'd)

- ½ cup (125 mL) sugar + 6 tbsp (90 mL) honey, maple syrup, or corn syrup (in baking, reduce liquid in recipe by 2 tbsp/25 mL, or add 2 tbsp/25 mL flour if there is no other liquid in recipe; reduce oven temperature by 25°F/14°C)
- ½ cup (125 mL) granulated sugar + ½ cup (125 mL) molasses + ½ tsp (2 mL) baking soda (reduce liquid in recipe by 2 tbsp/25 mL, or add 2 tbsp/25 mL flour if there is no other liquid in recipe)
- ¾ cup (175 mL) granulated sugar + ¼ cup (50 mL) maple sugar

For Better Health
Substitute ¼ tsp (1 mL) liquid stevia with:
- 1 cup (250 mL) Sucanat (powdered organic sugarcane juice, which retains all its vitamins and minerals)
- ½ cup (125 mL) granulated sugar + ½ cup (125 mL) sugar-free sugar substitute such as sucralose, Splenda© or DiabetiSweet© (for best balance of reduced calories, flavor, and browning in baking)
- 1 cup (250 mL) sugar-free sugar substitute such as sucralose, Splenda© or DiabetiSweet© (calorie-free; may leave slight aftertaste and browning will not occur in baking because there is no sugar to caramelize)

Sticky Rice

See VARIETIES OF RICE (PAGE 591).

Stilton

A superstar of the cheese world, Stilton is a golden, rich, crumbly British blue-veined cheese. Purists say it should be savored alone with only a glass of port or dry red wine for accompaniment.

4 oz (125 g) = 1 cup (250 mL) crumbled

If You Don't Have It
Substitute 1 oz (30 g) Stilton with:
- 1 oz (30 g) Shropshire Blue (more pungent; bright orange color)
- 1 oz (30 g) Roquefort (slightly softer; more pungent)
- 1 oz (30 g) Gorgonzola (creamier; more pungent)
- 1 oz (30 g) Cashel Blue
- 1 oz (30 g) Maytag Blue

To Vary the Flavor
Substitute 1 oz (30 g) Stilton with:
- 1 oz (30 g) Huntsman cheese (a layer of Stilton sandwiched between two layers of Double Gloucester)

Stinging Nettles

See NETTLES.

Stock, Beef

Few home cooks these days go to the time, effort, and expense to make stocks from scratch; but fortunately, many commercial renderings are available. Most of these products tend to be salty, so adjust additional salt in the recipe accordingly. Liquid broths are available in supermarkets packed in steel cans or aseptic packages. Concentrated forms of stock, which have the advantage of requiring less storage space, include bouillon cubes and granules as well as jarred or frozen concentrated meat pastes, also known as stock base. The paste is reconstituted with water to create stock.

If You Don't Have It

Substitute 1 cup (250 mL) beef stock with:

- 1 cup (250 mL) boiling water + 1 tsp (5 mL) beef base or instant beef bouillon granules, 1 beef bouillon cube, or 1 envelope beef bouillon (may be higher in sodium and less flavorful)
- 1 cup (250 mL) aseptically packaged or canned beef broth (may be higher in sodium and less flavorful)
- 1 cup (250 mL) cold or room temperature aseptically packaged or canned beef broth + $\frac{1}{8}$ to $\frac{1}{4}$ tsp (1 mL) unflavored powdered or granulated gelatin, mixed in saucepan then reheated until gelatin dissolves (improves texture)

To Vary the Flavor

Substitute 1 cup (250 mL) beef stock with:

- 1 cup (250 mL) red wine or beer (to replace up to half of beef stock in sauces and stews)
- 1 cup (250 mL) vegetable stock, broth, or reconstituted base or bouillon (may be less robust in flavor; use roasted vegetable stock to intensify flavor)

For Better Health

- 1 cup (250 mL) low-sodium beef broth

Stock, Chicken

The natural choice of flavoring liquid for poultry soups, braised dishes, stews, gravies, and sauces. Low-salt versions allow you to salt to taste or reduce the broth to a glaze without it becoming overly salty.

If You Don't Have It

Substitute 1 cup (250 mL) chicken stock with:

- 1 cup (250 mL) boiling water + 1 tsp (5 mL) chicken base or instant chicken bouillon granules, 1 chicken bouillon cube, or 1 envelope chicken bouillon (may be higher in sodium and less flavorful)
- 1 cup (250 mL) aseptically packaged or canned chicken broth (may be higher in sodium and less flavorful)
- 1 cup (250 mL) cold or room temperature aseptically packaged or canned chicken broth + $\frac{1}{8}$ to $\frac{1}{4}$ tsp (0.5 to 1 mL) unflavored powdered or granulated gelatin, mixed in saucepan then reheated until gelatin dissolves (improves texture of broth)

Stock, Chicken (cont'd)

- 1 cup (250 mL) aseptically packaged or canned chicken broth + 2 tbsp (25 mL) chopped leftover chicken bones, brought to a boil in a saucepan then gently simmered for 30 minutes and strained before using (improves texture and flavor of broth)

To Vary the Flavor
Substitute 1 cup (250 mL) chicken stock with:
- 1 cup (250 mL) dry white wine, vermouth or sherry (to replace up to half of chicken stock in sauces and stews)
- 1 cup (250 mL) vegetable stock, broth, or reconstituted base or bouillon (may be less robust in flavor; use roasted vegetable stock to intensify flavor)

For Better Health
- 1 cup (250 mL) low-sodium chicken broth

Stock, Fish

Also known as fish fumet. From the home cook's perspective, the easiest, fastest stock to make from scratch. Only the frames of white-fleshed fish should be used. Oilier fish such as bluefish or mackerel would overpower the flavor.

If You Don't Have It
Substitute 1 cup (250 mL) fish stock with:
- 1 cup (250 mL) Homemade Fish Stock: Combine ¾ cup (175 mL) bottled clam juice, ½ cup (125 mL) water, ½ cup (125 mL) dry white wine, ½ tsp (2 mL) sliced onion, and 2 to 3 sprigs parsley in a saucepan. Simmer over medium heat until reduced to 1 cup (250 mL), about 30 minutes, then strain. Makes about 1 cup (250 mL).
- 1 cup (250 mL) boiling water + ½ tsp (2 mL) lobster, clam, or chicken base or instant fish or chicken bouillon granules, ½ tsp (2 mL) fish or chicken bouillon cube, or ½ tsp (2 mL) envelope fish or chicken bouillon

To Vary the Flavor
Substitute 1 cup (250 mL) fish stock with:
- ½ cup (125 mL) aseptically packaged or canned chicken broth + ½ cup (125 mL) water (less flavorful)
- 1 cup (250 mL) dry white wine, vermouth, or sherry (to replace up to half of fish stock in sauces and stews)
- 1 cup (250 mL) reconstituted instant dashi or dashi-no-moto (more fishy, less fresh flavor)

- 1 cup (250 mL) chicken stock or broth + 2 tbsp (25 mL) dulse (seaweed) flakes or a 1-inch (2.5 cm) square of kombu, brought to a boil, removed from heat and cooled for 5 minutes, then strained (not as flavorful)
- 1 cup (250 mL) vegetable stock, broth, or reconstituted base or bouillon (less aromatic and flavorful)

Stock, Veal

Brown veal stock is the most flavorful and versatile stock of the French repertoire. A properly made veal stock will acquire a deep golden brown color from oven-roasting the bones before they are simmered with water and aromatic vegetables and herbs. It will also jell when refrigerated. It is the basis for numerous gravies, sauces, soups, and stews. Bones with a good proportion of meat and cartilage, such as veal breast, are essential.

If You Don't Have It

Substitute 1 cup (250 mL) veal stock with:

- 1 cup (250 mL) cold or room temperature aseptically packaged or canned chicken or beef broth + $\frac{1}{8}$ to $\frac{1}{4}$ tsp (0.5 to 1 mL) unflavored powdered or granulated gelatin, mixed in saucepan then reheated until gelatin dissolves (improves texture of broth)
- 1 cup (250 mL) aseptically packaged or canned chicken broth + 2 tbsp (25 mL) chopped leftover chicken bones, brought to a boil in a saucepan then gently simmered for 30 minutes and strained before using (improves texture and flavor of broth)
- 1 cup (250 mL) boiling water + 1 tsp (5 mL) chicken or beef base or instant chicken or beef bouillon granules, 1 chicken or beef bouillon cube, or 1 envelope chicken or beef bouillon (less rich; less flavorful)
- 1 cup (250 mL) aseptically packaged or canned chicken or beef broth (may be higher in sodium and less flavorful)
- 1 cup (250 mL) dry white wine, vermouth or sherry (to replace up to half of veal stock in sauces and stews)
- 1 cup (250 mL) vegetable stock, broth, or reconstituted base or bouillon (may be less robust in flavor; use roasted vegetable stock to intensify flavor)

Stock, Vegetable

For vegetarians or those just trying to cut down on meat consumption, a tasty vegetable stock will add immeasurable flavor to many dishes. When making your own stock, try adding vegetables or herbs to match the flavor of the dishes you'll be making. For instance, add ginger to the stock to complement Asian dishes. Or add a few sprigs of fresh cilantro to the stock to marry with Mexican dishes. Experiment with vegetables and seasonings, but avoid very strong-tasting vegetables such as broccoli.

If You Don't Have It

Substitute 1 cup (250 mL) vegetable stock with:

- 1 cup (250 mL) Homemade Vegetable Stock: Combine 2 cups (500 mL) chopped onions, 2 cups (500 mL) chopped carrots, 1 cup (250 mL) chopped celery, 4 halved garlic cloves, 4 sprigs parsley, 1 to 2 bay leaves, and a few sprigs of thyme in a large saucepan. Cover with cold water by 1 inch (2.5 cm). Simmer over medium heat until vegetables are tender, about 1 hour. Pour through a fine-mesh strainer into a heatproof container, pressing on solids. Discard solids. Season to taste with salt and pepper. Let cool. Refrigerate in airtight containers for 1 week or freeze for up to 6 months. Makes about 4 cups (1 L).
- 1 cup (250 mL) boiling water + 1 tsp (5 mL) vegetable or chicken base or instant vegetable or chicken bouillon granules, 1 vegetable or chicken bouillon cube, or 1 envelope vegetable or chicken bouillon
- 1 cup (250 mL) aseptically packaged or canned vegetable broth (may be higher in sodium and less flavorful)
- 1 cup (250 mL) roasted vegetable stock (roast vegetables at 475°F/240°C until well-browned before making stock; intensifies flavors)
- 1 cup (250 mL) cold or room temperature aseptically packaged or canned vegetable or chicken broth + ⅛ to ¼ tsp (0.5 to 1 mL) unflavored powdered or granulated gelatin, mixed in saucepan then reheated until gelatin dissolves (improves texture of broth)

To Vary the Flavor

Substitute 1 cup (250 mL) vegetable stock with:

- 1 cup (250 mL) aseptically packaged or canned chicken broth (may be higher in sodium and less flavorful; adds chicken flavor)
- 1 cup (250 mL) dry white wine, vermouth or sherry (to replace up to half of vegetable stock in sauces and stews)

For Better Health

- 1 cup (250 mL) low-sodium vegetable broth

Stone Crab

See CHOOSING AMONG CRABS (PAGE 597)

Stoneware

A sturdy type of cookware made from glazed pottery that's fired at temperatures of up to 2200°F (1204°C). After passing the test of fire, these chip-resistant pans are ideal for slow cooking and baking in either conventional or microwave ovens.

If You Don't Have It
Substitute stoneware with:
- earthenware
- porcelain
- heatproof glass

Stout

See BEER.

Stracchino

Also known as stracchino di crescenza. Various types of cheeses in Northern Italy are made from cows' milks combined from morning and evening milkings and called stracchino. Gorgonzola and taleggio are both stracchino cheeses. Crescenza or stracchino di crescenza is another type.

If You Don't Have It
Substitute 1 oz (30 g) young stracchino di crescenza with:
- 1 oz (30 g) mascarpone (creamier)
- 1 oz (30 g) cream cheese (creamier)

For Better Health
Substitute 1 oz (30 g) young stracchino with:
- 1 oz (30 g) Neufchâtel (creamier)

Strainer

Also known as Chinese spider strainer or a sieve. They can be shaped as cones, drums, or bowls, but strainers all have a mesh bottom designed to strain liquids from solids or sift dry ingredients.

If You Don't Have It
Substitute a strainer with:
- colander
- tongs, pasta spoon, or slotted spoon (for plucking or scooping foods out of hot liquid)
- Chinese spider strainer (for skimming or scooping foods out of hot liquid)
- sifter (for sifting ingredients)
- fine-holed shaker (for quickly sifting small amounts of a single ingredient such as confectioner's sugar or cocoa powder)

See also COLANDER.

Strawberry

Wild strawberries are indigenous to both the Old and New Worlds. In 19th century England, Michael Keens produced the Keens' Seedling, a strawberry variety of remarkable size and taste. Almost all varieties in cultivation today are descended from it.

> 1 pint = 24 medium =
> 36 small = 2½ cups
> (625 mL) whole =
> 1¾ cups (425 mL) sliced
> = 1¼ cups (300 mL)
> puréed
>
> 20 oz (600 g) pkg frozen
> whole strawberries =
> 4 cups (1 L) = 2¼ cups
> (550 mL) puréed
>
> 10 oz (300 g) pkg in
> syrup = 1¼ cups (300 mL)

If You Don't Have It

Substitute 1 pint strawberries with:
- 1 pint raspberries (red color; slightly more tart)
- 1 pint loganberries (red color; slightly more tart)
- 1 pint tayberries (red color; slightly more tart)
- 1 pint blueberries (purple color; slightly more tart)
- 2 cups (500 mL) guava pulp (pinkish orange color)
- 2 cups (500 mL) peeled kiwifruit (green color; slightly more tart)

See also FRAISES DES BOIS.

Strawberry Liqueur

See CRÈME DE FRAISE.

Strawberry Preserves

One of many attempts to extend our enjoyment of stawberries beyond their botanical seasons.

If You Don't Have It

Substitute ½ cup (125 mL) strawberry preserves with:
- ½ cup (125 mL) raspberry or blueberry preserves
- ½ cup (125 mL) quava paste
- ½ cup (125 mL) other tropical fruit preserves

Strega

Made from more than 70 herbs, this anise-tasting liqueur is named "witch" but that doesn't seem to deter the many Italians who enjoy it. Strega may be clear or a glistening yellow green color.

If You Don't Have It

Substitute 2 tbsp (25 mL) Strega with:
- 2 tbsp (25 mL) Chartreuse (green or yellow color)
- 2 tbsp (25 mL) Izarra (green or yellow color)
- 2 tbsp (25 mL) Liqueur d'Or (includes gold flakes)
- 2 tbsp (25 mL) Bénédictine (deep amber color)
- 2 tbsp (25 mL) sambuca (colorless; licorice flavor)

String Bean

See GREEN BEAN.

String Cheese

Semihard, mild white cheese that's typically formed into strips. It's popular for snacking because it's easy to eat out-of-hand.

If You Don't Have It
Substitute 1 oz (30 g) string cheese with:
- 1 oz (30 g) firm mozzarella, cut into strips
- 1 oz (30 g) Scamorza, cut into strips
- 1 oz (30 g) Caciocavallo, cut into strips

Striped Bass

Also known as rock, rockfish, and striper. A highly sought after true bass of the eastern U.S. coast. The white flesh is firm, well-flavored, and only moderately high in fat. Wild striped bass has olive green, silvery skin marked by up to 8 longitudinal black stripes. Less flavorful farmed striped bass is a hybrid of wild striped bass and white bass. It's easy to distinguish the farmed striped because of its shorter stubbier body and a stripe pattern that appears broken up.

If You Don't Have It
Substitute 1 lb (500 g) striped bass with:
- 1 lb (500 g) blackfish
- 1 lb (500 g) rockfish
- 1 lb (500 g) black sea bass
- 1 lb (500 g) grouper
- 1 lb (500 g) red snapper
- 1 lb (500 g) swordfish

Strudel Dough

A central European gossamer pastry dough similar to phyllo. Typically, many layers are piled on one another to create a crescendo of crispness after baking.

If You Don't Have It
Substitute 1 lb (500 g) strudel dough with:
- 1 lb (500 g) phyllo dough
- 1 lb (500 g) puff pastry (less crisp)

Stuffing Cubes

See CROUTONS.

Sturgeon

Fine-tasting fish that has been compared in flavor and texture to veal. Sturgeon, particularly from the Black Sea and the Caspian Sea, is most sought after for its caviar.

If You Don't Have It

Substitute 1 lb (500 g) sturgeon with:

- 1 lb (500 g) swordfish
- 1 lb (500 g) tuna
- 1 lb (500 g) mahi-mahi
- 1 lb (500 g) halibut
- 1 lb (500 g) smoked sturgeon

See also CHANGING ROE (PAGE 594).

Sucanat

Also known as granulated sugarcane juice, dehydrated sugarcane juice, and unrefined natural sugar. "Su-ca-nat" is short for sugarcane natural. Unlike commercial "brown sugar" which is molasses-flavored granulated sugar, Sucanat is comprised of brown porous granules that result from crushing the sugarcane, extracting the juice, and rapidly evaporating the syrup. It retains most of the nutrients that are naturally occurring in the sugarcane.

> 1 lb (500 g) = 2¼ cups (550 mL) packed

If You Don't Have It

Substitute 1 cup (250 mL) Sucanat with:

- 1 cup (250 mL) granulated sugar (more highly refined; fewer nutrients and minerals)
- 1¾ cups (425 mL) unsifted confectioner's (icing) sugar
- 1 cup (250 mL) packed light or dark brown sugar (more highly refined; fewer nutrients and minerals)
- 1 cup (250 mL) superfine (castor) sugar
- 1 cup (250 mL) turbinado sugar
- 1 cup (250 mL) date sugar
- ⅔ cup (150 mL) granulated fructose or fruit sugar (fructose tends to make baked goods moister, darker, and chewier)
- 1 cup (250 mL) minus 2 tbsp (25 mL) honey (for baking, reduce liquid in recipe by 3 tbsp/45 mL; add ¼ tsp/1 mL baking soda to neutralize acidity of honey)
- ¾ cup (175 mL) maple syrup (for baking, reduce liquid in recipe by 3 to 4 tbsp/45 to 60 mL; add scant ¼ tsp/1 mL baking soda to neutralize acidity of maple syrup)
- ½ cup (125 mL) granulated sugar + 6 tbsp (90 mL) honey, maple syrup, or corn syrup (in baking, reduce liquid in recipe by 2 tbsp/25 mL, or add 2 tbsp/25 mL flour if there is no other liquid in recipe; reduce oven temperature by 25°F/14°C)

- ½ cup (125 mL) granulated sugar + ½ cup (125 mL) molasses + ½ tsp (2 mL) baking soda (reduce liquid in recipe by 2 tbsp/25 mL, or add 2 tbsp/ 25 mL flour if there is no other liquid in recipe)
- ¾ cup (175 mL) granulated sugar + ¼ cup (50 mL) maple sugar

For Better Health

Substitute 1 cup (250 mL) Sucanat with:

- ½ cup (125 mL) Sucanat + ½ cup (125 mL) sugar-free sugar substitute such as sucralose, Splenda© or DiabetiSweet© (for balance of reduced calories, flavor, and browning in baking)
- 1 cup (250 mL) sugar-free sugar substitute such as sucralose, Splenda© or DiabetiSweet© (calorie-free; may leave slight aftertaste and browning will not occur in baking because there is no sugar to caramelize)
- ⅛ to ¼ tsp (0.5 to 1 mL) liquid stevia (calorie-free; probiotic, which promotes growth of healthy bacteria in digestive system; may leave slight licorice-like aftertaste and browning will not occur in baking because there is no sugar to caramelize)

Sucralose

A calorie-free sweetener made from sugar by a chemical process that replaces three hydrogen-oxygen groups on the sugar molecule with three chlorine atoms. Because the body does not recognize sucralose as a carbohydrate, it passes through the body without being broken down for energy. It is stable and can be used in cooking and baking. The most widely available brand, Splenda®, is interchangeable with sucralose in all the following substitutions.

If You Don't Have It

Substitute 1 cup (250 mL) sucralose with:

- 1 cup (250 mL) granulated sugar (adds calories; aids in browning)
- 1¾ cups (425 mL) unsifted confectioner's (icing) sugar (adds calories; aids in browning)
- 1 cup (250 mL) packed light or dark brown sugar (adds calories; aids in browning; makes baked goods moister and chewier)
- 1 cup (250 mL) superfine (castor) sugar (adds calories; aids in browning)
- 1 cup (250 mL) turbinado sugar (adds calories; aids in browning)
- 1 cup (250 mL) date sugar (adds calories; aids in browning)
- ⅔ cup (150 mL) granulated fructose or fruit sugar (adds calories; fructose tends to make baked goods moister, darker, and chewier)

Sucralose (cont'd)

- 1 cup (250 mL) minus 2 tbsp (25 mL) honey (adds calories; for baking, reduce liquid in recipe by 3 tbsp/45 mL; add ¼ tsp/1 mL baking soda to neutralize acidity of honey; makes baked goods moister and chewier; reduce oven temperature by 25°F/14°C)
- ¾ cup (175 mL) maple syrup (adds calories; for baking, reduce liquid in recipe by 3 to 4 tbsp/ 45 to 60 mL; add scant ¼ tsp/1 mL baking soda to neutralize acidity of maple syrup)
- ½ cup (125 mL) granulated sugar + 6 tbsp (90 mL) honey, maple syrup, or corn syrup (adds calories; for baking, reduce liquid in recipe by 2 tbsp/25 mL, or add 2 tbsp/25 mL flour if there is no other liquid in recipe; reduce oven temperature by 25°F/14°C)
- ½ cup (125 mL) granulated sugar + ½ cup (125 mL) molasses + ½ tsp (2 mL) baking soda (adds calories; for baking, reduce liquid in recipe by 2 tbsp/25 mL or add 2 tbsp/25 mL flour if there is no other liquid in recipe)
- ¾ cup (175 mL) granulated sugar + ¼ cup (50 mL) maple sugar (adds calories)

For Better Health

Substitute 1 cup (250 mL) sucralose with:

- 1 cup (250 mL) Sucanat (adds calories; powdered organic sugarcane juice, which retains all its vitamins and minerals)
- ½ cup (125 mL) granulated sugar + ½ cup (125 mL) sugar-free sugar substitute such as Splenda® or DiabetiSweet® (adds calories; for best balance of reduced calories, flavor, and browning in baking)
- 1 cup (250 mL) sugar-free sugar substitute such as DiabetiSweet© (calorie-free; may leave slight aftertaste and browning will not occur in baking because there is no sugar to caramelize)
- ¼ tsp (1 mL) liquid stevia (calorie-free; probiotic, which promotes growth of healthy bacteria in digestive system; may leave slight licorice-like aftertaste and browning will not occur in baking because there is no sugar to caramelize)

Suet

The solid, white fat found around the kidneys and loins of beef and other animals. Suet is a traditional component of many British recipes for pastries, puddings, and mincemeats.

1 lb (500 g) ground =
3¾ cups (925 mL)

If You Don't Have It

Substitute ½ cup (125 mL) suet with:

- ½ cup (125 mL) vegetarian suet such as Atora (made from vegetable fat; same calories and fat content as beef suet; suitable for vegetarians)
- ½ cup (125 mL) vegetable shortening (moister)
- ½ cup (125 mL) rendered and solidified beef, chicken, or pork fat (moister)
- ½ cup (125 mL) butter (moister)

Suey Gow Wrappers

See WON TON SKINS.

Sugar Apple

See SWEETSOP.

Sugar, Chinese

See SUGAR, ROCK.

Sugar, Confectioner's

Also known as powdered sugar and icing sugar. Granulated sugar that's pulverized to a powder and mixed with about 3% cornstarch to prevent clumping. It dissolves almost instantly in icings and frostings. It's also sprinkled on pastries for decorative effect. The number of Xs on the package indicates the degree of fineness. XXXX is finer than XXX.

1 lb (500 g) = 3½ to
4 cups (875 mL to 1 L)
unsifted = 4½ to 5 cups
(1.125 to 1.25 L) sifted

If You Don't Have It

Substitute 1 cup (250 mL) confectioner's sugar with:

- ½ cup (125 mL) plus 1½ tbsp (22 mL) granulated sugar plus ¾ tsp (4 mL) cornstarch (optional) finely ground in a blender or small food processor

See also SUGAR, GRANULATED.

Sugar, Dark Brown

Use dark brown sugar instead of light brown sugar for a deeper molasses flavor in cooking, baking, spice rubs, and marinades. To measure accurately, always pack the sugar firmly into a measuring cup.

> 1 lb (500 g) = 2¼ cups (550 mL) packed

If You Don't Have It

Substitute 1 packed cup (250 mL) dark brown sugar with:

- 1 packed cup (250 mL) light brown sugar + 1 tbsp (15 mL) molasses
- 1 cup (250 mL) granulated sugar + 2 to 3 tbsp (25 to 45 mL) molasses
- 1 cup (250 mL) turbinado sugar
- 1 cup (250 mL) chopped jaggery (more firm)
- 1 cup (250 mL) chopped piloncillo (more firm)

For Better Health

Substitute 1 packed cup (250 mL) dark brown sugar with:

- 1 cup (250 mL) sugar-free sugar substitute such as sucralose, Splenda© or DiabetiSweet© + ¼ cup (50 mL) molasses (fewer calories; may leave slight aftertaste and browning will not occur in baking because there is less sugar to caramelize)

See also JAGGERY; PILONCILLO; SUGAR, GRANULATED.

Sugar, Decorating

Also known as coarse sugar, crystal sugar, and sugar crystals. Sparkling clear pellets that are four times as large as those in granulated sugar are employed for decorating pastries. They are sold in cake-decorating supply shops, specialty pastry catalogs, online, and some supermarkets.

If You Don't Have It

Substitute 1 cup (250 mL) decorating sugar with:

- 1 cup (250 mL) Homemade Colored Decorating Sugar: Put 1 cup (250 mL) decorating or granulated sugar in a glass jar with a tight-fitting lid. Add 8 to 10 drops food coloring, seal, and shake immediately and vigorously until sugar is evenly color. Makes 1 cup (250 mL).
- 1 cup (250 mL) turbinado sugar (slightly smaller, blond-color crystals)
- 1 cup (250 mL) Demerara sugar (slightly smaller, light brown color crystals)

To Vary the Flavor

Substitute 1 cup (250 mL) decorating sugar with:

- 1 cup (250 mL) Homemade Cinnamon Sugar (adds cinnamon flavor; smaller crystals; see recipe, page 486)
- 1 cup (250 mL) Homemade Vanilla Sugar (adds vanilla flavor; smaller crystals; see recipe, page 485)
- 1 cup (250 mL) nonpareils (solid white color)
- 1 cup (250 mL) jimmies (various colors and flavors)

Sugar, Granulated

Also known as white sugar. These medium-size white crystals are processed from sugarcane and also, to a lesser degree in the marketplace, from sugar beets. Some product labels specify "pure cane sugar" while others do not. Although scientists detect no chemical difference between the two, many bakers and jam makers contend that cane sugar produces more consistent results. Many vegetarians prefer beet sugar because some cane sugar is whitened using animal bones. Aside from its obvious role as a sweetener, sugar helps maintain moisture in baked goods, stabilizes egg whites for meringue, prevents some food from spoilage, and gives many cooked foods a golden color. Sugar cubes are granulated sugar that is "glued" together with syrup and molded in tiny blocks.

---

1 lb (500 g) = 2 to 2¼ cups (500 to 550 mL)

1 tsp (5 mL) = two ½-inch (1 cm) sugar cubes

If You Don't Have It

Substitute 1 cup (250 mL) granulated sugar with:

- 1¾ cups (425 mL) unsifted confectioner's (icing) sugar (may make baked goods less crisp)
- 1 cup (250 mL) packed light or dark brown sugar (slightly higher calories, minerals, and other nutrients; makes baked goods moister and chewier)
- 1 cup (250 mL) superfine or castor sugar (smaller crystals)
- 1 cup (250 mL) turbinado sugar (larger crystals)
- ⅔ cup (150 mL) granulated fructose or fruit sugar (fructose tends to make baked goods moister, darker, and chewier)

To Vary the Flavor

Substitute 1 cup (250 mL) granulated sugar with:

- 1 cup (250 mL) date sugar
- 1 cup (250 mL) minus 2 tbsp (25 mL) honey or brown rice syrup (for baking, reduce liquid in recipe by 3 tbsp/45 mL; add ¼ tsp/1 mL baking soda to neutralize acidity; makes baked goods moister and chewier; reduce oven temperature by 25°F/14°C)
- ¾ cup (175 mL) maple syrup (for baking, reduce liquid in recipe by 3 to 4 tbsp/45 to 60 mL; add scant ¼ tsp/1 mL baking soda to neutralize acidity of maple syrup)
- ¾ cup (175 mL) barley malt syrup (for baking, reduce liquid in recipe by 3 to 4 tbsp/45 to 60 mL)
- ½ cup (125 mL) granulated sugar + 6 tbsp (90 mL) honey, maple syrup, or corn syrup (in baking, reduce liquid in recipe by 2 tbsp/25 mL, or add 2 tbsp/25 mL flour if there is no other liquid in recipe; reduce oven temperature by 25°F/14°C)
- ½ cup (125 mL) granulated sugar + ½ cup (125 mL) molasses + ½ tsp (2 mL) baking soda (for baking, reduce liquid in recipe by 2 tbsp/25 mL, or add 2 tbsp/25 mL flour if there is no other liquid in recipe; adds molasses flavor)
- ¾ cup (175 mL) granulated sugar + ¼ cup (50 mL) maple sugar
- 1 cup (250 mL) Homemade Vanilla Sugar: Combine 2 whole vanilla beans and 2 cups (500 mL) granulated sugar in an airtight container and store at room temperature indefinitely. Shake the

Sugar, Granulated (cont'd)

container occasionally. The vanilla beans will flavor the sugar within 1 to 2 weeks. Remove vanilla sugar as necessary and replace with an equal amount of granulated sugar. Replace vanilla beans when they give up their flavor. Makes 2 cups (500 mL). To substitute 1 cup (250 mL) vanilla sugar, use 1 cup (250 mL) sugar + ½ tsp (2 mL) vanilla extract.

- 1 cup (250 mL) Homemade Cinnamon Sugar: Combine 1 cup (250 mL) granulated sugar and 2 to 3 tbsp (25 to 45 mL) cinnamon in an airtight container and store at room temperature indefinitely. Or combine 6 cinnamon sticks and 4 cups (1 L) sugar in an airtight container and store at room temperature indefinitely. Shake the container occasionally. The cinnamon sticks will flavor the sugar within 1 to 2 weeks. Remove cinnamon sugar as necessary and replace with an equal amount of granulated sugar. Replace cinnamon sticks when they give up their flavor. Makes 4 cups (1 L).

For Better Health

Substitute 1 cup (250 mL) granulated sugar with:

- ¾ cup (175 mL) granulated sugar (fewer calories; sugar can often be reduced by one-quarter of the amount called for; makes baked goods slightly less sweet and more pale and dry)
- 1 cup (250 mL) Sucanat (powdered organic sugarcane juice, which retains all its vitamins and minerals)
- ½ cup (125 mL) granulated sugar + ½ cup (125 mL) sugar-free sugar substitute such as Splenda® or DiabetiSweet® (for best balanced of reduced calories, flavor and browning in baking)
- 1 cup (250 mL) sugar-free sugar substitute such as sucralose, Splenda© or DiabetiSweet© (calorie-free; may leave slight aftertaste and browning will not occur in baking because there is no sugar to caramelize)
- ⅛ to ¼ tsp (0.5 to 1 mL) liquid stevia (calorie-free; probiotic, which promotes growth of healthy bacteria in digestive system; may leave slight licorice-like aftertaste and browning will not occur in baking because there is no sugar to caramelize)

See also DATE SUGAR; MAPLE SUGAR.

Sugar, Light Brown

Made by mixing granulated sugar with molasses. Generally, the lighter the brown color, the less molasses is added. To keep the sugar soft after opening a package, place a strip of orange zest, about 3 inches by 1 inch (7.5 by 2.5 cm) in the bag. Seal tightly and store inside a resealable plastic bag.

> 1 lb (500 g) =
> 2¼ cups (550 mL) packed

If You Don't Have It

Substitute 1 packed cup (250 mL) light brown sugar with:

- 1 cup (250 mL) granulated sugar + 1 to 2 tbsp (15 to 25 mL) molasses
- ½ cup (125 mL) dark brown sugar + ½ cup (125 mL) granulated sugar
- 1 cup (250 mL) turbinado sugar (less moist; larger crystals)

For Better Health

- ¾ cup (175 mL) light brown sugar (sugar can often be reduced by one-quarter of the amount called for; makes baked goods slightly less sweet and more pale and dry)
- ½ cup (125 mL) light brown sugar + ½ cup (125 mL) sugar-free brown sugar substitute such as Brown Sugar Twin© (for best balance of reduced calories, flavor and browning in baking)
- 1 cup (250 mL) sugar-free brown sugar substitute such as Brown Sugar Twin© (may leave slight aftertaste and browning will not occur in baking because there is no sugar to caramelize)

See also SUGAR, DARK BROWN; SUGAR, GRANULATED.

Sugar, Palm

Also known as coconut sugar, gur, and jaggery. Coarse dark sugar derived from the sap of various palm trees or from sugarcane juice. Some manufacturers classify palm sugar as gur and sugarcane as jaggery. This sweetener adds complex wine-like flavor and aroma to many dishes.

If You Don't Have It

Substitute 1 cup (250 mL) palm sugar with:

- 1 cup (250 mL) jaggery
- 1 cup (250 mL) piloncillo
- 1 cup (250 mL) dark brown sugar + 2 tsp (10 mL) molasses

See also JAGGERY; PILONCILLO.

Sugar, Raw

Resembling brown sugar in looks only, raw sugar is the residue remaining after cane sugar is processed to remove molasses and refine the sugar crystals. In its natural state, raw sugar may contain fibers, molds, and other contaminants, therefore commercially marketed raw sugar is purified. Demerara sugar is dry and coarse, Barbados sugar is more fine and moist, and turbinado sugar is cleaned by a steaming process.

1 lb (500 g) =
3 to 3¼ cups
(750 to 800 mL)

If You Don't Have It
Substitute 1 cup (250 mL) raw sugar with:
- 1 cup (250 mL) light or dark brown sugar (moister)
- 1 cup (250 mL) granulated sugar (drier; less molasses-like flavor)

Raw Sugar Varieties
Choose 1 cup (250 mL) raw sugar from these varieties:
- 1 cup (250 mL) turbinado sugar (steam-cleaned raw sugar; coarse, blond-color crystals; mild molasses flavor)
- 1 cup (250 mL) Demerara sugar (from Guyana; dry, coarse crystals; slightly stronger molasses flavor)
- 1 cup (250 mL) Barbados sugar (moist, fine crystals; slightly stronger molasses flavor)

For Better Health
Substitute 1 cup (250 mL) raw sugar with:
- 1 cup (250 mL) Sucanat (powdered organic sugarcane juice, which retains all its vitamins and minerals)

See also SUGAR, DARK BROWN; SUGAR, GRANULATED; SUGAR, LIGHT BROWN.

Sugar, Rock

Also known as Chinese sugar. The largest-size crystals of decorating sugar.

If You Don't Have It
Substitute 1 rock sugar crystal with:
- 2 to 3 tsp (10 to 15 mL) granulated sugar (sweeter; less caramelized flavor)

See also SUGAR, DECORATING; SUGAR, GRANULATED.

Sugar Snap Pea

See PEAS, EDIBLE POD.

Sugar, Superfine

Also known as bar sugar, caster sugar, and castor sugar (British). Ground finer than granulated sugar, superfine sugar dissolves more easily.

1 lb (500 g) =
2⅓ cups (575 mL)

If You Don't Have It
Substitute 1 cup (250 mL) superfine sugar with:
- 1 cup (250 mL) + 1 tsp (5 mL) granulated sugar finely ground in a blender or small food processor

See also SUGAR, GRANULATED.

Sugar Syrup

Also known as simple syrup. A solution of sugar and water cooked just until the sugar crystals dissolve. These syrups can be of thin, medium, or heavy consistency depending upon the ratio of sugar to water. They have many applications in confectionery and beverages.

If You Don't Have It

Substitute 1 cup (250 mL) sugar syrup with:

- 1 cup (250 mL) Homemade Simple Syrup: Combine 1 cup (250 mL) water and 1 cup (250 mL) granulated sugar in a small saucepan. Bring to a boil over high heat. Then reduce heat to medium or medium-low and gently simmer until sugar is dissolved and mixture is syrupy, 3 to 5 minutes. Let cool and refrigerate in an airtight container for up to 6 months. Makes about 1 cup (250 mL).
- 1 cup (250 mL) Homemade Extra-Light Syrup: Combine 1 cup (250 mL) water and ¼ cup (50 mL) granulated sugar in a small saucepan. Bring to a boil over high heat. Then reduce heat to medium or medium-low and gently simmer until sugar is dissolved and mixture is syrupy, 3 to 5 minutes. Let cool and refrigerate in an airtight container for up to 6 months. Makes about 1 cup (250 mL).
- 1 cup (250 mL) Homemade Light Syrup: Combine 1 cup (250 mL) water and ½ cup (125 mL) granulated sugar in a small saucepan. Bring to a boil over high heat. Then reduce heat to medium or medium-low and gently simmer until sugar is dissolved and mixture is syrupy, 3 to 5 minutes. Let cool and refrigerate in an airtight container for up to 6 months. Makes about 1 cup (250 mL).
- 1 cup (250 mL) Homemade Heavy Syrup: Combine 1 cup (250 mL) water and 1⅓ cups (325 mL) granulated sugar in a small saucepan. Bring to a boil over high heat. Then reduce heat to medium or medium-low and gently simmer until sugar is dissolved and mixture is syrupy, 3 to 5 minutes. Let cool and refrigerate in an airtight container for up to 6 months. Makes about 1 cup (250 mL).

Sugar, Turbinado

See SUGAR, RAW.

Sujuk

Also known as soujouk and yershig. Spicy Lebanese beef sausage.

If You Don't Have It

Substitute 1 lb (500 g) sujuk with:
- 1 lb (500 g) pepperoni
- 1 lb (500 g) sopressata (made with pork; slightly flattened shape; dry and well-seasoned with black pepper)
- 1 lb (500 g) Neapolitan or Napoli salami (made with pork and beef; long and thin; spicy with red and black pepper)
- 1 lb (500 g) Sardinian or Sardo salami (made with pork; spicy with red pepper)
- 1 lb (500 g) Calabrian or Calabrese sausage or salami (made with pork; short and squat; dry and spicy with red pepper)
- 1 lb (500 g) other spicy salami

Sultana

See RAISIN.

Sumac

The tart berries of the Sicilian or elm-leafed sumac are used whole or powdered in Middle Eastern cookery, particularly in parts of Syria, northern Iraq, and other remote areas where fresh lemons are rare.

1 tsp (5 mL) whole berries = 1½ tsp (7 mL) ground sumac

If You Don't Have It

Substitute 1 tsp (5 mL) ground sumac with:
- ¾ tsp (4 mL) whole sumac berries
- 1 tsp (5 mL) finely grated lemon zest
- 1 to 2 tsp (5 to 10 mL) lemon juice
- 1 to 2 tsp (5 to 10 mL) cider vinegar
- 1 tsp (5 mL) za'atar (combines sumac, thyme, sesame seeds, and salt)
- 1 tsp (5 mL) salt-free lemon pepper seasoning
- 1 tsp (5 mL) herbal salt substitute (most have high proportion of lemon)

Summer Sausage

The generic term for any semidry sausage that does not require refrigeration. Contrary to its name, summer sausage is traditionally prepared in the autumn during hunting seasons in North America and Europe.

If You Don't Have It

Substitute 1 lb (500 g) summer sausage with:
- 1 lb (500 g) salami or other dry sausage
- 1 lb (500 g) pepperoni
- 1 lb (500 g) Bierwurst
- 1 lb (500 g) Blockwurst
- 1 lb (500 g) bologna

Summer Sausage Varieties

Choose 1 lb (500 g) summer sausage from these varieties:

- 1 lb (500 g) Thuringer (smoked; made with beef and ham or pork fat; mildly tangy flavor)
- 1 lb (500 g) Lebanon bologna (heavily smoked and dark; made with coarsely chopped beef; tart, tangy flavor)
- 1 lb (500 g) Landjäger (heavily smoked and dark; made with beef; links are slightly flattened in shape; tart flavor)

See also CERVELAT; LANDJÄGER; LEBANON BOLOGNA; THURINGER.

Summer Squash

See PATTYPAN SQUASH; YELLOW SQUASH; ZUCCHINI.

Sunchoke

Also known as Jerusalem artichoke and topinambou. A mild and crisp, native North American tuber that can be eaten raw in salads or cooked as a side dish.

> 1 lb (500 g) =
> 12 medium = 2½ cups
> (625 mL) peeled
> and sliced

If You Don't Have It

Substitute 1 lb (500 g) sunchokes with:

- 1 lb (500 g) oca
- 1 lb (500 g) arrowhead
- 1 lb (500 g) arracacha
- 1 lb (500 g) salsify
- 1 lb (500 g) artichoke hearts (softer texture)
- 1 lb (500 g) water chestnuts (sweeter)
- 1 lb (500 g) jicama (sweeter)
- 1 lb (500 g) potatoes (drier texture; less complex flavor)

Sun-Dried Tomato

Best quality sun-dried tomatoes should be deep red in color, fleshy and flexible with a rich piquant tomato flavor.

> 1 lb (500 g) = 2¾ cups
> (675 mL) sun-dried
> tomato halves
>
> 1 tbsp (15 mL) sun-dried
> tomato paste = 3 to 5
> sun-dried tomatoes

If You Don't Have It

Substitute 3 to 5 sun-dried tomatoes with:

- 1 tbsp (15 mL) sun-dried tomato paste
- 1 tbsp (15 mL) tomato paste (less intense tomato flavor)
- 1 to 2 fresh plum tomatoes (less intense tomato flavor; more watery)

Sunflower Oil

See SUBSTITUTING OILS (PAGE 598).

Sunflower Seeds

Iron-rich seeds of the sunflower plant are eaten as a snack, a condiment, or an addition to breads and other baked goods. They are sold plain and salted.

> 7 oz (210 g) unshelled = 2½ cups (625 mL) unshelled = ¾ cup (175 mL) kernels

If You Don't Have It
Substitute 1 cup (250 mL) sunflower seeds with:
- 1 cup (250 mL) pumpkin seeds (larger; green)
- 1 cup (250 mL) sesame seeds (smaller)
- 1 cup (250 mL) pine nuts (larger)
- 1 cup (250 mL) almonds, peanuts, or other snacking nuts

Sunflower Sprouts

Hulled sunflower kernels that are soaked for a day or so to sprout.

If You Don't Have It
Substitute 1 cup (250 mL) sunflower sprouts with:
- 1 cup (250 mL) mung bean sprouts
- 1 cup (250 mL) soybean sprouts
- 1 cup (250 mL) julienned snow peas

Superfine Sugar

See SUGAR, SUPERFINE.

Surimi

Japanese-style fake shellfish is made by an ancient method dating back to 1100 AD. Mild white-fleshed fish is processed into a flavorless paste then seasoned with natural or artificial shellfish flavoring.

If You Don't Have It
Substitute 1 lb (500 g) surimi with:
- 1 lb (500 g) real crabmeat (much better flavor)
- 1 lb (500 g) lobster (firmer)
- 1 lb (500 g) shrimp (firmer)
- 1 lb (500 g) scallops
- 1 lb (500 g) monkfish
- 1 lb (500 g) cod

Sushi Mat

Also known as a sushi roller or sudare. Looks like a place mat made of tiny bamboo slats. It is used to roll and shape the hot cooked seasoned rice for sushi.

If You Don't Have It
Substitute a sushi mat with:
- flexible plastic place mat
- flexible silicone baking sheet

Sushi Nori

See NORI.

Suze

A French bittersweet herbal liqueur. Its most pronounced essence is gentian, also one of the flavors in angostura bitters.

If You Don't Have It

Substitute 2 tbsp (25 mL) Suze with:
- 2 tbsp (25 mL) Punt e Mes
- 2 tbsp (25 mL) Amer Picon
- 2 tbsp (25 mL) Byrrh
- 2 tbsp (25 mL) Campari

Swedish Limpa Bread

See LIMPA BREAD.

Sweet Acidophilus Milk

See MILK, WHOLE.

Sweet Basil

See BASIL.

Sweet Bean Sauce

See BEAN SAUCE.

Sweet Cherry

See CHERRY, SWEET.

Sweet Cicely

See CHERVIL; CICELY.

Sweet Dumpling Squash

Pretty, little winter squash with green stripes on a cream rind when harvested but turning pale orange in storage. The cooked flesh is mealier than other squash, with a fresh taste hinting of corn. Unlike most winter squashes, the skin is thin enough to eat.

1 lb (500 g) =
1 cup (250 mL)
cooked and mashed

If You Don't Have It

Substitute 1 cup (250 mL) chopped sweet dumpling squash with:
- 1 cup (250 mL) chopped delicata squash
- 1 cup (250 mL) chopped butternut squash (tougher peel)
- 1 cup (250 mL) chopped buttercup squash (tougher peel)
- 1 cup (250 mL) chopped pumpkin (tougher peel)
- 1 cup (250 mL) chopped sweet potato

Sweetened Condensed Milk

Milk reduced by evaporation then sweetened. A 14-oz (398 mL) can is made from 1 quart (1 L) whole milk and 7 ounces (210 g) of granulated sugar. An essential ingredient for genuine Key lime pie.

> 14-oz (398 mL) can =
> 1¼ cups (300 mL)

If You Don't Have It
Substitute 1 14-oz (398 mL) can sweetened condensed milk (8% to 10% fat) with:
- 1 cup (250 mL) evaporated milk + 1¼ cups (300 mL) granulated sugar, heated until sugar dissolves

For Better Health
Substitute 1 14-oz (398 mL) can sweetened condensed milk with:
- 1 14-oz (398 mL) can fat-free sweetened condensed milk

Sweet Gherkin

Pickles that are named for a variety of tiny cucumbers.

If You Don't Have It
Substitute 1 cup (250 mL) sweet gherkins with:
- 1 cup (250 mL) cornichons (more tart)
- 1 cup (250 mL) bread and butter pickles
- 1 cup (250 mL) small whole or sliced dill pickles (more tart)

Sweet Marjoram

See MARJORAM.

Sweet Pepper

Pod vegetables that are called sweet to distinguish them from their hot cousins, the chile peppers. Sweet peppers include red pimientos, Cubanelles, yellow banana peppers, and the most common bell peppers. Freshly picked peppers keep fine at room temperature for several days. For longer storage, refrigerate in a perforated plastic bag.

If You Don't Have It
Substitute 1 cup (250 mL) chopped fresh sweet peppers with:
- 1 cup (250 mL) chopped fresh Anaheim peppers (spicier)
- 1 cup (250 mL) chopped fresh poblano peppers (spicier)
- ½ cup (125 mL) dried bell peppers

Sweet Pepper Varieties
Choose 1 cup (250 mL) chopped fresh sweet peppers from these popular varieties:
- 1 cup (250 mL) chopped fresh bell peppers (bell-shaped; sweet and juicy with thick walls; green, red, yellow, orange, purple, or brown colors; the most popular sweet pepper variety)

1 lb (500 g) bell peppers
= 2 large = 2½ cups
(625 mL) chopped =
3 cups (750 mL) sliced

1 lb (500 g) Cubanelles,
banana peppers or
pimientos = 2½ cups
(625 mL) chopped

- 1 cup (250 mL) chopped fresh, canned, or bottled pimiento (heart-shaped; sweet, juicy, and more complex flavor than bell peppers; red color; often used fresh to stuff olives or dried to make paprika)
- 1 cup (250 mL) chopped fresh banana peppers (long and banana-shaped; sweet and slightly less juicy than bell peppers; pale yellow color)
- 1 cup (250 mL) chopped fresh Cubanelle peppers (long and banana-shaped but more tapered than banana peppers; sweet and slightly less juicy but more complex flavor than bell peppers; yellow to red color)
- 1 cup (250 mL) chopped fresh bull's horn peppers (thin, curved shape; sweet and less juicy than bell peppers; green color)

See also BELL PEPPER; CHILE PEPPER; PIMIENTO.

Sweet Potato

"Sweet potatoes, potatoes, and yams are not *related," writes produce authority Elizabeth Schneider. Orange-fleshed sweet potatoes, such as the Beauregard, Jewel, and Garnet, are preferred only in North America and Europe. In Asia, where sweet potatoes are a major food crop, varieties are typically ivory in color with a medium sweet flavor and creamy texture. Yams, the name U.S. markets commonly misapply to sweet potatoes, are large white-fleshed bland tropical tubers.*

If You Don't Have It
Substitute 1 cup (250 mL) chopped sweet potatoes with:
- 1 cup (250 mL) chopped sweet pumpkin
- 1 cup (250 mL) chopped butternut squash (more firm)
- 1 cup (250 mL) chopped buttercup squash (more firm)
- 1 cup (250 mL) chopped dumpling squash (lighter orange flesh)
- 1 cup (250 mL) chopped white or cushcush yams (white flesh; more starchy; less sweet)
- 1 cup (250 mL) chopped russet potatoes (white flesh; more starchy; less sweet)

Sweet Potato Varieties
Choose 1 cup (250 mL) chopped sweet potatoes from these varieties:
- 1 cup (250 mL) chopped orange-flesh sweet potatoes (the most common variety; brown or reddish skin; orange flesh; soft and sweet flesh when cooked)
- 1 cup (250 mL) chopped white-flesh sweet potatoes (tan skin; cream-color flesh; soft and sweet flesh when cooked)

Sweet Potato (cont'd)

1 lb (500 g) fresh =
3 medium = 3½ to
4 cups (875 mL to 1 L)
chopped or sliced

15½ oz (440 mL) can =
1½ to 1¾ cups
(375 to 425 mL)

- 1 cup (250 mL) chopped boniato (red or brown skin; sometimes more lumpy in shape than orange-flesh sweet potatoes; white flesh; less sweet and more dry, starchy flesh than orange-flesh sweet potatoes)
- 1 cup (250 mL) chopped Asian, Japanese, or Korean sweet potatoes (reddish skin; cream-color flesh; slightly less sweet and slightly drier than orange-flesh sweet potatoes)

See also BONIATO; YAM.

Sweet Rice Flour

See RICE FLOUR, SWEET.

Sweetsop

Also known as sugar apple. This fruit of a tropical American tree is popular in Latin America, the West Indies, and India. The scaly, green skin protects the luscious custard-like fruit within. The seeds are poisonous and should not be eaten.

1 sweetsop = 12 oz to
1 lb (375 to 500 g)

If You Don't Have It
Substitute 1 lb (500 g) sweetsop with:
- 1 lb (500 g) cherimoya (larger)
- 1 lb (500 g) atemoya (hybrid of sweetsop and cherimoya)
- 1 lb (500 g) soursop (larger)

See also ATEMOYA; CHERIMOYA; SOURSOP.

Swiss Chard

See CHARD.

Swiss Cheese

Also known as American-style Swiss cheese. Countless generic cheeses — pale yellow, nutty flavored, riddled with holes — attempt to recreate Switzerland's esteemed Emmental and Gruyère.

1 lb (500 g) = 4 cups
(1 L) shredded

If You Don't Have It
Substitute 1 oz (30 g) Swiss cheese with:
- 1 oz (30 g) Emmental
- 1 oz (30 g) Gruyère
- 1 oz (30 g) Jarlsberg
- 1 oz (30 g) slice provolone (to replace slices of Swiss for sandwiches)

Swordfish

The "steak" of seafood, the firm, succulent, mild flesh of this large sea fish has become very popular with diners.

If You Don't Have It
Substitute 1 lb (500 g) swordfish with:
- 1 lb (500 g) marlin
- 1 lb (500 g) tuna
- 1 lb (500 g) shark
- 1 lb (500 g) mahi-mahi
- 1 lb (500 g) grouper
- 1 lb (500 g) halibut

Syrup

See SPECIFIC TYPES.

Szechuan Pepper

Also known as Chinese pepper, flower pepper, and sansho pepper. Dried berries of the prickly ash tree with a peppery taste, citrus aroma, and lingering fizzy sensation on the tongue. The dried and powdered leaves of the same tree are called sansho and used in Japanese cooking.

If You Don't Have It
Substitute 1 tbsp (15 mL) Szechuan peppercorns with:
- 2 tsp (10 mL) black peppercorns + 1 tsp (5 mL) finely grated lemon zest
- 1 tbsp (15 mL) salt-free lemon-pepper seasoning

To Vary the Flavor
Substitute 1 tbsp (15 mL) Szechuan peppercorns with:
- 1 to 1½ tbsp (15 to 22 mL) shichimi togarashi (spicier; combines Szechuan peppercorns, dried red chiles, sesame and/or poppy seeds, dried orange peel, and nori)

See also PEPPERCORN; SANSHO.

Tabasco to Tybo

Tabasco®

See HOT PEPPER SAUCE.

Tabil

A blazing Tunisian spice paste that's similar to harissa but even hotter. Among its components are cilantro, coriander seeds, caraway seeds, garlic, sweet peppers, and chile peppers.

If You Don't Have It

Substitute 1 tbsp (15 mL) tabil with:
- 1 tbsp (15 mL) Homemade Tabil: Toast 1 tsp (5 mL) caraway seeds and 1 tsp (5 mL) coriander seeds in a dry skillet over medium heat until fragrant, about 2 minutes. Grind to a powder in a spice grinder, blender, or with a mortar and pestle (preferred method). If using a spice grinder, transfer to a blender or small food processor and add 1 large chopped garlic clove, 1 to 1½ tsp (5 to 7 mL) cayenne pepper, and 1 tbsp (15 mL) vegetable oil. Grind to a paste and add salt to taste. Makes about ¼ cup (50 mL).

To Vary the Flavor

Substitute 1 tbsp (15 mL) tabil with:
- 1 tbsp (15 mL) harissa (a similar spice paste from Tunisia; adds paprika and cumin flavors)
- 1 tbsp (15 mL) chile paste
- 1 tbsp (15 mL) berbere
- 1 to 3 tsp (5 to 15 mL) hot sauce (less aromatic)

See also HARISSA.

Taco Sauce

A bottled condiment that is the Mexican-American adaptation of a traditional Mexican sauce made from roasted tomatoes, hot chiles, onion, garlic, and sometimes spices such as cumin.

If You Don't Have It

Substitute 1 cup (250 mL) taco sauce with:
- 1 cup (250 mL) enchilada sauce (often spicier)
- 1 cup (250 mL) tomato salsa (chunkier)
- 1 cup (250 mL) chili sauce

Taco Seasoning Mix

Americanized Mexican spice blend typically used to season ground beef for tacos.

1¼ oz (35 g) pkg =
¼ cup (50 mL)

If You Don't Have It

Substitute 1 tbsp (15 mL) taco seasoning mix with:
- 1 tbsp (15 mL) Homemade Taco Seasoning Mix: Combine 2 tsp (10 mL) pure chile powder, ¼ tsp (1 mL) dried oregano, ¼ tsp (1 mL) ground cumin, ⅛ tsp (0.5 mL) garlic powder, ⅛ tsp (0.5 mL) onion powder, and a pinch of cayenne pepper. Add salt to taste. Makes about 1 tablespoon (15 mL).
- 1 tbsp (15 mL) chili powder

Taco Shell

See TORTILLA, CORN.

Tahini

Thick paste of ground sesame seeds that's essential in many Middle Eastern specialties, including baba ghanoush and hummus.

If You Don't Have It

Substitute 1 cup (250 mL) tahini with:
- 1 cup (250 mL) sesame seeds ground in a blender with enough untoasted sesame oil, peanut oil, or vegetable oil to create a smooth paste
- ¾ cup (175 mL) peanut butter, almond butter, or cashew butter + ¼ cup (50 mL) untoasted sesame oil (more peanutty flavor)
- 1 cup (250 mL) peanut butter, almond butter, or cashew butter

See also SESAME SEEDS.

Taleggio

A soft, buttery Stracchino-style Italian cheese made from cow's milk in the Taleggio Valley near Bergamo in the Lombardy region.

If You Don't Have It

Substitute 1 oz (30 g) Taleggio with:
- 1 oz (30 g) Robiola Lombardia
- 1 oz (30 g) Fontina
- 1 oz (30 g) Beaumont
- 1 oz (30 g) Reblochon

See also STRACCHINO.

Tamari

See SOY SAUCE.

Tamarillo

Also known as tree tomato. A gorgeous tree fruit indigenous to South America, this pointed egg-shaped fruit has glossy red or golden skin and deep apricot flesh marked by whorls of purple seeds.

> 1 lb (500 g) = 5 medium
> = 2 cups (500 mL)
> chopped

If You Don't Have It
Substitute 1 lb (500 g) tamarillos with:
- 1 lb (500 g) pepinos
- 1 lb (500 g) babacos (less flavorful)
- 1 lb (500 g) papaya (less tart)
- 1 lb (500 g) plum tomatoes (less tart)

Tamarind Concentrate

Also known as tamarind paste. The tart dried pulp of the pods from an Asian shade tree. Tamarind concentrate is the most widely used form. From it, tamarind "juice" is made by soaking 1 cup (250 mL) of tamarind concentrate in 4 cups (1 L) hot water then straining and pressing on the solids to extract the juice.

If You Don't Have
Substitute 1 tbsp (15 mL) tamarind concentrate or paste with:
- 1½ tbsp (22 mL) mango powder or amchur (for acidity)
- 1 to 1½ tbsp (15 to 22 mL) lime or lemon juice (for acidity)
- 1 tbsp (15 mL) Worcestershire sauce (less acidic; adds other flavors, including vinegar, molasses, anchovies, onion, and garlic)

Tandoori Paste

Also known as tandoori coloring. A seasoning and coloring mixture of herbs, aromatics and spices that give tandoori chicken its distinctive reddish hue and spicy flavor. The paste is often mixed with yogurt to make a marinade for chicken prior to roasting in a tandoor.

If You Don't Have It
Substitute 1 cup (250 mL) tandoori paste with:
- 1 cup (250 mL) Homemade Tandoori Paste: Combine 8 to 10 finely minced garlic cloves, ¼ cup (50 mL) finely minced fresh ginger, 1 tbsp (15 mL) garam masala (see page 200), 1 tbsp (15 mL) paprika, 2 tsp (10 mL) ground coriander, 1 tsp (5 mL) ground cumin, ½ to 1 tsp (2 to 5 mL) cayenne pepper, and 2 to 3 tbsp (25 to 45 mL) vegetable oil or enough to make a thick paste. If you like, stir in ½ tsp (2 mL) yellow food coloring and ¼ tsp (1 mL) red food coloring for color.

Tandoor Oven

A style of clay oven found in countries from the Middle East to India. It is a large clay jar with an opening at the bottom for adding and removing fuel. Flatbreads are slapped onto the heated vertical walls of the tandoor where they quickly bake by a combination of radiant heat and convection. As the heat subsides somewhat, casseroles and other dishes are placed in the oven to bake.

If You Don't Have It

Substitute a tandoor oven with:
- brick oven
- charcoal or gas grill (to help get a crisp crust, use a ceramic-type grill such as the Big Green Egg; or use any other grill and a pizza stone or unglazed quarry tiles to absorb moisture)

Tangelo

A cross between the pummelo and the tangerine, this citrus has juicy, tart-sweet flesh with few seeds. The skin is loose and size varies from that of a tangerine to a small grapefruit. The Minneola is the most common variety in the U.S.

> 1 lb (500 g) = 4 medium
> = 2 cups (500 mL)
> sections

If You Don't Have It

Substitute 1 tangelo with:
- 1 mandarin orange (typically orange flesh; sweet flavor with honey aromas)
- 1 Moro or blood orange (red flesh; sweet-tart, complex flavor)
- 1 navel orange (orange flesh; sweeter)
- 1 Rangpur or mandarin lime (sweet-tart; complex mandarin and lime aromas)
- 1 calamondin (orange flesh; acidic)
- ½ to 1 grapefruit (typically pink or white flesh; sweetly tart flavor)

Tangelo Varieties

Choose 1 tangelo from these varieties:
- 1 Minneola (orange flesh; sweet-tart flavor with honey aromas)
- 1 Nocatee (white to yellow flesh; sweetly tart like grapefruit)
- 1 Sampson (yellow orange flesh; tart flavor; best for juicing or as an ornamental)

Tangerine

See MANDARIN ORANGE.

Tapenade

Intense paste of ripe olives, capers, anchovies, olive oil, lemon juice and seasonings is one of the glories of Provençal cooking. It enlivens raw vegetables, cooked fish or seafood, various meats, and other preparations.

If You Don't Have It

Substitute 1 cup (250 mL) tapenade with:

- 1 cup (250 mL) Homemade Tapenade: Put 1 cup (250 mL) pitted black olives (oil-cured, Niçoise, or Kalamata), 1 cup (250 mL) loosely packed fresh parsley leaves, 3 tbsp (45 mL) extra virgin olive oil, 2 tbsp (25 mL) drained capers, 5 anchovy fillets or 2½ tsp (12 mL) anchovy paste, 1 chopped garlic clove, 2 tsp (10 mL) chopped fresh thyme leaves, 2 tsp (10 mL) lemon juice, and ¼ tsp (1 mL) ground black pepper in a small food processor, blender or large mortar. Pulse or grind until finely minced but not completely puréed. Refrigerate for up to 1 month. Makes about 1½ cups (375 mL).

To Vary the Flavor

Substitute 1 cup (250 mL) tapenade with:

- 1 cup (250 mL) basil pesto
- 1 cup (250 mL) sun-dried tomato paste
- 1 cup (250 mL) roasted red pepper pesto

Tapioca

From the roots of the cassava plant comes pearl tapioca, which looks like beads and is often used to make tapioca pudding. Granulated quick-cooking or instant tapioca is convenient for thickening fruit pies to a clear gel. Ground tapioca flour or starch thickens pies, puddings, stews, and sauces without leaving behind any swollen beads.

1 lb (500 g) pearl tapioca = 2¾ cups (675 mL) = 7½ cups (1.875 L) cooked

1 lb (500 g) quick-cooking tapioca = 3 cups (750 mL) = 7½ cups (1.875 L) cooked

If You Don't Have It

Substitute 1 tbsp (15 mL) quick-cooking tapioca (for thickening) with:

- 1½ to 2 tsp (7 to 10 mL) sweet rice flour (does not separate when frozen)
- 2 to 3 tsp (10 to 15 mL) tapioca flour or cassava flour (does not separate when frozen)
- 2 tbsp (25 mL) small pearl tapioca, soaked (or, to approximate tapioca flour, ground in a clean spice grinder or with a mortar and pestle; does not separate when frozen)
- 2 to 3 tsp (10 to 15 mL) gari (fermented, roasted, and ground cassava; best for thickening stews)
- 2 to 3 tsp (10 to 15 mL) sago flour or pearls
- 2 tsp (10 mL) arrowroot powder (separates when frozen)
- 1 heaping tbsp (15 mL) all-purpose flour (cook a few minutes after thickening to cook out raw flour taste; separates when frozen)
- 1½ to 2 tsp (7 to 10 mL) cornstarch, potato starch, or rice starch (separates when frozen)

Taro

Also known as dasheen and malanga. Small, dark, rough-skinned cormels of taro have a moist bland flesh. The larger barrel-shaped dark shaggy roots have dense flesh that tastes of coconut, potato, and chestnut.

> 1 lb (500 g) = 3½ to 4 cups (875 mL to 1 L) chopped or sliced = 2 cups (500 mL)

If You Don't Have It

Substitute 1 lb (500 g) taro with:
- 1 lb (500 g) yautía or malanga
- 1 lb (500 g) cassava
- 1 lb (500 g) boniato
- 1 lb (500 g) potatoes
- 1 lb (500 g) parsnips

See also CALLALOO.

Tarragon

The distinctive anise flavor of this herb is most associated with the French kitchen in dishes where it flavors vinegar and seasons dishes such as poulet à l'estragon *and* sauce béarnaise.

> 1 oz (30 g) fresh leaves = ⅔ cup (150 mL)
>
> 1 oz (30 g) dried leaves = 1 cup (250 mL)

If You Don't Have It

Substitute 1 tbsp (15 mL) chopped fresh tarragon with:
- 1 tbsp (15 mL) chopped fresh cicely
- 1 tbsp (15 mL) chopped fresh chervil (milder anise flavor)
- 1 tbsp (15 mL) chopped fresh fennel leaves (milder anise flavor)
- 1 tbsp (15 mL) chopped fresh fines herbes (usually includes tarragon, chervil, chives, and parsley)
- 1 tbsp (15 mL) chopped fresh parsley
- 1 tsp (5 mL) dried tarragon (much less flavorful)
- 1 tbsp (15 mL) chopped fresh dill (particularly with chicken, fish, eggs, and cheese)

Tartar Sauce

See MAYONNAISE.

Tasso

Spiced and smoked piece of pork or beef used in Cajun cooking as a seasoning ingredient.

If You Don't Have It

Substitute 4 oz (125 g) tasso with:
- 4 oz (125 g) smoked ham, Canadian bacon, slab bacon, or hog jowl + 1 tbsp (15 mL) Cajun seasoning
- 4 oz (125 g) Cajun andouille
- 4 oz (125 g) spicy smoked sausage

Tatsoi

Also known as flat cabbage and rosette bok choy. Sometimes growing flat, sometimes in a bouquet, this variety of bok choy has celery-color stems and dark green puckered leaves. More strongly flavored than other bok choy. Young tiny leaves are good in salads. Larger leaves are wonderful in soups and stir-fries.

> 1 lb (500 g) =
> 6 cups (1.5 L) chopped

If You Don't Have It
Substitute 1 lb (500 g) tatsoi with:
- 1 lb (500 g) Shanghai or baby bok choy (for cooking; not fresh salads)
- 1 lb (500 g) mizuna
- 1 lb (500 g) baby spinach leaves
- 1 lb (500 g) arugula (more bitter and peppery, less cabbagey flavor)
- 1 lb (500 g) escarole
- 1 lb (500 g) broccoli raab (for cooking)
- 1 lb (500 g) mustard greens (for cooking)

See also BOK CHOY.

Tautog

See BLACKFISH.

Tayberry

Named after the Tay River in Scotland, where this blackberry-raspberry hybrid was developed in the late 1970s, the tayberry tastes similar to a loganberry with a bit more zest.

> 1 pint fresh =
> 2 cups (500 mL)

If You Don't Have It
Substitute 1 cup (250 mL) tayberries with:
- 1 cup (250 mL) loganberries (hybrid of blackberries and raspberries; dark red color)
- 1 cup (250 mL) boysenberries (hybrid of blackberries, raspberries, and loganberries; reddish purple color)
- 1 cup (250 mL) olallieberries (hybrid of youngberries and loganberries; dark purple color; larger; sweeter)
- 1 cup (250 mL) blackberries (larger; darker purple color)
- 1 cup (250 mL) youngberry (larger; red color)
- 1 cup (250 mL) raspberries (sweeter; red color)

Teewurst

A smoky, spreadable sausage similar to liverwurst. Germans enjoy it spread on bread or crackers at teatime.

If You Don't Have It
Substitute 1 lb (500 g) Teewurst with:
- 1 lb (500 g) Braunschweiger
- 1 lb (500 g) liverwurst
- 1 lb (500 g) Mettwurst
- 1 lb (500 g) pâté

Teff

Also known as tef. The seeds of a North African species of lovegrass. Similar to millet but much tinier. Teff is high in protein, containing all eight essential amino acids. It is extensively cultivated in Ethiopia, India, and Australia.

> 2 cups (500 mL) =
> 4 cups (1 L) cooked

If You Don't Have It

Substitute 1 cup (250 mL) teff with:

- 1 cup (250 mL) quinoa
- 1 cup (250 mL) millet
- 1 cup (250 mL) couscous, especially whole wheat (cooks more quickly)
- 1 cup (250 mL) bulgur
- 1 cup (250 mL) cracked wheat (takes longer to cook)
- 1 cup (250 mL) brown rice (takes longer to cook)
- 1 cup (250 mL) kasha (roasted buckwheat groats; takes longer to cook)

Teff Flour

See CHOOSING AMONG WHOLE-GRAIN AND ALTERNATIVE FLOURS (PAGE 586).

Teleme

A soft and tangy cow's milk cheese associated with Northern California. As it ages, the flavor becomes more assertive and the texture more runny.

If You Don't Have It

Substitute 1 oz (30 g) Teleme with:

- 1 oz (30 g) Touloumi (made with goat's milk)
- 1 oz (30 g) Monterey Jack

See also TOULOUMI.

Tempeh

Also known as tempe. Made from fermented cooked soybeans, this meat replacement has a mild mushroom-like aroma, earthy flavor, and toothsome texture. Because it holds its shape well and absorbs seasonings, it is used as the base for numerous vegetarian prepared foods.

If You Don't Have It

Substitute 1 lb (500 g) tempeh with:

- 1 lb (500 g) firm tofu, drained and pressed (softer and moister; more bland)
- 1 lb (500 g) seitan (chewier; more bland)
- 1 lb (500 g) vegetarian meat substitutes (available in the frozen section of most grocery stores)
- 1 cup (250 mL) textured vegetable protein, reconstituted in 1½ to 2 cups (375 to 500 mL) vegetable stock (to replace crumbled tempeh; less chewy; less flavorful)

Temperature

See TEMPERATURE EQUIVALENTS (PAGE 605).

Temple Orange

See MANDARIN ORANGE.

Tempura Oil

A combination of safflower oil and untoasted sesame oil traditionally used in Japan for deep-frying pieces of batter-dipped vegetables and fish.

If You Don't Have It
Substitute 1 cup (250 mL) tempura oil with:
- ½ cup (125 mL) safflower or soybean oil + ½ cup (125 mL) untoasted sesame oil
- 1 cup (250 mL) safflower oil

Tenderizer

See MEAT TENDERIZER, POWDERED.

Tentsuyu

Japanese dipping sauce that cools and flavors foods hot from the fryer such as tempura. Typically, a mixture of mirin, dashi, soy sauce, and sugar.

If You Don't Have It
Substitute 1 cup (250 mL) tentsuyu with:
- 1 cup (250 mL) Homemade Tentsuyu: Combine 1 cup (250 mL) heated dashi or reconstituted dashi-no-moto, ¼ cup (50 mL) tamari or soy sauce, 2 tbsp (25 mL) mirin (or 1 to 2 tsp/5 to 10 mL granulated sugar plus 2 tbsp/25 mL sake), 2 tbsp (25 mL) sake or dry vermouth or sherry, and 1 to 2 tsp (10 mL) freshly grated ginger. Makes about 1½ cups (375 mL).
- 1 cup (250 mL) teriyaki sauce
- 1 cup (250 mL) soy sauce

Tepin

See CHOOSING DRIED CHILES (PAGE 578); CHOOSING FRESH CHILES (PAGE 582).

Tequila

A distinctive Mexican liquor produced by fermenting and distilling the sweet sap of the blue agave cactus. Not to be confused with mezcal, a very similar liquor, which may be made from any mixture of agave species, anywhere in Mexico. By law, tequila can only be made in the states of Guanajuato, Jalisco, Michoacan, Mayarit, and Tamaulipas and must contain 51% blue agave

If You Don't Have It
Substitute 2 tbsp (25 mL) tequila with:
- 2 tbsp (25 mL) pulque (thicker; milky-white; lower in alcohol)
- 2 tbsp (25 mL) vodka (less flavorful)
- 2 tbsp (25 mL) light rum
- 2 tbsp (25 mL) grappa

Tequila Varieties
Choose 2 tbsp (25 mL) tequila from these varieties:
- 2 tbsp (25 mL) tequila blanco, white, or silver tequila (colorless; unaged or aged 1 to 2 months; fiery and peppery with gasoline aromas in lesser-quality versions; often used for mixed drinks)

(the remainder is mostly sugarcane). Tequilas labeled 100% blue agave are often of better quality. Four categories exist. Blanco, also known as white, plata, or silver, captures the herbaceous character of the newly distilled liquor. Joven abocado, also known as gold, is a colored and flavored blanco. Resposado may also be colored and flavored but must be aged in wood for between 2 and 12 months, a process that contributes hints of vanilla and spice. Añejo is aged for 1 to 3 years to create a tequila complex and elegant enough for sipping.

- 2 tbsp (25 mL) tequila joven abocado or gold tequila (gold color; silver tequila with added coloring and flavoring; often used for mixed drinks)
- 2 tbsp (25 mL) tequila reposado or rested tequila (pale straw to gold color; aged 2 to 12 months; spirited yet softer, mellowed flavor, often with aromas of vanilla; may contain added coloring and flavoring; good for sipping or uncomplicated mixed drinks such as margaritas)
- 2 tbsp (25 mL) añejo or aged tequila (gold to deep amber color; aged at least 1 year but preferably longer; smooth, complex flavor often with hints of vanilla and mild oak; best for sipping)
- 2 tbsp (25 mL) mezcal (clear or pale straw and potent; harsh, smoky flavor that's often sweetened or softened with fruits, herbs, or nuts; made from any mixture of agave, anywhere in Mexico; often marketed with a worm in the bottle; often used for mixed drinks or shots)

Testerbranntwein

See GRAPPA.

Tetragonia

See NEW ZEALAND SPINACH.

Textured Vegetable Protein

Also known as TVP, textured soy protein (TSP), and vegetable protein. A neutrally flavored dried granular ingredient produced from refined soybean meal. It's used as a ground meat extender in many processed foods. Vegetarians often cook it as a meat substitute. It's most commonly available as granules but also comes in chunks and flakes. It's sold in natural food stores.

If You Don't Have It
Substitute 1 cup (250 mL) reconstituted textured vegetable protein granules with:

- 1 lb (500 g) vegetarian ground beef or crumbles (often a mix of textured vegetable protein, tofu, and seitan; more flavorful)
- 1 lb (500 g) firm tofu, frozen, thawed, and crumbled with a few quick pulses in a food processor (less chewy; less flavorful)
- 1 lb (500 g) tempeh (stronger flavor)
- 1 lb (500 g) prepared seitan (more chewy)
- 1 lb (500 g) ground beef, pork, turkey, or chicken

Thai Basil

See BASIL.

Thai Fish Sauce

See FISH SAUCE.

Thai Ginger

See GALANGAL.

Thai Sweet Black Soy Sauce

See SOY SAUCE.

Thermometer

Meat thermometers take the guesswork out of knowing when roasts, poultry, and even bread are cooked through but not overdone. The older style thermometer is inserted into the food at the beginning of the cooking time and remains throughout the cooking process. More recent advancements have brought us instant-reading and digital thermometers, which only need to be inserted when checking the temperature.

If You Don't Have It

Substitute a meat thermometer with:

- The touch test (for steaks): Press your fingertip into the meat. If it's soft, the meat is most likely medium-rare (about 145°F/63°C); if it springs back a bit, the meat is most likely medium (about 160°F/71°C); if it is stiff, the meat is most likely well-done (about 165°F/74°C). These are inexact doneness tests; if the quality or cleanliness of your meat is questionable, use a thermometer to be sure the meat is properly cooked.

See also TEMPERATURE EQUIVALENTS (PAGE 605).

Thimbleberry

See RASPBERRY.

Thompson Grape

See GRAPE, TABLE; RAISIN.

Thuringer

A group of semidry summer sausages often made with beef, ham, pork fat, and mild spices such as coriander.

If You Don't Have It

Substitute 1 lb (500 g) Thuringer with:

- 1 lb (500 g) Landjäger
- 1 lb (500 g) Lebanon bologna
- 1 lb (500 g) other semidry or summer sausage
- 1 lb (500 g) salami or other dry sausage
- 1 lb (500 g) pepperoni

See also CERVELAT; SUMMER SAUSAGE.

Thyme

"Sun loving, tiny leafed but tough, thyme tastes and smells warm, earthy and flowery. Use it in every kind of long-simmered and red-wine dish, with rabbit, veal and chicken in all their tomatoey forms, in a bouquet garni and marinades and — instead of rosemary — with lamb." — The Cook Book *by Terence and Caroline Conran.*

1 oz (30 g) fresh leaves = ⅔ cup (150 mL)

1 oz (30 g) dried leaves = ½ cup (125 mL)

If You Don't Have It

Substitute 1 tbsp (15 mL) fresh thyme leaves with:

- ¾ to 1 tsp (4 to 5 mL) dried thyme
- 1 tbsp (15 mL) chopped fresh marjoram
- 1 tbsp (15 mL) chopped fresh oregano
- 1 tbsp (15 mL) chopped fresh basil
- 1 tbsp (15 mL) chopped fresh summer savory
- 1 to 2 tsp (5 to 10 mL) chopped fresh sage
- 2 to 3 tsp (10 to 15 mL) chopped fresh rosemary (more pine-like resinous aromas)
- 1 tsp (5 mL) dried Italian seasoning (usually combines thyme, oregano, and basil)
- 1 tsp (5 mL) dried poultry seasoning (usually combines dried thyme, sage, and marjoram)
- 1 tsp (5 mL) Herbes de Provence (often combines thyme, savory, marjoram, lavender, rosemary, fennel seeds, and bay leaves)
- 2 tsp (10 mL) dried ajwain (a southern Indian spice with aromas similar to thyme)

Thyme Varieties

Choose 1 tbsp (15 mL) fresh thyme leaves from these varieties:

- 1 tbsp (15 mL) fresh garden thyme leaves (small, gray-green leaves with a warming, citrus-like sharpness; includes narrow-leafed French thyme and broad-leafed English thyme)
- 1 tbsp (15 mL) fresh lemon thyme leaves (hybrid of garden thyme and wild thyme; small green leaves; less pungent and more lemony aroma than garden thyme)

Tía Maria

See COFFEE LIQUEUR.

Tilapia

Also known as St. Peter's fish. A mild and versatile white-fleshed fish originating in East Africa. It's now a major aqua-cultured specimen.

If You Don't Have It

Substitute 1 lb (500 g) tilapia with:

- 1 lb (500 g) porgy
- 1 lb (500 g) black sea bass
- 1 lb (500 g) red snapper
- 1 lb (500 g) orange roughy
- 1 lb (500 g) ocean perch
- 1 lb (500 g) sole
- 1 lb (500 g) flounder

Ti Leaves

The shiny green leaves of a tropical Asian/Polynesian plant are used as a pot herb or food wrapper.

If You Don't Have It

Substitute ti leaves (as a food wrapper) with:

- banana leaves (adds mild herby-green aroma)
- corn husks (much smaller; adds mild corn aroma)
- hoja santa leaves (much smaller; adds aromas of root beer and fennel)
- parchment paper (no flavor)
- aluminum foil (no flavor; reduce cooking time slightly)

Tilefish

Although he tastes good, it's the North Atlantic tilefish's looks that get him noticed. He is one of the most brilliantly colored fish found outside of the tropics. Various body parts are colored bluish green, pinkish purple, yellow, rose, white, red, and spotted yellow.

If You Don't Have It

Substitute 1 lb (500 g) tilefish with:

- 1 lb (500 g) blackfish
- 1 lb (500 g) croaker
- 1 lb (500 g) black sea bass
- 1 lb (500 g) halibut
- 1 lb (500 g) grouper
- 1 lb (500 g) red snapper
- 1 lb (500 g) turbot
- 1 lb (500 g) weakfish
- 1 lb (500 g) cod
- 1 lb (500 g) haddock

Tilsit

Also known as tilsiter. In the mid-1800s, Dutch settlers in East Prussia had their Gouda cheese hijacked by local molds, yeast, and bacteria. The resulting semisoft, tangy Tilsit cheese is ivory or butter colored with tiny holes.

> 1 lb (500 g) = 4 cups (1 L) shredded

If You Don't Have It

Substitute 1 oz (30 g) Tilsit with:

- 1 oz (30 g) Havarti (milder)
- 1 oz (30 g) Esrom (stronger)
- 1 oz (30 g) Fontina (more nutty)
- 1 oz (30 g) Monterey Jack
- 1 oz (30 g) brick cheese

Timbale

Named after its drum shape, this baking mold is usually high-sided and tapered at the bottom.

If You Don't Have It

Substitute a timbale with:

- custard cup
- deep muffin cup
- tall-sided ramekin

Tiramisù Liqueur

See CHOCOLATE LIQUEUR.

Toasted Sesame Oil

See SESAME OIL, TOASTED; SUBSTITUTING OILS (PAGE 598).

Tocino

See PANCETTA.

Tofu

Also known as bean curd and soybean curd. Think of tofu as "cheese" made from "milk" extracted from cooked soybeans instead of cows. Those who love to hate tofu complain that it is bland, but that is one of tofu's strengths. It absorbs flavors beautifully and adapts to numerous ethnic seasonings. It's processed into a variety of textures — silken, soft, firm and extra-firm. It can be found in supermarkets, water-packed in sealed containers, vacuum-packed without water, aseptically packaged, or freeze-dried. In some Asian markets, it is displayed in tubs of water.

If You Don't Have It

Substitute 1 lb (500 g) tofu with:
- 1 lb (500 g) tempeh (stronger flavor)
- 1 lb (500 g) prepared seitan (more chewy)
- 1 cup (250 mL) reconstituted textured vegetable protein granules (to replace crumbled tofu)
- 1 lb (500 g) panir (to replace cubed tofu in savory dishes)
- 1 lb (500 g) vegetarian beef, pork, or chicken products (often a mix of textured vegetable protein, tofu, and seitan; more flavorful; available in the frozen section of most grocery stores)
- 1 lb (500 g) beef, pork, turkey, or chicken

Tofu Varieties

Choose 1 lb (500 g) tofu from these varieties:
- 1 lb (500 g) extra-firm tofu (sold in tubs of water; very firm texture; holds its shape well; good for marinating, grilling, broiling, baking, sautéing, and stir-frying)
- 1 lb (500 g) firm tofu (sold in tubs of water; firm texture; holds its shape fairly well; good for marinating, grilling, broiling, baking, sautéing, and stir-frying; can be mashed and used like ricotta cheese)
- 1 lb (500 g) soft tofu (sold in tubs of water; soft texture; does not hold its shape well; good for baking, sautéing, and stir-frying; can be mashed and used like ricotta cheese)
- 1 lb (500 g) silken tofu (often sold in small aseptic boxes; available in soft and firm varieties; lower in fat than other varieties; very soft, almost creamy texture; does not hold its shape well; best for soups or puréed and used like sour cream, yogurt, or mayonnaise)

Tofu (cont'd)

- 1 lb (500 g) marinated or flavored tofu (firm or extra-firm tofu marinated with Chinese five-spice powder or other flavors)
- 1 lb (500 g) baked tofu (firm or extra-firm tofu that is baked and usually flavored)
- 1 lb (500 g) smoked tofu (firmer texture; smoke flavor; excellent for grilling)
- 1 lb (500 g) deep-fried tofu (firmer texture; chewy surface; excellent for stir-frying)
- 1 lb (500 g) extra-firm tofu, frozen, thawed, and crumbled with a few quick pulses in a food processor (do this at home to make tofu more firm, chewy, and absorbent)
- 1 lb (500 g) pressed tofu (do this at home to make tofu more firm and chewy; cut the block of tofu into slabs, lay the slabs flat and put a heavy weight on top for 20 minutes to press out excess liquid)

For Better Health
Substitute 1 lb (500 g) tofu with:
- 1 lb (500 g) reduced-fat tofu

See also SOY ICE CREAM; SOY SOUR CREAM.

Togarashi

See SZECHUAN PEPPER; CHOOSING DRIED CHILES (PAGE 578); CHOOSING FRESH CHILES (PAGE 582).

Tomatillo

Also known as Mexican green or husk tomato. Tomatillo is not a green tomato, but it does resemble a small green tomato, if a small green tomato had a papery husk surrounding it. Widely used in Mexican and Guatemalan cooking, tomatillos must be husked and cooked briefly to bring out their full, tart flavor in "green" dishes and sauces.

1 lb (500 g) = 12 to 16 medium tomatillos

If You Don't Have It
Substitute 1 lb (500 g) tomatillos with:
- 1 lb (500 g) green or red cherry tomatoes (add lime or lemon juice to help mirror the aroma of tomatillos)
- 1 lb (500 g) cape gooseberries (more tart)

Tomato

"The total number of dishes around the world in which tomato is the or a main ingredient must amount to thousands," writes Alan Davidson in The Oxford Companion to Food. *"For a foodstuff which has come up to the front from almost nowhere in under two centuries, the tomato has proved to have astonishingly vigorous penetrative qualities, so that it is as close to being ubiquitous in the kitchens of the world as any plant food."*

---

1 lb (500 g) = 3 to 4 medium tomatoes = 2 cups chopped

If You Don't Have It
Substitute 1 lb (500 g) fresh tomatoes with:
- 1½ cups (375 mL) canned whole tomatoes (for cooking, not salads)
- 6 to 8 sun-dried tomato halves, reconstituted in hot water (more chewy; more intense tomato flavor; less watery; for cooking, not salads)
- 3 tbsp (45 mL) tomato paste (to replace cooked tomatoes; more concentrated tomato flavor; add liquid as necessary)
- 1 lb (500 g) tomatillos (slightly more tart; adds apple and citrus aromas; for cooking or salads)
- 1 lb (500 g) red bell peppers + 1 tsp (5 mL) lemon juice (to replace cooked-down tomatoes for sauce, roast, peel, and seed red bell peppers or use jarred roasted red peppers then purée the pepper flesh and add a splash of lemon juice)

Tomato Varieties
Choose 1 lb (500 g) fresh tomatoes from these varieties:
- 1 lb (500 g) globe or slicing tomatoes (familiar, medium, round tomatoes such as red Early Boy and Early Girl; heirloom varieties may be red, pink, purple, orange, yellow, or green; yellow tomatoes tend to be sweeter and less acidic than red varieties; tender, juicy flesh that's good both raw and cooked)
- 1 lb (500 g) beefsteak tomatoes (similar to globe tomatoes, but larger; includes many heirloom varieties such as the red Mortgage Lifter)
- 1 lb (500 g) plum or Roma tomatoes (oblong, red or yellow tomatoes with thick, dry, flesh; best for sauces or preparations where you don't want a lot of juice)
- 1 lb (500 g) grape tomatoes (baby plum tomatoes; best for snacking and salads)
- 1 lb (500 g) cherry, pear, or currant tomatoes (round or teardrop shaped, red or yellow tomatoes ranging in diameter from the tiny, ½-inch (1 cm) currants to larger 1-inch (2.5 cm) cherries; sweet, juicy flesh; best for snacking, salads, or light sautéing)
- 1 lb (500 g) green tomatoes (unripe tomatoes; firm, slightly acidic flesh; best for frying, broiling, and salsas, chutneys, and relishes)

See also SUN-DRIED TOMATO; TOMATO JUICE; TOMATO PASTE; TOMATO PURÉE; TOMATO SAUCE; TOMATO SOUP.

Tomato Juice

The official state beverage of Ohio and solace to Bloody Mary lovers everywhere who can rationalize that at least they're imbibing vitamin A, lycopene, and other health-giving compounds with their vodka.

If You Don't Have It

Substitute 1 cup (250 mL) tomato juice with:

- ½ cup (125 mL) tomato purée or tomato sauce + ½ cup (125 mL) water
- ¼ cup (50 mL) tomato paste + ¾ cup (175 mL) water

To Vary the Flavor

Substitute 1 cup (250 mL) tomato juice with:

- 1 cup (250 mL) V8® juice (more complex flavor)
- 1 cup (250 mL) carrot juice (sweeter; orange color)

Tomato Paste

If you typically use only small amounts of tomato paste to thicken a sauce, look for it packed in a squeezable tube. Because the tube is virtually air tight, the paste can be refrigerated for months without spoiling.

If You Don't Have It

Substitute 1 tbsp (15 mL) tomato paste with:

- 2 to 3 tbsp (25 to 45 mL) tomato purée or tomato sauce (reduce liquid in recipe by 2 to 3 tbsp/25 to 45 mL; or boil tomato purée or sauce until reduced to 1 tbsp/15 mL)

Tomato Purée

Briefly cooked tomatoes puréed through a food mill to remove the skin and seeds.

12 cups (3 L) tomato purée = 10 lbs (5 kg) plum tomatoes

If You Don't Have It

Substitute 1 cup (250 mL) tomato purée with:

- ⅓ cup (75 mL) tomato paste + ⅔ cup (150 mL) water
- 1 cup (250 mL) tomato sauce (slightly thicker; adds other seasonings)

See also FOOD MILL.

Tomato Sauce

Sauce based on chunky or puréed tomatoes with the addition of aromatics and other seasonings. Vodka is a "secret" ingredient in many chefs' tomato sauces.

If You Don't Have It

Substitute 1 cup (250 mL) tomato sauce with:

- ½ cup (125 mL) tomato paste + ½ cup (125 mL) water
- 1 cup (250 mL) seasoned tomato purée
- 1 cup (250 mL) canned stewed tomatoes, blended in a blender until smooth

Tomato Soup

Soulmate of the grilled cheese sandwich, icon to pop artist Andy Warhol, and tummy warmer to generations of kids. Two factions square off in the preparation of condensed tomato soup: the milk people and the water people.

If You Don't Have It
Substitute 1 (10¾ oz/305 g) can tomato soup with:
- 1 cup (250 mL) tomato sauce + ¼ cup (50 mL) water or milk

Tomme de Savoie

From the French Alps, a semifirm, disc-shaped, pale cow's milk cheese that's mild, a bit salty, and fruity with a hint of grass. The rind is thick and gray brown.

If You Don't Have It
Substitute 1 oz (30 g) Tomme de Savoie with:
- 1 oz (30 g) Saint Nectaire
- 1 oz (30 g) Beaumont
- 1 oz (30 g) Reblochon

Tongue Sausage

Pork, lamb, veal, or beef tongue pieces that have been cooked, pressed into loaves, jellied, and, sometimes, smoked.

If You Don't Have It
Substitute 1 lb (500 g) tongue sausage with:
- 1 lb (500 g) Zungenwurst (tongue blood sausage)

Tonic Water

Also known as quinine water. A beverage mixer, this carbonated water gets its bitter note from quinine, an alkaloid derived from the bark of the evergreen cinchona tree. Tonic water is also sweetened and flavored with fruit extracts.

If You Don't Have It
Substitute 2 tbsp (25 mL) tonic water with:
- 2 tbsp (25 mL) ginger ale (makes an interesting gin and tonic)
- 2 tbsp (25 mL) lemon-lime soda

For Better Health
Substitute 2 tbsp (25 mL) tonic water with:
- 2 tbsp (25 mL) low-calorie tonic water

Tortilla Chips

Deep-fried or baked tortilla wedges come packaged in a variety of seasoning styles. Usually served with salsa, guacamole, or other dips.

If You Don't Have It

Substitute 1 lb (500 g) tortilla chips with:

- 1 lb (500 g) Homemade Tortilla Chips: Cut a stack of 5 corn tortillas into 8 wedges like a pizza to make 40 wedges. Spread in a single layer on a large baking sheet (or two small ones) and coat generously with cooking spray. Sprinkle with $\frac{1}{4}$ to $\frac{1}{2}$ tsp (1 to 2 mL) salt and $\frac{1}{4}$ to $\frac{1}{2}$ tsp (1 to 2 mL) pure chile powder or other seasonings if you like. Bake at 375°F (190°C) until crisp, about 10 minutes. Makes 40 chips (about 4 oz/125 g).

To Vary the Flavor

Substitute 1 lb (500 g) tortilla chips with:

- 1 lb (500 g) corn chips
- 1 lb (500 g) potato chips
- 1 lb (500 g) sweet potato or other vegetable chips
- 1 lb (500 g) bagel chips

For Better Health

Substitute 1 lb (500 g) tortilla chips with:

- 1 lb (500 g) pretzels

Tortilla, Corn

The staff of daily life for Mexicans, these flavorful corn flatbreads are used as wrappers, scoops for eggs and beans, and thickeners for soups and stews. For a change of texture, they are fried and then folded so they harden in a U-shape to make taco "shells."

If You Don't Have It

Substitute 8 corn tortillas with:

- 8 Homemade Corn Tortillas: Mix 1 cup (250 mL) minus 2 tbsp (25 mL) masa harina with $\frac{1}{2}$ cup (125 mL) hot water and set aside to reconstitute for 30 minutes. Or use 8 oz (250 g) of fresh masa. Gently work cold water into the dough, teaspoon by teaspoon until it is soft and pliable but not sticky. Shape the dough into 7 to 8 balls and cover with plastic wrap. Working with 1 ball at a time and a tortilla press lined with plastic wrap on the top and bottom, press each ball to a thin circle about 6 inches (15 cm) in diameter and no more than $\frac{1}{8}$-inch (3 mm) thick. Peel off the top layer of plastic and flip the tortilla into your hand. Peel off the remaining layer of plastic and quickly flip the tortilla onto a dry griddle or heavy skillet preheated to medium. Cook until lightly browned, about 30 seconds per side. Repeat with remaining dough. Makes 7 to 8 tortillas.

To Vary the Flavor

Substitute 8 corn tortillas with:

- 8 arepas (Venezuelan corn flatbread; thicker and softer)
- 8 chalupas (thicker; softer)
- 8 gorditas (thicker; softer)
- 8 flour tortillas (slightly thinner; softer)

See also MASA; MASA HARINA.

Tortilla, Flour

Griddle flatbreads made from all-purpose flour and, traditionally, lard or shortening. Most common in the northern states of Mexico.

If You Don't Have It

Substitute 8 flour tortillas with:

- 8 corn tortillas (firmer; can be more brittle)
- 8 pieces of soft lavash (chewier)
- 8 chapati (chewier)
- 8 naan (puffier)
- 8 rounds of pita bread (puffier)

Tortoise

See TURTLE.

Touloumi

Semisoft, tart goat cheese made on the island of Crete. Greek immigrants in Northern California started making a similar cheese using cow's milk, and it came to be called Teleme.

If You Don't Have It

Substitute 1 oz (30 g) Touloumi with:

- 1 oz (30 g) Teleme (made with cow's milk)
- 1 oz (30 g) Monterey Jack

See also TELEME.

Toulouse

French pork sausage flavored with garlic, wine, and other seasonings. It contributes character to cassoulet and other braises.

If You Don't Have It

Substitute 1 lb (500 g) Toulouse with:

- 1 lb (500 g) French andouillette (made with tripe)
- 1 lb (500 g) kielbasa
- 1 lb (500 g) Spanish chorizo
- 1 lb (500 g) Portuguese chouriço or linguiça
- 1 lb (500 g) other mild sausage such Italian sweet sausage

Treacle

Also known as black or dark treacle. The British term for the syrup left over after sugar is refined. Very close to molasses with a slightly bitter note.

If You Don't Have It

Substitute 1 cup (250 mL) dark treacle with:
- 1 cup (250 mL) molasses (especially blackstrap molasses)
- 1 cup (250 mL) dark corn syrup (slightly thinner; sweeter)
- 1 cup (250 mL) golden syrup or light treacle (lighter color and flavor; less bitter)

See also GOLDEN SYRUP.

Treacle, Light

See GOLDEN SYRUP.

Tree Ear

See SHUFFLING MUSHROOMS (PAGE 572).

Treemelon

See PEPINO.

Tree Tomato

See TAMARILLO.

Triple Sec

See ORANGE LIQUEUR.

Triticale Flour

See CHOOSING AMONG WHOLE-GRAIN AND ALTERNATIVE FLOURS (PAGE 586).

Trivet

Ceramic or metal stand on which to sit hot pans or dishes.

If You Don't Have It

Substitute a trivet with:
- cooling rack
- oven mitt
- pizza stone or unglazed quarry tiles

Trompette de la Mort

See SHUFFLING MUSHROOMS (PAGE 572).

Trout

One of the most common and well-liked fish in the world. Includes brown trout (also known as sea trout), rainbow trout (also known as steelhead), cutthroat trout, brook trout, and lake

If You Don't Have It

Substitute 1 lb (500 g) trout with:
- 1 lb (500 g) salmon (especially to replace rainbow trout)
- 1 lb (500 g) char (especially to replace rainbow trout)

trout. Trout respond to a variety of cooking methods including poaching, grilling, broiling, frying, and en papillote.

- 1 lb (500 g) shad
- 1 lb (500 g) sablefish
- 1 lb (500 g) ocean perch

Trout Varieties

Choose 1 lb (500 g) trout from these popular varieties:

- 1 lb (500 g) smoked trout (usually rainbow trout)
- 1 lb (500 g) rainbow trout (freshwater species; light purple band along body; black spots on tail fin; often farmed; prepare like salmon)
- 1 lb (500 g) steelhead or salmon trout (a large, saltwater subspecies of rainbow trout that migrates to freshwater to spawn; prepare like salmon)
- 1 lb (500 g) brown, river, or lake trout (freshwater species; greenish brown skin with black spots or mottling; excellent flavor; best cooked simply)
- 1 lb (500 g) brook or speckled trout (freshwater species; smaller than rainbow trout; excellent flavor; best cooked whole and simply)
- 1 lb (500 g) sea trout (include several subspecies, most of which are milder in flavor than freshwater varieties and have white to pale pink flesh)

Truffle

The fruiting body of a fungus that grows under certain trees in a mycorrhizal relationship that benefits both parties. Truffles, which can only be foraged in the wild, cost a fortune for those enamored of their pungent, earthy, mysterious essence. Black truffles are found in France, Spain, and Italy. The best are said to come from Périgord in France. The Piedmontese town of Alba claims dominance in the white truffle arena.

If You Don't Have It

Substitute 1 oz (30 g) truffles with:

- 1 to 2 tbsp (15 to 25 mL) truffle oil
- 1 to 2 oz (30 to 60 g) fresh porcini mushrooms (less complex flavor)

Truffle Varieties

Choose 1 oz (30 g) truffles from these popular varieties:

- 1 oz (30 g) black truffles (complex earthy, floral, mushroom-like aroma; best paired with somewhat strongly flavored foods)
- 1 oz (30 g) white truffles (complex, earthy, garlicky, mushroom-like aroma; best paired with delicately flavored foods)
- 1 oz (30 g) summer truffles (complex, woodsy, mushroom-like, relatively delicate aroma and crisp texture; best paired with delicately flavored food)

Tuaca

An Italian brand herbal liqueur with the dominant note coming from vanilla.

If You Don't Have It
Substitute 2 tbsp (25 mL) Tuaca with:
- 2 tbsp (25 mL) Licor
- 2 tbsp (25 mL) crème de vanille or other vanilla liqueur
- 2 tbsp (25 mL) vanilla vodka (less sweet)

Tuna, Canned

Likely the most abundant canned seafood in the world, cooked tuna comes packed in either water or oil. Canned "white tuna" is albacore tuna while "chunk light" is yellowfin or skipjack tuna, which has a slightly stronger flavor. The highest grade, consisting of large pieces, is called "solid" or "fancy." "Chunk" grade is smaller pieces.

> 6 oz (170 g) can =
> ⅔ to ¾ cup
> (150 to 175 mL) drained

To Vary the Flavor
Substitute 1 (6-oz/170 g) can tuna with:
- 1 (6-oz/170 g) can salmon
- 1 (6-oz/170 g) can mackerel

For Better Health
Substitute 1 (6-oz/170 g) can tuna in oil with:
- 1 (6-oz/170 g) can tuna in water (fewer calories)

Tuna, Fresh

Also known as tunny. Tuna's muscles are red, textured, and hearty — much more meat-like than other fish — because tuna's muscles are so powerful. Tuna is a warm-blooded fish that must swim continuously to draw oxygen-rich water over its gills.

If You Don't Have It
Substitute 1 lb (500 g) fresh tuna with:
- 1 lb (500 g) swordfish
- 1 lb (500 g) marlin
- 1 lb (500 g) shark
- 1 lb (500 g) bluefish
- 1 lb (500 g) blackfish
- 1 lb (500 g) mahi-mahi
- 1 lb (500 g) striped bass
- 1 lb (500 g) mackerel
- 1 lb (500 g) salmon

Tuna Varieties
Choose 1 lb (500 g) fresh tuna from these varieties:
- 1 lb (500 g) skipjack, aku, katsuwo, or watermelon (weighs 6 to 40 lbs/3 to 20 kg; parallel dark blue

stripes on body; relatively lean, pale pink flesh; sometimes canned; sometimes used for sashimi)

- 1 lb (500 g) albacore (weighs 10 to 60 lbs/5 to 30 kg; dark blue black back and silver-gray sides; long pectoral fins; relatively rich, pale pink or white flesh; often canned; sometimes used for sashimi)
- 1 lb (500 g) yellowfin or ahi (weighs up to several hundred pounds; has yellow fins; relatively lean, pink flesh; sometimes canned; sometimes used for sashimi)
- 1 lb (500 g) bigeye or ahi (weighs up to several hundred pounds; dark blue black back; yellow pectoral fins and relatively large eyes; relatively rich, crimson flesh; sometimes used for sashimi)
- 1 lb (500 g) bluefin (weighs up to a ton; includes northern and southern varieties; rich, deep crimson flesh; used for high-quality sashimi; endangered by overfishing)

See also BONITO.

Turban Squash

Also known as Turk's cap. An old variety of winter squash cultivated mostly for its dramatic appearance. The flesh is yellow and mild. The rind is very tough, but if the squash is baked or steamed whole, the top can be sliced off and the insides scooped out to make soup. The empty squash shell then makes a beautiful tureen.

1 lb (500 g) =
1 cup (250 mL)
cooked and mashed

If You Don't Have It
Substitute 1 cup (250 mL) chopped turban squash with:

- 1 cup (250 mL) chopped butternut squash (more easily peeled; creamier)
- 1 cup (250 mL) chopped buttercup squash (smaller; similar turban cap)
- 1 cup (250 mL) chopped pumpkin (creamier)
- 1 cup (250 mL) chopped delicata squash (moister)
- 1 cup (250 mL) chopped sweet potato (sweeter; moister)

See also BUTTERCUP SQUASH.

Turbinado Sugar

See SUGAR, RAW.

Turbot

An esteemed European flatfish, almost on a par with Dover sole. Demand exceeds the catch, which is mostly from the Atlantic North Sea.

If You Don't Have It
Substitute 1 lb (500 g) turbot with:
- 1 lb (500 g) halibut
- 1 lb (500 g) Dover sole
- 1 lb (500 g) brill

Turkey

Dark meat has slightly more fat, calories, and flavor than white meat. To reduce calories by up to 30% in dark meat parts, use skinless turkey or don't eat the skin (leave the skin on during cooking, particularly the breast, to help keep the meat moist). Use bone-in turkey pieces for slightly more flavor.

> 1 lb (500 g) boneless turkey = 3 cups (750 mL) cubed

If You Don't Have It
Substitute 1 lb (500 g) turkey with:
- 1 lb (500 g) chicken
- 1 lb (500 g) rabbit
- 1 lb (500 g) emu
- 1 lb (500 g) ostrich
- 1 lb (500 g) pheasant

For Better Health
Substitute 1 lb (500 g) turkey with:
- 1 lb (500 g) kosher turkey (raised more humanely with tighter bacterial controls; brined, which makes the meat slightly more salty)
- 1 lb (500 g) free-range turkey (raised more humanely; often fed a vegetarian diet; meat may be slightly less tender but more flavorful)
- 1 lb (500 g) pasture-raised turkey (raised outdoors on a diet with a high percentage of natural forage; meat may be slightly less tender but more flavorful)
- 1 lb (500 g) organic turkey (fed an organic diet)
- 1 lb (500 g) vegetarian turkey products (made with soy protein)
- 1 lb (500 g) extra-firm tofu (more tender; less flavorful; press to extract excess liquid)

Turkey, Ground

Fresh or frozen ground turkey is a blend of white and dark turkey meat or all dark turkey meat with natural portion of skin that is at least 85% lean. Some supermarkets also grind whole boneless, skinless turkey breast that is up to 99% fat-free.

If You Don't Have It
Substitute 1 lb (500 g) ground turkey with:
- 1 lb (500 g) ground chicken
- 1 lb (500 g) ground veal
- 1 lb (500 g) ground beef

For Better Health
- 1 lb (500 g) ground turkey breast (less fat and fewer calories)

Turmeric

Also known as Indian or yellow ginger and Indian saffron. A southeast Asian/Indian rhizome that can be used fresh or ground after it's dried. It's valued as much for its intense reddish golden color as for its astringent flavor. Turmeric is frequently presented as a cheaper alternative to saffron, although it lacks saffron's complexity.

1 tbsp (15 mL) minced fresh = 1/8 to 1/4 tsp (0.5 to 1 mL) ground

If You Don't Have It

Substitute 2 tbsp (25 mL) chopped fresh turmeric with:
- 1/4 to 1/2 tsp (1 to 2 mL) ground turmeric

To Vary the Flavor

Substitute 1/4 to 1/2 tsp (1 to 2 mL) ground turmeric with:
- 5 to 7 crushed saffron threads (more expensive; more complex floral aroma)
- 1/2 to 3/4 tsp (2 to 4 mL) annatto seeds steeped in oil or other liquid for 15 minutes, then discarded (for yellow orange color; less pungent flavor)
- 1/2 tsp (2 mL) crushed dried safflower florets (for yellow orange color)
- 1 drop yellow food coloring + 1 small drop red food coloring mixed into water or other liquid (for yellow orange color)
- 1/2 tsp (2 mL) curry powder (includes other ground spices such as coriander, cumin, fenugreek seeds, black pepper, mustard seeds, allspice, cayenne pepper, ginger, and salt)

Turner

Typically a flat piece of metal, nylon, or acrylic attached to a long handle, turners flip and/or lift burgers, pancakes, cutlets, cookies, eggs, and more. Some turners are slotted so that fat can drain from the food as it's lifted.

If You Don't Have It

Substitute a turner with:
- wide spatula
- clean flexible spackling knife or dough scraper

Turnip

A root vegetable related to broccoli and Brussels sprouts. Although turnips can be cultivated in a rainbow of colors, the most common is the lilac and white variety. A small, white Japanese turnip is also appearing in some supermarkets. Turnips

If You Don't Have It

Substitute 1 cup (250 mL) chopped turnips with:
- 1 cup (250 mL) chopped rutabaga (less sweet)
- 1 cup (250 mL) chopped kohlrabi bulb (sweeter)
- 1 cup (250 mL) chopped parsnips (sweeter)
- 1 cup (250 mL) chopped salsify (milder)
- 1 cup (250 mL) chopped celeriac (stronger flavor with celery aromas)
- 1 cup (250 mL) chopped parsley root (stronger flavor)

Turnip (cont'd)

can be eaten raw, steamed, or roasted and have a delightful sweet pungency when not overcooked.

1 lb (500 g) = 3 to 4 medium = 2½ cups (625 mL) chopped and cooked

- 1 cup (250 mL) chopped broccoli stems (sweeter, milder)
- 1 cup (250 mL) chopped Asian radishes such as daikon (more peppery)
- 1 cup (250 mL) chopped black radishes (much sharper and hotter flavor)

Turnip Greens

The leaves that top turnip bulbs can be cooked like mustard leaves, beet leaves, or any other green.

1 lb (500 g) fresh = 1⅓ to 2 cups (325 to 500 mL) cooked

If You Don't Have It
Substitute 1 lb (500 g) turnip greens with:
- 1 lb (500 g) mustard greens
- 1 lb (500 g) dandelion greens
- 1 lb (500 g) kohlrabi greens
- 1 lb (500 g) collards
- 1 lb (500 g) kale
- 1 lb (500 g) beet greens
- 1 lb (500 g) green chard leaves (milder)
- 1 lb (500 g) mature spinach (milder)

Turtle

The availability of the meat of several varieties of hard-shelled reptiles has been limited by conservation measures. The sea or green turtle is found in temperate salt water. The white or, the preferred, green flesh is often simmered into turtle soup. A smaller species called the terrapin inhabits fresh or brackish water. Its meat is highly regarded, sometimes pounded into a cutlet. Less desirable as food are tortoises, which live on land.

If You Don't Have It
Substitute 1 lb (500 g) turtle meat with:
- 1 lb (500 g) alligator or crocodile tail meat
- 1 lb (500 g) chicken or turkey (less chewy)

Turtle Bean

See THE WIDE WORLD OF DRIED BEANS (PAGE 566).

TVP

See TEXTURED VEGETABLE PROTEIN.

Tybo

Mild, Danish cow's milk cheese is the color of cream and dotted with holes. The mild taste is similar to Samsoe. Some versions contain caraway seeds.

1 lb (500 g) = 4 cups (1 L) shredded

If You Don't Have It

Substitute 1 oz (30 g) Tybo with:

- 1 oz (30 g) Samsoe (slightly more flavorful)
- 1 oz (30 g) Danbo (may add caraway flavor)
- 1 oz (30 g) Emmental (drier; more complex flavor)
- 1 oz (30 g) Gouda

See also SAMSOE.

Udo to Unsweetened Cocoa Powder

Udo

Just like asparagus in the West, the young stalks of this plant, which taste like fennel, are a springtime delicacy in Japan.

> 1 lb (500 g) = 3½ cups (875 mL) chopped

If You Don't Have It

Substitute 1 lb (500 g) udo with:
- 1 lb (500 g) fennel bulb (crunchier)
- 1 lb (500 g) bok choy stems (preferably, add 1 tsp/5 mL crushed fennel seeds or 1 tbsp/15 mL anise liqueur such as Pernod or Ricard to add anise flavor)
- 1 lb (500 g) asparagus (preferably, add 1 tsp/5 mL crushed fennel seeds or 1 tbsp/15 mL anise liqueur such as Pernod or Ricard to add anise flavor)

Udon

See A SNAPSHOT OF ASIAN NOODLES (PAGE 588).

Ugli™ Fruit

Also known as uniq fruit. A trademarked name for a thick-skinned Jamaican citrus that's thought to be a cross between the mandarin and a grapefruit or pummelo.

> 1 medium ugli = 10 oz (300 g) = 1 cup (250 mL) segments

If You Don't Have It

Substitute 1 cup (250 mL) Ugli™ fruit segments with:
- 1 cup (250 mL) pummelo segments (less sweet)
- 1 cup (250 mL) grapefruit segments (more acidic)
- 1 cup (250 mL) sweet orange segments (sweeter)
- 1 cup (250 mL) tangelo segments (sweeter)

Uhu

See PARROT FISH.

Umeboshi

Japanese pickled plums made from ume or green plums that are salt-cured and sun-dried by a time-consuming, complicated process that starts during the rainy season in June and concludes with sunny August days. It is the leaves of the reddish purple variety of shiso that color the plums crimson. Umeboshi are eaten in onigiri, *stuffed rice balls, and many other dishes. Umeboshi are among the most concentrated sources of citric acid, a natural energizer. Samurai of the Edo Period (1600-1868) are said to have always carried a supply of umeboshi so they could be alert and ready for action.*

If You Don't Have It

Substitute 1 umeboshi plum with:
- 1 tsp (5 mL) umeboshi paste or bainiku

To Vary the Flavor

Substitute 1 umeboshi plum with:
- 6 to 10 vinegar-brined sloes
- 1 tbsp (15 mL) miso
- 1 tsp (5 mL) soy sauce
- ½ tsp (2 mL) sea salt

See also SHISO.

Uni

See CHANGING ROE (PAGE 594).

Uniq Fruit

See UGLI™ FRUIT.

Unsalted Butter

See BUTTER.

Unsweetened Cocoa Powder

See COCOA POWDER, UNSWEETENED.

V8 Juice to Vodka

V8® Juice

A blend of tomato, spinach, celery, carrot, beet, lettuce, watercress, and parsley juices.

If You Don't Have It
Substitute 1 cup (250 mL) V8® Juice with:
- 1 cup (250 mL) tomato juice (less complex flavor)
- ½ cup (125 mL) tomato purée or tomato sauce + ½ cup (125 mL) water (less complex flavor)
- ¼ cup (50 mL) tomato paste + ¾ cup (175 mL) water (less complex flavor)

To Vary the Flavor
Substitute 1 cup (250 mL) V8® Juice with:
- 1 cup (250 mL) carrot juice (orange color; sweeter)

Vacherin Fribourgeois

A Swiss cow's milk cheese with a soft, smooth consistency. It is cured in very damp conditions in order to promote the growth of surface mold.

If You Don't Have It
Substitute 1 oz (30 g) Vacherin Fribourgeois with:
- 1 oz (30 g) Fontina
- 1 oz (30 g) Vacherin d'Abondance
- 1 oz (30 g) Morbier
- 1 oz (30 g) Appenzeller

See also VACHERIN MONT D'OR.

Vacherin Mont d'Or

Also known as Vacherin du Haut-Doubs (a French cheese that is very similar). A traditional Swiss cow's milk cheese that is so soft, it can be eaten with a spoon.

If You Don't Have It
Substitute 1 oz (30 g) Vacherin Mont d'Or with:
- 1 oz (30 g) Vacherin du Haut-Doubs
- 1 oz (30 g) Reblochon

See also VACHERIN FRIBOURGEOIS.

Vandermint

See CHOCOLATE LIQUEUR.

Vanilla Bean

One of the most wonderfully aromatic and complex flavorings in the world comes from the only orchid vanilla planifolia *(out of some 20,000 varieties) that has an edible long, thin pod. Vanilla bean is expensive due to the labor and time required to cultivate and process it. Three types of bean are most common. The rich, thin Bourbon-Madagascar vanilla bean, accounting for 75% of the world's supply, comes from islands of Madagascar and Réunion. The thicker Mexican vanilla bean is smooth and rich but scarcer in supply. The Tahitian vanilla bean is the thickest and darkest. It is intensely aromatic, though not as flavorful as the others. Vanilla bean is available whole or as vanilla powder.*

If You Don't Have It
Substitute 1 8-inch (20 cm) vanilla bean with:
- 2 to 3 tsp (10 to 15 mL) vanilla extract (for the most flavor, add to custards or other cooked mixtures toward the end of cooking rather than at the beginning)
- 2 to 2½ tsp (10 to 12 mL) vanilla powder (good for baking, because its flavor does not dissipate as readily as vanilla extract when exposed to heat)
- 8 to 12 drops vanilla essence
- 1½ to 2 tbsp (22 to 25 mL) imitation vanilla extract
- 3 tbsp (45 mL) vanilla liqueur (adds alcohol)

Vanilla Bean Varieties
Choose 1 8-inch (20 cm) vanilla bean from these varieties:
- 1 8-inch (20 cm) Bourbon or Madagascar vanilla bean (robust aroma and dark, smooth, sweet flavor that hints of fermented fruit; best for baking and long-cooking because the strong flavors withstand heat better than other varieties)
- 1 8-inch (20 cm) Mexican vanilla bean (strong, delicately complex floral aroma and sweet flavor with hints of chocolate and warm spices; good for both hot and cold dishes; buy from a reputable merchant or check the label, as some lesser-quality Mexican vanilla products may contain coumarin, a potential toxin banned by the U.S. Food and Drug Administration)

Vanilla Bean (cont'd)

> 1 8-inch (20 cm) vanilla bean = 1 tbsp (15 mL) vanilla extract
> 1 2-inch (5 cm) piece vanilla bean = 1 tsp (5 mL) vanilla extract

- 1 8-inch (20 cm) Tahitian vanilla bean (intense floral aroma with sweet flavor and hints of cherry and anise; best for cold preparations such as pastry cream because the strong aroma dissipates with prolonged heat)
- 1 8-inch (20 cm) Java or Indonesian vanilla bean (relatively mild aroma and flavor; these smaller, less expensive beans are often used to make mass-market vanilla extract)

See also VANILLA ESSENCE; VANILLA EXTRACT; VANILLA POWDER.

Vanilla Essence

Highly concentrated extract of vanilla. Not to be confused with the British vanilla essence or imitation vanilla essence, both of which are synonymous with vanilla extract and imitation vanilla extract, respectively.

If You Don't Have It

Substitute 2 drops concentrated vanilla essence with:
- 1-inch (2.5 cm) piece vanilla bean (split or beans scraped from pod; add early in the recipe to allow the most flavor extraction)
- ½ tsp (2 mL) vanilla extract
- ½ tsp (2 mL) vanilla powder (good for baking because its flavor does not dissipate as readily as vanilla extract when exposed to heat)
- ¾ tsp (4 mL) imitation vanilla extract

See also VANILLA BEAN; VANILLA EXTRACT; VANILLA POWDER.

Vanilla Extract

Also known as vanilla essence (British). Pure vanilla extract is extracted by soaking vanilla beans in alcohol. Imitation vanilla extract has a vaguely similar flavor but is entirely artificial and often manufactured from the paper industry's wood-pulp by-products.

If You Don't Have It

Substitute 1 tsp (5 mL) pure vanilla extract with:
- 3-inch (7.5 cm) piece vanilla bean (split or beans scraped from pod; add early in the recipe to allow the most flavor extraction)
- 1 to 1½ tsp (5 to 7 mL) Homemade Vanilla Extract: Combine ¾ cup (175 mL) vodka and 1 to 2 split vanilla beans in a large glass jar. Seal and store in a cool, dark place for at least 4 months or indefinitely. To use sooner, jump-start the mixture with 3 tbsp (45 mL) pure vanilla extract and store for at least 2 months. Remove extract as necessary, replacing the vanilla beans when they give up their flavor and the vodka when it begins to run low.
- ½ tsp (2 mL) double-strength vanilla extract
- ¼ tsp (1 mL) triple-strength vanilla extract

- 3 to 5 drops vanilla essence
- ¾ to 1 tsp (4 to 5 mL) vanilla powder (good for baking because its flavor does not dissipate as readily as vanilla extract when exposed to heat)
- 1½ tsp (7 mL) imitation vanilla extract
- 1 tbsp (15 mL) vanilla liqueur

To Vary the Flavor

Substitute 1 tsp (5 mL) vanilla extract with:

- ½ tsp (2 mL) almond, orange, or lemon extract
- ¼ tsp (1 mL) peppermint extract
- 1 tbsp (15 mL) rum
- 1 tbsp (15 mL) almond liqueur
- ¼ tsp (1 mL) Fiori di Sicilia (a Sicilian flower essence with vanilla and citrus aromas)

See also VANILLA BEAN.

Vanilla Liqueur

The generic term for a French sweetened spirit flavored with vanilla.

If You Don't Have It

Substitute 2 tbsp (25 mL) vanilla liqueur with:

- 2 tbsp (25 mL) crème de vanille (may be thicker; sweeter)
- 2 tbsp (25 mL) vanilla vodka (less sweet)
- 2 tbsp (25 mL) Tuaca
- 2 tbsp (25 mL) Licor 43

Vanilla Powder

Dried vanilla beans that are finely ground. Because the powder holds its flavor when exposed to heat, it is excellent for flavoring baked goods, custards, and other cooked dishes. It is sold in specialty cake decorating supply shops (also catalogs and online), as well as some gourmet markets.

If You Don't Have It

Substitute 1 tsp (5 mL) vanilla powder with:

- 1 to 1½ tsp (5 to 7 mL) vanilla extract
- 1½ to 2 tsp (7 to 10 mL) imitation vanilla extract
- 4 to 6 drops vanilla essence

See also VANILLA BEAN; VANILLA ESSENCE; VANILLA EXTRACT.

Vanilla Sugar

See SUGAR, GRANULATED.

Veal

The meat of a young calf, generally no older than 3 months. "Milk-fed veal" comes from calves that have not been weaned so the flesh remains soft and creamy-white with perhaps a pale pink tinge. "Formula-fed veal" can come from calves as old as 4 months, fed on milk solids, fats, nutrients, and water. This type is not as delicate as milk-fed.

If You Don't Have It

Substitute 1 lb (500 g) veal with:
- 1 lb (500 g) pork
- 1 lb (500 g) chicken
- 1 lb (500 g) turkey

Vegemite©

See YEAST EXTRACT.

Vegetable Oil

See SUBSTITUTING OILS (PAGE 598).

Vegetable Oil Spray

A commercial product of vegetable oil, lecithin, and a harmless propellant packed into a spray can. It is used to coat cooking and baking pans with the minimum amount of oil to make the surface nonstick. To make your own oil spray, fill a plastic pump spray bottle with your favorite cooking oil. Adding 2 tablespoons (25 mL) of liquid lecithin per ½ cup (125 mL) of oil helps create a smoother spray but is not absolutely necessary.

> 10- to 15-second spray =
> 1 tsp (5 mL) oil

If You Don't Have It

Substitute a 10- to 15-second spray of vegetable oil spray with:
- 1 tsp (5 mL) vegetable oil (to use the least amount, spread to a fine film using a paper towel or pastry brush)
- 1 tsp (5 mL) butter or margarine
- nonstick silicone bakeware (for baking; available as baking sheets or molds in the shapes of most baked goods such as breads, muffins, and cakes; reusable; flexible; does not need to be greased; highly recommended)

Vegetable Oil Spray Varieties

Choose a 10- to 15-second spray of vegetable oil spray from these varieties:
- 10- to 15-second spray of olive oil spray
- 10- to 15-second spray of butter-flavored vegetable oil spray

See also BUTTER.

Vegetable Peeler

This handy sharp-bladed tool is indispensable for cooks who peel apples for pies or potatoes for mashing. If possible, purchase a peeler from a cookware shop that will let you test drive the implement to make sure it fits your hand well.

If You Don't Have It

Substitute a vegetable peeler with:
- paring knife
- countertop peeling-coring-slicing machine
- slicing side of a box grater (to remove vegetable or fruit peels in small pieces)
- citrus zester (to remove small thin strips of peel from fruit or vegetables)

Vegetable Protein

See TEXTURED VEGETABLE PROTEIN.

Vegetable Shortening

Also known as Crisco and solid shortening. Produces light and tender baked goods because, unlike butter, it is free of water. But it lacks buttery flavor. A combination of shortening and butter works best for many baked goods.

1 lb (500 g) = 2⅓ cups (575 mL)

If You Don't Have It

Substitute 1 cup (250 mL) vegetable shortening with:
- 1 cup (250 mL) lard
- 1 cup plus 2 tbsp (275 mL) unsalted butter (adds butter flavor; makes softer cookies)
- 1 cup plus 2 tbsp (275 mL) margarine (makes softer cookies; decrease salt by ⅛ tsp/0.5 mL)
- 1 cup (250 mL) bacon fat (for sautéing and frying)

To Vary the Flavor

Substitute 1 cup (250 mL) vegetable shortening with:
- ½ cup (125 mL) vegetable shortening + ½ cup (125 mL) unsalted butter (for both flakiness and flavor in biscuits, pie crust and pastries)

See also BUTTER.

Velveeta

See PROCESSED CHEESE.

Venison

The meat of deer is dark red, finely grained, typically lean, and often delicious. The term venison is often used to refer to the meat of related animals such as elk, caribou, moose, and reindeer.

If You Don't Have It

Substitute 1 lb (500 g) venison with:
- 1 lb (500 g) antelope
- 1 lb (500 g) gazelle
- 1 lb (500 g) buffalo
- 1 lb (500 g) beef (richer; less gamey tasting)

See also CARIBOU; DEER; ELK; MOOSE; REINDEER.

Ventrèche

See PANCETTA.

Verbena

See LEMON VERBENA.

Vermouth

Fortified white wine liqueurs that some historians date back as medicinals to 400 BC. The name derives form the German for wormwood (wermut or vermut), which was a primary ingredient until, fortunately, someone discovered that it is poisonous. Today, vermouths are concocted with countless herbs, flowers, seeds, and other botanicals. Two basic types exist. Sweet vermouth, developed in Italy in the 1700s, can be clear or tinted reddish brown with caramel. Dry vermouth, also known as French Vermouth, dates from around 1800. Both are enjoyed as apéritifs and as ingredients in various cocktails.

If You Don't Have It
Substitute 2 tbsp (25 mL) vermouth with:
- 2 tbsp (25 mL) dry sherry (to replace dry vermouth, especially for sauces and soups)
- 2 tbsp (25 mL) dry white wine (to replace dry vermouth, especially for sauces and soups)
- 2 tbsp (25 mL) Punt e Mes (to replace dry vermouth; red color; more bitter)
- 2 tbsp (25 mL) Madeira (to replace dry vermouth)
- 2 tbsp (25 mL) sake (to replace dry vermouth)
- 2 tbsp (25 mL) Shaoxing wine (to replace dry vermouth)
- 2 tbsp (25 mL) Lillet blanc (to replace sweet vermouth)
- 2 tbsp (25 mL) medium-dry white wine (to replace sweet vermouth)

Vermouth Variety
Substitute 2 tbsp (25 mL) vermouth with:
- 1 tbsp (15 mL) dry or French vermouth + 1 tbsp (15 mL) sweet or Italian vermouth (to make "perfect" cocktails such as a perfect Manhattan)

For Better Health
Substitute 2 tbsp (25 mL) vermouth with:
- 2 tbsp (25 mL) chicken, fish, or vegetable stock (no alcohol; to replace vermouth in sauces or soups)

Viande

See GLACE DE VIANDE.

Vienna Sausage

Tiny wieners that are typically available in cans.

If You Don't Have It

Substitute 1 lb (500 g) Vienna sausage with:
- 1 lb (500 g) cocktail wieners
- 1 lb (500 g) frankfurters (cut to size as necessary)
- 1 lb (500 g) Bockwurst (made with veal; cut to size as necessary)
- 1 lb (500 g) kielbasa (larger; cut to size as necessary)
- 1 lb (500 g) chipolata (spicier; cook first)

Vietnamese Fish Sauce

See FISH SAUCE.

Vietnamese Mint

Also known as Cambodian mint, daun kesom, hot mint, laksa leaf, Vietnamese coriander, and water pepper. Each stem sprouts many pointy leaves with a strong, minty, peppery essence. The herb seasons Vietnamese soups, rice paper rolls, and other dishes.

> 2 oz (60 g) = 1½ cups (375 mL) chopped

If You Don't Have It

Substitute 1 tbsp (15 mL) chopped fresh Vietnamese mint with:
- 1½ tsp (7 mL) chopped fresh cilantro + 1½ tsp (7 mL) chopped fresh peppermint or lemon basil

Vinegar

While vinegar ("sour wine" in French) probably produced itself naturally from wine exposed to air, vinegar can be made from any sugary or starchy liquid that can be induced to ferment. It is used prolifically around the world as a flavoring and pickling agent.

If You Don't Have It

Substitute 2 tbsp (25 mL) vinegar with:
- 2 tbsp (25 mL) lemon juice or lime juice (for acidulated water, dressings, marinades, sauces, and deglazing pans)
- 2 tbsp (25 mL) mango powder (as a souring agent in curries, chutneys, and soups)
- 1½ to 2 tsp (7 to 10 mL) tamarind concentrate or paste (as a souring agent in curries, chutneys, and soups)
- 2 tbsp (25 mL) wine, sherry, brandy, or port (for deglazing pans)

See also CHOOSING VINEGAR (PAGE 600).

Viola

See PICKING EDIBLE FLOWERS (PAGE 604).

Violet

See PICKING EDIBLE FLOWERS (PAGE 604).

Virginia Ham

A class of fine American hams noted for their lean meat. The superb example is Smithfield ham, which is processed from razorback pigs. The ham is dry-rubbed with salt and pepper, smoked over hickory and apple wood, and then aged for at least a year.

If You Don't Have It
Substitute 4 oz (125 g) Virginia ham with:
- 4 oz (125 g) Smithfield ham (the most famous and often the best Virginia ham)
- 4 oz (125 g) Kentucky ham (also smoked over hickory and apple woods)
- 4 oz (125 g) York ham (lighter smoke flavor)
- 4 oz (125 g) Yunnan ham (lean, dry-cured Chinese ham)
- 4 oz (125 g) Westphalian ham (adds juniper flavor)
- 4 oz (125 g) Ardennes ham
- 4 oz (125 g) Bayonne ham
- 4 oz (125 g) serrano or Iberico ham (lacks smoke flavor)
- 4 oz (125 g) prosciutto (lacks smoke flavor)

Vodka

A clear, colorless distilled liquor. The finest come from grains such as barley and wheat. Vegetables, such as potatoes and beets, can also be used to make vodka. Vodka is purified by distillation at high proof levels followed by filtration through activated charcoal. Some vodkas are embellished with fruits, peppers, or other flavorings.

If You Don't Have It
Substitute 2 tbsp (25 mL) vodka with:
- 1 tbsp (15 mL) neutral spirits (increase liquid in recipe by 1 tbsp/15 mL)
- 1 tbsp (15 mL) grain spirits (wood-aged; mellow flavor; increase liquid in recipe by 1 tbsp/15 mL)
- 2 tbsp (25 mL) gin (adds other flavors such as juniper)
- 2 tbsp (25 mL) white rum (slightly sweeter; mellower, richer flavor if aged)
- 2 tbsp (25 mL) aquavit (adds caraway flavor)
- 2 tbsp (25 mL) tequila (more peppery, herbaceous flavor; mellower, richer flavor if aged)

To Vary the Flavor
Substitute 2 tbsp (25 mL) vodka with:
- 2 tbsp (25 mL) flavored vodka such as lemon, pepper, or vanilla (some flavored vodkas may be sweeter than unflavored vodka)

See also NEUTRAL SPIRITS.

Wahoo to Worcestershire Sauce

Wahoo

Also known as ono (Hawaiian). A Pacific game fish with sweet, fine, moderately high-fat flesh. The flavor is often compared to albacore.

If You Don't Have It
Substitute 1 lb (500 g) wahoo with:
- 1 lb (500 g) king mackerel
- 1 lb (500 g) mahi-mahi (moister; sweeter)
- 1 lb (500 g) swordfish
- 1 lb (500 g) mako shark
- 1 lb (500 g) tuna

See also MACKEREL.

Wakame

A delicate, brown seaweed that is very important in Japanese cooking for soups and salads. Available fresh in spring, it is semidried or dried for year-round consumption.

If You Don't Have It
Substitute 1 oz (30 g) wakame with:
- 1 oz (30 g) dulse (similar brine flavor; maroon-brown color)
- 1 oz (30 g) arame (similar brine flavor; reddish or greenish brown color; long, slender shape)
- 1 oz (30 g) kombu or kelp (stronger brine flavor; dark brown to black color)
- 1 oz (30 g) hijiki (stronger brine flavor; black color; long, slender shape)

Walla Walla

See ONION, SWEET.

Walleye

See PIKE.

Walnut

The most common commercially grown walnuts are the English (Persian), which are marketed in the shell, as halves, and as pieces. American black walnuts are a different species, with a thick, blackish brown shell and a much more pronounced taste. Predominantly used for desserts and baked goods, walnuts are also delicious in many savory dishes.

> 1 lb (500 g) in shell =
> 2 cups (500 mL) nuts
>
> 1 lb (500 g) shelled =
> 3¾ cups (925 mL) halves
> = 3½ cups (875 mL)
> chopped

If You Don't Have It
Substitute 1 cup (250 mL) walnuts with:
- 2 to 4 tbsp (25 to 60 mL) walnut oil (for baking and cooking; will add nut flavor but not texture of whole nuts; reduce fat in recipe by 2 to 4 tbsp/ 25 to 60 mL)
- 2 to 4 tbsp (25 to 60 mL) walnut liqueur (for baking and cooking; adds nut flavor and alcohol but not texture of whole nuts; reduce liquid in recipe by 2 to 4 tbsp/25 to 60 mL)

To Vary the Flavor
Substitute 1 cup (250 mL) walnuts with:
- 1 cup (250 mL) butternuts
- 1 cup (250 mL) pine nuts
- 1 cup (250 mL) pecans
- 1 cup (250 mL) almonds
- 1 cup (250 mL) hazelnuts

Walnut Varieties
Choose 1 cup (250 mL) walnuts from these popular varieties:
- 1 cup (250 mL) Persian or English walnuts (the most common type)
- 1 cup (250 mL) American black walnuts (thicker, harder shell; stronger, more complex, and slightly more bitter flavor that withstands heat better than English walnuts)

See also BUTTERNUT; NUT MEAL; NUTS.

Walnut Liqueur

Traditionally, Italian nocino, a walnut liqeur made from green walnuts, is consumed on November 2, All Souls' Day, to honor the departed. A similar liqueur is now mass produced by several popular brands including Nocciole, Nocello, and Nocino.

If You Don't Have It
Substitute 2 tbsp (25 mL) walnut liqueur with:
- 2 tbsp (25 mL) crème de noix (thicker; sweeter)
- 2 tbsp (25 mL) water + ½ to ¾ tsp (2 to 4 mL) walnut extract (or skip the water and reduce liquid in recipe by a scant 2 tbsp/25 mL)

To Vary the Flavor
Substitute 2 tbsp (25 mL) walnut liqueur with:
- 2 tbsp (25 mL) almond liqueur, hazelnut liqueur, coffee liqueur, or chocolate liqueur

Walnut Oil

See SUBSTITUTING OILS (PAGE 598).

Wasabi

The root of a Japanese herb, grated into a fine pale green paste, adds hot pungency to sushi, sashimi, and other dishes. The fresh root is rarely available outside of Japan. When buying wasabi paste or powder, look for the words "100% grated hon-wasabi" on the label. Lesser quality imitation "wasabi" paste and powder are made with horseradish, mustard, and colorings such as spinach powder.

If You Don't Have It

Substitute 1 tbsp (15 mL) freshly grated wasabi with:
- 1 tbsp (15 mL) wasabi paste
- 1 tbsp (15 mL) wasabi powder + 2 to 3 tsp (10 to 15 mL) water (mix, cover, and let rest for 15 minutes)
- 1 tbsp (15 mL) finely grated fresh horseradish (white color; less pungent; mix with a ¼ drop of green food coloring if you like)
- 1 tbsp (15 mL) well-drained prepared horseradish (white color; coarser texture; less pungent; mild vinegar flavor; mix with a ¼ drop of green food coloring if you like)
- 1 tbsp (15 mL) mustard powder + 1 tsp (5 mL) water (mix, cover, and let rest for 15 minutes; yellow color; hotter at the back of the throat and less aromatically pungent)

Water

See BOILING WATER; SPARKLING MINERAL WATER.

Water Chestnut

Look for fresh water chestnuts in Asian markets. The pale, sweet flesh tastes of apple, sunchoke, and sugarcane.

> 8 oz (250 g) can =
> 24 to 28 water chestnuts
> = 1 cup (250 mL) sliced

If You Don't Have It

Substitute 1 cup (250 mL) fresh water chestnuts with:
- 1 cup (250 mL) canned water chestnuts (less sweet, less crisp, and less nutty)
- 1 cup (250 mL) chopped jicama (less nutty)
- 1 cup (250 mL) chopped cooked or canned lotus root
- 1 cup (250 mL) chopped sunchokes (less sweet and nutty)
- 1 cup (250 mL) chopped cooked or canned bamboo shoots (for stir-fries; less crisp)

Water Chestnut Powder

Also known as water chestnut flour. Dried and ground water chestnuts are used in Asian cooking for thickening or for dredging foods. It is available in Asian markets and some natural food stores.

If You Don't Have It

Substitute 1 tbsp (15 mL) water chestnut powder (for thickening) with:
- 1 tbsp (15 mL) cornstarch
- 2 tbsp (25 mL) all-purpose flour (cook a few minutes after thickening to cook out raw flour taste)
- 2 tsp (10 mL) arrowroot (a better choice if thickened food will be frozen or cooked for a long time; also makes sauces more glossy)

Watercress

See CRESS.

Watermelon

Cleopatra probably enjoyed cool, sweet, refreshing slices of watermelon on many a sweltering afternoon. The melon was cultivated in Egypt for a good 2,000 years before she ascended the throne.

2 lbs (1 kg) =
3 cups (750 mL) diced

If You Don't Have It

Substitute 1 cup (250 mL) chopped watermelon with:

- 1 cup (250 mL) chopped honeydew melon (less crisp; less watery)
- 1 cup (250 mL) chopped Galia melon (less crisp; less watery)

Water Spinach

Also known as swamp cabbage. A thick-stemmed, green-leafed water plant that's common in China and Southeast Asia, prepared in stir-fries or with highly seasoned sauces. It's relatively high in protein and iron.

If You Don't Have It

Substitute 1 lb (500 g) water spinach shoots and leaves with:

- 1 lb (500 g) sweet potato shoots and leaves

Wax Bean

See GREEN BEAN.

Wax Paper

Also known as greaseproof paper and waxed paper. Thomas Alva Edison, inventor of the phonograph, light bulb, and motion picture camera, also created wax paper.

If You Don't Have It

Substitute wax paper with:

- parchment paper (for lining baking pans)
- aluminum foil (for lining baking pans and wrapping food)
- plastic wrap (for wrapping food)

Weakfish

See CROAKER.

Wehani Rice

See VARIETIES OF RICE (PAGE 591).

Weisswurst

Also known as white sausage. Mildly seasoned fresh German veal sausages. Often paired with potato salad.

If You Don't Have It

Substitute 1 lb (500 g) Weisswurst with:
- 1 lb (500 g) French boudin blanc (delicate flavor)
- 1 lb (500 g) Cajun boudin blanc (spicier, more complex flavor)
- 1 lb (500 g) white Bratwurst (mild flavor)
- 1 lb (500 g) Bockwurst (mild flavor)

Wensleydale

A British whole milk cheese with a flavor akin to a sour version of Cheddar. A renowned blue Wensleydale is more rare and expensive.

1 lb (500 g) = 4 cups
(1 L) shredded

If You Don't Have It

Substitute 1 oz (30 g) Wensleydale with:
- 1 oz (30 g) Cheshire
- 1 oz (30 g) Cheddar

West Indian Cherry

See ACEROLA.

Westphalian Ham

A notable German ham that is dry-salted, soaked in salt brine, and then scrubbed with fresh water to remove excess sodium. The ham is smoked over beech and juniper wood.

If You Don't Have It

Substitute 4 oz (125 g) Westphalian ham with:
- 4 oz (125 g) York ham (mild flavor; may be lightly or heavily smoked)
- 4 oz (125 g) Virginia ham such as Smithfield ham (smoked over hickory and apple woods)
- 4 oz (125 g) Kentucky ham (smoked over hickory and apple woods)
- 4 oz (125 g) Bradenham ham (sweeter; black exterior)
- 4 oz (125 g) Black Forest ham (stronger flavor; black exterior)
- 4 oz (125 g) Ardennes ham
- 4 oz (125 g) Bayonne ham

Wet-Cured Ham

See HAM, WET-CURED.

Wheat Beer

See BEER.

Wheat Berries

Whole wheat kernels with only the inedible hull removed. Soaking wheat berries for several hours in cold water significantly reduces the cooking time. They make a chewy, nutritious addition to cooked grain salads.

1 cup (250 mL) whole wheat berries = 2½ cups (625 mL) cooked

If You Don't Have It

Substitute 1 cup (250 mL) wheat berries with:
- 1 cup (250 mL) cracked wheat (takes less time to cook)
- 1 cup (250 mL) bulgur (takes less time to cook)
- 1 cup (250 mL) rye berries (takes less time to cook)
- 1 cup (250 mL) kasha (takes less time to cook)
- 1 cup (250 mL) triticale berries or groats
- 1 cup (250 mL) spelt berries or groats
- 1 cup (250 mL) Kamut® berries or groats

Wheat Bran

The rough covering of wheat berries is a wealth of dietary fiber. The bran is packaged and sold in supermarkets and can be used to add fiber to a variety of dishes, from meat loaf to breads.

If You Don't Have It

Substitute 1 cup (250 mL) wheat bran with:
- 1 cup (250 mL) oat bran
- 1 cup (250 mL) rice bran
- 1 cup (250 mL) wheat germ

Wheat Germ

The most nutritious part of the wheat berry contains vitamins, minerals, and protein. Wheat germ is sold in its natural form as well as toasted. Because of its high natural oil content, it should be stored in the refrigerator or freezer to delay rancidity.

If You Don't Have It

Substitute 1 cup (250 mL) wheat germ with:
- 1 cup (250 mL) wheat bran
- 1 cup (250 mL) oat bran
- 1 cup (250 mL) rice bran

Wheatmeal Biscuit

See GRAHAM CRACKER.

Whelk

A large marine snail with a decorative shell and large foot muscle that is typically pounded into steaks to tenderize before cooking.

If You Don't Have It

Substitute 1 lb (500 g) whelks with:
- 1 lb (500 g) periwinkles
- 1 lb (500 g) limpets
- 1 lb (500 g) conch
- 1 lb (500 g) snails

Whipped Cream

Whipped cream is not what it used to be. Prior to the Second World War, raw heavy cream could be frothed into unctuous drifts almost by stirring alone. Cream is more difficult to whip today because it is pasteurized or ultra-pasteurized, a procedure that destroys an enzyme that encourages the fat globules to clump together. To get the best possible results from supermarket creams, choose fresh whipping cream that is at least 30% fat. If possible, buy heavy cream that is 36% fat or more. Chill the bowl, beaters, and cream in the freezer for 15 minutes before whipping.

½ cup (125 mL) heavy or whipping cream = 1 cup (250 mL) whipped

If You Don't Have It

Substitute 1 cup (250 mL) freshly whipped cream with:
- 1 cup (250 mL) canned whipped cream
- 1 cup (250 mL) frozen nondairy whipped topping, thawed
- 1 envelope nondairy whipped topping mix, prepared according to instructions

For Better Health

Substitute 1 cup (250 mL) freshly whipped cream with:
- 12-oz (375 g) can Milnot evaporated milk (at room temperature or chilled), whipped
- 12-oz (375 g) can evaporated milk, chilled overnight, mixed with 1 tbsp (15 mL) lemon juice, and whipped until stiff (less fat; to flavor, beat in 1 tsp/5 mL vanilla extract and ¼ cup/50 mL confectioner's sugar)
- 1 cup (250 mL) canned reduced-fat whipped cream
- 1 cup (250 mL) frozen light nondairy whipped topping, thawed
- 1 cup (250 mL) Homemade Whipped Cream Substitute: Combine 1 cup (250 mL) dry whole milk and ⅔ cup (150 mL) cold water in a glass bowl. Freeze until beginning to ice over. Beat with chilled beaters on high speed until soft peaks form when beaters are lifted. Add 1 tbsp (15 mL) lemon juice and beat until stiff peaks form when beaters are lifted. To flavor, beat in 1 tsp (5 mL) vanilla extract and ¼ cup (50 mL) confectioner's (icing) sugar. Chill until serving. Makes about 1½ cups (375 mL).

Whipped Topping

Also known as nondairy whipped topping. A packaged fluffy whipped cream replacement manufactured from processed vegetable oils and high fructose corn syrup.

If You Don't Have It
Substitute 1 cup (250 mL) frozen nondairy whipped topping with:
- 1 envelope nondairy whipped topping mix, prepared according to package instructions

To Vary the Flavor
Substitute 1 cup (250 mL) frozen nondairy whipped topping with:
- 1 cup (250 mL) whipped cream (richer, fresher flavor)

For Better Health
Substitute 1 cup (250 mL) frozen nondairy whipped topping with:
- 1 cup (250 mL) light frozen nondairy whipped topping

Whipping Cream

See CREAM.

Whisk

Also known as a whip. A utensil that beats ingredients as it whips air into the mixture. The tool is comprised of looped wires attached to a handle.

If You Don't Have It
Substitute a whisk with:
- electric mixer with beaters
- rotary beater
- fork (for light whisking)
- pastry blender (for light whisking)

Whiskey

Also known as whisky (Canada and British Isles). "The water of life" in Ireland and Scotland traveled to North America with immigrants. Barley, rye, or corn is fermented and distilled to produce this amber liquor. Factors affecting the final quality and taste are the type of grain, the water source, the yeast, the distillation method, and the aging. "Straight whiskey," such as

If You Don't Have It
Substitute 2 tbsp (25 mL) whiskey (for cooking and baking) with:
- 2 tbsp (25 mL) cognac, brandy, or rum
- 1 to 1½ tsp (5 to 7 mL) vanilla extract (add 4½ to 5 tsp/22 to 25 mL water or apple cider if necessary to replace lost liquid volume)
- ¾ to 1 tsp (4 to 5 mL) rum extract or brandy extract (add 5 to 5¼ tsp/25 to 26 mL water or apple cider if necessary to replace lost liquid volume)

Whiskey Varieties
Choose 2 tbsp (25 mL) whiskey from these varieties:
- 2 tbsp (25 mL) bourbon (includes small-batch bourbon blended from select barrels and single-barrel bourbon made from a single barrel; bourbon is straight whiskey made from a mash of 51 to

bourbon, Tennessee whiskey, and rye whiskey, must contain 51% of a single grain and cannot be higher than 160 proof. It is aged in oak for 2 years and may be diluted with water to no less than 80 proof. "Blended whiskey" is a mix of at least two 100-proof straight whiskeys blended with neutral spirits, grain spirits, or light whiskeys. "Light whiskey," generally used for blending, is distilled to more than 160 proof then diluted with water. It acquires distinction from aging in charred oak barrels. "Single-malt whiskey" is made exclusively with malted barley by a single distiller. Single malt Scotch whiskeys and Irish Whiskeys are richly flavored and tend to be pricey.

79% corn; aged in new, charred, white-oak barrels for at least 2 years; bottled at 80 to 125 proof; amber color; lightly sweet, smoky flavor)

- 2 tbsp (25 mL) Tennessee whiskey (straight whiskey similar to bourbon; made from a mash of at least 51% corn or another single grain; filtered through sugar-maple charcoal, which imparts a sweeter flavor than bourbon)
- 2 tbsp (25 mL) corn whiskey, moonshine, or white lightning (similar to bourbon and Tennessee whiskey; made from a mash of more than 80% corn; less smooth flavor)
- 2 tbsp (25 mL) rye whiskey (similar to bourbon; made from a mash of at least 51% rye, often with barley and wheat comprising the rest; the predominance of rye gives it a strong, spicy flavor)
- 2 tbsp (25 mL) Scotch whiskey (includes single-malt Scotch, made only from malted barley; and blended Scotch, made from malted barley and unmalted barley, corn, and wheat; Scotch is smokier than other whiskeys because the malted barley is dried over burning peat or turf)
- 2 tbsp (25 mL) Irish whiskey (includes single-malt and blended Irish whiskeys; typically blended and made from malted or unmalted barley, corn, rye, oats, or other grains; aged in wood for at least 4 years in used casks, which impart unique aromas; exceptionally smooth and light flavor resulting from three distillations)
- 2 tbsp (25 mL) Canadian whiskey (blended whiskey made from rye, corn, barley, and wheat; aged in wood for at least 3 years in used casks, which impart unique aromas; smooth, light flavor)

White Chocolate

See CHOCOLATE, WHITE.

White Currant

See CURRANT, FRESH.

Whitefish

A North American lake fish with delicate flavor is marketed either as whole fish or in fillets. Smoked whitefish is also produced as is the roe for caviar.

If You Don't Have It
Substitute 1 lb (500 g) whitefish with:
- 1 lb (500 g) pike
- 1 lb (500 g) perch
- 1 lb (500 g) walleye
- 1 lb (500 g) lake trout

See also CHANGING ROE (PAGE 594).

Whitefish Caviar

See CHANGING ROE (PAGE 594).

White Pepper

See PEPPERCORN.

White Pudding

British sausage that contains chicken or pork, a grain such as oatmeal, and seasonings. In the butcher's case, white pudding is the counterpoint to black pudding (blood sausage).

If You Don't Have It
Substitute 1 lb (500 g) white pudding with:
- 1 lb (500 g) French boudin blanc (delicate flavor)
- 1 lb (500 g) Cajun boudin blanc (spicier, more complex flavor)
- 1 lb (500 g) German Weisswurst (mild flavor)
- 1 lb (500 g) white Bratwurst (mild flavor)

White Sapote

See SAPOTE, WHITE.

White Walnut

See BUTTERNUT.

Whiting

A name applied to different fish in North Atlantic/European and Indo-Pacific waters. The European fish is digestible but dull. The species that are caught near India and Australia are an important food source, offering better flavor and a delicate texture.

If You Don't Have It
Substitute 1 lb (500 g) whiting with:
- 1 lb (500 g) hake
- 1 lb (500 g) cod
- 1 lb (500 g) pollock
- 1 lb (500 g) flounder or other flatfish
- 1 lb (500 g) ocean perch
- 1 lb (500 g) red snapper
- 1 lb (500 g) tilefish

Whole Wheat Flour

See FLOUR, WHOLE WHEAT.

Whortleberry

See BILBERRY.

Wild Rice

A cereal grass that grows wild in water in parts of North America, Africa, Southeast Asia, and China. It is not closely related to rice and doesn't lend itself to cultivation. In the upper Midwest U.S., and in several Canadian provinces, the grains are traditionally harvested by Native Americans paddling in canoes through the rice beds.

> 1 cup (250 mL) =
> 3½ to 4 cups
> (875 mL to 1 L) cooked

If You Don't Have It

Substitute 1 cup (250 mL) uncooked wild rice with:
- 1 cup (250 mL) uncooked brown rice (less chewy; less complex flavor; decrease liquid and cooking time slightly)
- 1 cup (250 mL) uncooked brown basmati rice (less chewy; more aromatic, nutty flavor; decrease liquid and cooking time slightly)
- 1 cup (250 mL) wild pecan rice (less chewy; more aromatic, popcorn-like flavor; decrease liquid and cooking time slightly)
- 1 cup (250 mL) uncooked bulgur (less chewy; less complex flavor; decrease liquid and cooking time slightly)

Wine, Dessert

Sweet and luscious, perfect as a finale to a great meal or a delightful treat in itself. The finest dessert wines are those that nature sweetens by concentrating the grape sugars in late-harvested grapes infected with the Botrytis cinerea *mold, known as "noble rot." French Sauternes is an eminent example of a late-harvest dessert wine. Fortified wines, such as port and sherry are also often*

If You Don't Have It

Substitute 1 cup (250 mL) dessert wine with:
- 1 cup (250 mL) sparkling grape juice (nonalcoholic)
- 1 cup (250 mL) sparkling cider (nonalcoholic)
- 1 cup (250 mL) grape juice (nonalcoholic)

To Vary the Flavor

Substitute 1 cup (250 mL) dessert wine with:
- 1 cup (250 mL) coffee or espresso (to accompany dessert)

Dessert Wine Varieties

Choose 1 cup (250 mL) dessert wine from these popular varieties:
- 1 cup (250 mL) sparkling wine such as asti spumante (sweet, musky flavor from Muscat grapes)

Wine, Dessert (cont'd)

classified as dessert wines. Fortified wines are made by adding grape brandy to wine to increase the amount of alcohol.

- 1 cup (250 mL) demi-sec or doux champagne (sweet champagnes with more than 3% sugar)
- 1 cup (250 mL) late-harvest wine such as Riesling, Gewürztraminer, Sauvignon Blanc, and Sauternes (sweet wines with a relatively high alcohol content; made from late-harvest grapes infected with a beneficial mold that shrivels the grapes and concentrates their sugar content)
- 1 cup (250 mL) ice wine (sweet wines made from grapes frozen on the vine and pressed while still frozen, which produces a richly flavored, high-sugar wine)
- 1 cup (250 mL) sherry, especially oloroso, Amoroso, or cream sherry (sweet, medium- to full-bodied, and golden in color; full flavor)
- 1 cup (250 mL) Madeira, especially Boal or Malmsey (medium-sweet to sweet and golden in color with rich flavor)
- 1 cup (250 mL) port (sweet; light amber to reddish color; mild or full flavor depending on age and vintage)

See also PORT; SHERRY.

Wine, Red

To make red wine, the juice of crushed grapes is left in contact with the skins to extract color. Tannin is another important component of the extraction. It contributes structure and body as well as aging potential. The amount of color will depend on the grape type and the length of time that maceration on the skins is permitted. Red wines are typically more robust than whites.

750 mL bottle = 25.4 oz
= 5 (5-oz) servings

If You Don't Have It
Substitute 1 cup (250 mL) red wine (for cooking) with:
- ¾ cup (175 mL) red grape juice + ¼ cup (50 mL) red wine vinegar or lemon juice (for marinades)
- 1 cup (250 mL) beef stock (for sauces and stews)
- 1 cup (250 mL) soaking liquid from sun-dried tomatoes or dried mushrooms (for sauces and stews)
- 1 cup (250 mL) beer (for stews)
- 1 cup (250 mL) Madeira (for sauces and stews; pale to tawny color and dry to sweet flavor)
- 1 cup (250 mL) port (for sauces and stews; sweeter)

For Better Health
Substitute 1 cup (250 mL) red wine with:
- 1 cup (250 mL) nonalcoholic red wine (sweeter)

Wine, Sparkling

Wines made effervescent by the presence of carbon dioxide bubbles.

If You Don't Have It
Substitute 1 cup (250 mL) sparkling wine with:
- 1 cup (250 mL) sparkling grape juice (nonalcoholic)
- 1 cup (250 mL) sparkling cider (nonalcoholic)
- 1 cup (250 mL) grape juice (nonalcoholic)

See also CHAMPAGNE; WINE, DESSERT.

Wine, White

In the making of white wine, after the juice is squeezed from the grapes, it has only the briefest contact with the grape skins. (Some white wines are actually made from red-skinned grapes.) Virtually no color and very little tannin is extracted. While tannins add structure and body to red wines, they may overpower the delicate flavors and aromas of white wines. Depending upon the varietal, white wines should be served chilled, at temperatures ranging from 36° to 50°F (2° to 10°C).

750 mL bottle = 25.4 oz = 5 (5-oz) servings

If You Don't Have It
Substitute 1 cup (250 mL) white wine (for cooking) with:
- 1 cup (250 mL) sherry or vermouth (especially for sauces and stews)
- 1 cup (250 mL) sake (especially for sauces and stews)
- 1 cup (250 mL) mirin (especially for sauces and stews; sweeter)
- 1 cup (250 mL) Madeira (for sauces and stews; pale to tawny color and dry to sweet flavor)
- 1 cup (250 mL) chicken or vegetable stock (for sauces and stews)
- 1 cup (250 mL) fish stock (for sauces, soups, and stews; adds briny, fish flavor)
- 1 cup (250 mL) veal stock (for sauces, soups, and stews; adds rich texture)
- ¾ cup (175 mL) white grape juice, apple juice, or apple cider + ¼ cup (50 mL) white wine vinegar or lemon juice (for marinades)

For Better Health
Substitute 1 cup (250 mL) white wine with:
- 1 cup (250 mL) nonalcoholic white wine (sweeter)

See also MIRIN; SAKE.

Winged Bean

Also known as goa bean. A nourishing tropical vegetable with edible pods that taste like a combination of pod beans and green beans.

1 lb (500 g) fresh = 3½ cups (875 mL) whole

If You Don't Have It
Substitute 1 lb (500 g) winged bean pods with:
- 1 lb (500 g) yard-long beans
- 1 lb (500 g) fresh cranberry beans
- 1 lb (500 g) green beans (less starchy and beany-tasting; sweeter)

Winter Melon

Also known as ash gourd, Chinese preserving melon, dung gua (Chinese), jundol (Philippine), petha (India), wax gourd, and white gourd. Winter melons are eaten throughout the summer in China. The icy white flesh, akin in taste to cucumber and summer squash, has a cooling effect. It is also simmered into delightful winter melon soup. In India, it is crystallized into fruit candy. Winter melons can weigh from 5 to 50 pounds (2.5 to 25 kg) and have a dark green skin with a lovely frosty finish.

> 2 lbs (1 kg) =
> 3 cups (750 mL) diced

If You Don't Have It
Substitute 1 lb (500 g) winter melon with:
- 1 lb (500 g) cucuzza
- 1 lb (500 g) bottle gourd
- 1 lb (500 g) chayote
- 1 lb (500 g) zucchini
- 1 lb (500 g) yellow squash

Winter Squash

See ACORN SQUASH; BANANA SQUASH; BUTTERCUP SQUASH; BUTTERNUT SQUASH; CALABAZA; DELICATA SQUASH; HUBBARD SQUASH; KABOCHA SQUASH; PUMPKIN; SPAGHETTI SQUASH; SWEET DUMPLING SQUASH.

Wok

A round-bottomed pan popular in Asian cooking.

If You Don't Have It
Substitute a wok with:
- slope-sided sauté pan (preferably heavy and nonstick or well-seasoned)

Won Ton Skins

Also known as potsticker wrappers and won ton wrappers. Square or round sheets of dough, in varying thicknesses, purchased ready-made to make won tons, egg rolls, and other

If You Don't Have It
Substitute 1 lb (500 g) won ton skins with:
- 1 lb (500 g) egg roll wrappers (relatively thick; often used for egg rolls)
- 1 lb (500 g) empanada wrappers (round)
- 1 lb (500 g) rolled pasta (cut to desired shape)
- 1 lb (500 g) rice paper (thinner; larger; cut to desired shape; makes crispy dumplings)

dough-encased dishes. Thinner varieties are best cooked in liquid, such as wontons cooked in soup. Thicker varieties, such as gyoza wrappers, are best fried.

Won Ton Skin Varieties

Choose 1 lb (500 g) won ton skins from these varieties:

- 1 lb (500 g) water dumpling wrappers (relatively thin; round; often used for soups or cooked in liquid)
- 1 lb (500 g) shao mai skins (relatively thin; round; often used for steamed dumplings)
- 1 lb (500 g) gyoza wrappers (thicker; round; often used for pot stickers)
- 1 lb (500 g) suey gow wrappers (may be thin or thick; used for dumplings)

Wood Ear

See SHUFFLING MUSHROOMS (PAGE 572).

Worcestershire Sauce

This dark and complex liquid condiment is modeled after an Indian sauce that was fancied by the former governor of Bengal Lord Marcus Sandys. It was in the early 1800s that Sandys commissioned two Worcester (UK) chemists, John Lea and William Perrins, to create a large batch to replicate the Indian sauce. Lord Sandys said the result "tasted filthy" and was nothing like the Indian sauce. A few months later, Lea and Perrins rechecked the mixture to discover it had fermented and matured into a piquant, spicy flavoring. They purchased the recipe from Sandys and began to manufacture the now internationally famous Worcestershire Sauce.

If You Don't Have It

Substitute 1 tbsp (15 mL) Worcestershire sauce with:

- 1 tsp (5 mL) tamarind concentrate or paste + 1 tsp (5 mL) soy sauce + 1 tsp (5 mL) apple cider vinegar + dash of hot pepper sauce + small pinch of ground cloves
- 1 tbsp (15 mL) HP sauce (thicker; sweeter)
- 2 tsp (10 mL) soy sauce + 4 drops hot pepper sauce + $\frac{1}{4}$ tsp (1 mL) lemon juice + $\frac{1}{4}$ tsp (1 mL) granulated sugar
- 1 tbsp (15 mL) steak sauce (thicker; sweeter; usually lacks the sour tang of tamarind)
- 1 tbsp (15 mL) vegetarian Worcestershire sauce (made without anchovies)

Yam to Yuzu

Yam

Also known as igname (French) and ñame (Spanish). A bland and starchy tropical tuber that nourishes many of the world's people. Most yams have dark brown, shaggy skin, but types can differ in size and shape from large tubes to small rounds. These include the white yam, purple yam, Chinese yam, and cushcush yam. In the U.S., the term "yam" is often misapplied to sweet potatoes, to which yams bear no resemblance.

1 lb (500 g) =
3½ to 4 cups
(875 mL to 1 L)
chopped or sliced

If You Don't Have It

Substitute 1 lb (500 g) yams with:
- 1 lb (500 g) boniato
- 1 lb (500 g) cassava
- 1 lb (500 g) mandiba
- 1 lb (500 g) yautía
- 1 lb (500 g) starchy potatoes such as russets
- 1 lb (500 g) taro
- 1 lb (500 g) oca
- 1 lb (500 g) arracacha
- 1 lb (500 g) arrowhead
- 1 lb (500 g) unripe green plantains
- 1 lb (500 g) orange-flesh sweet potatoes (much softer, moister, sweeter, orange-color flesh)

Yam Varieties

Choose 1 lb (500 g) yams from these varieties:
- 1 lb (500 g) white or water yams (the most common true yam; white, crisp, mildly sweet flesh)
- 1 lb (500 g) African white yams (similar to white yams; white to pale yellow, crisp, mildly sweet flesh; often used to make the African mash called fufu)
- 1 lb (500 g) purple yams (uncommon variety of white yam; pinkish purple, crisp, mildly sweet flesh; color deepens after cooking)

- 1 lb (500 g) cushcush or mapuey yams (cream-color, firm, starchy, mildly sweet flesh; more flavorful and delicately textured than other yams)
- 1 lb (500 g) Chinese yams (cream to yellow color, very mild, dry flesh)

See also SWEET POTATO.

Yankee Bean

See THE WIDE WORLD OF DRIED BEANS (PAGE 566).

Yard-Long Bean

These skinny flexible pods are at their best when stir-fried, sautéed, pan fried, or deep fried.

1 lb (500 g) fresh =
3½ cups (875 mL) sliced

If You Don't Have It

Substitute 1 lb (500 g) yard-long beans with:
- 1 lb (500 g) green beans (sweeter, less starchy, and more crisp)
- 1 lb (500 g) winged-bean pods
- 1 lb (500 g) fresh shelled black-eyed peas or cranberry beans

Yau Choy

Also known as yau tsoi, you cai, yu choy, and yu choy sum. A type of bok choy that looks like a thinner-stemmed version of Chinese broccoli with pretty yellow flower buds.

1 lb (500 g) fresh =
3½ cups (875 mL) chopped

If You Don't Have It

Substitute 1 lb (500 g) yau choy with:
- 1 lb (500 g) choy sum or flowering Chinese cabbage (similar to bok choy but slightly smaller stems and leaves; often blossoms with clusters of small yellow flowers)
- 1 lb (500 g) Taiwan bok choy (thinner stems; more delicate leaves; very mild cabbage flavor)
- 1 lb (500 g) Shanghai bok choy (short, squat, green stems; often sold as "baby" bok choy; mellow cabbage flavor)
- 1 lb (500 g) Canton bok choy (slightly stronger cabbage flavor)
- 1 lb (500 g) mature bok choy (the variety of bok choy that is common in American markets; sweet; juicy; mild cabbage flavor)
- 1 lb (500 g) Chinese broccoli or gai lan (darker green stems and sweeter, less cabbagey flavor)
- 1 lb (500 g) Napa cabbage (paler green yellow color; more tender; great for stir-frying)
- 1 lb (500 g) Green chard (less cabbagey flavor)
- 1 lb (500 g) collards (firmer, greener stems; larger leaves)

See also BOK CHOY.

Yautía

Also known as coco, cocoyam, malanga (Cuban), tanier, tannia, taro, yautía amarilla, yautía blanca, and yautía lila. The Puerto Rican name of a root vegetable that's native to New World tropics. The cormels are typically long and tapered, with dark shaggy skin that sometimes doesn't completely cover the flesh. Yautía (malanga) is a boiled staple in many countries, eaten with spicy sausages, pungent dried fish, or peppery stews.

1 lb (500 g) = 3½ to 4 cups (875 mL to 1 L) chopped or sliced = 2 cups (500 mL) cooked and mashed

If You Don't Have It

Substitute 1 lb (500 g) yautía or malanga with:
- 1 lb (500 g) taro
- 1 lb (500 g) cassava
- 1 lb (500 g) mandiba
- 1 lb (500 g) boniato
- 1 lb (500 g) oca
- 1 lb (500 g) arracacha
- 1 lb (500 g) arrowhead
- 1 lb (500 g) unripe green plantains
- 1 lb (500 g) potatoes
- 1 lb (500 g) parsnips
- 1 lb (500 g) orange-flesh sweet potatoes (much softer, moister, sweeter, orange-color flesh)

Yautía Varieties

Choose 1 lb (500 g) yautía or malanga from these varieties:
- 1 lb (500 g) white yautía or malanga blanca (white flesh with potato-like texture; mild to earthy flavor; the most common variety in North America)
- 1 lb (500 g) purple yautía or malanga lila (light purple flesh with dense, potato-like texture; earthy flavor; color fades to grayish when cooked)
- 1 lb (500 g) yellow yautía or malanga amarilla (pale yellow orange flesh with very dense, potato-like texture; sweet, nutty flavor; often mixed with other ingredients to make pasteles, fufu, and other Latin American dishes)

See also TARO.

Yeast, Baker's

Microscopic single-celled organism that causes breads and other baked goods to rise. As it feasts upon flour, and perhaps sugar, in the dough, yeast (through fermentation) converts that food into carbon dioxide.

If You Don't Have It

Substitute ¼ oz (8 g) pkg or 2¼ tsp (11 mL) active dry yeast or 0.6 oz (17 g) cake compressed fresh yeast with:
- 2 cups (500 mL) yeast starter (adds flavor of starter, such as tartness of sourdough starter)

¼ oz (8 g) pkg active dry yeast = 2¼ tsp (11 mL) = 0.6 oz (17 g) cake compressed fresh yeast

1 large (2 oz/60 g) cake compressed fresh yeast = 3 small (0.6 oz/17 g) cakes compressed fresh yeast = 3 tbsp (45 mL) active dry yeast

To Save Time
Substitute ¼ oz (8 g) pkg active dry yeast with:

- 2¼ tsp (11 mL) instant or quick-rising yeast (needs only one rise; reduce rising time by 40 to 50%; add to dry ingredients; flavor of bread may be slightly diminished)
- 2¼ tsp (11 mL) bread machine yeast (fine texture; needs only one rise; reduce rising time by 40 to 50%; add to dry ingredients; flavor of bread may be slightly diminished)

Yeast, Brewer's

Particular strains of yeast used in beer making. Because it is rich in B vitamins, it is also eaten as a nutritional supplement. It is sold in natural food stores and beer-making equipment shops.

1 tbsp (15 mL) powdered = 2 tbsp (25 mL) flakes

If You Don't Have It
Substitute 1 tbsp (15 mL) brewer's yeast with:

- 1 to 1½ tbsp (15 to 25 mL) nutritional yeast (pale yellow color; less bitter and more cheesy flavor)
- 2 to 3 tsp (10 to 15 mL) yeast extract (dark brown paste; stronger, saltier flavor)

To Vary the Flavor
Substitute 1 tbsp (15 mL) brewer's yeast with:

- 1 tbsp (15 mL) debittered brewer's yeast (less bitter flavor)

See also YEAST, NUTRITIONAL.

Yeast Extract

A combination of liquids extracted from fresh yeast and fresh vegetables. It can be pourably thin or as thick as paste. It's rich in B vitamins and can be used as a seasoning. Also the base for pungent, salty brown spreads such as Marmite© and Vegemite©.

If You Don't Have It
Substitute 1 tbsp (15 mL) yeast extract with:

- 1 tbsp (15 mL) brewer's yeast (flakes or powder)
- 1 tbsp (15 mL) nutritional yeast (milder, more cheesy flavor)
- 1 tbsp (15 mL) dark or hatcho miso (saltier)
- 1 tbsp (15 mL) peanut butter (for spreading on bread; sweeter and milder flavor)

Yeast Extract Varieties
Choose 1 tbsp (15 mL) yeast extract from these commercial varieties:

- 1 tbsp (15 mL) Vegemite© (pungent and slightly salty; popular in Australia)
- 1 tbsp (15 mL) Marmite© (pungent, salty, and slightly sweet; popular in Britain)
- 1 tbsp (15 mL) Promite© (pungent and slightly sweet)

Yeast, Nutritional

A dietary supplement from the same strain as brewer's yeast but with a less bitter flavor. It has a nutty-cheesy taste and is packed with protein and B vitamins. Sold as flakes or powder in natural food stores, nutritional yeast is favored among vegans, who use it to for a dairy-free cheesy flavor in many dishes. Also makes a good popcorn topping.

1 tbsp (15 mL) powdered = 2 tbsp (25 mL) flakes

If You Don't Have It

Substitute 1 tbsp (15 mL) nutritional yeast with:
- 2 to 3 tsp (10 to 15 mL) brewer's yeast (darker color; more bitter and less cheesy flavor)
- 2 to 3 tsp (10 to 15 mL) yeast extract (dark brown paste; stronger, saltier flavor)
- 1 tbsp (15 mL) grated Parmesan or Cheddar cheese (for cheesy flavor)

See also YEAST, BREWER'S.

Yellow Berry

See CLOUDBERRY.

Yellowfin Tuna

See TUNA, FRESH.

Yellow Squash

A sunny-skinned summer marrow that can have either a straight, semistraight or crooked neck that is narrower than the base.

1 lb (500 g) = 3 medium = 3 cups (750 mL) sliced

If You Don't Have It

Substitute 1 lb (500 g) yellow squash with:
- 1 lb (500 g) zucchini (yellow or green color)
- 1 lb (500 g) pattypan squash (yellow or green color)
- 1 lb (500 g) Zephyr summer squash (hybrid of yellow crookneck, Delicata, and acorn squashes; yellow on one end and green on the other)
- 1 lb (500 g) cucuzza (pale green)
- 1 lb (500 g) bottle gourd (pale green)
- 1 lb (500 g) chayote (cream to pale green)

Yellow Squash Varieties

Choose 1 lb (500 g) yellow squash from these varieties:
- 1 lb (500 g) yellow crookneck squash (warty and curved near stem end; slightly sweeter than straightneck yellow squash)
- 1 lb (500 g) straightneck yellow squash (smooth and tapered near stem end; milder, less sweet flavor than crookneck squash)

Yellow Storage Onion

See ONION, STORAGE.

Yellowtail

See POMPANO.

Yerba Buena

See MINT.

Yogurt

Also known as yoghurt. The Turkish name for this healthful fermented milk product has been adopted into English. Refreshing, protein-rich, and easy to digest, yogurt is even reputed to increase longevity. In its myriad mass-produced incarnations, with the addition of sugar and other empty calorie add-ons, yogurt often strays from its healthful roots.

If You Don't Have It

Substitute 1 cup (250 mL) yogurt with:

- 1 cup (250 mL) sour cream (thicker; less tart)
- 1 cup (250 mL) soy sour cream (contains soy milk; thicker; less tart)
- 1 cup (250 mL) crème fraîche (thicker; less tart)
- 1 cup (250 mL) silken tofu, blended until smooth (thicker; less tart)
- 1 cup (250 mL) buttermilk (thinner; best for baking, dressings, and gently cooked or uncooked sauces)
- 1 cup (250 mL) kefir (traditionally contains camel's milk; these days, usually contains cow's milk; thinner; more sour-tasting)
- 1 cup (250 mL) quark (richer texture)
- 1 cup (250 mL) mayonnaise (contains eggs; richer texture)

Yogurt Varieties

Choose 1 cup (250 mL) yogurt from these varieties:

- 1 cup (250 mL) flavored yogurt (sweeter)
- 1 cup (250 mL) soy yogurt (contains soy milk)
- 1 cup (250 mL) low-lactose yogurt (for the lactose intolerant)
- 1 cup (250 mL) goat's milk yogurt (for the lactose intolerant)

For Better Health

Substitute 1 cup (250 mL) yogurt with:

- 1 cup (250 mL) reduced-fat yogurt (less fat and fewer calories)

Yogurt Cheese

A delightfully tangy fresh cheese prepared by straining yogurt through cheesecloth to remove much of the liquid. It makes a delicious spread when mixed with fresh herbs, spices, or other seasonings.

If You Don't Have It

Substitute 1 oz (30 g) yogurt cheese with:

- 1 oz (30 g) Homemade Yogurt Cheese: Put 3 cups (750 mL) plain yogurt into a colander or sieve lined with cheesecloth or a thin kitchen towel. For extra-firm yogurt cheese, cover with a top layer of cheesecloth and weigh down with a bag of beans or another weight. Set the colander or sieve over a deep bowl, loosely cover, and refrigerate overnight or until the yogurt is reduced in volume by at least half (the excess liquid will drain into the bowl). Make about 1½ cups (375 mL).
- 1 oz (30 g) kefir cheese

To Vary the Flavor

Substitute 1 oz (30 g) yogurt cheese with:

- 1 oz (30 g) quark (richer texture)
- 1 oz (30 g) cream cheese
- 1 oz (30 g) mascarpone
- 1 oz (30 g) fromage blanc
- 1 oz (30 g) sour cream
- 1 cup (250 mL) crème fraîche
- 1 cup (250 mL) silken tofu, blended until smooth
- ½ oz (15 g) ricotta cheese + ½ oz (15 g) sour cream, blended
- ½ oz (15 g) cream cheese + ½ oz (15 g) sour cream, blended
- ½ oz (15 g) cottage cheese + ½ oz (15 g) yogurt, blended

Yogurt, Frozen

Similar in texture to soft ice cream, frozen yogurt took off in popularity in the 1980s as a healthier alternative to ice cream.

If You Don't Have It

Substitute 1 cup (250 mL) frozen yogurt with:

- 1 cup (250 mL) ice cream or soy ice cream

For Better Health

Substitute 1 cup (250 mL) frozen yogurt with:

- 1 cup (250 mL) reduced-fat frozen yogurt (less fat and fewer calories)

York Ham

Originally from York, England, this mild, lightly colored style of ham is delectable served hot or cold. It is dry-salted and smoked then aged for several months.

If You Don't Have It

Substitute 4 oz (125 g) York ham with:

- 4 oz (125 g) Virginia ham, such as Smithfield (more heavily smoked over hickory and apple woods)
- 4 oz (125 g) Kentucky ham (more heavily smoked over hickory and apple woods)
- 4 oz (125 g) Yunnan ham (lean, dry-cured Chinese ham)
- 4 oz (125 g) Westphalian ham (adds juniper flavor)
- 4 oz (125 g) Ardennes ham
- 4 oz (125 g) Bayonne ham
- 4 oz (125 g) serrano or Iberico ham (lacks smoke flavor)
- 4 oz (125 g) prosciutto (lacks smoke flavor)

Youngberry

Distinctively flavored, tart, dark red berry. A cross between the Phenomenal berry (a blackberry/ raspberry hybrid) and the Austin Mayes dewberry developed in Morgan City, Louisiana by B.M. Young in 1905.

> 1 pint fresh =
> 2 cups (500 mL)

If You Don't Have It

Substitute 1 cup (250 mL) youngberries with:

- 1 cup (250 mL) dewberries (close relative of blackberry)
- 1 cup (250 mL) loganberries (hybrid of blackberries and raspberries; dark red color)
- 1 cup (250 mL) boysenberries (hybrid of blackberries, raspberries, and loganberries; reddish purple color)
- 1 cup (250 mL) olallieberries (hybrid of youngberries and loganberries; dark purple color; larger; sweeter)
- 1 cup (250 mL) tayberries (hybrid of blackberries and raspberries; larger; red color)
- 1 cup (250 mL) blackberries (larger; darker purple color)
- 1 cup (250 mL) raspberries (sweeter; red color)

See also DEWBERRY.

Yuca

See CASSAVA.

Yu Choy Sum

See YAU CHOY.

Yunnan Ham

A lean, dry-cured Chinese ham similar to Virginia ham.

If You Don't Have It

Substitute 4 oz (125 g) Yunnan ham with:

- 4 oz (125 g) Smithfield ham or other Virginia ham
- 4 oz (125 g) Westphalian ham (adds juniper flavor)
- 4 oz (125 g) Ardennes ham
- 4 oz (125 g) Bayonne ham
- 4 oz (125 g) York ham
- 4 oz (125 g) serrano or Iberico ham (lacks smoke flavor)
- 4 oz (125 g) prosciutto (lacks smoke flavor)

Yuzu

A tangerine-size citrus much loved in Japan. Bright green in summer, yuzu turns yellow when it ripens in the fall. The tart zest and juice flavor many dishes, particularly ponzu dressing, in which it is combined with rice vinegar, mirin, soy sauce, and fish broth.

If You Don't Have It

Substitute 1 tbsp (15 mL) yuzu with:

- 1 tbsp (15 mL) grated lemon or lime zest (to replace grated yuzu zest)
- 1½ tsp (7 mL) lime juice + 1½ tsp (7 mL) orange or grapefruit juice (to replace yuzu juice)

Za'atar to Zwieback

Za'atar

Also known as zahtar. A Middle Eastern spice blend of dried marjoram, toasted sesame seeds, dried thyme, and sumac. It enhances dips, meats, and vegetables. Often, it's blended with olive oil and salt to accompany hot bread.

If You Don't Have It

Substitute 1 tbsp (15 mL) za'atar with:

- 1 tbsp (15 mL) Homemade Za'atar: Combine 2 tsp (10 mL) dried thyme, ¾ tsp (4 mL) sumac (optional), ½ tsp (2 mL) toasted sesame seeds, and ⅛ tsp (0.5 mL) salt in a mortar and pestle and coarsely grind.

Zester

A tiny-toothed cutting instrument that removes citrus zest in filament-like strands.

If You Don't Have It

Substitute a zester (for zesting citrus fruit) with:

- fine holes of a box grater
- Microplane® or rasp grater
- paring knife

See also GRATER.

Zucchini

Also known as courgette (Britain). Tender-skinned summer squash with mild buttery flavor. In U.S.

If You Don't Have It

Substitute 1 lb (500 g) zucchini with:

- 1 lb (500 g) yellow squash (yellow color)
- 1 lb (500 g) pattypan squash (green or yellow color)
- 1 lb (500 g) Zephyr summer squash (hybrid of

Zucchini (cont'd)

markets, zucchini is almost always the dark green or cylindrical squash but many other flavorful types exist. Vegetable marrow or marrow squash refers to a large zucchini.

> 1 lb (500 g) =
> 3 medium zucchini =
> 3 cups (750 mL) sliced

yellow crookneck, Delicata, and acorn squashes; yellow on one end and green on the other)
- 1 lb (500 g) cucuzza or bottle gourd (pale green)
- 1 lb (500 g) chayote (cream to pale green)

Zucchini Varieties

Choose 1 lb (500 g) zucchini from these varieties:
- 1 lb (500 g) straightneck or classic zucchini (deep green skin; mild flavor)
- 1 lb (500 g) golden or yellow zucchini (straightneck; bright yellow skin; sweeter than classic zucchini)
- 1 lb (500 g) Costata Romanesca, Roman zucchini, or cocozelle (thick straightneck; dark green and speckled white with raised lengthwise ridges; sweet and juicy)
- 1 lb (500 g) Lebanese or Middle Eastern zucchini (bell-shaped; pale green and shiny skin; firm, sweet, and juicy)
- 1 lb (500 g) round zucchini or globe squash (round balls; dark green skin; few or no seeds; firm, sweet, and juicy)
- 1 lb (500 g) oval or Tatume zucchini (egg-shaped; pale green speckled skin; few or no seeds; very firm and sweet; popular in Mexico)

Zungenwurst

Also known as blood tongue sausage. A German blood sausage studded with chunks of pickled tongue meat.

If You Don't Have It

Substitute 4 oz (125 g) zungenwurst with:
- 4 oz (125 g) Blutwurst (German)
- 4 oz (125 g) boudin rouge (Cajun)
- 4 oz (125 g) morcilla (Spanish)
- 4 oz (125 g) tongue sausage (no blood)

Zwieback

Also known as biscotte and rusk. "Twice-baked" German bread that comes in the form of long thin crackers.

If You Don't Have It

Substitute 1 lb (500 g) zwieback with:
- 1 lb (500 g) graham crackers
- 1 lb (500 g) bagel chips
- 1 lb (500 g) crostini or bruschetta
- 1 lb (500 g) Melba toasts
- 1 lb (500 g) dense crackers
- 1 lb (500 g) crisp lavash

Ingredient Guides and **Measurement Equivalents**

USE THE CHARTS ON THE FOLLOWING PAGES when substituting one variety of a particular food for another variety of the same food. The charts provide basic information about each food variety, including alternate names for the food, its texture and flavor characteristics, and its best uses or substitutes. A few charts do not include substitutes. For instance, substitutes are not included in the apple chart because so many different apple varieties can be substituted for one another that it would be unhelpful to list them all. In these charts, the food's best uses are offered instead of a lengthy list of substitutes.

A SERIES OF MEASUREMENT EQUIVALENCY TABLES begins on page 605. This reference section includes international equivalents for temperatures, pan sizes, Imperial-to-Metric conversions, and common cooking measures such as weight and volume. It also offers charts of the stages of cooked sugar for candy making and suggested adjustments for cooking and baking at high altitude.

Picking Apples

Choosing the right apple is generally a matter of matching its texture and flavor to its intended use. Crisp, juicy, sweet apples tend to work best for eating out of hand. Tart apples with a more firm texture are better suited for cooking and baking. Some varieties, such as Gala, taste good both raw and cooked. Small crabapples, considered a different species, are very tart and high in pectin making them ideal for jellies, jams, and chutneys. Experiment with different varieties using the table below as a guide. See also Apple (page 25).

Apple	Texture and Flavor	Best Uses
Arkansas Black	Crisp, firm, juicy	Eating, sauce
Baldwin	Crisp, rough-textured, juicy, spicy	Pie, sauce, eating
Braeburn	Crisp, firm, sweet-tart	Eating, sauce, pie
Bramley	Firm, rough-textured, juicy, tangy-sweet	Baking, sauce
Cortland	Crisp, juicy, tangy, aromatic	Salad, eating, pie, sauce
Cox's Orange Pippin	Firm, juicy, tangy, aromatic	Eating, pie, sauce
Crispin (Mutsu)	Crisp, juicy, spicy, sweet-tart	Eating, sauce
Empire	Crisp, delicate-textured, juicy, sweet-tart	Eating, salad
Fuji	Crisp, fine-textured, juicy, tangy, sweet, aromatic	Eating
Gala	Crisp, mildly tart, aromatic	Eating, baking, sauce
Golden Delicious	Juicy, sweetly aromatic	Eating, salad, sauce, baking
Granny Smith	Crisp, firm, juicy, tart	Pie, baking, sauce, eating
Gravenstein	Crisp, fine-textured, juicy, mildly tart	Pie, baking, sauce, eating
Greening (Rhode Island)	Crisp, juicy, tart	Pie, sauce, eating
Idared	Soft-textured, juicy, mildly tart	Pie, sauce, baking
Jonagold	Crisp, juicy, sweet-tart	Eating, pie, baking
Jonathan	Crisp, fine-textured, juicy, mildly tart	Eating, sauce, pie
Lady (Christmas) Apple	Crisp, juicy, intensely sweet	Eating, baking
Macoun	Firm, juicy, aromatic	Eating, pie, sauce
McIntosh	Soft-textured, juicy, tart, spicy, aromatic	Eating, sauce, pie
Newton Pippin	Firm, somewhat fine-textured, tart, aromatic	Eating, pie, sauce

Apple	Texture and Flavor	Best Uses
Northern Spy	Extra-firm, extra-juicy, sweet	Pie, sauce, eating, baking
Red Delicious	Crisp, juicy, mildly tart	Eating
Rome Beauty	Crisp, firm, juicy, mildly tart	Baking
Spartan	Crisp, fine-textured, sweet-tart	Eating
Winesap	Firm, juicy, winey-tasting	Eating, sauce

Picking Pears

While pear varieties number in the thousands, the fruit is so fragile that far fewer varieties are commonly available. Use the guide below to find the most popular eating and cooking pears. See also Asian pear (page 32) and Pear (page 359).

Pear	Characteristics	Best Uses	Substitutes
Anjou	Pale green yellow skin, often russeted; velvety, juicy white flesh; mild and sweet	Eating, cooking	Bartlett, Comice
Bartlett	Yellow speckled skin blushed pink; juicy, sweet flesh	Eating, cooking	Red Bartlett, Anjou
Bartlett, Red	Shiny, speckled red skin; buttery-soft, sweet and juicy flesh	Eating, cooking	Bartlett, Anjou
Bosc	Golden or light brown russeted skin; juicy, firm yet tender white flesh; sweet and mildly tart	Cooking, eating	Seckel (smaller)
Comice	Yellow green, speckled, russeted skin; soft, velvety, juicy, white flesh; sweet, rich, and aromatic	Eating	Anjou, Red Bartlett, Packham's Triumph
Forelle	Red speckled skin; firm, grainy, sweet flesh	Cooking	Winter Nellis
Packham's Triumph	Green yellow speckled skin, sometimes russeted; soft, smooth, succulent flesh; sweet and mildly tart	Eating, cooking	Comice, Anjou, Bartlett
Seckel	Very small, rounded pear with thick, green and red skin; firm yet tender, juicy flesh; sweet, spicy, and aromatic	Cooking, eating	Bosc (larger)
Winter Nellis	Small, rounded pear with green or red, russeted skin; firm, grainy, sweet flesh	Cooking	Forelle

The Wide World of Dried Beans

Freshly cooked dried beans taste richer, less salty, and less mushy than canned beans. But the two can be used interchangeably in many recipes. To remove the salty canning liquid, rinse canned beans in a sieve under running water before using. If cooking dried beans, plan on 1 pound (500 g), (about 2 cups/500 mL), expanding to 4 to 6 cups (1 to 1.5 L) total volume when cooked. To substitute one variety of dried bean for another, see the suggestions below. For information on lentil varieties, see Switching Lentils (page 569). For other legumes, see Beans, Dried (page 45); Legume (page 261); and Peas, Split (page 361).

Dried Bean	Characteristics	Substitutes
Adzuki (azuki)	Small, round-oval, maroon red, fine-textured, mildly sweet	Black adzuki beans (similar but black color), pink beans (slightly larger), red kidney beans (larger)
Anasazi	Medium, oval kidney shape, brick-red spotted with white (deep pink when cooked), mildly sweet	Pink beans, red kidney beans, cranberry beans
Appaloosa	Medium, oval kidney shape, white or cream spotted with black or brown	Pink beans, red kidney beans, pinto beans, black beans, tepary beans
Black (turtle)	Medium-small, oval kidney shape, black with coarse-textured, cream-color interior	Appaloosa beans, calypso beans (milder), black soybeans, small red beans, pink beans, pinto beans
Black-eyed pea	Small, oval kidney shape, cream with black dot, mildly sweet	Yellow-eye, lady, crowder or other cowpeas, pigeon peas
Calypso	Small, oval kidney shape, white with black splotch, fine-textured	Cannellini beans, white kidney beans, black beans (stronger flavor)
Cannellini	Medium, elongated oval kidney shape, white, fine-textured	White kidney beans, Great Northern beans (larger), navy beans (smaller), calypso beans, flageolets (fresher taste)
Chickpea (garbanzo)	Small, round, bumpy, beige, coarse-textured	Tan tepary beans, white kidney beans, Great Northern beans, large lima beans
Cranberry (borlotti)	Medium, oval kidney shape, cream speckled with chianti red	Tongues of fire beans, Anasazi beans, pink beans, red beans, pinto beans
European Soldier	Large, oval kidney shape, ivory with reddish brown markings, mildly sweet	White kidney beans, cannellini beans, red kidney beans, Anasazi beans

Dried Bean	Characteristics	Substitutes
Fava (broad)	Large, flat, earlobe-shape, light brown, mildly bitter	Ful (smaller, rounder fava bean variety used to make the Egyptian dish *ful medames*; takes longer to cook), lima beans
Flageolet (immature kidney bean)	Medium, oval kidney shape, white or light green, delicate texture	Cannellini beans, Great Northern beans, calypso beans, white tepary beans
Great Northern	Medium, oval kidney shape, white, coarse-textured	White kidney beans, cannellini beans, navy beans (smaller), lima beans, flageolets (more tender)
Jackson Wonder	Medium-large, flattened oval kidney shape, reddish brown speckled with dark brown	Red kidney beans, pink beans, pinto beans, red beans, cranberry beans
Lima (baby or sieva)	Medium, round kidney shape, white, delicate texture, sweet	Cannellini beans, navy beans, black-eyed peas, ful (small, round fava beans)
Lima (butter or Fordhook)	Extra-large, kidney shape, white, sweet	Christmas limas (brick red marking), Great Northern beans, white kidney beans, cannellini beans, fava beans
Marrow	Medium-large, oval, putty-color, creamy texture	Great Northern beans, cannellini beans, white kidney beans, navy beans (smaller)
Mung	Small, round-oval, green (yellow interior), soft texture, sweet	Small flageolets, pigeon peas
Navy (pea bean or Yankee bean)	Small, round-oval, white, dense texture	French navy beans (egg shape with light green marking), baby lima beans, cannellini beans, Great Northern beans, white kidney beans, white tepary beans
Pigeon pea	Small, round, beige or yellow spotted with reddish brown	Yellow-eye, black-eye, lady, crowder or other cowpeas
Pink (chili bean)	Medium, round kidney shape, pale reddish brown	Small red beans, pinto beans, rattlesnake beans, red kidney beans, cranberry beans
Pinto	Medium, kidney shape, light brown speckled with brown or pink, coarse texture	Pink beans, small red beans, rattlesnake beans, red kidney beans, Anasazi beans, cranberry beans

continued on next page…

Dried Bean	Characteristics	Substitutes
Rattlesnake	Medium, round kidney shape, brown speckled with dark brown, smooth texture	Pinto beans, pink beans, small red beans, red kidney beans, Anasazi beans, cranberry beans
Red (small Mexican chili bean)	Medium-small, oval kidney shape, reddish brown, dense texture	Red kidney beans, pink beans, pinto beans, red kidney beans, Anasazi beans, cranberry beans
Red kidney	Medium, kidney shape, deep reddish brown, coarse texture	Small red beans, pink beans, pinto beans, Anasazi beans, cranberry beans
Scarlet Runner	Large, oval kidney shape, mottled black and lavender, fluffy texture	White, black or other runner beans, cranberry beans, pinto beans, red kidney beans
Soybean	Small, round, pale yellow, very dense texture	Chickpeas, navy beans
Spanish Tolosana	Medium, kidney shape, mottled tan and reddish purple	Jackson Wonder beans, red kidney beans, pinto beans, pink beans, cranberry beans
Steuben Yellow-eye	Medium, oval kidney shape, half cream and half light brown, coarse texture	Navy beans, white kidney beans, Great Northern beans, cannellini beans, baby lima beans
Swedish Brown	Medium-small, oval shape, caramel brown	Pinto beans, cranberry beans, Great Northern beans, navy beans
Tepary	Medium-small, flattened oval, tan or white or gold or black color	Navy beans, pinto beans, rattlesnake beans, black beans
Tongues of Fire	Medium, oval, mottled beige and reddish brown	Cranberry beans, rattlesnake beans, pinto beans, pink beans
Trout (Jacob's Cattle)	Medium-large, kidney shape, white speckled with brownish purple, coarse texture	Pinto beans, pink beans, Spanish Tolosana beans, white kidney beans
White kidney	Medium, kidney shape, white, coarse texture	Cannellini beans (creamier), Great Northern beans, navy beans (smaller), flageolets (more tender)

Switching Lentils

In botanical terms, lentils include several varieties of the Lens culinaris family, all of which are small, flat, disc-shaped legumes. However, in culinary parlance, Indian cooks also use the term "lentils" or "dal" to refer to similar skinned and split peas or beans that cook relatively quickly and do not need to be soaked, such as split mung beans (moong dal). Unsplit whole beans are often referred to by Indian cooks as "gram." The chart below includes substitutes for popular lentils and other split peas or beans that are cooked like lentils. To find substitutes for other legumes, see specific entries listed alphabetically in the A to Z section.

	Legume	Interior Color	Substitutes
Lentils	**Beluga lentil**	Black	French green lentils
	Brown lentil (green lentil)	Brown or green	French green lentils (firmer), yellow lentils
	French green lentil (Puy lentils)	Brown or green	Beluga lentils, brown lentils (softer)
	Red lentil	Orange pink	Masoor dal (cooks faster), yellow lentils
	Yellow lentil	Yellow	Yellow moong dal, yellow split peas, toor dal (firmer), channa dal (firmer)
Dal	**Channa dal (split chickpea relative)**	Pale yellow	Toor dal, yellow split peas, yellow lentils (softer), yellow moong dal (cooks faster)
	Masoor dal (split red lentils)	Orange pink	Red lentils (takes longer to cook), yellow lentils
	Matar dal (split green or yellow peas)	Green or pale yellow	Yellow moong dal, yellow lentils, channa dal
	Moong dal (split mung beans)	Cream (green skins)	Yellow moong dal (cooks faster), brown lentils, yellow lentils
	Moong dal, yellow (split and husked mung beans)	Yellow	Yellow split peas, yellow lentils, toor dal (firmer), moong dal (takes longer to cook)
	Toor dal (split pigeon peas)	Yellow	Channa dal, yellow split peas, yellow lentils
	Urad dal (split black lentils)	Cream (black skins)	Whole pigeon peas, split black-eyed peas, beluga lentils (softer)
	Urad dal chilka (split and husked black lentils)	Cream	Val dal (larger)
	Val dal (split lablab beans)	Ivory	Urad dal chilka (smaller), split black-eyed peas

Choosing Among Olives

Olives are variously marketed by their country of origin (Greece), curing method (oil-cured), and/or the varietal of the fruit itself (Picual). Color also comes into play, as green olives often taste slightly bitter, while black olives tend to taste richer. For simplicity's sake, the chart below groups olives by the most widely used curing methods: dry-curing and brine-curing. Dry-cured olives are cured in salt, which typically leaves them wrinkled, soft, and salty. They are sometimes packed with oil or herbs. Oil-cured olives are similarly wrinkled and soft, but less salty-tasting. Brine-cured olives are firmer with a sharp, salty flavor due to the salt, vinegar or wine in the brine. Some recipes call for specific olive varieties, while others call for generic categories of olives such as black Greek olives or French oil-cured olives. Use the guide below to choose or substitute olive varieties that have the characteristics you seek.

	Olive	Characteristics	Substitutes
Dry-Cured Olives	Aleppo	Black, Middle Eastern, slightly bitter	Moroccan, Nyons
	Gaeta	Black, small, Italian, often rubbed with oil and flavored with herbs	Niçoise
	Moroccan	Black, Moroccan, shiny and slightly bitter	Aleppo, Nyons
	Niçoise	Black, French, small, oily, chewy, sometimes flavored with lemon and garlic	Gaeta
	Nyons	Black brown, French, shiny, salty, bitter, often packed in oil	Moroccan, Aleppo
Brine-Cured Olives	Agrinion	Green, Greek, large, soft, cracked, tart	Atalanta, Naphlion, Kura
	Aleppo	Green, Middle Eastern, salty, bitter	Kura, Naphlion
	Alphonso	Purple black, Chilean, large, soft, tart, slightly bitter	Kalamata, Gaeta
	Amphissa	Purple black, Greek, large, soft	Kalamata, Gaeta, Alphonso
	Arauco	Green, Spanish, large, flavored with rosemary	Manzanilla
	Arbequina	Green, Spanish, small, mild flavor	Manzanilla (larger)
	Atalanta	Green brown, Greek, soft	Royal, Agrinion
	Calabrese	Green brown, Italian, sharp, often flavored with chile peppers and herbs	Sicilian, Kalamata
	Cerignola	Green (sometimes black), Italian, very large, meaty, mildly sweet	Sicilian (more tart), Calabrese (sharper)

Olive	Characteristics	Substitutes
Gaeta	Brownish purple black, Italian, small, soft, nutty, salty	Ponentine, Kalamata, Alphonso
Kalamata (Calamata)	Purple black, Greek, almond-shaped, soft, rich, fruity	Royal, Gaeta, Amphissa
Kura	Green, Middle Eastern, cracked, bitter	Naphlion (more fruity), Agrinion
Ligurian	Black brown, Italian, small, tart and piquant, sometimes includes stems	Niçoise, Gaeta
Lugano	Black, Italian, firm and salty	Picual, Ligurian
Manzanilla	Green, Spanish, crisp, often pitted and stuffed with pimiento or garlic	Arauco, Arbequina, Sevillano, Naphlion
Mission	Black, Californian, soft, mild, watery flavor	Alphonso (more bitter), Gaeta (more flavorful), Kalamata (more firm and flavorful)
Naphlion	Dark green, Greek, cracked, crisp, fruity	Agrinion, Kura (more bitter), Aleppo, Manzanilla, Picholine
Niçoise	Black brown, French, small, chewy and meaty, tart and rich	Ligurian, Kalamata, Gaeta
Picholine	Green, French, oblong, crisp, tart, sometimes flavored with herbes de Provence	Sevillano, Manzanilla, Naphlion
Picual	Black, Spanish, firm, nutty	Lugano, Ligurian
Ponentine	Black, Italian, mild flavor	Gaeta, Cerignola (black), Amphissa, Kalamata
Royal (Victoria)	Reddish brown, Greek, large, chewy	Kalamata, Atalanta
Sevillano (Queen, Super-Colossal)	Pale green, Californian, very large, crisp	Manzanilla, Naphlion, Picholine
Sicilian	Green, large, Sicilian, tart, meaty, often flavored with red pepper or fennel	Calabrese, Manzanilla

Brine-Cured Olives

Shuffling Mushrooms

Mushrooms are the fruiting bodies of edible fungi. Most have a similar flavor chemistry based on glutamate, the savory flavor component that is now understood as umami, the fifth detectable flavor after sweet, sour, salty, and bitter. For this reason, many mushrooms are interchangeable for flavor purposes. But each mushroom has a unique flavor, texture, and color. Use the guide below to make more accurate fresh mushroom substitutions. Keep in mind that many dried and reconstituted mushrooms, such as porcinis and morels, make a fair substitute for fresh. In general, 1 pound (500 g) fresh mushrooms equals 2 to 3 ounces (60 to 90 g) dried. For more information on dried mushrooms, see Mushrooms, Dried (page 307) and Mushrooms, Powdered (page 308).

Mushroom	Characteristics	Substitutes
Beech (Brown Clamshell, Hon-Shimeji)	White to light brown clustered caps; firm, crunchy texture; mild, nutty flavor	Enoki (more delicate), oyster, white button
Blewit (Blue Foot)	Violet gray cap and stem; meaty texture; earthy, somewhat spicy flavor	Matsutake (spicier), shiitake
Cauliflower	Large, pale yellow white, cauliflower-like, ruffled, layered lobes on a rooting stalk; firm, yet supple texture; nutty, sweet flavor	Pom pom (firmer)
Chanterelle, Black Trumpet (Trompette de la Mort)	Charcoal to black trumpet-shaped caps on thick white stems; delicate texture; rich, smoky, fruity flavor	Golden chanterelle (more delicate flavor), hedgehog
Chanterelle, Golden (Egg Mushroom, Girolle, Pfifferling)	Golden yellow funnel-shaped caps on tapered, hollow, yellow stems; firm, yet supple texture; earthy, nutty flavor and apricot-like aroma	White chanterelle, yellow foot chanterelle (less flavorful), hedgehog, royal trumpet or king oyster
Chanterelle, White	Pale white, funnel-shaped caps on pale white stems; firm, yet supple texture; earthy, nutty flavor with fruity aroma	Golden chanterelle, hedgehog, royal trumpet or king oyster
Chanterelle, Yellow Foot	Brown, funnel-shaped caps on yellow stems; firm, yet supple texture; earthy flavor with plum-like aroma	Golden chanterelle (more flavorful), hedgehog, royal trumpet or king oyster
Chicken-of-the-Woods	Yellow orange overlapping, tiered fruitbody; firm texture (similar to chicken); mild, earthy flavor and citrus-like aroma	Porcini (richer flavor), portobello (richer flavor), shiitake (more woodsy flavor)
Cinnamon Cap	Tawny-color clustered caps; firm, yet supple texture; earthy, sweet flavor	Nameko, shiitake, matsutake, golden chanterelle

Mushroom	Characteristics	Substitutes
Crimini (Italian brown)	Tan to brown cap; similar to white mushrooms but with denser texture and deeper flavor	White mushrooms, baby portobellos, shiitakes
Enoki (snow puff)	Several tiny, white caps joined at the base; delicate, nearly crunchy texture; mild, aromatic flavor	Oyster, white button
Fairy-Ring	Smooth, tawny, conical caps on long beige stem; firm, yet supple texture; mild, earthy flavor	Nameko, cinnamon cap, white button, chanterelle
Hedgehog	Creamy white, slightly funnel-shaped caps on white stem; delicate texture; earthy, nutty, flavor	White or golden chanterelle, nameko
Honey	Large, amber or light brown, clustering caps on light brown stems; firm, yet supple texture; earthy flavor	Cinnamon cap, nameko, hedgehog, shiitake (richer flavor)
Maitake (Hen of the Woods)	Grayish brown, layered cluster of fungus petals fused to a central stalk; firm, yet supple texture; aromatic, woodsy flavor	Oyster, shiitake
Matsutake (Pine Mushroom)	Light to dark brown caps; dense, meaty texture; rich, spicy aroma	Blewit (blue color), portobello (more earthy), shiitake
Morel	Beige, yellow or black sponge-like, pointed, honeycomb caps on thick, hollow stems; delicate texture; rich, woodsy, nutty flavor	Dried and reconstituted morel, oyster, shiitake, portobello
Nameko	Shiny, orange brown clustered caps; firm, yet supple texture; earthy, sweet flavor	Cinnamon cap, shiitake, matsutake, golden chanterelle
Oyster (Pleurotus)	Light brown to gray to red flattened caps; velvety, oyster-like texture; mild flavor	White chanterelle, enoki (slightly more crunchy texture)
Oyster (Royal trumpet or king oyster)	Light brown trumpet-shaped caps on tender, white stem; delicate texture; mild flavor	Oyster, white chanterelle, matsutake, shiitake
Pom Pom (Yamabushitake, bear's head)	White ball-shaped cap with no stem; velvety texture; mild, sweet flavor	King oyster or royal trumpet, white chanterelle, small puffball (firmer)

continued on next page…

Mushroom	Characteristics	Substitutes
Porcini (Cèpe, King Bolete, Steinpilze)	Smooth, light to dark brown, bun-shaped cap on thick barrel-shaped stem; dense, meaty texture; rich, woodsy, complex flavor	Dried and reconstituted porcini, matsutake, portobello (less complex flavor), hedgehog
Portobello (mature crimini)	Dark brown caps up to 6 inches (15 cm) in diameter; meaty texture; rich woodsy flavor	Large crimini (milder), jumbo white mushrooms (even milder), porcini, matsutake
Puffball	White ball-shaped cap with no stem; firm texture; mild, earthy flavor	Pom Pom (more delicate), jumbo white
Shiitake (Oak, Chinese or black forest)	Golden to dark brown umbrella-shaped caps; spongy, yet meaty texture; rich, woodsy flavor	Golden chanterelle, crimini, oyster, straw
Straw	Small, light brown to dark charcoal, conical cap; firm, yet supple texture; mild, earthy, musty flavor	Canned straw mushrooms (less firm), enoki, white button
White (Button)	Small (button) to large (jumbo) white to light brown bun-shaped caps; mild, earthy flavor	Crimini (more flavorful), oyster (more delicate)
Wood Ear	Earthy flavor; includes tree ear (thick), cloud ear (thin), and silver ear (white)	Dried and reconstituted wood ear, maitake (more flavorful), shiitake (more flavorful)

Choosing Among Potatoes

Potatoes come in three basic types, which determine their best uses. High-starch potatoes, such as russets, are called baking potatoes due to their low-moisture content, which makes them light and fluffy when baked. High-starch potatoes also make excellent mashed potatoes and french fries. Low-starch or waxy potatoes, such as round red-skinned potatoes, are called boiling potatoes because they retain their shape when boiled, which makes them a good choice in salads and stews. New potatoes are also low-starch because they are harvested young before the starch develops. Some low-starch varieties are called creamers due to their moist, firm texture. Medium-starch potatoes, such as Yukon Gold, are called all-purpose potatoes because their starch content falls somewhere in between the two extremes. Fingerlings are named for their small, finger-like shape and may have high-, medium-, or low-starch content. Use the guide below to substitute potatoes within and outside of the three main categories: high-starch, medium-starch, and low-starch. Varieties or alternate names for certain potatoes are listed in parentheses.

	Potato	Characteristics	Substitutes
High-Starch Potatoes	**Russet (Arcadia, Burbank, Butte, Idaho)**	Oval, netted brown skin, white flesh that is mealy and fluffy when cooked	White Rose or other long white (for baking or frying), Yellow Finn, Yukon Gold, or other yellow flesh (for baking, mashing, or frying)
Medium-Starch Potatoes	**All Blue**	Round, dense, somewhat waxy bluish purple flesh	Purple Peruvian, Peruvian Blue, Russian Blue
	Austrian Crescent	Fingerling shape, smooth golden skin, somewhat waxy, pale yellow flesh	Banana, Ratte, Ruby Crescent (rosy skin), Bintje
	Banana (Russian Banana)	Fingerling shape, smooth, golden skin, somewhat waxy, pale yellow flesh	Austrian Crescent, Ratte, Ruby Crescent (rosy skin), Bintje
	Bintje	Golden skin, somewhat waxy, creamy yellow flesh	Charlotte, Austrian Crescent, Banana, Ratte, Ruby Crescent (rosy skin), Yukon Gold, White Rose or other long white
	California White (Long white)	Oval, light tan, thin skin, somewhat starchy, somewhat waxy white flesh	White Rose or other long white, Irish Cobbler or other round white
	Caribe	Purplish blue skin, somewhat starchy, white flesh	Purple Viking, Bintje, Yellow Finn, Yukon Gold, Irish Cobbler or other round white

continued on next page...

Potato	Characteristics	Substitutes
Charlotte	Oval, thin golden skin, somewhat starchy, somewhat waxy, yellow flesh	Yellow Finn, Yukon Gold, White Rose or other long white, Kennebec or other round white
Desiree	Oval, thin red skin, somewhat waxy, creamy yellow flesh	Rose Finn Apple, Ruby Crescent, Russian Red, Red Bliss (white flesh), La Soda (white flesh), Bintje (gold skin), Yellow Finn (gold skin), Yukon Gold (gold skin)
German Butterball	Rounded, golden skin, somewhat starchy yellow flesh	Yukon Gold, Yellow Finn, Charlotte, Irish cobbler or other round white (white flesh)
Irish Cobbler (Round white)	Tan, thin skin, somewhat starchy white flesh	Katahdin or other round white, German Butterball, White Rose or other long white
Katahdin (Round white)	Light brown skin, somewhat starchy white flesh	Kennebec or other round white, German Butterball, White Rose or other long white
Kennebec (Round white)	Light tan skin, somewhat starchy, somewhat waxy white flesh	Katahdin or other round white, German Butterball, White Rose or other long white
Peruvian Blue	Oval, dark blue skin, somewhat starchy, somewhat waxy, deep purple flesh with sweet, nutty flavor	All Blue, Russian Blue, Purple Peruvian
Purple Peruvian	Fingerling shape, shiny, thick purple skin, somewhat waxy purple flesh	All Blue, Russian Blue, Peruvian Blue
Purple Viking	Striking purple and pink skin, somewhat starchy, white flesh	Caribe, White Rose or other long white, Irish Cobbler or other round white, Bintje, Yellow Finn, Yukon Gold
Ratte	Fingerling shape, golden skin, somewhat waxy, buttery, pale yellow flesh	Austrian Crescent, Banana, Bintje
Red Gold	Oblong, red skin, somewhat waxy, creamy, yellow flesh	Desiree, Ruby Crescent, Bintje (gold skin), Austrian Crescent (gold skin), Banana (gold skin), Ratte (gold skin)
Russian Blue	Blue skin, somewhat waxy, blue flesh with white ring just inside	All Blue, Purple Peruvian, Peruvian Blue

Medium-Starch Potatoes

	Potato	Characteristics	Substitutes
Medium-Starch Potatoes	**White Rose (Long white)**	Oval, light tan, thin skin, somewhat starchy, somewhat waxy white flesh	California White or other long white, Kennebec or other round white, Purple Viking (purple and pink skin)
	Yellow Finn	Golden skin, somewhat starchy, buttery-sweet, yellow flesh	Yukon Gold, German Butterball, Caribe (purplish blue skin)
	Yukon Gold	Golden skin, somewhat starchy, yellow flesh	Yellow Finn, German Butterball, Caribe (purplish blue skin)
Low-Starch Potatoes	**All Red**	Round or oblong, thin red skin, red flesh	Purple Peruvian (purple flesh), Russian Blue (blue flesh)
	Anoka	Oblong, pale yellow skin, white flesh	White rose or other long white, Kennebec or other round white, La Soda (rosy skin), Red Bliss (red skin)
	La Soda	Small, round, smooth, rosy skin, white flesh	Red Bliss, Desiree (yellow flesh), Rose Finn Apple (yellow flesh), Ruby Crescent (yellow flesh), Russian Red (yellow flesh)
	Red Bliss (Round red)	Red, thin skin, white flesh	La Soda, White Rose or other long white (tan skin), Kennebec or other round white (tan skin), Rose Finn Apple (yellow flesh), Ruby Crescent (yellow flesh), Russian Red (yellow flesh)
	Rose Finn Apple	Fingerling shape, rosy skin, yellow, fruity-sweet flesh	Ruby Crescent, Russian Red, La Soda, Desiree, Austrian Crescent (gold skin), Banana (gold skin), Ratte (gold skin), Bintje (gold skin), Red Bliss (white flesh)
	Ruby Crescent	Fingerling shape, rosy skin, yellow flesh	Russian Red, La Soda, Desiree, Austrian Crescent (gold skin), Banana (gold skin), Ratte (gold skin), Bintje (gold skin), Red Bliss (white flesh)
	Russian Red	Fingerling shape, red skin, yellow flesh	Ruby Crescent, La Soda, Desiree, Austrian Crescent (gold skin), Banana (gold skin), Ratte (gold skin), Bintje (gold skin), Red Bliss (white flesh)

Choosing Dried Chiles

There is widespread confusion about chile nomenclature due the massive variety of chiles grown around the world. The same chile pepper may have five different names, depending on where it was grown. Fresh chiles are often given a different name when dried, adding to the confusion. In the chart below, I have included alternate names whenever possible. All chiles referred to here are dried or they are the dried versions of fresh chiles that have the same name. The heat level of chiles is measured on a scale from 0 to 16,000,000 "Scoville units." For more information on Scoville heat units, see Choosing Fresh Chiles (page 582).

Pepper	Characteristics	Scoville Units	Substitutes
African Bird's Eye	$\frac{1}{2}$ to 1 inches (1 to 2.5 cm) long, blunt point, red	100,000 to 200,000	Thai, Charleston hot cayenne, tepín, piquin
Ají Amarillo (cuzqueño)	4 inches (10 cm) long, $\frac{3}{4}$ inch (2 cm) wide, pointed, orange, fruity	30,000 to 50,000	Ají colorado, cayenne, tabasco, arbol
Ají Colorado (cuzqueño)	4 inches (10 cm) long, $\frac{3}{4}$ inch (2 cm) wide, pointed, red, fruity	30,000 to 50,000	Ají amarillo, cayenne, tabasco, arbol
Ají Mirasol (cuzqueño)	3 to 5 inches (7.5 to 12.5 cm) long, 1 inch (2.5 cm) wide, tapered point, reddish orange, fruity	1,000 to 3,000	Ancho, New Mexico, ají panca
Ají Panca (cuzqueño)	3 to 5 inches (7.5 to 12.5 cm) long, 1 inch (2.5 cm) wide, tapered point, ruddy brown, fruity	500 to 1,000	Ancho, New Mexico, ají mirasol
Aleppo (Halaby)	4 to 6 inches (10 to 15 cm) long, $\frac{1}{2}$ inch (1 cm) wide, pointed, red	6,000 to 10,000	Cayenne, serrano, costeño rojo
Ancho (dried poblano)	4 inches (10 cm) long, 3 inches (7.5 cm) wide, heart-shaped, reddish brown or mahogany, earthy and fruity	1,250 to 2,500	Mulato, pasilla, chilhuacle rojo, costeño amarillo, New Mexico
Arbol (de Arbol)	2 to 3 inches (5 to 7.5 cm) long, $\frac{1}{4}$ inch (0.5 cm) wide, pointed, shiny red, grassy-hot	15,000 to 30,000	Pico de pajaro, serrano, cayenne
Cascabel (bola)	$1\frac{1}{2}$ inch (4 cm) diameter, round, reddish brown	1,250 to 2,500	Chilhuacle rojo, costeño amarillo, guajillo, catarina, Hungarian cherry pepper

Pepper	Characteristics	Scoville Units	Substitutes
Catarina	1½ to 2 inches (4 to 5 cm) long, ¾ inch (2 cm) wide, blunt point, red	2,000 to 4,000	Costeño amarillo, chilhuacle rojo, guajillo, Hungarian cherry pepper, New Mexico
Cayenne (Ginnie)	2 to 4 inches (5 to 10 cm) long, ½ inch (1 cm) wide, pointed, shiny red	10,000 to 40,000	Arbol, serrano, ají colorado, Thai
Chilcostle	3 to 5 inches (7.5 to 12.5 cm) long, ½ inch (1 cm) wide, pointed, deep red	3,500 to 5,000	Catarina, chilhuacle amarillo, costeño amarillo, pepperoncini, puya
Chilhuacle Amarillo	2 to 3 inches (5 to 7.5 cm) long, 1½ inches (4 cm) wide, blunt point, orange red	1,250 to 2,000	Chilhuacle negro, chilhuacle rojo, cascabel, catarina, guajillo, costeño amarillo
Chilhuacle Negro	2 to 3 inches (5 to 7.5 cm) long, 2 to 3 inches (5 to 7.5 cm) wide, heart-shaped, deep purplish brown, earthy, fruity	1,250 to 2,000	Mulato, pasilla, pátzcuaro, ancho
Chilhuacle Rojo	2 to 3 inches (5 to 7.5 cm) long, 1½ inches (4 cm) wide, blunt point, reddish brown	1,250 to 2,000	Chilhuacle amarillo, cascabel, catarina, guajillo, costeño amarillo
Chipotle (smoked jalapeño)	2 to 4 inches (5 to 10 cm) long, 1 inch (2.5 cm) wide, blunt point, grayish chocolate brown	5,000 to 10,000	Pasilla de Oaxaca, mora or morita, serrano (a drop of liquid smoke adds smoke flavor)
Costeño (rojo or bandeño)	2 to 3 inches (5 to 7.5 cm) long, ½ inch (1 cm) wide, pointed, orange red	5,000 to 10,000	Costeño amarillo, chilhuacle rojo, serrano, cayenne, arbol, puya, pico de pajaro
Costeño Amarillo	2 to 3 inches (5 to 7.5 cm) long, ¾ inch (2 cm) wide, pointed, yellow-red	1,250 to 2,500	Costeño rojo, chilhuacle amarillo, cascabel, guajillo, puya, catarina, New Mexico
Guajillo	4 to 6 inches (10 to 15 cm) long, 1 inch (2.5 cm) wide, blunt point, shiny brownish orange red	2,000 to 4,500	New Mexico, puya, ají mirasol, chilhuacle amarillo or rojo, costeño amarillo, cascabel, ancho, mulato

continued on next page…

Pepper	Characteristics	Scoville Units	Substitutes
Habanero	1½ inches (4 cm) long, 1 inch (2.5 cm) wide, lantern shape, yellow, orange, red or green, fruity	100,000 to 500,000	Scotch bonnet, Thai, African bird's eye, Charleston hot cayenne
Mora or morita	1 to 2 inches (2.5 to 5 cm) long, ¼ to ¾ inch (0.5 to 2 cm) wide, blunt point, reddish brown	5,000 to 10,000	Chipotle, pasilla de Oaxaca, serrano (a drop of liquid smoke adds smoke flavor)
Mulato (dried poblano)	4 inches (10 cm) long, 2 to 3 inches (5 to 7.5 cm) wide, blunt point, chocolate brown	1,250 to 2,500	Ancho, pasilla, chilhuacle rojo, costeño amarillo, New Mexico
New Mexico (roasted green or Anaheim)	5 inches (12.5 cm) long, 1 inch (2.5 cm) wide, blunt point, brownish green	500 to 1,500	New Mexico red, Hungarian cherry pepper
New Mexico (red or Colorado)	6 inches (15 cm) long, 1½ inches (4 cm) wide, blunt point, red	1,000 to 2,500	Guajillo, ají mirasol, catarina, costeño amarillo, ancho
Onza (rojo)	3 inches (7.5 cm) long, ½ inch (1 cm) wide, pointed, brick red	2,500 to 5,000	Chilhuacle rojo, catarina, cascabel, chilcostle, costeño rojo, guajillo, New Mexico
Pasilla (negro)	6 inches (15 cm) long, 1½ inches (4 cm) wide, blunt point, raisin brown	1,000 to 1,500	Mulato, ancho, pasilla de Oaxaca, pátzcuaro, cascabel, chilhuacle negro, costeño amarillo, guajillo
Pasilla de Oaxaca	4 inches (10 cm) long, 1 inch (2.5 cm) wide, blunt point, mahogany red	4,000 to 8,000	Pátzcuaro, puya, cascabel, chilcostle, serrano
Pátzcuaro	5 inches (12.5 cm) long, 1 inch (2.5 cm) wide, blunt point, purplish red	3,000 to 8,000	Pasilla de Oaxaca, puya, cascabel, chilcostle, serrano
Pico de Pajaro	1 inch (2.5 cm) long, ¼ inch (0.5 cm) wide, pointed, dark orange red	40,000 to 80,000	Piquin, tepín, arbol, Thai, ají colorado
Piquin (pequín)	½ inch (1 cm) long, ¼ inch (0.5 cm) wide, oval blunt point, orange red	50,000 to 100,000	Tepín, pico de pajaro, cayenne, serrano, arbol

Pepper	Characteristics	Scoville Units	Substitutes
Piri-piri (pili pili)	1/4 to 1/2 inch (0.5 to 1 cm) long, 1/4 inch (0.5 cm) wide, blunt point, red	30,000 to 60,000	Pico de pajaro, piquin, ají colorado, arbol, cayenne, Thai, serrano
Puya (pulla)	4 to 5 inches (10 to 12.5 cm) long, 3/4 inch (2 cm) wide, pointed, purplish red	5,000 to 15,000	Chilcostle, cascabel, costeño rojo, pátzcuaro, guajillo (milder)
Serrano	1 1/2 inches (4 cm) long, 1/2 inch (1 cm) wide, blunt point, orange red	10,000 to 25,000	Arbol, cayenne, costeño rojo
Tepín (chiltepín)	1/2 inch (1 cm) diameter, round or oval, red	40,000 to 80,000	Pico de pajaro, piquin, piri-piri, ají colorado, cayenne
Thai	1 to 2 inches (2.5 to 5 cm) long, 1/4 inch (0.5 cm) wide, pointed, various colors	15,000 to 30,000	Hontaka, Santaka, serrano, cayenne
Togarashi (ichimi)	1/2 to 1 1/2 inches (1 to 4 cm) long, 1/4 to 1/2 inch (0.5 to 1 cm) wide, pointed, red	10,000 to 40,000	Cayenne, Thai, arbol, serrano

Choosing Fresh Chiles

The Scoville heat scale, developed in 1912 by pharmacist Wilbur Scoville, measures a pepper's pungency. Bell or sweet peppers have 0 Scoville heat units; jalapeños have 5,000 to 10,000; and pure capsaicin, the heat-producing substance in chile peppers, clocks in at 16 million Scoville units. The chiles below include composite Scoville ratings from several authoritative sources. Keep in mind that a chile pepper's heat and flavor often fluctuate according to the variety of seeds used and the particular conditions under which the pepper was grown.

Pepper	Characteristics	Scoville Units	Substitutes
African Bird's Eye	1/2 to 1 inch (1 to 2.5 cm) long, blunt point, red	100,000 to 200,000	Thai, Charleston hot cayenne
Ají (green or red)	4 inches (10 cm) long, 3/4 inch (2 cm) wide, pointed, green or red, fruity	30,000 to 50,000	Cayenne, tabasco, arbol
Anaheim (green California, red Colorado)	6 to 8 inches (15 to 20 cm) long, 1 to 1 1/2 inches (2.5 to 4 cm) wide, blunt point, green or red	500 to 1,500	New Mexico, poblano, Hungarian cherry pepper, pepperoncini
Banana (Sweet)	5 inches (12.5 cm) long, 1 to 1 1/2 inches (2.5 to 4 cm) wide, blunt point, pale yellow to orange red	0 to 250	Bell, cubanelle, mexi-bell, pimiento, Anaheim
Bell	4 to 5 inches (10 to 12.5 cm) long, 3 to 4 inches (7.5 to 10 cm) wide, bell or elongated bell shape, various colors	0	Banana, cubanelle, mexi-bell, pimiento, Anaheim
Cachucha	2 to 3 inches (5 to 7.5 cm) long, 1 1/2 to 2 inches (4 to 5 cm) wide, bell shape, various colors	0 to 250	Bell, banana, cubanelle, mexi-bell, pimiento, Anaheim
Cayenne (Ginnie)	4 to 6 inches (10 to 15 cm) long, 1/2 inch (1 cm) wide, pointed, green or red	10,000 to 40,000	Serrano, tabasco, ají Colorado, Thai
Cherry (Hungarian)	1 inch (2.5 cm) long, 1 1/2 inches (4 cm) wide, cherry shape, green or red	100 to 500	Mexi-bell, pepperoncini, pimiento, Anaheim, New Mexico
Chilaca	8 inches (20 cm) long, 1 inch (2.5 cm) wide, twisted blunt point, dark purple green	1,000 to 1,500	Poblano, New Mexico, Anaheim

Pepper	Characteristics	Scoville Units	Substitutes
Cubanelle (Italian frying)	6 inches (15 cm) long, 2 inches (5 cm) wide, elongated bell shape, yellow green or orange red	0	Bell, banana, pimiento, mexi-bell, Anaheim
Fresno (caribe)	3 inches (7.5 cm) long, 1½ inches (4 cm) wide, blunt point, green to red, floral	5,000 to 8,000	Jalapeño, Santa Fe grande, yellow wax, serrano
Güero	3 to 5 inches (7.5 to 12.5 cm) long, 1 to 1½ inches (2.5 to 4 cm) wide, blunt point, pale yellow	3,000 to 8,000	Hungarian wax, Santa Fe grande, Fresno, jalapeño
Habanero	1½ inches (4 cm) long, 1 inch (2.5 cm) wide, lantern shape, yellow, orange, red or green, fruity	100,000 to 500,000	Scotch bonnet, Thai, African bird's eye, Charleston hot cayenne
Holland (Dutch)	4 inches (10 cm) long, 1 to 1½ inches (2.5 to 4 cm) wide, pointed, red	4,000 to 6,000	Fresno, jalapeño, yellow wax
Hontaka (Japones)	1 to 2 inches (2.5 to 5 cm) long, ¼ inch (0.5 cm) wide, pointed, red	15,000 to 30,000	Santaka, Thai, serrano, cayenne
Jalapeño	2 to 4 inches (5 to 10 cm) long, 1 inch (2.5 cm) wide, blunt point, green or red	5,000 to 10,000	Fresno, Sante Fe grande, Holland, serrano, cayenne
Malagueta pepper	1 to 2 inches (2.5 to 5 cm) long, ¾ inch (2 cm) wide, pointed, yellow orange or green, fruity	8,000 to 30,000	Thai, Hontaka, Santaka, serrano, cayenne, tabasco
Mexi-bell	3 to 5 inches (7.5 to 12.5 cm) long, 3 to 4 inches (7.5 to 10 cm) wide, bell shape, various colors	100 to 400	Pimiento, New Mexico, Hungarian cherry, bell, banana
Mirasol	4 inches (10 cm) long, ¾ inch (2 cm) wide, pointed, red, fruity	2,500 to 5,000	Hungarian wax, jalapeño, serrano
New Mexico (green or red)	6 to 8 inches (15 to 20 cm) long, 1½ to 2 inches (4 to 5 cm) wide, blunt point, green or red	500 to 1,500	Anaheim, poblano, Hungarian cherry, pepperoncini

continued on next page…

Pepper	Characteristics	Scoville Units	Substitutes
Pepperoncini	3 inches (7.5 cm) long, ¾ inch (2 cm) wide, pointed, pale green to red	100 to 500	Hungarian wax or cherry, Anaheim, mexi-bell, New Mexico, pimiento
Pimiento	3 to 5 inches (7.5 to 12.5 cm) long, 2 to 3 inches (5 to 7.5 cm) wide, pointed bell shape, red	0 to 500	Bell, mexi-bell, Hungarian cherry, banana, New Mexico
Poblano	4 to 5 inches (10 to 12.5 cm) long, 2 to 3 inches (5 to 7.5 cm) wide, dimpled pointed bell shape, dark green or red	1,250 to 2,500	Chilaca, Hungarian wax, New Mexico, Anaheim
Rocoto (manzano or péron)	2 to 3 inches (5 to 7.5 cm) long, 2 to 2½ inches (5 to 6 cm) wide, bell or lantern shaped, yellow orange or red	20,000 to 50,000	Tabasco, serrano, jalapeño, Thai, Hontaka, Santaka
Santaka (Japones)	1 to 2 inches (2.5 to 5 cm) long, ¼ inch (0.5 cm) wide, pointed, red	15,000 to 30,000	Hontaka, Thai, serrano, cayenne
Sante Fe Grande	3 to 5 inches (7.5 to 12.5 cm) long, 1 to 1½ inches (2.5 to 4 cm) wide, blunt point, pale yellow	3,000 to 8,000	Güero, Fresno, jalapeño, Hungarian wax
Scotch Bonnet	1½ inches (4 cm) long, 1 inch (2.5 cm) wide, lantern shape, yellow green, orange, or red, fruity	200,000 to 325,000	Habanero, Thai, African bird's eye, Charleston hot cayenne
Serrano	1 to 3 inches (2.5 to 7.5 cm) long, ½ inch (1 cm) wide, blunt point, green or red	10,000 to 25,000	Cayenne, Hontaka, Santaka, Thai
Tabasco	1 to 1½ inches (2.5 to 4 cm) long, ¼ to ½ inch (0.5 to 1 cm) wide, blunt point, yellow orange or red	30,000 to 50,000	Rocoto, Thai, serrano, cayenne, malagueta, Hontaka, Santaka
Tepín (chiltepin)	½ inch (1 cm) diameter, round or oval, red	40,000 to 80,000	Thai, Tabasco, Serrano, rocoto

Pepper	Characteristics	Scoville Units	Substitutes
Thai	1 to 2 inches (2.5 to 5 cm) long, ¼ inch (0.5 cm) wide, pointed, various colors	15,000 to 30,000	Hontaka, Santaka, serrano, cayenne
Togarashi (ichimi)	½ to 1½ inches (1 to 4 cm) long, ¼ to ½ inch (0.5 to 1 cm) wide, pointed, red	10,000 to 40,000	Hontaka, Santaka, cayenne, Thai, serrano
Wax (yellow or Hungarian)	4 to 6 inches (10 to 15 cm) long, 1 to 1½ inches (2.5 to 4 cm) wide, blunt point, pale yellow green	5,000 to 15,000	Santa Fe grande, güero, serrano, jalapeño, mirasol

Choosing Among Wheat Flours

Different varieties of wheat flour produce different textures in baked goods. When choosing among flours, consider the protein content. Generally, you can substitute up to half of the flour called for with another flour of similar protein content. For yeast breads requiring a sturdy structure, choose high-protein flour (12 to 14% protein). For quick breads and pastry requiring a lighter structure, choose lower-protein flour (7 to 11% protein). Here's a guide based on the percentage of protein in common types of wheat flour.

Flour Type	% Protein	Best Uses
Cake	7 to 9	Cakes, particularly those high in sugar
Pastry	8 to 9	Biscuits, cookies, pie crusts, pastries
Whole wheat pastry	9 to 10	Quick breads
All-purpose	8 to 11	Quick breads, yeast breads, cakes, cookies, and everyday baking
Self-rising	8 to 11	Quick breads
Bread	12 to 14	Pizza crusts, yeast breads, and bread machine recipes
Semolina	12 to 16	Pasta
Durum	12 to 16	Pasta
Graham	14	Combine with other flours in breads
Whole wheat	14	Combine with other flours in breads

Choosing Among Whole-Grain and Alternative Flours

Generally, a whole-grain or alternative flour can be substituted for up to half of the all-purpose flour called for in quick bread and yeast bread recipes. Whole-grain flours add fiber while varying the flavor and texture of baked goods. Use the guide below to replace all-purpose flour with alternative flours. To make homemade flour from whole grains such as barley, millet, oats, quinoa, rice, and teff, grind the grain in a food processor to the texture of flour.

Flour	Protein Content	Gluten Content	Taste	Best Uses
Amaranth	High	Gluten-free	Assertive, nutty	Quick breads
Barley	Low	Low-gluten	Earthy, mild, sweet flavor, chewy texture	Quick breads, some cookies
Buckwheat	Low	Gluten-free	Earthy and mild or strong (if buckwheat groats are roasted)	Quick breads (especially pancakes), dumplings, noodles (soba); creates tender baked goods; pairs well with fruits like apples, cherries, and pumpkin; gray color
Chestnut	Low	Gluten-free	Nutty, smoky (if chestnuts are roasted)	Quick breads, noodles, pizza dough
Chickpea (garbanzo, gram)	High	Gluten-free	Mild, not beany	Quick breads, yeast breads
Corn	Low	Gluten-free	Nutty, corn flavor	Quick breads, yeast breads; pairs well with higher-gluten flours
Kamut©	Low	Medium Low-gluten	Nutty, earthy	Quick breads, yeast breads, substitute 1:1 for all-purpose flour
Millet	High	Gluten-free	Mild, slightly nutty	Quick breads, makes baked goods very crumbly; pairs well with cornmeal, oat flour, or rye flour
Oat	High	Gluten-free	Sweet, earthy	Quick breads, cookies, yeast breads (in combination with high-gluten flour); creates moister more chewy texture; pairs well with whole wheat flour, rye flour, millet flour

Flour	Protein Content	Gluten Content	Taste	Best Uses
Potato	Low	Gluten-free	Mild potato flavor	Yeast breads (in combination with high-gluten flour)
Pumpernickel	Low	Low-gluten	Earthy and strong	Yeast breads (this flour is coarsely ground, dark rye flour used to make pumpernickel bread)
Quinoa	High	Gluten-free	Mild, nutty	Quick breads, yeast breads (in combination with high-gluten flour); pairs well with cornmeal, oat flour, barley flour, and buckwheat flour
Rice	Low	Gluten-free	Mild, earthy (white rice flour) or nutty (brown rice flour)	Quick breads, dumplings, noodles; makes baked goods more crumbly; pairs well with oat flour
Rye	Low	Low-gluten	Earthy and mild to strong (depending upon fineness of grind)	Quick breads, yeast breads (in combination with high-gluten flour); knead gently and increase yeast to improve rise in yeast breads
Soy	Very high	Gluten-free	Mild, slightly beany	Quick breads, yeast breads (in combination with high-gluten flour); adds moisture to baked goods; high in fat
Spelt	High	Low-gluten	Mild, nutty	Quick breads, yeast breads
Teff	High	Gluten-free	Mild to rich molasses flavor (depending on whether light or dark)	Quick breads, especially spice breads; yeast breads (in combination with high-gluten flour)
Triticale	High	Low	Mild, earthy	Quick breads, yeast breads (in combination with high-gluten flour); hybrid of rye and wheat; knead yeast breads gently

A Snapshot of Asian Noodles

Sheets, ribbons, strands and nests of noodles from China, Japan, Korea, Thailand, Vietnam, Laos, Malaysia, and other Asian countries are made from a variety of starches and vegetables including rice, wheat, buckwheat, soybeans, mung beans, arrowroot, cornstarch, tapioca, seaweed, and sweet potatoes. Noodles often have various names in different languages, many of which are listed below. When substituting one noodle for another, keep in mind that dried rice noodles are usually soaked in cold water then briefly boiled or added to soups during the few minutes of cooking, while dried wheat noodles are boiled like Italian pasta. As with Italian pasta, there are two basic types of Asian wheat noodles: those made with egg, such as lo mein and ramen, and those made with only water, such as chow fun, soba, somen, and udon.

	Noodle	Characteristics	Substitutes
Rice Noodles	**Laksa noodles (Lei fun)**	Thick, white strands	Wide rice noodles, Chinese wheat noodles
	Rice noodles, wide (Jantaboon, sha he fan, sen chan)	Thick, flat ribbons	Medium rice sticks, somen, linguine or fettuccine
	Rice sticks, medium (Banh pho, ho fun, lai fen, sen lek, kway teow)	Opaque ribbons	Wide rice noodles, linguine, somen
	Rice sticks, thin (Bun, pancit palabok, sen yai)	Very thin, opaque or white strands	Cellophane noodles, rice vermicelli, vermicelli
	Rice vermicelli (Sen mee, mi fen, mai fun, pancit bijon, banh hoi, bee hoon)	Very thin, delicate strands sold in nests	Thin rice sticks, cellophane noodles, wide rice noodles (thicker), vermicelli
Wheat Noodles	**Chinese egg noodles**	Chewy, round, yellowish strands or flat ribbons	Chinese wheat noodles, egg roll wrappers (sliced into noodles), strand or ribbon pasta such as spaghetti or fettuccine
	Chinese wheat noodles	Tender round strands	Chinese egg noodles (not as delicate), ramen, strand pasta such as spaghetti
	Chow fun	Flat, wide wheat noodles	Wide Chinese egg noodles, linguine or fettuccine
	Chow mein	Thin, round egg noodle strands	Chinese wheat noodles, strand pasta such as thin spaghetti

	Noodle	Characteristics	Substitutes
Wheat Noodles	**Chow mein, fried**	Crunchy, round strands	Ramen, boiled and fried strand pasta such as thin spaghetti
	Hiyamugi	Narrow, wheat ribbons	Somen, udon
	Hokkien noodles (Mee)	Thick, round yellow egg noodle strands	Laksa noodles, Shanghai noodles
	Kishimen	Flat, wide wheat noodle ribbons with slippery texture	Udon, linguine
	Korean wheat noodles (Gook soo)	Flat wheat ribbons	Somen, fettuccine
	Lo mein	Round or flat egg noodle strands or ribbons	Ramen, chow mein, spaghetti, fettuccine
	Ramen	Thin, egg noodle strands	Lo mein, chow mein, spaghetti
	Shanghai noodles	Thick, oval wheat noodle strands	Perciatelli, spaghetti, laksa noodles
	Soba	Strands made with wheat and buckwheat	Whole wheat vermicelli, Korean buckwheat noodles (naeng myun)
	Somen	Thin, delicate wheat noodle strands	Hiyamugi, vermicelli, rice sticks
	Udon (Kal guksu)	Thick, flat, slippery ribbons	Kishimen, linguine
	Wonton noodles	Thin, wide egg noodles	Egg roll wrappers (sliced into noodles)
Other Asian Noodles	**Arrowroot vermicelli**	Thin, opaque strands made with arrowroot starch	Cellophane noodles, cornstarch noodles
	Bean curd noodles (Gan si, soybean noodles)	Thin, chewy strands made from tofu	Chinese egg noodles such as chow mein
	Cellophane noodles (Bean threads, bai fun, Chinese vermicelli, fen si, fen szu, glass noodles, sai fun, soo hoon, pancit sotanghon, woon sen, bun tao)	Thin, translucent, gelatinous strands made from mung bean starch	Harusame, rice vermicelli, thin rice sticks
	Cornstarch noodles (Pancit luglug)	Thin, gelatinous strands made from cornstarch	Cellophane noodles, arrowroot vermicelli

continued on next page…

	Noodle	Characteristics	Substitutes
Other Asian Noodles	**Harusame (Japanese vermicelli)**	Thin, translucent strands similar to cellophane noodles but sometimes made from potato, sweet potato, or rice starch	Cellophane noodles, arrowroot vermicelli, cornstarch noodles
	Korean buckwheat noodles (Naeng myun)	Thin strands made with buckwheat flour and potato starch	Soba, whole wheat vermicelli
	Korean sweet potato vermicelli (Dang myun)	Chewy strands made from sweet potato starch	Harusame, cellophane noodles, arrowroot vermicelli
	Seaweed noodles	Long, thin strands made from seaweed	Cellophane noodles, arrowroot vermicelli
	Tapioca sticks (Hu tieu bot loc)	Thin strands made from tapioca starch	Cellophane noodles, arrowroot noodles
	Yam noodles (Shirataki, ito konnyaku)	Gelatinous strands made from yams	Cellophane noodles, harusame

Varieties of Rice

Rice is generally classified by grain length. Long-grain rice is four to five times as long as it is wide. When cooked, the grains are separate and fluffy. Medium-grain rice is two to three times longer than its width. Cooked medium-grain rice is more moist, tender, and apt to cling together more than long-grain rice. Short-grain rice has a plump, almost round shape. When cooked, short-grain rice is very soft and clings together. Within each length, varieties of rice are generally interchangeable. Other categories of rice include aromatic rice, which often has a nutty flavor, risotto rice, a short-grain variety that gets creamy on the surface when cooked, and glutinous rice, a mildly sweet, sticky rice often used to make sushi. "Popcorn" rice is a sub-category of aromatic rice that includes wild pecan, wehani, and Texmati varieties, all of which have a popcorn-like flavor. See also Rice (page 407) and Wild Rice (page 547).

	Rice	Characteristics	Substitutes
Long-Grain Rices	**Basmati**	Aromatic, nutty-tasting grains that are dry and fluffy when cooked, available brown or white, often used in Indian cooking	Patna rice (less nutty tasting), Texmati, wehani, wild pecan or other "popcorn" rice, jasmine rice (more floral aroma)
	Converted (Parboiled)	Husked white rice that is briefly steamed	White rice, brown rice (takes longer to cook)
	Himalayan Red	Red, chewy, whole-grain rice	Long-grain brown rice
	Jasmine (Thai Basmati)	Aromatic, floral-perfumed grains that are fluffy when cooked, available brown or white, often used in Thai cooking	Basmati (more nutty tasting), Texmati, wehani, wild pecan or other "popcorn" rice, patna rice (less aromatic)
	Patna	Aromatic rice often used in Indian cooking	Basmati rice (more nutty tasting), Texmati, wehani, wild pecan or other "popcorn" rice, jasmine rice (more floral aroma)
	Texmati	Aromatic, Texan cross between basmati and American long-grain rice, available brown or white	Wild pecan, wehani, other "popcorn" rice, basmati rice (more nutty tasting), patna rice, jasmine rice (more floral aroma)
	Wehani	Aromatic, terra cotta colored, whole-grain (brown) rice with popcorn-like flavor that becomes slightly cracked when cooked	Brown basmati rice, brown rice, wild pecan rice, brown Texmati rice, wild rice
	Wild Pecan	Aromatic, Louisianian, chewy, nutty-tasting rice with popcorn-like flavor	Wehani, Texmati, or other "popcorn" rice, brown basmati rice, brown rice

continued on next page...

	Rice	Characteristics	Substitutes
Medium-Grain Rices	**Bahia**	Spanish, slightly sticky, often used for paella	Bomba, granza, Valencia or other Spanish rice; Arborio, Carnaroli or other risotto rice
	Black Japonica	Aromatic, spicy, mushroom-like flavor	Wehani rice, wild pecan rice, wild rice
	Bomba	Spanish, slightly sticky, often used for paella	Bahia, granza, Valencia or other Spanish rice; Arborio, Carnaroli or other risotto rice
	Granza	Spanish, slightly sticky, often used for paella	Bahia, bomba, Valencia or other Spanish rice; Arborio, Carnaroli or other risotto rice
	Shinma	Tender, sweet Japanese rice harvested in early autumn, cooks quickly	Botan rice
	Valencia	Spanish, slightly sticky, often used for paella	Bomba, granza, or other Spanish rice; Arborio, Carnaroli or other risotto rice
Short-Grain Rices	**Arborio**	Fat, ivory grains that release creamy starch when cooked, often used for risotto	Baldo, Carnaroli, nano, Roma or other risotto rice; Bahia, bomba, granza, Valencia or other Spanish rice; pearl barley (chewier, less starchy, makes passable risotto)
	Baldo	Fat, ivory grains that release creamy starch when cooked, often used for risotto	Arborio, Carnaroli, nano, Roma or other risotto rice; Bahia, bomba, granza, Valencia or other Spanish rice; pearl barley (chewier, less starchy, makes passable risotto)
	Bhutanese red rice	Red short-grain rice, a staple in rural areas of Bhutan, a small kingdom nestled high in the Himalayas, with a strong, nutty flavor, best served with other assertive ingredients. It cooks much faster than brown rice.	Himalayan red rice, wehani rice, brown rice
	Botan rice	Ivory-color, mildly sweet, glutinous rice	Shinma or other glutinous rice Baldo; Carnaroli, nano, Roma or other risotto rice; Bahia, bomba, granza, Valencia or other Spanish rice

Rice	Characteristics	Substitutes
Carnaroli	Fat, ivory grains that release creamy starch when cooked, often used for risotto	Arborio, Carnaroli, nano, Roma or other risotto rice; Bahia, bomba, granza, Valencia or other Spanish rice; pearl barley (chewier, less starchy, makes passable risotto)
Glutinous (Mochi, Sticky, Sweet, or Sushi Rice)	Mildly sweet, sticky rice that releases some starch when cooked, available white or russet	Thai Purple rice (purple color); Baldo, Carnaroli, nano, Roma or other risotto rice; Bahia, bomba, granza, Valencia or other Spanish rice
Nano	Fat, ivory grains that release creamy starch when cooked, often used for risotto	Arborio, baldo, Carnaroli, Roma or other risotto rice; Bahia, bomba, granza, Valencia or other Spanish rice; pearl barley (chewier, less starchy, makes passable risotto)
Risotto rice	See Arborio, Baldo, Carnaroli, Nano, Roma	
Roma	Fat, ivory grains that release creamy starch when cooked, often used for risotto	Arborio, baldo, Carnaroli, nano or other risotto rice; Bahia, bomba, granza, Valencia or other Spanish rice; pearl barley (chewier, less starchy, makes passable risotto)
Thai Purple (Thai Black Sticky Rice)	Purple-color, mildly sweet, sticky rice that releases some starch when cooked	Botan or other glutinous rice; Baldo, Carnaroli, nano, Roma or other risotto rice; Bahia, bomba, granza, Valencia or other Spanish rice

Short-Grain Rices

Changing Roe

Varieties of fish roe are available in three general categories: hard roe (female eggs), white or soft roe (the milt of male fish), and true caviar (salted eggs of certain varieties of sturgeon). The best caviar is harvested from sturgeon in the Caspian and Black Seas. The term malassol (Russian for "lightly salted") often appears on the finest caviar taken early in the spawning season. The term "pressed caviar" refers to the ripest, most strongly flavored sturgeon eggs, which are taken late in the season and pressed together. Pasteurized roe have been heated to improve shelf life, which creates a slightly firmer texture. Some roe not labeled "caviar" is quite good and can be substituted for true sturgeon caviar, especially when a splash of lemon juice is added. Some connoisseurs prefer these less-expensive substitutes in order to allow overfished sturgeon to recover in the Caspian Sea.

Roe	Characteristics	Substitutes
Bottarga (Sardinian Caviar)	Amber, salted and sun-dried gray mullet (bottarga di muggine) or tuna (bottarga di tonno) roe, sold in a sausage-like "baffa" or sack to be sliced, shaved, or grated	Tara, cod roe
Bowfin Roe (Choupique, Cajun Caviar)	Black, small, shiny, firm	Beluga caviar, sevruga caviar, American hackleback roe, paddlefish roe
Capelin Roe (Masago)	Orange, somewhat translucent, very small, often served with sushi	Smelt roe, flying fish roe, orange lumpfish roe, whitefish roe
Caviar, American Hackleback Sturgeon (Black Pearl Caviar)	Black, small, buttery, sweet	Beluga caviar, sevruga caviar, black lumpfish roe, paddlefish roe, bowfin roe
Caviar, American Lake Sturgeon	Light to dark gray, large, soft, mildly sweet	Beluga caviar, American hackleback caviar, paddlefish roe
Caviar, Beluga	Light to dark gray, large, velvety soft, mildly sweet, from Huso huso sturgeon	American lake sturgeon caviar, American hackleback sturgeon caviar, osetra caviar, sevruga caviar, black lumpfish roe, paddlefish roe, bowfin roe
Caviar, Mandarin	Grayish green, large, from Chinese white sturgeon	Osetra caviar, beluga caviar , sevruga caviar
Caviar, Osetra (Oscietra)	Gray to brown, strong flavor, from Acipenser guldenstaedti sturgeon; also includes the rare and superior golden brown grains of "golden," "Imperial," or "sterlet" caviar from the albino sturgeon of this species	Golden paddlefish roe (to replace Imperial osetra), sevruga caviar, beluga caviar, Mandarin caviar, American hackleback caviar, bowfin roe, black lumpfish roe

Roe	Characteristics	Substitutes
Caviar, Sevruga	Gray to greenish black, small, very strong flavor	Paddlefish roe, American hackleback caviar, osetra caviar, beluga caviar, Mandarin caviar, bowfin caviar, black lumpfish roe
Cod Roe	Pale pink, salty, sometimes sold as a paste in tubes, also available smoked	Lobster roe, sea urchin roe, herring roe, tara, bottarga
Flying Fish Roe (Tobiko)	Red orange, crunchy	Capelin roe (smaller), smelt roe, golden caviar, salmon roe, trout roe
Herring Roe (Kazunoko)	Pink yellow, often pickled, salty, and sold in a shaped mass	Cod roe, shad roe, sea urchin roe
Lobster Roe (Coral)	Coral pink when heated	Sea urchin roe, cod roe
Lumpfish Roe	Red, orange, or black, small, firm	Beluga caviar, osetra caviar, salmon roe or capelin roe or smelt roe (to replace orange lumpfish roe)
Paddlefish Roe	Light to dark steel gray or golden	Sevruga caviar, osetra caviar, beluga caviar , American hackleback roe, bowfin roe
Salmon Roe (Red Caviar, Ikura)	Red orange, large, translucent, juicy, also available smoked	Trout roe, orange lumpfish roe, flying fish roe
Sea Urchin Roe (Uni)	Red orange to yellow, velvety soft, often served with sushi	Flying fish roe (for sushi), salmon roe, lobster roe
Shad Roe	Small roe swaddled in two oblong, translucent membranes	Herring roe
Smelt Roe	Orange, somewhat crunchy	Flying fish roe, orange lumpfish roe, capelin roe, trout roe
Tara	Salted and dried gray mullet roe; rare; puréed to make Greek taramasalata spread	Cod roe, bottarga
Trout Roe	Golden brown orange, firm, sticky, salty	Whitefish roe, salmon roe, flying fish roe, smelt roe, orange lumpfish roe
Whitefish Roe (American Golden Caviar)	Pale orange or iridescent gold, crunchy, mild flavor	Trout roe, salmon roe, smelt roe, orange lumpfish roe

Swapping Clams

Numbering in the hundreds, clam varieties fall into two main categories: hard-shell clams, which may be eaten raw, and soft-shell clams, which are generally eaten cooked. The soft-shell varieties are named for their thin, brittle shells and long necks that are used to siphon ocean water. While each clam variety has its own taste and texture, substitutions can be made within each of the two main categories.

	Clam	Shell Diameter	Substitutes
Hard Shell (Quahog)	Butter	3 to 5 inch (7.5 to 12.5 cm)	Chowder
	Cherrystone	2 to 3 inches (5 to 7.5 cm)	Littleneck
	Chowder (large)	3 to 6 inches (7.5 to 15 cm)	Butter, manila
	Littleneck (Atlantic and Pacific)	1 to 2 inches (2.5 to 5 cm)	Cherrystone
	Manila (Japanese Littleneck)	3 to 4 inches (7.5 to 10 cm)	Littleneck, cherrystone
	Pismo	5 to 7 inches (7.5 to 17.5 cm)	Cherrystone, littleneck
	Ocean Quahog (Mahogany)	2 to 3 inches (5 to 7.5 cm)	Cherrystone, littleneck
	Surf (bar or hen clam)	4 to 8 inches (10 to 20 cm)	Ocean quahog
Soft Shell (Longneck)	Geoduck (mirugai)	6 to 8 inches (15 to 20 cm)	Surf clam, abalone
	Razor	5 to 8 inches (12.5 to 20 cm) long, 1/4 to 1/2 inch (0.5 to 1 cm) wide	Manila, geoduck (for chowder)
	Steamer	1 to 2 inches (2.5 to 5 cm)	Razor

Choosing Among Crabs

Crab devotees often prefer either she-crabs or he-crabs, but both can be delicious. To tell a male from a female, turn a whole crab over and look at the underside of the shell. On she-crabs, you'll see a wide, triangular, off-white "apron" on the underside of the shell. Males (also called jimmies) have a longer, more narrow, T-shaped apron on the underside.

Crab	Shell Diameter	Substitutes
Blue (Chesapeake blue)	4 to 6 inches (10 to 15 cm)	Dungeness
Dungeness	6 to 8 inches (15 to 20 cm)	Blue
King	5 to 7 inches (12.5 to 17.5 cm)	Snow
Peekytoe	3 to 6 inches (7.5 to 15 cm)	Dungeness, blue
Snow	3 to 5 inches (7.5 to 12.5 cm)	King
Stone (morro)	3 to 6 inches (7.5 to 15 cm)	Blue crab claws

Substituting Oils

There are two main categories of oils: frying oils and salad oils. Within each category, the oils are generally interchangeable. Frying oils tend be mild in flavor yet they can withstand the high temperatures needed for sautéing and frying. When sautéing or frying with "vegetable oil," corn oil, canola oil, and soybean oil all make good choices. Choose a frying oil with a high smoke point for extended deep-fat frying. To help you choose, the sautéing and frying oils listed below are arranged according to smoke point from lowest to highest. The salad oils, on the other hand, are arranged alphabetically. Salad oils tend to have pronounced flavors that dissipate when exposed to heat. Full-flavored salad oils work best in uncooked or gently heated dishes like dressings, sauces, and desserts. Choose a salad oil with a color and flavor that best complements the dish you are making.

Sautéing and Frying Oils	Smoke Point	Characteristics
Coconut Oil	350°F (180°C)	Mild to rich coconut flavor; light color; fat content is 89% saturated, 3% polyunsaturated, and 8% monounsaturated
Corn oil	410°F (210°C)	Mild flavor; yellow color; fat content is 13% saturated, 62% polyunsaturated, and 25% monounsaturated
Olive oil	410°F (210°C)	Mild to rich olive flavor; pale yellow to deep green color; fat content is 14% saturated, 10% polyunsaturated, and 76% monounsaturated
Sesame seed oil (untoasted)	415°F (213°C)	Mild nutty flavor; light yellow color; fat content is 18% saturated, 41% polyunsaturated, and 41% monounsaturated
Canola (rapeseed) oil	435°F (224°C)	Flavorless; light yellow color; fat content is 6% saturated, 32% polyunsaturated, and 62% monounsaturated
Grapeseed oil	445°F (229°C)	Mild flavor; fat content is 13% saturated, 70% polyunsaturated, and 17% monounsaturated
Palm oil	450°F (230°C)	Mild flavor; red orange color; fat content is 50% saturated, 10% polyunsaturated, and 40% monounsaturated
Peanut oil	450°F (230°C)	Neutral yet rich flavor; golden color; fat content is 17% saturated, 35% polyunsaturated, and 48% monounsaturated
Safflower oil	450°F (230°C)	Flavorless; light texture; fat content is 9% saturated, 76% polyunsaturated, and 15% monounsaturated
Soybean oil	450°F (230°C)	Light color; fat content is 14% saturated, 61% polyunsaturated, and 25% monounsaturated

Salad, Sauce, and Flavoring Oils	Characteristics
Almond oil	Toasted almond flavor; light yellow color; breaks down with heat; also great in cold desserts
Avocado oil	Rich buttery flavor; light yellow to green color; breaks down with heat
Grapeseed oil	Mild flavor; pale yellow to green color
Hazelnut oil	Toasted hazelnut flavor; light golden color; breaks down with heat; also good for baking
Macadamia oil	Mild to rich macadamia flavor; light color; breaks down with heat
Olive oil	Mild to rich olive flavor; pale yellow to deep green color; can be used for baking; use extra virgin for uncooked or gently cooked dishes
Pecan oil	Mild to rich pecan flavor; light golden color; breaks down with heat
Pistachio oil	Toasted pistachio flavor; deep green color; breaks down with heat
Pumpkin seed oil	Toasted pumpkin seed flavor; green color; breaks down with heat
Sesame oil (toasted)	Concentrated toasted sesame flavor; dark amber color; breaks down with heat
Sunflower oil	Mild flavor; light yellow color; breaks down with heat
Truffle oil	Mild (white truffle oil) to rich (black truffle oil) and complex, mushroom-like flavor; light amber color; breaks down with heat
Walnut oil	Rich walnut flavor; amber color; breaks down with heat

Choosing Vinegar

Vinegars are made from various foods such as fermented grains (rice vinegar, malt vinegar), fermented grapes (balsamic, champagne, sherry, and wine vinegar), and other fermented fruits (apple cider vinegar, umeboshi plum vinegar). When choosing or substituting vinegars, try to match color and flavor of the vinegar with the color and flavor of the food. Use the chart below as a guide. See also the entry for Vinegar (page 535).

Vinegar	Characteristics	Substitutes
Apple cider	Amber, tart, mildly fruity-tasting vinegar made from fermented apples, often used with pork, for salads, or to make pickles	Malt vinegar, white wine vinegar, rice vinegar
Balsamic	Brownish black, mildly acidic, sweet and fruity-tasting vinegar made from concentrated Trebbiano white grape juice, aged in wood barrels for at least 10 years, also available as white balsamic, often used to make vinaigrettes and sauces	Red or white wine vinegar, Chinese black vinegar (more strongly flavored), raspberry or other fruit vinegar (lighter body, less complex taste, more fruity aroma)
Cane	Light-color, mildly sweet, made from sugar cane syrup	Champagne vinegar, sherry vinegar, white rice vinegar, coconut vinegar (stronger flavor)
Champagne	Light-bodied, mildly flavored, often used with seafood, chicken, or salads	White wine vinegar, raspberry or other fruit vinegar, rice vinegar
Chinese black (Chekiang)	Black rice vinegar often used in Asian cooking	Balsamic vinegar, red rice vinegar, white rice vinegar
Coconut (Suka ng niyog)	Strong vinegar used sometimes in Southeast Asian and Indian cooking	Cane vinegar, white wine vinegar
Distilled white	Harsh-tasting white vinegar made from grain alcohol, often used for cleaning and acidulated water	Apple cider vinegar, malt vinegar, lemon juice
Malt	Amber, mild-tasting vinegar usually made from beer	Cider vinegar, white wine vinegar, lemon juice

Vinegar	Characteristics	Substitutes
Raspberry	White wine vinegar infused with raspberries	Other fruit vinegar such as blueberry or pineapple, herb vinegar such as tarragon, champagne vinegar, white balsamic vinegar
Red rice (Chinese red vinegar)	Reddish, salty-tasting rice vinegar often used in Asian cooking	Chinese black vinegar (sweeter), red wine vinegar, white rice vinegar
Red wine	Reddish, mildly sweet vinegar with pronounced flavor, often used to make vinaigrettes and sauces	White wine vinegar, sherry vinegar, champagne vinegar, balsamic vinegar
Rice	Mildly sweet, mildly acidic vinegar made from white rice	Red rice vinegar (red color), champagne vinegar, white wine vinegar
Sherry (Jerez Vinegar)	Amber, mildly acidic, mildly sweet and fruity-tasting vinegar, aged in barrels for at least 6 years, often used to make vinaigrettes and sauces	Red or white wine vinegar, champagne vinegar, raspberry or other fruit vinegar (lighter body, less complex taste, more fruity aroma), balsamic vinegar (darker, richer)
Tarragon	White wine vinegar infused with fresh tarragon	Other herb vinegar such as rosemary, fruit vinegar such as raspberry
Umeboshi (Plum Vinegar)	Salty, somewhat tart and fruity vinegar made from umeboshi plums, often used in Japanese cooking	Red rice vinegar
White wine	Light-bodied, mildly flavored vinegar, often used with seafood, chicken, or salads	Champagne vinegar, raspberry or other fruit vinegar, rice vinegar, red white vinegar (stronger flavor)

Trading Salts

There are two basic types of salts: those mined from the earth and those evaporated from the sea. Mined salts are usually refined and include common table salt, kosher salt, pickling salt, rock salt, and the less common, unrefined black salt used in Indian cooking. Sea salts are those evaporated from bay or ocean waters bordering various lands around the world such as France and Hawaii. Use the less-expensive, fine-grained table or sea salts for baking. Use coarse-grained sea salt or Kosher salt for cooking, especially because the coarse grains can be pinched up more easily. Reserve the most expensive coarse sea salts for sprinkling onto foods at the last minute so you will taste their complex flavors before the salt completely dissolves. Use the guide below for other substitutions among types of mined and sea salts.

	Salt	Characteristics	Substitutes
Mined Salts	Black salt (kala namak, sanchal)	Brown black in lump form, purple pink in powder form, unrefined mineral salt often used in Indian cooking, assertive sulfuric aroma with pleasant smoky taste	Other sea salt or table salt (may need to use 1½ to 2 times as much)
	Kosher salt	Coarse salt free of additives	Coarse or flaked sea salt such as Maldon, pickling salt, margarita salt, table salt (finer, use a bit less due to the fine grind)
	Margarita salt	Coarse salt used to salt rims of Margarita glasses	Kosher salt, coarse sea salt, table salt
	Pickling salt (Canning salt)	Fine, non-iodized, additive-free salt similar to table salt	Kosher salt (use a bit more due to the coarser grind), non-iodized table salt
	Popcorn salt	Fine table salt used for salting snacks	Table salt
	Pretzel salt	Coarse, white salt used to salt pretzels	Kosher salt, margarita salt
	Rock salt	Coarse salt used for making ice cream	Kosher salt, margarita salt
	Table salt	Fine, iodized or non-iodized salt used for all-purpose cooking and flavoring	Kosher salt (coarser, use a bit more due to the coarse grind), fine sea salt

	Salt	Characteristics	Substitutes
Sea Salts	**Bamboo salt (Jukyom)**	Sea salt roasted in bamboo cylinders with yellow mud, smoky, mineral-rich flavor	Other smoked sea salt, black salt, kosher salt, table salt
	Celtic salt	Light gray, moist, complex mineral flavor	Sel gris, fleur de sel, kosher salt
	Fleur de Sel (French, flower of the sea)	White, somewhat moist, complex mineral flavor	Sel gris, Celtic salt, Maldon salt, kosher salt
	Hawaiian salt	Pink or brown, complex mineral flavor	Fleur de sel, sel gris, other sea salt, kosher salt
	Maldon salt	White, thin flakes (sometimes crystals)	Fleur de sel, celtic salt, sel gris, other sea salt, Kosher salt
	Sel Gris (French gray salt)	Gray, moist, complex mineral flavor	Celtic salt, fleur de sel, other sea salt, kosher salt

Picking Edible Flowers

Most edible flowers make beautiful garnishes. They can also bring color and flavor to salads, soups, sauces, desserts, and beverages. Only use edible flowers that have not been sprayed with harmful chemicals. Look for them in gourmet shops and farmer's markets (or your own organic garden) rather than in florist shops.

Flower	Color	Flavor	Best Uses
Begonia	Shades of white, yellow, or red	Sweet and lemony	Fruit salads, desserts
Borage	Blue or pink	Cool, refreshing, and cucumber-like	Salads, cold soups, beverages, crystallized
Calendula	Yellow orange	Earthy and saffron-like	Crumbled like saffron
Carnation (Dianthus)	Shades of white, pink, or red	Peppery like cloves or nutmeg	Desserts, wine, crystallized
Chive Blossom	Pink or lavender	Mild onion flavor	Salads, soups, fish or egg dishes
Daisy	Yellow and white	Mild clover or mint flavor	Salads
Dandelion	Yellow	Honey flavor (when young) or bitter (when old)	Salads, infusions, wine
Daylily	Various colors	Sweet and crunchy	Salads, stuffed as an appetizer, desserts
Johnny Jump-Up (Viola)	White, yellow, or purple	Wintergreen flavor	Salads, cold soups, desserts, beverages
Lavender	Light purple	Sweet and citrusy	Desserts, baking, beverages, soups, salads, sauces
Lilac	Light purple	Lemony	Salads
Marigold	Yellow or orange	Spicy and citrusy, sometimes bitter	Salads, soups
Nasturtium	Various colors	Peppery like watercress	Salads, sandwiches, egg dishes
Pansy	White, yellow, or purple	Mildly grassy	Salads, soups, fruit salads, desserts
Rose	Various colors	Sweet and fruity	Salads, fruit salads, desserts, syrups, sweet sauces, jams
Squash Blossom	Yellow or orange with green	Mildly sweet squash flavor	Salads, egg dishes, stuffed as an appetizer
Violet	Purple and white	Sweet wintergreen flavor	Salads, desserts, beverages, crystallized

Temperature Equivalents

An oven's actual temperature often varies from the temperature to which the oven has been set. To be absolutely sure your oven temperature is correct, buy an inexpensive oven thermometer at a cookware store and keep it in your oven for reference. For any temperature conversions not listed below, convert Fahrenheit to Celsius by subtracting 32, multiplying by 5, then dividing by 9. To covert Celsius to Fahrenheit, multiply by 9, divide by 5, then add 32.

Temperature Description	Fahrenheit	Celsius	Gas Mark
Freezer storage	0°	-18°	N/A
Water freezes	32°	0°	N/A
Refrigerator storage	40°	4°	N/A
Wine storage	55°	13°	N/A
Butter is ready for creaming	67°	19°	N/A
Room temperature	68° to 72°	20° to 22°	N/A
Yeast dough will rise properly	85°	30°	N/A
Water is lukewarm	95°	35°	N/A
Poaching temperature	160° to 180°	70° to 82°	N/A
Water simmers	185° to 205°	85° to 95°	N/A
Water boils	212°	100°	N/A
Very cool oven	225°	110°	$\frac{1}{4}$
Cool oven	250°	120°	$\frac{1}{2}$
Very slow oven	275°	140°	1
Slow oven	300°	150°	2
Low oven	325°	160°	3
Moderate oven	350°	180°	4
Moderately hot oven	375°	190°	5
Hot oven	400° to 425°	200° to 220°	6 to 7
Very hot oven	450° to 475°	230° to 240°	8 to 9
Extremely hot oven	500°	260°	9+
Broil			Grill

Pan Size Equivalents

When substituting one pan for another, choose a pan with a similar shape and size. If your substitute pan is deeper than the one you are replacing, increase the cooking time to allow heat to reach the interior. If the substitute pan is shallower, reduce the cooking time. To get accurate width dimensions, measure pans from inside edge to inside edge. For volume, fill the pan with water then measure the water in a measuring cup to the top of the pan. In general, fill pans no more than two-thirds full to allow for expansion when baking.

Pan Size	Pan Type	Approximate Filled Volume
1¾-by ¾-inch (4.5 by 2 cm)	Mini muffin cup	2 tbsp (25 mL)
2¾-by 1⅛-inches (7 by 2.8 cm)	Muffin cup	¼ cup (50 mL)
2¾-by 1⅜-inches (7 by 3.4 cm)	Deep muffin cup	7 tbsp (105 mL)
3-by 1¼-inches (7.5 by 3 cm)	Jumbo muffin cup	10 tbsp (150 mL)
3½-by 1¾-inches (8.5 by 4.5 cm)	Round ramekin or custard cup	¾ cup (175 mL)
5½-by 3-by 2½-inches (14 by 7.5 by 6 cm)	Loaf	2 cups (500 mL)
1 quart (1 L)	Casserole	4 cups (1 L)
8-by 1½-inches (20 by 4 cm)	Pie or round cake	4 cups (1 L)
11-by 1-inch (27.5 by 2.5 cm)	Tart	4 cups (1 L)
9-by 1½-inches (23 by 4 cm)	Pie or round cake	5 cups (1.25 L)
7½-by 3-inches (19 by 7.5 cm)	Bundt	6 cups (1.5 L)
8-by 2-inches (20 by 5 cm)	Round cake	6 cups (1.5 L)
8-by 8-by 1½-inches (20 by 20 by 4 cm)	Square	6 cups (1.5 L)
10-by 1½-inches (25 by 4 cm)	Pie	6 cups (1.5 L)
11-by 7-by 2-inches (27.5 by 18 by 5 cm)	Rectangular	6 cups (1.5 L)
8½-by 4½-by 2½-inches (21 by 11 by 6 cm)	Loaf	6 cups (1.5 L)
2 quart (2 L)	Casserole	8 cups (2 L)

Pan Size	Pan Type	Approximate Filled Volume
8-by 8-by 2-inches (20 by 20 by 5 cm)	Square	8 cups (2 L)
9-by 2-inches (23 by 5 cm)	Deep-dish pie or round cake	8 cups (2 L)
9-by 5-by 3-inches (23 by 13 by 7.5 cm)	Loaf	8 cups (2 L)
9-by 9-by 1½-inches (23 by 23 by 4 cm)	Square	8 cups (2 L)
9¼-by 2¾-inches (23.5 by 7 cm)	Ring mold	8 cups (2 L)
8-by 3-inches (20 by 7.5 cm)	Tube	9 cups (2.25 L)
9-by 3-inches (23 by 7.5 cm)	Bundt	9 cups (2.25 L)
9-by 9-by 2-inches (23 by 23 by 5 cm)	Square	10 cups (2.5 L)
9½-by 2½-inches (24 by 6 cm)	Springform	10 cups (2.5 L)
15-by 10-by 1-inch (38 by 25 by 2.5 cm)	Jelly Roll	10 cups (2.5 L)
10-by 2-inches (25 by 5 cm)	Round cake	11 cups (2.75 L)
10-by 2½-inches (25 by 6 cm)	Springform	12 cups (3 L)
10-by 3½-inches (25 by 8.5 cm)	Bundt	12 cups (3 L)
3 quart (3 L)	Casserole	12 cups (3 L)
13-by 9-by 2-inches (33 by 23 by 5 cm)	Rectangular	12 cups (3 L)
10-by 4-inches (25 by 10 cm)	Tube	16 cups (4 L)
14-by 10½-by 2½-inches (35 by 26 by 6 cm)	Roasting	18 cups (4.5 L)

Weight Equivalents

Weight conversions from Imperial (U.S.) to metric are not always precise. The equivalents below have been rounded slightly to make measuring easier and avoid odd numerical measurements. For more precise conversions, see the formulas on page 609.

Ounces	Pounds	Grams	Kilograms
1 oz		30 g	
2 oz		60 g	
3 oz		90 g	
3.5 oz		100 g	
4 oz	¼ lb	125 g	
5 oz	⅓ lb	150 g	
6 oz		175 g	
7 oz		210 g	
8 oz	½ lb	250 g	
10 oz		300 g	
12 oz	¾ lb	375 g	
14 oz		400 g	
16 oz	1 lb	500 g	
24 oz	1½ lbs	750 g	
	2 lbs		1 kg
	3 lbs		1.5 kg
	3½ lbs		1.75 kg
	4 lbs		2 kg

Quarts	Pecks	Gallons	Bushels
8 quarts (dry)	1 peck		
	4 pecks (dry)	8 gallons	1 bushel

Metric Conversions

Use the following formulas for precise conversions from Imperial (U.S) to metric measurements. To convert from metric to Imperial, use the same formulas but work backward, dividing by instead of multiplying by the number in the center column. For a list of common weight and volume conversions, see the tables on pages 608 and 610. Note that the measurements on those pages have been slightly rounded, while the formulas below will yield more precise conversions.

To Convert	Multiply By	To Determine
Teaspoon	4.93	Milliliter
Tablespoon	14.79	Milliliter
Fluid ounce	29.57	Milliliter
Cup	236.59	Milliliter
Cup	0.236	Liter
Pint	473.18	Milliliter
Pint	0.473	Liter
Quart	946.36	Milliliter
Gallon	3.785	Liter
Ounce	28.35	Gram
Pound	0.454	Kilogram
Inch	2.54	Centimeter

Volume Equivalents

Volume conversions from Imperial (U.S.) to metric are not always precise. The equivalents below have been rounded slightly to make measuring easier and avoid odd numerical measurements. For more precise conversions, see the formulas on page 609.

	IMPERIAL				
Descriptive Measures	**Teaspoons**	**Tablespoons**	**Fluid Ounces**	**Cups**	
Dash or pinch	less than ⅛ tsp (dry)		0.015 fl oz		
20 drops	¼ tsp		0.03 fl oz		
40 drops	½ tsp		0.06 fl oz		
	¾ tsp	¼ tbsp	0.12 fl oz		
	1 tsp	⅓ tbsp	0.15 fl oz		
	1½ tsp	½ tbsp	0.25 fl oz		
	3 tsp	1 tbsp	0.5 fl oz		
	6 tsp	2 tbsp	1 fl oz	⅛ cup	
1 jigger	9 tsp	3 tbsp	1.5 fl oz		
	12 tsp	4 tbsp	2 fl oz	¼ cup	
		5 tbsp + 1 tsp	3 fl oz	⅓ cup	
	24 tsp	8 tbsp	4 fl oz	½ cup	
		10 tbsp + 2 tsp	5 fl oz	⅔ cup	
	36 tsp	12 tbsp	6 fl oz	¾ cup	
	42 tsp	14 tbsp	7 fl oz	⅞ cup	
	48 tsp	16 tbsp	8 fl oz	1 cup	
		32 tbsp	16 fl oz	2 cups	
			32 fl oz	4 cups	
			64 fl oz	8 cups	
			128 fl oz	16 cups	

IMPERIAL			METRIC	
Pints	**Quarts**	**Gallons**	**Milliliters**	**Liters**
			0.5 mL	
			1 mL	
			2 mL	
			4 mL	
			5 mL	
			7 mL	
			15 mL	
			25 mL	
			45 mL	
			50 mL	
			75 mL	
			125 mL	
			150 mL	
			175 mL	
			220 mL	
½ pint			250 mL	0.25 L
1 pint	½ quart		500 mL	0.5 L
2 pints	1 quart	¼ gallon	1,000 mL	1 L
4 pints	2 quarts	½ gallon	2,000 mL	2 L
8 pints	4 quarts	1 gallon	4, 000 mL	4 L

Baking at High Altitude

At high altitudes, foods dry out more quickly due to lower air pressure and thinner, drier air. For yeast breads, no ingredient adjustments are necessary but allow the dough to rise twice before the final rising to develop flavor and texture. Also, keep an eye on yeast dough as it rises to avoid letting it rise beyond the point of doubling. To prevent overrising of yeast dough in the oven, increase the baking temperature by 25°F (14°C) at least during the first 15 minutes. Quick breads require a few more adjustments. Depending on the recipe, you may need to use slightly more liquid, less leavener, less flour, a higher oven temperature, and/or a reduced cooking time for cake batters and

Altitude Above Sea Level	Sugar (reduce each cup/mL by)	Baking Powder or Soda (reduce each tsp/mL by)
3,000 ft (915 m)	½ to 1 tbsp (7 to 15 mL)	⅛ tsp (0.5 mL)
5,000 ft (1,525 m)	½ to 2 tbsp (7 to 25 mL)	⅛ to ¼ tsp (0.5 to 1 mL)
7,000 ft + (2,135 m +)	1 to 3 tbsp (15 to 45 mL)	¼ tsp (1 mL)

Cooking at High Altitude

At altitudes above sea level, atmospheric pressure steadily decreases. The lower air pressure causes liquids in food to heat more slowly because there is less pressure on the surface to retain the heat. For instance, at sea level, water boils at 212°F (100°C). For every 1,000 feet (305 meters) above sea level, the boiling point of water reduces by about 2°F (about 1°C). Thus, at 5,000 feet (1,525 meters), water boils at 203°F (95°C).

Altitude Above Sea Level	Vegetables and Dried Beans (increase cooking time by)	Stewing and Braising (on low heat, increase cooking time by)
3,000 ft (915 m)	20 to 30%	30 mins
5,000 ft (1,525 m)	40 to 50%	1 hr
7,000 ft + (2,135 m +)	60 to 70%	2 to 3 hrs

cookie doughs to achieve the right texture. Use the basic adjustments in the table below then refine your adjustments as necessary. Also, use extra-large eggs, which have additional moisture that compensates for the drier air at high altitudes. Due to the lower air pressure, beat egg whites no further than the soft-peak stage to prevent baked goods from overrising. It also helps to let cake and quick bread batters stand for 15 minutes before baking to allow some of the leavening gases to escape. Fill baking pans only halfway to allow more room for rising.

Liquid (for each cup/mL add)	Temperature and Time (increase temperature and reduce time by)
1 to 2 tbsp (15 to 25 mL)	10° to 15°F (5.5° to 8°C); 2 mins
2 to 4 tbsp (25 to 60 mL)	25°F (14°C); 5 mins
3 to 4 tbsp (45 to 60 mL)	25° to 30°F (14° to 17°C); 5 to 10 mins

To compensate for the lower boiling points and thinner, drier air, foods cooked above sea level generally require higher temperatures, longer cooking times, and/or more water. Contact your local Cooperative Extension Service or municipal government office to determine the altitude of your kitchen and use the general guide below to make adjustments as necessary.

Roasting (increase cooking temperature by)	Deep Frying (slightly increase cooking and reduce oil temperature by)
10° to 20°F (5.5° to 11°C)	8° to 10°F (4° to 5.5°C)
20° to 30°F (11° to 17°C)	10° to 15°F (5.5° to 8°C)
30° to 50°F (17° to 28°C)	15° to 25°F (8° to 14°C)

Stages of Cooked Sugar

Use a candy thermometer to test the doneness of cooked sugar syrup, which progresses in stages as its temperature rises. If you don't have a thermometer, use a visual test by dropping a small amount of the sugar syrup into ice-cold water (without ice cubes) then observing it or removing it to feel its texture.

Stage	Temperature	When dropped into ice-cold water:	Common Uses
Thread	223° to 234°F (106° to 112°C)	Spins a soft thread	Flavored syrups, jellies, icings
Soft ball	234° to 240°F (112° to 116°C)	Forms a soft, flat ball	Fondant, fudge, buttercreams
Firm ball	242° to 248°F (117° to 120°C)	Forms a firm but pliable ball	Soft caramels, toffee
Hard ball	250° to 265°F (120° to 129°C)	Forms a hard, compact ball	Hard caramels, nougat, marshmallow
Soft crack	270° to 290°F (132° to 143°C)	Separates into firm yet pliable threads	Butterscotch, taffy
Hard crack	300° to 310°F (150° to 154°C)	Separates into hard, brittle threads	Toffee, nut brittle, lollipops
Light caramel	320° to 338°F (160° to 170°C)	Appears light amber in color	Nut brittle, flan
Medium caramel	340° to 356°F (171° to 180°C)	Appears medium amber to brown in color	Praline, caramel cages
Dark caramel	357° to 374°F (181° to 190°C)	Appears dark brown in color	Dark-color sauces

Acknowledgments

WRITING THIS BOOK HAS BEEN a years-long journey. It took about one year just to develop the list of entries. The substitutions themselves were developed in various ways over several years. Most came from my own experience tinkering in the kitchen. But many came from suggestions given by colleagues, friends, and family. I owe a huge debt of gratitude to all those who generously contributed substitution ideas, including Mark Bowman, Christine Bucher, Bob Dees, Lisa Ekus, Judith Finlayson, Beatrice Flint, Raghavan Iyer, Bonnie Joachim, Jon and Michelle Joachim, Normand LeClair, Karen Levin, Janine MacLachlan, Nick Malgieri, Sharon Sanders, Andrew Schloss, Mark Taylor, and Marc Vetri.

I tested many substitutions with ingredients from local food producers and purveyors. Thanks to George and Melanie DeVault, Rod Wieder, and the other farmers at the Emmaus Farmers Market for carefully growing and producing such wonderful ingredients with which to work. Thanks also to Barbara Hoback at the Allentown Wegman's Cheese Shop for helpful advice and tasty samples of cheeses.

I have combed through and combined a great deal of information in this book, some of which came from well-known and lesser-known books on a variety of cuisines and styles of cooking around the world. Several substitution suggestions appeared in these books, and I would like to thank the authors for offering their wonderful ideas. Please see the Bibliography on page 618 for a list of these authors and their books. I am also grateful for the background information provided by many organizations, including the Almond Board of California, the American Egg Board, the Florida Fish and Wildlife Conservation Commission, the Food and Agricultural Organization of the United Nations, the Horseradish Information Council, the Mushroom

Council, the National Hot Dog and Sausage Council, the National Potato Promotion Board, the Oregon Raspberry and Blackberry Commission, the Trade Commission of Spain, the U.S. Apple Association, the USA Rice Federation, and the United States Department of Agriculture.

It's amazing how many people it takes to publish a book of this size — or of any size for that matter. Like building a house, creating a book typically involves dozens of people with very specialized skills. There are project managers who oversee production and keep the book on schedule, writers who transform raw materials into a new edifice and editors who make sure that it is structurally sound, copy editors who check to see that everything is properly and consistently aligned, designers who make the book beautiful, publicity people who market it, and agents who negotiate the deals. Every one of these folks contributes greatly to the book and deserves special mention.

But before I get to that, I must to tell you about a dream I had several months ago. In the dream, I was sitting in my home office writing these acknowledgments and some kind of linguistic blackout prevented me from using any proper names. Instead, I had to use little descriptive snapshots that captured the thanked person in words. I began with my publisher at Robert Rose, Bob Dees. He became "a pleasure to dine with," "a nimble raconteur," and "See also Visionary Thinker." My agent, Lisa Ekus, was, "bursts of brilliant energy," "a wonderful friend and counselor," and "a keen businesswoman." For my editor Carol Sherman, I wrote "patient, steady hand," "thoughtful re-organizer," and "supreme mover of bean sprouts." The phrases "delicious sense of humor," "creative researcher," and "Campari connoisseur," stood in for Sharon Sanders, who helped write the entry introductions. I'm not sure why, but in the dream, all of these descriptive phrases came in sets of three. My wife Christine's triad of unusually long phrases was: "the only person in the world who would put up with weird substitution experiments in our kitchen laboratory," "iron legs and an iron stomach strong enough to watch me sip tamari and Maggi seasoning side by side," and "her veiled look of horror as I mixed yeast extract and barbecue sauce to approximate hoisin sauce." My two sons, August and Maddox, were briefly characterized as "jumping monkeys," "messy eaters," and "willing subjects in the experiment of life."

And so it went with the other unfortunate souls whose names were replaced by phrases, including scores of publishing people such as sales & marketing manager Marian Jarkovich, designers Andrew Smith, Joseph Gisini, Kevin Cockburn, Daniella Zanchetta and Caroline Bright, and copy editors Karen Campbell-Sheviak and Jennifer MacKenzie.

I awoke, rubbed the sleep from my eyes, and wrote down bits and pieces of this bizarre dream. Soon, it became clear that not using names wasn't such a hardship. The substitutes worked just fine.

Bibliography

Books

Aaron, Chester. *The Great Garlic Book*. Ten Speed Press, 1997.

Amendola, Joseph. *The Bakers' Manual (Fourth Edition)*. John Wiley & Sons, Inc., 1993.

Anderson, Jean. *The Food of Portugal*. William Morrow, 1994.

Ayto, John. *An A-Z of Food & Drink*. Oxford University Press, 2002.

Barrett, Judith. *Fagioli: The Bean Cuisine of Italy*. Rodale, 2004.

Bartlett, Jonathan. *The Cook's Dictionary and Culinary Reference*. Contemporary Books, 1996.

Bayless, Rick. *Authentic Mexican: Regional Cooking from the Heart of Mexico*. William Morrow, 1987.

_____. *Rick Bayless's Mexican Kitchen*. Scribner, 1996.

Beard, James. *James Beard's American Cookery*. Little, Brown and Company, 1972.

_____. *Beard on Food*. Alfred A. Knopf, 1974.

Beard, James, Milton Glaser, and Burton Wolf. *The Cooks' Catalogue*. Avon Books, 1975.

Beranbaum, Rose Levy. *The Cake Bible*. William Morrow and Company, Inc., 1988.

_____. *The Pie and Pastry Bible*. Scribner, 1998.

Bissell, Frances. *The Book of Food*. Henry Holt and Company, 1994.

Bittman, Mark. *How to Cook Everything*. Macmillan, 1998.

_____. *Fish: The Complete Guide to Buying and Cooking*. Macmillan, 1994.

_____. *Leafy Greens*. Macmillan, 1995.

Bloom, Carole. *The International Dictionary of Desserts, Pastries, and Confections*. Hearst Books, 1995.

Brennan, Jennifer. *The Cuisines of Asia*. St. Martin's Press, 1984.

Brillat-Savarin, Jean Anthelme. *The Physiology of Taste*. Counterpoint, 1949.

Brown, Marlene. *The International Produce Cookbook & Guide*. HP Books, 1989.

Casas, Penelope. *The Foods and Wines of Spain*. Alfred A. Knopf, 1982.

Child, Julia. *The Way to Cook*. Alfred A. Knopf, 1989.

_____. *Mastering the Art of French Cooking (Revised Edition)*. Alfred A. Knopf, 2001.

Clingerman, Polly. *The Kitchen Companion*. The American Cooking Guild, 1994.

Conran, Terence and Caroline. *The Cook Book*. Crown Publishers, 1980.

Cost, Bruce. *Asian Ingredients*. William Morrow, 1988.

Culinary Institute of America. *The New Professional Chef (Seventh Edition)*. John Wiley & Sons, 2001.

Davidson, Alan. *Seafood: A Connoisseur's Guide and Cookbook*. Simon & Schuster, 1989.

_____. *The Oxford Companion to Food*. Oxford University Press, 1999.

De'Medici, Lorenza. *A Passion for Fruit*. Abbeville Press Publishers, 1999.

DeWitt, Dave. *The Chile Pepper Encyclopedia*. William Morrow, 1999.

Epstein, Becky Sue and Hilary Dole Klein. *Substituting Ingredients (Third Edition)*. Globe Pequot Press, 1996.

Farmer, Fannie Merritt. *The Original Boston Cooking-School Cook Book 1896 (facsimile)*. Crown Publishers, 1973.

Field, Carol. *The Italian Baker*. Harper & Row, 1985.

Friberg, Bo. *The Professional Pastry Chef (Third Edition)*. Van Nostrand Reinhold, 1996.

Gardiner, Anne and Sue Wilson. *The Inquisitive Cook*. Owl Books, 1998.

Goldman, Amy. *The Compleat Squash: A Passionate Grower's Guide to Pumpkins, Squash, and Gourds*. Artisan, 2004.

Green, Karen. *The Great International Noodle Experience*. Atheneum, 1977.

Greene, Bert. *The Grains Cookbook*. Workman, 1988.

Griffith, Fred. *Nuts*. St. Martin's Press, 2003.

Grigson, Jane. *Jane Grigson's Fruit Book*. Atheneum, 1982.

_____. *Jane Grigson's Vegetable Book*. Macmillan, 1979.

Guzman, Elmer. *The Shoreline Chef*. Watermark Publishing, 2003.

Harrison, S.G., G.B. Masefield, and M. Wallis. *The Oxford Book of Food Plants*. Oxford University Press, 1969.

Hawkes, Alex D. *The Flavors of the Caribbean & Latin America.* Viking Press, 1978.

Hazan, Marcella. *Essentials of Classic Italian Cooking.* Alfred A. Knopf, 1998.

Hemphill, Ian. *The Spice and Herb Bible.* Robert Rose, 2000.

Herbst, Sharon Tyler. *The New Food Lover's Companion (Third Edition).* Barron's Educational Series, 2001.

_____. *The New Food Lover's Tiptionary.* William Morrow, 2002.

Hibler, Janie. *The Berry Bible.* HarperCollins, 2004.

Hill, Tony. *Contemporary Encyclopedia of Herbs and Spices.* John Wiley & Sons, 2004.

Hillman, Howard. *Kitchen Science (Revised Edition).* Houghton Mifflin, 1989.

Hoffman, Matthew and David Joachim (eds). *Prevention's The Healthy Cook.* Rodale, 1997.

Hom, Ken. *Ken Hom's Asian Ingredients.* Ten Speed Press, 1996.

Hosking, Richard. *A Dictionary of Japanese Food.* Tuttle Publishing, 1997.

Iyer, Raghavan. *Betty Crocker's Indian Home Cooking.* Hungry Minds, Inc., 2001.

Jackson, Michael. *Michael Jackson's Beer Companion (Second Edition).* Running Press, 1997.

Jenkins, Nancy Harmon. *The Essential Mediterranean.* HarperCollins, 2003.

Jenkins, Steven. *Cheese Primer.* Workman, 1996.

Joachim, David. *Brilliant Food Tips and Cooking Tricks.* Rodale, 2001.

_____. *Fresh Choices.* Rodale, 2004.

Kamman, Madeleine. *The New Making of a Cook.* William Morrow, 1997.

Kasper, Lynne Rosetto. *The Splendid Table.* William Morrow, 1993.

Kennedy, Diana. *The Cuisines of Mexico.* Harper & Row, 1972.

Kiple, Kenneth F. and Kriemhild Coneè Ornelas (eds). *The Cambridge World History of Food.* Cambridge, Cambridge University Press, 2000.

Kirby, Jane, R.D. and David Joachim. *Eat Great Lose Weight.* Rodale, 2000.

Kochilas, Diane. *The Glorious Foods of Greece.* Morrow, 2001.

Kowalchik, Claire and William H. Hylton (eds). *Rodale's Illustrated Encyclopedia of Herbs.* Rodale Press, 1987.

Labensky, Steven, Gaye G. Ingram, and Sarah R. Labensky. *Webster's New World Dictionary of Culinary Arts (Second Edition).* Prentice Hall, 2000

Laessøe, Thomas and Anna Del Conte. *The Mushroom Book.* Dorling Kindersley, 1996.

Lee, Mercédès (ed). *Seafood Lover's Almanac.* National Audubon Society Living Oceans Program, 2000.

Levy, Paul. *The Penguin Book of Food and Drink.* Penguin Books, 1996.

Lichine, Alexis. *Alexis Lichine's New Encyclopedia of Wines & Spirits.* Alfred A. Knopf, 1979.

Lo, Eileen Yin-Fei. *The Chinese Kitchen.* Morrow, 1999.

MacNeil, Karen. *The Wine Bible.* Workman, 2001.

Madison, Deborah. *Vegetarian Cooking for Everyone.* Broadway, 1997.

Malgieri, Nick. *How to Bake.* HarperCollins, 1995.

Mallet, Gina. *Last Chance to Eat: The Fate of Taste in a Fast Food World.* W.W. Norton & Company, 2004.

Mariani, John F. *The Dictionary of Italian Food and Drink.* Broadway Books, 1998.

_____. *The Dictionary of American Food and Drink (Revised Edition).* Hearst Books, 1994.

May, Tony. *Italian Cuisine.* Italian Wine & Food Institute, 1990.

Mayes, Kathleen and Sandra Gottfried. *Boutique Bean Pot.* Woodbridge, 1992.

McGee, Harold. *The Curious Cook.* North Point Press, 1990.

_____. *On Food and Cooking (Revised Edition).* Scribner, 2004.

Miller, Mark. *The Great Chile Book.* Ten Speed Press, 1991.

Montagné, Prosper (ed). *Larousse Gastronomique.* Clarkson Potter, 2001.

Morton, Mark. *Cupboard Love: A Dictionary of Culinary Curiosities.* Bain & Cox Publishers, 1996.

Newman, Bettina and David Joachim. *Lose Weight the Smart Low-Carb Way.* Rodale, 2002.

Oliver, Garrett. *The Brewmaster's Table*. Ecco, 2003.

Ortiz, Elizabeth Lambert. *The Encyclopedia of Herbs, Spices, and Flavorings*. Dorling Kindersley, 1992.

Patent, Greg. *Baking in America*. Houghton Mifflin, 2002.

Peterson, James. *Vegetables*. William Morrow, 1998.

_____. *Fish & Shellfish*. William Morrow, 1996.

_____. *Sauces: Classic and Contemporary Sauce Making (Second Edition)*. John Wiley & Sons, 1998.

Prudhomme, Paul. *Chef Paul Prudhomme's Louisiana Kitchen*. William Morrow, 1984.

Raichlen, Steven. *Steven Raichlen's Healthy Latin Cooking*. Rodale, 1998.

Reardon, Joan and Ruth Ebling. *Oysters: A Culinary Celebration*. Parnassus Imprints, 1984.

Resnik, Linda and Dee Brock. *Food FAQs*. FAQs Press, 2000.

Revsin, Leslie. *Great Fish, Quick*. Doubleday, 1997.

Roden, Claudia, *Mediterranean Cookery*. Alfred A. Knopf, 1987.

_____. *The New Book of Middle Eastern Food (Revised Edition)*. Alfred A. Knopf, 2000.

Rogers, Ford. *Olives: Cooking with Olives and Their Oils*. Ten Speed, 2002.

Rolland, Jacques L. *The Cook's Essential Kitchen Dictionary*. Robert Rose, 2004.

Rombauer, Irma S., Marion Rombauer Becker, and Ethan Becker. *The Joy of Cooking*. Scribner, 1997.

Rombauer, Irma S. and Marion Rombauer Becker, *The Joy of Cooking*. Bobbs-Merrill, 1975.

Root, Waverley. *Food*. Fireside, 1980.

Sahni, Julie. *Classic Indian Cooking*. Morrow, 1980.

Sass, Lorna. *Lorna Sass' Complete Vegetarian Kitchen*. Hearst Books, 1992.

Schneider, Elizabeth. *Vegetables from Amaranth to Zucchini*. William Morrow, 2001.

_____. *Uncommon Fruits & Vegetables: A Commonsense Guide*. William Morrow, 1986.

Schwartz, Arthur. *Naples at Table*. HarperCollins, 1998.

Sheraton, Mimi. *The German Cookbook*. Random House, 1965.

Shimbo, Hiroko. *The Japanese Kitchen*. Harvard Common Press, 2000.

Simmons, Marie. *The Good Egg*. Houghton Mifflin, 2000.

Simonds, Nina. *Classic Chinese Cuisine*. Houghton Mifflin, 1982.

_____. *Asian Noodles*. Morrow, 1997.

Susser, Alan. *The Great Citrus Book*. Ten Speed Press, 1997.

Suzuki, Tokiko. *The Essentials of Japanese Cooking*. Japan Publications, 1995.

Taylor, John Martin. *Hoppin' John's Low Country Cooking*. Bantam, 1992.

Teubner, Christian. *The Cheese Bible*. Penguin Studio, 1998.

_____. *The Vegetable Bible*. Penguin Studio, 1998.

_____. *The Chicken and Poultry Bible*. Penguin Studio, 1997.

Thompson, David. *Thai Food*. Ten Speed Press, 2002.

Thorne, John, *Simple Cooking*. Viking, 1987.

Trang, Corinne. *Essentials of Asian Cuisine*. Simon & Schuster, 2003.

Tribole, Evelyn. *More Healthy Homestyle Cooking*. Rodale Inc., 2000

Tropp, Barbara. *The Modern Art of Chinese Cooking*. Hearst, 1996.

Tsuji, Shizuo. *Japanese Cooking: A Simple Art*. Kodansha International, 1980.

Underwood, Greer. *The New Gourmet Light (Third Edition)*. Globe Pequot Press, 1999.

Waldron, Maggie. *Potatoes: A Country Garden Cookbook*. HarperCollins, 1993.

Weinzweig. Ari. *Zingerman's Guide to Good Eating*. Houghton Mifflin, 2003.

Whiteman, Kate. *The New Guide to Fruit*. Lorenz Books, 1999.

Willan, Anne. *LaVarenne Pratique*. Crown Publishers, 1989.

Williams, Chuck. *Williams-Sonoma Kitchen Companion*. Time Life Books, 2000.

Wolf, Burt. *The New Cooks' Catalogue*. Alfred A. Knopf, 2000.

Wolfert, Paula. *World of Food*. Harper & Row, 1988.

_____. *Mediterranean Grains and Greens.* HarperCollins, 1998.

_____. *The Cooking of the Eastern Mediterranean.* HarperCollins, 1994.

_____. *Mediterranean Cooking (Revised Edition).* Perennial Currents, 1994.

Wright, Clifford A. *Mediterranean Vegetables.* Harvard Common Press, 2001.

Yepsen, Roger. *Apples.* W.W. Norton & Company, 1994.

Websites

Agence Partenaire. **www.francefromages.com**

Alberto-Culver Company. Mrs. Dash® Products. **www.mrsdash.com**

Almond Board of California. California Almonds Are In! **www.almondsarein.com**

Amazon. **www.amazon.com**

American Egg Board. **www.aeg.org**

Baking 911. **www.baking911.com**

Barilla Group. **www.barilla.com**

The Chemical Heritage Foundation. **www.chemheritage.org**

The Cincinnati Enquirer. **www.enquirer.com**

Cocktail DB. **www.cocktaildb.com**

Columbia Encyclopedia, Sixth Edition. **www.encyclopedia.com**

Cooking.com. **www.cooking.com**

The Cook's Thesaurus. **www.foodsubs.com**

Diversified Business Communications. SeaFood Business. **www.seafoodbusiness.com**

Drinks Mixer. **www.drinksmixer.com**

Durkee-Mower Inc. **www.marshmallowfluff.com**

Espana. **www.spain.info**

Fiery Foods. **www.fiery-foods.com**

Florida Fish and Wildlife Conservation Commission. **www.marinefisheries.org**

Food and Agricultural Organization of the United Nations. **www.fao.org**

The Fruit Pages. **www.thefruitpages.com**

Gammel Dansk. **www.gammeldansk.dk**

GourmetSleuth.com. **www.GourmetSleuth.com**

Greek Products.com. **www.greekproducts.com**

Harper, Douglas. Online Etymology Dictionary. **www.etymonline.com**

Hellenic Electronic Center. **www.greece.org**

Hormel Foods. **www.hormel.com**

Innvista. **www.invista.com**

Internet Movie Database. **www.universal.imdb.com**

Joy of Baking. **www.joyofbaking.com**

Kraft Foods. **www.kraft.com**

LeRoy Historical Society. **www.jellomuseum.com**

McCormick & Co. **www.mccormick.com**

Microsoft Corporation. **www.encarta.msn.com**

Mushroom Council. **www.mushroomcouncil.org**

National Hot Dog and Sausage Council. **www.hot-dog.org**

National Potato Promotion Board. **www.potatohelp.org**

Ochef. **www.ochef.com**

Oregon Raspberry and Blackberry Commission. **www.oregon-berries.com**

Primedia. **www.about.com**

Rieger, Mark. Mark's Fruit Crops. **www.uga.edu/fruit**

Spice Advice. **www.spiceadvice.com**

Trade Commission of Spain. **www.cheesefromspain.com**

Truestar Health. **www.truestarhealth.com**

U.K. Chile Head. **www.g6csy.net**

Unilever UK. **www.uniliver.co.uk/**

United States Department of Agriculture, Food Safety and Inspection Service. **www.fsis.usda.gov**

University of Florida. **www.news.ifas.ufl.edu**

University of Massachusetts Medical School. **www.umassmed.edu**

U.S. Apple Association. **www.usapple.org**

USA Rice Federation. **www.usarice.com**

USDA National Nutrient Database for Standard Reference. **www.nal.usda.gov**

View London. **www.viewlondon.co.uk**

The Webtender. **www.webtender.com**

What's Cooking America. **www.whatscookingamerica.net**

Whyte and Mackay, Ltd. **www.glayva.com**

Wilton Industries, Inc. **www.wilton.com**

Wines on the Internet. **www.wines.com**

More Great Books from Robert Rose

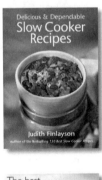

Appliance Cooking

- 125 Best Microwave Oven Recipes
  by Johanna Burkhard
- The Blender Bible
  by Andrew Chase and Nicole Young
- The Mixer Bible
  by Meredith Deeds and Carla Snyder
- The 150 Best Slow Cooker Recipes
  by Judith Finlayson
- Delicious & Dependable Slow Cooker Recipes
  by Judith Finlayson
- 125 Best Vegetarian Slow Cooker Recipes
  by Judith Finlayson
- 125 Best Rotisserie Oven Recipes
  by Judith Finlayson
- 125 Best Food Processor Recipes
  by George Geary
- The Best Family Slow Cooker Recipes
  by Donna-Marie Pye
- The Best Convection Oven Cookbook
  by Linda Stephen
- 125 Best Toaster Oven Recipes
  by Linda Stephen
- 250 Best American Bread Machine Baking Recipes
  by Donna Washburn and Heather Butt
- 250 Best Canadian Bread Machine Baking Recipes
  by Donna Washburn and Heather Butt

Baking

- 250 Best Cakes & Pies
  by Esther Brody
- 500 Best Cookies, Bars & Squares
  by Esther Brody
- 500 Best Muffin Recipes
  by Esther Brody
- 125 Best Cheesecake Recipes
  by George Geary
- 125 Best Chocolate Recipes
  by Julie Hasson
- 125 Best Chocolate Chip Recipes
  by Julie Hasson
- 125 Best Cupcake Recipes
  by Julie Hasson
- Complete Cake Mix Magic
  by Jill Snider

Healthy Cooking

- 125 Best Vegetarian Recipes
  by Byron Ayanoglu with contributions from Algis Kemezys
- America's Best Cookbook for Kids with Diabetes
  by Colleen Bartley
- Canada's Best Cookbook for Kids with Diabetes
  by Colleen Bartley
- The Juicing Bible
  by Pat Crocker and Susan Eagles
- The Smoothies Bible
  by Pat Crocker

125 Best Vegan
Recipes
*by Maxine Effenson Chuck
and Beth Gurney*

500 Best Healthy
Recipes
Edited by Lynn Roblin, RD

125 Best Gluten-Free
Recipes
*by Donna Washburn
and Heather Butt*

125 Best Gluten-Free
Family Cookbook
*by Donna Washburn
and Heather Butt*

America's Everyday
Diabetes Cookbook
*Edited by Katherine
E. Younker, MBA, RD*

Canada's Everyday
Diabetes Choice
Recipes
*Edited by Katherine
E. Younker, MBA, RD*

Canada's Complete
Diabetes Cookbook
*Edited by Katherine
E. Younker, MBA, RD*

The Best Diabetes
Cookbook (U.S.)
*Edited by Katherine
E. Younker, MBA, RD*

The Best Low-Carb
Cookbook
from Robert Rose

Recent Bestsellers

125 Best Soup Recipes
*by Marylin Crowley
and Joan Mackie*

The Convenience Cook
by Judith Finlayson

125 Best Ice
Cream Recipes
*by Marilyn Linton
and Tanya Linton*

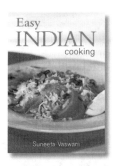

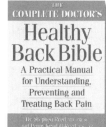

Easy Indian Cooking
by Suneeta Vaswani

Simply Thai Cooking
*by Wandee Young
and Byron Ayanoğlu*

Health

The Complete
Natural Medicine
Guide to the
50 Most Common
Medicinal Herbs
*by Dr. Heather Boon,
B.Sc.Phm., Ph.D. and
Michael Smith, B.Pharm,
M.R.Pharm.S., ND*

The Complete
Kid's Allergy and
Asthma Guide
Edited by Dr. Milton Gold

The Complete Natural
Medicine Guide to
Breast Cancer
by Sat Dharam Kaur, ND

The Complete
Doctor's Stress
Solution
*by Penny Kendall-Reed,
MSc, ND and Dr. Stephen
Reed, MD, FRCSC*

The Complete Doctor's
Healthy Back Bible
*by Dr. Stephen Reed, MD
and Penny Kendall-Reed,
MSc, ND with Dr. Michael
Ford, MD, FRCSC and
Dr. Charles Gregory,
MD, ChB, FRCP(C)*

Everyday Risks
in Pregnancy
& Breastfeeding
*by Dr. Gideon Koren,
MD, FRCP(C), ND*

Help for Eating
Disorders
*by Dr. Debra Katzman,
MD, FRCP(C), and
Dr. Leora Pinhas, MD*

Also Available
from Robert Rose

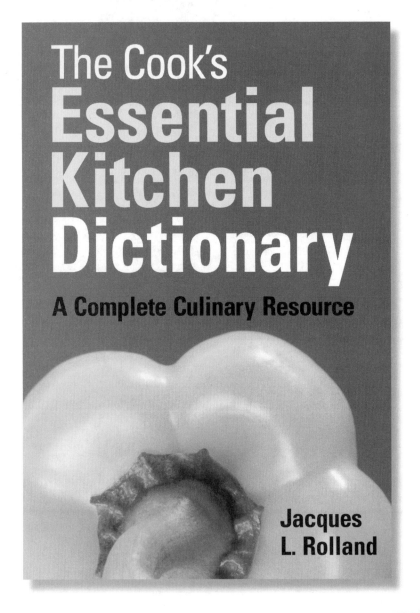

The Cook's
Essential
Kitchen
Dictionary

A Complete Culinary Resource

Jacques
L. Rolland